Foundations of Marketing

Third Edition
Essentials

Part 2   Planning the Marketing Effort

Part 3   Consumer Behaviour

Part 4   Products

Part 7   Promotion

Preface

The mid-1980s is both a trying and exciting time in which to begin a study of marketing. Organizations—both profit and nonprofit—are engaged in intense competition for customers, audiences, and clients. The marketplace has grown rapidly. Rising costs, increased scarcity of energy and other needed resources have resulted in increasingly complex decision-making. Marketing will play an important role in the Canadian economy. Organizations ranging from the local symphony orchestra to the Federal Government are attempting to employ marketing concepts and techniques in their operations. Politicians, hospital administrators, accountants, financial institutions, and provincial tourism offices are studying—and applying — marketing knowledge in their attempts to identify their clients and provide them with needed services.

Foundations of Marketing is designed to be the textbook for such an environment. It provides the reader with the following features that we believe make it one of the most thorough and comprehensive textbooks available.

• Comprehensive coverage of marketing planning and strategy and of orthodox marketing subjects

Foundations of Marketing is written with a strong marketing planning/strategy orientation. Several chapters deal with the vital subjects of marketing planning, forecasting, evaluation, and control. Two chapters are devoted to market segmentation. Since planning occurs at the beginning of the marketing effort, coverage of marketing planning and forecasting begins in Chapter 3.

• Major emphasis on consumer behaviour and elements of the marketing mix

Although the text does emphasize the importance of marketing planning, this is not done at the expense of coverage of essential marketing concepts. The vital subjects of consumer behaviour and the elements of the marketing mix are stressed throughout the book. *Foundations* devotes two entire chapters to the critical subject of consumer behaviour. In addition, at least two chapters are devoted to each of the elements of marketing mix, and separate chapter treatment of retailing, wholesaling, and physical distribution is provided.

- Separate chapter coverage of the marketing of services.

This textbook pays special attention to this emerging area of marketing in chapter 11.

- Readable text with marketing concepts emphasized by real-world examples

Foundations of Marketing is comprehensive, systematic, and rigorous. We hope it is also both practical and written in a lively, engaging manner that avoids tedious, boring prose. Readily identifiable cases and real-world examples are included to illustrate the application — correct and incorrect — of fundamental marketing concepts discussed in the text. Opening vignettes provide the reader with a flavour of the marketing concepts to be treated in each chapter. Examples following the explanation of each concept reinforce student learning. The book avoids sexist language and portrays women in realistic roles.

- Comprehensive teaching-learning package

Foundations of Marketing is available in a complete educational package, designed for both instructor and student. The package includes:

Study Guide: a totally rewritten comprehensive aid for students. It includes review exercises to be done by the students as well as many study questions and cases that can be discussed in class. The study guide also includes an extensive and comprehensive marketing project that unfolds with the textual materials. This provides a thread that requires students to tie theory and practice together.

Instructor's Manual: the most complete manual available with any basic marketing text. The *Manual* includes lecture suggestions, a film guide, reference materials, and suggestions for using the transparency masters and acetates.

Transparencies: a complete transparency package, prepared with the help of Jim Forbes of The University of British Columbia, is available to adapters on request.

Test Bank: over 2000 items organized into quiz-type and comprehensive exam-type questions. Prepared by Ann Walker, of the Ryerson Polytechnical Institute, the *Test Bank* is available on floppy disk and in printed format.

Acknowledgements

The authors gratefully acknowledge the contributions of a large number of persons — colleagues, students, professional marketers in businesses and nonprofit organizations, and the fine professionals at Holt, Rinehart and Winston of Canada, Limited for their invaluable critiques, questions, and advice in making **Foundations of Marketing** a reality. In particular, our thanks go to Mike Roche and Jacqueline Kaiser for their tireless efforts. We would like to express our special appreciation to Professor Jim Forbes of the University of British Columbia for his comprehensive suggestions. For their reviews on all or part of the manuscript we would like to express our appreciation to:

Karen Karpuk, Southern Alberta Institute of Technology
Don Yurchuk, Northern Alberta Institute of Technology
Jay Rubinstein, Vanier College, Snowdon Campus

Padraig Cherry, British Columbia Institute of Technology
Knud Jenson, Ryerson Polytechnical Institute
William Lyon, Fanshawe College
J.L. Zoellner, Seneca College
Byron Collins, Humber College
J. Steen, Georgian College
Lewis A. Presner, Durham College
Gordon Thomas, University of Manitoba

M. Dale Beckman
Professor and Head, Department of Business Administration
Univeristy of Manitoba
Winnipeg, Manitoba

David L. Kurtz
The University Professor of Business
Seattle University
Seattle, Washington

Louis E. Boone
The Ernest G. Cleverdon Chair of Business and Management
University of South Alabama
Mobile, Alabama

January, 1986

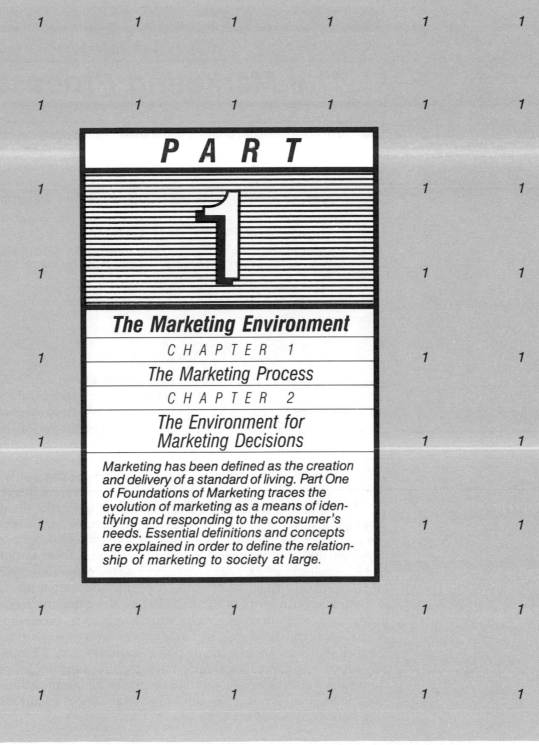

PART

1

The Marketing Environment

CHAPTER 1

The Marketing Process

CHAPTER 2

The Environment for Marketing Decisions

Marketing has been defined as the creation and delivery of a standard of living. Part One of Foundations of Marketing traces the evolution of marketing as a means of identifying and responding to the consumer's needs. Essential definitions and concepts are explained in order to define the relationship of marketing to society at large.

The Marketing Process

1. *To explain the types of utility and the role played by marketing in their creation.*

2. *To relate the definition of marketing to the concept of the exchange process.*

3. *To contrast marketing activities in each of the three eras in the history of marketing.*

4. *To explain the concept of marketing myopia.*

5. *To identify the variables involved in marketing decision-making and the environments in which these decisions must be made.*

Would you predict success for a retailer with a fanatical dedication to quality of products offered to its customers? Marks and Spencer of Canada spends about $1 million a year in trying to achieve this. A staff of twenty technologists and quality control persons ensure that textiles used in their clothing are made to rigorous standards, monitoring all steps of the manufacturing process. Similarly, a staff of eight tastes every new item of food sold by the company, while senior technologists regularly visit food plants to make quality checks.

Marks and Spencer, Britain's most successful retailer discovered that quality products and methods that worked in Britain were not enough to make the firm successful in Canada. They ignored the fundamental fact that marketing success comes from finding out which products and services *customers* want, providing these, and then communicating the benefits offered to these customers.

After several years of financial losses, the company has finally added new and interesting styles and colours to its product assortment, and renovated stores to make them more interesting. It has also changed its no-advertising policy and allocated $1 million to an advertising campaign to inform people about the unique quality and values offered by this very interesting retail organization. Such an application of marketing thinking and practices augurs well for the future success of the company.[1]

The Conceptual Framework

All business organizations perform two basic operating functions — they produce a good or a service, and they market it. This is true of all firms — from giant corporations such as Canada Packers and Canadian Pacific to the neighbourhood convenience store. Production and marketing are the very essence of economic life in any society.

Production and Marketing Create Utility for the Consumer

Through the production and marketing of desired goods and services, businesses fulfill the needs of society, their customers, and their owners. They create **utility**, which may be defined as *the want-satisfying power of a product or service*. There are four basic kinds of utility — form, time, place, and ownership.

Form utility is created when the firm converts raw materials and component inputs into finished products and services. Glass, steel, fabrics, rubber, and other components are combined to form a new Peugeot or Firebird. Cotton, thread, and buttons are converted into GWG jeans. Sheet music, musical instruments, musicians, a conductor, and the facilities of Roy Thomson Hall are converted into a performance by the Toronto Symphony. Although marketing inputs may be important in specifying consumer and audience preferences, the actual creation of form utility is the responsibility of the production function of the organization.

Time, place, and *ownership utility* are created by marketing. They are created when products and services are available to the consumer when the person wants to purchase them, at a convenient location, and where facilities are available whereby title to the product or service may be transferred at the time of purchase.

Chapter 1 sets the stage for the entire text by examining the meaning of marketing and its importance to organizations — both profit-seeking and nonprofit. The chapter examines the development of marketing in our society and its contributions. The marketing variables utilized in a marketing strategy are also introduced.

What Is Marketing?

All organizations must create utility if they are to survive. The design and marketing of want-satisfying products, services, and ideas is the foundation for the creation of utility. However, the role of marketing in the success of an organization has only recently been recognized. An expert on business management, Peter F. Drucker, emphasized the importance of marketing in his book, *The Practice of Management*:

If we want to know what a business is we have to start with its purpose. And its purpose must lie outside the business itself. In fact, it must lie in society since a business enterprise is an organ of society. There is one valid definition of business purpose: to create a customer.[2]

How does an organization "create" a customer? As Professors Guiltinan and Paul explain:

Essentially, 'creating' a customer means identifying needs in the marketplace, finding out which needs the organization can profitably serve, and developing an offering to convert potential buyers into customers. Marketing managers are responsible for most of the activities necessary to create the customers the organization wants. These activities include:
- identifying customer needs
- designing products and services that meet those needs
- communicating information about those products and services to prospective buyers
- making the products or services available at times and places that meet customers' needs
- pricing the products to reflect costs, competition, and customers' ability to buy
- providing for the necessary service and follow-up to ensure customer satisfaction after the purchase.[3]

Marketing Defined

Ask five persons to define marketing and you are likely to get five definitions. Due to the continuing exposure to advertising and personal selling, most respondents are likely to link marketing and selling. The Definitions Committee of the American Marketing Association, the international professional association in the marketing discipline, has attempted to standardize marketing terminology by proposing the following definition: "*Marketing is the process of planning and executing the conception, pricing, promotion, and distribution of ideas, goods, and services to create exchanges that satisfy individual and organizational objectives.*"[4]

This definition shows the wide-ranging dimensions of marketing. It encompasses more than products, or even businesses; it can also involve the activities of a nonprofit organization or the marketing of an idea or service. The firm should be viewed as an organized behaviour system designed to generate outputs of value to consumers. In profit-making organizations profitability is achieved through creating customer satisfaction. Marketing activities begin with new product concepts and designs analysed and developed to meet specific unfilled consumer needs — not with finished goods ready for shipment. Thus, a properly oriented marketing system reflects consumer and societal needs.[5]

This concept of marketing activities should permeate all activities of an organization. It assumes that true marketing effort is in accordance with ethical business practices and that it is effective from the standpoint of both society and the individual firm. It also emphasizes the need for efficiency in distribution although the nature and degree of efficiency is dependent upon the kind of business environment within which the firm must operate. The final assumption included in the definition is that those consumer segments to be satisfied through production and marketing activities of the firm have already been selected and analysed *prior to* production. In other words, the customer, client, or public determines the marketing program.

However not all companies have a market orientation. In addition to market-oriented firms, there are still some which are *product-oriented* and/or *production-oriented*. In a product-oriented firm, the emphasis is on the product itself rather than the consumer's needs, while in the production-oriented firm, the dominant considerations in product design are those of ease or cheapness of production. In either case, market considerations are ignored or de-emphasized.[6]

The Origins of Marketing

The essence of marketing is the **exchange process**. This is the process by which two or more parties give something of value to one another to satisfy felt needs.[7] In many cases, the item is a tangible good, such as a newspaper, a hand calculator, or a pair of shoes. In other cases, intangible services, such as a car wash, transportation, or a concert performance, are exchanged for money. In still other instances, funds or time donations may be offered to political candidates, a Red Cross office, or a church or synagogue.

The marketing function is both simple and direct in subsistence-level economies. For example, assume that a primitive society consists solely of Person A and Person B. Assume also that the only elements of their standard of living are food, clothing, and shelter. The two live in adjoining caves on a mountainside. They weave their own clothes and tend their own fields independently. They are able to subsist even though their standard of living is minimal.

Person A is an excellent weaver but a poor farmer, while Person B is an excellent farmer but a poor weaver. In this situation, it would be wise for each to specialize in the line of work that he or she does best. The net result would then be a greater total production of both clothing and food. In other words, specialization and division of labour will lead to a production surplus. But neither A nor B is any better off until they *trade* the products of their individual labour, thereby creating the exchange process.

Exchange is the origin of marketing activity. In fact, marketing has been described as "the process of creating and resolving exchange relationships."[8] When there is a need to exchange goods, the natural result is marketing effort on the part of the people involved.

Wroe Alderson, a leading marketing theorist, said, "It seems altogether reasonable to describe the development of exchange as a great invention which helped to start primitive man on the road to civilization."[9]

While the cave dweller example is simplistic, it does point up the essence of the marketing function. Today's complex industrial society may have a more complicated exchange process, but the basic concept is the same: production is not meaningful until a system of marketing has been established. Perhaps the adage "Nothing happens until somebody sells something"[10] sums it up best.

Three Eras in the History of Marketing

Although marketing has always been present in businesses, its importance has varied greatly. Three historical eras can be identified: the production era, the sales era, and the marketing era.

The Production Era

One hundred years ago, most firms were production-oriented. Manufacturers stressed production of products and then looked for people to purchase them. The Pillsbury Company of this period is an excellent example of a production-oriented company. Here is how the company's board chairman, the late Robert J. Keith, described the Pillsbury of the early years:

> We are professional flour millers. Blessed with a supply of the finest North American wheat, plenty of water power, and excellent milling machinery, we produce flour of the highest quality. Our basic function is to mill high-quality flour, and, of course (and almost incidentally), we must hire salesmen to sell it, just as we hire accountants to keep our books.[11]

The prevailing attitude of this era was that a good product (defined in terms of physical quality) would sell itself. This production orientation dominated business philosophy for decades. Indeed, business success was often defined in terms of production victories.

Although marketing had emerged as a functional activity within the business organization prior to the twentieth century, management's orientation remained with production for quite some time. In fact, what might be called industry's production era did not reach its peak until the early part of this century. The apostle of this approach to business operations was Frederick W. Taylor, whose

Principles of Scientific Management was widely read and accepted at that time. Taylor's approach reflected his engineering background by emphasizing efficiency in the production process. Later writers, such as Frank and Lillian Gilbreth, the originators of motion analysis, expanded on Taylor's basic concepts.

Henry Ford's mass production line serves as a good example of this orientation. Ford's slogan, "They [customers] can have any colour they want, as long as it's black," reflected a prevalent attitude toward marketing. Production shortages and intense consumer demand were the rule of the day. It is no wonder that production activities took precedence.

A production orientation still exists in many businesses today. Often a firm does not consider changing from this outdated approach until it runs into trouble.

The Sales Era
As production techniques became more sophisticated and as output grew, manufacturers began to increase the emphasis on an effective sales force to find customers for their output. This era saw firms attempting to match customers to their output. A sales orientation assumes that customers will resist purchasing products and services not deemed essential, and that the task of personal selling and advertising is to convince them to buy. Marketing efforts were also aimed at wholesalers and retailers in an attempt to motivate them to stock greater quantities of the manufacturer's output.

Although marketing departments began to emerge during the sales era, they tended to remain in a subordinate position to production, finance, and engineering. Many chief marketing executives held the title of sales manager. Here is how Pillsbury was described during the sales era:

> We are a flour-milling company, manufacturing a number of products for the consumer market. We must have a first-rate sales organization which can dispose of all the products we can make at a favourable price. We must back up this sales force with consumer advertising and market intelligence. We want our sales representatives and our dealers to have all the tools they need for moving the output of our plants to the consumer.[12]

But selling is only one component of marketing. As marketing expert Theodore Levitt has pointed out: ". . . marketing is as different from selling as chemistry is from alchemy, astronomy from astrology, chess from checkers."[13]

The Marketing Era
As personal income and consumer demand for goods and services dropped rapidly during the Great Depression of the 1930s, marketing was thrust into a more important role. Organizational

survival dictated that managers pay closer attention to the markets for their products. This trend was halted by the outbreak of World War II, when rationing and shortages of consumer goods were commonplace. The war years, however, were an atypical pause in an emerging trend that was resumed almost immediately after the hostilities ceased. An important new philosophy known as the marketing concept was about to emerge.

Emergence of the Marketing Concept

What was the setting for the crucial change in management philosophy? Perhaps it can best be explained by the shift from a **seller's market** (*one with a shortage of goods and services*) to a **buyer's market** (*one with an abundance of goods and services*). When World War II ended, factories stopped manufacturing tanks and jeeps and started turning out consumer goods again—an activity that had for all practical purposes stopped in 1940.

Once the pent-up demand created by the war had been satisfied, Canadian businesses found themselves operating in a buyer's market. It was no longer possible to sell just anything they chose to produce. In fact, it was not good enough to put special emphasis on selling or advertising. Buyers were becoming choosy, and purchased the products and services that *they* perceived would serve their needs.

Firms began to discover their principal task was to understand, and then make the business serve the interests of the customers rather than trying to make the customer buy what the business wanted to produce. A sincere customer orientation was required.

The realization that emerged has been identified as *the marketing concept*. The recognition of the marketing concept and its dominating role in business can be dated from 1952, when General Electric Company's annual report heralded a new management philosophy:

> [The concept] . . . introduces the marketing man at the beginning rather than at the end of the production cycle and integrates marketing into each phase of the business. Thus, marketing, through its studies and research, will establish for the engineer, the design and manufacturing man, what the customer wants in a given product, what price he is willing to pay, and where and when it will be wanted. Marketing will have authority in product planning, production scheduling, and inventory control, as well as in sales distribution and servicing of the product.[14]

In other words, marketing would no longer be regarded as a supplemental activity to be performed after the production process had been accomplished. For instance, the marketer would now play the lead role in product planning. Marketing and selling were no longer synonymous.

In a marketing-oriented firm, the decisions are based upon the analysis of market needs and demands. The objective is to take the opportunities the market offers. This approach can produce any of the good effects of the other two orientations, and avoids their drawbacks. More important, it can identify new opportunities.[15]

Optimal success for all products requires effective marketing based on a thorough understanding of what consumers want and need. Therefore, marketing is a primary function of any organization.

The marketing concept may be defined as *a company-wide consumer orientation with the objective of achieving long-run profits*. The key words are "company-wide consumer orientation." All facets of the business must be involved with assessing and then satisfying customer wants and needs. This is not something to be left just to the marketers. Accountants working in the credit office and the engineers employed in product design in the credit office and the engineers employed in product design also play important roles. Consumer orientation must indeed be company-wide.

The words "with the objective of achieving long-run profits" are used in order to differentiate the marketing concept from policies of short-run profit maximization. The marketing concept is a modern philosophy for dynamic business growth. Since the continuity of the firm is an assumed part of the concept, such a company-wide consumer orientation will lead to greater long-run profits than would be the case for other managerial philosophies geared to reaching short-run goals.

Avoiding Marketing Myopia

The emergence of the marketing concept has not been without setbacks. One troublesome situation has been what Theodore Levitt called "marketing myopia."[16] According to Levitt, **marketing myopia** is *the failure of management to recognize the scope of its business*. Future growth is endangered when management is product-oriented rather than customer-oriented. Levitt cited many service industries — dry cleaning, electric utilities, movies, and railways — as examples of companies which defined their business too narrowly. Railways thought of themselves as being in the "railway business" rather than the "transportation business," and thus lost much to the trucking industry.

Organizational goals must be broadly defined and oriented toward consumer needs. One air carrier, for example, has redefined its business from that of air transportation to travel. This allows the firm to offer complete travel services, such as hotel accommodations, credit, and ground transportation, as well as air travel. Texas Instruments, a firm known for its technological innovations, completely reorganized in 1982 in an attempt to mesh its capabilities with consumer needs instead of trying to *sell* what it could produce. As one observer noted, "The company has always developed products from a technology point of view, as opposed to what the market wanted. What we see happening now is a corporate determination to match technology prowess with what will sell."[17] Such efforts illustrate how firms may overcome marketing myopia.

Broadening the Marketing Concept for the 1980s

Industry has been responsive to the marketing concept as an improved method of doing business. Consideration of the consumer is now well accepted in many organizations. Today the relevant question is an inquiry into what the nature and extent of the concept's parameters should be.

Can nonbusiness organizations like art galleries, churches, and charities benefit from the application of marketing principles? Some marketers argue that the marketing discipline should be substantially broadened to include many areas formerly not concerned with marketing efforts. Others contend that the application of marketing has been extended too far. Certainly, recent experience has shown that many nonprofit organizations have accepted the marketing concept. For instance, the Canadian government is Canada's leading advertiser and spends approximately $54.5 million in advertising annually.[18] The Canadian Forces advertise to recruit volunteers; the United Way and other charitable groups have developed considerable marketing expertise; some police departments have used marketing-inspired strategies to improve their image with the public; and we are all familiar with the marketing efforts employed in a political campaign.

It would be difficult to envisage business returning to an era when engineering genius prevailed at the expense of consumer needs. It would be equally difficult for nonprofit organizations to return to a time when they lacked the marketing skills necessary to present a message of vital public importance. Marketing is a dynamic function, and it will no doubt be subject to continuous change. But in one form or another marketing is playing an ever more important role in all organizations and in our daily lives.

Introduction to the Marketing Process

The starting place for effective marketing is the consumer. The marketer sets out to make profits by satisfying customer needs with a firm's products and services. (Consumer analysis is treated in detail in a later chapter.)

However, since people's wants and needs vary so greatly, it is unlikely that any particular product or service can adequately serve everyone. For this reason, one of the first tasks in marketing planning is to divide the market into relatively homogeneous segments. Once a particular customer group has been identified and analysed, the marketing manager can direct company activities to profitably satisfy this segment.

Figuratively speaking, management asks itself the following questions:

1. What problems do our customers or potential customers have that our products or services can solve better than those of other suppliers?
2. Who has these problems?
3. What are the particular circumstances, actual or potential, that would suggest modifications in our products, prices, distribution, or promotion?

The idea of thinking in terms of providing *solutions* to *problems* is a very useful one in marketing. It helps considerably in identifying new markets, finding new products for existing customers, finding new customers for existing products, and very importantly, discovering potential and possibly unsuspected competition.[19]

Although thousands of variables are involved, marketing decision-making can be conveniently classified into four strategy elements:

1. Product strategy
2. Pricing strategy
3. Distribution strategy
4. Promotional strategy

Product strategy includes *decisions about the product and its uses, package design, branding, trademarks, warranties, guarantees, product life cycles, and new product development.* The marketer's concept of product strategy involves more than just the *physical* product. It also considers the satisfaction of all consumer needs in relation to a good or service.

Pricing strategy, one of the most difficult parts of marketing decision-making, deals with *the methods of setting profitable and justified prices.* Most prices are freely set in Canada. However some prices, such as those for public utilities, airlines, and some food products, are regulated and subject to public scrutiny.

Distribution strategy involves *the selection and management of marketing channels and the physical distribution of goods.* **Marketing channels** are *the steps or handling organizations that a good or service goes through from producer to final consumer.* Channel decision-making involves establishing and maintaining the institutional structure in marketing channels. This includes retailers, wholesalers, and other institutional middlemen.

Promotional strategy involves *personal selling, advertising, sales promotion tools, and publicity.* The various aspects of promotional strategy must be blended together in order to communicate effectively with the marketplace.

Figure 1-1   Elements of the Marketing Mix

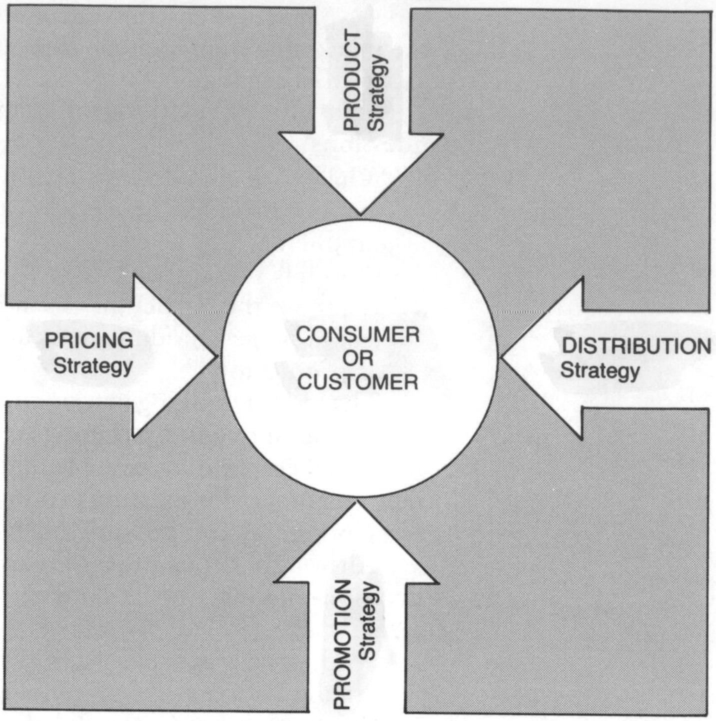

The total package forms the **marketing mix** — *the blending of the four strategy elements of marketing decision-making to satisfy chosen consumer segments*. Each of the strategies is a variable in the mix (see Figure 1–1). While that fourfold classification may be useful for the purpose of study and analysis, it is the total package (or mix) that determines the degree of marketing success. As Figure 1-1 shows, the central focus of the marketing concept is the consumer. A closer examination of the variables in the marketing mix forms a major part of this text (Chapters 9 to 20).

The Marketing Environment

Marketing decisions are not made in a vacuum. Marketers cannot make changes to marketing mix variables without recognizing that a change made to one variable will likely require an adjustment to one or more of the others to produce a balanced, effective marketing mix.

Furthermore, to be successful marketing decisions must take into account environmental factors over which the decision maker has little or no control — competition, political and legal considerations, the economy, technology, and the socio-cultural environment.

These five environmental factors require a great deal of attention when making marketing decisions. They are examined in detail in Chapter 2.

The Study of Marketing

Marketing is a pervasive element in contemporary life. In one form or another, it is close to every person. Three of its most important concerns for students are the following:

1. Marketing costs may be the largest item in the personal budget. Numerous attempts have been made to determine these costs, and most estimates have ranged between 40 and 60 percent. Regardless of the exact cost, however, marketing is obviously a key item in any consumer's budget.

   Cost alone, however, does not indicate the value of marketing. If someone says that marketing costs are too high, that person should be asked, "Relative to what?" The standard of living in Canada is in large part a function of the country's efficient marketing system. When considered in this perspective, the costs of the system seem reasonable. For example, marketing expands sales, thereby spreading fixed production costs over more units of output and reducing total output costs. Reduced production costs offset many marketing costs.

   Eight **marketing functions** occur in the marketing process: *buying, selling, transporting, storing, grading, financing, risk taking, and information collection and disemination.* These are inherent to a greater or lesser degree in all marketing transactions. They may be shifted to various members of the channel, or to the customer, but they cannot be eliminated.

2. Marketing-related occupations account for 25 to 33 percent of the nation's jobs, so it is likely that many students will become marketers. Indeed, marketing opportunities remained quite strong even during recent periods when many graduates could not find jobs. History has shown that the demand for effective marketers is relatively unaffected by cyclical economic fluctuations.

3. Marketing provides an opportunity to contribute to society as well as to an individual company. Marketing decisions affect everyone's welfare. Furthermore, opportunities to advance to decision-making positions come sooner in marketing than in most occupations.

Why study marketing? The answer is simple: marketing affects numerous facets of daily life as well as individuals' future careers and economic well-being. The study of marketing is important because it is relevant to students today and tomorrow. It is little wonder that marketing is now one of the most popular fields of academic study.

Summary   This overview of the marketing process has pointed out that the two primary functions of a business organization are production and marketing. Traditionally, industry emphasized production efficiency, often at the expense of marketing. Sometime after World War II the marketing concept became the accepted business philosophy. The change was caused by the economy shifting from a seller's market to a buyer's market.

Marketing is the development and efficient distribution of goods, services, issues, and concepts for chosen consumer segments, and marketing decision-making has been classified into four strategy elements: 1) product strategy, 2) pricing strategy, 3) distribution strategy, and 4) promotional strategy. The combination of these four variables forms the total marketing mix. It has been stressed that marketing decisions must be made in a dynamic environment determined by competitive, legal, economic, and social functions.

Three basic reasons for studying marketing are:
1. Marketing costs may be the largest item in your personal budget.
2. There is a good chance you may become a marketer.
3. Marketing provides an opportunity to make a real contribution not only to your business, but to society as a whole.

CHAPTER 2

The Environment for Marketing Decisions

1. *To identify the environmental factors that affect the consumer and the marketing mix.*

2. *To explain the types of competition faced by marketers and how an organization develops a competitive strategy.*

3. *To trace the legal framework within which marketing decisions are made.*

4. *To outline the economic factors that affect marketing strategy.*

5. *To explain the impact of the technological environment on a firm's marketing activities.*

6. *To explain how the socio-cultural environment influences marketing.*

A changing environment, important political decisions and rapid advances in technology have created enormous challenges and opportunities for Canada's two major telecommunications companies. They have leapt ahead in a seven-year rush to the top of the telephone world. Northern Telecom Ltd. of Toronto and Mitel Corp. of Ottawa are currently ranked two and four respectively in North America in regard to the numbers of sales of private branch exchanges (PBXs), the internal switching systems that channel telephone calls within companies and to the outside world.

Recent political decisions in the United States introduced the most feverish marketing competition in history in this billion-dollar-a-year market. The U.S. government decided that one of the world's largest companies, American Telephone and Telegraph Co. was too large to assure real competition in the marketplace. Therefore, AT&T was forced to divest itself of 22 operating subsidiaries which were then grouped into seven regional operating companies. These were given freedom to buy and market telephone equipment as they pleased. The impact of this was phenomenal, considering that the average assets of each of the seven were about U.S. $17 billion, roughly 1.5 times the size of Bell Canada. Since it was expected that the new companies would try to establish a clean break with their former parent company, Northern Telecom and Mitel saw great potential for sales of their equipment in this new market.

Technology was a critical factor for Mitel. Mitel's founders, Michael Cowpland and Terry Matthews, had left Northern Telecom in 1973 to start their own company. As a result of their expertise, technological innovation and sound marketing pushed Mitel's sales to a staggering $255 million over a ten-year period. However, by 1983 technology was becoming a potential problem. Technical hitches forced the postponement of the introduction of the company's long-awaited SX-2000 switching system. This system, handling up to 10 000 lines and heralded by Mitel executives as the firm's entry into the big league of digital switching, was more than a year overdue. It was to allow Mitel to compete directly with Northern Telecom's SL1, which had similar capabilities.

Competition was another important concern. Despite its rapid growth, and large resource base, Mitel was still a modest firm compared with its chief Canadian rival. Sales of $255 million did not seem so large alongside Northern Telecom's $3 billion. Furthermore, Northern Telecom was shortly expected to announce an advanced version of its SL1.[1]

The Conceptual Framework

The changing environment is constantly creating and destroying business opportunities. The battle between Northern Telecom and Mitel reveals the importance of environmental factors to the success of any organization. A combination of political, technological, and competitive forces has led to great opportunities in their industry. These forces must be identified and analyzed, and the marketing decision-makers must determine their impact upon a particular marketing situation. Although they cannot be controlled by the marketing manager, they must be considered in the development of marketing strategies together with the more controllable variables of the marketing mix.

Chapter 1 introduced marketing and the elements of the marketing mix used to satisfy chosen market targets. But the blending of a successful marketing mix must be based upon thorough analysis of environmental forces. The marketer's product, distribution, promotion, and pricing strategies must filter through these forces before they reach their goal: the consumers who represent the firm's market target. In this chapter we will examine how each of the environmental variables can affect a firm's marketing strategy.

As Figure 2-1 indicates, the environment for marketing decisions may be classified into five elements: the *competitive* environment, the *political and legal* environment, the *economic* environment, the *technological* environment, and the *social and cultural* environment. The forces are important because they provide the frame of reference within which marketing decisions are made. However, since they represent outside factors, they are *not* considered marketing mix components.

Figure 2-1   Elements of the Marketing Mix as They Operate within an Environmental Framework

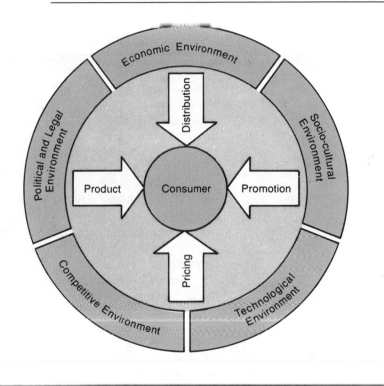

In addition to their importance in affecting current marketing decisions, their dynamic nature means that management at every level must continually reevaluate marketing decisions in response to changing environments. Even modest environmental shifts can alter the results of marketing decisions. Polaroid Corporation's failure to recognize the flexibility, ease of use, and rapidly declining prices of videocassette cameras and recorders contributed to disappointing sales for their Polavision instant movies that required users to purchase a display unit and lacked the re-recording features of the videocassette competition.

The Competitive Environment

The interactive process that occurs in the marketplace as competing organizations seek to satisfy markets is known as the **competitive environment**. Marketing decisions by an individual firm influence consumer responses in the marketplace; they also affect the marketing strategies of competitors. As a consequence, marketers must continually monitor the marketing activities of competitors—their products, channels, prices, and promotional efforts.

In a few instances, organizations enjoy a monopoly position in the marketplace. Utilities, such as natural gas, electricity, water, and cable television service, accept considerable regulation from government in such marketing-related activities as rates, service levels, and geographic coverage in exchange for exclusive rights to serve a particular group of consumers. However, such instances are rare. In addition, portions of such traditional monopoly industries as telephone service have been deregulated in recent years, and telephone companies currently face competition in such areas as the sale of telephone receivers, some long distance services, and installation and maintenance of telephone systems in larger commercial and industrial firms.

Sporting goods provide an illustration of the importance of the competitive environment. Sports and recreation fads result in boom periods for the manufacturers of the equipment involved. Bowling boomed in the early 1960s, snowmobiles in 1971, skiing in 1973, tennis in 1975, and aerobic dancing in 1980. Each of these periods has been followed by a terrific expansion of the related segment of the sporting goods industry. Excess supply soon develops, and the net result is that some firms try to compete by cutting prices. Other firms are then forced to make similar reductions to remain competitive. Tensor sold its metal tennis racquets for $25 in 1968 and for $9 by the mid-1970s. Eventually, many of the marginal competitors are forced out of the industry, and production and marketing resume normal patterns, although the industry may be vastly restructured.

Jogging and racquetball are among the sports fads today that have given rise to industries serving the participants. Many companies now make running shoes or "training flats" for joggers. Racquetball courts dot the landscape of most suburban areas and smaller cities. Today, supplying racquetball equipment and accessories is a major industry. But the signs of change are already here. Joggers can choose from more than a hundred different models of jogging shoes. And racquetball courts face increased competition in many major metropolitan areas. The competitive environment is a fact of life even in recreation and leisure activities.

Types of Competition

Marketers actually face three types of competition. The most direct form of competition occurs between marketers of similar products.

Xerox photocopiers compete with models offered by Canon, Sharp, and Olivetti. Massey-Ferguson tractors face competition from Ford Motor Company's farm equipment division, Case, and John Deere.

A second type of competition is competition between products that can be substituted for one another. In the construction industry and in manufacturing, steel products by Stelco may compete with similar products made of aluminum by Alcan. Cast-iron pipes compete with pipes made of such synthetic materials as polyvinyl chloride (PVC). In instances where a change such as a price increase or an improvement in the strength of a product occurs, demand for substitute products is directly affected.

The final type of competition involves all organizations that compete for the consumer's purchases. Traditional economic analysis views competition as a battle between companies in the same industry or between substitutable products and services. Marketers, however, accept the argument that *all* firms are competing for a limited amount of discretionary buying power. Restaurants compete with microwave ovens and gourmet delicatessens. The Mazda GLC competes with a vacation in the Bahamas and the local live theatre centre competes with pay television and the Leafs, Blue Bombers, or Expos for the consumer's entertainment dollars.

Since the competitive environment often determines the success or failure of the product, marketers must continually assess marketing strategies of competitors. New product offerings with technological advances, price reductions, special promotions, or other competitive actions must be monitored in order to adjust the firm's marketing mix in light of such changes. Among the first purchasers of any new product are the product's competitors. Careful analysis of its components — physical components, performance attributes, packaging, retail price, service requirements, and estimated production and marketing costs — allows the marketer to forecast its likely competitive impact. If necessary, adjustments to one or more marketing mix components may take place as a result of the new market entry.

Developing a Competitive Strategy

All marketers must develop an effective strategy for dealing with the competitive environment. Some will compete in a broad range of product markets in many areas of the world. Others prefer to specialize in particular market segments such as those determined by geographical, age, or income factors. Essentially, the determination of a competitive strategy involves three questions.
1. Should we compete?
2. If so, in what markets should we compete?
3. How should we compete?

The first question—should we compete?—should be answered based on the resources and objectives of the firm and expected profit potential for the firm. In some instances, potentially successful ventures are not considered due to a lack of a match between the venture and the overall organizational objectives. For example, a clothing manufacturer may reject an opportunity to diversify through the purchase of a profitable pump manufacturer. Or a producer of industrial chemicals might refrain from entering the consumer market and instead sell chemicals to another firm familiar with serving consumers at the retail level.

In other cases a critical issue is expected profit potential. If the expected profits are insufficient to pay an adequate return on the required investment, then the firm should consider other lines of business. Many organizations have switched from less profitable ventures quite efficiently. This decision should be subject to continual reevaluation so that the firm avoids being tied to traditional markets with declining profit margins. It is also important to anticipate competitive responses.

The second question concerns the markets in which to compete. This decision acknowledges that the firm has limited resources (engineering and productive capabilities, sales personnel, advertising budgets, research and development, and the like) and that these resources must be allocated to the areas of greatest opportunity. Too many firms have taken a "shotgun" approach to market selection and thus do an ineffective job in many markets rather than a good one in selected markets.

"How should we compete?" is the third question. It requires the firm's marketers to make the tactical decisions involved in setting up a comprehensive marketing strategy. Product, pricing, distribution, and promotion decisions, of course, are the major elements of this strategy.

The Political and Legal Environment

Before you play the game, learn the rules! It would be absurd to start playing a new game without first understanding the rules, yet some businesspeople exhibit a remarkable lack of knowledge about marketing's **political and legal environment**—*the laws and interpretation of laws that require firms to operate under competitive conditions and to protect consumer rights*.[2] Ignorance of laws, ordinances, and regulations could result in fines, embarrassing negative publicity, and possibly civil damage suits.

It requires considerable diligence to develop an understanding of the legal framework of marketing. Numerous laws, often vague and legislated by a multitude of different authorities, characterize the legal environment for marketing decisions. Regulations affecting marketing have been enacted at the federal, provincial, and local levels as well as by independent regulatory agencies. Our existing legal framework was constructed on a piecemeal basis, often in response to a concern over current issues.

Canada has tended to follow a public policy of promoting a competitive marketing system. To maintain such a system, competitive practices within the system have been regulated. Traditionally, the pricing and promotion variables have received the most legislative attention.

Society's Expectations Create the Framework

We live in and desire a "free enterprise society" — or do we? The concept of free enterprise is not clear, and has been gradually changing. At the turn of the century the prevalent attitude was to let business act quite freely. As a result, it was expected that new products and jobs would be created and the economy would develop and prosper.

This provided great freedom for the scrupulous and the unscrupulous. Although most businesses sought to serve their market targets in an equitable fashion, abuses did occur. Figure 2-2 is an example of questionable marketing practices. Such advertisements were not unusual in the late 1800s and early 1900s. Advancing technology led to the creation of a multitude of products in many fields. Often the buying public did not possess the expertise needed to choose among them.

With the increasing complexity of products, the growth of big, impersonal business, as well as the unfair or careless treatment of

Figure 2-2   An Example of Questionable Advertising

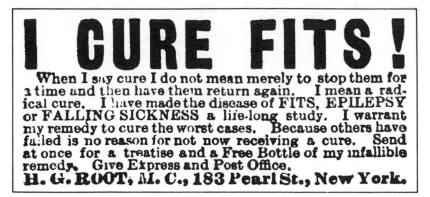

Source: S. Watson Dunn and Arnold M. Barban, *Advertising: Its Role in Modern Marketing* (Hinsdale, Ill.: Dryden Press, 1982), p. 84. Reprinted by permission.

consumers by a few, the values of society changed. "Government should regulate business more closely," we said. Over time, governments at the federal and provincial levels have responded until many laws have been passed to protect consumers, and to attempt to maintain a competitive environment for business. Large bureaucracies have grown with this increase in market regulation.

A significant development in the legal environment at the federal level was the consolidation in 1967 of consumer and business regulation programs into Consumer and Corporate Affairs Canada, and the appointment of a cabinet minister to represent these interests at the highest level. Previously these functions had been scattered among several different government departments. Following the lead of the federal government, most provinces have established consumer and corporate affairs branches and have generally streamlined the regulation of these sectors. Figure 2-3 lists some of

---

Figure 2-3   Legislation Administered by Consumer and Corporate Affairs Canada

1. Fully Administered by CCA
- Bankruptcy Act and Bankruptcy Rules
- Boards of Trade Act
- Canada Cooperative Associations Act
- Canada Corporations Act
- Combines Investigation Act
- Consumer Packaging and Labelling Act
- Copyright Act
- Department of Consumer and Corporate Affairs Act
- Electricity Inspection Act
- Farmer's Creditors Arrangement Act
- Gas Inspection Act
- Hazardous Products Act
- Industrial Design Act
- National Trade Mark and True Labelling Act
- Patent Act
- Precious Metals Marking Act
- Textile Labelling Act
- Timber Marking Act
- Trade Marks Act
- Weights and Measures Act

2. Administered Jointly with Other Departments
- Canada Agricultural Products Standards Act (with Agriculture)
- Canada Dairy Products Act (with Agriculture)
- Fish Inspection Act (with Environment)
- Food and Drugs Act (with Health and Welfare)
- Maple Products Industry Act (with Agriculture)
- Shipping Conferences Exemption Act (with Transport)
- Winding-up Act (with Finance)

the significant federal legislation that affects business today. The detailed study of provincial laws and regulations is beyond the scope of this text.

The Combines Investigation Act Sets the Standards

Of all the legislation mentioned in Figure 2-3, the Combines Investigation Act has the most significance in the legal environment for marketing decisions. The Act dates back to 1889, when it was enacted to protect the public interest in free competition.[3] Since then, various revisions have occurred in response to changes in social values and in business practices (Figure 2-4).

The Act prohibits rather than regulates. That is, it does not spell out in detail the activities that industry may undertake, but greatly discourages certain activities through the threat of penal consequences.

The provisions of the Act fall into three main classes. Generally speaking, they prohibit the following:

1. Combinations that prevent, or lessen unduly, competition in the production, purchase, sale, storage, rental, transportation, or supply of commodities, or in the price of insurance.
2. Mergers or monopolies that may operate to the detriment of the public.
3. Deceptive trade practices, including price discrimination, predatory pricing, certain promotional allowances, false and misleading advertising, misrepresentation of the regular price, resale price maintenance, false statements in door-to-door selling, double ticketing, pyramid sales, and referral selling.

Despite the long history of the Combines Act, it has proved remarkably powerless in prosecuting those who appear to contravene either of the first two categories. The Act is criminal law, requiring proof of guilt beyond any reasonable doubt. This means that government prosecutors must prove about 98 percent of their case, instead of the 51 percent that might suffice in a civil action.[4]

Combines and Restraint of Trade

It is an offence to conspire, combine, agree, or arrange with another person to prevent or lessen competition unduly. The most common types of combination relate to price fixing, bid rigging, and market sharing and group boycotting of competitors, suppliers, or customers.

While this covers much territory, it should be noted that in the following circumstances agreements between business persons are *not* unlawful.

1. The exchange of statistics.
2. Definition of product standards.
3. The exchange of credit information.

Figure 2-4   Evolution of Major Combines Legislation

Date	Legislation	Reason for Legislation
1888	Combines Investigation Commission	To protect small businesses who suffered from monopolistic and collusive practices in restraint of trade by large manufacturers.
1889	Act for the Prevention and Suppression of Combinations Formed in Restraint of Trade	To declare illegal monopolies and combinations in restraint of trade.
1892	Above Act incorporated into the Criminal Code as Section 502	To make the above a criminal offence.
1900	Above Act amended	To make the Act effective because, as it stood, an individual would first have to commit an illegal act within the meaning of common law. Now, any undue restriction of competition became a criminal offence.
1910	Additional legislation passed to complement the Criminal Code and assist in the application of the Act	To stop a recent rush of mergers that had involved some 58 firms.
1919	The Combines and Fair Prices Act	To prohibit undue stockpiling of the "necessities of life" and prohibit the realization of exaggerated profits through "unreasonable prices."
1923	Combines Investigation Act	To consolidate combines legislation.
1952, 1960	Amendments to the above	
1976	Bill C-2; amendments	To include the service industry within the Act; to prohibit additional deceptive practices; to give persons the right to recover damages; to protect rights of small businesses.

4. Definition of trade terms
5. Co-operation in research and development.
6. Restriction of advertising.

Consequently, it is possible to report statistics centrally for the purpose of providing analysis of factors relating to industrial operation and marketing, as long as competition is not lessened unduly.

Mergers

Since there is very little legal precedent with respect to the merger provisions of the Combines Investigation Act, little is understood of the implications of the law. Generally speaking the primary test that would be applied is whether competition is likely to be lessened over a substantial segment of the market as a result of a merger. This applies to both vertical and horizontal integration. Therefore, it appears that mergers are not illegal *per se*. The government and the courts have been reluctant to prevent mergers, and this section of the Act has not been effective.

Deceptive Trade Practices

This is an extremely important section for marketing decision-makers, as it contains a number of directly related provisions. There are real teeth in the legislation which the marketer should be aware of. Many successful prosecutions have been made under this section.

Misleading Advertising

False statements of every kind (even in the picture on a package) made to the public about products or services are prohibited. Not only the literal meaning of the statements will be taken into account, but also the general impression they give. For example, on December 10, 1972, Colgate Palmolive Ltd. was convicted of publishing statements designed to mislead the public.[5] The company was charged under the Combines Investigation Act after an investigator from the Department of Consumer and Corporate Affairs purchased a package of toothpaste at an Ottawa drugstore. The advertising on the package indicated that a felt pen would be given free with the purchase of the toothpaste. However, upon opening the package, the buyer found that a further purchase was necessary to get the pen. Specifically, the package read, "Free felt pens, see details inside."

The company was found guilty and fined $1500. However, the presiding judge said he was satisfied that the offending offer was the result of an error by the company and did not represent an *intent* to mislead the public. Often carelessness has been seen as responsible for the offence, and over the years, numerous advertisers have been prosecuted under the misleading advertising provisions of the Combines Investigation Act. The fines meted out have been surprisingly small.

A greater level of determination to discourage deceptive advertising was signalled in 1983 when a fine levied against Simpsons-Sears sent shock waves through the entire advertising industry. Simpsons-Sears had been found guilty of advertising through its catalogues and through newspapers between 1975 and 1978 diamond rings that it claimed had been appraised at values significantly higher than those given by bona fide diamond appraisers consulted by

Consumer and Corporate Affairs Canada. The fine imposed was a million dollars! — the highest ever levied under the Act. This set a precedent for vigorous prosecution of violaters of the Act.[6]

Another important facet of misleading advertising legislation concerns pricing. Many businesses seem to be unaware that much care needs to be taken when advertising comparative prices. It is, for example, considered misleading for a retailer to advertise a television set as follows:

Manufacturer's suggested list price	$680.00
On sale for	$500.00

if the manufacturer's suggested list price is not normally followed in this area of activity, and the usual price is normally around $600. Thus, while the retailer is offering a bargain, the magnitude of it is not indicated accurately.

Retailers may try to get around this provision by choosing different comparative expressions such as "regular price," "ordinarily $ . . . ," "list price," "hundreds sold at," "compare with," "regular value," and the like. However, the business person who genuinely seeks to comply with this provision should ask two questions:

1. Would a reasonable shopper draw the conclusion from the expression used that the figure named by way of comparison is a price at which goods have been, are, or will ordinarily be sold?
2. If the answer is yes, would such a representation be true?

Pricing Practices   It is an offence for a supplier to make a practice of discriminating in price among purchasers who are in competition with one another and who are purchasing like quantities of goods. Selling above the advertised price is also prohibited. Furthermore, the lowest of two or more prices must be used in the case of double-ticketed products. This latter provision has led to the development of easy-tear-off, two-price stickers, so that the sale price can readily be removed after a sale.

If you are a ski manufacturer and wish all ski shops to sell your skis at your suggested list price, can you force them to do so? No; it is an offence under the Act to deny supplies to an outlet that refuses to maintain the resale price. Thus, resale price maintenance is illegal, and a retailer is generally free to set whatever price is considered to be appropriate.

The Combines Investigation Act includes several other prohibitions, including ones against bait-and-switch selling, pyramid selling, and some types of referral selling and promotional contests.

Other Provisions
of the Combines
Investigation Act

**Protection Against
Foreign Laws and
Directives**

Foreign companies doing business in Canada sometimes have been constrained by laws or judgments in their home country to the detriment of competition in Canada, or of opportunities for Canadian international trade. For example, Canadian subsidiaries of American companies have felt constraints of American law against doing business with Cuba. This is theoretically no longer the case because the Restrictive Trade Practices Commission (established under the anti-combines provisions of the Combines Investigation Act) has been given power to rule against such interference in Canadian affairs.

Civil Damages

A new and important provision gives persons the right to recover damages incurred as a result of a violation by others. This has profound implications. In some jurisdictions, not only can an individual sue for damages, but if the person wins, that judgment will apparently serve as evidence for anyone else who has experienced a similar loss. Would this mean that a company could face the possibility of virtually every purchaser of a product claiming damages? Consider the millions of dollars involved for an automobile manufacturer, for example. To our knowledge, there have been no such cases in Canada.

Regulation, Regulation,
and . . . More
Regulation

So far, only some of the provisions from the most important federal Act have been cited. Figure 2-3 shows that the federal government has a virtual sea of regulations that marketers must be aware of. Provincial governments are also very active in this area. Fortunately, each marketer need not be aware of all provisions, for many are specific to situation, time, place, and products.

In addition, provincial and municipal governments have other laws that must be considered when developing marketing plans. For example, regulations vary from province to province concerning the amount and nature of advertising directed at children. Some other significant laws or regulations relate to bilingual specifications for packaging and labelling; there are special language requirements in Quebec.

From a broad point of view, the legal framework for relations between business and consumers is designed to encourage a competitive marketing system employing fair business practices. In many respects the action taken by the federal government in 1967 has resulted in more effective competition, although there are many who feel business is over-regulated and others who think that more regulations are needed. There is little doubt that consumers in Canada are protected as well as or better than consumers in any other country in their dealings with sellers, especially regarding truth in advertising. The total number of files opened on cases of misleading advertising was 15 in 1967, when Consumer and Corporate Affairs Canada was formed; it rose to 9782 in 1981–82. While many of these files came to naught, 2319 investigations were conducted, resulting in 95 convictions. Prosecutions for noncompetitive activities (excluding advertising and deceptive marketing practices) have risen from an average of five a year to close to 24 a year. These are more complex cases such as conspiracy, merger and monopoly, and resale price maintenance.[7]

What marketing's legal future will be is of course open to debate, as is the question of whether business is overregulated. However, federal and provincial laws requiring truth and high standards in dealings between consumers and sellers are not likely to be changed, nor do federal efforts to maintain a competitive environment appear to be lessening. Deregulation of airline services is evidence of this latter point.

The Economic Environment

In addition to the competitive and political and legal environments, marketers must understand the economic environment and its impact upon their organizations. Three economic subjects of major concern to marketers in recent years have been recession, unemployment, and inflation.

Clearly, in a deteriorating economic environment many firms experience a decline. However, it is good news for some companies. As inflation and unemployment go up and production declines, consumer buying patterns shift. Flour millers note that flour sales go up. Automobile repairs and home improvements also increase. Greeting card firms report that consumers buy fewer gifts, but more expensive cards. Hardware stores show higher sales. The economic environment will considerably affect the way marketers operate.

Stages of the Business Cycle

The **economic environment** is *a complex setting operating within which are dynamic business fluctuations that tend to follow a cyclical pattern* composed of four stages:

1. recession (sometimes involves such factors as inflation and unemployment)
2. depression
3. recovery
4. prosperity

No marketer can disregard the economic climate in which a business functions, for the type, direction, and intensity of a firm's marketing strategy depends upon it. In addition, the marketer must be aware of the economy's relative position in the business cycle and how it will affect the position of the particular firm. This requires the marketer to study forecasts of future economic activity.

Of necessity, marketing activity differs with each stage of the business cycle. During prosperous times, consumers are usually more willing to buy than when they feel economically threatened. For example, during the recent recession, personal savings climbed to high levels as consumers (fearing possible layoffs and other workforce reductions) cut back their expenditures for many products they considered nonessential. Marketers must pay close attention to the consumer's relative willingness to buy. The aggressiveness of one's marketing strategy and tactics is often dependent upon current buying intentions. More aggressive marketing may be called for in periods of lessened buying interest, as when automakers use cash rebate schemes to move inventories. Such activities, however, are unlikely to fully counteract cyclical periods of low demand.

While sales figures may experience cyclical variations, the successful firm has a rising sales trend line. This depends upon management's ability to foresee, correctly define, and reach new market opportunities. Effective forecasting and research is only a partial solution. Marketers must also develop an intuitive awareness of potential markets. This requires that one be able to correctly delineate opportunities.

Inflation   Another economic factor that critically influences marketing strategy is **inflation**, which can occur during any stage in the business cycle. Inflation is *a rising price level resulting in reduced purchasing power for the consumer*. A person's money is devalued (in terms of what it can buy). Traditionally, this circumstance has been more prevalent in countries outside of North America. However, in the late 1970s and early 1980s Canada experienced "double digit inflation" (an inflation rate of over 10 percent a year). Although the rate of inflation has declined considerably during the mid-1980s, the recent experiences led to widespread concern over political approaches to controlling interest rates and stabilizing price levels, and over ways in which the individual can adjust to such reductions in the spending power of the dollar.

Stagflation is a word that has been coined to describe a peculiar brand of inflation that characterized some of the recent Canadian economic experience. It is a situation where an economy has *high unemployment and a rising price level at the same time*. Formulation of effective strategies is particularly difficult under these circumstances.

Unemployment   Another significant economic problem that has affected the marketing environment in recent years is unemployment. The ranks of the
unemployed — officially defined as people actively looking for work
who do not have jobs — swelled to 12.4 percent of the Canadian
labour force by January 1984. By contrast the unemployment rate
was 5.9 percent in January 1965.

In the severe recession of the early 1980s, numerous businesses
failed, production slowed, many factories ceased operation entirely,
and thousands of workers found themselves out of work. The consequences of reduced income and uncertainty about future income
were reflected in the marketplace in many ways.

Government Tools for   The government can attempt to deal with the twin economic prob-
Combatting Inflation   lems of inflation and unemployment by using two basic approaches:
and Unemployment   fiscal policy and monetary policy. **Fiscal policy** concerns *the receipts
and expenditures of government.* To combat inflation, an economy
could reduce government expenditures, raise its revenue (primarily
taxes), or do a combination of both. It could also use direct controls such as wage and price controls. **Monetary policy** refers to *the
manipulation of the money supply and market rates of interest.* In
periods of rising prices monetary policy may dictate that the government take actions to decrease the money supply and raise interest
rates, thus restraining purchasing power.

Both fiscal and monetary policy have been used in our battles
against inflation and unemployment. Their marketing implications
are numerous and varied. Higher taxes mean less consumer purchasing power, which usually results in sales declines for nonessential goods and services. However, some taxes which have been
collected may find their way into various job-creation programs.
Income earned from these will tend to be spent on basic goods and
services. Lower federal expenditure levels make the government a
less attractive customer for many industries. A lowered money supply means less liquidity is available for potential conversion to purchasing power. High interest rates often lead to a significant slump
in the construction and housing industry.

Both unemployment and inflation affect marketing by modifying consumer behaviour. Unless unemployment insurance, personal
savings, and union supplementary unemployment benefits are sufficient to offset lost earnings, the unemployed individual has less
income to spend in the marketplace. Even if the individual is
completely compensated for lost earnings, his or her buying
behaviour is likely to be affected. As consumers become more
conscious of inflation, they are likely to become more price conscious
in general. This can lead to three possible outcomes, all important
to marketers. Consumers can (1) elect to buy now in the belief that

prices will be higher later (automobile dealers often use this argument in their commercial messages); (2) decide to alter their purchasing patterns; or (3) postpone certain purchases.

The Technological Environment

The **technological environment** consists of *the applications to marketing of knowledge based upon scientific discoveries, inventions, and innovations.* It results in new products for consumers and improves existing products. It is a frequent source of price reduc tions through the development of new production methods or new materials. It also can make existing products obsolete virtually overnight—as slide rule manufacturers would attest. Technological innovations are exemplified in the container industry, where glass and tinplate containers have faced intense competition from such innovations as aluminum, fiberfoil, and plastics.

Marketing decision makers must closely monitor the technological environment for a number of reasons. New technology may be the means by which they remain competitive in their industries. It may also be the vehicle for the creation of entirely new industries. For example, the development of the microchip and lasers has resulted in the development of major industries during the past 25 years.

In the case of high technology products such as computers and related items, marketers face real challenges in keeping up with the pace of change. They not only have to maintain an understanding of the industry, but must somehow try to communicate totally new concepts and ways of solving problems to potential customers. As Francis McInerney, president of Northern Business Information says, "The time it takes to explain a product may be longer than the time it takes to introduce a whole new generation of products."[8]

In addition, marketers must anticipate the effect such technological innovations are likely to have upon the lifestyles of consumers, the products of competitors, the demands of industrial users, and the regulatory actions of government. The advent of videocassette recorders, videodiscs, and lower cost satellite receiving stations may adversely affect concert attendance and movie ticket sales. A longer lasting engine may reduce industrial purchases. A new process may result in reduction of pollution and produce changes in local ordinances.

A major source of technological innovations has been the space program. Hundreds of industrial applications of space technology have been made, and private enterprise has been encouraged to make use of these innovations. Figure 2-5 reveals some applications, not all of them obvious, that have already been implemented.

Figure 2-5 Technological Spinoffs from the Space Program

Orbiting satellites that can monitor the earth and provide valuable data on crops, weather, and earthquakes.

Carbon fibers used in jet aircraft, golf clubs, and tennis rackets. They are lighter than steel, but they are stronger and stiffer.

Advances in health and medical areas, such as improved splints for broken limbs and more effective cancer detection devices.

New alloys used in tools, kitchenware, and household appliances.

Trajectory and moon landing analyses have resulted in a fully computerized auto traffic control system for at least one city. The system calculates the best traffic light sequence during rush hour traffic. Mobility has been increased by 15 percent during tests, resulting in gas consumption savings and reduced air pollution.

Wind deflectors for trucks have been developed to reduce wind resistance by 24 percent, resulting in a 10 percent fuel savings.

Life rafts equipped with radar reflective canopies greatly increase their visibility from the air.

Orbiting satellites have been responsible for the virtual elimination of the screwworm. The worm destroys cattle, poultry, and wildlife.

Land surveying satellites can spot 99 percent of the fresh water sources currently not being used.

Aluminized plastic used to keep fluids cold in space programs is used in lightweight jackets, sleeping bags, and parkas.

Silicone plastic from airplane seats has been used in football helmet liners.

A computer image process used to enhance satellite photos can indicate missing chromosomes in fetuses, thus identifying possible inherited diseases before the infant is born.

Source: Richard T. Hise, Peter L. Gillett, and John K. Ryans, Jr., *Basic Marketing* (Boston, Mass.: Little, Brown & Co., 1979), p. 121. Reprinted by permission.

Demarketing—Dealing with Shortages

Shortages — temporary or permanent — can be caused by several factors. A brisk demand may exceed manufacturing capacity or outpace the response time required to gear up a production line. Shortages may also be caused by a lack of raw materials, component parts, energy, or labour. Regardless of the cause, shortages require marketers to reorient their thinking.

Demarketing, a term that has come into general use in recent years, refers to the process of *cutting consumer demand for a product back to a level that can reasonably be supplied by the firm.* Some oil companies, for example, have publicized tips on how to cut gasoline consumption during the recent problems with energy. Utility companies have encouraged homeowners to install more insulation to lower heating bills. And many cities have discouraged central business district traffic by raising parking fees and violation penalties.

Shortages sometimes force marketers to be allocators of limited supplies. This is in sharp contrast to marketing's traditional objective of expanding sales volume. Shortages require marketers to decide whether to spread a limited supply over all customers so that none are satisfied, or to back-order some customers so that others may be completely supplied. Shortages certainly present marketers with a unique set of marketing problems.

The Social Environment

The Chevalline Meat Company knows that the social environment works against them. When you try to get someone to eat somebody's pony, you've got trouble. Chevalline is trying to induce Canadians to eat more horsemeat, despite a social environment that views horses as pets and companions, not livestock for slaughter. Canadians consume virtually no horsemeat, although in France and other European countries the meat is highly thought of.

Chevalline even had some difficulty obtaining a licence to open a horsemeat market. The company wishes to sell to Canadians, rather than rely on overseas markets for its customers. Whether the firm will ever change Canadian opinion is a moot question. But its problems dramatize the importance of understanding and assessing the social environment when making marketing decisions.

The socio-cultural environment is *the marketer's relationship with the society and culture in which the company operates.* Obviously, there are many different facets of significance. One important category is the general readiness of society to accept a marketing idea, as discussed above.

Another important category is the trust and confidence of the public in business as a whole. Such relationships have been on the decline since the mid-1960s. Opinion polls suggest that people have lost confidence in major companies (although they maintain faith in the private enterprise system). These declines should, however, be viewed in perspective. All institutions have lost public confidence to some degree. In fact, some would argue that governments and labour unions are even less popular than business.

The socio-cultural environment for marketing decisions has both expanded in scope and increased in importance. Today no marketer can initiate a strategy without taking the social environment into account. Marketers must develop an awareness of the manner in which it affects their decisions.[9] The constant flux of social issues requires that marketing managers place more emphasis on solving these questions instead of merely concerning themselves with the standard marketing tools.[10] Some firms have created a new position — manager of public policy research — to study the changing social environment's future impact on the company.

One question facing contemporary marketing is how to measure the accomplishment of socially oriented objectives. A firm that is attuned to its social environment must develop new ways of evaluating its performance. Traditional income statements and balance sheets are no longer adequate. This issue will be further developed in a later chapter as one of the most important problems facing contemporary marketing.

Importance in International Marketing Decisions

The societal context for marketing decision-making is often more crucial in the international sphere than in the domestic. Marketers must be cognizant of social differences in the way that business affairs are conducted abroad. Consider the following case:

> The stereotype of the North American male — hail-fellow-well-met, cordial, friendly, outgoing and gregarious — does not mesh with the discomfort he feels and often shows in his contacts with Latin Americans and Middle Easterners. These people crowd close to him to talk, and in Latin America his host is likely to greet him with a warm *abrazo*, suggesting unfamiliar intimacy. Anyone who has ever attended a party or a reception in Latin America must surely have observed the self-consciousness of the uninitiated . . . visitor, who keeps backing away from his native host, to whom it is natural to carry on a conversation separated by inches. Last year at a businessman's club in Brazil, where many receptions are held for newly arrived executives, the railings on the terrace had to be reinforced because so many businessmen fell into the garden as they backed away.[11]

Consumer behaviour and tastes also differ from place to place, as is suggested by these situations.[12]

1. In Thailand Helene Curtis sells black shampoo because Thai women feel it makes their hair look glossier.
2. Nestlé, a Swiss multinational company, now brews more than 40 varieties of instant coffee to satisfy different national tastes.
3. General Foods Corp. entered the British market with its standard powdered Jell-O only to find that British cooks prefer the solid-wafer or cake form, even if it takes more time to prepare. After several frustrating years, the company gave up and pulled out of the market.
4. In Italy a United States company that set up a corn-processing plant found that its marketing effort failed because Italians think of corn as "pig food."

Many marketers recognize societal differences between countries, but assume that a homogeneous social environment exists domestically. Nothing could be farther from the truth! Canada is a mixed society composed of varied submarkets. These submarkets can be classified by age, place of residence, sex, ethnic background, and numerous other determinants.

For example, the Quebec market segment has historically been ignored by too many firms. In recent years, however, Quebec has been recognized as a distinct market within itself. The culture and values of this market require more careful treatment than merely translating English into French.

Sex is another increasingly important social factor. The feminist movement has had a decided effect on marketing, particularly promotion. Television commercials now feature women in less stereotyped roles than in previous years.

Since social variables change constantly, marketers must continually monitor their dynamic environment. What appears to be out-of-bounds today may be tomorrow's greatest market opportunity. Consider the way that previously taboo subjects such as feminine hygiene products are now commonly advertised.

The social variables must be recognized by modern business executives since they affect the way consumers react to different products and marketing practices. One of the most tragic — and avoidable — of all marketing mistakes is the failure to appreciate social differences within our own domestic market.

The rise of consumerism can be partially traced to the growing public concern with making business more responsible to its constituents. Consumerism, which is discussed in detail in a later chapter, is an evolving aspect of marketing's social environment. Certainly the advent of this movement has influenced the move toward more direct protection of consumer rights in such areas as product safety and false and misleading advertising. These concerns will undoubtedly be amplified and expanded in the years ahead.

Role of the Marketing Manager

As a conclusion to this look at the marketing environment, Figure 2-6 illustrates how the marketing manager works, controlling marketing elements in relation to the forces bearing on a firm's marketing mix. In light of the opportunities and constraints perceived in the environmental framework, as well as the objectives and resources of the firm, the manager develops a marketing program (marketing strategy). The elements or tools of the marketing strategy are product, pricing, distribution, and promotion strategies. These are blended together in a unique manner to make up the marketing mix. The result wins customers, sales, and profits for the firm.

Figure 2-6   The Marketing Manager Controls Marketing Elements

While this concept is simple in itself, it is extremely complicated in practice and difficult to do well. The rest of this text will elaborate on the process. The next chapters start with marketing planning and discuss some important basic concepts that must be considered.

Summary

A consideration of several environmental variables is of paramount importance in making marketing decisions. Five specific environments should be considered: competitive, political and legal, economic, technological, and social and cultural. These are important to the study of marketing because they provide the framework within which marketing strategies are formulated. Environmental factors are among the most dynamic aspects of contemporary business.

The competitive environment is the interactive process that occurs in the marketplace. Marketing decisions influence the market and are, in turn, affected by the counterstrategies of competition. The legal segment attempts to maintain a competitive environment as well as regulate specific marketing practices. The economic environment often influences the manner in which consumers will behave toward varying marketing appeals. Socio-cultural aspects, however, may become the most important to marketers. The matter of adapting to a changing social environment, both domestically and internationally, has advanced to the forefront of marketing thought.

2 2 2 2 2 2 2

2 2 2 2 2 2 2

2 2 2 2 2 2 2

2 2 2 2 2 2 2

2 2 2 2 2 2 2

2 2 2 2 2 2 2

2 2 2 2 2 2 2

2 2 2 2 2 2 2

2 2 2 2 2 2 2

PART

2

Planning The Marketing Effort

CHAPTER 3

Marketing Planning and Forecasting

CHAPTER 4

Market Segmentation

CHAPTER 5

Market Segmentation Strategies

CHAPTER 6

Marketing Research and Information Systems

The focus on the four chapters in Part Two is planning—anticipating the future and determining the courses of action designed to achieve organizational objectives. The chapters treat such vital subjects as development of marketing strategies, sales forecasting, use of market segmentation in selecting market targets, and provision of needed, decision-relevant marketing information. This part provides a foundation for the development of appropriate marketing programs for profitably serving chosen market segments.

CHAPTER 3

Marketing Planning and Forecasting

1. *To distinguish between strategic planning and tactical planning.*

2. *To explain how marketing planning differs at different levels of the organization.*

3. *To identify the steps in the marketing planning process.*

4. *To explain the portfolio and the BCG growth-market matrix approaches to marketing planning.*

5. *To identify the alternative marketing strategies available to marketers.*

6. *To identify the major types of forecasting methods.*

7. *To explain the steps involved in the forecasting process.*

Rex Faithfull and Herman Herbst had a plan to break into the electric kettle market. However, given the tough competition from Canadian General Electric, Sunbeam, and others, many businesspeople would not have given them much of a chance. Careful marketing planning and aggressive marketing implementation resulted in their company, Creative Appliance Corp., growing from nothing to 24 percent of the Canadian market in four years. Today, the company is the largest manufacturer of kettles in Canada next to Canadian General Electric.

The Creative story started when industrial consultant Faithfull teamed up with Herbst, the former owner of a tool-and-die metal stamping business. Their new company began by turning out metal parts for small appliances. This put them in an ideal position to take advantage of a strategic window that soon appeared in the electric kettle market. In 1975 Consumer and Corporate Affairs Canada declared that kettles using lead solder were a health hazard and these kettles, most at the low end of the price range, were withdrawn from the Canadian market.

Faithfull and Herbst believed that they could design their own kettle, and make it better and cheaper. They felt this was an opportunity waiting for a marketing strategy. They decided to deal with large retailers directly, rather than marketing their product through middlemen.

Herbst designed a kettle using silver solder and an innovative plastic upper section. The plastic looked nice, and the design cost less than the traditional steel. This allowed the kettle to retail initially at what one competitor calls "the magic price-point of $9.99."

The partners took a wooden model of their proposed kettle to Canadian Tire and Woolco and got orders for more than 50 000 units. Tooling up for production cost $100 000, and as the company had sales of only $800 000 a year at the time, the partners went on what Faithfull calls "minimum wage." They put all the money they had or could borrow — mainly from the Federal Business Development Bank — into preparing steel dies and getting production established in order to fill the orders. In that first year they sold more than 100 000 units to Woolco, Canadian Tire, Zellers, and Towers stores.

In 1980 they added a second kettle to the product line. The first export order of this "international" model was shipped to Trinidad in 1981. Faithfull predicted the company's total export sales in 1983 to France, Trinidad, Jamaica, South Africa, Chile, Japan, Hong Kong, the United States, and Britain would be worth at least $800 000.

Creative's marketing and production have obviously been very successful. The biggest problem has been the generation of sufficient funds to finance their successful marketing venture. Rex Faithfull and Herman Herbst have found that sound marketing planning pays off![1]

The Conceptual Framework

"Should we grant a licence for our new liquid-crystal display watch to a Japanese firm or simply export our models to Japan?"

"Will changing the performance time and date affect concert attendance?"

"Should we use company sales personnel or independent agents in the new territory?"

"Should discounts be offered to cash customers? What impact would such a policy have on our credit customers?"

These questions are examples of thousands of both major and minor decisions that regularly face the marketing manager. Continual changes in the marketplace resulting from changing consumer expectations, competitive actions, economic trends, political and legal changes, as well as developments in such areas as product innovations or pressures from distribution channel members, are likely to have substantial impact on the operations of any organization. Although such changes are often beyond the control of the marketing manager, effective planning can prepare the manager by anticipating many changes and focusing upon possible actions to take should such changes occur. Effective planning is often a major factor in the difference between success and failure. Figure 3-1 summarizes the major benefits of planning for an organization.

Planning is *the process of anticipating the future and determining the courses of action to achieve organizational objectives.* In other words, planning is a continuous process that includes the specification of objectives and the actions required to achieve them. The planning process results in the creation of a blueprint that not only specifies the means of achieving organizational objectives but also includes checkpoints where actual performance can be compared with expectations in order to determine whether the organizational activities are moving the organization in the direction of its objectives. Such checkpoints are important means of *control.*

Marketing planning — *the implementation of planning activities as they relate to the achievement of marketing objectives* — is the basis for all marketing strategies. Product lines, pricing decisions, selection of appropriate distribution channels, and decisions relating to promotional campaigns all depend upon the plans that are formulated within the marketing organization.

Strategic Planning vs. Tactical Planning

Planning is often classified on the basis of scope or breadth. Some plans are quite broad and long-range, focusing on major organizational objectives with major impact on the organization for a period of five or more years. Such plans are typically called strategic plans. **Strategic planning** can be defined as *the process of determining the primary objectives of an organization, and the adoption of courses of action and the allocation of resources necessary to achieve those objectives.*[2]

The word *strategy* is derived from a Greek term meaning "the general's art." Strategic planning has a critical impact on the destiny of the organization since it provides long-run direction for decision-makers. At K-Mart, the strategic plan calls for marketers to use low prices on commodity type items to attract customers who may also buy merchandise with higher margins.

By contrast, **tactical planning** focuses on *the implementation of those activities specified by the strategic plans.* Tactical plans typically have a shorter term than strategic plans, focusing more on current and near-term activities that must be executed in order to implement overall strategies. Resource allocation is a common decision area for tactical planning. The decision by a car-rental firm to counter special offers by a competitor would be the result of tactical planning.

Figure 3-1   What Planning Can Accomplish for a Firm

1. It leads to a better position or standing for the organization.
2. It helps the organization progress in the ways that its management considers most suitable.
3. It helps every manager think, decide, and act more effectively for progress in the desired direction.
4. It helps keep the organization flexible.
5. It stimulates a co-operative, integrated, enthusiastic approach to organizational problems.
6. It indicates to management how to evaluate and check up on progress toward the planned objectives.
7. It leads to socially and economically useful results.

Source: Subhash, C. Jain, *Marketing Planning and Strategy* (Cincinnati: Southwestern Publishing Co., 1981), p. 5.

Planning at Different Levels in the Organization

Planning is a major responsibility for every manager. Although managers at all levels within an organization devote some of their workdays to planning, the relative proportion of time spent in planning activities and the types of planning vary at different organization levels.

Top management of a corporation — the board of directors, president, and functional vice-presidents such as the chief marketing officer — spend greater proportions of their time engaged in planning than do middle- and supervisory-level managers. In fact, one company president recommends that 30 to 50 percent of a chief executive's time should be spent on strategic planning.[3] Also, top management are more likely to devote more of their planning activities to longer-range strategic planning, while middle-level managers (such as the director of the advertising department, regional sales managers, or the physical distribution manager) tend to focus on narrower, tactical plans for their departments, and supervisory management are more likely to engage in developing specific programs designed to meet the goals for their responsibility areas. Figure 3-2 indicates the types of planning engaged in at the various organizational levels.

Steps in the Planning Process

As Figure 3-3 indicates, the *objectives* of the organization are the starting point for marketing planning. These basic goals of the organization are the guideposts from which marketing objectives and plans are derived. They provide direction for all phases of the organization and serve as standards in evaluating performance. For Nike,

Figure 3-2   Types of Plans Prepared by Different Levels of Management

Management Level	Type of Plan	General Content
Top board of directors, president, operating division vice-presidents including marketing	strategic planning	objectives of organization; fundamental strategies; total budget
Middle general sales manager, marketing research director, head of advertising department	tactical planning	quarterly and semi-annual plans; subdivision of budgets; policies and procedures for each individual's department
Supervisory district sales manager, supervisors	tactical planning derived from planning at higher organization levels	daily and weekly plans; unit budgets

Source: Adapted from William F. Glueck, *Management* (Hinsdale, Ill.: Dryden Press, 1980), p. 246. Copyright 1980 by Dryden Press, a division of Holt, Rinehart and Winston. Adapted by permission of Holt, Rinehart and Winston.

Inc., the overall objective is to be the leading firm in the quality athletic-shoe market. Nike's marketing plans — both strategic and tactical — are based on this objective.

Marketing *opportunities* arise from a number of circumstances. The dramatic increase in prices for oil and natural gas has given rise to new ventures such as firms which specialize in finding air leaks in your home so that you can reinsulate it. Other companies are marketing solar heating products or are developing a new breed of windmills for many different energy applications. Opportunities often arise from improved technology, for example, the digital record industry.

The *environmental forces* described in Chapter 2 — competitive, political and legal, economic, technological, and social and cultural — are forces which affect marketing opportunities. For instance, environmental factors have decreased the market for afternoon papers. Such papers, frequently called PMs, were very popular when people went to work in the predawn hours and returned home sometime in the afternoon. The PM environment has changed in recent times. The white-collar labour force now reports for work at 9 a.m. rather than 6 a.m. Approximately 60 percent of all married women now work, so that families are more likely to shop during the evening hours, when they used to read PMs. Furthermore,

Figure 3-3   Steps in the Marketing Planning Process

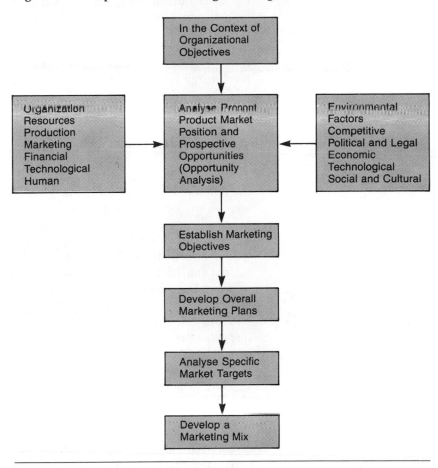

television is rapidly becoming the most popular source of news. The PMs are attempting to counter this trend by improving their suburban, entertainment, and special-interest sections. Some are even beginning to offer morning editions.

Another major influence on a firm's decision to take advantage of marketing opportunities is the *resources of the organization*. Resources include marketing strengths, production strengths, financial position, research and development capability, and quality of management. When Bic, a French manufacturer of inexpensive ballpoint pens, decided to enter the North American market, it recognized the problems caused by its lack of an effective distribution system. Its decision was to purchase Waterman, a firm that manufactured and marketed refillable fountain pens. Although Bic discontinued the Waterman pen line four years later, it had acquired the distribution system it previously lacked.

Marketing *objectives* and *plans* result from overall organizational objectives and marketing opportunity analysis. The environmental factors have different impacts upon the organization at different times. Derek Abell has suggested the term **strategic window** to define *the limited periods during which the key requirements of a market and the particular competencies of a firm best fit together.*[4] Pontiac's decision to develop and market the Fiero in 1983, the first sports car built in North America for more than two decades, was in response to its marketers' decision that organizational and environmental factors resulted in a strategic window.

General Electric has made a number of major contributions to the concept of strategic planning. In 1970, General Electric underwent a major reorganization by separating planning- and policy-oriented activity from administration. GE is now regarded as having outstanding long-range planning functions. Often labelled the world's most diversified company, the following year GE decided to reorganize its nine product groups and 48 divisions into a portfolio of businesses called **strategic business units** (SBUs). For instance, responsibility for various GE food preparation appliances had been scattered through three separate divisions; they were merged into a housewares SBU. The GE reorganization forced the firm's personnel to focus on customer needs, rather than on internal divisions.

The SBU concept of *related product groupings within a multi-product firm* was quickly adopted by such major firms as Union Carbide and International Paper. Although such early experimenters as General Foods have already returned to traditional organizational structure, the SBU concept is utilized currently in about 20 percent of the largest manufacturing corporations.[5]

The Portfolio Approach to Marketing Planning

Portfolio analysis is a very useful tool in developing marketing plans. The criteria used can provide valuable insights into the effects of past planning and the needs for future decisions. Portfolio analysis across the entire range of products or product lines helps to assure that no marketing plan will be based solely on the merits of an individual item considered in isolation from others. Instead, the key elements of any marketing plan are likely to be pre-positioned within the portfolio framework of management's deliberations on how best to allocate resources between all of its product offerings.[6]

The BCG Matrix

The work of the Boston Consulting Group (BCG) is widely known in industry. BCG has developed a four-quadrant matrix, shown in

Figure 3-4, that is useful in understanding the strategic planning-marketing strategy interface. The **BCG growth-share matrix** *plots market share*, the percentage of a market controlled by a firm, *against market growth potential*. All of a firm's various businesses can be plotted in one of the four quadrants. The resulting quadrants are labeled cash cows, stars, dogs, and question marks, and each one has a unique marketing strategy. Marketers employ varying strategies for each category of business.

Cash Cows (dominant market share in a market with low growth): Cash cows are the main source of earnings and cash to support growth areas. Marketing planners want to maintain this situation for as long as possible since it produces a strong cash flow. The objective is to maximize cash flow while maintaining market share.

Stars (dominant market share in a market with high growth): While this type of business produces profits, it requires heavy cash consumption in order to maintain a leading market position. If this share can be maintained until growth of the market slows, stars may become high dollar earners. In the meantime stars may even produce a negative cash flow. Such products require considerable management attention.

Dogs (small market share in a market with low growth): This type of business generally consumes far more than an equitable

Figure 3-4   A Matrix for Marketing Planning

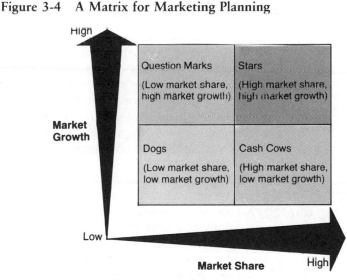

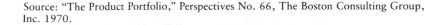

Source: "The Product Portfolio," Perspectives No. 66, The Boston Consulting Group, Inc. 1970.

amount of management attention. Usually, the company should minimize its position in this market area, pulling investment from it and withdrawing completely if possible.

Question Marks (small market share in a market with high growth): Question mark enterprises must achieve a dominant position before growth slows, or they will be frozen in a marginal position and become dogs. Because they demand a heavy commitment from limited financial and management resources, their number in the portfolio should be restricted. These situations require that marketers make a basic go/no go decision. Unless question marks can be converted to stars the firm should pull out of these markets.[7]

The BCG matrix highlights the importance of creating a mix that positions the firm to its best advantage. A portfolio approach to the setting of business strategies has won a growing number of adherents during recent years. Numerous variations of this basic approach are now in use. The BCG matrix highlights the importance of creating a mix that positions the firm to best advantage. It is largely the result of the BCG's pioneering work with the experience curve first identified in 1966. The **experience curve** indicates that the highest market-share competitor will have a cost advantage over others. BCG reports that higher market shares reduce costs because of factors like learning advantages, increased specialization, higher investment, and economies of scale. Doubling the experience factor can cut product costs by 25 to 30 percent. The consultants suggest that market share is a better measure of performance than profitability.

Critics of the BCG approach often point to the tendencies of some marketers to apply it in a largely mechanistic manner. In an attempt to develop a product line of stars, marketers may ignore possible methods of converting products and services labelled as dogs. Critics also suggest that the firm with no stars may successfully find means of expanding market and sales opportunities of an existing product regardless of the label attached to it. The advantages of following the matrix approach must be balanced against the potential shortcomings by each organization.[8]

The Strategic Planning/ Marketing Strategy Interface

The net result of strategic planning is marketing planning designed to achieve corporate objectives. This transaction requires that marketing planning efforts be directed toward the establishment of marketing strategies that are resource-efficient, flexible, and adaptable. **Marketing strategy** describes *the overall company program for selecting a particular market segment and then satisfying the consumers in that segment through careful use of the elements of the marketing mix.* Planning is an integral part of marketing strategy formulation and is the basis of effective strategy.

**Need for a Compre-
hensive Marketing
Program**

A productive marketing strategy requires that all aspects of the marketing mix be considered. The components of an overall marketing strategy are product planning, pricing, distribution, and promotion. An advertising strategy by itself is not a marketing strategy. Marketing mix components are subsets of the overall marketing strategy.

A strategy may emphasize one mix component more than others. For example, a discount store may depend primarily on its pricing strategy, but it must also maintain adequate product selection and efficient distribution and promotion. One industrial goods manufacturer may emphasize its advanced product technology, while a competitor may stress its superior field sales force. But neither can totally neglect the other elements of marketing strategy.

Marketers must also be prepared to alter their strategy. When S. C. Johnson introduced Pledge, the first aerosol furniture polish, most competitors felt certain that it would fail because its quality was believed lower than some competitive products, including Johnson's own Old English brand. But Pledge proved a major sales success when Johnson carefully positioned it as an easy-to-use dusting product rather than a furniture polish. Johnson succeeded because it adapted its marketing strategy with the "waxed beauty instantly as you dust" advertising theme.[9]

**Alternative Marketing
Strategies**

An essential first step in the marketing management decision process is an assessment of the marketing strategy positions already taken by the company, and an assessment of the new situations into which it might move. A firm entering a new market with a new product or service faces a substantially different marketing challenge than one operating in an existing market with a line of established products.

A number of alternative strategies are available for the marketing manager. The selection of any given strategy is based upon market and product factors, competition, and other environmental influences. In large, multiproduct firms, more than one strategy may be used for different products and services. The five alternative marketing strategies are: (1) balancing strategy, (2) market retention strategy, (3) market development strategy, (4) growth strategy, and (5) new venture strategy.[10] Examples of businesses employing the five strategy positions are given in Figure 3-5.

Balancing Strategy

A balancing strategy is used for mature products in established markets where the competition is well known. The strategy here is for the company to balance revenues and costs in order to generate profits. The emphasis for management is control rather than

---

Figure 3-5   The Five Alternative Strategy Positions Put to Use

Balancing Strategy
Strategy position occupied by railways, electric utilities, and various other mature industries.
Holiday Inn's provision of motel services to its existing markets.

Market Retention Strategy
Annual model changes of appliance manufacturers aimed at retaining market share.
Introduction of ribs to the Chicken Chalet food line.
Modification of styles and models by automobile manufacturers.

Market Development Strategy
Procter & Gamble's development of "Pringles" potato chips.
Efforts of public transportation firms to lure people away from use of the automobile through modification of services.
Movement of the large aluminum companies into the automobile and beverage can markets for their products.

Growth Strategy
Offering first-run movies at a fee on private TV channels in hotels and motels.
Texas Instruments' move into consumer electronic calculator markets.
Designing and marketing a low-premium $1-million umbrella personal liability insurance policy for individuals.

New-Venture Strategy
Polaroid's introduction of the original Land camera.
Xerox's pioneering development and marketing of copying equipment.
Initial publication and marketing of *Playgirl* magazine.

Source: Adapted from David W. Cravens, "Marketing Strategy Positioning," *Business Horizons* (December 1975), p. 57. Copyright © 1975 by the Foundation of the School of Business at Indiana University. Reprinted by permission.

---

planning. A broad base of knowledge and experience about familiar markets and products exists, and the focus of environmental analysis is on monitoring external influences to identify possible opportunities and threats. Only modest changes are normally made to marketing programs.

Market Retention Strategy   Market retention is probably the most typical strategy followed by established firms. It is based on the desire to improve corporate performance. Such a strategy relies on product modifications and adaptations and/or expansion of current markets. It is the next step beyond a balancing strategy.

**Market Development
Strategy**

Pursuit of a market development strategy may extend an enterprise beyond existing market-product capabilities, and is likely to require realignments of resources, personnel, product lines, and organizational structure. It requires a major effort on the part of the organization. Caution is needed in undertaking such a venture.

Growth Strategy

A growth strategy is riskier than the alternatives already described. The company offers a new product or enters a new market while expanding its existing markets and adapting its products. Major new resources are needed to pursue this strategy. In this strategy position, design of the marketing program presents a major challenge to management. The growth strategy can probably not be launched from the firm's existing marketing program base. Texas Instruments' decision to move into consumer electronic calculators is an illustration of growth strategy.

New-Venture Strategy

When a firm decides to follow a new-venture strategy, it is making an effort in an entirely new area for the company. While risks are high, so are business opportunities. Competition is usually limited. The development of an effective marketing program is a difficult aspect of this strategy.

Firms often follow multiple marketing strategies. However, it is extremely useful to analyse the strategies followed because the characteristics and demands of widely separated strategies may vary significantly. Attempting to launch a growth strategy through marketing organization built around a balancing strategy is a clear mismatch of capabilities and needs. Furthermore, marketing decisions that lead an organization to try to use several strategies at once may require more resources and skills than the firm can muster. Thus, considerable insight into the marketing task can be gained by determining what a firm's marketing strategy is. Analysis of its current strategy and evaluation of possible shifts may lead to the development of a sound basis for making needed changes.

**The Importance of
Flexibility**

The need for adaptable marketing planning is evident in the abundant examples provided by a variety of industries and firms. Toyota's management recognizes the challenge faced by the company in the North American market. The highly profitable Japanese firm knows that several factors are working against further increases in automobile imports to North America. Slower sales have led North American firms to offer small cars to compete with the Japanese compacts. And the rising value of the yen relative to the Canadian dollar forced Toyota to raise its retail price by more than 20 percent in a recent year.

What has Toyota done to counter the possibility of a slowdown in new car sales? It has begun to produce and market prefabricated houses and commercial buildings through its strong domestic dealer network. Although the new products represent a very small percentage of total sales, the move into a completely different industry illustrates Toyota's marketing planning adaptability.[11]

When a Kentucky Fried Chicken franchise opened in Harlan, Kentucky (population 3300), some customers waited in line 1½ hours to purchase their chicken. Over a ton of fried chicken was sold on the opening day despite the fact that the store did no advertising. Kentucky Fried Chicken's move to a community of 3300 people illustrates a dramatic change taking place in fast-food franchising. KFC Corporation once preferred *not* to operate in areas of under 35 000 population. Now, 890 of its 4000 units are located in towns with fewer than 10 000 residents.

Other fast-food franchisers are also revamping their distribution plans. Pizza Hut is considering areas of under 4000 population, and Burger King has plans for reduced-size units for smaller towns. These fast-food franchisers have found that smaller communities sometimes offer less competition than do larger areas. The franchise operators can benefit from changed consumer preferences and national advertising. The move to smaller towns illustrates how fast-food franchisers have modified their marketing planning to cope with the modern business environment.

Potential Influences on Marketing Planning

Various factors will influence marketing planning in the future. Some current trends will likely accelerate in the years ahead and will play a critical role in new marketing strategies. Other anticipated changes will take some factors out of marketing decision-making. Many potential influences cluster around a few basic areas: structural changes in the marketing system, public and legal pressures, market changes, and technological changes. Environmental forecasting is an integral component of good strategic marketing planning.

Structural Changes

Some structural changes in the marketing system have had a pronounced effect on marketing decisions. The franchise system has altered concepts of small-business ownership. Collective marketing organizations such as OPEC have certainly influenced the world markets for their products, as have Common Market trade practices, restricting access to historical sales outlets for Canadian exports. Executives must constantly evaluate the changes taking place in the marketing system. Even slight and gradual changes can have a profound effect on sales and profits.

Public and Legal Pressures

Future marketing planning is very subject to public and legal decisions. Actions such as the deregulation of the airline industry may shake many of the basic foundations upon which marketers in that industry have always operated. Legislative controls of business practices gradually increase as all levels of government strive to fill what some critics see as loopholes in the system. There is a real need for self-regulation in marketing if restrictive legislation is to be avoided.

Market Changes

Market changes are perhaps the most obvious potential influence on strategic plans. Market potentials for various goods and services shift with changes in geographical patterns of population and income. Lifestyle preferences also influence marketing. Record inflation rates affect marketers of recreational equipment, bank services, and real estate. Often this impact is negative. Monitoring market shifts is vital to successful marketing.

Technological Changes

The goods and services that are marketed in the relatively free competitive system of Canada are affected by technological changes. Since technological shifts can make a product obsolete overnight, marketers must be assured of a constant new-product development effort. Marketing planning requires that products and services be effectively matched with consumer desires.

Change is inevitable. A permanent part of contemporary marketing, it must be dealt with constantly. Marketers know that changes in the structure of the marketing system, the public and legal framework, markets, and technology can alter the very foundation of today's marketing discipline. Successful future marketers will be those who are best able to cope with these changes.

Sales Forecasting

The basic building block of marketing planning is the **sales forecast** — *the estimate of company sales for a specified future period*. In addition to its use in marketing planning, the sales forecast also plays an instrumental role in production scheduling, financial planning, inventory planning and procurement, and in the determination of personnel needs. An inaccurate forecast will result in incorrect decisions in each of these areas. The sales forecast is also an important tool for marketing control because it produces standards against which actual performance can be measured. Without such standards, no comparisons can be made — if there exists no criterion of success, there is also no definition of failure.

Sales forecast periods vary in length. Short-run forecasts are usually for a period of up to one year, while long-run forecasts tend to look several years ahead. Since all forecasts are developed in basically the same manner, and since more firms forecast sales for the coming year, short-run forecasting will be discussed here.

Types of Forecasting Methods

Although forecasters utilize dozens of techniques of divining the future (ranging from complex computer simulations to crystal-ball gazing by professional futurists), two broad categories exist. *Quantitative* forecasting methods employ such statistical techniques as trend extensions based upon past data; computer simulation; and econometrics to produce numerical forecasts of future events. The second type, *qualitative* forecasting techniques, are more subjective in nature. They include surveys of consumer attitudes and intentions, estimates by the field sales force, predictions of key executives in the firm and in the industry. Since each method has its advantages, most organizations use both in their attempts to predict future events and to provide a range into which they expect actual performance to fall.

A survey of forecasting techniques used in 175 firms revealed that qualitative measures such as estimates by the sales force and a jury of executives are most commonly used. The techniques used on a regular basis by the respondent firms are shown in Figure 3-6.

Qualitative Forecasting Techniques[12]

Qualitative techniques include the jury of executive opinion and estimates by the sales force. Both rely upon experience and expectations. The **jury of executive opinion** method consists of *combining and averaging the forecasts of top executives from such areas as finance,*

Figure 3-6 Sales Forecasting Methods Used Regularly in 175 Firms

Method	Percentage
Jury of Executive Opinion	52%
Sales Force Composite	48%
Trend Projections	28%
Industry Survey	22%
Intention-to-Buy Survey	15%
Simulation Models	8%
Input-Output Models	6%

Source: Reported in Douglas J. Dalrymple, "Sales Forecasting Methods and Accuracy," *Business Horizons* (December 1975), p. 71.

production, marketing, and purchasing. It is particularly effective when top management is experienced and knowledgeable about situations which influence sales, open-minded concerning the future, and aware of the bases for their judgments.

The **sales force composite** is *a forecast based on the combined estimates of the firm's salespeople* on the assumption that organizational members closest to the marketplace — those with specialized product, customer, and competitor knowledge — are likely to have better insight concerning short-term future sales than any other group. This approach is a *bottom-up method* since the salespeoples' estimates are usually combined at the district level, the regional level, and the national level to obtain an aggregate forecast of sales. Few firms rely upon the sales force composite solely, however. Since salespeople recognize the role of the sales forecast in determining expected performance in their territories, they are likely to estimate conservatively. Moreover, their narrow perspectives on their limited geographic territories may prevent them from being knowledgeable about developing trends in other territories, forthcoming technological innovations, or major changes in company marketing strategies. Consequently, the sales force composite is typically combined with other forecasting techniques in developing the final forecast.

A third method of forecasting is through **surveys of buyer intentions**. *Mail questionnaires, telephone polls, or personal interviews may be used in attempting to determine the intentions of a representative group of present and potential consumers.* This technique is obviously limited to situations where customers are willing to confide their buying intentions. Moreover, customer expectations do not necessarily result in actual purchases.

Quantitative Forecasting Techniques[12]

Quantitative techniques, which make use of past data to predict future performance, attempt to eliminate the guesswork of the qualitative forecasting methods. They include such techniques as market tests, trend projections, and input-output models.

Market tests are frequently used in *assessing consumer response to new product offerings*. The procedure typically involves establishing a small number of test markets to gauge consumer responses to a new product under actual conditions. Such tests also permit evaluation of different prices, different promotional strategies, and other marketing mix variations through comparisons in different test markets. The primary advantage of market tests is the realism it provides for the marketer. On the other hand, it is an expensive and time-consuming approach that communicates marketing plans to competitors before a product is introduced to the market. Test marketing is discussed in more detail in Chapter 10.

Trend analysis involves *forecasting future sales by analysing the historical relationship between sales and time*. It is based upon the assumption that the factors which collectively determined past sales will continue to exert similar influence in the future. If historical data is available, it can be performed quickly and inexpensively.

An example will make this clear. If sales were X last year and have been increasing at Y percent for the past several years, the sales forecast for next year would be calculated as follows:

$$\text{Sales Forecast} = X + XY.$$

In actual numbers, if last year's sales totalled 280 000 units and the average sales growth rate has been 5 percent, the sales forecast would be:

$$\text{Sales Forecast} = 280\ 000 + (280\ 000 \times .05)$$
$$= 294\ 000.$$

The danger of trend analysis lies in its underlying assumption that the future is a continuation of the past. Any variations in the influences that affect sales will result in an incorrect forecast. In addition, historical data may not be readily available in some instances; in the case of new products it may not exist.

During periods of steady growth, the trend extension method of forecasting produces satisfactory results, but it implicitly assumes that the factors contributing to a certain level of output in the past will operate in the same manner in the future. When conditions change, the trend extension method often produces incorrect results. For this reason, forecasters are increasingly turning to more sophisticated techniques and more complex mathematical models.

Input-output models, *which depict the interactions of various industries in producing goods*, are being developed by the various government and private agencies. Since outputs (sales) of one industry are the inputs (purchases) of another, a change of inputs in one industry affects the outputs of other industries. Input-output models show the impact on supplier industries of changing production in a given industry and can be used to measure the impact of increasing or decreasing demand in any industry throughout the economy.

Steps in Sales Forecasting

Although sales forecasting methods vary, the most typical method begins with a forecast of general economic conditions which the marketer uses to forecast industry sales and to develop a forecast of company and product sales. This approach can be termed the *top-down method*.

**Forecasting General
Economic Conditions**

The most common measure of economic output is *gross national product* (GNP), the market value of all final products produced in a country in a given year. Trend extension is the most frequently used method of forecasting increases in GNP.

Since many federal agencies and other organizations develop regular forecasts of the GNP, a firm may choose to use their estimates. These forecasts are regularly reported in such publications as *The Financial Post* and *The Globe & Mail.*

**Developing the Industry
Sales Forecast**

Once the economic forecast has been produced, the next step is developing an industry sales forecast. Since industry sales may be related to GNP or some other measure of the national economy, a forecast may begin by measuring the degree of this relationship, then applying the trend extension method to forecast industry sales. More sophisticated techniques, such as input-output analysis or multiple regression analysis, may also be used.

**Forecasting Company
and Product Sales**

Once the industry forecast has been made, the company and product forecasts are developed. They begin with a detailed trend analysis. The firm's past and present market shares are reviewed, and product managers and regional and district sales managers are consulted to produce a sales force composite. Since an accelerated promotional budget or the introduction of new products may stimulate additional demand, the marketing plan for the coming year is also considered.

The product and company forecast must evaluate many aspects of company sales including sales of each product; future trends; sales by customer, territory, salesperson, and order size; financial arrangements; and other aspects. Once a preliminary sales forecast has been developed, it is reviewed by the sales force and by district, regional, and national sales managers.

**New Product Sales
Forecasting**

Forecasting sales for new products is an especially hazardous undertaking since no historical data is available for analysis. Companies often ask consumer panels for reactions to the products in order to assess probable purchase behaviour. They may also use test market data.

Since few products are totally new, forecasts carefully analyse the sales of competing products that may be displaced by the new entry. A new type of fishing reel, for example, will compete in an established market with other reels. This substitute method provides the forecaster with an estimate of market size and potential demand.

Summary   Planning is the process of anticipating the future and determining the courses of action to achieve company objectives, and it is the basis for all strategy decisions. Strategic planning refers to the primary objectives of the organization and the ways they will be implemented. Marketing planning is the implementation of strategic planning as it relates to the achievement of marketing objectives.

The marketing planning process is based upon the overall organizational objectives. Opportunity analysis is a continual process of assessing environmental factors and comparing them with the objectives of the organization and its resources. Marketing objectives are based upon organizational objectives and result in the development of marketing plans. Market target analysis and the development of a marketing mix to position products and services to satisfy chosen targets make up the marketing strategy of the organization.

The strategic business unit (SBU) concept and the market/growth matrix developed by the Boston Consulting Group are frequently used by marketing planners.

Effective strategic planning is now regarded as a prerequisite to survival. It is an organization-wide responsibility involving chief executive officers, heads of operating units, and corporate strategic planning personnel. Strategic planning provides a basis for marketing planning, which is then translated into the development of marketing strategies.

Five marketing strategies can be identified: (1) balancing strategy, (2) market retention strategy, and (3) market development strategy, (4) growth strategy, and (5) new venture strategy. Potential future influences on the planning/strategy interface are the marketing system itself, public and legal pressures, market changes, and technological changes.

Sales forecasting is an important component of both planning and controlling marketing programs. Forecasting techniques may be categorized as quantitative or qualitative. The most common approach to sales forecasting is to begin with a forecast of the national economy and use it to develop an industry sales forecast, which is then used to develop a company and product forecast.

Market Segmentation

1. To relate market segmentation to the marketing mix
2. To explain what is meant by a market.
3. To outline the role of market segmentation in the development of a marketing strategy.
4. To discuss the four bases for segmenting consumer markets.
5. To describe the three bases for segmenting industrial markets.

The Canadian consumer magazine industry has gone through a number of changes in the past twenty years or so. In the 1960s the market was dominated by a few mass-market magazines such as *Maclean's*, *Time*, and *Reader's Digest*. However, the position of these products in the marketplace was gradually eroded by a number of specialty magazines which concentrated on specific market groups. This "vertical specialization" enabled publishers to produce a magazine product that was specially geared for a particular interest group. Thus magazines were developed which dealt with sports, hobbies, and other interests. Publishers discovered that they could serve smaller interest groups in depth, and therefore generate loyalty, circulation, and subscription and advertising revenues.

Now there is a "specialty, broad interest" magazine which is focussed on yet another market segment. This is the city magazine. While city magazines have been around for some years, they appear to be rapidly gaining in popularity. Examples of such magazines are *Toronto Life*, *Calgary*, and *Vancouver*. These provide superior graphics, full-colour presentation, and good paper quality, as well as well-written articles. Many deal with items of interest to each particular city. Readers relate to such magazines because they provide quality, in-depth coverage of their cities. Advertisers like them because of their popularity, and the ability to reach a specific geographical and income level-market, as well as the quality of advertisements such magazines can produce.

There are a remarkable number of different market segments for consumer magazines, and a similar number of magazines which have been specifically designed to serve the needs of each of these segments. The same type of specialization has also occurred to an extensive degree in the industrial market; there is a special trade magazine for virtually every industry segment in the country. The magazine industry is thus a good example of the concept of market segmentation.

The Conceptual Framework

Although marketers may face hundreds of decisions in developing an effective plan for achieving organizational objectives, these decisions may be summarized as two fundamental tasks:

1. They must identify, evaluate, and ultimately select a market target.
2. Once the market target has been selected, they must develop and implement a marketing mix designed to satisfy the chosen target group.

These two tasks reflect the philosophy of consumer orientation in action. The choice of a market target is based on recognition of differences among consumers and organizations within a heterogeneous market. The starting point is to understand what is meant by a *market*.

What Is a Market?

A market is *people*. It is also business, nonprofit organizations, and government — local, provincial, and federal purchasing agents who buy for their "firms." But people alone do not make a market. The local dealer for foreign automobiles is unimpressed by news that 60 percent of the marketing class raise their hands in response to the question, "Who wants to buy a new XKE?" The next question is, "How many of them are waving cheques in their outstretched hands?" A **market** *requires not only people and willingness to buy, but also purchasing power and the authority to buy.*

One of the first rules that the successful salesperson learns is to determine who in the organization or household has the authority to make particular purchasing decisions. Too much time has been wasted convincing the wrong person that a product or service should be bought.

Types of Markets

Products may be classified as consumer or industrial goods. **Consumer goods** are *those products and services purchased by the ultimate consumer for personal use*. **Industrial goods** are *those products purchased to be used, either directly or indirectly, in the production of the other goods or for resale.* Most of the products you buy — books, clothes, milk — are consumer goods. Refined nickel is an industrial good for the mint; rubber is a raw material for the B.F. Goodrich Company.

Sometimes the same product is destined for different uses. The new set of tires when purchased by your neighbour are clearly consumer goods; yet when bought by Chrysler Corporation, they become part of a new Horizon and are classified as industrial goods, since they become part of another good destined for resale. The key to the proper classification of goods lies in the purchaser and *the reasons for buying the good*.

Market Segmentation   The world is too large and filled with too many diverse people and firms for any single marketing mix to satisfy everyone. Unless the product or service is an item such as an unbranded, descriptive-label detergent aimed at the mass market, an attempt to satisfy everyone may doom the marketer to failure. Even a seemingly functional product like toothpaste is aimed at a specific market segment. Stripe was developed for children; Crest focuses on tooth-decay prevention; Ultra Brite hints at enhanced sex appeal; and Aqua Fresh promises both protection and teeth whiteners.

The auto manufacturer who decides to produce and market a single automobile model to satisfy everyone will encounter seemingly endless decisions to be made about such variables as the number of doors, type of transmission, colour, styling, and engine size. In its attempt to satisfy everyone, the firm may be forced to compromise in each of these areas and, as a result, may discover that it does not satisfy anyone very well. Other firms appealing to particular segments — the youth market, the high-fuel-economy market, the large family market, and so on — may capture most of the total market by satisfying the specific needs of these smaller, more homogeneous market targets. *The process of dividing the total market into several homogeneous groups with similar interests in a particular product or service category* is called **market segmentation**.

Once a specific market segment has been identified, the marketer can design an appropriate marketing mix to match its needs, improving the chance of sales to that segment. Market segmentation can be used by both profit-oriented and nonprofit organizations.

Segmenting
Consumer Markets   Market segmentation results from a determination of factors that distinguish a certain group of consumers from the overall market. These characteristics—such as age, sex, geographic location, income and expenditure patterns, and population size and mobility, among others — are vital factors in the success of the overall marketing strategy. Toy manufacturers such as Ideal, Hasbro, Mattel, and Kenner study not only birthrate trends, but also shifts in income and expenditure patterns. Colleges and universities are affected by such factors as the number of high school graduates, changing atti-

tudes toward the value of college educations, and increasing enrolment of older adults. Figure 4-1 identifies four commonly used bases for segmenting consumer markets.

Figure 4-1   Bases for Market Segmentation

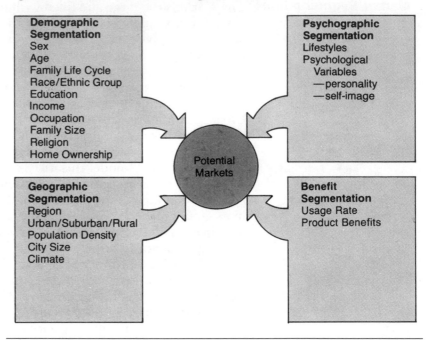

Geographic segmentation, the dividing of an overall market into homogeneous groups based on population location, has been used for hundreds of years. The second basis for segmenting markets is *demographic segmentation*—dividing an overall market on the basis of characteristics such as age, sex, and income level. Demographic segmentation is the most commonly used method of subdividing total markets.

The third and fourth bases represent relatively recent developments in market segmentation. *Psychographic segmentation* utilizes behavioural profiles developed from analyses of the activities, opinions, interests, and lifestyles of consumers in identifying market segments. The final basis, *benefit segmentation*, focuses on benefits the consumer expects to derive from a product or service. These segmentation bases can be important to marketing strategies provided they are significantly related to differences in buying behaviour.

Geographic Segmentation

A logical starting point in market segmentation is to find out where buyers are. It is not surprising, therefore, that one of the earliest bases for segmentation was geographic. Regional variations in consumer tastes often exist. Per capita consumption of seafood, for example, is higher in the Maritimes than in Alberta. Brick and stone construction, a mainstay in many homes in Ontario, is much less common in the West.

Geographic Location of the Canadian Population

Canada has grown tremendously from a population of 3 million in 1867 to about 25 million in 1985. The Canadian population, like that of the rest of the world, is not distributed evenly. In fact, it is extremely uneven; large portions of this country are uninhabited.[1]

The term used to describe settled areas is "ecumene," literally meaning inhabited space.[2] In Canada less than 8 percent of the land surface is occupied farmland. The ecumene in Canada is depicted in Figure 4-2. This dramatically shows that a relatively small strip lying adjacent to the American border is the land area most heavily settled and utilized. Business and social activities therefore must operate in an east–west manner, over tremendous distances. It is not surprising, therefore, to see the emergence of various distinct market segments, such as central Canada (Ontario and/or Quebec), the Maritimes, the Prairies, or British Columbia.

Not only do provinces vary widely in total population (see Figures 4-3 and 4-4), but pronounced shifts are also evident. People tend to move where work and opportunities exist. Thus, Ontario and British Columbia have been continuously attractive to those on the move. More recently, Alberta has experienced large population influxes because of the oil-induced prosperity there. However, the marketer should realize that the bulk of the country's sales potential is still in Ontario and Quebec. In fact, better than three-fifths, 62%, still lives in the two provinces.

Natural factors and immigration also influence population. Growth has occurred as a result of natural increase (births minus deaths) and net migration (immigration minus emigration). Overall, the rate of natural increase has been considerably higher than net migration. In fact, the Atlantic provinces and Saskatchewan depend on natural increase to restore population levels lost by emigration. On the other hand, Ontario, Alberta, and British Columbia have shown significant total population increases because they have received migration flows plus a natural increase. In recent years natural increases have been declining.

Immigration has had a tremendous impact on Canadian society. The injection of a steady stream of British immigrants and short bursts of central, eastern, and southern Europeans and southeast Asians into the Canadian population have created immense social

Figure 4-2   The Canadian Ecumene, 1985

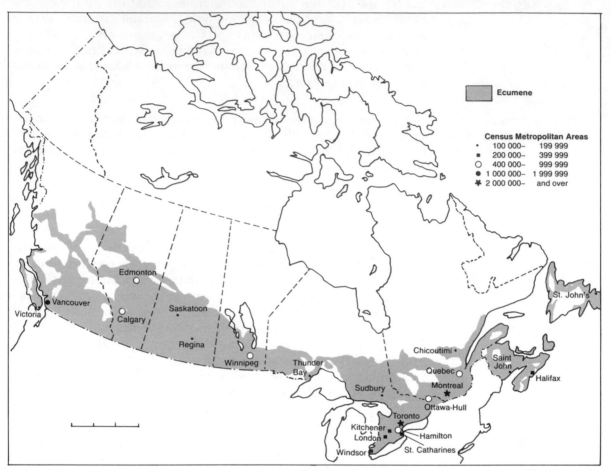

Source: *Perspective Canada: A Compendium of Social Statistics* (Ottawa: Information Canada, 1974). Reproduced by permission of the Minister of Supply and Services Canada. Updated.

pressures in assimilation and citizenship. Some areas have attracted much more immigration. In fact, Ontario contains 51.8 percent of Canada's living foreign-born people. The western provinces contain the greatest percentages of foreign-born who are "old-timers" (immigrated prior to 1946).

Postwar immigration tended to be from European urban centres to Canadian cities, whereas immigration before World War II was largely from European rural locations to Canadian rural areas.

A remarkable influence has been the immigration–emigration flow in Canada. Despite the fact that 8 million people entered the

**Figure 4-3   Percentage Distribution of the Population of Canada
by Province as of July 1983**

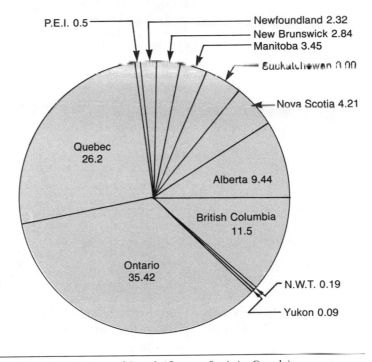

Source: Adapted from *1976 Census of Canada* (Ottawa: Statistics Canada),
Cat. 92-807. By permission of the Minister of Supply and Services Canada.

country through immigration between 1851 and 1961, it is estimated
that more than 6 million *left*. From Confederation to 1967, Canada's
growth was due largely to natural increase (14.5 million), whereas
net migration produced only a 2.4-million increase.[3]

It is estimated that emigration has decreased in recent years.
However, the tremendous immigration and emigration in proportion
to the size of Canada's population has resulted in a somewhat
unstable set of common goals and ends for society. The character of
Canadian society has continually been pulled in various directions
through the infusion of different ethnic groups at varying periods of
history via immigration.

The large-scale migration flow from the East to Alberta and
British Columbia in the late 1970s and 1980s is the latest significant
population flow. In fact, its size rivals the immigration flows that
occurred when the West was first settled.

Figure 4-4   Provincial and Territorial Populations, 1971, 1980, 1983

	1971	1980	1983
Newfoundland	522 105	582 900	578 600
Prince Edward Island	111 640	124 000	124 200
Nova Scotia	788 960	855 000	860 100
New Brunswick	634 560	708 700	707 800
Quebec	6 027 765	6 310 800	6 524 700
Ontario	7 703 105	8 587 300	8 822 200
Manitoba	988 245	1 028 000	1 048 300
Saskatchewan	926 245	973 000	994 000
Alberta	1 627 875	2 113 300	2 350 100
British Columbia	2 184 620	2 662 000	2 826 800
Yukon	18 390	21 600	22 200
Northwest Territories	34 810	43 000	48 400
TOTAL	21 568 310	24 009 600	24 907 100

Sources: Statistics Canada Catalogue 91–001 and 91–201 June, 1983. By permission
of the Minister of Supply and Services Canada.

These factors have traditionally affected the political outlook of Canada's geographic regions. Marketers also recognize that they must take geographical market segments into account.

People Are in the Cities

It is a myth that Canada's population is rural and agricultural. People have been migrating to the cities for many years. Figure 4-5 shows that the percentage of farm dwellers has dropped to 4.5 percent, whereas 75.5 percent of the population is urban. Figure 4-6 shows population and growth rate for the 23 largest metropolitan areas. The three largest, Toronto, Montreal, and Vancouver, already contained approximately 28 percent of Canada's total population by 1983 and approximately 55 percent of Canada's population lived in cities of 100 000 and over.

The Canadian population, along with the American and the Australian, is one of the most mobile in the world. The average Canadian moves 12 times in a lifetime, as compared to eight times for the average English citizen and five for the typical Japanese.[4] However, this trend may be waning. The slowdown may be due to a number of factors: poor job prospects elsewhere; the tendency of wage earners in two-income families to refuse transfers; an aging population; a heightened concern for the quality of one's life.

Using Geographic Segmentation

There are many instances where markets for products and services may be segmented on a geographic basis. Regional variations in taste often exist. Quebec has long been known for its interest in fine and varied foods.

Figure 4-5   Approximate Percentage Distribution, Canadian Urban and Rural Populations, 1983

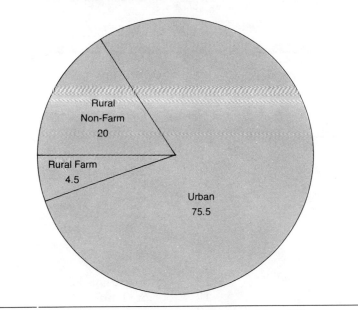

Source: *Canada Year Book 1978/79* (Ottawa: Statistics Canada), p. 158.
By permission of the Minister of Supply and Services Canada. Updated.

Residence location within a geographic area is another important geographic variable. Urban dwellers may eat more meals in restaurants than their suburban and rural counterparts, while suburban dwellers spend proportionally more on lawn and garden care than do people in rural or urban areas. Both rural and suburban dwellers may spend more of their household income on gasoline and automobile needs than urban households.

Climate is another important factor. Snow blowers, snowmobiles, and sleds are popular products in many parts of Canada. Residents of southwestern British Columbia may spend proportionately less of their total income on heating and heating equipment than other Canadians. Climate also affects patterns of clothing purchases.

Geographic segmentation is useful only when true differences in preference and purchase patterns for a product emerge along regional lines. Geographic subdivisions of the overall market tend to be rather large and often too heterogeneous for effective segmentation without careful consideration of additional factors. In such cases, it may be necessary to use several segmentation variables.

Figure 4-6   The 25 Largest Metropolitan Areas in 1983

Rank	Area	1983 Population (in thousands)	Ten-Year Growth Rate
1	Toronto	3034	14%
2	Montreal	2831	2
3	Vancouver	1292	19
4	Ottawa-Hull	722	7
5	Edmonton	673	38
6	Calgary	614	13
7	Winnipeg	588	56
8	Quebec	582	3
9	Hamilton	544	13
10	St. Catharines-Niagara	305	5
11	Kitchener	291	1
12	London	286	12
13	Halifax	280	10
14	Windsor	246	8
15	Victoria	237	15
16	Regina	167	-1
17	Oshawa	158	18
18	Saskatoon	158	-9
19	St. John's	156	33
20	Sudbury	148	29
21	Chicoutimi-Jonquière	136	10
22	Thunder Bay	122	3
23	Saint John	114	2
24	Sherbrooke	112	12
25	Trois Rivières	105	10

Source: *The Financial Post Survey of Markets*, 1983.

Demographic Segmentation

The most common approach to market segmentation is to divide consumer groups according to demographic variables. These variables—age, sex, income, occupation, education, household size, and others—are typically used to identify market segments and to develop appropriate market mixes. Demographic variables are often used in market segmentation for three reasons:

1. They arc casy to identify and measure.
2. They are associated with the sale of many products and services.
3. They are typically referred to in describing the audiences of advertising media, so that media buyers and others can easily pinpoint the desired market target.[5]

Vast quantities of data are available to assist the marketing planner in segmenting potential markets on a demographic basis.

Sex is an obvious variable for segmenting many markets, since many products are sex-specific. Electric razor manufacturers have utilized sex as a variable in the successful marketing of such brands as Lady Remington. Diet soft drinks have often been aimed at female markets. Even deodorants are targeted at males or females.

Age, household size, stage in the family life cycle, and income and expenditure patterns are important factors in determining buying decisions. The often distinct differences in purchase patterns based upon such demographic factors is justification for their frequent use as a basis for segmentation.

Age—An Important Demographic Segmentation Variable

The population of Canada is expected to grow by 16 percent between 1981 and 2001, but this growth will be concentrated in two age groups — adults between 35 and 54, and persons aged 65 and older. Both of these markets represent potentially profitable market targets.

The young to middle-aged adult segment includes family households with demand for goods such as houses, furniture, recreation, clothes, toys and food. The older and senior middle-aged adult segment (45–64) includes households where the children have grown up and most have left home. For many, housing costs are lower because mortgages are paid off. In general, this group finds itself with substantial disposable income because it is in a peak earning period, and many basic purchases for everyday living have been completed. This disposable income is often used for luxury goods, new furniture, and travel. While this segment currently represents 19 percent of the Canadian population, it will account for 50 percent of the growth in population between 1981 and 2001.

Not so many years ago, there was no such thing as a senior citizen market, since few people reached old age. Now, however, some 9 percent of the total population is 65 or older. Not only is it comforting for this year's retiree to learn that at age 65 his or her average life expectancy is at least another 13 years, but the trend also creates a unique and potentially profitable segment for the marketing manager. The manager of course will not ignore the youth segment, which will decline in proportion to the whole population, but remain large. Figure 4-7 shows the changing profile of the Canadian population.

Each of the age groups in Figure 4-7 represents different consumption patterns and each serves as the market target for particular firms. For instance, Gerber Products Company has been extremely successful in aiming at the infant market and prepacked tours appeal to older consumers. Figure 4-8 lists some of the types of merchandise often purchased by the various age groups.

Figure 4-7   Population Projections by Age Groups

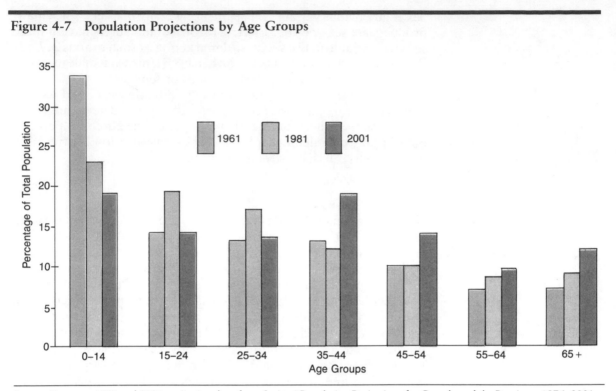

Source: For years 1981 and 2001 projection data from Series 4 Population Projections for Canada and the Provinces 1976–2001 Cat. No. 91520 Stats Canada.

Figure 4-8   Buying Patterns for Different Age Groups

Age	Name of Age Group	Merchandise
0–5	Young Children	Baby food, toys, nursery furniture children's wear
6–19	School Children (including teenagers)	Clothing, sports equipment, records, school supplies, food, cosmetics, used cars
20–34	Young Adult	Cars, furniture, houses, clothing, recreational equipment, purchases for younger age segments
35–49	Younger Middle-Aged	Larger homes, better cars, second cars, new furniture, recreational equipment
50–64	Older Middle-Aged	Recreational items, purchases for young marrieds and infants
65 +	Senior Adults	Medical services, travel, drugs, purchases for younger age groups

Segmenting by Family Life Cycle

The **family life cycle** *is the process of family formation, development, and dissolution.* Using this concept the marketing planner combines the family characteristics of age, marital status, presence or absence of children, and ages of children in developing the marketing strategy. Patrick E. Murphy and William A. Staples have proposed a six-stage family life cycle with several subcategories. The stages of the family life cycle are shown in Figure 4-9.

The behavioural characteristics and buying patterns of persons in each life cycle stage often vary considerably. Young singles have relatively few financial burdens; tend to be early purchasers of new fashion items; are recreation oriented; and make purchases of basic kitchen equipment, cars, and vacations. By contrast, young marrieds with young children tend to be heavy purchasers of baby products, homes, television sets, toys, and washers and dryers. Their liquid assets tend to be relatively low, and they are more likely to watch television than young singles or young marrieds without children. The empty-nest households in the middle-aged and older categories with no dependent children are more likely to have more disposable income; more time for recreation, self-education, and travel; and more than one member in the labour force than their full-nest counterparts with younger children. Similar differences in behavioural and buying patterns are evident in the other stages of the family life cycle as well.

Figure 4-9   Family Life Cycle Stages

1. Young Single
2. Young Married without Children
3. Other Young
   a. Young divorced without children
   b. Young married with children
   c. Young divorced with children
4. Middle-Aged
   a. Middle-Aged married without children
   b. Middle-Aged divorced without children
   c. Middle-Aged married with children
   d. Middle-Aged divorced with children
   e. Middle-Aged married without dependent children
   f. Middle-Aged divorced without dependent children
5. Older
   a. Older married
   b. Older unmarried (divorced, widowed)
6. Other
   All adults and children not accounted for by family life cycle stages

Source: Adapted with permission from Patrick E. Murphy and William A. Staples, "A Modernized Family Life," *Journal of Consumer Research* (June 1979), p. 16.

Analysis of life cycle stages often gives better results than reliance on single variables such as age. The buying patterns of a 25-year-old bachelor are very different from those of a father of the same age. The family of five headed by parents in their forties is a more likely prospect for the World Book Encyclopedia than the childless 40-year-old divorced person.

Marketing planners can use published data such as census reports and divide their markets into more homogeneous segments than would be possible if they were analyzing single variables. Such data is available for each classification of the family life cycle.

The Changing Household

Half the households in Canada are composed of only one or two persons, and the average household size is 3.3 persons. This development is in marked contrast to households that averaged more than four persons before World War II. Married couples still form the largest segment of households, but in relative terms their numbers are decreasing.

There are several reasons for the trend toward smaller households. Among them are lower fertility rates; the tendency of young people to postpone marriage; the increasing desire among younger couples to limit the number of children; the ease and frequency of divorce; and the ability and desire of many young single adults and the elderly to live alone.

Over 1.6 million people live alone today — approximately 20 percent of all households. The single-person household has emerged as an important market segment with a special title: **SSWD** (*single, separated, widowed, and divorced*). SSWDs buy approximately 25 percent of all passenger cars, but a much higher proportion of specialty cars. They are also customers for single-serving food products, such as Campbell's Soup-for-One and Green Giant's single-serving casseroles.

Segmenting Markets on the Basis of Income and Expenditure Patterns

Earlier, markets were defined as people and purchasing power. A very common method of segmenting consumer markets is on the basis of income. Fashionable specialty shops stocking designer label clothing obtain most of their sales from high-income shoppers.

Between 1970 and 1980 a large proportion of families moved from the lower to higher income groups. This is apparent from Figure 4-10 which displays family incomes in 1980 dollars. Over the decade, the number of families increased by 25 percent, but this increase is not distributed equally among the different income brackets. In fact, the number of families with incomes under $20 000 declined by 13 percent, while that of families with incomes of $20 000 or over increased by 73 percent. The number of families with an income of at least $35 000 nearly tripled over the decade.

Figure 4-10   Percentage Distribution by 1970 and 1980 Family Income Groups of Census Families in Private Households, Canada

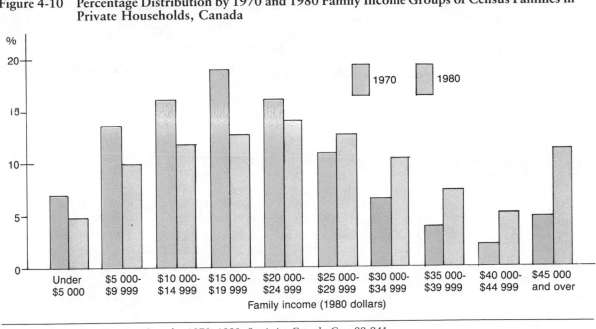

Source: Changes in Income in Canada, 1970–1980, Statistics Canada Cat. 99-941.

Income statistics can be better understood by examining family structures more closely. Families can be divided into two groups: husband-wife families and lone-parent families. The latter can be further subdivided by sex of the parent. Significant changes have occurred in the structure of families over the decade. The number of husband-wife families increased by 22 percent, while that of male lone-parent families increased by 25 percent. However, the number of female lone-parent families increased by 59 percent. The three groups fared differently with respect to their incomes over the decade as can be seen in Figure 4-10a. The husband-wife families increased their average income by 30 percent and male lone-parent families by 35 percent. The average income of female lone-parent families increased by only 18 percent.[6]

A household's expenditures may be divided into the two categories: 1) basic purchase of essential household needs, and 2) other purchases that can be made at the discretion of the household members once the necessities have been purchased (disposable income). Total Canadian disposable income is estimated to have tripled in constant dollars since 1961.[7] This is a substantial increase, despite the inflation rate.

Figure 4-10a   Percentage Distribution by 1970 and 1980 Family Income Groups of Families by Family Structure, Canada

Family income group (1980 dollars)		All families		Husband-wife families		Male lone-parent families		Female lone-parent families	
		1970	1980	1970	1980	1970	1980	1970	1980
Under $5 000		7.1	4.8	5.5	3.1	13.3	7.6	26.2	19.9
$ 5 000-$ 9 999		13.6	9.8	12.4	8.1	17.1	12.3	27.4	26.8
10 000- 14 999		16.0	11.7	15.7	11.0	19.6	13.0	19.0	17.5
15 000- 19 999		19.0	12.7	19.5	12.6	19.3	15.5	11.9	13.0
20 000- 24 999		16.0	14.1	16.8	14.6	12.4	15.4	6.6	8.7
25 000- 34 999		17.4	23.0	18.5	24.6	11.0	19.2	5.8	8.9
35 000- 44 999		6.1	12.6	6.5	13.6	3.8	9.1	1.8	3.2
45 000 and over		4.8	11.3	5.2	12.4	3.5	7.9	1.3	2.1
Total		100.0	100.0	100.0	100.0	100.0	100.0	100.0	100.0
Number	'000	5 055	6 325	4 585	5 612	99	124	370	589
Average income	$	20 820	26 748	21 631	28 186	17 286	23 243	11 714	13 790
Median income	$	18 447	23 894	1 210	25 250	15 002	20 468	9 246	10 890

Source: Changes in Income In Canada, 1970-1980, Statistics Canada, Catalogue 99–941.

How do expenditure patterns vary with increased income? More than a hundred years ago a German statistician named Ernst Engel published three general statements — **Engel's Laws** — based upon his studies of spending behaviour. According to Engel, *as family income increases*:

1) A smaller *percentage* of expenditures goes for food.
2) The *percentage* spent on housing and household operations and clothing will remain constant.
3) The *percentage* spent on other items (such as recreation, education, etc.) will increase.

Are Engel's Laws still valid today? Figure 4-11 supplies the answers.

A steady decline in the percentage of total income spent for food occurs from low to high incomes. Note the emphasis on the word *percentage*. The high-income families will spend a greater absolute amount on food purchases, but their purchases will represent a smaller percentage of their total expenditures than will be true of low-income households. The second law also appears partially correct since percentage expenditures for housing and household operations are relatively unchanged in all but the very lowest income group. The percentage spent on clothing, however, *increases* with increased income. The third law is also true. All groups spend somewhat more proportionately than the lowest income group.

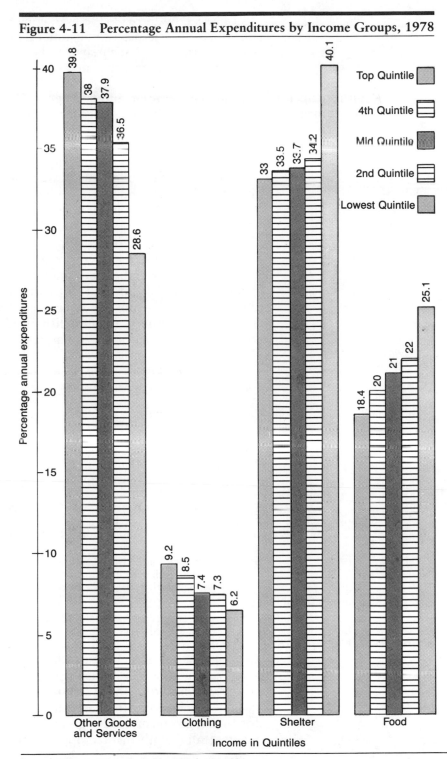

Figure 4-11   Percentage Annual Expenditures by Income Groups, 1978

Source: Statistics Canada Daily, March 15, 1984

Engel's Laws provide the marketing manager with useful generalizations about types of consumer demand that will evolve with increased income. They may also be useful when evaluating a foreign country as a potential market target.

Psychographic Segmentation

Although geographic and demographic segmentation traditionally have been the primary bases for dividing consumer and industrial markets into homogeneous segments to serve as market targets, marketers have long recognized the need for fuller, more lifelike portraits of consumers for use in developing marketing programs. Even though traditionally used variables such as age, sex, family life cycle, income, and population size and location are important in segmentation, lifestyles of potential consumers may prove equally important.

Lifestyle refers to *the mode of living* of consumers. Consumers' lifestyles are regarded as a composite of their individual behaviour patterns and psychological makeups — their needs, motives, perceptions, and attitudes. A lifestyle also bears the mark of many other influences — those of reference groups, culture, social class, and family members. A frequently used classification system for lifestyle variables is shown in Figure 4-12.

Figure 4-12   Lifestyle Dimensions

Activities	Interests	Opinions	Demographics
Work	Family	Themselves	Age
Hobbies	Home	Social issues	Education
Social events	Job	Politics	Income
Vacation	Community	Business	Occupation
Entertainment	Recreation	Economics	Family size
Club membership	Fashion	Education	Dwelling
Community	Food	Products	Geography
Shopping	Media	Future	City size
Sports	Achievements	Culture	Stage in life cycle

Source: Joseph T. Plummer, "The Concept and Application of Life-style Segmentation," *Journal of Marketing* (January 1974), p. 34. Reprinted from the *Journal of Marketing* published by the American Marketing Association.

Using Psychographics

In recent years, a new technique has been developed that promises to elicit more meaningful bases for segmentation. Although definitions vary among researchers, **psychographics** generally refers to *the behavioural profiles of different consumers*. These profiles are usually developed from quantitative research by asking consumers for their agreement or disagreement with several hundred statements dealing with the activities, interests, and opinions listed in

Figure 4-12. Because of the basis of the statements, many writers refer to them as **AIO statements** *(activities, interests, and opinions).*

Hundreds of psychographic studies have been conducted on products and services ranging from soap to air travel. A study of household food buying identified four distinct segments based on psychographic research. Of the 1800 adults interviewed, 98 percent were categorized by the researcher as falling into one of the following groupings:

Hedonists, who represent 20 percent of the population, want the good life — foods that taste good, are convenient, and inexpensive. They aren't worried about sugar, fat, cholesterol, salt, calories, additives, or preservatives. They are most likely young, male, and child-free. Hedonists are above average consumers of regular soft drinks, beer, margarine, presweetened cereal, candy, and gum.

Don't Wants, another 20 percent of the population, are the opposite extreme from the Hedonists. They avoid all the "no-no" ingredients in some processed foods. They will sacrifice taste and convenience and will pay more to obtain foods without sugar, artificial ingredients, cholesterol, and fat. They are concerned about calories and nutrition. Their avoidance behaviour is more health oriented than diet conscious. This segment is older; more than half are over age 50. They tend to be better educated, live in large urban areas, and don't have children at home. The Don't Wants are major consumers of decaffeinated coffee, fruit juices, wine, unsalted butter, corn oil margarine, nutritionally fortified cereal, yogurt, and sugar free foods and beverages.

The Weight Conscious, who comprise about one-third of the population, are primarily concerned about calories and fat. They like convenience foods, but try to avoid cholesterol, sugar, and salt. They're not particularly nutrition or taste conscious and don't avoid foods simply because they have artificial ingredients or preservatives. Members of this segment tend to have higher incomes and many are women employed full time. Given their concern for calories, the Weight Conscious are above average consumers of iced tea, diet soft drinks, diet margarine, and sugar-free candy and gum.

The Moderates, the final 25 percent of the population, are average in everything. They balance the trade-offs they make in food selection and don't exhibit strong concerns about the avoidance factors. Their profile closely fits that of the general population, and their consumption levels are average for the foods and beverages listed in the study.[8]

As the profiles of two very different market groups in Figure 4-13 suggest, the marketing implications of psychographic seg-

Figure 4-13   Profile of Heavy Users: Eye Makeup and Shortening

Heavy User of Eye Makeup	Heavy User of Shortening

Demographic Characteristics

Young, well-educated, lives in metropolitan areas	Middle-aged, medium to large family, lives outside metropolitan areas

Product Use

Also a heavy user of liquid face makeup, lipstick, hair spray, perfume, cigarettes, gasoline	Also a heavy user of flour, sugar, canned lunch meat, cooked pudding, ketchup

Media Preferences
Agrees more than average with

Fashion magazines, *The Tonight Show*, adventure programs	*Reader's Digest*, daytime TV serials, family-situation TV comedies

Activities, Interests, and Opinions
Agrees more than average with

"I often try the latest hairdo styles when they change."	"I love to bake and frequently do."
"An important part of my life and activities is dressing smartly."	"I save recipes from newspapers and magazines."
"I like to feel attractive to all men."	"I love to eat."
"I want to look a little different from others."	"I enjoy most forms of housework."
"I like what I see when I look in the mirror."	"Usually I have regular days for washing, cleaning, etc., around the house."
"I take good care of my skin."	"I am uncomfortable when my house is not completely clean."
"I would like to spend a year in London or Paris."	"I try to arrange my home for my children's convenience."
"I like ballet."	"Our family is a close-knit group."
"I like to serve unusual dinners."	"Clothes should be dried in fresh air and out-of-doors."
"I really do believe that blondes have more fun."	"I would rather spend a quiet evening at home than go out to a party."

Disagrees more than average with

"I enjoy most forms of housework."	"My idea of housekeeping is once over lightly."
"I furnish my home for comfort, not for style."	"Classical music is more interesting than popular music."
"If it was good enough for my mother, it's good enough for me."	"I like ballet."
	"I'd like to spend a year in London or Paris."

Source: William D. Wells and Arthur D. Beard, "Personality and Consumer Behavior," in Scott Ward and Thomas S. Robertson, eds., *Consumer Behavior*, © 1973, pp. 195–96. Reprinted by permission of Prentice-Hall, Inc. Englewood Cliffs, N.J.

mentation are considerable. Psychographic profiles produce a much richer description of a potential market target, and should assist promotional decision-makers in matching the image of the company and its product offerings with the type of consumer using the product.

Psychographic segmentation often serves as a component of an overall segmentation strategy in which markets are also segmented on the basis of demographic/geographic variables. These more traditional bases provide the marketer with accessibility to consumer segments through orthodox communications channels such as newspapers, radio and television advertising, and other promotional outlets. Psychographic studies may then be implemented to develop lifelike, three-dimensional profiles of the lifestyles of the firm's market target. When combined with demographic/geographic characteristics, psychographics emerges as an important tool in understanding the behaviour of present and potential market targets.

Benefit Segmentation

A fourth approach to market segmentation is to focus on such attributes as product usage rates and the benefits derived from the product. These factors may reveal important bases for pinpointing prospective market targets. One analysis of 34 segmentation studies indicated that benefit analysis provided the best predictor of brand use, level of consumption, and product type selected in 51 percent of the cases.[9] Many marketers now consider benefit segmentation the most useful approach to classifying markets.

Usage Rates   Marketing managers may divide potential segments into two categories: 1) users and 2) nonusers. Users may be further divided into heavy, moderate, and light users.

In some product categories, such as air travel, car rentals, dog food, and hair colouring, less than 20 percent of the population accounts for more than 80 percent of the total purchases. Even for such widely used products as coffee and soft drinks, 50 percent of all households account for almost 90 percent of the total usage.[10]

An early study of usage patterns by Dik Warren Twedt divided users into two categories: 1) light and 2) heavy. Twedt's analysis of consumer-panel data revealed that 29 percent of the sample households could be characterized as heavy users of lemon-lime soft drinks. This group represented 91 percent of sales in the product category.[11] It is, therefore, not surprising that usage rates are important segmentation variables for Coca-Cola, Pepsi-Cola, and 7-Up.

Heavy users often can be identified through analysis of internal records. Retail stores and financial institutions have records of charge-card purchases and other transactions. Warranty records may also be used.[12]

Product Benefits   Market segments may also be identified by the *benefits* the buyer expects to derive from a product or brand. In a pioneering investigation, Daniel Yankelovich revealed that much of the watch industry operated with little understanding of the benefits watch buyers expect in their purchases. At the time of the study, most watch companies were marketing relatively expensive models through jewellery stores and using prestige appeals. However, Yankelovich's research revealed that less than one-third of the market was purchasing a watch as a symbol. In fact, 23 percent of his respondents reported they purchased the lowest-price watch and another 46 percent focused on durability and overall product quality. The Timex Company decided to focus its product benefits on those two categories and market its watches in drugstores, variety stores, and discount houses. Within a few years of adopting the new segmentation approach, it became the largest watch company in the world.[13]

Figure 4-15 illustrates how benefit segmentation might be applied to the toothpaste market. The table reveals that some consumers are primarily concerned with price; some with tooth decay, some

Figure 4-15   Benefit Segmentation of the Toothpaste Market

	Segment name			
	The sensory segment	*The sociables*	*The worriers*	*The in-dependent segment*
Principal benefit sought	Flavour, product appearance	Brightness of teeth	Decay prevention	Price
Demographic strengths	Children	Teens, young people	Large families	Men
Special behavioural characteristics	Users of spearment-flavoured toothpaste	Smokers	Heavy users	Heavy users
Brands dis-proportionately favoured	Colgate, Stripe	MacLean's, Plus White, Ultra Brite	Crest	Brands on sale
Personality characteristics	High self-involvement	High sociability	High hypo-chondriasis	High autonomy
Lifestyle characteristics	Hedonistic	Active	Conserva-tive	Value-oriented

Source: Reprinted by permission from Russell I. Haley, "Benefit Segmentation: A Decision-Oriented Research Tool," *Journal of Marketing* (July 1968), p. 33, published by the American Marketing Association.

with taste, and others with brightness. Also included are the demographic and other characteristics utilized in focusing on each subgrouping.

Segmenting Industrial Markets

While the bulk of market segmentation research has concentrated on consumer markets, the concept can also be applied to the industrial sector. The overall process is similar. Three industrial market segmentation approaches have been identified: geographic segmentation, product segmentation, and segmentation by end-use application (See Figure 4-16).

Geographic Segmentation

Geographic segmentation is useful in industries where the bulk of the customers are concentrated in specific geographical locations. This approach can be used in such instances as the automobile industry, concentrated in the central Ontario area, or the lumber industry, centered in British Columbia and Quebec. It might also be used in cases where the markets are limited to just a few locations. The oil-field equipment market, for example, is largely concentrated in cities like Calgary and Edmonton.

Product Segmentation

Product segmentation can be used in the industrial marketplace. Industrial users tend to have much more precise product specifications than ultimate consumers do. Thus, industrial products often fit narrower market segments than consumer products. Designing

Figure 4-16   Segmentation Bases for Industrial Markets

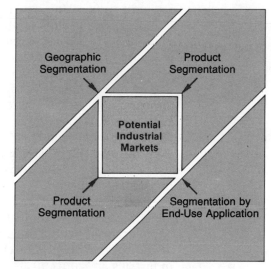

an industrial good or service to meet specific buyer requirements is a form of market segmentation.

Segmentation by End-Use Applications

A third segmentation base is end-use applications or precisely how the industrial purchaser will use the product. (This is similar to benefits segmentation in consumer markets.) A manufacturer of, say, printing equipment may serve markets ranging from a local utility to a bicycle manufacturer to Agriculture Canada. Each end-use may dictate unique specifications of performance, design, and price. The market for desk-top computers provides a good example. Xerox is targeting its 820-II model to the office market, rather than the home market. Technology Group Inc.'s BMC computer is being offered for end-use applications in accounting and blood diagnostics.[14] Regardless of how it is done, market segmentation is as vital to industrial marketing as it is in consumer markets.

Summary

A market consists of people or organizations with the necessary purchasing power and willingness to buy. The authority to buy must also exist. Markets can be classified by the type of products they handle. Consumer goods are products purchased by the ultimate consumer for personal use. Industrial goods are products purchased for use either directly or indirectly in the production of other goods and services for resale. Products are typically targeted at specific market segments. The process of dividing the total market into several homogeneous groups is called market segmentation.

Consumer markets can be divided on the bases of geographic, demographic, psychographic, or benefit segmentation. Geographic segmentation is the process of dividing the overall market into homogeneous groups on the basis of population location. It is one of the oldest forms of segmentation. The most commonly used form is demographic segmentation, which classifies the overall market into homogeneous groups based upon characteristics such as age, sex, and income levels. Psychographic segmentation is a relatively new approach. It uses behavioural profiles developed from analyses of the activities, opinions, interests, and lifestyles of consumers to identify market segments. The fourth approach, benefit segmentation, may be the most useful. It segments markets on the basis of the perceived benefits consumers expect to derive from a product or service.

Benefit segmentation is also useful in industrial markets. There are three bases for industrial market segmentation: geographic segmentation, product segmentation, and segmentation by end-use applications. Geographic segmentation is commonly used since many industries are concentrated in a few locations. A second industrial market segmentation base is by product. Industrial markets are characterized by precise product specifications, making this approach feasible. Segmentation by end-use applications is the final base. This approach is predicated upon the use that the industrial purchasers will make of the good or service.

This chapter has examined the various bases for segmenting both consumer and industrial markets. Chapter 5 examines how these concepts may be applied to market segmentation strategies. This section concludes with Chapter 6 on marketing research and information systems.

Market Segmentation Strategies

1. *To explain the rationale for and process of developing market matching strategies.*

2. *To outline the stages in the market segmentation process.*

3. *To present the concept of market positioning in developing market matching strategies.*

4. *To show how market target decision analysis can be used in market segmentation.*

5. *To show how market target decision analysis can be used to assess a product mix.*

Most major bakeries have been losing market share, but Corporate Foods Ltd. of Toronto has made its sales rise. Companies such as General Bakeries and Weston Bakeries have lost ground to in-store bakeries and to a growing list of specialized franchise bakeries. However, the strategy adopted by Corporate Foods has helped them to overcome such changes in the industry.

Corporate Foods' success lies in its ready willingness to recognize and cater to the growing fragmentation of the bread market through an intelligent market segmentation strategy. Corporate Foods delivers different types of fresh baked bread and rolls throughout Ontario under the brands Dempster's, Toastmaster, and Bamby, and under specialty labels such as Hollywood, Brownberry, and Sun-Maid Raisin Bread.

Through its Gainsborough division, it produces frozen pastry products for distribution across Canada. A 25 percent interest in the Quebec firm Unipain gives it a share of that market. This willingness to serve a variety of market segments has resulted in a 13 percent climb in sales over the past three years, compared with a 30 percent decline in market share by the major bakeries.

President Norman Currie concedes that "in-store bakeries do affect markets, as do neighbourhood bakeries and bakery franchises. "On the other hand, we sell products they cannot and do not produce. It's a very segmented market; it isn't a mass market. You have to design the product to meet each of those segments."

The company also plans to continue serving market segments through specialty product lines such as the newly introduced Gainsborough frozen croissant. Corporate Foods last summer bought a 49 percent interest in the pita and croissant baker Dough Delight of Toronto.

"I don't think there has been any decline in consumption of bakery products," Currie says. "Bread consumption hasn't changed; the market just shifts . . ."[1]

Market targets that are viable under current economic and competitive conditions must be identified and monitored continuously. The marketing planner must be prepared to make dramatic switches when necessary.

The Conceptual Framework

Chapter 5 takes the discussion of market segmentation further. Chapter 4 discussed the role of market segmentation in developing a marketing strategy and the bases for segmenting consumer markets (geographic, demographic, psychographic, and benefit segmentation) and industrial markets (geographic, product, and segmentation by end-use application). Here the emphasis shifts to the strategies associated with the concepts of market segmentation.

This chapter looks at the rationale for and process of matching product offerings to specific market segments. The selection of the appropriate market matching strategy is dependent upon a variety of internal and external variables facing the firm.

Next, the chapter outlines the various stages that exist in the segmentation process. The starting point is to identify the dimension that can be used to segment markets. The process ends with the decision on the actual market target segments. Chapter 5 concludes with a separate section on market target decision analysis, the procedure for selecting targeted market segments.

Alternative Market Matching Strategies

Market segmentation may take many forms, theoretically ranging from treating the entire market as a single homogeneous entity to subdividing it into several segments and providing a separate product and marketing mix for each segment.

The very core of the firm's strategies is to match product offerings with the needs of particular market segments. To do so successfully the firm must take the following factors into consideration:

1) *Company resources* must be adequate to cover product development and other marketing mix costs.

2) *Differentiability of products*. Some products can be easily differentiated from others. Some can be produced in versions designed specially for individual segments.
3) *Stage in the product life cycle*. As a product matures, different marketing mix emphases are required to fit market needs.
4) *Competitors' strategies*. Strategies and product offerings must be continually adjusted in order to be competitive.

Essentially, the firm makes a number of product/service offerings to the market in light of these determinants. One firm may decide on a **single-offer strategy**. This is defined as *the attempt to satisfy a large or a small market with one product and a single marketing mix*. Such a strategy may be adopted for different reasons. A small manufacturer of wheelbarrows might concentrate on marketing one product to retailers in one city only because it does not have the resources to serve a mass market. A large producer of drafting equipment might offer a single product line with a marketing mix aimed at draftspersons because it believes that only this limited segment would be interested in the product. A single-offer strategy aimed at one segment is often called *concentrated marketing*; aimed at mass markets it is often called *undifferentiated* or *mass marketing*. The marketing of Coca-Cola is an example of the latter.

On the other hand, another company with greater resources may recognize that there are several segments of the market that would respond well to specifically-designed products and marketing mixes. It adopts a **multi-offer strategy**. This is defined as *the attempt to satisfy several segments of the market very well with specialized products or services and unique marketing mixes aimed at each segment*. A bank designs particular services to fit the unique needs of different consumer and commercial market segments. A multi-offer strategy is also called *differentiated marketing*.

When these determinants are combined with markets segmented on the dimensions discussed in Chapter 4, the firm is able to develop a market matching strategy. A successful match of products to segments through the development of a marketing mix with appropriate product design, pricing strategy, distribution strategy, and promotion strategy is vital to the market success of the firm.

Many firms, large and small, practise a multi-offer strategy in today's environment. Procter & Gamble markets Tide, Dash, Duz, Cheer, Bold, Gain, Oxydol, and Bonus among other detergents to meet the desires of specific groups of detergent buyers. Lever Brothers offers two brands of complexion soap (Dove and Lux) and two brands of deodorant soap (Lifebuoy and Phase III).

Generally speaking, the company with a multi-offer marketing strategy should produce more sales by providing increased satisfaction for each of several market targets than would be possi-

Figure 5-1   Market Matching Strategies

	Product Offerings			
	Ford Motor Company		Audi/Volkswagen/Porsche	
	1908	1985	1955	1985
Market Segment	Single-Offer Strategy	Multi-Offer Strategy	Single-Offer Strategy	Multi-Offer Strategy
General Purpose Cars				
Small	Model T	Escort Lynx	"Beetle"	Golf
Medium	Model T	LTD Tempo Topaz		Jetta Rabbit
Large		LTD Crown Marquis		
Sport Cars				
Low-priced		EXP		
Medium-priced		Mustang Capri		Scirocco
High-priced		Thunderbird Cougar		Porsche 911, 944
Luxury Cars				
Medium-priced		Lincoln		Audi Quattro Audi 4000
High-priced		Continental		Audi 5000
Trucks				
Small	Model T (truck)	Ford		Vanagon
Medium		Ford		

Source: Adapted from *Canadian Consumer*, Vol. 14, No. 4, April 1984, and *Consumer Reports*, Vol. 49, No. 4, April 1984.

ble with only a single-offer strategy. However, whether a firm should choose a single- or multi-offer strategy depends on the economics of the situation — whether the company has the resources, and whether greater profits can be expected from the additional expense of a multi-offer strategy.

The Market Segmentation Process

The marketer has a number of potential bases for determining the most appropriate market-matching strategy. Geographic, demographic, product attributes, and psychographic bases are often utilized in converting heterogeneous markets into specific segments that serve as market targets for the consumer-oriented marketer. The industrial marketer segments geographically, by product, or by end-use application. In either case, a systematic five-stage decision process is followed. This framework for market segmentation is shown in Figure 5-2.

Since no single base for segmentation is necessarily the best, the analyst should segment the market in a way that will make the marketing mix easy to apply and that will achieve results. For example, demographic segmentation may be used in planning a print advertising campaign because magazines are normally aimed at specific demographic segments. The analyst thus often experiments with segmenting markets in several ways in the process of discovering which of the mix elements can be changed for greatest effect. (Similarly, marketing opportunities are sometimes discovered by rating how well competitors have served segments differentiated on a particular dimension.) This is part of the interactive process of analysis. Figure 5-2 shows a systematic, five-stage decision process that lends form to what are otherwise often complex and unstructured problems.[2]

Stage I: Select Market Segmentation Bases

The decision process begins when a firm seeks characteristics of potential buyers as bases that will allow the marketer to classify them into market segments. Segmentation bases should be selected so that each segment contains customers who respond similarly to specific marketing mix alternatives. For example, before Procter & Gamble decides to market Crest to a segment made up of large families, management should be confident that most large families are interested in preventing tooth decay so they will be receptive to the Crest marketing offer. In some cases, this objective is difficult to achieve. Consider the marketer seeking to reach the consumer segment that is over 50 years of age. Saturday evening television commercials can reach this group, but much of the expenditure may be wasted since the other major viewer group is comprised of teenagers.[3]

Stage II: Develop Relevant Profiles for Each Segment

Once segments have been identified, marketers should seek to understand the customer in each segment.

Segmentation bases provide some insight into the nature of customers, but typically not enough for the kinds of decisions that marketing managers must make. Managers need more precise descriptions of customers in order to match marketing offers to their

Figure 5-2   The Market Segmentation Decision Process

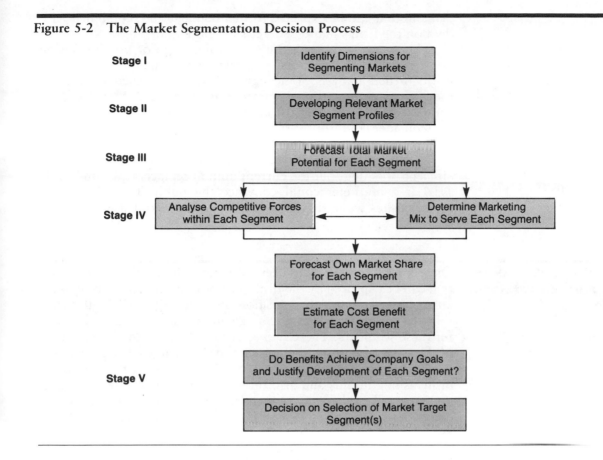

needs. Such descriptions can explain the similarities among customers within each segment as well as account for differences among segments. In other words, the task at this stage is to develop profiles of the typical customer in each segment with regard to lifestyle patterns, attitudes toward product attributes and brands, brand preferences, product use habits, geographic location, demographic characteristics, and so on. For example, one regional retail chain surveyed female customers and identified the following profile: age 25–55; 147–160 cm tall; 38–55 kg; career oriented, and having a $20 000 plus household income. The retailer used this profile to set up separate petite sections, one of the fastest growing segments of the women's fashion industry.[4]

Stage III: Forecast Market Potentials   In the third stage, market segmentation and market opportunity analysis are used together to produce a forecast of market potential within each segment. Market potential is the upper limit on the demand that can be expected from a segment and, combined with data on the firm's market share, sales potential.

This stage is management's preliminary go or no-go decision point as to whether the sales potential in a segment is sufficient to justify further analysis. Some segments will be screened out because they represent insufficient potential demand; others will be sufficiently attractive for the analysis to continue.

Consider the toothbrush part of the dental supply and mouthwash market—a multi-million dollar annual market. Dentists say that people should buy three or four toothbrushes a year for efficient brushing, but the current annual replacement rate is only 1.3.[5] If a marketer could convince the public to replace their toothbrushes when they should, market potential should almost triple.

Stage IV: Forecast Probable Market Share

Once market potential has been estimated, the share of that market that can be captured by the firm must be determined. This requires an analysis of competitors' positions in target segments. At the same time the specific marketing strategy and tactics should be designed for these segments. These two activities should lead to an analysis of the costs of tapping the potential demand in each segment.

Colgate once trailed Procter & Gamble nearly two to one in dishwashing liquids and also ran behind in heavy duty detergents and soaps. A realistic assessment indicated that for most directly competitive products they had little chance of overtaking P & G. So Colgate diversified its product line. Today, 75 percent of the firm's offerings do not face a directly competitive Procter & Gamble product, and those that do compete effectively.[6]

Stage V: Select Specific Market Segments

Finally the information, analyses, and forecasts accumulated through the process allow management to assess the potential for the achievement of company goals and justify the development of one or more market segments. Demand forecasts combined with cost projections are used to determine the profit and return on investment that can be expected from each segment. Analysis of marketing strategy and tactics will determine the degree of consistency with corporate image and reputation goals as well as with unique corporate capabilities that may be achieved by serving a segment. These assessments will, in turn, determine management's selection of specific segments as market targets.

At this point of the analysis the costs and benefits to be weighed are not just monetary, but include many difficult-to-measure but critical organizational and environmental factors. For example, the firm may not have enough experienced personnel to launch a successful attack on what clearly could be an almost certain monetary success. Similarly, a firm with 80 percent of the market may face legal problems with the federal Combines Branch if it increases its market concentration. The public utility may decide not to encourage higher electricity consumption because of environmental and political repercussions. The assessment of both financial and non-financial factors is a vital and final stage in the decision process.

There is not, and should not be, any simple answer to the market segmentation decision. The marketing concept's prescription to serve the customer's needs and to earn a profit while so doing implies that the marketer has to evaluate each possible marketing program on how it achieves this goal in the marketplace. By performing the detailed analysis outlined in Figure 5-2, the marketing manager can increase the probability of success in profitably serving consumers' needs.

Market Target Decision Analysis

Identifying specific market targets is an important aspect of overall marketing strategy. Clearly delineated market targets allow management to employ marketing efforts effectively like product development, distribution, pricing, and advertising to serve these markets.

Market target decision analysis, *the evaluation of potential market segments*, is a useful tool in the market segmentation process. Targets are chosen by segmenting the total market on the basis of any given characteristics (as described in Chapter 4). The example that follows illustrates how market target decision analysis can be applied.[7]

A Useful Method of Identifying Target Markets

One method of identifying target markets is simply to divide the total market into a number of boxes or cells. Each cell represents a potential target market. The definition of the cells can be based on consumer benefits desired, or geographic, demographic and psychographic characteristics, or some combination of these. While this concept is simple, it can be extremely complex in practice, and creativity is often required.

Consider the decisions of an airline company marketing manager wishing to analyse the market potential for various levels of passenger service. The company wants to delineate all possible market targets, and to assess the most profitable multi-offer strategy.

As a tool to outline the scope of the market, the marketing manager devises a grid like the one in Figure 5-3. This enables the company to match the possible types of service offerings with various customer classifications. The process of developing the target market grid forces the decision-maker to consider the entire range of possible market matching strategies. New or previously underserved

Figure 5-3   Market for Airline Passenger Travel

Type of Service

Market	First Class	Extra Service Business Class	Regular Tourist Class	Seat Sale Class	Age Specials	Charter
Senior Executives	X	X	?			X
Employees of large firms		X	X	?		X
Employees of small business		X	X	X		
Wealthy Individuals	X	X				?
Other Individuals			X	X		X
Senior Citizens			?	X	X	X
Youth			X	X	X	X

X = Probable demand for service
? = Uncertain or limited demand

segments may be uncovered. The framework also encourages an assessment of the sales potential in each of the possible segments, and aids in the proper allocation of marketing efforts to areas of greatest potential.

Having the cells of the grid identified helps the marketer to evaluate the wants, needs, and motivations of each market segment. For example, it appears that senior executives would be the appropriate targets for first-class service and extra-service categories. Further research could confirm or modify these evaluations and enable the marketer to determine whether the market size is worth developing a special offering for, and if so, what the marketing mix should be. *Market segmentation thus enables appropriate marketing mix design.*

The cross-classification in Figure 5-4 shows that the matrix can be further subdivided to gather more specific data about the characteristics of the proposed market target and to accurately develop a suitable marketing mix. The potential bases for segmenting markets is virtually limitless. For exmple, the segments might have been based on psychographic data, or on the basis of benefits sought. In the latter instance, prestige, comfort, and basic transporta-

Figure 5-4   Employees of Large Firms Extra Service Class

Service Benefit Desired	Heavy Traffic Regions	Southern Canada	North. Canada
Schedules	X		
Food			
Attendant service			
Leg Room			

tion might be some benefits which would assist in designing market offerings. Such divisions are sometimes made intuitively in the first place, but the final decisions are usually supported by concrete data.[8]

Using Market Target Decision Analysis in Assessing a Product Mix

Product mix, a concept in Chapter 10, refers to *the assortment of product lines and individual offerings available from a marketer.* Market target decision analysis can be used to assess a firm's product mix and to point up needed modifications. For example, one telephone company has used the concept to evaluate its product offerings.[9] The company segments the total market by psychographic categories as shown in Figure 5-5. Two of these categories are "belongers," and "achievers." Belongers were defined in this instance as those who are motivated by emotional and group influences. Achievers were defined as those whose dominant characteristic is the need to get ahead.

Figure 5-5   Using Market Target Decision Analysis to Evaluate a Product Mix

	Belongers	Achievers	Etc.
Romantic	Phone M Phone A Phone C		
Character		Phone R Phone Y	
Message-Centre Contemporary	Phone T		

Source: Reprinted from "Properly Applied Psychographics Add Marketing Luster," *Marketing News* (November 12, 1982), p. 10.

The telephone company's rule is to offer two and only two types of telephone sets in a given market segment in order not to have too complicated a market offering. The belonger segment was thus offered a regular phone and a romantic-type telephone to appeal to their sentiments. Achievers were offered the regular phone plus one designed to connote the idea of efficiency and character. This analysis helped to select a product from the assortment shown in Figure 5-5.

Market target decision analysis can go beyond merely identifying market targets. It can play a crucial role in actually developing marketing strategies such as product mixes.

Product Positioning

After a target market has been selected, the next task is to develop a market mix that will enable your product to compete effectively against others which are already in that market segment. It is unlikely that success will be achieved with a mix that is virtually identical to competitors for they already have attained a place in the minds of individuals in the target market and are used by a portion of them. Since people have a variety of needs and tastes, market acceptance is more easily achieved by **positioning** — *shaping the product and developing a market mix in such a way that the product is perceived to be* (and actually is) *different from competitors' products.*

This process requires a careful analysis of the features and strengths of competitive offerings, as well as a good understanding of the needs and wants of the target market. From comparing the two, the marketer tries to find a significant sized niche which is presently poorly served, and develops a marketing mix to fit that opportunity. Positioning generally goes beyond the simple use of promotion to differentiate a product or service in the mind of the customer, although this is often an important aspect.

Seven-Up used promotion as the sole element in positioning. The firm discovered that its product was missing the primary market for soft drinks — children, teenagers and young adults — because 7-Up's image was a mixer for older people's drinks. The firm used its now well-known "Uncola" campaign, first to identify the product as a soft drink, and then to position it as an alternative to colas in the soft drink market.

Another classic positioning campaign was Avis positioning itself against Hertz with the theme, "Avis is only number two, so why go with us? Because we try harder." In this instance, the service was also adjusted to make the claim true.

An example of the use of a total marketing mix package in market positioning is the case of Digital Equipment Corporation (DEC). This firm successfully carved out a niche in the small computer marketplace by identifying a competitive gap in IBM's domination of the computer market. IBM had concentrated on large mainframe applications, and had paid little attention to smaller business applications. The computer giant had easily fended off the efforts of many other major marketers such as Xerox, General Electric, and Singer, to crack IBM's hold on computer sales. A major error by these firms was their attempt to position their products in direct competition to IBM's mainframe computers. However, IBM's image as "the major computer producer" was too strongly entrenched in the minds of potential purchasers. They were unwilling to risk a major expenditure on a large computer from a newcomer.

All of these new competitors eventually pulled out of the mainframe market. However, by designing a minicomputer to fit the market niche it had discovered, and supporting it with a complementary marketing mix, DEC was able to capture a portion of the small computer market. Whether it can remain in that market over the long run remains to be seen. However, the use of product positioning to evaluate and develop marketing strategies in light of competitive offerings in the market is a useful and basic concept. It should follow naturally from the market segmentation decision.

Summary

This chapter continues the discussion of market segmentation introduced in Chapter 4. Various strategies associated with the market segmentation concept are considered here.

Correct strategy decisions are dependent upon a host of situational variables. The basic determinants of market matching strategy are: 1) company resources, 2) degree of product homogeneity, 3) stage in the product life cycle, and 4) competitors' strategies.

In light of an analysis of the market potential as well as these situational variables, the firm determines whether to adopt a single or multi-offer strategy. It then proceeds to position its offering(s) in the market with a marketing mix that will make it the most competitive.

The market segmentation process follows a sequential framework consisting of five stages. These stages can be outlined as follows:

- Stage 1. Determine the bases upon which markets can be segmented.
- Stage 2. Develop consumer profiles for the appropriate market segments.
- Stage 3. Assess the overall market potential for the relevant market segments.
- Stage 4. Estimate market share and cost benefit of each market segment given the existing competition and the marketing mix that is selected.

- Stage 5. Select the segments that will become the firm's market targets.

Market target decision analysis is a useful tool in the market segmentation process. A grid is developed that outlines the various market segments by their distinguishing characteristics. All bases for segmentation can be employed in market target decision analysis. In addition to selecting the actual market target segments, the type of analysis can also be used for assessing the firm's current and planned product mix.

Part Two began with a chapter on marketing planning and forecasting. This chapter dealt with the concept of market segmentation. In the next chapter, attention shifts to the research procedures and techniques used to acquire information for building effective marketing strategies. Chapter 6 covers marketing research and information systems and concludes Part Two.

Marketing Research and Information Systems

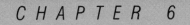
1. *To relate marketing research and information systems to the elements of the marketing mix.*

2. *To describe the development and current status of the marketing research function.*

3. *To list the steps in the marketing research process.*

4. *To differentiate the types and sources of primary and secondary data.*

5. *To identify the methods of collecting survey data.*

6. *To explain the various sampling techniques.*

7. *To distinguish between marketing research and marketing information systems.*

8. *To describe the current status of marketing information systems.*

Marketing research played a vital role in the design, development, and marketing of Kodak's successful Disc Camera, says John J. Powers, vice president–director of marketing communications, Eastman Kodak Co. Essentially, careful marketing research discovered a market segment that could be better served with new technology.

The photographic industry enjoys widespread consumer satisfaction with existing products. Simple-to-use, cartridge-loading cameras were extremely popular in the late 1970s. However, sales peaked in 1978 because the market was saturated. Consumers were generally very happy with the cameras they had already bought, and were willing to live with their limitations. Only those in the ranks of advanced amateurs invested significantly more time and money in the more complex world of 35 mm photography.

This situation challenged Kodak to restimulate the amateur photographic market. Kodak already knew that adding new features to its basic camera would not make it more attractive. After a point, more features interfered with an automatic camera's simplicity and resulted in unwanted complexities for the picture-taker. So Kodak marketing researchers were given a two-fold objective: to determine under what conditions consumers were and more importantly *were not* taking pictures.[1]

Marketing Research and the Marketing Information System

With the answers to the second part of the question, Kodak set out to develop a photographic system that could function well under the conditions that made photography unappealing to consumers. From a technical viewpoint they were looking at a total systems approach to solving a photographic problem uncovered by behavioural research. The result was the disc format and a number of breakthroughs in optics, electronics, and manufacturing technology, which Kodak utilized to produce its Disc Camera. The product is compact, easy to load and to use, and fits the picture-taking needs of a substantial segment of casual picture-takers.

From conception to introduction, marketing research played a key role in this innovative product line. Research findings were instrumental in determining the need for the products, in designing them to meet specific consumer wants and ultimately selling them. At later stages, research indicated a very high intent to purchase, and Kodak was able to set some high sales goals. Actual sales of film, cameras, and photofinishing equipment far exceeded the firm's most optimistic projections.

The Conceptual Framework

It has been said that the recipe for effective decisions is 90 percent information and 10 percent inspiration. All marketing strategy decisions depend on the type, quantity, and quality of the information on which they are based. A variety of sources of marketing information are available to the decision-maker. Some are well-planned investigations designed to elicit specific information. Other valuable sources are sales force reports, accounting data, or published reports. Controlled experiments or computer simulations can elicit still more information.

A major source of information takes the form of market research. **Marketing research** has been defined as *"the systematic gathering, recording, and analysing of data about problems relating to the marketing of goods and services."*[2]

The critical task of the marketing manager is decision-making. Managers earn their salaries by making effective decisions that enable their firms to solve problems as they arise, and by anticipating and preventing the occurrence of future problems. Many times though, they are forced to make decisions with limited information of uncertain accuracy and with inadequate facts. Marketing research aids the decision-maker by presenting pertinent facts, analysing them and suggesting possible action.

Chapter 6 deals with the marketing research function. Marketing research is closely linked with the other elements of the marketing planning process. All marketing research should be done within the framework of the organization's strategic plan. Research projects should be directed toward the resolution of marketing decisions that conform to an overall corporate strategy. Alfred S. Boote, the marketing research director for the Singer Company, estimates that research costs 50 to 60 percent more for firms that lack a strategic marketing plan because too much useless information is collected.[3]

Much of the material outlined in Chapters 4 and 5 on market segmentation and market target analysis is based on information collected through marketing research. Clearly, marketing research is the primary source of the information needed to make effective marketing decisions.

An Overview of the Marketing Research Function

Before looking at how marketing research is actually done, it is important to get an overall perspective of the field. What activities are considered part of the marketing research function? How did the field develop? Who is involved in marketing research?

Marketing Research Activities

All marketing decision areas are candidates for marketing research investigations. As Figure 6-1 indicates, marketing research efforts are commonly centred on developing sales forecasts for the firm's products, determining market and sales potential, designing new products and packages, analysing sales and marketing costs, evaluating the effectiveness of the firm's advertising, and determining consumer motives for buying products.

Marketing research in Canada may be said to have existed since there first were buyers and sellers. However, the day on which marketing research became a full-time profession was January 2, 1929. On that day, Henry King became the first full-time marketing researcher in Canada. His employer was an advertising agency, Cockfield Brown.[4]

In 1932, through the encouragement of Cockfield Brown, the first independent research company — Ethel Fulford and Associates — was founded in Toronto. In 1937, the Fulford company became known as Canadian Facts. By the end of World War II, four other major research companies had been established — Elliott-Haynes (now Elliott Research), the Canadian Institute of Public Opinion (Gallup Poll of Canada), A. C. Nielsen, and International Surveys. Since 1945, the number of research firms across Canada has grown dramatically.[5]

Figure 6-1   Marketing Research Activities of 798 Companies

Research Activity	Percentage of Companies Conducting the Activity
Advertising Research	
Motivation research	48
Copy research	49
Media research	61
Studies of advertising effectiveness	67
Business Economic and Corporate Research	
Short-range forecasting (up to a year)	85
Long-range forecasting (over a year)	82
Plant and warehouse location studies	71
Export and international studies	51
Corporate Responsibility Research	
Consumers' "right-to-know" studies	26
Ecological impact studies	33
Studies of legal constraints on advertising and promotion	51
Social values and policies studies	40
Product Research	
New-product acceptance and potential	84
Competitive product studies	85
Product testing	75
Packaging research	60
Sales and Market Research	
Measurement of market potentials	93
Market share analysis	92
Determination of market characteristics	93
Sales analyses	89
Establishment of sales quotas, territories	75
Distribution channel studies	69
Test markets, store audits	54
Consumer panel operations	50

Source: Dik Warren Twedt, ed., *1978 Marketing Research* (Chicago: American Marketing Association, 1978), p. 41. Reprinted by permission.

Participants in the Marketing Research Function

Many of the nation's leading manufacturing firms have established their own formal marketing research departments. Although such operations are found mostly in companies manufacturing consumer products, a substantial increase in marketing research departments has occurred recently in financial service firms, such as banks, trust companies, other lending institutions, insurance companies, and major nonprofit organizations.[6] Total expenditures for marketing research in 1985 are estimated at more than $70 million. Many smaller firms depend on independent marketing research firms to conduct their research studies. Even large firms typically rely on outside agencies to provide interviews, and they often farm out some research studies to independent agencies as well. The decision whether to conduct a study internally or through an outside organization is usually based on cost and the reliability of the information collected by the agency.

Research is likely to be contracted to outside groups when:

1) Problem areas can be defined in terms of specific research projects that can easily be delegated.
2) There is a need for specialized know-how or equipment.
3) Intellectual detachment is important.[7]
   A marketing research firm is often able to provide technical assistance and expertise not available within the firm. Also, the use of outside groups helps ensure that the researcher is not conducting the study only to validate the wisdom of a favourite theory or a preferred package design.

Marketing research companies can be classified as either syndicated services, full-service suppliers, or limited-service suppliers depending upon the primary thrust of the organization.[8]

Syndicated Service   A **syndicated service** is *an organization that offers to provide a standardized set of data on a regular basis to all who wish to buy it.* The Consumer Panel of Canada gathers information on consumer purchases of food and other household items from 3400 households that periodically report a detailed list of all food and other household products purchased during a particular time. This information can be extremely useful in determining brand preferences, the effects of various promotional activities on retail sales in one region or among a particular age group, and the degree of brand switching that occurs with certain products.

Full-Service Research Suppliers   **Full-service research suppliers** *contract with a client to conduct the complete marketing research project.* Full-service research suppliers start at the problem definition or conceptualization stage; work through the research design, data collection, and analysis stages; and prepare the final report to management. Full-service research suppliers literally become the client's marketing research arm.

Limited-Service Research Suppliers   **Limited-service research suppliers** are *organizations that specialize in a limited number of marketing research activities.* Companies that provide field interviews are the best example. Still others might provide data processing services. A syndicated service is a particular type of limited-service research supplier.

The Marketing Research Process

How is marketing research actually conducted? The starting point, of course, is the need for information on which to base a marketing decision, whether it be a specific question or an ongoing set of decisions. If need for information is perceived, the marketing research process can be invoked.

Figure 6-2   The Marketing Research Process

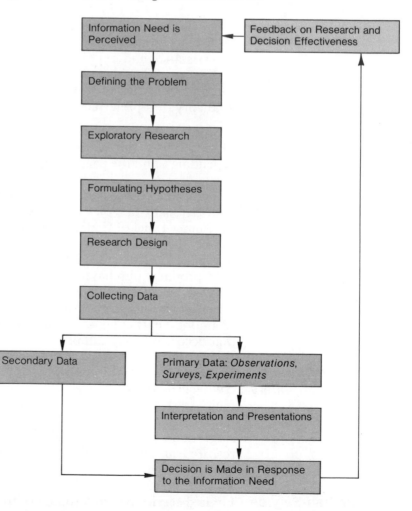

The marketing research process can be divided into six specific steps: 1) defining the problem; 2) exploratory research; 3) formulating a hypothesis; 4) research design; 5) collecting data; and 6) interpretation and presentation.

Figure 6-2 diagrams the marketing research process from information need to the research-based decision.

Problem Definition
Someone once remarked that well-defined problems are half solved. Problems are barriers that prevent the accomplishment of organizational goals. A clearly defined problem permits the researcher to focus the research process to secure the data necessary to solve the problem. Sometimes it is easy to pinpoint problems. Top executives at one airline company stood in airport line-ups in order to spot passenger complaints. The two most common gripes were inadequate flight information and cold in-flight coffee.[9] Once these problems were identified, they were corrected without further research.

However, it is often difficult to determine the specific problem, since what the researcher may be confronted with may be only symptoms of an underlying problem. In the late 1970s, Ciba-Geigy was stunned when its newly acquired Airwick Industries suffered $2 million loss on sales of such products as liquid room fresheners. When the parent firm investigated the problem, it recognized the losses as symptoms of a bitter price war in this market and that Airwick needed a more systematic method of developing and introducing product innovations to keep pace with competition. In order to solve the problems facing the firm, management had to look *beyond* the symptoms.

Exploratory Research
In searching for the cause of a problem the researcher will learn about the problem area and begin to focus on specific areas for study. This search, often called **exploratory research**, consists of discussing the problem with informed sources within the firm and with wholesalers, retailers, customers and others outside the firm, and examining secondary sources of information. Marketing researchers often refer to internal data collection as the *situation analysis* and to exploratory interviews with informed persons outside the firm as the *informal investigation*. Exploratory research also involves evaluating company records, such as sales and profit analyses of its own and its competitors' products. Figure 6-3 provides a checklist of topics to be considered in an exploratory analysis.

Formulating Hypotheses
After the problem has been defined and an exploratory investigation conducted, the marketer should be able to formulate a **hypothesis,** *a tentative explanation about the relationship between variables as a starting point for further testing.*

Figure 6-3   Topics for the Exploratory Analysis

The Company and Industry	1. Company objectives 2. The companies in the industry (size, financial power) and industry trends 3. Geographic locations of the industry 4. The company's market share as compared with competitors' 5. Marketing policies of competitors
The Market	1. Geographic location 2. Demographic characteristics of the market 3. Purchase motivations 4. Product use patterns 5. Nature of demand
Products	1. Physical characteristics 2. Consumer acceptance — strengths and weaknesses 3. Package as a container and as a promotional device 4. Manufacturing processes, production capacity 5. Closeness and availability of substitute products
Marketing Channels	1. Channels employed and recent trends 2. Channel policy 3. Margins for resellers
Sales Organization	1. Market coverage 2. Sales analysis by number of accounts per salesperson, size of accounts, type of account, etc. 3. Expense ratios for various territories, product types, account size, etc. 4. Control procedures 5. Compensation methods
Pricing	1. Elasticity 2. Season or special promotional price cuts 3. Profit margins of resellers 4. Legal restrictions 5. Price lines
Advertising and Sales Promotion	1. Media employed 2. Dollar expenditures as compared with competitors 3. Timing of advertising 4. Sales promotional materials provided for resellers 5. Results from previous advertising and sales promotional campaigns

A marketer of industrial products might formulate the following hypothesis:

Failure to provide 36-hour delivery service will reduce our sales by 20 percent.

Such a statement may prove correct or incorrect. The formulation of this hypothesis does, however, provide a basis for investigation and an eventual determination of its accuracy. It also allows the researcher to move to the next step: development of the research design.

Lever Brothers' Pepsodent toothpaste had been on the market since 1944, but by the mid-1960s surveys were indicating that young consumers were dissatisfied with current offerings in two areas: tooth whitening and breath freshening. Lever Brothers began to work on a hypothesis that a combination toothpaste and mouth-wash could become a successful market entry. The end result of the firm's hypothesis testing was Close-up toothpaste.[10]

Research Design   The research design should be a comprehensive plan for testing the hypotheses formulated about the problem. **Research design** refers to *a series of advance decisions that, taken together, make up a master plan or model for the conduct of the investigation.* Development of such a plan allows the researcher to control each step of the research process. Figure 6-4 lists the steps involved in the research design.

Data Collection   A major step in the research design is the determination of what data are needed to test the hypotheses. Two types of data are typically used: primary data and secondary data. **Primary data** refer to *data being collected for the first time* during a marketing research study, and for reasons that will become apparent will be discussed at length later in the chapter.

Secondary data are *previously published matter*. They serve as an extremely important source of information for the marketing researcher.

Collecting Secondary Data   Not only are secondary data important, they are also abundant in many areas that the marketing researcher may need to investigate. In fact, the overwhelming quantity of secondary data available at little or no cost often challenges the researcher in the selection of only pertinent information.

Secondary data consists of two types: internal and external. *Internal secondary data* include records of sales, product performances, sales force activities, and marketing costs. *External data* are obtained from a variety of sources. Governments—local, provincial, and federal — provide a wide variety of secondary data. Private sources also supply secondary data for the marketing decision-maker.

Figure 6-4 Sixteen Steps in the Research Design

Questions Faced	Steps to Take or Choices
1. What is needed to measure the outcome of the alternative solutions?	1. Decide the subjects on which data are needed.
	2. Examine the time and cost considerations.
2. What specific data are needed for that approach?	3. Write exact statements of data to be sought.
3. From whom are such data available?	4. Search and examine relevant secondary data.
	5. Determine remaining data gaps.
4. How should primary data be obtained?	6. Define the population from which primary data may be sought.
a. What are the types of data?	7. Determine the various needed facts, opinions, and motives.
b. What general collection methods shall be used?	8. Plan for obtaining data by survey, observational, or experimental methods.
c. How shall the sources be contacted?	9. If using a survey, decide whether to contact respondents by telephone, by mail, or in person.
d. How may the data be secured from the sources?	10. Consider the questions and forms needed to elicit and record the data.
e. Shall there be a complete count of the population or a sample drawn from it? How chosen?	11. Decide on the coverage of the population:
	a. Choose between a complete enumeration and a sampling.
	b. If sampling, decide whether to select from the whole population or restricted portions of it.
	c. Decide how to select sample members.
f. How will the fieldwork be conducted?	12. Map and schedule the fieldwork.
5. How will the data be interpreted and presented?	13. Plan the personnel requirements of the field study.
	14. Consider editing and tabulating requirements.
	15. Anticipate possible interpretation of the data, and be sure it can answer the research questions which need answering.
	16. Consider the way the findings may be presented.

Source: Adapted from David J. Luck, Hugh G. Wales, and Donald A. Taylor, *Marketing Research*, 3rd ed. (Englewood Cliffs, N.J.: Prentice-Hall, Inc., 1970), p. 87. Reprinted by permission.

Government Sources The federal government provides the country's most important sources of marketing data, the most frequently used being census data. Although the government spent millions of dollars in conducting the various Censuses of Canada, the information is available at no charge at local libraries and Statistics Canada offices, or it can be purchased at a nominal charge on computer tapes for instant electronic access. In fact, Statistics Canada produces several different censuses. Figure 6-5 briefly describes the main ones.

The 1981 data are so detailed for large cities that breakdowns of population characteristics are available for a few city blocks (census tracts). Thus local retailers or shopping centre developers can easily gather detailed information about the immediate neighbourhoods that will constitute their customers without spending time or money in conducting a comprehensive survey.

So much data is produced by the federal government that the marketing researcher often purchases summaries such as the *Canada Year Book* or *Market Research Handbook* or subscribes to *Statistics Canada Daily*. It is also possible to receive *Informat Weekly*, which provides a listing of new releases by Statistics Canada. A further

---

Figure 6-5 Census Data Collected by Statistics Canada

Census of Canada. Conducted once each decade, with certain categories checked every five years. It provides a count of all residents of Canada by province, city or town, county or other suitable division, and, in large cities, by census tract. Particularly useful to marketers is the data provided by economic rather than political boundaries, such as greater metropolitan areas. Data is also gathered on age, sex, race, citizenship, educational levels, occupation, employment status, income and family status of inhabitants. A less detailed census is conducted at the half-way point in the decade.

Census of Housing. Provides information regarding the housing conditions of Canadians, such as value of the dwelling, number of rooms, type of structure, ethnic origin of occupants, and year built.

Census of Manufacturers. Annual coverage of major industries revealing the value of products produced by industry, cost of materials and equipment, number of establishments, and wages paid.

Census of Agriculture. Conducted every five years. Data regarding the number of farms, number of persons residing on farms (by age and sex), value of farm products sold, area of each major crop, number of tractors, number of livestock, presence of electricity and running water.

Census of Minerals. Data on employees, wages, quantities produced, cost of materials and supplies, types of equipment used, and hours worked.

source of Statistics Canada data is the *Statistics Canada Catalogue*, which lists major data published by the agency. Furthermore, the researcher can gain access to unpublished data through on-line terminals at Statistics Canada User Advisory Services Centres.

Provincial and city governments are other important sources of information on employment, production, and sales activities within a particular province.

Private Sources   Numerous private organizations provide information for the marketing executive. In the *Handbook of Canadian Consumer Markets* published by The Conference Board of Canada the marketer will find a wide range of illuminating and valuable data. Figure 6-6 illustrates the type of information collected for each of the provinces. Another excellent source is *Canadian Markets* published by *The Financial Post*. Other good summary data can be found in the annual survey of buying power published by *Sales & Marketing Management* magazine. For activities in a particular industry, trade associations are excellent resource sources. Advertising agencies continually collect information on the audiences reached by various media.

Figure 6-6   A Page From Handbook of Canadian Consumer Markets. It Provides Many Types of Data for the Marketing Researcher

Family Expenditures on Food at Home and Away
Average annual urban family[1] expenditure on food, 1978 = 100%

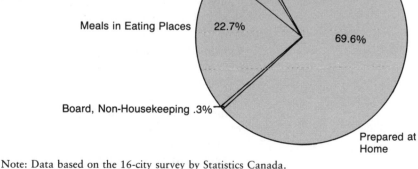

Note: Data based on the 16-city survey by Statistics Canada.
[1]Includes all families and unattached individuals.

Source: Statistics Canada; The Conference Board of Canada.

Family Expenditures on Food at Home and Away (FEXF)

Average annual expenditures on food, urban families[1]

	Expenditures (Dollars)		Percentage Distribution	
Item	1974	1978	1974	1978
	A		**B**	
1. Total Food................	2,412.3	3,063.8	100.0	100.0
2. Prepared at Home..........	1,920.2	2,131.5	79.6	69.6
3. Board, Non-Housekeeping...	15.6	9.8	0.6	0.3
4. Meals in Eating Places.......	333.9	694.7	13.8	22.7
5. At work................	174.5	n.a.	7.2	n.a.
6. At school..............	20.2	n.a.	0.8	n.a.
7. Other..................	139.2	n.a.	5.8	n.a.
8. Between-Meal Food.........	46.6	n.a.	1.9	n.a.
9. Food in Eating Places, Away from Home.............	85.9	199.2	3.6	6.5
10. At school or college.......	5.4	8.8	0.2	0.3
11. On a job...............	6.5	25.0	0.3	0.8
12. On vacation.............	74.0	165.4	3.1	5.4
13. Meals Prepared on a Trip.....	10.0	28.1	0.4	0.9

Note: The 1978 data were based on the Survey of Urban Family Expenditure carried out
       by Statistics Canada in 16 major cities across Canada (see note to table on page 134).
       The 1974 data were based on a similar survey carried out in 14 of the 16 cities
       included in the 1978 survey, but excluding Charlottetown and Summerside (P.E.I.).
n.a. — Not available.

[1]Includes all families and unattached individuals.

Source: Statistics Canada; The Conference Board of Canada.

Source: *Handbook of Canadian Consumer Markets*, 1982, 2nd Edition (Ottawa: The
Conference Board of Canada, 1982), p. 140.

Several national firms offer information to business firms on a
subscription basis. The largest of these, A. C. Nielsen Company,
collects data every two months on product sales, retail prices, display
space, inventories, and promotional activities of competing brands
of food and drug products from a substantial sample of food stores
and drugstores. The Consumer Panel of Canada (International
Surveys), mentioned earlier, gathers information on consumer
purchases.

Advantages and
Limitations of
Secondary Data

The use of secondary data offers two important advantages over that of primary data:

1) The assembly of previously collected data is almost always less expensive than the collection of primary data.

2) Less time is involved in locating and using secondary data. Figure 6-7 shows the estimated time involved in completing a research study requiring primary data. The time involved will naturally vary considerably depending on such factors as the research subject and the scope of the study.

The researcher must be aware of two potential limitations to the use of secondary data: 1) the data may be obsolete, or 2) the classifications of the secondary data may not be usable in the study. Published information has an unfortunate habit of rapidly going out of date. A marketing researcher analysing the population of the Calgary metropolitan market in 1985 discovers that much of the 1981 census data is already obsolete due to the influx of people attracted by the development of the oil and gas industry.

Data may also have been collected previously on such bases as county or city boundaries, when the marketing manager requires it broken down by city blocks or census tracts. In such cases the marketing researcher may not be able to rearrange the secondary data in a usable form and must begin the collection of primary data.

Figure 6-7   Time Requirements for a Primary Data Research Project

Step	Estimated Time Required For Completion
Problem Definition	Several Days
Development of Methodology	One Week
Questionnaire Design	One Week
Questionnaire Pretest and Evaluation of Pretest Results	Two Weeks
Field Interviews	One to Six Weeks
Coding of Returned Questionnaires	One week
Data Transfer to Computer Tape	One Week
Data Processing and Statistical Analysis	Seven to Ten Days
Interpretation of Output	One Week
Written Report and Presentation of Findings	Two Weeks
Total Elapsed Time	**12 to 17 Weeks**

Source: Estimates by Alfred S. Boote, Corporate Director of Market Research, The Singer Company. Quoted in "Everyone Benefits from Closer Planning, Research Ties," *Marketing News* (January 9, 1981), p. 30. Used by permission of the American Marketing Association.

Collecting Primary Data   When secondary data is incomplete or does not relate to the problem at hand, the research design must call for a direct test of a hypothesis. Producers at Paramount Pictures were fearful that the death of Mr. Spock in *Star Trek II — The Wrath of Khan* would turn "Trekkies" against it, so the movie was shown to participants at a science-fiction meeting. The audience loved the movie, and Paramount Pictures decided to leave Mr. Spock dead.[11]

As Figure 6-4 indicated, the marketing researcher has three alternative methods for collecting primary data: observation, survey, or controlled experiment. No one method is best in all circumstances.

The Observation Method   Observational studies are conducted by actually viewing (either by visual observation or through mechanical means such as hidden cameras) the overt actions of the respondent. This may take the form of traffic counts at a potential location for a fast-food franchise, a check of licence plates at a shopping centre to determine the area from which shoppers are attracted, or the use of supermarket scanners to record sales of certain products viewed.

The observation method has both advantages and drawbacks. Merits are that observation is often more accurate than questioning techniques like surveys and interviews, and that it may be the only way to get information such as actual shopping behaviour in a supermarket. It may also be the easiest way to get specific data. Limitations include observer subjectivity and errors in interpretation. For instance, the researchers might incorrectly classify people's economic status because of the way they were dressed at the time of observation.[12]

Eastman Kodak used the observation method in evaluating advertisements it scheduled for the launch of the Ektra camera. Perception Research Service was hired to study patterns of viewer eye movements when looking at advertisements featuring television actor Michael Landon. The eye-tracking tests resulted in Eastman Kodak's moving the headline "Kodak introduces the Ektra pocket camera" from the bottom of the ad to the top, since a majority of eye movements flowed to the top.[13]

The Survey Method   The amount and type of information that can be obtained through mere observation of overt consumer acts is limited; the researcher must ask questions to obtain information on attitudes, motives, and opinions. The survey method is the most widely used approach to collecting primary data. There are three kinds of surveys: telephone, mail, and personal interviews.

Telephone interviews are inexpensive and fast in obtaining small quantities of relatively impersonal information. Many firms have leased WATS services, which reduce considerably the cost of surveys by allowing unlimited long-distance calls at a fixed rate per region.

Telephone interviews account for 55 to 60 percent of all primary marketing research.[14] They are limited to simple, clearly worded questions. Such interviews have two drawbacks: it is extremely difficult to obtain personal characteristics of the respondent, and the survey may be prejudiced since two groups will be omitted — those households without telephones and those with unlisted numbers. One survey reported that alphabetical listings in telephone directories excluded one-fourth of large-city dwellers, and that they underrepresented service workers and separated and divorced persons. In addition, the mobility of the population creates problems in choosing names from telephone directories. As a result, a number of telephone interviewers have resorted to using digits selected at random and matched to telephone prefixes in the geographic area to be sampled. This technique is designed to correct the problem of sampling those with new telephone listings and those with unlisted numbers.[15]

Mail interviews allow the marketing researcher to conduct national studies at a reasonable cost. While personal interviews with a national sample may be prohibitive, by using the mail, the researcher can reach each potential respondent for the price of a postage stamp. Costs may be misleading, however, since *returned* questionnaires for such a study may average only 40 to 50 percent, depending upon the length of the questionnaire and respondent interest. When returns are even lower, the question arises as to the opinions of the majority who did not respond. Also, some surveys use a coin or other device to gain the reader's attention which further increases costs. Unless additional information is obtained from nonrespondents, the results of the study are likely to be biased, since there may be important differences between the characteristics of these people and of those who took the time to complete and return the questionnaire. For this reason a follow-up questionnaire is sometimes mailed to nonrespondents, or telephone interviews may be used to gather additional information.[16]

Personal interviews are typically the best means of obtaining more detailed information since the interviewer has the opportunity to establish rapport with the respondent. The interviewer can also explain questions that might be confusing or vague to the respondent. Mail questionnaires must be carefully worded and pretested to eliminate any potential misunderstanding by respondents. But misunderstandings can occur with even the most clearly worded questions. When a truck operated by a government agency accidentally killed a cow, an official responded with an apology and a form to be filled out. It included a space for "disposition of the dead cow." The farmer responded "kind and gentle."[17]

Personal interviews are slow and the most expensive method of collecting data. However, their flexibility coupled with the detailed information that can be collected often offset these limitations. Recently marketing research firms have rented locations in shopping centres where they have greater access to potential buyers of the products in which they are interested. Downtown retail districts and airports are other on-site locations for marketing-research.

Focus group interviews have been widely used in recent years as a means of gathering preliminary research information. In a **focus group interview** eight to 12 people are brought together to discuss a subject of interest. Although the moderator typically explains the purpose of the meeting and suggests an opening discussion topic, he or she is interested in stimulating interaction among group members in order to develop the discussion of numerous points about the subject. Focus group sessions, which are often one to two hours long, are usually taped so the moderator can devote full attention to the discussion. This process gives the researcher an idea of how consumers view a problem. Often it uncovers points of view that the researcher had not thought of.

The Experimental Method   The final and least-used method of collecting marketing information is through the use of *controlled experiments*. An experiment is a scientific investigation in which the researcher controls or manipulates a test group that did not receive the controls or manipulations. Such experiments can be conducted in the field or in a laboratory setting.

Although a number of experiments have been conducted in the controlled environment of a laboratory, most have been conducted in the field. To date, the most common use of this method has been in **test marketing**.

Marketers face great risks in introducing products to the Canadian market. They often attempt to reduce this risk by *introducing the new, untried product into a particular metropolitan area and then observing its degree of success*. Frequently used cities include Calgary, Lethbridge, and Winnipeg. Consumers in the test-market city view the product as they do any other new product since it is in retail outlets and is advertised in the local media. The test-market city becomes a small replica of the total market.The marketing manager can then compare actual sales with expected sales and can project them on a nationwide basis. If the test results are favourable, the risks of a large-scale failure are reduced. Many products fail at the test-market stage, and thus consumers who live in these cities may purchase products that no one else will ever buy.

The major problem with controlled experiments is the difficult task of controlling all variables in a real-life situation. The laboratory scientist can rigidly control temperature and humidity, but how can the marketing manager determine the effect of varying the retail price through refundable coupons when the competition decides to retaliate or deliberately confuse the experiment by also issuing competitive coupons?

In the future, experimentation will become more frequent as firms develop more sophisticated simulated competitive models requiring computer analysis. Simulation of market activities promises to be one of the great new developments in marketing.

Sampling Techniques

Sampling[18] is one of the most important aspects of marketing research. *The total group that the researcher wants to study* is called the **population** or **universe**. For a political campaign, the population would be all eligible voters. For a new cosmetic line, it might be all women in a certain age bracket. If this total group is contacted, the results are known as a **census**. Unless the group is small, the cost will be overwhelming. Even the federal government only attempts a full census once every ten years.

Information, therefore, is rarely gathered from the total population during a survey. Instead, researchers select a representative group called a sample. Samples can be classified as either probability samples or nonprobability samples. A **probability sample** *is one in which every member of the population has an equal chance of being selected*. **Nonprobability samples** are *arbitrary*, and standard statistical tests cannot be applied. Marketing researchers usually base their studies on probability samples, but it is important to be able to identify all types of samples. Some of the best known sampling plans are outlined below.

Convenience Sample

A **convenience sample** is *a nonprobability sample based on the selection of readily available respondents*. Broadcasting's "on-the-street" interviews are a good example. Marketing researchers sometimes use it in exploratory research, but not in definitive studies.

Judgment Sample

Nonprobability samples of people with a specific attribute are called **judgment samples**. Election-night predictions are usually based on polls of "swing voters" and are a type of judgment sample.

Quota Sample

A **quota sample** is *a nonprobability sample that is divided so that different segments or groups are represented in the total sample*. An example would be a survey of auto import owners that included 33 Nissan owners, 31 Toyota owners, 7 BMW owners, and so on.

Referral Sample

Sometimes called a snowball sample, a **referral sample** *is done in waves as more respondents with the characteristics are identified*. An industrial goods manufacturer might poll its customer list about a new cutting machine it will introduce. The survey might also ask respondents to identify other businesses who might use such a machine. The referrals would then be the target of a second stage of the research.

Simple Random Sample   The basic type of probability sample is the **simple random sample** where *every item in the relevant universe has an equal opportunity of being selected*. Provincial lotteries are an example. Each number that appears on a ticket has an equal opportunity of being selected and each ticket holder an equal opportunity of winning. Using a computer to select 200 respondents randomly from a mailing list of 1000 would give every name on the list an equal opportunity of being selected.

Systematic Sample   A *probability sample that takes every Nth item on a list, after a random start*, is called a **systematic sample**. Sampling from a telephone directory is a common example.

Figure 6-8   Manager and Researcher Complaints

Management complaints about marketing researchers:

1. Research is not problem-oriented. It tends to provide a plethora of facts, not actionable results or direction.
2. Researchers are too involved with techniques. They tend to do research for research's sake and they appear to be reluctant to get involved in management "problems."
3. Research is slow, vague, and of questionable validity. It depends too much on clinical evidence.
4. Researchers can't communicate; they don't understand; and they don't talk the language of management. In many cases, researchers are inexperienced and not well rounded.

Marketing researcher complaints about management:

1. Management doesn't include research in discussions of basic fundamental problems. Management tends to ask only for specific information about parts of problems.
2. Management pays no more than lip service to research and doesn't really understand or appreciate its value. Research isn't given enough corporate status.
3. Management has a propensity to jump the gun — not allowing enough time for research. Management draws preliminary conclusions based on early or incomplete results.
4. Management relies more on intuition and judgement than on research. Research is used as a crutch, not a tool. Management tends to "typecast" the marketing researcher.

Source: Reprinted by permission from "Communication Gap Hinders Proper Use of Market Research," *Marketing Insights* (February 19, 1968), p. 7. Copyright 1968 by Crain Communications Inc.

Interpreting Research Findings

The actual design and execution of a survey seeking primary data are beyond the scope of this book. A number of marketing research books contain solutions to the many problems involved in surveying the public. Among these problems are designing the questionnaires; selecting, training, and controlling the field interviewers; editing, coding, tabulating, and interpreting the data; presenting the results; and following up on the survey.

It is crucial that marketing researchers and research users cooperate at every stage in the research design. Too many studies go unused because marketing management views the results as too restricted due to the lengthy discussion of research limitations that accompanies the data, or the use of unfamiliar terminology such as "levels of confidence" and "Type 1 errors." Occasional misunderstandings between researchers and the manager-user may lead to friction and failure to make effective use of the findings. Figure 6-8 lists several complaints that each party may express about the other.

These complaints reflect lack of understanding of the needs and capabilities of both parties. They can often be settled by involving both managers and researchers in specifying needed information, developing research designs, and evaluating the findings of the research. The research report should include recommendations and, whenever possible, an oral report should explain, expand upon, or clarify the written summary. These efforts increase the likelihood of management's utilizing the research findings.

Marketing Information Systems

Many marketing managers discover that their information problems result from an overabundance — not a paucity — of marketing data. Their sophisticated computer facilities provide them daily with a deluge of printouts about sales in 30 different market areas, a hundred different products, and 6400 customers. A marketing manager may solve the crisis of too much information of the wrong kind in the wrong form each morning by gently sliding the ominous stack of computer printouts to the edge of the desk, where it quietly falls into the wastebasket. Data and information are not necessarily synonymous terms. *Data* refer to statistics, opinions, facts, or predictions categorized on some basis for storage and retrieval. *Information* is data relevant to the marketing manager in making decisions.

The solution to the problem of obtaining relevant information appears simple — establish a systematic approach to information management through the installation of a planned marketing information system. Establishment of an effective marketing information system (MIS) is, however, much easier said than done, as documented by the large number of firms who have attempted to develop an MIS and have only succeeded in increasing the amounts of irrelevant data.

The ideal **marketing information system** should be *a designed set of procedures and methods for generating an orderly flow of pertinent information for use in making decisions, providing management with the current and future states of the market with indications of market responses to company actions as well as to the actions of competitors.*[19]

Properly constructed, the MIS could serve as the nerve centre for the company, providing instantaneous information suitable for each level of management. It would act as a thermostat, monitoring the marketplace continuously so that management can adjust its actions as conditions change.

The analogy of an automatic heating system shows the role of marketing information in a firm's marketing system (see Figure 6-9). Once the objective of a temperature setting (perhaps 20°C) has been established, information about the actual temperature in the house is collected and compared with the objective, and a decision is made based upon this comparison. If the temperature drops below an estab-

Figure 6-9   The Decision — Turn the Furnace On or Off

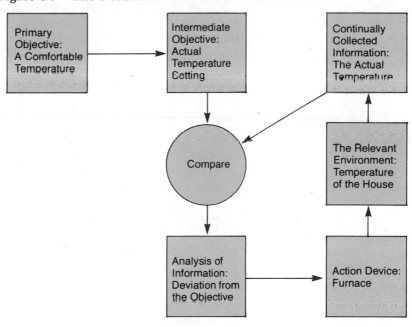

Source: Reprinted by permission from Bertram Schoner and Kenneth F. Uhl, *Marketing Research: Information Systems and Decision Making* (New York: Wiley, 1975), p. 10.

lished figure, the decision is made to activate the furnace until the temperature reaches some established amount. On the other hand, a high temperature may require a decision to turn off the furnace.

Deviation from the firm's goals of profitability, return on investment, or market share may necessitate changes in price structures, promotional expenditures, package design, or numerous marketing alternatives. The firm's MIS should be capable of revealing such deviations and possibly suggesting tactical changes that will result in attaining the established goals.

Many marketing executives feel that their company does not need a marketing information system, for various reasons. Two arguments are most often given: 1) the size of the company operations does not warrant such a complete system, and 2) the information provided by an MIS is already being supplied by the marketing research department.

These contentions arise from a misconception of services and functions performed by the marketing research department. Marketing research has already been described as typically focusing on a specific problem or project; the investigations have a definite beginning, middle, and end.

Marketing information systems, on the other hand, are much wider in scope and involve the continual collection and analysis of marketing information. Figure 6-10 indicates the various information inputs — including marketing research studies — that serve as components of the firm's MIS.

Robert J. Williams, creator of the first and still one of the most notable marketing information systems in 1961 at the Mead Johnson division of Edward Dalton Company explains the difference in this manner:

> The difference between marketing research and marketing intelligence is like the difference between a flash bulb and a candle. Let's say you are dancing in the dark. Every 90 seconds you're allowed to set off a flash bulb. You can use those brief intervals of intense light to chart a course, but remember everybody is moving, too. Hopefully, they'll accommodate themselves roughly to your predictions. You may get bumped and you may stumble every so often, but you can dance along.
>
> On the other hand, you can light a candle. It doesn't yield as much light, but it's a steady light. You are continually aware of the movements of the other bodies. You can adjust you own course to the courses of the others. The intelligence system is a kind of candle. It's no great flash on the immediate state of things, but it provides continuous light as situations shift and change.[20]

By focusing daily on the marketplace, the MIS provides a continuous systematic and comprehensive study of areas that indicate devi-

Figure 6-10   Information Components of a Firm's MIS

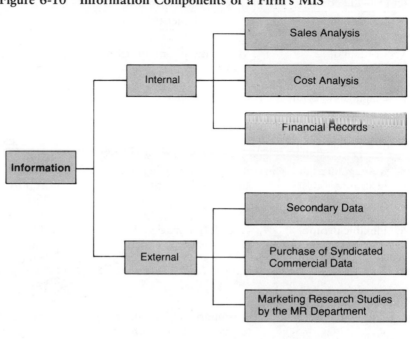

ations from established goals. The up-to-the minute data allows problems to be corrected before they adversely affect company operations. Figure 6-11 summarizes many of the applications and possible benefits of a sophisticated information system.

Current Status of Marketing Information Systems   Marketing information systems have progressed a long way from the days when they were primarily responsible for clerical activities — and usually at an increased cost over the old method! Today, managers have available special computer programs, remote access consoles, better data banks, direct communication with the computer, and assignment of authority to the computer for periodic review and referral. In some instances, the computer simulates various market conditions and makes decisions based on the results of the model. But just how common are these computer-based marketing information systems in company offices?

Some larger Canadian companies have had well-developed MIS for several years. While statistics are lacking, it is thought that the use of *marketing* information systems is not widespread. It appears that finance and production currently receive most of the overall *management* system's resources. It is logical that a growing proportion of resources will be devoted to marketing systems during the next few years.

Figure 6-11   Benefits Possible With an Information Sytem

Typical Applications	Benefits	Examples
Control Systems		
1. Control of marketing costs	1. More timely computerized reports	1. Undesirable cost trends are spotted more quickly so that corrective action may be taken sooner.
2. Diagnosis of poor sales performance	2. Flexible on-line retrieval of data	2. Executives can ask supplementary questions of the computer to help pinpoint reasons for a sales decline and reach an action decision more quickly.
3. Management of fashion goods	3. Automatic spotting of problems and opportunities	3. Fast-moving fashion items are reported daily for quick reorder, and slow-moving items are also reported for fast price reductions.
4. Flexible promotion strategy	4. Cheaper, more detailed, and more frequent reports	4. Ongoing evaluation of a promotional campaign permits reallocation of funds to areas behind target.
Planning Systems		
1. Forecasting	1. Automatic translation of terms and classifications between departments	1. Survey-based forecasts of demand for complex industrial goods can be automatically translated into parts requirements and production schedules.
2. Promotional planning and corporate long-range planning	2. Systematic testing of alternative promotional plans and compatibility testing of various divisional plans	2. Complex simulation models, developed and operated with the help of data bank information, can be used for promotional planning by product managers and for strategic planning by top management.
3. Credit manager	3. Programmed executive decision rules can operate on data bank information	3. Credit decisions are automatically made as each order is processed.
4. Purchasing	4. Detailed sales reporting permits automation of management decisions	4. Computer automatically repurchases standard items on the basis of correlation of sales data with programmed decision rules.
Research Systems		
1. Advertising strategy	1. Additional manipulation of data is possible when stored for computers in an unaggregated file.	1. Sales analysis is possible by new market segment breakdowns.
2. Pricing strategy	2. Improved storage and retrieval capability allows new types of date to be collected and used.	2. Systematic recording of information about past R & D contract bidding situations allows improved bidding strategies.

Figure 6-11   continued

Typical Applications	Benefits	Examples
3. Evaluation of advertising expenditures	3. Well-designed data banks permit integration and comparison of different sets of data.	3. Advertising expenditures are compared to shipments by district to provide information about advertising effectiveness.
4. Continuous experiments	4. Comprehensive monitoring of input and performance variables yields information when changes are made.	4. Changes in promotional strategy by type of customer are matched against sales results on a continuous basis.

Source: Reprinted by permission of the *Harvard Business Review*. Exhibit from "How to Build a Marketing Information System," by Donald F. Cox and Robert E. Good, *Harvard Business Review* (May–June 1967), p. 146 Copyright © 1967 by the President and Fellows of Harvard College; all rights reserved.

Successful Marketing Information Systems

Although only a few large companies have sophisticated, computer-based marketing information systems, considerable attention is being focused on their contributions. By the end of the decade many of the larger companies will establish their own information systems. The Monsanto Company and General Mills Incorporated are examples of firms with a successful MIS in operation.

Monsanto has designed one of the most advanced marketing information systems in operation. The system provides detailed sales analyses by product, sales, district, type of mill, and end use. Computer analyses are obtained from a continuing panel of households who represent a cross-section of the national market. Information is collected on purchase patterns by socio-economic group and is then analysed to determine current buying trends.

Monsanto also collects survey data to record the actions of competitors. In addition the system generates short-, medium-, and long-range forecasts for the company and industry. Short-term forecasts are developed for each of 400 individual products.

The General Mills computer supplies each zone, regional, and district manager with a daily teletype report on the previous day's orders by brand and a comparison of current projections of monthly sales with the monthly total projected the week before. Each of 1700 individual products is analysed in terms of current profitability and projected annual profitability as compared with target projections made at the beginning of the year. The "problem" products requiring management attention are then printed out on the daily reports. A similar report looks for problem areas in each region and breaks down the nature of the problem according to cause (for example, profit margins, over- or underspending on advertising and sales promotion).[21]

Developing an MIS   The first step in the construction of the MIS is obtaining the total support of top management. Management not only must be truly enthusiastic about the potential of the system, but also must maintain the belief that it is top management's place to oversee its development. Too often the technical staff are left to build such a system.

The next step involves a review and appraisal of the entire marketing organization and of the policies that direct it. The marketing managers' responsibilities must be clearly defined. If the system is to measure their performance against plans, then it is necessary to specify precisely each person's areas of accountability.

Once the organization is readied for the development of the system, the level of sophistication of the MIS must be determined. Before this can be done the company needs and the costs of meeting these needs must be carefully considered. The abilities of managers to develop and use a sophisticated system effectively must also be considered. Managers must be able to define their specific information needs. A questionnaire, such as the one in Figure 6-12, may be used to pinpoint specific information requirements.

Management must also be able to state explicitly its planning, decision-making, and control processes and procedures. For example, an automated exception reporting system may be developed for the manager who is able to verbalize a specific set of deci-

---

Figure 6-12   Sample Questionnaire for Determining Market Information Needs

1. What types of decisions are you regularly called upon to make?
2. What types of information do you need to make the decision?
3. What types of information do you regularly get?
4. What types of special studies do you periodically request?
5. What types of information would you like to get but are not currently receiving?
6. What information would you like to receive daily? weekly? monthly? yearly?
7. What magazines and trade journals would you like to receive regularly?
8. What types of data analysis programs would you like to receive?
9. What are four improvements you would like to see made in the present marketing information stystem?

Source: Philip Kotler, "A Design for the Firm's Marketing Nerve Center," *Business Horizons* (Fall 1966), p. 70. Copyright 1966 by The Foundation for the School of Business at Indiana University. Reprinted by permission.

sion rules, such as " I always like to know about all situations in which sales, profits, or market shares are running 4 percent or more behind plan. Furthermore, in any exceptional cases I also require the following diagnostic information: prices, distribution levels, advertising, and consumer attitude."[22]

A Futuristic Perspective for MIS

As marketing research becomes increasingly scientific and is combined by a growing number of organizations into fully functional information systems, decision-makers benefit by making informed decisions about problems and opportunities. Sophisticated computer simulations make it possible to consider alternative courses of action by posing a number of "what if?" situations. These developments may convert the scenario we imagine in 1995 into reality in a much shorter time.

Summary

Information is vital for marketing decision making. No firm can operate without detailed information of its market. Information may take several forms: one-time marketing research studies, secondary data, internal data, subscriptions to commercial information sources, and the output of a marketing information system.

Marketing research, an important source of information, deals with studies that collect and analyse data relevant to marketing decisions. It involves the specific delineation of problems, research design, collection of secondary and primary data, interpretation of research findings, and presentation of results for management action.

The most common market research activities are determining market potential, developing sales forecasts for the firm's products and services, competitive product analysis, new product estimates, studies related to marketing mix decisions and international trade, and social and cultural research. Annual expenditures for marketing research now exceed $70 million and most large companies have internal market research departments. However, outside suppliers still remain vital to the research function. Some of these outside research suppliers perform the complete research task, while others specialize in limited areas or provide syndicated data services.

The marketing research process can be divided into six specific steps: 1) defining the problem; 2) exploratory research; 3) formulating hypotheses; 4) research design; 5) collecting data; and 6) interpretation and presentation. A clearly defined problem allows the researcher to obtain the relevant decision-oriented information. Exploratory research refers to information gained both outside and inside the firm. Hypotheses—tentative explanations of some specific event — allow the researcher to set out a specific research design, the series of decisions that, taken together, comprise a master plan or model for the conduct of the investigation.

The data collection phase of the marketing research process can involve either or both primary data (original data) and secondary data (previously published data). Primary data can be collected by three alternative methods: observation, survey, or experimental. Once the data are collected, it is important that researchers interpret and present them in a way that is meaningful to management.

An increasing number of firms have installed planned marketing information systems. Properly designed, the MIS will generate an orderly flow of decision-oriented information as the marketing executive needs it. The number of firms with planned information systems will grow during the 1980s as more managers recognize their contribution to dealing with the information explosion.

Chapter 6 concludes the section on planning the marketing effort. Attention now shifts to the marketing mix variables: product, price, distribution, and promotion. The next section discusses products and services.

3 3 3 3 3 3 3

3 3 3 3 3 3 3

3 3 3 3 3 3 3

3 3 3 3 3 3 3

3 3 3 3 3 3 3

3 3 3 3 3 3 3

3 3 3 3 3 3 3

3 3 3 3 3 3 3

3 3 3 3 3 3 3

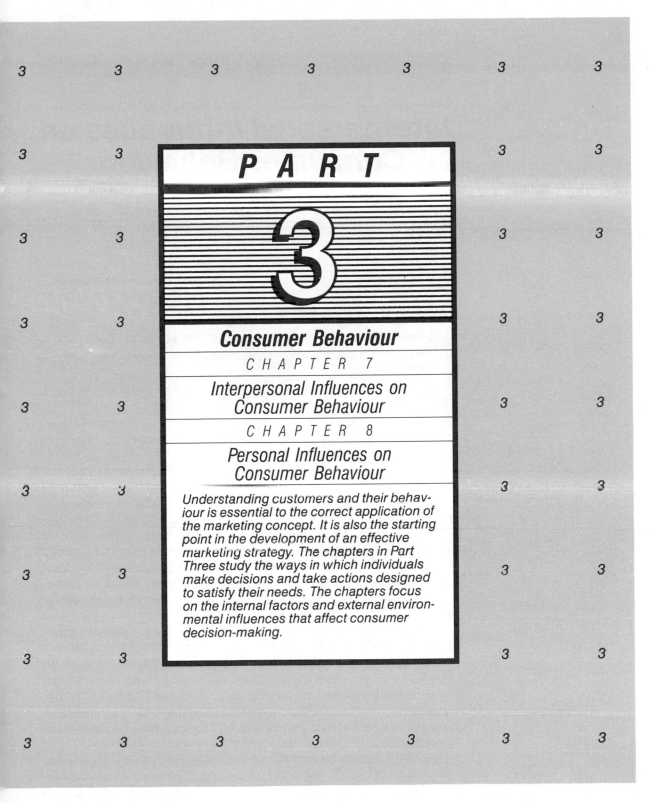

P A R T

3

Consumer Behaviour

C H A P T E R   7

Interpersonal Influences on Consumer Behaviour

C H A P T E R   8

Personal Influences on Consumer Behaviour

Understanding customers and their behaviour is essential to the correct application of the marketing concept. It is also the starting point in the development of an effective marketing strategy. The chapters in Part Three study the ways in which individuals make decisions and take actions designed to satisfy their needs. The chapters focus on the internal factors and external environmental influences that affect consumer decision-making.

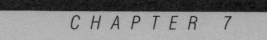

Interpersonal Influences on Consumer Behaviour

CHAPTER OBJECTIVES

1. To relate interpersonal influences on consumer behaviour to the variables of the marketing mix.

2. To explain the classification of behavioural influences.

3. To outline steps in the consumer decision process.

4. To identify the interpersonal determinants of consumer behaviour.

5. To explain the role of culture and subculture in consumer behaviour.

6. To describe the Asch phenomenon.

7. To know the impact of reference groups on consumer behaviour.

8. To explain the importance of social class in the study of consumer behaviour.

9. To describe family influences on consumer behaviour and how they are changing.

Li Shuang, Ke Ming, Li Yong, and Tan Yun Wei from the People's Republic of China learned a lot about the "different" behaviour of American consumers in Cleveland. The four accountants were on a six-month assignment with Ernst & Whinney, a Cleveland-based accounting firm. Their visit was part of an agreement whereby one of the firm's partners would go to China, while two teams of Chinese accountants would study American accounting practices in Cleveland and Chicago. But the foursome were probably more struck by North American consumption behaviour than the way they treat their debits and credits.

Some of their experiences were perhaps more amusing than shocking: on the way from Peking to San Francisco, Li Shuang was puzzled by the cup of salad dressing and glass of water on his airplane tray. So he mixed them together and drank it. Li later remarked in his limited English: "It wasn't very delicious." Similarly, his companion Tan Yun Wei was a bit surprised over the "sour oranges" he got when he ordered grapes — which he called grapefruit — for breakfast.

Li Yong admits he had heard a rumour that North Americans

actually sell dog food in their supermarkets. He was amazed when told it was true: "It's unbelievable. The dogs and cats in America eat better than people in some Asian countries." Li points out that most Chinese do not keep dogs as pets; indeed dogs are more likely to be eaten than provided for by consumers. Li also did not understand the strange custom of a buyer tipping a seller of a service. He wanted to know why North Americans did not tip before rather than after the fact, if they wanted better service.

While Ernst was renting a suite for the men in a downtown high rise, the rental agent launched into a long discourse on the garbage disposal, dishwasher, and so on. The four clients were oblivious to her spiel because they had never felt the need for such features before.[1]

The Conceptual Framework

Consumer behaviour consists of *the acts of individuals in obtaining and using goods and services, including the decision processes that precede and determine these acts.*[2] This definition includes both the ultimate consumer and the purchaser of industrial products. A major difference in the purchasing behaviour of industrial consumers and ultimate consumers is that additional influences from within the organization may be exerted on the industrial purchasing agent.

This chapter assesses interpersonal influences on consumer behaviour, while the next chapter explores personal influences.

Classifying Behavioural Influences: Personal and Interpersonal

The field of consumer behaviour borrows extensively from other areas like psychology and sociology. The work of Kurt Lewin, for instance, provides an excellent classification of influences on buying behaviour. Lewin's proposition was:

$$B = f(P, E)$$

where behaviour (B) is a function (f) of the interactions of personal influences (P) and the pressures exerted upon them by outside forces in the environment (E).

This statement is usually rewritten for consumer behaviour as follows:

$$B = f(I, P)$$

where consumer behaviour (B) is a function (f) of the interaction of interpersonal determinants (I), like reference groups and culture, and personal determinants (P), like attitudes, on the consumer. Understanding consumer behaviour requires an understanding of both the individual's psychological makeup and the influences of others.

The Consumer Decision Process

Consumer behaviour may be viewed as a decision process and the act of purchasing is merely one point in the process. To understand consumer behaviour, the events that precede and follow the purchase must be examined. Figure 7-1 identifies the steps in the consumer decision process: problem recognition, search, evaluation of alternatives, purchase decision, purchase act, and postpurchase evaluation. The consumer uses the decision process to solve problems and to take advantage of opportunities that arise. Through this process consumers correct differences between their actual and desired states. Feedback from each decision serves as additional experience to rely upon in subsequent decisions.

The process can be illustrated by the young couple whose only television set has been declared irreparable by the service representative. They clearly need to purchase a new set since television is a primary form of recreation for their young children (*problem recognition*). The couple questions their friends and acquaintances who have bought televisions recently. They pore over consumer-oriented reports on new models (*search*). Once they have collected all the necessary information the couple consider the various models on the basis of what is important to them—reliability and price (*evaluation*). They decide to buy a new set the next weekend (*purchase decision*). They do so at a local discount store the next

Figure 7-1   Steps in the Consumer Decision Process

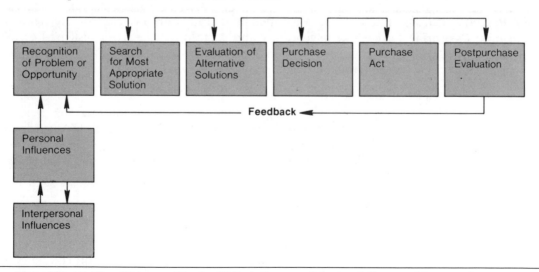

Source: Adapted from C. Glenn Walters and Gordon W. Paul, *Consumer Behavior: An Integrated Framework* (Homewood, Ill.: Richard D. Irwin, Inc., 1970), p. 18 © 1970 by Richard D. Irwin, Inc. and John Dewey, *How We Think* (Boston, Mass.: D. C. Heath, 1910), pp. 101-105. Similar steps are also discussed in Del I. Hawkins, Roger J. Best, and Kenneth A. Coney, *Consumer Behavior: Implications for Marketing Strategy*, revised ed. (Plano, Texas: Business Publications, Inc., 1983), pp. 447–606.

Saturday (*purchase act*). The new set is hooked up, and the young family sits back to enjoy their purchase (*post purchase evaluation*) and check out its special features.

This process is common to consumer purchase decisions. It is introduced here to provide an advance perspective of the field of consumer behaviour. An expanded discussion of the model concludes Chapter 8, after the reader has an overview of the various factors that affect consumer behaviour.

Interpersonal Determinants of Consumer Behaviour

People are social animals. They often buy products and services that will enable them to project a favourable image to others. Cultural environment, membership of reference groups, and family may influence such purchase decisions. A general model of the interpersonal (or group) determinants of consumer behaviour is shown in Figure 7-2. It indicates that there are three categories of interpersonal determinants of consumer behaviour: cultural influences, social influences, and family influences. (The model will be expanded to include personal influences in Chapter 8.)

Figure 7-2   Interpersonal Determinants of Consumer Behaviour

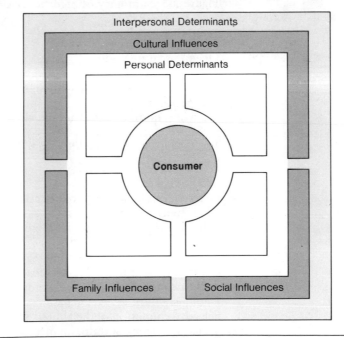

Source: Adapted with permission from C. Glenn Walters and Gordon W. Paul, *Consumer Behavior: An Integrated Framework* (Homewood Ill.: Richard D. Irwin, 1970), p. 16. © 1970 by Richard D. Irwin, Inc.

Cultural Influences

Culture is the broadest environmental determinant of consumer behaviour. Sometimes it is a very elusive concept for marketers to handle. General Mills knew that few Japanese homes had ovens, so it designed a Betty Crocker cake mix that could be made in the electric rice cookers widely used in that country. The product failed because of a cultural factor. Japanese homemakers regard the purity of their rice as very important, so they were afraid that a cake flavour might be left in their cookers.[3]

Culture can be defined as "*the complex of values, ideas, attitudes, institutions, and other meaningful symbols created by people to shape human behaviour and the artifacts of that behaviour, transmitted from one generation to the next.*"[4] It is the way of life learned and handed down through generations that gives each society its own peculiar characteristics and values.

Core Values in the Canadian Culture

The list in Figure 7-3 provides a useful summary of characteristics significant to the Canadian culture today. There are trends and shifts in cultural values, yet traditionally these changes have been gradual, unlike the revolutionary 1960s when some people felt overwhelmed by the pace of change. Rapid technological shifts may alter the pace

Figure 7-3 Summary of Significant Canadian Characteristics

As a function of being a part of the North American reality:

Modern orientation
Openness to new ideas
Egalitarianism
A rich developing society with many needs and high materialistic
    expectations
Growing, more diffuse "middle class"

In relation to the United States:

Conservative tendencies
Traditional bias
Greater confidence in bureaucratic institutions
Collectivity orientation—reliance on institutions such as state, big
    business, and the church vs. personal risk-taking
Less achievement-oriented
Lower optimism — less willing to take risks
Greater acceptance of hierarchical order and stratification
Tolerance for diversity — acceptance of cultural mosaic
Family stability
Selective emulation of the United States—resistance to some American
    characteristics and dominance, yet willingness to emulate
Elitist and ascriptive tendencies

once again in the future, so marketers must constantly assess cultural norms.[5] One of the most recent cultural trends is the search for more interpersonal relationships, rather than the self-centered orientation that characterized recent value structures. In other words, many people want greater friendship.[6] This trend has been noted by marketers who now feature more family and friendship groups in their scenarios for commercials. Restaurant and soft drink commercials often provide good examples.

**Cultural Influences:
An International
Perspective**

An awareness of cultural differences is particularly important for international marketers. Different attitudes, mores, and folkways all have an impact on marketing strategy. Examples of cultural influences on marketing strategy are abundant in the international environment. Look at the marketing implications of the following situations:

- Because of inept translation, Schweppes Tonic Water was advertised in Italy as "bathroom water," and in South America, Parker Pen Company unwittingly indicated that its product would prevent unwanted pregnancies.[7]
- A Goodyear advertisement demonstrated the strength of its "3T" tire cord by showing a steel chain breaking. When the commercial was shown in West Germany, however, it was perceived as an insult to steel chain manufacturers.[8]
- The headline for a series of advertisements shown in Japan to introduce Seiko's new line of coloured dial watches read as follows: "Like a Wind, I am the Colour of a Bird." To people in North America it was meaningless. But to Japanese consumers it meant something like: "This watch is light and delicate. It floats on your hand like a seedpod on the wind. Or a bird. A hummingbird with its jewel-like colours, the colours of the watch itself.[9]
- Deodorant usage among men ranges from 80 percent in the United States to 55 percent in Sweden, 28 percent in Italy, and 8 percent in the Philippines.[10]
- White is the colour of mourning in Japan. The colour purple is associated with death in many Latin American countries.
- Feet are regarded as despicable in Thailand. Athlete's-foot remedies with packages featuring a picture of feet will not be well received.[11]
- In Ethiopia the time required for a decision is directly proportional to its importance. This is so much the case that the low-level bureaucrats there attempt to elevate the prestige of their work by taking a long time to make decisions. North Americans there are innocently prone to downgrade their work in the local people's eyes by trying to speed things up.[12]

Often a marketing program that has been proven successful in Canada cannot be applied directly in international markets because of cultural differences. Real differences exist among different countries, and the differences must be known and evaluated by the international firm. When Helene Curtis introduced its Every Night shampoo line in Sweden, it renamed the product Every Day, since Swedes usually wash their hair in the morning.[13]

Denture makers are aware of the impact of cultural difference on tastes in false teeth. The people of Thailand are extremely fond of betel nuts, which stain their teeth black. For many years, once their original teeth wore out, they were replaced with black dentures. After World War II, however, fashions changed, and the Thais began using abrasives to scrub off the black stains. Abrasives are now popular items in Thailand. Scandinavians like greyish false teeth, mostly because nature has blessed them with naturally grey teeth. The Japanese select false teeth noticeably longer than their natural ones.[14]

World marketers face competition from firms in Germany, France, the Soviet Union, Japan, and a dozen other countries as well as firms in the host nation, and they must become intimately familiar with all aspects of the local population — including their cultural heritage. The local market segments in each country must be thoroughly analysed prior to the development of a marketing plan just as they are at home.

Subcultures

Within each culture are numerous **subcultures**, *subgroups with their own distinguishing modes of behaviour*. Any culture as heterogeneous as that existing in Canada is composed of significant subcultures based on such factors as race, nationality, age, rural-urban location, religion, and geographic distribution. The size of such subculture groups can be very significant. For example, the Italian population in the Toronto area is about 500 000 — larger than most Canadian cities.

Many people on the West Coast display a lifestyle emphasizing casual dress, outdoor entertaining, and water recreation. Mormons refrain from purchasing tobacco and liquor; orthodox Jews purchase kosher or other traditional foods; Chinese may exhibit more interest in products and symbols of their Chinese heritage.

The French-Canadian Market

Although Canada has many subcultures, in fact, the two founding cultures — English and French — are the most influential through sheer force of numbers. The francophone population is a significant market in Canada. Twenty-five percent of the Canadian population identify French as their mother tongue. While most of this population is in Quebec, there are significant French segments in other provinces. Proportionately, the largest is in New Brunswick where 33.6 percent of the population, or 224 000, have French as their mother tongue.[15] Numerically, Ontario has the larger group with 462 000.

The Quebec market is large enough and different enough to create an entire advertising industry of its own. Quebec constitutes about 27 percent of the total Canadian market for goods and services, and is the second largest market in Canada.[16] Personal disposable income in 1982 was over $48 billion, and retail sales were estimated at $23.5 billion.[17]

While there is no doubt that the Quebec market is substantially different from the rest of Canada, it is difficult to define those differences precisely. Considerable research over the years has pointed out many characteristics specific to the area — French Canadians, for example, are more fond of sweets than other Canadians. However, other data can usually be found to contest any such finding or show that it is at least not true any longer.

Such statements only reflect measurement of traits in the Quebec culture at one particular period. These measurements may be legitimate and necessary for a firm wishing to market a product in that segment at a particular point in time. However, similar differences can probably be detected between consumers in Nova Scotia and British Columbia, if you look for them.

Attention should not be concentrated on *specific* differences between the Quebec market and the rest of Canada, but rather on the fact that there is a basic cultural difference between the two markets. "Culture is a way of being, thinking and feeling. It is a driving force animating a significant group of individuals united by a common tongue, and sharing the same customs, habits and experiences."[18] Because of this cultural difference, some marketing programs may be distinctly different in Quebec than in the rest of Canada.

In the French-Canadian market, it is not the products that are different, it is the state of mind.[19] For example, Renault achieved a Quebec market penetration 10 times greater than in the rest of Canada. Since the product and price is the same, the difference must lie in the marketing program attuned to the Quebec market. In English Canada, Renault used the same campaign theme as in the U.S.: "Le Car." That was considered unsuitable for Quebec, where "Le Car" would have created negative feelings. The image of Renault was not good enough to be called the tops, the absolute Number One, which is what "Le Car" would mean in French. It would not be credible. Therefore, the Quebec agency for Renault chose "le chameau," a theme that humorously emphasized economy and fitted the needs of Quebec consumers (see Figure 7-4).

Current Characteristics of the Quebec Market   Nevertheless there

**Figure 7-4   Taking Cultural Differences into Consideration
in Advertising**

Advertisement used in French Canada.

are current differences between the Quebec market and the English-
Canadian market.[20] First, except for Atlantic Canada, income levels are somewhat lower in Quebec, although the differences are being
quite rapidly eliminated.

Second, food consumption patterns differ significantly. French
Canadians spend substantially more on food than English Canadians.

Figure 7-4   Continued

Advertisement used in English Canada.

Introducing the new 5-door Renault Le Car. Advantage, yours!

Renault has just made Europe's number one car even better. And the advantages of this newest Renault Le Car are all yours!

Easy access and passenger comfort.
Advantage, yours! *Four wide opening doors for easy entry and exit, reclining front bucket seats, plus a large rear hatch that opens to 9.1 cubic feet of covered cargo space. (The rear seat folded more than triples the capacity to 31.5 cu. ft.!)*

Remarkable fuel economy. Advantage, yours!
A responsive 1.4 litre 4-cylinder engine and all-synchromesh 4-speed manual transmission deliver a Transport Canada rating of 6.5 L/100 km or 43 mpg with a highway fuel consumption of 53 mpg*. That's performance you'll feel in your wallet!

Front-wheel drive. Advantage, yours! *On the open road the 5-door Renault Le Car is uncommonly quick, smooth and maneuverable, thanks to front-wheel drive, rack-and-pinion steering, 4-wheel independent torsion bar suspension and Michelin radial tires.*

Built by Renault. Advantage, yours!
Renault is one of the largest automobile manufacturers in the world and has been developing and building front-wheel drive automobiles for more than 20 years. In fact, over 18 million front-wheel drive Renault cars have been sold around the world. The new 5-door Renault Le Car. Spirited performance, precise handling, remarkable fuel economy and now the extra advantage of five doors.

◊ and Renault are trade marks of Régie Nationale des Usines Renault

* Transport Canada Fuel Consumption Guide, February 1981. (Fuel consumption rating 6.6 L/100 km, Highway 5.3 L/100 km, Urban 8.1 L/100 km). Ratings are only for comparison between various makes and models. Your actual fuel consumption may vary depending on road conditions, driving habits, road, weather and vehicle condition.

At over 200 Renault and American Motors Dealers across Canada.

Source: Courtesy of American Motors (Canada) Inc.

These cultural patterns are reflected in the type and quantities of food and ancillary items purchased.

French Canadians use their leisure differently also. More go to the movies and attend plays, concerts, opera, or ballet. However, more anglophones read books. Francophones spend less on travel than anglophones, although this is changing rapidly.

French Canadians watch slightly more television per week than English Canadians. Naturally they watch mainly French-language television, which has stimulated a large television and cinema industry in the province.

Michel Cloutier argues that many differences between French- and English-Canadian cultures are the result of education and income.[21] As the gap between these factors narrows, and as cultures are affected by similar political and technological influences, so will the differences in values and consumption patterns narrow. Nevertheless, it appears that frames of reference and significant cues will continue to be different, requiring the marketer to be astute in dealing with these market segments. This is shown in Figure 7-5.

The key to success in this important Canadian market is having marketing specialists who understand people, and understand how to deal in that specific market. Sophisticated marketers now realize this. That is why there are so many Quebec advertising agencies.

A final unique aspect of the Quebec market is the influence of the provincial government. Numerous special laws have been passed or are being proposed. Most notable is Bill 101, which makes French the official language of the province. The marketing communications implications of this appear in the design of signs and billboards, where it is illegal to use any language but French. The Quebec government is also probably more protective of the consumer than any other provincial government. For example, advertising to children is strictly regulated and restricted.

Figure 7-5   Cultural Characteristics of English- and French-speaking Canadians

	English-speaking	French-speaking
Ethnic origin	Anglo-Saxon	Latin
Religion	Protestant	Catholic
Intellectual attitude	Pragmatic	Theoretical
Family	Matriarchy	Patriarchy
Leisure time	In function of the professional class	In function of the family circle
Individual vis-à-vis the environment	More social	More individualistic
Business management	Administrator	Innovator
Political tendencies	Conservative	Liberal
Consumption attitudes	Propensity to save; conformist; financier more than financed	Propensity to spend; innovator; financed more than a financier

Source: Georges Hénault, "Les conséquences du biculturalisme sur la consommation," *Commerce* (septembre 1971).

Social Influences

The earliest awareness of children confirms that they are members of a very important group — the family — from whom they seek total satisfaction of their physiological and social needs. As they grow older, they join other groups — neighbourhood play groups, school groups, the Cub Scouts, Brownies, minor hockey — as well as groups of friends. From these groups they acquire both status and role. **Status** refers to their *relative position in the group*. **Role** refers to the *rights and duties expected by other members of the group of the individual in a certain position in the group*. Some of these are formal groups (the Cub Scouts) and others are quite informal (the friendship groups). But both types supply their members with status and roles and, in doing so, influence the activities, including the consumer behaviour, of each member.

The Asch Phenomenon: Group Influence Effects on Conformity

Although most persons view themselves as individuals, groups are often highly influential in purchase decisions. In situations where individuals feel that a particular group or groups are important, they tend to adhere in varying degrees to the general expectations of that group.

The surprising impact that groups and group norms can exhibit on individual behaviour has been called the *Asch phenomenon*. The phenomenon was first documented in the following study conducted by the psychologist S. E. Asch:

> Eight subjects are brought into a room and asked to determine which of a set of three unequal lines is closest to the length of a fourth line shown some distance from the other three. The subjects are to announce their judgments publicly. Seven of the subjects are working for the experimenter and they announce incorrect matches. The order of announcement is arranged such that the naive subject responds last. In a control situation, 37 naive subjects performed the task 18 times each without any information about others' choices. Two of the 37 subjects made a total of 3 mistakes. However, when another group of 50 naive subjects responded *after* hearing the unanimous but *incorrect* judgment of the other group members, 37 made a total of 194 errors, all of which were in agreement with the mistake made by the group.[22]

This widely replicated study illustrates the role of groups upon individual choice-making. Marketing applications range from the choice of automobile models and residential locations to the decision to purchase at least one item at a Tupperware party.

Reference Groups

In order for groups to exert such influence on individuals, they must be categorized as **reference groups,** or groups whose *value structures and standards influence a person's behaviour.* Consumers usually try to keep their purchase behaviour in line with what they perceive to be the values of their reference group.

The status of the individual within the reference group produces three subcategories: **membership group**, where *the person actually belongs* to, say, a country club; **aspirational group**, a situation where *a person desires to associate with a group*; and a **disassociative group**, one *with which the individual does not want to be identified by others*. For example, teenagers are unlikely to enjoy the middle-of-the-road music played on radio stations catering to their parents' generation.

It is obviously not essential that the individual be a member in order for the group to serve as a point of reference. This partially explains the use of athletes in advertisements. Even though few

Figure 7-6   Extent of Reference Group Influence on Product and Brand Decision

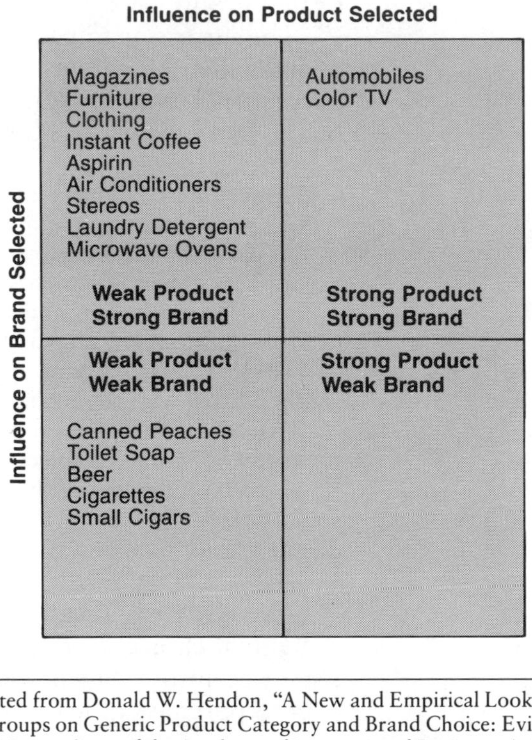

Influence on Product Selected

	Weak Product	Strong Product
Strong Brand	Magazines Furniture Clothing Instant Coffee Aspirin Air Conditioners Stereos Laundry Detergent Microwave Ovens **Weak Product Strong Brand**	Automobiles Color TV **Strong Product Strong Brand**
Weak Brand	**Weak Product Weak Brand** Canned Peaches Toilet Soap Beer Cigarettes Small Cigars	**Strong Product Weak Brand**

Influence on Brand Selected

Source: Reprinted from Donald W. Hendon, "A New and Empirical Look at the Influence of Reference Groups on Generic Product Category and Brand Choice: Evidence from Two Nations," *Proceedings of the Academy of International Business: Asia-Pacific Dimensions of International Business* (Honolulu: College of Business Administration, University of Hawaii, December 18–20, 1979), pp. 752–761. Based on Francis S. Bourne, *Group Influence in Marketing and Public Relations* (Foundation for Research on Human Behavior, 1956), p. 8.

possess the skills necessary to pilot a racer, all racing fans can identify with the Mosport winner by injecting their engines with STP.

The extent of reference-group influence varies widely among purchases. For reference-group influence to be great, two factors must be present:

1. The item must be one that can be seen and identified by others.
2. The item must also be conspicuous in the sense that it stands out, is unusual, and is a brand or product that not everyone owns.

Figure 7-6 shows the influence of reference groups on both the basic decision to purchase a product and the decision to purchase a particular brand. The figure shows that reference groups had a significant impact on both the decision to purchase an automobile and the type of brand that was actually selected. By contrast, reference groups had little impact on the decision to purchase canned peaches or the brand that was chosen. Figure 7-6 was derived from a survey which updated a widely cited 1956 study. A comparison with the earlier study shows that over time the extent of reference group influence can vary for both types of decisions.[23]

Social Classes

Although North Americans prefer to think of their society as open with equality for all, a well-structured class system exists on this continent as it does in all parts of the world. Research conducted during the 1940s by W. Lloyd Warner and during the late 1950s in Chicago by Pierre Martineau identified a six-class system within the social structure of both small and large cities. A description of the members of each class and an estimate of the population percentage in each class is shown in Figure 7-7. John Porter performed a similar analysis of social class in Canada and reported comparable findings in his classic book, *The Vertical Mosaic*.

Membership in a **social class** is determined by *occupation, source of income (not amount), education, family background, and dwelling areas*. Income is not the main determinant, and the view that "A rich person is a poor person with more money" is incorrect. Pipefitters paid at union scale will earn more money than many college professors, but their purchase behaviour may be quite different.

Richard Coleman illustrates the behaviour of three families, all earning less than $25 000 a year (in the mid 1970s), but each decidedly in a different social class. An upper-middle-class family in this income bracket — a young lawyer or a college professor and his or her family — is likely to spend its income to live in a prestige neighbourhood, buy expensive furniture from "quality stores," and join social clubs.

The lower-middle-class family — headed by a grocery store owner or a sales representative — buys a good house in a less expensive neighbourhood. They buy more furniture from less expensive stores and typically have a savings account at the local bank.

Figure 7-7   The Warner Social Class Hierarchy

Social Class	Membership	Population Percentage (Estimated)
Upper-upper	Locally prominent families, third- or fourth-generation wealth. Merchants, financiers, or higher professionals. Wealth is inherited. Do a great amount of travelling.	1.5
Lower-upper	Newly arrived in upper class; "nouveau riche." Not accepted by upper class. Executive elite, founders of large businesses, doctors, lawyers.	1.5
Upper-middle	Moderately successful professionals, owners of medium-sized businesses, and middle management. Status conscious. Child- and home-centred.	10.0
Lower-middle	Top of the average world. Nonmanagerial office workers, small-business owners, and blue-collar families. Described as "striving and respectable." Conservative.	33.0
Upper-lower	Ordinary working class. Semiskilled workers. Income often as high as the next two classes above. Enjoy life. Live from day to day.	38.0
Lower-lower	Unskilled, umemployed, and unassimilated groups. Fatalistic. Apathetic.	16.0
Total		100.0

Source: Adapted from Charles B. McCann, *Women and Department Store Newspaper Advertising* (Chicago: Social Research, Inc., 1957). Reprinted by permission. (The estimates are based on Warner and Hollings's distributions in rather small communities. However, an estimate of social class structure for the U.S. and Canada approximates these percentages.)

The lower-class family — headed by a truck driver or welder — spends less money on the house but buys one of the first new cars sold each year and owns one of the largest colour television sets in town. The working-class family stocks its kitchen with appliances — its symbols of security. The husband spends relatively more money on tickets to sporting events and more time hunting and bowling.

Usage of the same product or service may vary among social classes. A study of commercial bank credit-card holders uncovered social class variations in how the cards were used. Lower-class families were more likely to use their credit cards for instalment purchases, while upper-class families used them mainly for convenience as a cash substitute.[24]

Figure 7-8   Direct, Two-Step, and Multi-Step Communication Flows

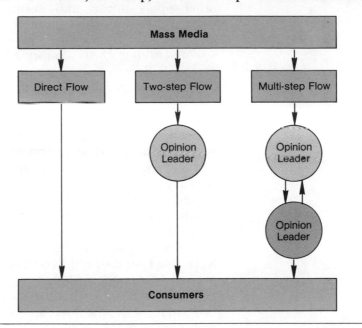

The role of social class in determining consumer behaviour continues to be a source of debate in the field of marketing. Some have argued against using social class as a market segmentation variable. Others disagree as to whether income or social class is the best base for market segmentation. The findings tend to be mixed. One recent study found that social class was the superior segmentation variable for food and nonsoft drink/nonalcoholic beverage markets. Social class also influenced shopping behaviour and evening television watching. Income was the superior segmentation variable for major appliances, soft drinks, mixes, and alcoholic beverages. For other categories, like clothing, a combination of the two variables was the best approach.[25]

Opinion Leaders   Each group usually contains a few members who can be considered **opinion leaders** or trend setters. These individuals are more likely to purchase new products early and to serve as information sources for others in the group. Their opinions are respected, and they are often sought out for advice.

Generalized opinion leaders are rare. Individuals tend to be opinion leaders in specific areas. Their considerable knowledge and interest in a particular product or service motivates them to seek out further information from mass media, manufacturers, and other supply sources; and, in turn, they transmit this information to their associates through interpersonal communications. Opinion leaders are found within all segments of the population.

Communication Flows   Information about products, retail outlets, and ideas flow through a number of channels. In some instances, the information flow is direct. Continuing access to radio, television and other mass media allows much information to be transmitted directly to individuals who represent the organization's market target with no intermediaries. Preliminary findings indicating some success in the use of the experimental drug Interferon, in treating certain types of cancer, were quickly disseminated to the general public by the mass media. Researchers were forced to utilize the same channels in an attempt to dispel the general public's belief that the new drug was a miracle cure.

In some cases, the flows are from the media to opinion leaders, and then from opinion leaders to the masses of the population. Elihu Katz and Paul Lazarfeld referred to this channel as the *two-step process* of communication.[26]

Another possible channel for information flows is a multistep flow. In this case, the flows are from mass media to opinion leaders and then on to other opinion leaders before being disseminated to the general public. Figure 7-8 illustrates the types of communication flows.

Applying the Opinion Leadership Concept   Opinion leaders play a crucial role in interpersonal communication. The fact that they distribute information and advice to others indicates their potential importance to marketing strategy. Opinion leaders can be particularly useful in the launching of new products.

General Motors once provided Chevettes to college marketing classes as a basis for a course project. Rock stations have painted teenagers' cars for them. Of course, the paint job includes the stations' call letters and slogans. Politicians sometimes hold issues forums for community leaders. All of these efforts are directed at the opinion leaders in a particular marketplace. These people play an important role in how successful a new or established product, idea, or political candidacy is communicated to consumers.

Family Influences

The family is an important interpersonal determinant of consumer behaviour. The close, continuing interactions among family members are the strongest group influences for the individual consumer.

Most people in our society are members of two families during their lifetime: the family into which they are born, and the family they eventually form as they marry and have children. With divorce an increasingly common phenomenon, many people become involved with three or more families.

The establishment of a new household upon marriage produces marketing opportunities. A new household means a new home and accompanying furniture. The need for refrigerators, vacuum cleaners, and an original oil painting for the living room is dependent

Figure 7-9   Marital Roles in 25 Decisions

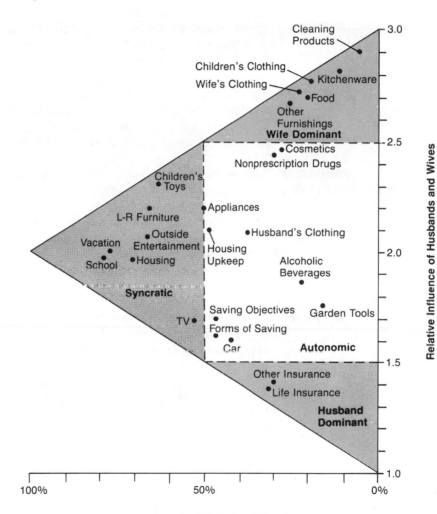

Source: Harry L. Davis and Benny P. Rigaux, "Perception of Marital Roles in Decision Processes," *Journal of Consumer Research* (June 1974), p. 57. Reprinted by permission from the *Journal of Consumer Research*, published by the Journal of Consumer Research, Inc.

not upon the number of persons in the household but upon the number of *households* themselves.

As children are added to the household, sizes of products purchased naturally increase. Two litres of milk will be purchased instead of one. Some larger families will purchase station wagons, or larger cars. Many other child-related purchases will be made over the period of time they remain in the home. Marketers find many opportunities in this market segment. For example, Nissan Motors was able to expand the market for its Datsun Z-cars greatly by adding a four-seat "2 + 2" series to meet the needs of family purchasers who are sports car enthusiasts.

Another market evolves as parents are left alone when the children move away from home. These parents find themselves with a four-bedroom "empty nest" and a sizeable lawn to maintain each week. Lacking assistance from their children and no longer needing the extra space, they become customers for town houses, condominiums, and high-rise luxury apartments in the larger cities. This market segment also eventually purchases bifocals, and is a good target for organized tour packages.

Traditional Household Roles

Although an infinite variety of roles are played in household decision-making, four role categories are often used: 1) *autonomic* — situations where an equal number of decisions is made by each partner, but each decision is made individually by one partner or the other; 2) *male-dominant*; 3) *female-dominant*; and 4) *syncratic* — situations where decisions are made jointly by male and female.[27] Figure 7-9 shows the roles commonly played by household members in the purchase of a number of products.

Changing Family Roles

Two forces have changed the female's role as sole purchasing agent for most household items. First, a shorter work week provides each wage-earning household member with more time for shopping. Second, a large number of women are now in the work force. In 1950, only about a quarter of married women were also employed outside the home; by 1981 that figure had doubled. Currently, over half of all married women with school-age children hold jobs outside the home. Studies of family decision-making have shown that working wives tend to exert more influence than nonworking wives. Households with two wage earners also exhibit a larger number of joint decisions and an increase in night and weekend shopping.

These changing roles of household members have led many marketers to adjust their marketing programs. Men's clothing stores, such as Stollery's in Toronto, now offer suits and accessories for the career woman. Although demand for men's suits has been sluggish in recent years, sales of women's suits increased 70 percent in 1980. Meanwhile a survey of 1000 married men revealed that 77 percent participate in grocery shopping and 70 percent cook. A Del Monte promotional campaign recognized these changes and de-emphasized women as the sole meal preparer. Its theme, "Good things happen when you bring Del Monte home," is applicable to both male and female food shoppers.[28]

Children's Roles in Household Purchasing

The role of the children evolves as they grow older. Their early influence is generally centred on toys to be recommended to Santa Claus and the choice of brands of cereals. Younger children are important to marketers of fast-food restaurants. Even though the parents may decide when to eat out, the children often select the restaurant.[29] As they gain maturity, they increasingly influence their clothing purchases.

One study revealed that thirteen to fifteen-year-old teenage boys spend most of their money on food, snacks, movies, and entertainment. Girls in this same age group buy clothing, food and snacks, tickets for movies and entertainment, and cosmetics and fragrances. Sixteen to nineteen-year-old boys spend most of their money on entertainment, dating, movies, automobiles and gasoline, clothing, food, and snacks while girls of the same age buy clothing, cosmetics, fragrances, automobiles and gasoline, and movie and entertainment tickets.[30]

Summary

Consumer behaviour refers to the way people select, obtain, and use goods and services. Both interpersonal and personal factors determine patterns of consumer behaviour, but the consumer decision process itself can be divided into six steps: problem recognition, search, evaluation, purchase decision, purchase act, and post-purchase evaluation. The consumer decision process has been introduced here to provide an overall perspective. It is explained in detail at the end of Chapter 8.

There are three interpersonal determinants of consumer behaviour: cultural influences, social influences, and family influences. Culture is the broadest of these three influences. Culture refers to behavioural values that are created and inherited by a society. Cultural norms can change over time, although traditionally the pace of change is slow. However, it may occur at a faster pace in the future.

Cultural influences are particularly significant in international marketing, but they are also a crucial factor in domestic marketing. Increased attention is being devoted to the consumption behaviour patterns of subcultures. Canada's two founding cultures, English and French, have a significant effect on the design of marketing programs in various regions, as do the presence of other cultural groups.

Social influences are described as the nonfamily group influences on consumer behaviour. The role that groups play in individual decision making was demonstrated by research conducted by S. E. Asch. If a group's values or standards influence an individual's behaviour, the group may be called a reference group for that person. The importance of reference groups on specific product and brand decision varies.

Social class ranking also influences consumer behaviour. The existence of a class structure was demonstrated by W. Lloyd Warner years ago. The reaction of opinion leaders or trend setters to new products is highly influential in the future success of the good or service. Marketers must make special efforts to appeal to these bellwethers of consumer behaviour.

Family influences are the third major interpersonal determinant of consumer behaviour. Family purchasing patterns vary. In some cases, the female is dominant; in others, the male. Some purchase decisions are made jointly, while in other situations, the decisions are made separately, but the number of such decisions is roughly equal between male and female. The traditional role for the female as the family's purchasing agent is now in flux.

CHAPTER 8

Personal Influences on Consumer Behaviour

1. To relate personal influences on consumer behaviour to the variables of the marketing mix.

2. To identify the personal determinants of consumer behaviour.

3. To distinguish between needs and motives.

4. To explain perception.

5. To describe how attitudes influence consumer behaviour.

6. To demonstrate how learning theory can be applied to marketing strategy.

7. To explain the self-concept.

8. To outline the steps in the consumer decision process.

9. To differentiate among routinized response behaviour, limited problem solving, and extended problem solving.

At Paul Magder Furs in Toronto it was business as usual one recent Sunday. As it does most Sundays the store racked up more than a quarter of the week's sales, and for the 34th time in the past two years, the furrier was charged with violating Ontario's Retail Business Holidays Act.

Even retailers strongly opposed to the idea of Sunday shopping concede that pressure to change Canada's so-called blue laws may win out in the end. However, retailers are divided on the advantages, if any, of opening Sunday. Those in favour argue that business is now lost because retailers have failed to adapt to changing lifestyles and shopping patterns to fit consumer shopping preferences. The additional sales generated by opening on Sunday combined with revamping shopping hours on Monday to Friday will, they say, more than offset costs. "Traditional shopping habits and patterns are changing and whenever that happens, everything has to change," says Rubin Stahl, executive vice-president of Edmonton-based Triple Five Corp., owners of the giant 426 West Edmonton Mall. "Retailers must find all sorts of ways to retail—be it on a Sunday, or a Saturday, or evenings, or whatever."

Opponents deny that opening an extra day will mean a corresponding increase in sales. "It's been proven as you open up more nights that that is not the case," argues Grant MacLaren, president of Woodward Stores Ltd. of Vancouver.

Until now, there has been little firm evidence to support either side of the debate. Even the experience in the U.S. where shopping seven days a week is widespread, has been less than conclusive. There are more sales on Sunday, but whether the sales are new ones is questionable. It is clear however, that the behaviour of consumers is changing, and the issue is how marketers should adjust given the social considerations that surround the decision.[1]

The Conceptual Framework

Chapter 7 defined consumer behaviour as the acts of individuals in obtaining and using goods and services, including the decision processes that precede and determine these acts. The chapter introduced the concept of the consumer decision process and explained the interpersonal determinants of consumer behaviour.

This chapter is a continuation of the discussion of consumer behaviour. It concentrates on the personal determinants of consumer behaviour such as needs and motives which are affecting retail shopping behaviour, for example. The chapter concludes by reintroducing and expanding the discussion of the consumer decision process.

Personal Determinants of Consumer Behaviour

Consumer behaviour is a function of both interpersonal and personal influences. The personal determinants of consumer behaviour include the individual's needs, motives, perceptions and attitudes, and self-concept. Figure 8-1 shows how these determinants operate within the framework of interpersonal influences discussed in Chapter 7, and that together these factors cause the individual to act.

Needs and Motives

The starting point in the purchase decision process is the recognition of a felt need. A **need** is simply *the lack of something useful*. The consumer is typically confronted with numerous unsatisfied needs. It is important to note that a need must be sufficiently aroused before it may serve as a motive.

Motives are *inner states that direct us toward the goal of satisfying a felt need*. The individual is *moved* (the root word of motive) to take action to reduce a state of tension and to return to a condition of equilibrium.

Although psychologists disagree on specific classifications of needs, a useful theory that may apply to consumers in general has been developed by A. H. Maslow.[2] He proposes a classification of needs (sometimes referred to as a hierarchy), as shown in Figure 8-2. It is important to recognize that Maslow's hierarchy may not apply

Figure 8-1   Personal and Interpersonal Determinants of Consumer Behaviour

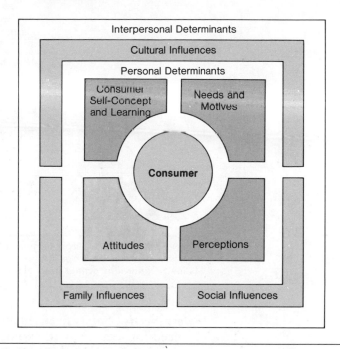

Source: C. Glenn Walters and Gordon W. Paul, *Consumer Behavior: An Integrated Framework* (Homewood, Ill.: Richard D. Irwin, 1970), p. 14 © by Richard D. Irwin, Inc. Reprinted by permission.

to each individual, but seems to be true of groups in general. His list is based upon two important assumptions:

1. People are wanting animals, whose needs depend upon what they already possess. A satisfied need is not a motivator; only those needs that have not been satisfied can influence behaviour.
2. Once one need has been largely satisfied, another emerges and demands satisfaction.

Physiological Needs   The primary needs for food, shelter, and cloth ing normally must be satisfied before the higher-order needs are considered. A hungry person is possessed by the need to obtain food. Other needs are ignored. Once the physiological needs are at least partially satisfied, other needs come into the picture.

Figure 8-2 Need Classification Structure

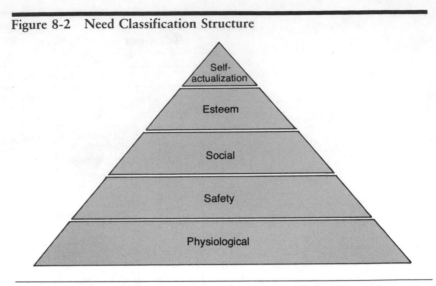

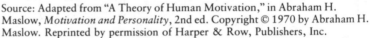

Source: Adapted from "A Theory of Human Motivation," in Abraham H.
Maslow, *Motivation and Personality*, 2nd ed. Copyright © 1970 by Abraham H.
Maslow. Reprinted by permission of Harper & Row, Publishers, Inc.

Safety Needs   Safety needs include protection from physical harm,
the need for security, and avoidance of the unexpected. Gratifica-
tion of these needs may take the form of a savings account, life
insurance, the purchase of radial tires, or membership in the local
health club. American Express advertisements target this need.

Social Needs   Satisfaction of physiological and safety needs may
be followed by the desire to be accepted by members of the family
and other individuals and groups — that is, the social needs. Individuals may be motivated to join various groups, to conform to
their standards of dress, purchases, and behaviour, and become interested in obtaining status as a means of fulfilling these social needs.
Chapter 7 pointed out that social needs seem to be becoming a more
important cultural value.

Esteem Needs   The higher-order needs are prevalent in the developed countries where a sufficiently high per capita income has
allowed most families to satisfy the basic needs and to concentrate
on the desire for status, esteem, and self-actualization. These needs
are more difficult to satisfy. At the esteem level is the need to feel a
sense of accomplishment, achievement, and respect from others.
The competitive need to excel—to better the performance of others
and "stand out" from the crowd — is an almost universal human
trait.

Esteem needs are closely related to social needs. At this level, however, the individual desires not just acceptance but also recognition and respect in some way.

Self-Actualization Needs   Self-actualization needs are the desire for fulfilment, for realizing one's own potential, for using one's talents and capabilities totally. Maslow defines self-actualization this way: "The healthy man is primarily motivated by his needs to develop and actualize his fullest potentialities and capacities. What man can be, he must be."[3] The author Robert Louis Stevenson was describing self-actualization when he wrote, "To be what we are, and to become what we are capable of becoming, is the only end of life."

Maslow argues that a satisfied need is no longer a motivator. Once the physiological needs are satiated, the individual moves on to the higher-order needs. Consumers are periodically motivated by the need to relieve thirst or hunger, but their interests are most often directed toward satisfaction of safety, social, and other needs.

Caution must be used in applying Maslow's theory. Empirical research shows little support for a universal hierarchical ordering of needs in *specific individuals*.[4] It would therefore be unsafe to use the theory to explain a particular purchase. The need hierarchy and motive strength concept may be useful in considering the behaviour of consumers *in general*, however. It has been verified that in consumer buying, previously ignored desires often surface only after a purchase has satisfied a predominant (and *perhaps* lower-order) motive.[5]

Self-Actualization   The Need for Fulfilment

Source: © 1970 United Feature Syndicate, Inc.

Perception   Several years ago, a pharmaceutical firm developed Analoze, a cherry-flavoured combination painkiller and stomach sweetener that could be taken without water. The product failed because consumers associated the ritual of taking pills and a glass of water with pain relief.[6] Analoze was not perceived as an effective remedy because it violated their experience with other pain killers. Individual behaviour resulting from motivation is affected by how we perceive stimuli. **Perception** is *the meaning that each person attributes to incoming stimuli received through the five senses.*

Psychologists previously assumed that perception was an objective phenomenon, that is, that the individual perceived what was there to be perceived. Only recently have researchers recognized that what we perceive is as much a result of what we *want* to perceive as of what is actually there. This does not mean that people view dogs as pigeons. We can distinguish shopping centres from churches, but a retail store stocked with well-known brand names and staffed with helpful, knowledgeable sales personnel is perceived differently from a largely self-serve discount store. The Dodge Colt and the BMW 320 are both important automobiles, but they carry quite different images.

Our perception of an object or event is the result of the interaction of two types of factors:

1. Stimulus factors, which are characteristics of the physical object such as size, colour, weight, or shape.
2. Individual factors, which are characteristics of the perceiver. These factors include not only sensory processes but also past experiences with similar items and basic motivations and expectations.

Selective Perception   The individual is continually bombarded with a myriad of stimuli, but most are ignored. In order to have time to function, each of us must respond selectively to stimuli. What stimuli we respond to, then, is the problem of all marketers. How can they gain the attention of the individual so that he or she will read the advertisement, listen to the sales representative, react to a point-of-purchase display?

Even though studies have shown that the average consumer is exposed to more than a thousand ads daily, most of them never break through our *perceptual screen*, the filter through which messages must pass. Sometimes breakthroughs may be accomplished in the printed media through larger ads, since doubling the size of the ad increases the attention value by approximately 50 percent. Colour ads in the newspaper, in contrast with the usual black and white ads, are another device to break the reader's perceptual screen. However, the colour ad must produce enough additional readers to justify the extra cost, which is considerable. Another method of using contrast is to include a large amount of white space to draw attention to the ad, or the use of white type on a black background.

In general, the marketer seeks to make the message stand out, to be sufficiently different from other methods in order to gain the attention of the prospective customer. Menley & James Laboratories followed the practice of running hay-fever radio commercials for their Contac capsules only on days when the pollen count was above specified minimum levels. Each commercial was preceded by live announcements of the local pollen count.

Piercing the perceptual screen can be a frustrating task. Consider the problem of getting consumers to try a product for the first time. The manufacturer bombards people with television and magazine advertising, sales promotion discounts and premiums, and point-of-purchase displays, often with little change in sales. Follow-up research shows that many consumers have no knowledge of the product or promotion. Why? Because this information simply never penetrated their perceptual screens.

With such selectivity at work, it is easy to see the importance of the marketer's efforts to obtain a "consumer franchise" in the form of brand loyalty to a product. Satisfied customers are less likely to seek information about competing products. Even when it is forced on them, they are not as likely as others to allow it to pass through their perceptual screens. They simply tune out information that is not in accord with their existing beliefs and expectations.

Weber's Law Affects Perception

The relationship between the actual physical stimulus such as size, loudness, or texture, and the corresponding sensation produced in the individual is known as *psychophysics*, which can be expressed as a mathematical equation:

$$\frac{\Delta I}{I} = k$$

where ΔI = the smallest increase in stimulus that will be noticeably different from the previous intensity

I = the intensity of the stimulus at the point where the increase takes place

k = a constant (that varies from one sense to the next)

In other words, *the higher the initial intensity of a stimulus, the greater the amount of the change in intensity that is necessary in order for a difference to be noticed.*

This relationship, known as **Weber's Law**, has some obvious implications in marketing. A price increase of $300 for a Chevette is readily apparent for prospective buyers; the same $300 increase on a $45 000 Mercedes seems insignificant. A large package requires a much greater increase in size to be noticeable than a smaller-sized package requires. People perceive *by exception*, and the change in stimuli must be sufficiently great to gain the individual's attention.[7]

Subliminal Perception   Is it possible to communicate with persons without their being aware of the communication? In other words, is there **subliminal perception** — *a subconscious level of awareness*? In 1957 the words "Eat popcorn" and "Drink Coca-Cola," were flashed upon the screen of a New Jersey movie theatre every five seconds for 1/300th of a second. Researchers then reported that these messages, although too short to be recognizable at the conscious level, resulted in a 58 percent increase in popcorn sales and an 18 percent increase in the sale of Coca-Cola. After the publication of these findings, advertising agencies and consumer protection groups became intensely interested in subliminal perception.[8] Later attempts to duplicate the test findings have, however, invariably been unsuccessful.

Subliminal advertising is aimed at the subconscious level of awareness to avoid the perceptual screens of viewers. The goal of the original research was to induce consumers to purchase without being aware of the source of the motivation. Although subliminal advertising has been universally condemned (and declared illegal in Canada and California), it is exceedingly unlikely that such advertising can induce purchases anyway. There are several reasons for this: 1) strong stimulus factors are required to even gain attention, as discussed earlier; 2) only a very short message can be transmitted; 3) individuals vary greatly in their thresholds of consciousness. Messages transmitted at the threshold of consciousness for one person will not be perceived at all by some people and will be all too apparent for others. When exposed subliminally, the message "Drink Coca-Cola" might go unseen by some viewers while others read it as "Drink Pepsi-Cola", "Drink Cocoa," or even "Drive Slowly";[9] 4) perceptual defenses *also* work at the subconscious level.

Contrary to earlier fears, research has shown that subliminal messages cannot force the receiver to purchase goods that he or she would not consciously want.

Attitudes   Perception of incoming stimuli is greatly affected by attitudes regarding these stimuli. In fact, decisions to purchase products are based upon currently held attitudes about the product, the store, or the salesperson.

Attitudes may be defined as *a person's enduring favourable or unfavourable evaluations, emotional feelings, or pro or con action tendencies toward some object or idea.*[10] Attitudes are formed over a period of time through individual experiences and group contacts and are highly resistant to change.

Components of an Attitude   Attitudes consist of three related components: cognitive, affective, and behavioural. The *cognitive* component is the information and knowledge one has about an object or concept. The *affective* component is one's feelings or emotional reactions. The *behavioural* component is the way one tends to act or to behave. In considering the decision to shop at a warehouse-type food store, a person obtains information from advertising, trial visits, and input from family, friends, and associates (cognitive). A consumer also receives inputs from others about their acceptance of shopping at this new type of store, as well as impressions about the type of people who shop there (affective). The shopper may ultimately decide to make some purchases of canned goods, cereal, and bakery products there, but continue to rely upon a regular supermarket for major food purchases (behavioural).

As Figure 8-3 illustrates, the three components exist in a relatively stable and balanced relationship to one another and combine to form an overall attitude about an object or idea.

Figure 8-3   Three Components of an Attitude

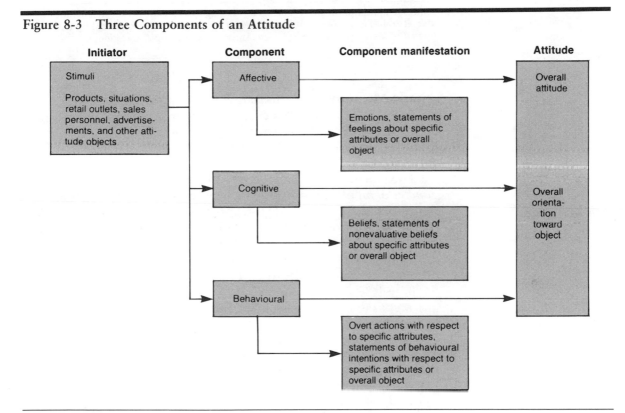

Source: Del I. Hawkins, Kenneth A. Coney, and Roger J. Best, *Consumer Behaviour: Implications for Marketing Strategy* (Dallas, Tex.: Business Publications, Inc. 1980), p. 334. The figure is adapted from M. J. Rosenberg and C. I. Hovland, *Attitude Organization and Change* (New Haven, Conn.: Yale University Press, 1960), p. 3. Reprinted by permission.

Figure 8-4   Product Images of Brands X, Y, and Z

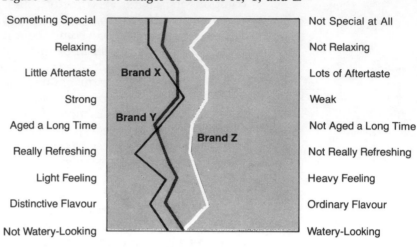

Source: Adapted from William A. Mindak, "Fitting the Semantic Differential to the Market Problem," *Journal of Marketing* (April 1961), pp. 28–33. Reprinted from *Journal of Marketing*, published by the American Marketing Association.

Attitude Measurement   Since favourable attitudes are likely to be conducive to brand preference, marketers are interested in determining consumer attitudes toward their products. Although numerous attitude scaling devices have been developed, the **semantic differential** is probably the most commonly used technique.[11]

The semantic differential is *an attitude scaling device that uses a number of bipolar adjectives* — such as new–old, reliable–unreliable, sharp–bland. The respondent records an evaluation of the product by checking a point on a seven-point scale between the extremes. The average rankings of all respondents then become a profile of the product. One test comparing three unidentified product brands produced the profiles illustrated in Figure 8-4.

Brands X and Y dominated the local market and enjoyed generally favourable ratings. Brand Z, a newly introduced product, was less well known and was reacted to neutrally. A comparison of Brands X and Y can be made, and weak areas in the brand image can be noted for possible remedial action. The semantic differential scale provides management with a more detailed picture of the direction and intensity of opinions and attitudes about a product than could be obtained through a typical research questionnaire. It supplies a comprehensive multidimensional portrait of brand images and is often used in deciding how to position or reposition a brand in the market.

Producing Attitude Change   Given that a favourable consumer attitude is a prerequisite to market success, how can a firm lead prospective buyers to adopt a more favourable attitude toward its products? The marketer has two choices: either attempt to change attitudes to make them consonant with the product or determine consumer attitudes and then change the product to match them.[12]

If consumers view the product unfavourably, the firm may choose to redesign the product to better conform with their desires. To accommodate the consumer, the firm may make styling changes, variations in ingredients, changes in package size, and changes in retail stores handling the product.

The other course of action—changing consumer attitudes toward the product without changing the product—is much more difficult. A famous study using two imaginary shopping lists (see Figure 8-5) revealed surprisingly negative attitudes toward homemakers who served instant coffee. Half of a sample of 100 homemakers were shown List 1 and the other half were shown List 2. Each respondent was asked to describe the hypothetical shopper.

The only difference in the lists was in the form of coffee, but the shopper who bought instant coffee was described as lazy by 48 percent of those evaluating List 1; only 24 percent of those evaluating List 2 described the shopper as lazy. Forty-eight percent described the instant coffee purchaser as failing to plan household purchases and schedules well; only 12 percent described the homemaker who purchased regular coffee this way.

But consumer attitudes often change with time. The shopping list study was repeated 20 years later, and this time revealed that much of the stigma attached to buying and using instant coffee had disappeared. Instead of describing the instant coffee purchaser as lazy and a poor planner, most respondents felt that the writer of

---

Figure 8-5   Shopping Lists Used in the Haire Study

Shopping List 1	Shopping List 2
1 kg of hamburger	1 kg of hamburger
2 loaves of Wonder bread	2 loaves of Wonder Bread
Bunch of carrots	Bunch of carrots
1 can Rumford's Baking Powder	1 can Rumford's Baking Powder
Nescafé Instant Coffee	500 g Maxwell House coffee (drip grind)
2 cans Del Monte peaches	2 cans Del Monte peaches
2 kg potatoes	2 kg potatoes

Source: Mason Haire, "Projective Techniques in Marketing Research," *Journal of Marketing* (April 1950), pp. 649–656. Reprinted from *Journal of Marketing*, published by the American Marketing Association.

List 1 was a working woman.[13] Nonetheless General Foods took no chances when it introduced its new freeze-dried Maxim as a coffee that "tastes like *regular* and has the convenience of *instant*."

Modifying the Attitudinal Components   Attitude change frequently occurs when inconsistencies are introduced among the three attitudinal components. The most common examples of such inconsistencies are changes to the cognitive component of an attitude as a result of new information.

The Pepsi Challenge showed consumers that a larger-than-expected group would prefer Pepsi if they tried it. This new information was expected to lead to increased sales. A recent Life Savers advertising campaign was built around the theme that a Life Saver contains only ten calories, in order to correct misconceptions in the minds of many consumers about the candy's high caloric content.

The affective component may be altered by relating the use of the new product or service to desirable consequences for the user. The growth of health clubs can be attributed to the successful promotion of the benefits of being trim and physically fit.

The third alternative in attempting to change attitudes is to focus upon the behavioural component by inducing someone to engage in behaviour that is contradictory to the person's currently held attitudes. Attitude-discrepant behaviour of this type may occur if the consumer is given a free sample of a product. Such trials may lead to attitude change.

Learning

Since marketing is as concerned with the process by which consumer decisions change over time as with describing those decisions at one point in time, the study of how learning takes place is important. A useful definition of **learning** is *changes in behaviour, immediate or expected, as a result of experience.*

The learning process includes several components. The first component, **drive**, refers to any strong stimulus that impels action. Examples of drives include fear, pride, desire for money, thirst, pain avoidance, and rivalry.

Cues, the second component of the learning process, are any objects existing in the environment that determine the nature of the response to a drive. Cues might include a newspaper advertisement for a new French restaurant, an in-store display, or a Petrocan sign on a major highway. For the hungry person, the shopper seeking a particular item, or the motorist needing gasoline, these cues may result in a specific response to satisfy a drive.

A **response** is the individual's reaction to the cues and drive, such as purchasing a package of Gillette Trac II blades, dining at a Burger King, or deciding to enroll at a particular university or community college.

Reinforcement is the reduction in drive that results from a proper response. The more rewarding the response, the stronger the bond between the drive and the purchase of that particular item becomes. Should Trac II blades result in closer shaves through repeated use, the likelihood of their purchase in the future is increased.

Applying Learning Theory to Marketing Decisions

Learning theory has some important implications for marketing strategists.[14] A desired outcome such as repeat purchase behaviour has to be developed gradually. **Shaping** is *the process of applying a series of rewards and reinforcement so that more complex behaviour* (such as the development of a brand preference) *can evolve over time*. Both promotional strategy and the product itself play a role in the shaping process.

Figure 8-6 shows the application of learning theory and shaping procedures to a typical marketing scenario in which marketers attempt to motivate consumers to become regular buyers of a certain product. An initial product trial is induced by a free sample package that includes a substantial discount coupon on a subsequent purchase. This illustrates the use of a cue as a shaping procedure. The purchase response is reinforced by satisfactory product performance and a coupon for the next purchase.

The second stage is to entice the consumer to buy the product with little financial risk. The large discount coupon enclosed in the free sample prompts such an action. The package that is purchased has a smaller discount coupon enclosed. Again, the reinforcement is satisfactory product performance and the second coupon.

The third step would be to motivate the person to buy the item again at a moderate cost. The discount coupon accomplishes this objective, but this time there is no additional coupon in the package. The only reinforcement is satisfactory product performance.

The final test comes when the consumer is asked to buy the product at its true price without a discount coupon. Satisfaction with product performance is the only continuing reinforcement. Thus, repeat purchase behaviour has been literally shaped.

Kellogg used learning theory and shaping when it introduced its Nutri-Grain brand sugarless whole grain cereal. Coupons worth 40 cents off—about a third of the product's cost—were distributed to elicit trial purchases by consumers. Inside boxes of the new cereal were additional cents-off coupons of lesser value.[15] Kellogg was clearly trying to shape future purchase behaviour by effective application of learning theory within a marketing strategy context.

Figure 8-6   Application of Learning Theory and Shaping Procedure to Marketing

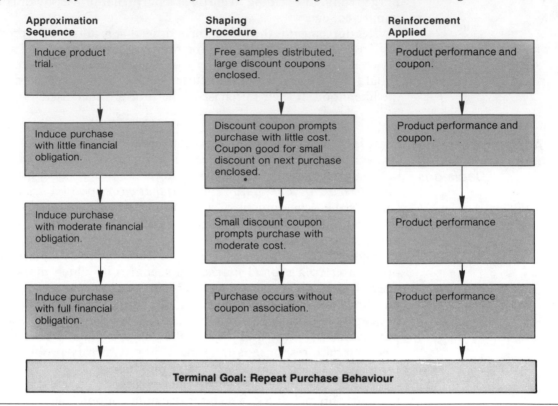

Approximation Sequence	Shaping Procedure	Reinforcement Applied
Induce product trial.	Free samples distributed, large discount coupons enclosed.	Product performance and coupon.
Induce purchase with little financial obligation.	Discount coupon prompts purchase with little cost. Coupon good for small discount on next purchase enclosed.	Product performance and coupon.
Induce purchase with moderate financial obligation.	Small discount coupon prompts purchase with moderate cost.	Product performance
Induce purchase with full financial obligation.	Purchase occurs without coupon association.	Product performance

Terminal Goal: Repeat Purchase Behaviour

Source: Adapted from Michael L. Rothschild and William C. Gaidis, "Behavioral Learning Theory: Its Relevance to Marketing and Promotions," *Journal of Marketing* (Spring 1981), p. 72.

Self-Concept Theory

Self-concept plays an important role in consumer behaviour. An individual is both a physical and mental entity. Each of us possesses a multifaceted picture of ourselves. We may view ourselves as intellectual, self-assured, moderately talented athletes, and rising young business executives. Our actions, including purchase decisions, are dependent upon our actual or desired *mental conception of self*. This is our **self-concept**. For example, the response to such direct questions as "Why do you buy Pierre Cardin cologne?" is likely to reflect our desired self-image. Personal needs, motives, perception, attitudes, and learning lie at the core of an individual's conception of self. So too do the environmental interpersonal factors of family, social, and cultural influences.

As Figure 8-7 indicates, the self may be regarded as having four components: real self, self-image, looking-glass self, and ideal self.

Figure 8-7 Components of Self

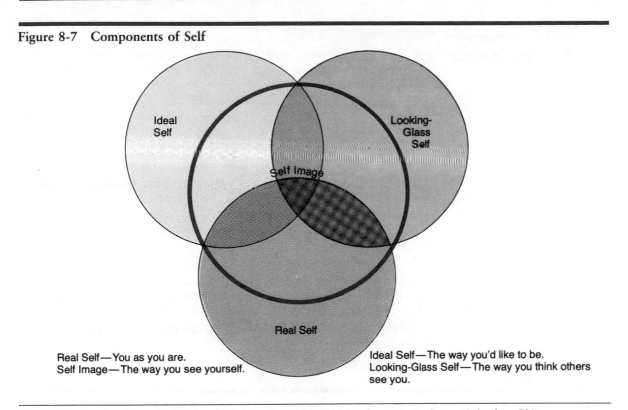

Ideal
Self

Looking-
Glass
Self

Self Image

Real Self

Real Self—You as you are.
Self Image—The way you see yourself.

Ideal Self—The way you'd like to be.
Looking-Glass Self—The way you think others
see you.

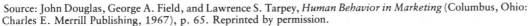

Source: John Douglas, George A. Field, and Lawrence S. Tarpey, *Human Behavior in Marketing* (Columbus, Ohio: Charles E. Merrill Publishing, 1967), p. 65. Reprinted by permission.

The *real self* is an objective view of the total person as he or she actually is. This image is partially distorted into the *self-image* — the way individuals view themselves. The *looking-glass self* — the way individuals think others see them — may also be quite different from their self-image since they may choose to project a different image to others. A person's *ideal self* serves as a personal set of objectives since it is the image to which he or she aspires. All of these affect self-concept.

In purchasing goods and services, people are likely to choose those products that will move them closer to their ideal selves. Persons who possess images of themselves as scholars are more likely to join the literary book club. The young woman who sees herself as a budding tennis star may become engrossed in evaluating the merits of graphite versus steel racquets and may view with disdain the cheaply made imports. The college graduate on the way up the organization ladder at the bank may hide a love for bowling and instead take up golf — believing that this is the typical sport for a banker.

**The Consumer
Decision Process**
Chapter 7 began with a discussion of the consumer decision process, using a schematic model showing six stages: problem recognition, search, evaluation of alternatives, the purchase decision, the purchase act, and postpurchase evaluation. For convenience, it is reproduced here as Figure 8-8.

Consumer behaviour research traditionally has focused on such specific areas as attitudes, personality, and the influence of reference groups on the individual. These fragments, however, should be seen in their proper perspective. This model allows us to integrate the various components of consumer behaviour and assists us in understanding the complex relationships among them. It also provides a means of integrating new research findings in the search for a more complete explanation of why consumers behave as they do. The total model approach can be used in major buying situations, such as a first-time purchase of a new product or the purchase of a high-priced, long-lived article. It can also be applied to routine purchases handled in a largely habitual manner, such as buying a newspaper or a particular brand of chewing gum.

The discussion that follows presents one generalized model of consumer behaviour.

Figure 8-8   Steps in the Consumer Decision Process

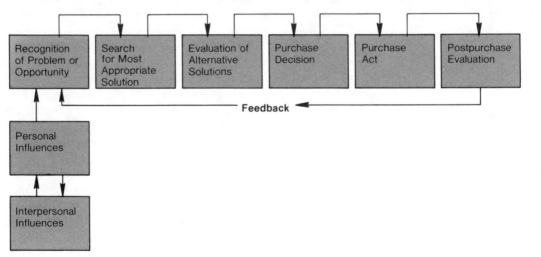

Source: Adapted from C. Glenn Walters and Gordon W. Paul, *Consumer Behavior: An Integrated Framework* (Homewood, Ill.: Richard D. Irwin, Inc., 1970), p. 18 © 1970 by Richard D. Irwin, Inc. and John Dewey, *How We Think* (Boston, Mass.: D. C. Heath, 1910), pp. 101–105. Similar steps are also discussed in Del I. Hawkins, Roger J. Best, and Kenneth A. Coney, *Consumer Behavior: Implications for Marketing Strategy*, revised ed. (Plano, Texas: Business Publications, Inc., 1983), pp. 447–606.

Problem Recognition   This first stage in the decision process occurs when the consumer becomes aware of a discrepancy of sufficient magnitude between the existing state of affairs and a desired state of affairs. Once the problem has been recognized, it must be defined in order that the consumer may seek out methods for its solution. Having recognized the problem, the individual is motivated to achieve the desired state.

What sort of problems might a person recognize? Perhaps the most common is a routine depletion of the stock of products. A large number of consumer purchases involve the replenishment of items ranging from gasoline to groceries. In other instances, the consumer may possess an inadequate assortment of products. The individual whose hobby is gardening may make regular purchases of different kinds of fertilizers, seeds, or gardening tools as the size of the garden grows.

A consumer may also be dissatisfied with a present brand or product type. This situation is a common factor in the purchase of a new automobile, new furniture, or a new fall wardrobe. In many instances, boredom with current products and a desire for novelty may be the underlying rationale for the decision process leading to new-product purchases.

Another important factor is changed financial status. The infusion of added financial resources from such sources as a salary increase, a second job, or an inheritance may permit the consumer to recognize desires and make purchases that previously had been postponed due to their cost.

Search   Search, the second stage in the decision process, is the gathering of information related to the attainment of a desired state of affairs. This stage involves the identification of alternative means of solving the problem.

Internal search is a mental review of the information that a person already knows relevant to the problem situation. This includes actual experiences and observations plus remembered reading or conversations and exposures to various persuasive marketing efforts.

External search is the gathering of information from outside sources. These may include family members, friends and associates, store displays, sales representatives, brochures, and such product-testing publications as *Canadian Consumer*.

In many instances, the consumer does not go beyond internal search but merely relies upon stored information in making a purchase decision. Achieving favourable results using Du Pont's Rain Dance car polish may sufficiently motivate a consumer to repurchase this brand rather than consider possible alternatives. Since external search involves both time and effort, the consumer will rely upon it only in instances in which for some reason information remembered is inadequate.

The search process will identify alternative brands for consideration and possible purchase. *The number of brands that a consumer actually considers in making a purchase decision* is known as the **evoked set**. In some instances, the consumer will already be aware of the brands worthy of further consideration; in others the external search process will permit the consumer to identify those brands. Not all brands will be included in the evoked set. The consumer may remain unaware of certain brands and others will be rejected as too costly or as having been tried previously and considered unsatisfactory. In other instances, unfavourable word-of-mouth communication or negative reactions to advertising or other marketing efforts will lead to the elimination of some brands from the evoked set. While the number of brands in the evoked set will vary by product categories, research indicates that the number is likely to be as few as four or five brands.[16]

Evaluation of Alternatives

The third step in the consumer decision process involves the evaluation of alternatives identified during the search process. Actually, it is difficult to completely separate the second and third steps since some evaluation takes place simultaneously with the search process as consumers accept, discount, distort, or reject some incoming information as they receive it.

Since the outcome of the evaluation stage is the choice of a brand or product in the evoked set (or, possibly, the search for additional alternatives should all those identified during the search process prove unsatisfactory), the consumer must develop a set of **evaluative criteria**, *features the consumer considers in making a choice among alternatives*. These criteria can either be *objective* (federal government automobile fuel consumption tests in litres per 100 kilometres, or comparison of retail prices) or *subjective* (favourable image of Calvin Klein sportswear). Commonly used evaluative criteria include price, reputation of the brand, perceived quality, packaging, size, performance, durability, and colour. Most research studies indicate that consumers seldom use more than six criteria in the evaluation process. Evaluative criteria for detergents include suds level and smell as indicators of cleaning power. High quality and potential for long wear were the underlying criteria in the choice of nylon stockings, according to one research study.[17]

The Purchase Decision and the Purchase Act

When the consumer has evaluated each of the alternatives in the evoked set, utilizing his or her personal set of evaluative criteria, and narrowed the alternatives to one, the end result is the purchase decision and the act of making the purchase.

The consumer must decide not only to purchase a product but also where to buy it. Consumers tend to choose the purchase location by considering such factors as ease of access, prices, assortment, store personnel, store image, physical design, and services provided. The product category will also influence the store selected. Some consumers will choose the convenience of in-home shopping by telephone or mail order rather than complete the transaction in a retail store.

Postpurchase Evaluation   The purchase act results in the removal of the discrepancy between the existing state and the desired state. Logically, it should result in satisfaction to the buyer. However, even in many purchase decisions where the buyer is ultimately satisfied, it is common for that person to experience some initial postpurchase anxieties. He or she often wonders if the right decision has been made. Leon Festinger refers to this postpurchase doubt as **cognitive dissonance**.[18]

Cognitive dissonance is a psychologically unpleasant state that occurs after a purchase when there exists a discrepancy among a person's knowledge and beliefs (cognitions) about certain attributes of the final products under consideration. This occurs because several of the final product choice candidates have desirable characteristics, making the final decision difficult. Consumers may, for example, experience dissonance after choosing a particular automobile over several alternative models, when one or more of the rejected models have some desired features that the purchased automobile does not.

Dissonance is likely to increase 1) as the dollar value of the purchase increases, 2) when the rejected alternatives have desirable features not present in the chosen alternative, and 3) when the decision is a major one. The consumer may attempt to reduce dissonance in a variety of ways. He or she may seek out advertisements and other information supporting the chosen alternative or seek reassurance from acquaintances who are satisfied purchasers of the product. At the same time the individual will avoid information favouring unchosen alternatives. The Toyota purchaser is more likely to read Toyota advertisements and to avoid Datsun and Volkswagen ads. The cigarette smoker may ignore the magazine articles reporting links between smoking and cancer.

Marketers should try to reduce cognitive dissonance by providing informational support for the chosen alternative. Automobile dealers recognize "buyer's remorse" and often follow up purchases with a warm letter from the president of the dealership, offering personal handling of any customer problems and including a description of the quality of the product and the availability of convenient, top quality service.

The consumer may ultimately deal with cognitive dissonance by changing opinions, deciding that one of the rejected alternatives would have been the best choice, and forming the intention of purchasing it in the future.

Should the purchase prove unsatisfactory, the consumer will revise purchase strategy to obtain need satisfaction. Feedback from the results of the decision process, whether satisfactory or not, will be called upon in the search and evaluation stages of similar buying situations.

Classifying Consumer Problem-Solving Processes

The consumer decision process is dependent on the type of problem-solving effort required. Problem-solving behaviour has been divided into three categories: routinized response, limited problem solving, and extended problem solving.[19]

Routinized Response

Many purchases are made as a routine response to a need. The selection is a preferred brand or from a limited group of acceptable brands. The consumer has set the evaluative criteria and identified the available options. The routine purchase of a particular newspaper or regular brands of soft drinks or toilet soap would be examples.

Limited Problem Solving

Consider the situation where the consumer has set evaluative criteria but encounters a new, unknown brand. The introduction of a new fragrance line might create a limited problem-solving situation. The consumer knows the evaluative criteria but has not assessed the new brand on the basis of these criteria. A certain amount of time and external search will be required. Limited problem solving is affected by the multitude of evaluative criteria and brands, the extent of external search, and the process by which preferences are determined.

Extended Problem Solving

Extended problem solving occurs in important purchase decisions when evaluative criteria have not been established for a product category, or where the individual wishes to review such criteria. Today many individuals are in the process of purchasing personal computers. Since most have never owned one before, they generally engage in an extensive search process. The main aspect of this is the determination of appropriate evaluative criteria which are relevant to the needs of the decision maker. How much computing power is required? Is portability important? What will be its main uses? What special features are required? As the criteria are being set, an evoked set of brands is also established. Most extended problem-solving efforts are lengthy, involving considerable external search.

Regardless of the type of problem solving, the steps in the basic model of the consumer decision process remain valid. The problem-solving categories described here relate only to the time and effort that is devoted to each step in the process.

Summary   Consumer behaviour is a function of both interpersonal and personal influences. The personal determinants of consumer behaviour have been identified as needs, motives, perception, attitudes, and self-concept. Learning theory also plays a role in consumer buying processes.

A need is the lack of something useful, while motives are the inner states that direct individuals to satisfy such needs. A. H. Maslow proposed a need classification structure that started with basic physiological needs and proceeded to progressively higher levels of needs — safety, social, esteem and self-actualization. Perception is the meaning that people assign to incoming stimuli received through the five senses. Most of these stimuli are screened or filtered out, so that the marketer must break through these screens to present the sales message effectively. Attitudes are a person's evaluations and feelings toward an object or idea. There are three components of attitudes: cognitive (what the person knows), affective (what the person feels about something), and behavioural (how the person tends to act). Learning refers to changes in behaviour, immediate or expected, as a result of experience. The learning theory concept can be useful in building a consumer franchise for a particular brand. Self-concept refers to an individual's conception of him- or herself. Self-concept theory has important implications for marketing tactics such as in targeting advertising messages.

The consumer decision process consists of six stages: problem recognition, search, evaluation of alternatives, the purchase decision, the purchase act, and postpurchase evaluation. Various types of problem-solving effort are required in the decision process. Routinized response, limited problem solving, and extended problem solving are the three categories of problem-solving behaviour.

4 4 4 4 4 4 4

4 4 4 4 4 4 4

4 4 4 4 4 4 4

4 4 4 4 4 4 4

4 4 4 4 4 4 4

4 4 4 4 4 4 4

4 4 4 4 4 4 4

4 4 4 4 4 4 4

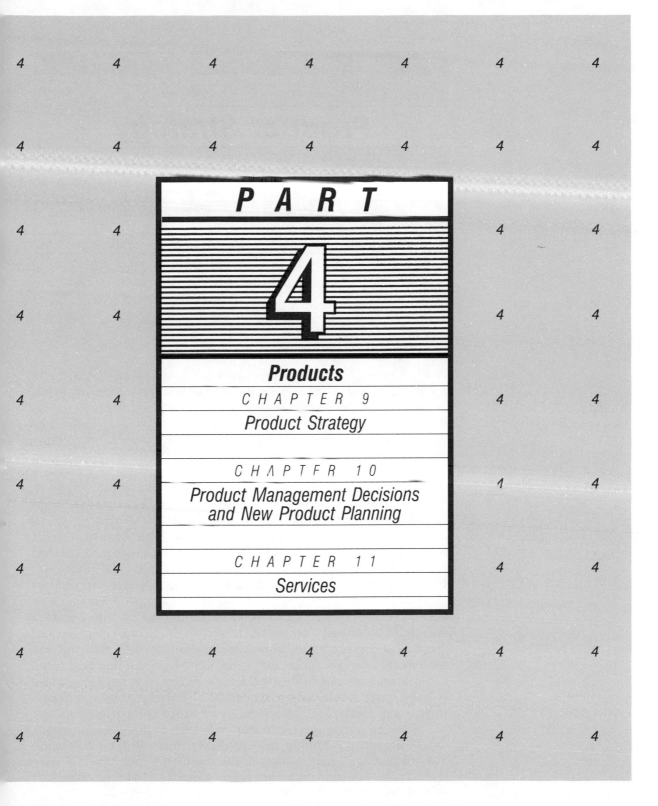

PART

4

Products

Product Strategy

1. *To relate product strategy to the other variables of the marketing mix.*

2. *To explain the concept of the product life cycle, as well as its uses and limitations.*

3. *To identify the determinants of the speed of the adoption process.*

4. *To explain the methods for accelerating the speed of adoption.*

5. *To identify the classifications for consumer goods and to briefly describe each category.*

6. *To classify the types of industrial goods.*

Product managers in the photocopier business are both excited and apprehensive these days. The separate technologies of copiers, printers and computers are merging into a new generation of super-machines complete with microprocessors and disk drives.[1] The managers are wondering whether their current lines of photocopy machines will soon be obsolete, and whether the technological path that they are following in developing new machines will produce winning products among the new generation of copiers.

When they arrive, these new "intelligent" machines may not even be called copiers, because they will be able to do so much — print, copy *and* transmit material.[2] However, a great deal of market segmentation exists in this field. It will be a real challenge to develop the right mix of products to fit existing and potential segments. Current market needs range from small offices which require less than 2000 copies per day, to those which require two or more copiers, each capable of volumes of 20 000 to 50 000 copies a month. Will the new copiers be chosen on the basis of number and speed of copies produced, or will the new information transmission technology be more important? What combinations, number, speed and transmission capabilities will serve which market segments? How will the ready availability of computers from micros to mainframe in virtually every office affect the demand for compatible copiers?

Marketing managers will not only face such decisions about designing and positioning new products, but will have to decide how to manage existing ones. Over the life of each product they will have to determine whether prices should be lowered or raised, whether money should be spent on redeveloping such older products, and how they should be promoted and distributed. Establishing strategies for new products, and managing older ones is a major aspect of marketing management.

The Conceptual Framework

Chapter 9 looks at product concepts, and Chapter 10 covers the product mix and new product planning. Planning efforts begin with the choice of products to offer the market target. Pricing structures, marketing channels, and promotional plans — the other variables of the marketing strategy — are all based on product planning. In a very real sense, the sole economic justification of the firm's existence is the production and marketing of want-satisfying products.

Designing services is similar to designing physical products. However, because some characteristics of services are unique, Chapter 11 is devoted exclusively to this class of want-satisfying items.

Products: A Definition

A narrow definition of the word *product* would focus on the physical or functional characteristics of a good offered to consumers. For example, a Sony videocassette recorder is a rectangular container of metal and plastic wires connecting it to a television set, accompanied by a series of special tapes for recording and viewing. This is the core product. But the purchaser has a much broader view of the recorder. He has bought the convenience of viewing television programs at his leisure, the warranty and service that Sony, the manufacturer, provides, the prestige of owning this relatively new product innovation, and the ability to rent or purchase recently released movies for home viewing. Thus the brand product image, warranty and service are also all parts of the product as seen by the consumer.

Marketing decision-makers must have this broader concept in mind and realize that people purchase more than just the physical features of products. *They are buying want satisfaction.* Most drivers know very little about the gasoline they so regularly purchase. If they bother to analyse it, they discover that it is almost colourless and emits a peculiar odour. However, most of them do not think of gasoline as a product at all — to them, gasoline is a tax. It is a payment that they must periodically make for the privilege of driving their cars on the streets and highways. And the friendly service station attendant is a tax collector. Petroleum retailers should be aware of this image in the minds of many customers before spending huge sums to promote dozens of secret ingredients designed to please the motorist.

The shopper's conception of a product may be altered by such features as packaging, labelling, or the retail outlets in which the product may be purchased. An image of high quality has been created for Maytag appliances, whose television commercials describe the Maytag repairer as "the loneliest person in town." Twenty-five years ago, the firm's president set a standard of "10 years of trouble-free operation" for automatic clothes washers. The company's success in achieving a reputation for high product quality is evident in Maytag's continued sales growth record, even though the washer's retail price is about $70 higher than the nearest competitor's.

Some products have no physical ingredients. A haircut and blow-dry at the local hair stylist produces only well-groomed hair. A tax counsellor produces only advice. Thus, a broader view of product must also include services.

A **product** then, may be defined as *a total bundle of physical, service, and symbolic characteristics designed to produce consumer want satisfaction.* Figure 9-1 reflects this broader definition by identifying the various components of the total product.

An important feature of many products is a product **warranty**. The warranty is *a guarantee to the buyer that the manufacturer will replace a defective product or refund its purchase price during a*

Figure 9-1   The Total Product Concept

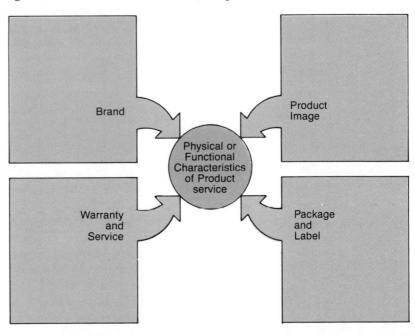

specified period of time. Such warranties serve to increase consumer purchase confidence and can prove to be an important means of stimulating demand. Zippo lighters used a warranty as one of the most important features of the firm's marketing strategy. The manufacturer agreed to a lifetime guarantee, promising to repair or replace any damaged or defective Zippo lighter regardless of age. Many retailers have a broad, unwritten but frequently honoured warranty of satisfaction or your money back.

The Product Life Cycle

Product types, like individuals, pass through a series of stages. As humans progress from infancy to childhood to adulthood to retirement to death, successful products also progress through stages before their death. This progression of *introduction, growth, maturity, and decline* is known as the **product life cycle**. The cycle is depicted in Figure 9-2, with examples of products currently at each stage of development.

Figure 9-2   Stages in the Product Life Cycle

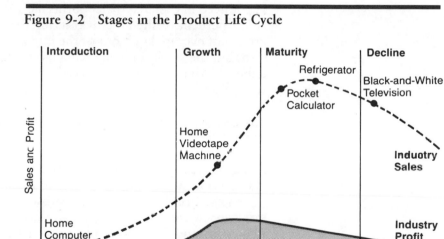

Stages of the Cycle

Introductory Stage   The firm's objective in the early stages of the product life cycle is to stimulate demand for the new market entry. Since the product is not known to the public, promotional campaigns stress information about its features. Promotion may also be directed toward middlemen in the channel to induce them to carry the product. In this initial phase the public is being acquainted with the merits of the new product and acceptance is being gained.

As Figure 9-2 indicates, losses are common during the introductory stage due to heavy promotion and extensive research and development expenditures. But the groundwork is being laid for future profits. Firms expect to recover their costs and to begin earning profits when the new product moves into the second phase of the cycle — the growth stage.

In the case of the videodisk, RCA Corporation and a joint team of the Dutch-based Philips and MCA, Inc., spent more than $200 million in the development expenses prior to its introduction. But the home videoplayer, which squeezes 30 minutes of movies or other entertainment or educational programs onto each side of a phonograph record-type disk, is aimed at a market with estimated annual sales of $500 million.[3]

Pressdent is an example of a product that recently entered the introductory stage. Pressdent is a pump-dispensed toothpaste that was originally discovered by a 10-year-old who dumped water and toothpaste into a liquid-soap container. The child's father decided to set up a company to market the new product. Pressdent was first introduced in Canada, then Southern California. The eventual goal is 3.5 percent of the North America dentifrice market. Whether Pressdent ever makes it out of the introductory stage remains to be seen, but the small company remains confident. The entrepreneurial father, Nathalie Goulet, remarked, "Eventually toothpaste in a tube will go the way of shaving cream in a tube."[4]

Growth Stage   Sales volume rises rapidly during the growth stage as new customers make initial purchases and repurchases are made by the early users of the product. Word-of-mouth and mass advertising induce hesitant buyers to make trial purchases. Videotape machines now seem to have entered this phase of the cycle.

As the firm begins to realize substantial profits from its investment during the growth stage, it attracts competitors. Success breeds imitation, and firms rush into the market with competitive products in search of profit during the growth stage. As soon as the dramatic market acceptance of the IBM personal computer was realized, many other manufacturers jumped into the market with "IBM compatible" versions of the IBM PC.

Maturity Stage   Industry sales continue to grow during the early portion of the maturity stage but eventually reach a plateau as the backlog of potential customers is exhausted. By this time a large number of competitors have entered the market, and profits decline as competition intensifies.

In the maturity stage differences among competing products have diminished as competitors have discovered the product and promotional characteristics most desired by the market. Heavy promotional outlays emphasize subtle differences among competing products, and brand competition intensifies.

For the first time, available products exceed industry demand. Companies attempting to increase sales and market share must do so at the expense of competitors. As competition intensifies, the tendency grows among competitors to cut prices in an attempt to attract new buyers. Even though a price reduction may be the easiest method of inducing additional purchases, it is also one of the simplest moves for competitors to duplicate. Reduced prices will result in decreased revenues for all firms in the industry unless the price cuts produce enough increased purchases to offset the loss in revenue on each product sold.

Decline Stage   In the final stage of the product's life, new innovations or shifting consumer preferences bring about an absolute decline in total industry sales. The safety razor and electric shavers replace the straight razor, *Pac-Man* replaces *Rubik's Cube* as the latest fad, and the black and white television is exchanged for a colour set. As Figure 9-3 indicates, the decline stage of the old product is also the growth stage for the new market entry.

Industry profits decline and in some cases actually become negative as sales fall and firms cut prices in a bid for the dwindling market. Manufacturers gradually begin to leave the industry in search of more profitable products.

Figure 9-3   Overlap of Life Cycle for Products A and B

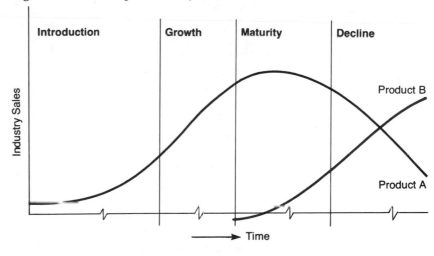

Departures from the Traditional Product Life-Cycle Model

The preceding discussion has examined what is considered the traditional product life cycle with its four clearly delineated stages. Some marketing theorists divide the life cycle into additional stages, but these four, identified in Figure 9-2, are generally accepted within the marketing discipline.

Yet despite the vast body of material written on the subject, considerable controversy surrounds the format and usefulness of product life-cycle theory. On the one hand, the concept has an enduring appeal because of the intuitive logic of the birth-to-decline biological analogy.[5] As such, it has considerable descriptive value when used as a systematic framework for explaining market dynamics.

However, the simplicity of the concept has led to simplistic uses and expectations for the model, and this has called the concept itself into question. Part of the problem lies in failing to distinguish between the life cycle of a product type and that of an individual brand within that generic product category. Life cycle theory is most applicable to product types. A truly new brand is obviously also the generic category for a while, but as competing brands are introduced, it becomes one of several brands within that category. The greatest misuse of product life-cycle theory is to consider it a predictive model for anticipating when changes will occur and to presume that one stage will always succeed another. Managers can make grave errors if they naively interpret a particular rise or fall in sales as a sign that a product has moved from one stage to another. Such an interpretation could lead to serious errors in strategy, such as concluding that a product was in decline and removing it from the market.

A second criticism is the use of the life cycle as a *normative* model which *prescribes* the alternative strategies which should be considered at each stage. As will be shown later, there are strategies which are generally appropriate at various stages of the life cycle of a product *category*. In the case of an individual brand *within* a product category, however, as Enis, LaGarce, and Prell argue, "the product life cycle [of a brand] is a *dependent* variable. . . . That is, the brand's stage in the product life cycle depends primarily upon the marketing strategy implemented for that product at a particular time."[6]

A more realistic view is that life cycle analysis serves several different roles in the formulation of strategy. In the case of both generic product type and individual brand the life cycle serves as an *enabling condition* in the sense that the underlying forces that inhibit or facilitate growth create opportunities and threats having strategic implications. The stage of the life cycle also acts as a *moderating variable* through its influence on the value of market share position and the profitability consequences of strategic decisions. In the case of an individual brand a stage in the life cycle is partially a *consequence* of managerial decisions. Its position is not necessarily a *fait accompli*, which can only be reacted to, but instead is only

Figure 9-4   Alternative Product Life Cycles

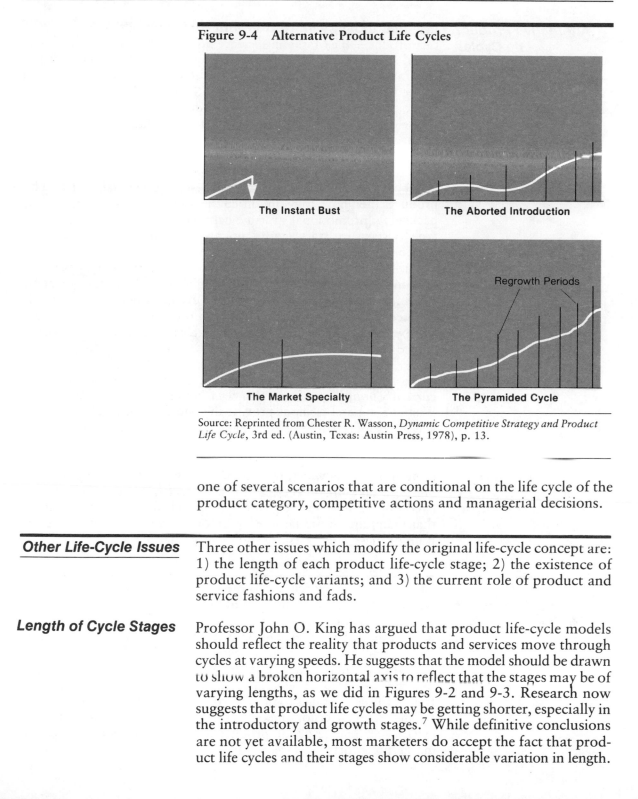

Source: Reprinted from Chester R. Wasson, *Dynamic Competitive Strategy and Product Life Cycle*, 3rd ed. (Austin, Texas: Austin Press, 1978), p. 13.

one of several scenarios that are conditional on the life cycle of the product category, competitive actions and managerial decisions.

Other Life-Cycle Issues

Three other issues which modify the original life-cycle concept are: 1) the length of each product life-cycle stage; 2) the existence of product life-cycle variants; and 3) the current role of product and service fashions and fads.

Length of Cycle Stages

Professor John O. King has argued that product life-cycle models should reflect the reality that products and services move through cycles at varying speeds. He suggests that the model should be drawn to show a broken horizontal axis to reflect that the stages may be of varying lengths, as we did in Figures 9-2 and 9-3. Research now suggests that product life cycles may be getting shorter, especially in the introductory and growth stages.[7] While definitive conclusions are not yet available, most marketers do accept the fact that product life cycles and their stages show considerable variation in length.

Alternative Product Life Cycles

In a study dealing with 100 categories of food, health, and personal care products, the Marketing Science Institute reported that the traditional life-cycle model was applicable for only 17 percent of the general categories and 20 percent of the specific brands.[8] Variants to the traditional model are shown in Figure 9-4.

As shown in Figure 9-4, some products simply do not make it. These can be labeled the "instant busts"; a failure simply does not go through the four steps of the traditional model. Still other products are introduced but information derived from test market situations indicates that changes will be necessary if the product launch is to be successful. (Test markets are described in Chapter 10.) The products then have to be modified in some way, such as in design, packaging, promotional strategy, before they are reintroduced. This type of start-up, start-again launch is labeled the "aborted introduction" in Figure 9-4.

Still other products become market specialty items (discussed later in the chapter), and provide long and stable maturity stages. A common variant is the "pyramided cycle," where the product is adapted through new technology or a revised marketing strategy. The pyramided cycle (also discussed later in the chapter) is characterized by a series of regrowth periods.

Fashions and Fads

Fashions and fads are also important to marketers. **Fashions** are *currently popular products that tend to follow recurring life cycles*. Women's apparel fashions provide the best examples. The miniskirt was reintroduced in 1982 after being out of fashion for over a decade.

By contrast, **fads** are *fashions with abbreviated life cycles*. Consider the case of popular music for teenagers. Disco gave way to punk and new wave, which has since been replaced by the *new music*, a take-off on rock and roll.[9] Most fads experience short-lived popularity and then fade quickly. However, there are some that maintain a residual market among certain market segments. Both of these fad cycles are shown in Figure 9-5.

Product Life Cycles Considerations in Marketing Strategy

Marketing strategy related to the product life cycle is most useful when carried out on an individual *brand* basis rather than a generic product category basis.[10] There are too many uncontrollable variables at the generic level. The product life cycle — with all its variants — is a useful tool in marketing strategy decision making. The knowledge that profits assume a predictable pattern through the stages and that promotional emphasis must shift from product information in the early stages to brand promotion in the later ones allows the marketing decision-maker to take advantage of conditions that exist in each stage of the product life cycle through appropriate marketing efforts.

Figure 9-5   Fad Cycles

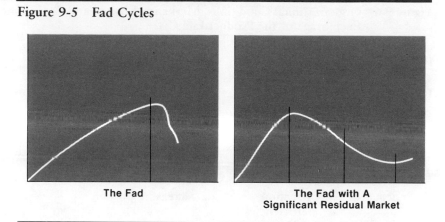

The Fad	**The Fad with A** **Significant Residual Market**

Source: Reprinted from Chester R. Wasson, *Dynamic Competitive Strategy and Product Life Cycle*, 3rd ed. (Austin, Texas: Austin Press, 1978), p. 13.

A firm's marketing efforts should emphasize stimulating demand at the introductory stage. The emphasis shifts to cultivating selective demand in the growth period. Market segmentation should be used extensively in the maturity period. During the decline, the emphasis again shifts to increasing primary demand. Figure 9-6 suggests possibilities for appropriate pricing, distribution, product development, and service and warranty strategies for each life-cycle stage. The reader is again cautioned that the life cycle does not determine the strategy. The market matching process suggested in chapter 5 is applicable for analysis in each situation.

Extending the Product Life Cycle

A good example of the concept that the product life cycle is often subject to managerial strategy is the practice of extending the cycle as long as possible. Marketing managers can accomplish this objective if they take action early in the maturity stage. Product life cycles can sometimes be extended indefinitely by actions designed to:
1. Increase the frequency of use by present customers.
2. Add new users.
3. Find new uses for the product.
4. Change package sizes, labels, or product quality.
Examples of such actions are cited below.

Increasing the Frequency of Use   Noxzema was originally intended as an occasional-use skin medicine but it was repositioned as a routine-use, beauty-care item. This substantially increased the rate of use — and amount purchased.

Figure 9-6   Organizational Conditions, Marketing Efforts, and Environmental Conditions at Each Stage of the Product Life Cycle

Introduction	Growth	Maturity		Decline
		Early Maturity	*Late Maturity*	*Decline*
Organizational Conditions				
High costs	Smoothing production	Efficient scale of operation	Low profits	
Inefficient production levels	Lowering costs	Product modification work	Standardized production	
Cash demands	Operation efficiencies Product improvement work	Decreasing profits		
Environmental Conditions				
Few or no competitors	Expanding markets	Slowing growth	Faltering demand	Permanently declining demand
Limited product awareness and knowledge	Expanded distribution	Strong competition Expanded market	Fierce competition Shrinking number of competitors	Reduction of competitors
Limited demand	Competition strengthens Prices soften a bit	Heightened competition	Established distribution patterns	Limited product offerings Price stabilization
Marketing Efforts				
Stimulate demand	Cultivate selective demand	Emphasize market segmentation	Ultimate in market segmentation	Increase primary demand
Establish high price	Product improvement	Improve service and warranty	Competitive pricing	Profit opportunity pricing
Offer limited product variety	Strengthen distribution	Reduce prices	Retain distribution	Prune and strengthen distribution
Increase distribution	Price flexibility			

Source: Adapted from Burton H. Marcus and Edward M. Tauber, *Marketing Analysis and Decision Making* (Boston: Little, Brown 1979), pp. 115–16. Copyright © 1979 by Burton H. Marcus and Edward M. Tauber. Reprinted by permission of Little, Brown and Company.

Add New Users Cadillac introduced its Cimarron to attract non-Cadillac buyers who usually purchased cars like BMW. Crest and Colgate were reintroduced as sweeter-tasting gels to appeal to younger consumers, further extending the life cycles of these well-known brands.[11] Finding new users is sometimes difficult. Gerber Products failed in attempts to sell its products to the 15 to 22 age group as desserts and snacks. Many still regarded Gerber as baby food.[12]

Find New Uses   Q-tips cotton swabs were originally sold as a baby-care item, but Chesebrough-Pond's Inc.'s marketers found a new use for them as makeup applicators. Cow Brand baking soda was used primarily in cooking until its product life cycle was extended by finding new uses as a denture cleaner, swimming pool pH adjuster, cleaning agent, flame extinguisher, first-aid remedy, and refrigerator freshener.[13]

Change the Package Size, Label, or Product Quality   Levi Strauss Canada Inc. has introduced a limited edition jean called 555. The straight-leg jean uses details of the original jean that Levi Strauss made during the California Gold Rush of 1849. Each pair carries a five-digit serial number. A postage-paid card is used to register each pair of the $33.95 jeans.[14] One of the best examples of a product that has been managed well and avoided the decline stage is Tide. This synthetic detergent, introduced nationally in 1947, continues to sell well in 1985. But more than 50 modifications of packaging, cleaning performance, sudsing characteristics, aesthetics, and physical properties have been made during its lifetime.[15]

Consumer Adoption Process

Once the product is launched, consumers begin a process of evaluating the new item. This evaluation is known as the **adoption process**, whereby potential consumers go through *a series of stages from learning of the new product to trying it and deciding to purchase it regularly or to reject it.* The process has some similarities to the consumer decision process discussed in chapters 7 and 8. These stages in the consumer adoption process can be classified as:
1. *Awareness:* individuals first learn of the new product but lack information about it.
2. *Interest:* they begin to seek out information about it.
3. *Evaluation:* they consider whether the product is beneficial.
4. *Trial:* they make a trial purchase in order to determine its usefulness.
5. *Adoption/Rejection:* if the trial purchase is satisfactory, they decide to make regular use of the product.[16] Of course, rejection may take place at any stage of the process.

The marketing managers need to understand the adoption process so that they can move potential consumers to the adoption stage. Once the manager is aware of a large number of consumers at the interest stage, steps can be taken to stimulate sales. For example,

Gillette introduced Aapri Apricot Facial Scrub by mailing 15 million samples to households in Canada and the United States. Total sample costs for the new skin product, designed to compete with Noxzema, Ponds, and Oil of Olay, were $4.1 million.[17] Sampling, if it is successful, is a technique that reduces the risk of evaluation and trial, moving the consumer quickly to the adoption stage.

Adopter Categories   Some people will purchase a new product almost as soon as it is placed on the market. Others wait for additional information and rely on the experiences of the first purchasers before making trial purchases. **Consumer innovators** are the *first purchasers* at the beginning of a product's life cycle. Some families are first in the community to buy colour television sets.[18] Some doctors are the first to prescribe new drugs,[19] and some farmers will use new hybrid seeds much earlier than their neighbours.[20] Some people are quick to adopt new fashions,[21] while some drivers are early users of automobile diagnostic centres.

A number of investigations analysing the adoption of new products has resulted in the identification of five categories of purchasers based upon relative time of adoption, which are shown in Figure 9-7.

The **diffusion process** refers to this *acceptance of new products and services by the members of a community or social system.* Figure 9-7 shows this process as following a normal distribution. A few people adopt at first, and then the number of adopters increases rapidly as the value of the innovation is apparent. The rate finally diminishes as fewer potential consumers remain in the nonadopter category.

Since the categories are based on the normal distribution, standard deviations are used to partition each category. Innovators are defined as the first 2.5 percent of the individuals to adopt the new product; laggards are the final 16 percent to adopt. Excluded from the figure are the nonadopters, persons who never adopt the innovation.

Identifying the   Locating first buyers of new products represents a challenge for the
First Adopters   marketing manager. If the right people can be reached early in the product's development or introduction, they may serve as a test market, evaluating the products and possibly making suggestions for modifications. Since early purchasers are frequently opinion leaders, from whom others seek advice, their attitudes toward new products are communicated in their neighbourhood and in clubs and organizations. Acceptance or rejection of the innovation by these purchasers may serve as a kind of signal for the marketing manager, indicating the probable success or failure of the new product.

Figure 9-7   Categories of Adopters on the Basis of Relative Time of Adoption

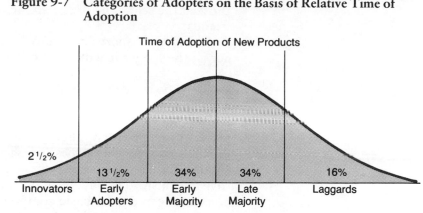

Time of Adoption of New Products

2 1/2%

13 1/2%   34%   34%   16%

Innovators   Early   Early   Late   Laggards
              Adopters   Majority   Majority

Source: Everett M. Rogers and F. Floyd Shoemaker, *Communication of Innovations* (New York: Free Press, 1971), p. 182. Copyright © 1971 by the Free Press of Glencoe. Reprinted by permission.

Unfortunately, persons who are first adopters of one new product may not necessarily be innovators for other products or services. A large number of research studies have, however, established some general characteristics possessed by most first adopters.

In general, first adopters tend to be younger, have a higher social status, be better educated, and enjoy a higher income. They are more mobile than later adopters and change both their jobs and their home addresses more often. They are more likely to rely upon impersonal information sources than later adopters who depend more on promotional information from the company and word-of-mouth communications.[22]

What Determines the Rate of Adoption?

The electronic calculator replaced the slide-rule as the engineering student's friend as soon as prices came within range of the student budget because of its versatility and ease of use. It took 13 years to convince most corn farmers to use hybrid seed corn — an innovation capable of doubling corn yields — even though some progressive farmers adopted it at once. The adoption rate is influenced by five characteristics of the innovation.

1. *Relative advantage:* the degree to which the innovation appears superior to previous ideas. The greater the relative advantage, whether manifested in terms of lower price, physical improvements, or ease of use, the faster the adoption rate.
2. *Compatibility:* the degree to which the innovation is compatible with existing facilities or consistent with the values and experiences of potential adopters. The business student who purchases a

personal computer will likely buy one that is compatible with those at the school he or she attends or with those of his or her friends.

3. *Complexity:* the more difficult to understand or use the new product is, the longer it will take to be generally accepted in most cases.

4. *Divisibility:* the degree to which the innovation may be used on a limited basis. First adopters face two types of risk — financial losses and the risk of ridicule by others — if the new product proves unsatisfactory. The option of sampling the innovation on a limited basis allows these risks to be reduced and, in general, should accelerate the rate of adoption. Computers can be divisible; instead of buying all of a new system on the market, a consumer can try the basic components using a home TV set, and do without a printer.

5. *Communicability:* the degree to which the results of the product may be observable or communicated to others. If the superiority of the innovation may be displayed in a tangible form, it will increase the adoption rate.

These five characteristics can be used, to some extent, by the marketing manager in accelerating the rate of adoption. First, will consumers perceive the product as complex, or will its use necessitate a significant change in typical behaviour patterns? Product complexity must be overcome by promotional messages of an informational nature. Products should be designed to emphasize their relative advantages and, whenever possible, be divisible for sample purchases. If divisibility is physically impossible, in-home demonstrations or trial placements in the home may be used. Positive attempts must also be made to ensure compatibility of the innovation with the adopters' value systems.

These actions are based on extensive research studies of innovators in agriculture, medicine, and consumer goods. They should pay off in increased sales by accelerating the rate of adoption in each of the adopter categories.

Consumer Goods and Industrial Goods: A Definition

How a firm markets its product depends largely on the product itself. For example, a perfume manufacturer stresses subtle promotions in prestige media such as *Chatelaine* and *Vogue* magazines, and markets the firm's products through exclusive department stores and specialty shops. Cadbury Schweppes Powell Ltd. markets its candy products through candy wholesalers to thousands of supermarkets, variety stores, discount houses, and vending machines. Its marketing objective is to saturate the market and to make its candy as convenient as possible for potential buyers. A firm manufacturing and marketing fork-lifts may use sales representatives to call on purchasing agents and ship its product either directly from the factory or from regional warehouses.

Product strategy differs for consumer goods and industrial goods. As defined earlier, consumer goods are products destined for use by the ultimate consumer, and industrial goods are products used directly or indirectly in producing other goods for resale. These two major categories can be broken down further.

Characteristics of Consumer Goods   Although a number of classification systems have been suggested, the system most often used is based on consumer buying habits. The three categories of consumer goods are convenience goods, shopping goods, and specialty goods.[23]

Convenience Goods   The *products that the consumer wants to purchase frequently, immediately, and with a minimum of effort* are called **convenience goods**. Consumers substitute if their desired brand is not available, or forego consumption. They do not make up lost consumption. Milk, bread, butter, and eggs (the staples of the 24-hour convenience food stores) are all convenience goods. So are newspapers, chewing gum, magazines, chocolate bars, and items found in most vending machines.

Convenience goods are usually branded and are low-priced. Many of them are staple items, such as bread, milk, and gasoline, and the consumer's supply must be constantly replenished. In most cases the buyer has already made a decision on a particular brand of gasoline or candy or a particular store and spends little time in conscious deliberation in making a purchase decision. The buyer has already decided on a specific gas station or brand of soft drink and makes a purchase of an item *through habit when supply is low.* Those *products often purchased on the spur of the moment* are referred to as **impulse goods**.

The consumer rarely visits competing stores or compares price and quality in purchasing convenience goods. The possible gains from such comparisons are outweighed by the costs of gaining the additional information. This does not mean, however, that the consumer is destined to remain permanently loyal to one brand of detergent, pop, or candy. The consumer is continually receiving new information inputs through radio and television advertisements, billboards, and word-of-mouth communications. Since the price of most convenience goods is low, trial purchases of competing brands or products can be made with little financial risk and can sometimes lead to new habits.

Since the consumer is unwilling to expend much effort in purchasing convenience goods, the manufacturer must strive to make them as convenient as possible. Newspapers, soft drinks, and candy are sold in almost every supermarket, variety store, service station, and restaurant. Where retail outlets are physically separated from a large number of consumers, the manufacturer constructs small "stores" in the form of vending machines and places them in office buildings and factories for the convenience of its customers. Coca-Cola distributors know that most of their customers will not leave the building in search of a Coke if the vending machine is completely stocked with Pepsi. They must protect this fragile brand loyalty by ensuring that their product is easily available.

Retailers usually carry several competing brands of convenience products and are unlikely to promote any particular brand. The promotional burden, therefore, falls on the *manufacturer.* The firm must advertise extensively to develop consumer acceptance for its product. The Coca-Cola promotional program, consisting of radio and television commercials, magazine ads, billboards, and point-of-purchase displays in the store designed to motivate the consumer to choose Coke over competing brands, is a good example of promotion by the manufacturer designed to stimulate consumer demand.

Shopping Goods   In contrast with convenience goods, **shopping goods** are usually purchased only *after the consumer has made comparisons of competing goods* on such bases as price, quality, style, and colour in competing stores. The consumer is willing to forego consumption for a period in order to evaluate product offerings because he or she anticipates monetary savings and/or greater satisfaction of needs by evaluating alternatives.

The purchaser of shopping goods lacks complete information prior to the actual purchase and gathers additional information during the shopping trip. A woman intent on adding a new dress to her wardrobe may visit many stores, try on perhaps 30 dresses, and may spend days in making the final decision. She may follow a regular route from store to store in surveying competing offerings and ultimately selects the dress that most appeals to her. New stores carrying assortments of shopping goods must ensure that they are located near other shopping goods stores so that they will be included in shopping expeditions.

Shopping goods are typically more expensive than convenience goods and are most often purchased by women. In addition to women's apparel, shopping goods include such items as jewellery, furniture, appliances, shoes, and used automobiles.

Some shopping goods, such as children's shoes, may be classed as *homogeneous* — that is, the consumer views them as essentially the same — while others, such as furniture and clothing, are *heterogeneous* — essentially different. Price is a more important factor in the purchase of homogeneous shopping goods while quality and styling are more important in the purchase of heterogeneous goods.

Brands are often less important for shopping than for convenience goods. Although some furniture brands may come to mind, they are typically less important than the physical attributes of the product, its price, styling, and even the retail store that handles the brand. Even though apparel companies have spent large amounts of money in promoting their brands, the dress buyer knows that the brand is inside the dress, and is more impressed with how the dress looks on her and its fit than with the hidden label.

Manufacturers of shopping goods utilize fewer retail stores than is common for convenience goods since purchasers can be expected to expend some effort in finding what they want to buy, and retailers will expend more effort on selling an exclusively distributed good. Thinness of the market may also affect the number of outlets. Retailers often purchase directly from the manufacturer or its representative rather than going through wholesalers. Fashion merchandise buyers for department stores and specialty shops make regular visits to Toronto, Montreal, New York, and Winnipeg on buying trips. Manufacturers often visit regional centres such as Vancouver, Edmonton, or Moncton to meet retailers there. Buyers for furniture retailers often go directly to the factories of furniture manufacturers or visit major furniture trade shows.

Specialty Goods   The specialty goods purchaser is well aware of what he or she wants and is willing to make a special effort to obtain it. The nearest Leica camera dealer may be 20 km away, but the camera enthusiast will go to that store to obtain what he or she may consider to be the ultimate in cameras. The Chicoutimi collector who longs for a $2500 *objet d'art* of Steuben glassware is willing to journey to Montreal to find the nearest Steuben dealer.

Specialty goods possess *some unique characteristics that cause the buyer to prize that particular brand.* The buyer possesses relatively complete information about the product prior to the shopping trip and is unwilling to accept substitutes.

Specialty goods are typically high-priced and frequently are branded. Since consumers are willing to exert a considerable effort in obtaining the good, fewer retail outlets are needed. Mercury outboard motors and Porsche sports cars may be handled by only one or two retailers for each 100 000 population.

Applying the Consumer Goods Classification System   The three-way classification system gives the marketing manager additional information for use in developing a marketing strategy. For example, if the new food product sells well in a test market as a convenience good, this provides insights about marketing needs in branding, promotion, pricing, and distribution methods. The impact of the goods classifications on their associated consumer factors and to marketing mix variables is shown in Figure 9-8.

Figure 9-8   The Marketing Impact of the Consumer Goods Classification

Factor	Convenience Goods	Shopping Goods	Specialty Goods
Consumer Factors			
Planning time involved in purchase	Very little	Considerable	Extensive
Purchase frequency	Frequent	Less frequent	Infrequent
Importance of convenient location	Critical Importance	Important	Unimportant
Comparison of price and quality	Very little	Considerable	Very little
Marketing Mix Factors			
Price	Low	Relatively high	High
Advertising	By manufacturer	By manufacturer and retailer	By manufacturer and retailer
Channel length	Long	Relatively short	Very short
Number of retail outlets	Many	Few	Very small number; often one per market area
Store image	Unimportant	Very important	Important

But the classification system also poses problems of which the marketing manager must be aware. One pitfall is that it suggests a neat, three-way series of demarcations into which all products can easily be fitted. Some products do fit neatly into one of the three classifications, but others fall into the grey areas between categories.

How should a new automobile be classified? It is expensive, is branded, and is handled by a few exclusive dealers in each city. But before it is classified as a specialty good, other characteristics must be considered. Most new-car buyers shop extensively among competing models and auto dealers before deciding on the best "deal." A more effective method of utilizing the classification system, therefore, is to consider it as a continuum representing degrees of effort expended by the consumer. The new-car purchase can then be located between the categories of shopping and specialty goods, but nearer the specialty-goods end of the continuum.

A second problem with the classification system is that consumers differ in their buying patterns. One person will make an unplanned purchase of a new Pontiac Firebird, while others will shop extensively before purchasing a car. One buyer's impulse purchase does not make the Firebird a convenience good. Goods are classified by the purchase patterns of the *majority* of buyers.

Classifying Industrial Goods

Industrial goods can be subdivided into five categories: installations, accessory equipment, fabricated parts and materials, raw materials, and industrial supplies. Industrial buyers are professional customers; their job is to make effective purchase decisions. Although details may vary, the purchase decision process involved in buying supplies of flour for General Mills, for example, is much the same as that used in buying the same commodity for Robin Hood. Thus the classification system for industrial goods must be based on product uses rather than on consumer buying patterns.

Installations

Installations are *major capital assets like factories and heavy machinery used to produce products and services.* Installations are the specialty goods of the industrial market. New aircraft for CP Air, locomotives for Canadian National, or a new pulp mill for Macmillan Bloedel, are examples of installations.

Since installations are relatively long-lived and involve large sums of money, their purchase represents a major decision for an organization. Sales negotiations often extend over a period of several months and involve the participation of numerous decision-makers. In many cases, the selling company must provide technical expertise. When custom-made equipment is involved, representatives of the selling firm work closely with the buyer's engineers and production personnel to design the most feasible product.

Price is almost never the deciding factor in the purchase of installations. The purchasing firm is interested in the product's efficiency and performance over its useful life. The firm also wants a minimum of breakdowns. "Down time" is expensive because employees are nonproductive (but still are paid) while the machinery is repaired.

Since most of the factories of firms purchasing installations are geographically concentrated, the selling firm places its promotional emphasis on well-trained salespeople who often have a technical background. Most installations are marketed directly on a manufacturer-to-user basis. Even though a sale may be a one-time transaction, contracts often call for regular product servicing. In the case of extremely expensive installations, such as computer and electronic equipment, some firms lease the installations rather than sell them outright and assign personnel directly to the lessee to operate or to maintain the equipment.

Accessory Equipment   Fewer decison-makers are usually involved in purchasing **accessory equipment**—*second-level capital items that are used in the production of products and services but are usually less expensive and shorter-lived than installations.* Although quality and service still remain important criteria in purchasing accessory equipment, the firm is likely to be much more price conscious. Accessory equipment includes such products as desk calculators, hand tools, portable drills, small lathes, and typewriters. Although these goods are considered capital items and are depreciated over several years, their useful life is generally much shorter than that of an installation.

Because of the need for continuous representation and the more widespread geographic dispersion of accessory equipment purchasers, a *wholesaler*, often called an **industrial distributor**, may be used to contact potential customers in each geographic area. Technical assistance is usually not necessary, and the manufacturer of accessory equipment often can effectively utilize such wholesalers in marketing the firm's products. Advertising is more important for accessory manufacturers then it is for installation producers.

Component Parts   While installations and accessory equipment are used in producing
and Materials   the final product, **component parts and materials** are the *finished industrial goods that actually become part of the final product.* Champion spark plugs make a new Chevrolet complete; nuts and bolts are part of a Peugeot bicycle; tires are included with a Dodge pickup truck. Some materials, such as flour, undergo further processing before producing a finished product.

Purchasers of component parts and materials need a regular continuous supply of uniform quality goods. These goods are generally purchased on contract for a period of one year or more. Direct sale is common, and satisfied customers often become permanent buyers. Wholesalers sometimes are used for fill-in purchases and in handling sales to smaller purchasers.

Raw Materials   *Farm products, such as cattle, wool, eggs, milk, pigs, and canola, and natural products, such as coal, copper, iron ore, and lumber,* constitute **raw materials**. They are similar to component parts and materials in that they become part of the final products.

Since most raw materials are graded, the purchaser is assured of standardized products with uniform quality. As with component parts and materials, direct sale of raw materials is common, and sales are typically made on a contractual basis. Wholesalers are increasingly involved in the purchase of raw materials from foreign suppliers.

Price is seldom a deciding factor in the purchase of raw materials, since it is often quoted at a central market and is virtually identical among competing sellers. Purchasers buy raw materials from the firms they consider most able to deliver in the quantity and the quality required.

Supplies   If installations represent the specialty goods of the industrial market, then operating supplies are the convenience goods. **Supplies** are *regular expense items necessary in the daily operation of the firm, but not part of the final product.*

Supplies are sometimes called **MRO items** because they can be divided into three categories: 1) *maintenance items*, such as brooms, floor-cleaning compounds, and light bulbs; 2) *repair items*, such as nuts and bolts used in repairing equipment; and 3) *operating supplies*, such as heating fuel, lubricating oil, and office stationery.

The regular purchase of operating supplies is a routine aspect of the purchasing agent's job. Wholesalers are very often used in the sale of supplies due to the items' low unit prices, small sales, and large number of potential buyers. Since supplies are relatively standardized, price competition is frequently heavy. However, the purchasing agent spends little time in making purchase decisions. He or she frequently places telephone orders or mail orders, or makes regular purchases from the sales representative of the local office-supply wholesaler.

Summary   A critical variable in the firm's marketing mix is the product it plans to offer its market target. The best price, most efficient distribution channel, and most effective promotional campaign cannot maintain continuing purchases of an inferior product.

Consumers view products not only in physical terms but more often in terms of expected want satisfaction. The broad marketing conception of a product encompasses a bundle of physical, service, and symbolic attributes designed to produce this want satisfaction. The total product concept consists of the product image, brand, package and label, and warranty and service.

Most successful products pass through the four stages of the product life cycle: introduction, growth, maturity and decline. The rate at which they pass through the cycle is affected partially by many external uncontrollable factors. It can also be affected in many instances by managerial decisions. Therefore, marketers should not simply view the product life cycle as a deterministic phenomenon to which they can only react.

Several departures from the traditional product life-cycle are noted. First there is evidence that product life cycles may be getting shorter, particularly in the introductory and growth stages. Second, research shows that a number of products do not actually conform to the standard product life cycle model, and several alternative product life cycles are outlined. Finally, there is the matter of fashions and fads. Fashions are currently popular products that tend to have recurring life cycles. By contrast, fads are fashions with abbreviated life cycles.

The product life-cycle concept provides significant opportunities to adjust marketing strategy. Pricing, distribution, and promotion strategies, as well as product strategy, may affect the life-cycle stage, and should also be appropriate to it. Marketers should also attempt to extend the life cycles of successful individual products. Of course, they generally have little control over the life cycle of a product *category*.

Consumers go through a series of stages in adopting new product offerings: initial product awareness, interest, evaluation, trial purchase, and adoption or rejection of the new product.

Although first adopters of new products vary among product classes, several common characteristics have been isolated. First adopters are often younger, better educated, and more mobile, and they have higher incomes and higher social status than later adopters.

The rate of adoption for new products depends on five characteristics: 1) relative advantage, the degree of superiority of the innovation over the previous product; 2) compatibility, the degree to which the new product or idea is consistent with existing operations or the value system of potential purchasers; 3) complexity of the new product; 4) divisibility, the degree to which trial purchases on a small scale are possible; and 5) communicability, the degree to which the superiority of the innovation can be transmitted to other potential buyers.

Products are classified as either consumer or industrial goods. Consumer goods are used by the ultimate consumer and are not intended for resale or further use in producing other products. Industrial goods are used either directly or indirectly in producing other products for resale.

Differences in consumer buying habits can be used to further classify consumer goods into three categories: convenience goods, shopping goods, and specialty goods. Industrial goods are classified on the basis of product uses. The five categories in the industrial goods classification are installations, accessory equipment, component parts and materials, raw materials, and industrial supplies.

CHAPTER 10

Product Management Decisions and New Product Planning

1. *To relate product-mix decisions and new product planning to the other variables of the marketing mix.*

2. *To explain the various product-mix decisions that must be made by marketers.*

3. *To explain why most firms develop a line of related products rather than a single product.*

4. *To outline alternative new product strategies and the determinants of their success.*

5. *To identify and explain the various organizational arrangements for new product development.*

6. *To list the stages in the product development process.*

7. *To explain the role of brands, brand names, and trademarks.*

8. *To define the package and its major functions.*

"We felt we had to get into it because that's our market, our business — home entertainment," says Philip Kives, president of K-Tel International Ltd. A continent-wide decline in the record industry has helped push K-Tel into the tough home video game business. With 1000 new games expected in the current year, the market is crowded and the fight for retail shelf space is ferocious.

Despite the competition, Mr. Kives believed that K-Tel's experience in mass distribution would enable the company to enter the market successfully. "Basically, we are distributing the merchandise in the same manner as we would records. And we can probably distribute merchandise better than any company that I know of," he said.

Kives, 54, has some unusual and extensive experience. A former door-to-door salesman of vacuum cleaners and cookware, he and his brother started K-Tel in 1962 and carved an empire out of gadgets such as the Veg-O-Matic, Hair Magician, and Miracle Lint Brush. The company now has subsidiaries in 16 countries and franchises in 31 others.

Since the mid-1970s, K-Tel has concentrated mostly on musical recordings, selling established hits performed by little-known artists and repackaged into theme albums. Supported by a barrage of television advertising, the company has sold 150 million albums in the past six years.

The video game industry is expected to be tough. A hit game often depends on the finicky whims of 12-year-olds. It will be tougher to forecast a popular video game than a popular record, at least until K-Tel gains more experience in the market. To be successful, the company must select the right products for the right market and then use its expertise to advertise in the right media.

Obtaining shelf space is another critical variable, but K-Tel will likely have little problem here since they have a proven track record for moving products. Furthermore, the company has developed a reputation for dependable delivery of merchandise. It appears that the key to K-Tel's success in this new venture will be the selection of appropriate products for the chosen target markets.[1]

The Conceptual Framework

Chapter 10 expands the discussion of products and services by examining the product mix and new product planning. A starting point is to consider the concept of a product mix.

A **product mix** is the *assortment of product lines and individual offerings available from a marketer.* Its two components are the **product line,** *a series of related products*, and the **individual offerings** or *single products* within those lines.

Figure 10-1   The Canada Packers Product Mix

Width of Assortment

Meats	Groceries	Non-edible
Fresh meats	Peanut butter	By-products
Bacon	Mincemeat	Soap
Pepperoni	Canned pumpkin	Hides
Wieners	Cheese	Pharmaceutical raw
Bologna	Lard	materials
Canned ham	Shortening	
Poultry		
Kolbassa		
Garlic sausage		

Product mixes are typically measured by width and depth of assortment. Width of assortment refers to the number of product lines that the firm offers, while depth of assortment refers to the extension of a particular product line. Canada Packers offers an assortment of consumer product lines — meats, and several unrelated grocery items such as peanut butter. These product lines would be considered the width of the Canada Packers product mix. The depth is determined by the number of individual offerings within each product line. For example, their meat line consists of fresh meats, smoked and processed meats, and the grocery line is represented by York peanut butter and several types of canned vegetables. The company also sells a non-edible line of by-products.

The Existing Product Mix

The starting point in any product planning effort is to assess the firm's current product mix. What product line does it now offer? How deep are the offerings within each of the product lines? The marketer wants to look for gaps in the assortment that can be filled by new products or modified versions of existing products.

Cannibalization

The firm wants to avoid a costly new-product introduction that will adversely affect sales of one of its existing products. *A product that takes sales from another offering in a product line* is said to be **cannibalizing** the line. Marketing research should ensure that cannibalization effects are minimized or at least anticipated. When Coke introduced Diet Coke they were resigned to the fact that the sales of their existing diet brand, Tab, would be negatively affected.

Line Extension

An important rationale for assessing the current product mix is to determine whether line extension is feasible. A **line extension** refers to *the development of individual offerings that appeal to different market segments, but are closely related to the existing product line*. If cannibalization can be minimized, line extension provides a relatively cheap way of increasing sales revenues at minimal risk. Oh Henry chocolate bars can now be purchased in ice cream bar format, in addition to their traditional form.[2] This illustrates the line extension of an existing Hershey product.

Once the assessment of the existing product mix has been made and the appropriate line extensions considered, marketing decision makers must turn their attention to product line planning and the development of new products.

The Importance of Product Lines

Firms that market only one product are rare today. Most offer their customers a product line — a series of related products. Polaroid Corporation, for example, began operations with a single product, a polarized screen for sunglasses and other products. Then, in 1948, it introduced the world's first instant camera. For the next 30 years, these products proved to be sufficient for annual sales and profit growth. By 1983, however, instant cameras accounted for only about two thirds of Polaroid's sales. The company had added hundreds of products in both industrial and consumer markets, ranging from nearly 40 different types of instant films for various industrial, medical, and other technical operations, to batteries, sonar devices, and machine tools.[3] Several factors account for the inclination of firms such as Polaroid to develop a complete line rather than concentrate on a single product.

Desire to Grow

A company places definite limitations on its growth potential when it concentrates on a single product. In a single 12-month period, Lever Brothers introduced 21 new products in its search for market growth and increased profits. A study by a group of management consultants revealed that firms expect newly developed products to account for 37 percent of their sales and 51 percent of their profits over the next five years.[4]

Firms often introduce new products to offset seasonal variations in the sales of their current products. Since the majority of soup purchases are made during the winter months, Campbell Soup Company has made attempts to tap the warm-weather soup market. A line of fruit soups to be served chilled was test-marketed, but results showed that consumers were not yet ready for fruit soups. The firm continued to search for warm-weather soups, however, and in some markets in the early 1980s, it added gazpacho and other varieties to be served chilled, to its product line.

Optimal Use of Company Resources

By spreading the costs of company operations over a series of products, it may be possible to reduce the average costs of all products. Texize Chemicals Company started with a single household cleaner and learned painful lessons about marketing costs when a firm has only one major product. Management rapidly added the products K2r and Fantastik to the line. The company's sales representatives can now call on middlemen with a series of products at little more than the cost for marketing a single product. In addition, Texize's advertising produces benefits for all products in the line. Similarly, production facilities can be used economically in producing related products. For example, Chrysler has produced a convertible, van, and sports car from the basic K car design.[5] Finally, the expertise of all the firm's personnel can be applied more widely to a line of products than to a single one.

Increasing Company Importance in the Market

Consumers and middlemen often expect a firm that manufactures and markets small appliances to also offer related products under its brand name. The Maytag Company offers not only washing machines but also dryers, since consumers often demand matching appliances. Gillette markets not only razors and blades but also a full range of grooming aids, including Foamy shave cream, Right

Guard deodorant, Gillette Dry Look hair spray and Super Max hair dryers.

The company with a line of products is often more important to both the consumer and the retailer than the company with only one product. Shoppers who purchase a tent often buy related items, such as tent heaters, sleeping bags and air mattresses, camping stoves, and special cookware. Recognizing this tendency, the Coleman Company now includes in its product line dozens of items associated with camping. The firm would be little known if its only product were lanterns. Similarly, new cameras from Eastman Kodak help the firm sell more film — a product that carries a 60 percent profit margin.[6]

Exploiting the Product Life Cycle

As its output enters the maturity and decline stages of the life cycle of a product category, the firm must add new products if it is to prosper. The regular addition of new products to the firm's line helps ensure that it will not become a victim of product obsolescence. The development of stereophonic sound in the 1950s shifted single-speaker high-fidelity phonographs from the maturity stage to the decline stage, and companies such as RCA and Zenith began to develop new products incorporating stereo.[7]

New-Product Planning

The product development effort requires considerable advance planning. New products are the lifeblood of any business firm, and a steady flow of new entries must be available if the firm is to survive. Some new products are major technological breakthroughs. For instance, Procter & Gamble has filed patent applications for a male baldness cure, a margarine that cuts cholesterol in the blood, and a plaque-eliminating dental product.[8] Other new products are simple product-line extensions. In other words a new product is simply a product new to either the company or the customer. One survey found that for products introduced between 1976 and 1981, about 85 percent were line extensions, and only 15 percent were truly new products.[9]

The Product Decay Curve

New-product development is risky and expensive. A Conference Board study of 148 medium and large North-American manufacturing companies revealed that one out of three new industrial and consumer products introduced within the past five years has failed. The leading cause of new product failure was insufficient and poor marketing research.[10]

Dozens of new-product ideas are required to produce even one successful product. Figure 10-2 depicts the product decay curve in a 1968 survey of 51 companies. Of every 58 ideas produced in these

Figure 10-2   Decay Curve of New-Product Ideas

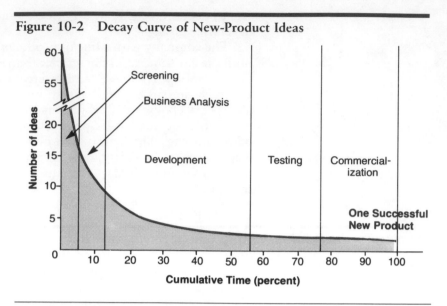

Source: Reprinted by permission from *Management of New Products* (New York: Booz, Allen & Hamilton, 1968), p. 9.

firms, only 12 passed the preliminary screening test designed to determine whether they were compatible with company resources and objectives. Of these 12, only 7 showed sufficient profit potential in the business analysis phase. Three survived the development phase, two made it through the test marketing stage, and only one, on the average, was commercially successful. Thus, less than 2 percent resulted in a successful product.

A 1981 follow-up study reported that while the success rate may be no better today, new-product development is becoming more cost effective. According to the new data, some 54 percent of total new-product expenditures are going to successes, compared with 30 percent in 1968. Capital investment in new products has fallen from 46 percent to 26 percent of total new-product spending.[11] These figures suggest that new-product development is now more efficient.

Determinants of Success for New Products

What determines the success or failure of a new product? A research effort known as Project New Product suggests the following six categories as determinants of new-product outcomes:[12]

1. the relative strengths of the new product and its marketplace launch
2. the nature and quality of the information available during the product development process
3. the relative proficiency of new-product development efforts

4. the characteristics of the marketplace at which the new product is aimed
5. the fit or compatibility of the new product and the firm's resource base
6. the specific characteristics of the new-product effort.

These hypothetical variables allowed Robert Cooper of McGill University to classify various types of new products. Cooper contends that the most important key to new-product success lies in the product strategy itself. In his research he found that in the cases he studied, the best 20 percent of the products had an astounding success rate of 82 percent. In contrast, the 20 percent at the other end of the scale (the "me-too" products) suffered a *failure* rate of 78 percent.

Characteristics of the Superior Product

What then is a superior product? Cooper found that a number of characteristics comprised the superior product dimension. In descending order of importance these critical characteristics are:
1. a product that meets customers' needs better than competing products
2. a product that offers features or attributes to the customer that competing products do not
3. a higher quality product than competitive products (one that has tighter specifications, is stronger, lasts longer, or is more reliable)
4. a product that does a special task or job for the customer — something that cannot be done with existing products
5. a product that is highly innovative, totally new to the market
6. a product that permits the customer to reduce his costs.[13]

Products with these characteristics supported by creative marketing strategies will greatly contribute to a profitable product line.

Product Development Strategies

The firm's strategy for new-product development should vary in accordance with the existing product mix and the determinants cited above. Marketing decision-makers also need to look at the firm's present market position. Figure 10-3 provides a means for looking at overall product development strategy. Four forms of product development are suggested: product improvement, market development, product development, and product diversification.

A *product improvement strategy* refers to modification in existing products. Product positioning often plays a major role in such strategy. **Product positioning** (discussed in Chapter 5) refers to *the consumer's perception of a product's attributes, use, quality, and advantages and disadvantages in relation to competing brands.* Good examples are the recent effort to reposition 7-Up as a caffeine-free soft drink[14] and Pacific Western's effort to get travellers to consider the airline as an alternative when planning a flight. To achieve this they positioned themselves as "the competition," in an extensive advertising campaign.

Figure 10-3   Forms of Product Development

	Old Product	New Product
Old Market	Product Improvement	Product Development
New Market	Market Development	Product Diversification

Source: Charles E. Meisch, "Marketers, Engineers Should Work Together in 'New Product' Development Departments," *Marketing News* (November 13, 1981), p. 10. Earlier discussion of these strategies is credited to H. Igor Ansoff, "Strategies for Diversification," *Harvard Business Review* (September-October 1957), pp. 113–124. See Philip Kotler, *Principles of Marketing*, 2nd ed. (Englewood Cliffs, N.J.: Prentice-Hall, Inc. 1983), pp. 34, 52.

A *market development strategy* concentrates on finding new markets for existing products. Market segmentation (discussed in Chapters 4 and 5) is a useful tool in such an effort. The penetration of new markets with Cow Brand baking soda, an established product, is illustrative of this strategy.

Product development strategy, as defined here, refers to the introduction of new products into identifiable or established markets. Sometimes, the new product is the firm's first entry in this particular marketplace. In other cases, firms choose to introduce new products into markets in which they have already established positions in an attempt to increase overall market share. These new offerings are called *flanker brands*.

Product diversification strategy refers to the development of new products for new markets. In some cases, the new market targets are complementary to existing markets; in others, they are not.

New products should be consistent with the firm's overall strategic orientation. Assume that a beverage firm has set four strategic requirements for a new product:

1. It must appeal to the under-21 age segment.
2. It must utilize off-season or excess capacity.
3. It must successfully penetrate a new product category for the firm.
4. It could simply be a cash cow that funds other new products.[15]

Each of these criteria would fit in well with the orientation, skills, and resources of the firm. As the above section indicates, new-product planning is a complex area. The critical nature of product planning decisions requires an effective organizational structure to make them.

The Organizational Structure for New-Product Development

A prerequisite for efficient product innovation is an organizational structure designed to stimulate and co-ordinate new-product development. New-product development is a specialized task and requires the expertise of many departments.[16] A company that delegates new-product development responsibility to the engineering department often discovers that engineers sometimes design good products from a structural standpoint but poor ones in terms of consumer needs. Many successful medium and large companies assign new-product development to one or more of the following: 1) new-product committees, 2) new-product departments, 3) product managers, or 4) venture teams.

New-Product Committees

The most common organizational arrangement for new-product development is the **new-product committee**. Such a committee is typically composed of representatives of top management in areas such as marketing, finance, manufacturing, engineering, research, and accounting. Committee members are less concerned with conception and development of new product ideas than with reviewing and approving new product plans.

Since key executives in the functional areas are committee members, their support for a new-product plan is likely to result in its approval for further development. However, new-product committees tend to be slow, are generally conservative, and sometimes compromise in order to expedite decisions so that members may get back to their regular company responsibilities.

New-Product Departments

To overcome the limitations of the new-product committee, a number of firms have established a separate, formally organized department responsible for all phases of the product's development within the firm, including making screening decisions, development of product specifications, and co-ordinating product testing. The head of the department is given substantial authority and usually reports to the president or to the top marketing officer.

Product Managers

Product managers (also called **brand managers**) are *individuals assigned one product or product line and given responsibility for determining its objectives and marketing strategies*. Procter & Gamble assigned the first product manager back in 1927 when they made one person responsible for Camay soap.[17] The role of product manager is now widely accepted by marketers. Johnson & Johnson, Canada Packers and General Mills are examples of firms employing product managers.

Product managers set prices, develop advertising and sales promotion programs and work with sales representatives in the field. Although product managers have no line authority over the field sales force, they share the objective of increasing sales for the brand, and managers try to help salespeople accomplish their task. In multiproduct companies, product managers are key people in the marketing department. They provide individual attention to each product, while the firm as a whole has a single sales force, marketing research department, and advertising department that all product managers can utilize.

In addition to product analysis and planning, the product manager uses interpersonal skills and salesmanship to gain the cooperation of people over which he has no authority. This occurs with levels above the manager, as well as with those in sales and advertising.

In addition to having primary responsibility for marketing a particular product or product line, the product manager is often responsible for new-product development, the creation of new-product ideas, and recommendations for improving existing products. These suggestions become the basis for proposals submitted to top management.

The product manager system is open to one of the same criticisms as the new-product committee: new-product development may get secondary treatment because of the manager's time commitments for existing products. Although a number of extremely successful new products have resulted from ideas submitted by product managers, it cannot be assumed that the skills required for marketing an existing product line are the same as those required for successfully developing new products.[18]

Venture Teams   An increasingly common technique for organizing new-product development is the use of **venture teams**.[19]

The venture-team concept is an organizational strategy to develop new-product areas through *the combination of the management resources of technologial innovations, capital, management, and marketing expertise*. Like new-product committees, venture teams are composed of specialists from different functions in the organization: engineering representatives for expertise in product design and the development of prototypes; marketing staff members for development of product-concept tests, test marketing, sales forecasts, pricing, and promotion; and financial accounting representatives for detail cost analyses and decisions concerning the concept's probable return on investment.

Unlike representatives on new-product committees, venture-team members do not disband after every meeting. They are assigned to the project as a major responsibility, and the team possesses the necessary authority to both plan and carry out a course of action.

As a means of stimulating product innovation, the team is typically separated from the permanent organization and is also linked directly with top management. One company moved its three-member venture team from its divisional headquarters to the corporate head office. Since the venture-team manager reports to the division head or to the chief administrative officer, communications problems are minimized and high-level support is assured.

The venture team usually begins as a loosely organized group of members with common interest in a new-product idea. Team members are frequently given released time during the workday to devote to the venture. If viable product proposals are developed, the venture team is formally organized as a task force within a venture department or as a task force reporting to a vice-president or the chief executive officer.

The venture team must meet such criteria as prospective return on investment, uniqueness of the product, existence of a well-defined need, degree of the product's compatibility with existing technology, and strength of patent protection. Although the organization is considered temporary, the actual life span of the venture team is extremely flexible and often extends over a number of years. When the commercial potential of new products has been demonstrated, the products may be assigned to an existing division, may become a division within the company, or may serve as the nucleus of a new company.

The flexibility and authority of the venture team allows the large firm to operate with the manoeuvrability of smaller companies. Venture teams established by Colgate-Palmolive Company have already broadened the base of the toiletries and detergents manufacturer into such products as freeze-dried flowers. Such teams also serve as an outlet for innovative marketing by providing a mechanism for translating research and development ideas into viable products.

> The venture team with its single mission, unstructured relationships, insulation from the daily routine, and entrepreneurial thrust is an organizational concept uniquely suited to the task of product innovation. For many companies whose future depends as much on the successful launching of new products as the successful marketing of existing ones, the venture team concept offers a promising mechanism for more innovative marketing and the growth which it makes possible.[20]

Stages in the New-Product Development Process

New-product development strategy should be built upon the existing business strategy of the company. Companies that have successfully launched new products are more likely to have had a formal new-product process in place for some time. They are also more likely to have a strategic plan, and be committed to growth through internally developed new products.[21]

Once the firm is organized for new-product development, it can establish procedures for evaluating new-product ideas. The product development process may be thought of as involving seven stages: 1) development of overall new-product strategy, 2) new-product idea generation, 3) screening, 4) business analysis, 5) final product development, 6) test marketing, and 7) commercialization. At each stage, management faces the decision to abandon the project, continue to the next stage, or seek additional information before proceeding further. The process is illustrated in Figure 10-4.

New-Product Strategy   New-product strategy links corporate objectives to the new-product effort, provides direction for the new-product process, and identifies the strategic roles in the product line that the new products should play. It also helps set the formal financial criteria to be used in measuring new-product performance and in screening and evaluating new-product ideas.[22]

Figure 10-4   Seven Stages of the New-Product Process

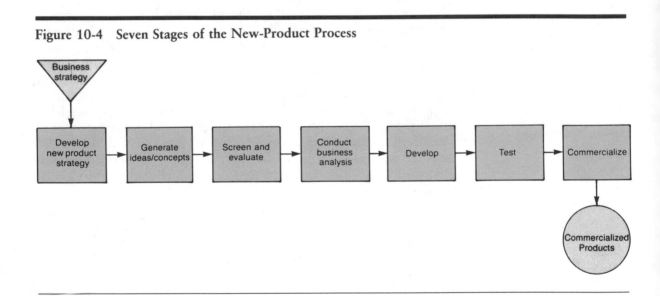

Idea Generation   New-product development begins with an idea. Ideas emanate from many sources: the sales force, marketing employees, research and development (R & D) specialists, competitive products, retailers, inventors outside the company, and customers who write letters asking "Why don't you . . . ?" It is extremely important for the firm to develop a system of stimulating new ideas and for rewarding persons who develop them.

Screening   This crucial stage involves separating ideas with potential from those incapable of meeting company objectives. Some organizations use checklists to determine whether product ideas should be eliminated or subjected to further consideration. These checklists typically include such factors as product uniqueness; availability of raw materials; and compatibility of the proposed product with current product offerings, existing facilities, and capabilities. In other instances, the screening stage consists of open discussions of new-product ideas among representatives of different functional areas in the organization. This is an important point in the product development process since any product ideas that go beyond this point will cost the firm valuable time and money. Figure 10-5 presents some basic criteria used in the screening process.

Business Analysis   Product ideas surviving the initial screening are then subjected to a thorough business analysis. This involves an assessment of the potential market, its growth rate, and the likely competitive strength of the new product. Decisions must be made in determining the compatibility of the proposed product with such company resources as financial support for necessary promotion, production capabilities and distribution facilities.

Concept testing, or the consideration of the product idea prior to its actual development, is an important aspect of the business analysis stage. **Concept testing** is *a marketing research project that attempts to measure consumer attitudes and perceptions relevant to the new product idea*. Focus groups (see Chapter 6) and in-store polling can be effective methods for assessing a new-product concept.

Figure 10-5   Basic Criteria for Preliminary Screening

1. The item should be in a field of activity in which the corporation is engaged.
2. If the idea involves a companion product to others already being manufactured, it should be made from materials to which the corporation is accustomed.
3. The item should be capable of being produced on the type and kind of equipment that the corporation normally operates.
4. The item should be easily handled by the corporation's existing sales force through the established distribution pattern.
5. The potential market for the product should be at least $_____.
6. The market over the next five years should be expected to grow at a faster rate than the GNP.
7. Return on investment, after taxes, must reach a minimum level of _____ percent.

Source: Reprinted from Willam S. Sachs and George Benson, *Product Planning and Management* (Tulsa, Okla.: PennWell Books, 1981), p. 231.

Product Development   Those product ideas with profit potential are then converted into
a physical product. The conversion process becomes the joint responsibility of development engineering, which is responsible for
developing the original concept into a product, and the marketing
department, which provides feedback on consumer reactions to alternative product designs, packages, features, colours, and other
physical appeals. Numerous changes may be necessary before the
original mock-up is converted into the final product.

The series of revisions, tests, and refinements should result in
the ultimate introduction of a product with a greater likelihood of
success. Some firms use their own employees as a sounding board
and obtain their reactions to proposed new-product offerings.
Employees at Levi Strauss & Company test new styles by wearing
them and providing feedback. A shoe manufacturer asks its workers
to report regularly over an eight-week testing period on shoe wear
and fit.[23]

But occasionally attempts to be first with a new product result
in the premature introduction of new products. Kellogg and several
other cereal-makers experienced this several years ago when they
all failed in attempts to introduce freeze-dried fruit cereal. In their
rush to be first on the market with the new offering, they failed to
perfect the product. The small, hard pellets of real fruit took too
long to reconstitute in the bowl. Millions of bowls of cereal went
into garbage cans.[24]

Test Marketing   To determine consumer reactions to their products under normal
shopping conditions, a number of firms test-market their new
offerings. Up to this point, consumer information has been obtained
by submitting free products to consumers who then gave their
reactions. Other information may have been gathered by asking shoppers to evaluate competitive products, but test marketing is the first
point where the product must perform in a "real life" environment.

Test marketing involves selecting usually one to three cities or
television-coverage areas considered reasonably typical of the total
market, and introducing the product in this area with a total marketing campaign. A carefully designed and controlled test allows
management to develop estimates of the effectiveness of marketing-
mix decisions and of sales on full scale introduction.

Some firms omit the test-marketing stage and move directly from
product development to full-scale production. They cite four problems with test marketing:

1. Test marketing is expensive. As one marketing executive pointed
out:

> It's very difficult to run a little [test market] for six months or a year
> in three or four markets across the [country] and then project what

your sales volume is going to be two or three years in the future, mainly because you're testing in such small localities, generally to keep your costs down.

You simply can't afford to test your product in markets like [Toronto or Montreal]. So you run your test in [smaller cities]. And your test costs are over $1 million even in places like that.[25]

2. Competitors who learn about the test market may disrupt the findings by reducing the price of their products in the test area, distributing cents-off coupons, installing attractive in-store displays, or giving additional discounts to retailers to induce them to display more of their products.

Test marketing a new product also communicates company plans to competitors prior to the product's introduction. The Kellogg Company discovered a new product with suspected sales potential by learning of a test marketing of a new fruit-filled tart designed to be heated in the toaster and served hot for breakfast. Kellogg rushed a similar product into full-scale production and became the first national marketer of the product they named Pop Tarts.

3. Long-lived durable goods, such as dishwashers, hair dryers, and VCRs, are seldom test marketed due to the major financial investment required for the development, the need to develop a network of dealers to distribute the products, and the parts and servicing required. A company such as Whirlpool invests from $1 million to $33 million in the development of a new refrigerator. To develop each silicon chip in an Apple microcomputer costs approximately $1 million and takes from one to 15 months. Producing a prototype for a test market is simply too expensive, so the "go/no go" decision for the new durable product is typically made without the benefit of test-market results.[26]

A decision to skip the test-marketing stage should be based on a very high likelihood of the product's success. The costs of developing a new detergent from idea generation to national marketing have been estimated at *$10 million*. Even though a firm will experience losses on any product that passes the initial screening process but is not introduced, it will still be much better off by stopping as soon as it discovers that the product cannot succeed, rather than being faced with a failure such as Corfam, an artificial leather that DuPont introduced and suffered losses of more than *$100 million* over the lengthy period they tried to make it a success.

Commercialization   The few product ideas that will survive all of the steps in the development process are now ready for full-scale marketing. Marketing programs must be established, outlays for necessary production facilities may be necessary, and the sales force, middlemen, and potential customers must become acquainted with the new product.

New product development should follow the step-by-step approach previously outlined in Figure 10-4. Systematic planning and control of all phases of development and introduction can be accomplished through the use of such scheduling methods as the Program Evaluation and Review Technique (PERT) and the Critical Path Method (CPM). These techniques map out the sequence in which each step must be taken and show the time allotments for each activity. Detailed PERT and CP flow charts will not only assist in coordinating all activities in the development and introduction of new products, but they can also highlight the sequence of events which will be the most critical in scheduling.

As Figure 10-6 indicates, new-product development and introduction can take many years. A study of the elapsed time between initial development and full-scale introduction of 42 products revealed a time lag ranging from six months for a new heavy-duty oil to 55 years for television. Since the time needed for orderly development of new products is longer than might be expected, the planning horizon for new-product ideas may have to be extended five to ten years into the future.[27]

Product Deletion Decisions

While many firms devote a great deal of time and resources to the development of new products, the thought of eliminating old products from the firm's line is painful for many executives. Often sentimental attachments to marginal products prevent objective decisions to drop products with declining sales. Management finds it difficult to bury an old friend.

If waste is to be avoided, product lines must be pruned, and old products must eventually be eliminated from the firm's line. This decision is typically faced in the late maturity and early decline stages of the product life cycle. Periodic reviews of weak products should be conducted in order to prune weak products or to justify their retention.

In some instances a firm will continue to carry an unprofitable product so as to provide a complete line of goods for its customers. Even though most supermarkets lose money on such bulky, low-unit-value items as salt, they continue to carry it to meet shopper demands.

Shortages of raw materials have prompted some companies to discontinue the production and marketing of previously profitable items. Du Pont dropped an antifreeze from its product line due to raw material shortages.

Other cases arise where profitable products are dropped because of failure to fit into the firm's existing product line. The development

Figure 10-6   Elapsed Time Between Initial Development and Full-Scale Introduction

Product	Years
Strained baby foods	1
Frozen orange juice	2
Filter cigarettes	2
Polaroid Land Camera	2
Dry dog food	4
Electric toothbrush	4
Stripe toothpaste	6
Roll-on deodorant	6
Plastic tile	6
Liquid shampoo	8
Freeze-dried instant coffee	10
Fluoride toothpaste	10
Penicillin	15
Xerox electrostatic copier	15
Polaroid Color-pack Camera	15
Transistors	16
Minute rice	18
Instant coffee	22
Zippers	30
Television	55

Source: Lee Adler, "Time Lag in New Product Development," *Journal of Marketing* (January 1966), pp. 17–21. Reprinted from *Journal of Marketing*, published by the American Marketing Association.

of automatic washing machines necessitated the developing of a low-sudsing detergent. The Monsanto Company produced the world's first low-sudsing detergent in the 1950s and named it All. All was an instant success, and Monsanto was swamped with orders from supermarkets throughout the nation. But the Monsanto sales force was primarily involved with the marketing of industrial chemicals to large-scale buyers. A completely new sales force was required to handle a single product. Nine months after the introduction of All, Procter & Gamble introduced the world's second low-sudsing detergent and named it Dash. The Procter & Gamble sales force handled hundreds of products and could spread the cost of contacting dealers over all of these products. Monsanto had only All. Rather than attempting to compete, Monsanto sold All in 1958 to Lever Brothers, a Procter & Gamble competitor with a marketing organization capable of handling it.[28]

Product Identification

Manufacturers identify their products through the use of brand names, symbols, and distinctive packaging. So also do large retailers such as Canadian Tire, with its line of Mastercraft products, and Simpsons and The Bay with their Beaumark Brand. Almost every product distinguishable from another contains a means of identification for the buyer. Even a 5-year-old can distinguish a Chiquita banana from other ones. And the California Fruit Growers Exchange literally brands its oranges with the name Sunkist. The purchasing agent for a construction firm can turn over an ordinary sheet of roofing and find the name and symbol for Domtar. The choice of means of identification for the firm's output is often a major decision area for the marketing manager.

Brands, Brand Names, and Trademarks

A **brand** is *a name, term, sign, symbol, design, or some combination used to identify the products of one firm and to differentiate them from competitive offerings*. A **brand name** is that part of the brand consisting of *words, letters or symbols making up a name used to identify and distinguish the firm's offerings from those of competitors*.[29] The brand name is, therefore, that part of the brand that may be vocalized. A **trademark** is *a brand that has been given legal protection and has been granted solely to its owner*. Thus, the term trademark includes not only pictorial design but also the brand name. Many thousands of trademarks are currently registered in Canada.

For the consumer, brands allow repeat purchases of satisfactory products. The brand assures a uniform quality and identifies the firm producing the product. The purchaser associates the satisfaction derived from a carbonated soft drink with the brand name Pepsi-Cola.

For the marketing manager, the brand serves as the cornerstone around which the product's image is developed. Once consumers have been made aware of a particular brand, its appearance becomes further advertising for the firm. The Shell Oil Company symbol is instant advertising to motorists who view it while driving. Well-known brands also allow the firm to escape some of the rigours of price competition. Although any chemist will confirm that all ASA tablets contain the same amount of the chemical acetylsalicylic acid, Bayer has developed so strong a reputation that it can successfully market its Aspirin at a higher price than competitive products. Similarly, McDonald's "golden arches" attract customers to their outlets.

What Constitutes a Good Brand Name?

Good brand names are easy to pronounce, recognize and remember. Short names like Coke, Gleem, Dash, and Kodak meet these requirements. Multinational marketing firms face a particularly acute problem in selecting brand names in that an excellent brand name in one country may prove disastrous in another.

For 21 years, Nissan Motor Corporation marketers struggled with an easily mispronounced brand name for Datsun cars and trucks. Nissan found that in English-speaking nations some people pronounced the *a* like the *a* in *hat*, while others pronounced it like the *o* in *got*, and the difference hindered brand recognition. Finally, Nissan marketers decided to change the name of all of its automobile products to Nissan beginning with its Stanza model in 1982. Total costs of the change — to be effected in more than 135 countries — are estimated as high as $150 million.[30]

Every language has "O" and "K" sounds, and "okay" has become an international word. Every language also has a short "a," so that Coca-Cola and Texaco are good in any tongue. An American advertising campaign for E-Z washing machines failed in the United Kingdom because the British pronounce "Z" as "zed," as we do in Canada.

The brand name should give the buyer the right connotation. Mercury Marine presents favourable images of boating pleasures. The Craftsman name used on the Sears line of quality tools also produces the correct image. Accutron suggests the quality of the high-priced and accurate timepiece by the Bulova Watch Company. But what can the marketing manager do if the brand name is based on a strange-sounding company name? Sometimes the decision may be to poke fun at this improbable name in a promotional campaign built around the theme "With a name like Koogle, it has to be good!"

The Brand Name Should Be Legally Protectable

S. C. Johnson and Son, makers of OFF, lost a court case against Bug Off since it was held that OFF was an improper trademark, because it was not unusual enough to distinguish it from other similar products.

When all offerings in a class of products become generally known by the brand name of the first or leading brand in that product class, the brand name may be ruled a descriptive **generic name**, and the original owner loses exclusive claim to it. Generic names like cola, nylon, zipper, kerosene, linoleum, escalator, and shredded wheat were once brand names.

Bayer's Aspirin is the only ASA tablet permitted to carry that protected trademark in Canada. All other acetylsalicylic acid tablets are called ASA. In the United States, because Bayer did not protect its trade name, the generic name "aspirin" is given to all acetylsalicylic acid tablets. Most drug purchasers there would not know what an ASA tablet is.

There is a difference between brand names that are legally generic and those that are generic in the eyes of many consumers. Jell-O is a brand name owned exclusively by General Foods. But to most grocery purchasers the name Jell-O is the descriptive generic name for gelatin dessert. Legal brand names, such as Formica, Xerox, Frigidaire, Kodak, Frisbee, Styrofoam, Coke, Kleenex, Scotch Tape, Fiberglas, Band-Aid, and Jeep, are often used by consumers as descriptive names. Xerox is such a well-known brand name that it is frequently used as a verb. British and Australian consumers often use the brand name Hoover as a verb for vacuuming.

To prevent their brand names from being ruled descriptive and available for general use, companies must take deliberate steps to inform the public of their exclusive ownership of brand names. They may resort to legal action in cases of infringement. The Eastman Kodak Company developed a series of advertisements around the theme "If it isn't an Eastman, it isn't a Kodak." The Coca-Cola Company uses the ® symbol for registration immediately after the names Coca-Cola and Coke and sends letters to newspapers, novelists, and other writers who use the name Coke with a lower-case first letter, informing them that the name is owned by Coca-Cola.[31] These companies face the pleasant dilemma of attempting to retain the exclusive rights to a brand name that is generic to a large part of the market.

Since any dictionary word may eventually be ruled to be a generic name, some companies create new words to use for brand names. Brand names such as Keds, Rinso, and Kodak have obviously been created by their owners.

Measuring Brand Loyalty

Brands vary widely in consumer familiarity and acceptance. While a boating enthusiast may insist on a Mercury outboard motor, one study revealed that 40 percent of homemakers could not identify the brands of furniture in their own homes.[32]

Brand loyalty may be measured in three stages: brand recognition, brand preference, and brand insistence.

Brand recognition is a company's first objective for newly introduced products — *to make them familiar to the consuming public*. Often the company achieves this through advertising. Sometimes it uses free samples or coupons offering discounts for purchases. Several new brands of toothpaste have been introduced on college campuses through free samples contained in Campus Pacs. Once the consumer has used the product, it moves from the "unknown" to the "known" category, and provided the consumer was satisfied with the trial sample, he or she is more likely to repurchase it.

Brand preference is the second stage of brand loyalty. Because of previous experience with the product, *consumers will choose it rather than competitors — if it is available*. Even if students in a classroom prefer Coca-Cola as a means of quenching their thirst, almost all of them will quickly switch to Pepsi-Cola or 7-Up when they discover the vending machine has no Coke and the nearest sup-

From Brand Name to Generic Name

Nylon
Aspirin
Escalator
Kerosene
Zipper
Addressograph

**Sometimes a company's product becomes
so well known that its name becomes generic.**

It's not going to happen to Addressograph, no sir. Even though some of our competitors have lately fallen into the unfortunate habit of using variations of our trademark to describe their equipment.

For 82 years, no one's beat us in offering you the broadest best line of addressing equipment. We make the addresser you need. We always will. And now we've added folders and inserters, too.

So the next time their salesman tells you he's got something that's "just like Addressograph", please help us protect our good name. Tell him that as far as you're concerned "there's nothing like Addressograph."

Then call your nearby AM Representative. He'll show you why you're right. Or write: Dept. M., 1800 W. Central Rd., Mt. Prospect, Ill. 60056.

We make you look better on paper.

ADDRESSOGRAPH MULTIGRAPH
MULTIGRAPHICS DIVISION

NOTE: Nylon, Aspirin, Escalator, Kerosene, and Zipper — all once registered trademarks — are now generic dictionary words. "Addressograph" remains a registered and protected trademark of Addressograph Multigraph Corp., as it has been since 1906.

Source: Courtesy of Addressograph Farrington Inc.

ply is two buildings away. Companies with products at the brand-preference stage are in a favourable position in competing in their industries.

The ultimate stage in brand loyalty is **brand insistence** when *consumers will accept no alternatives and will search extensively for the product.* Such a product has achieved a monopoly position with this group of consumers. Even though brand insistence may be the goal of many firms, it is seldom achieved. Only the most exclusive specialty goods attain this position with a large segment of the total market.

The Importance of Brand Loyalty   A study of 12 patented drugs including well-known drugs like Librium and Darvon illustrates the importance of brand loyalty. The research indicated that patent expiration had minimal effect on the drugs' market shares or price levels, a resiliency credited to the brand loyalty for the pioneer product in the field.[33] Another measure of the importance of brand loyalty is found in the Brand Utility Yardstick used by the J. Walter Thompson advertising agency. These ratings measure the percentage of buyers who remain brand loyal even if a 50-percent cost savings was available from generic products. Beer consumers were very loyal with 48 percent refusing to switch. Sinus-remedy buyers were also brand loyal with a 44 percent rating. By contrast, only 13 percent of the aluminum-foil buyers would not switch to the generic product.[34]

Some brands are so popular that they are carried over to unrelated products because of their marketing advantages. *The decision to use a popular brand name for a new product entry in an unrelated product category* is known as **brand extension**. This should not be confused with line extension, which refers to new sizes, styles, or related products. Brand extension, by contrast, refers only to carrying over the brand name.

Examples of brand extension are abundant in contemporary marketing. Deere & Co.'s insurance line prominently features the John Deere brand made famous in the farm machinery business. In fact, John Deere Insurance proudly notes: "Our name is the best insurance you can buy." Similarly, General Foods is extending its Jell-O brand. In some markets the company now has Jell-O Pudding Pops, Jell-O Slice Creme, and Jell-O Gelatin Pops.[35]

Choosing a Brand Strategy

Brands may be classified as family brands or individual brands. A **family brand** is *one brand name used for several related products.* E. D. Smith markets dozens of food products under the E. D. Smith brand. Canadian General Electric has a complete line of kitchen appliances under the CGE name. Johnson & Johnson offers parents a line of baby powder, lotions, plastic pants, and baby shampoo under one name.

On the other hand, manufacturers such as Procter & Gamble market hundreds of products with **individual brands,** such as Tide, Cheer, Crest, Gleem, Oxydol, and Dash. The item is *known by its own brand name rather than by the name of the company producing it or an umbrella name covering similar items.* Individual brands are more expensive to market since a new promotional program must be developed to introduce each new product to its market target.

The use of family brands allows promotional outlays to benefit all products in the line. The effect of the promotion is spread over each of the products. A new addition to the H. J. Heinz Company gains immediate recognition due to the well-known family brand. Use of family brands also facilitates the task of introducing the product—for both the customer and the retailer. Since supermarkets carry an average of nearly 10 000 items in stock, they are reluctant to add new products unless they are convinced of potential demand. A marketer of a new brand of turtle soup would have to promise the supermarket chain buyer huge advertising outlays for promotion and evidence of consumer buying intent before getting the product into the stores. The Campbell Soup Company, with approximately 85 percent of the market, would merely add the new flavour to its existing line and could secure store placements much more easily than could a company using individual brand names.

Family brands should be used only when the products are of similar quality—or the firm risks the danger of harming its product image. Use of the Mercedes brand name on a new, less expensive auto model might severely tarnish the image of the other models in the Mercedes product line.

Individual brand names should be used for dissimilar products. Campbell Soup once marketed a line of dry soups under the brand name Red Kettle. Large marketers of grocery products, such as Procter & Gamble, General Foods, and Lever Brothers, employ individual brands to appeal to unique market segments. Unique brands also allow the firm to stimulate competition within the organization and to increase total company sales. Product managers are also freer to try different merchandising techniques with individual brands. Homemakers who do not prefer Tide may choose Dash or Oxydol rather than purchase a competitor's brand.

National Brands or Private Brands?

Most of the brands mentioned in this chapter have been *manufacturers' brands*, commonly termed **national brands**. But, to an increasing extent, *large wholesalers and retailers operating over a regional or national market are placing their own brands on the products that they market*. These brands offered by wholesalers and retailers are usually called **private brands**. Eaton's carries its own brands such as Viking, Birkdale, Haddon Hall, Eatonia, and Teco. Safeway store shelves are filled with such company brands as Edwards, Town House, Empress, and Taste Tells. Safeway brands represent a large percentage of all products in an average Safeway supermarket.

For a large retailer such as Eaton's, The Bay, or Dominion, private brands allow the firm to establish an image and to attain greater control over the products that it handles. Quality levels, prices, and availability of the products become the responsibility of the retailer or wholesaler who develops a line of private brands.

Even though the manufacturers' brands are largely presold through national promotional efforts, the wholesaler and retailer may easily lose customers since the same products may be available in competing stores. But only Eaton's handles the Viking line of appliances. By eliminating the promotional costs of the manufacturers' brands, the dealer can often offer a private brand at a lower price than the competing national brands or make higher margins. Both consumers and the company benefit. As private brands achieve increasing brand loyalty they may even enable a retailer to avoid some price competition since the brand can only be sold by the brand owner.

Battle of the Brands   Competition between manufacturers' brands and the private brands offered by wholesalers and large retailers has been called the "battle of the brands." Although the battle appears to be intensifying, the marketing impact varies widely among industries. One survey showed that private brands represented 36 percent of the market in replacement tires but only 7 percent in portable appliances. Fifty-two percent of shoe sales are by private brands. For example, Agnew Surpass and Bata stores distribute their own private brands. Department stores capture about 53 percent of heavy appliance sales, most of which are private brands.[36]

The growh of private brands has paralleled the growth of chain stores in Canada. Most of the growth for both has occurred since the 1930s. The chains with their own brands become customers of the manufacturer, who will place the chains' private brands on the products that the firm produces. Such leading corporations as Westinghouse, Armstrong Rubber, and Heinz obtain an increasingly larger percentage of total sales through private labels.

Even though the battle of the brands is far from over, it is clear that great inroads have been made on the dominance of the manufacturers' national brands. Private brands have proven that they can compete with the national brands and have often succeeded in causing price reductions on the national brands to make them more competitive.

Generic Products   *Food and household staples characterized by plain labels, little or no advertising, and no brand names* are called **generic products**. Generic products were first sold in Europe, where their prices were as much as 30 percent below brand namc products. By 1979, they had captured 40 percent of total volume in European supermarkets.

This new version of private brands has received significant acceptance in Canada. Surveys indicate that both professional, college-educated consumers and lower-income, blue-collar consumers are heavy purchasers of generics. Canned vegetables are the most commonly purchased generic product, followed by fruits and paper goods. Shoppers are indicating some willingness to forgo the known quality levels of regular brands in exchange for the lower prices of the generics.

For all food categories in Ontario food chain stores generics represented 10.4 percent, private brands 10.8 percent, and national brands 78.8 percent of the volume. The proportion held by generics remained about constant over three years, but private labels lost about three points to national brands.[37] Thus in the retail food industry, private brands seem to be caught between the success of generic products and the continuing influence of national brands. According to Dominion Stores' director of advertising, Craig Hemming, private brands seem to have slipped from the minds of consumers. Since they are unique to each retail chain, firms like Dominion are beginning to develop special advertising campaigns to re-emphasize them.[38]

Packaging

In a very real sense the package is a vital part of the total product. Indeed, in an overcrowded supermarket, packaging very often *is* the significant difference between one product and another. Take Nabob, for example. Nabob coffee was packaged in a new type of tough, vacuum-seal package which gave the coffee greater freshness. "Five years ago our market share [of the ground coffee market] was 5%," says John Bell, vice-president of marketing. "Today we have 26%."[39]

Packaging represents a vital component of the total product concept. Its importance can be inferred from the size of the packaging industry. Approximately $50 billion is spent annually on packaging in Canada. A study of packaging costs in the food industry found that total packaging costs as a percentage of net processed food sales range from 4 to 59 percent, averaging about 22 percent. In the cases where packaging costs appear disproportionately high, ingredient costs were found to be very low (e.g. salt).

The package has several objectives that can be grouped into three general categories: 1) protection against damage, spoilage, and pilferage; 2) assisting to market the product; and 3) cost effectiveness.

Protection Against Damage, Spoilage, and Pilferage

The original purpose of packaging was to offer physical protection. The typical product is handled several times between manufacture and consumer purchase, and its package must protect the contents against damage. Perishable products must also be protected against spoilage in transit, in storage, or while awaiting selection by the consumer.

Another important role provided by many packages for the retailer is in preventing pilferage, which at the retail level, is very costly. Many products are packaged with oversized cardboard backings too large to fit into a shoplifter's pocket or purse. Large plastic packages are used in a similar manner on such products as eight-track and cassette tapes.

Assisting to Market the Product

Package designers frequently use marketing research in testing alternative designs. Increasingly scientific approaches are utilized in designing a package that is attractive, safe, and esthetically appealing. Kellogg's, for instance, tested the package for a new product as well as the product itself.[40]

In a grocery store containing as many as 15 000 different items, a product must capture the shopper's attention. Walter Margulies, chairman of Lippincott & Margulies advertising, summarizes the importance of first impressions in the retail store: "Consumers are more intelligent, but they don't read as much. They relate to pictures." Margulies also cites another factor: one of every six shoppers who needs eyeglasses does not wear them while shopping. Consequently, many marketers offering product lines are adopting similar package designs throughout the line in order to create more visual impact in the store. The adoption of common package designs by such product lines as Weight Watchers foods and Planter's nuts represent attempts to dominate larger sections of retail stores as Campbell's does.[41]

Packages can also offer the consumer convenience. Pump dispenser cans facilitate the use of products ranging from mustard to insect repellent. Pop-top cans provide added convenience for soft drinks, and other food products. The six-pack carton, first introduced by Coca-Cola in the 1930s, can be carried with minimal effort by the food shopper.

A growing number of firms provide increased consumer utility with packages designed for reuse. Peanut butter jars and jelly jars have long been used as drinking glasses. Bubble bath can be purchased in plastic bottles shaped like animals and suitable for bathtub play. Packaging is a major component in Avon's overall marketing strategy. The firm's decorative reusable bottles have even become collectibles.

Cost Effective Packaging

Although packaging must perform a number of functions for the producer, marketer, and consumer, it must accomplish them at a reasonable cost. Packaging currently represents the single largest item in the cost of producing numerous products. For example, it accounts for 70 percent of the total cost of the single-serving packets of sugar found in restaurants. However, restaurants continue to use the packs because of the saving in wastage and washing and refilling sugar containers.

An excellent illustration of how packaging can be cost effective is provided by the large Swedish firm, Tetra-Pak. They pioneered aseptic packaging for products like milk and juice. Aseptic packaging wraps a laminated paper around a sterilized product and seals it off. The big advantage of the packaging technology is that products can be kept unrefrigerated for months. Aseptically packed sterilized milk, for instance, will keep its nutritional qualities and flavour for six months. With 60 percent of a supermarket's energy bill going for refrigeration, aseptic packaging is certainly cost effective. The paper packaging is also cheaper and lighter than the cans and bottles used for unrefrigerated fruit juices. Handling cost can also be reduced in many cases.[42]

Labelling   Although in the past the label was often a separate item applied to the package, most of today's plastic packages contain the label as an integral part of the package. Labels perform both a promotional and an informational function. A **label** in most instances *contains 1) brand name or symbol, 2) name and address of the manufacturer or distributor, 3) product composition and size, and 4) recommended uses of the product.*

Government-set and voluntary packaging and label standards have been developed in most industries. The law requires a listing of food ingredients, in descending order of the amounts used, and labels of such companies as Del Monte Corporation now show specific food values and include a calorie count and a list of vitamins and minerals. In other industries, such as drugs, fur, and clothing, federal legislation requires the provision of various information and prevents false branding. The marketing manager in such industries must be fully acquainted with these laws and must design the package and label in compliance with these requirements.

The informational aspect of a label is particularly noteworthy. Figure 10-7 depicts the results of a study of consumer expectations for drug labels. People who condemn all types of elaborate or fancy packaging fail to realize that the information on the label and the nature of the container enhance the product itself. In some cases, the dispenser is almost as important as the contents and is really an integral part of the total "product." Furthermore, with the advent of self-service nearly everywhere, the information on the label takes the place of a salesperson. Self-service improves marketing efficiency and lowers costs.

Universal Product Code (UPC)   The Universal Product Code (UPC) designation is another very important point of a label or package. A great number of packages now display the zebra-stripe UPC on the label. In other cases, the code lines are printed right into the package, such as on a can of Tab.

The **Universal Product Code**, introduced as an attempt to cut expenses in the supermarket industry, is *a code read by optical scanners that can print the name of the item and the price on the cash*

Figure 10-7   What Consumers Want on Drug Labels

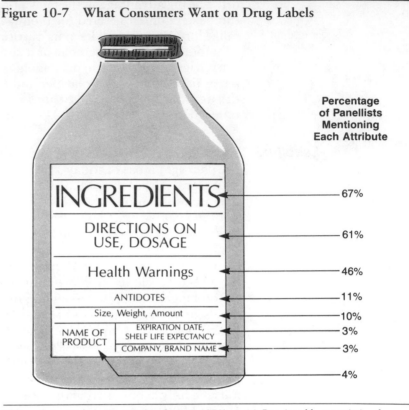

Percentage
of Panellists
Mentioning
Each Attribute

INGREDIENTS — 67%

DIRECTIONS ON
USE, DOSAGE — 61%

Health Warnings — 46%

ANTIDOTES — 11%

Size, Weight, Amount — 10%

NAME OF PRODUCT | EXPIRATION DATE, SHELF LIFE EXPECTANCY — 3%

COMPANY, BRAND NAME — 3%

— 4%

Source: *Sales Management* (September 15, 1970), p. 46. Reprinted by permission from *Sales Management, The Marketing Magazine*, copyright 1970.

register receipt. Some 95 percent of all packaged grocery items contain the UPC lines.

While the initial cost of UPC scanners is high — about $125 000 for a four-lane supermarket — they do permit considerable cost savings. The advantages include:

1. Labour saving because products are no longer individually priced.
2. Faster customer check-out.
3. Better inventory control since the scanners can be tied to inventory records.
4. Easier marketing research for the industries involved with it.
5. Fewer errors in entering purchases at the check-out counter.

Despite these and other advantages, UPC still faces several obstacles. Many consumers still do not understand the purpose and advantages of the UPC scanners. In some localities, regulations specifically require items to be individually priced, thus negating much of the labour savings advantage of UPC scanners. It is obvious, however, that the Universal Product Code is going to play an even greater role in product management over the next few years.

Product Safety

If the product is to fulfil its mission of satisfying consumer needs, it must above all be safe. Manufacturers must design their products in such a way as to protect not only children but all consumers who use them. Packaging can play an important role in product safety. The law requires that bottle tops of dangerous products such as pharmaceuticals be child-proof (some are virtually parent-proof). This safety feature has reduced by two-thirds the number of children under five years of age who swallow dangerous doses of ASA. Prominent safety warnings on the labels of such potentially hazardous products as cleaning fluids and drain cleaners inform users of the dangers of these products and urge purchasers to store them out of the reach of children. Changes in product design have reduced the dangers involved in the use of such products as lawn mowers, hedge trimmers, and toys.

The need for fire-retardant fabrics for children's sleepwear was recognized long before federal regulations were established. While fire-retardant fabrics were available, the problems lay in how to produce them to meet consumer requirements in the areas of softness, colour, texture, durability, and reasonable cost. Monsanto spent seven years and millions of dollars in research before introducing a satisfactory fabric in 1972. Today government flame-retardancy standards are strictly enforced.

Federal and provincial legislation has long played a major role in promoting product safety. The Hazardous Products Act, passed in 1969, was a major piece of legislation, consolidating previous legislation and setting significant new standards for product safety. The Act defines a hazardous product as any product that is included in a list called a schedule compiled by Consumer and Corporate Affairs Canada or Health and Welfare Canada. Any consumer product considered to be a hazard to public health or safety may be listed in the schedule. Figure 10-8 lists some of the main items and outlines the regulations that affect them.

The Act itself consists of just 15 clauses. Those relating to criminal penalties and seizure put sharp teeth in the law. Inspectors designated under the Act have powers of search and seizure. Hazardous products inspectors may enter, at any reasonable time, any place where they reasonably believe a hazardous product is manufactured, prepared, packaged, sold, or stored for sale. They may examine the product, take samples, and examine any records believed to contain

Figure 10-8   Some Hazardous Products Act Regulations

Bedding may not be highly flammable.

Children's sleepwear, dressing gowns, and robes must meet flammability standards.

Children's toys or equipment may not contain toxic substances, such as lead pigments beyond a prescribed limit.

Two plastic balloon-blowing kits containing organic solvents are banned.

Certain household chemical products must be labelled with appropriate symbols to alert consumers to their hazards.

Hockey helmets must meet safety standards to protect young hockey players.

Pencils and artists' brushes are regulated to limit lead in their decorative coating.

Matches must meet safety standards for strength and packaging.

Safety glass is mandatory in domestic doors and shower enclosures.

Liquid drain cleaners and furniture polishes containing petroleum solvents must be sold in child-proof packaging.

Toys and children's playthings must comply with safety standards.

Crib regulations provide for increased child safety.

information relevant to enforcement of the Act. Products that an inspector has reasonable grounds to believe are in contravention of the Act may be seized.

These regulatory activities have prompted companies voluntarily to improve safety standards for their products. For many companies, safety has become a very important ingredient in the broader definition of product.

Summary

A product mix is the assortment of product lines and individual offerings available from a marketer. A product line is a series of related products, and an individual offering is a single product offered within that line. Product mixes are assessed in terms of width and depth of assortment. Width of assortment refers to the variety of product lines offered, while depth refers to the extent of the line. Firms usually produce several related products rather than a single product in order to achieve the objectives of growth, optimal use of company resources, and increased company importance in the market.

New products experience a decay curve from idea generation to commercialization. Only one of 58 new product ideas typically makes it all the way to commercialization. The success of a new product depends on a host of factors and can be the result of four alternative product development strategies: product improvement, market development, product development, and product diversification.

The organizational responsibility for new products in most large firms is assigned to new-product committees, new-product departments, product managers, or venture teams. New product ideas evolve through seven stages before their market introduction: 1) development of new product strategy, 2) idea generation, 3) screening, 4) business analysis, 5) product development, 6) test marketing, and 7) commercialization.

While new products are added to the line, old ones may face deletion from it. The typical causes for product eliminations are unprofitable sales and failure to fit into the existing product line.

Product identification may take the form of brand names, symbols, distinctive packaging, and labelling. Effective brand names should be easy to pronounce, recognize, and remember; they should give the right connotation to the buyer; and they should be legally protectable. Brand loyalty can be measured in three stages: brand recognition, brand preference, and finally, brand insistence. Marketing managers must decide whether to use a single family brand for their product line or to use an individual brand for each product. Retailers have to decide the relative mix of national and private brands as well as generic products that they will carry.

Modern packaging is designed to: 1) protect against damage, spoilage, and pilferage; 2) assist in marketing the product; and 3) be cost effective. Labels identify the product, producer, content, size, and uses of a packaged product. Most products also contain a Universal Product Code designation so that optical check-out scanners can be used.

Product safety has become an increasingly important component of the total product concept. This change has occurred through voluntary attempts by product designers to reduce hazards and through strict requirements established by Consumer and Corporate Affairs Canada.

CHAPTER 11

Services

1. *To distinguish between products and services.*
2. *To relate services to other elements of the marketing mix.*
3. *To explain the nature and role of the service sector.*
4. *To identify the distinguishing features of services.*
5. *To discuss buyer behaviour as it relates to services.*
6. *To outline the similarities and differences in the environment for service firms.*
7. *To describe the marketing mix for service firms.*
8. *To suggest methods for increasing productivity for services.*

Suppose that you live in Victoria, and must have a meeting with several people in St. John's. A new service greatly expands your alternatives for holding that meeting. Traditionally, one would expect to take several days to fly to Newfoundland, hold the meeting and return. Conference 600 is a nation-wide, fully interactive, two-way videoconferencing service which can save direct costs of travel and hotels in addition to the time taken to travel.

Telecom Canada suggests that the benefits can be substantial. For example, for a meeting of six people in St. John's conferring with six others from Victoria, airfares and hotel bills alone would cost about $7600. A four-hour meeting on Conference 600 would come to about $4000.

The secret of Conference 600 is an advanced picture processor that converts the video signal to digital form and enables the signal to be compressed by as much as 60 times. The signal is transferred by Anik C, but the compression reduces demand on capacity of the satellite and thus on earthly costs.

The name of the company providing the service is also new. Telecom Canada used to be known as the TransCanada Telephone System. The advent of technology that goes beyond that of the telephone and the potential of a huge market has led to the change in name.[1]

A tremendous amount of economic activity is accounted for by service industries. These range from communications enterprises like Telecom Canada to life insurance, pizza restaurants, and cleaning services for office buildings. Marketing planning for services is similar to that for products, yet there are some important differences.

The Conceptual Framework

The first two chapters in this section on product/service strategy dealt with the basic concepts of this aspect of marketing. Product lines, product life cycles, branding, and classification systems are examples of some of these concepts.

Chapter 11 deals with services. In a fundamental sense, marketers approach the development of marketing programs for both products and services in the same manner. Such programs begin with an investigation, analysis, and selection of a particular market target and follow with the development of a marketing mix designed to satisfy the chosen target. Although tangible products and intangible services are similar in that both provide consumer benefits, there are significant differences in the marketing of the two. Both the similarities and differences are examined in this chapter. Services are treated in a special chapter because of two factors:

1) the immense size of the service industry market sector; and
2) the differences between marketing strategies for services and for tangible products.[2]

Services: A Definition

Services are troublesome to define. It is difficult to distinguish between certain kinds of goods and services. Personal services, such as hair styling and dry cleaning, are easily recognized as services, but these are only a small portion of the total service industry.

Some firms provide both goods and services. A protection specialist may market alarms and closed-circuit TVs (goods) as well as uniformed guards (a service). A dentist's business may also be divided into goods and service components. A bridge, crown, or filling is a good, while the dentist's professional skills are a service. Some services are an integral part of the marketing of physical goods. Thus, a computer sales representative may emphasize his or her firm's *service* capabilities to minimize machine down-time. These illustrations suggest that business needs some method to alleviate the problems of definition in the marketing of services.

One useful approach is a products spectrum, which shows most products to have both goods and services segments. Figure 11-1 presents a **goods-services continuum**, a method that is *useful in visualizing the differences and similarities among goods and services.* A tire is relatively a pure good, although services like balancing may be sold along with the product (or included in the total price). Hair styling, at the other end of the spectrum, is relatively a pure service. The middle of the continuum consists of products with both goods and services components. The satisfaction that comes from dining

Figure 11-1   Goods-Services Continuum

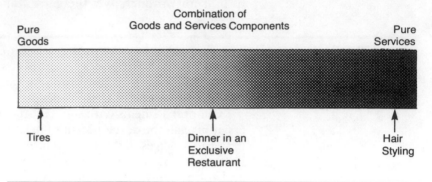

Source: After John M. Rathmell, "What Is Meant by Services?" in *Journal of Marketing* (October, 1966), published by the American Marketing Association.

in an exclusive restaurant is derived not only from the food and drink but also from the services rendered by the establishment's personnel.

While it is difficult, if not impossible, to describe in one definition all of the services that are available to consumers, a general definition can be developed. *A* **service** *is a product with no physical characteristics; it is a bundle of performance and symbolic attributes designed to produce consumer want satisfaction.*

The Nature of the Service Sector

There has been a considerable increase in expenditure for consumer services over the past decade. Services—ranging from such necessities as electric power and dry cleaning to such luxuries as foreign travel, backpacking guides, ski resorts, and hockey schools—now account for over 40 percent of the average consumer's total expenditures. Services also provide about two-thirds of all jobs. In fact, total employment in the Canadian economy more than doubled from 1950 to 1980 and nearly 90 percent of this increase took place in the service-producing sector. The distribution of personal consumption expenditures for goods and services is shown in Figure 11-2.

The increasing complexity of modern business has also provided substantial opportunities for business service firms such as Deloitte Haskins & Sells (public accountants), A. C. Nielsen (marketing research), and Brinks, Inc. (protection). For most consumer and business service firms, marketing is an emerging activity for two reasons: 1) the growth potential of the service market represents a vast marketing opportunity, and 2) increased competition is forcing traditional service industries to emphasize marketing in order to compete in the marketplace.

Figure 11-2   Personal Consumption Expenditures for Selected Years

			Actual			Forecast	
	1955	1960	1970	1981	1982	1985	1987
Durable Goods	14.1	11.6	13.2	13.8	12.3	15.0	15.2
Semidurable Goods	55.8	55.1	13.1	11.8	11.0	11.0	10.9
Nondurable Goods			31.8	31.1	32.0	31.8	32.0
Services	30.1	37.3	42.0	43.3	44.7	42.2	41.9

Source: Statistics Canada, *National Income and Expenditure Accounts*, Catalogue 13 001, 1983, pp. 42–43. Forecast adapted from *Market Research Handbook, 1983*, Catalogue 63-224, p. 344.

Features of Services   The preceding discussion suggests that services are varied and complex. Following are the four key features of services that have major marketing implications:
1. Services are intangible.
2. Services are perishable.
3. Services are often not standardized.
4. Buyers are often involved in the development and distribution of services.

Intangibility   Services do not have tangible features that appeal to consumers' senses of sight, hearing, smell, taste, and touch. They are therefore difficult to demonstrate at trade fairs, to display in retail stores, to illustrate in magazine advertisements, and to sample. Consequently, imaginative personal selling is usually an essential ingredient in the marketing of services.

Furthermore, buyers are often unable to judge the quality of a service before buying it. Because of this, the reputation of the service's vendor is often a key factor in the buying decision. Consumers are literally buying a promise, so it is important to "tangibilize" services. A good example is an architect's rendering of an office building that shows contented workers enjoying a casual lunch in a beautiful courtyard.[3]

Service marketers are sometimes perceived as more personal, friendlier, and more co-operative than goods marketers. These and other distinctive personal elements are a main component of interservice competition. Personal contact between salespeople and customers occurs in the marketing of goods as well as services; however, for service representatives it plays an even more important role. One writer described it in this way:

With service retailing there is a change in the sequence of events that occur — the sale must be made before production and consumption take place. Thus the truism that all customer contact employees are engaged in personal selling is much more real for the service firm than for the goods firm. With goods, the physical object can carry some of the selling burden. With services, contact personnel *are* the service. Customers, in effect, perceive them to be "the product." They become the physical representation of the offering. The service firm employees are both factory workers *and* salespersons because of the simultaneous production and consumption of most services.

Perishability   The utility of most services is short-lived; therefore, they cannot be produced ahead of time and stored for periods of peak demand. Vacant seats on an airplane, idle dance instructors, and unused electrical generating capacity represent economic losses that can never be recovered. Sometimes, however, idle facilities during slack periods must be tolerated so the firm will have sufficient capacity for peak periods. Electric and natural gas utilities, resort hotels, telephone companies, and airlines all face the problem of perishability.

Some service firms are able to overcome this problem with off-peak pricing. Resorts feature high and low season pricing schemes, the telephone company grants reduced rates on Sunday, and baseball teams offer low-priced general admission seats.

Difficulty of Standardization   Services are often dissimilar since it is frequently impossible to standardize offerings among sellers of the same service, or even to assure consistency in the services provided by one seller. For instance, no two hair styles from the same hairdresser are identical. Although the standardization of services is often desirable, it occurs only in the case of equipment-based firms, such as those offering automated banking services, car washes, and computer time-sharing. Creative marketing is needed to adapt satisfactorily a nonstandardized service to the needs of individual customers.

Involvement of Buyers   Buyers often play major roles in the marketing and production of services. The hair stylist's customer may describe the desired style and make suggestions at several stages during the styling process. Different firms often require unique blends of insurance coverage, and the final policy may be developed after several meetings between the purchaser and the insurance agent. Although purchaser specifications also play a role in the creation of major products such as installations, the interaction of buyer and seller at both the production and the distribution stages is a common feature of services.

Classifying Consumer and Industrial Services

Literally thousands of services are available to consumer and industrial users. In some instances, they are provided by specialized machinery with almost no personal assistance (such as an automated car wash). In other cases, the services are provided by skilled professionals with little reliance on specialized equipment (such as accountants and management consultants). Figure 11-3 provides a means of classifying services based on the following factors: the degree of reliance on equipment in providing the service, and the degree of skill possessed by the people who provide the service.

Buyer Behaviour

Important elements of buyer behaviour were discussed in Chapters 7 and 8. There are many similarities between buyer behaviour for goods and for services, yet some important differences exist. These differences may be grouped into three categories — 1) attitudes, 2) needs and motives, and 3) purchase behaviour. In most of these the personal element of the services is the key to the consumer's decision of which services to purchase.[4]

Attitudes

For almost any product or service a consumer's attitudes will directly influence his or her buying decision. Attitudes seem to be especially pertinent to the marketing of services since services are intangible. This probably causes buyers to emphasize their subjective impressions of a service and its seller when buying a service. This is less true in the purchase of tangible goods. Two attributes appear to represent important distinctions between goods and services: 1) services are perceived as being more personal than goods, and 2) consumers are sometimes less satisfied with purchases of services.

Dissatisfaction with the personal elements of a service, such as an unfriendly flight attendant or impolite bank teller, is likely to lead to an attitude of dissatisfaction with the entire service. For example, one woman reported that her Hawaii vacation was marred only by her annoyance with an airline's flight attendant. She expressed a preference for one airline over another because the latter's flight attendants "were not as competent." When pressed for a further explanation, it was learned that her annoyance resulted from one attendant's cold, distant attitude. This impression contrasted with the warm, friendly personalities of the personnel on another airline.

The comments of one young man sum up the outlook of many consumers. Although he is not satisfied with a local dry cleaner, this consumer has not bothered to consider others. Previous experience has convinced him that there are really no satisfactory dry cleaners, and that at least, "this is the best of the worst." He has

Figure 11-3   Types of Service Businesses

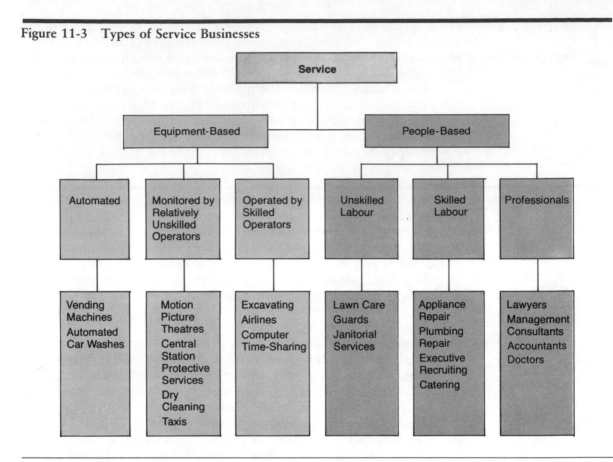

begun to purchase clothing that does not require dry cleaning. It is likely that consumers feel the same way about many other services and have taken steps to avoid the need for these services.

Needs and Motives   A comparison of needs and buying motives for goods and services suggests that there are more similarities than differences. Essentially the same types of needs are satisfied whether a person buys the materials for a home repair or hires a service organization to perform the task. Although service needs have increased in importance, these needs usually can be satisfied by new or modified goods as well as by services.

A need that often does stand out is the consumer's desire for personal attention. By appealing to this need, the hair stylist, the banker, or the insurance agent provides a form of satisfaction that the seller of a good cannot easily match. The desire for personal attention is often the dominant need satisfied by a service.

Purchase Behaviour

Research suggests that differences between goods and services are most noticeable in the case of purchase behaviour. Goods-selection decisions are normally concerned more with the question of whether to purchase, while service-selection decisions emphasize proper timing and selection of a source.[6] This situation suggests several distinctions between purchase behaviour for goods and for services. In particular, the degree of prepurchase planning may differ, influences on the buyer may differ, and the buyer may be more personally involved in a service purchase.

Consumers are influenced more by others — friends, neighbours, and salespeople — when buying services than when buying goods. Since services are intangible, it is difficult for the service buyer to judge quality and value. Buyers are usually unable to inspect or try out a service prior to purchase, so they may depend on the experiences and observations of others.

The dominant role of personal influence in the selection of services has two principal implications for services marketing: 1) added emphasis must be placed upon developing a professional relationship between service suppliers and their customers, and 2) promotional efforts must be aimed toward exploiting word-of-mouth promotion.

The service sector has traditionally been a cottage-type industry consisting of many small, independent firms. Some aspects still are, for example, the local hairdresser. Other service firms have become giant organizations. Scott's Restaurants started as a working-man's diner. When Colonel Harland Sanders walked into one of their outlets carrying a bag of chicken, another carrying a mixture of herbs and spices and a special cooking pot, management saw potential. They opened the world's first take-out location devoted exclusively to Kentucky Fried Chicken in northeastern Toronto. Scott's has opened other food chains and now owns Commonwealth Hospitality Inns of Canada.

The Status of Marketing in Service Firms

Although spending for services has grown substantially, the development of marketing as a major business activity has come slowly to most service industries. This is largely due to what Theodore Levitt has called *marketing myopia* (described in Chapter 1), the thesis that top executives in many industries have failed to recognize the scope of their businesses.[7] Future growth is endangered because management is product-oriented rather than customer-oriented. Levitt specifically mentions several service industries, including dry cleaning, motion pictures, railways, and electric utilities. The film studio president, for example, who defines the firm's activities as "making movies" instead of as "marketing entertainment" is suffering from marketing myopia, in Levitt's view.

Indicative of the low status of marketing in many service industries are the findings of a survey of manufacturing and service firms that concluded that "the marketing function appears to be less structured in service companies than in manufacturing firms."[8] The following major findings were reported:

> In comparison to manufacturing firms, service firms appear to be 1) generally less likely to have marketing mix activities carried out in the marketing department, 2) less likely to perform analysis in the offering area, 3) more likely to handle their advertising internally rather than go to outside agencies, 4) less likely to have an overall sales plan, 5) less likely to develop sales training programs, 6) less likely to use marketing research firms and marketing consultants, and 7) less likely to spend as much on marketing when expressed as a percentage of gross sales.[9]

For many service industries the shift to a marketing orientation will require a change from traditional ways of doing business. Fortunately, this change is already taking place in some of the leading service industries. Airlines have shifted their emphasis from the technical aspects of operation to marketing considerations. Long-range, high-capacity jets forced airline managements to think in terms of marketing as practised in goods industries. Banking and insurance are other service industries that have begun to emphasize marketing co-ordination.

The Marketing Environment for Service Industries

The environmental framework for marketing decisions was discussed in Chapter 2. In many ways the economic, social, legal, and competitive forces exert the same type of pressures on service firms as they exert on goods producers. However, certain features of the environment for service marketing should be highlighted.

Economic Environment

The growth of consumer expenditures for services has been accompanied by the further expansion of business and government services to keep pace with the increasing complexity of the Canadian economy. The sharp increase in spending for services and the development of the service industries as the major employer of labour is one of the most significant economic trends in our post-World War II economy. Most explanations of this trend are based upon changes associated with a maturing economy and the by-products of rapid economic growth. A theory developed by economist Colin Clark describes the growth of service industries.[10] In the first, most primitive, stage, the vast majority of an economy's population is engaged in farming, grazing, hunting, fishing, and forestry. As an economy becomes more advanced, emphasis shifts from agriculture to manufacturing activity. The final and most advanced stage occurs when the majority of labour is engaged in the so-called **tertiary industries**   industries engaged in *the production of services.*

Technological advances, population shifts, and changing consumer needs also contribute to increased spending for consumer services. The evolution of science and technology has altered productivity trends, and higher productivity in the manufacturing industries brought about the shift of workers to service industries. Technological advances have created a higher standard of living for the average person, who spends a larger portion of his or her increased discretionary income for services. In addition, population changes, particularly increased urbanization resulting from advanced technology, have widened the demand for personal and public services. Psychological and sociological factors are also relevant. The consumer's growing desire for personal service, for convenience, and for a wider range of services is an important economic trend.

Perhaps even more spectacular than the growth of consumer expenditures for services has been the increased spending for business services. Servicing other business has become big business, and companies in this field range from suppliers of temporary help to highly specialized consultation services.

Business services have grown rapidly for two reasons. First, business service firms are frequently able to perform a specialized function more cheaply than the purchasing company can do it itself. Enterprises providing maintenance, cleaning, and protection services to office buildings and industrial plants are common examples. For instance, the decorative plants in Ottawa's many federal buildings are cared for and maintained by a firm specializing in such services. Second, many companies are unable to perform certain services for themselves. Marketing research studies, for example, often require outside specialists.

Socio-cultural Environment   The socio-cultural environment has a significant impact on the marketing of services. Consumers are offered a wide array of services; some are accepted, others rejected. Tastes can also shift over time. For instance, the increased use of counsellors and consultants influences many aspects of modern personal, family, and work lives. A few years ago some of these services were not even available, let alone influential. Now there are even leisure consultants to advise consumers on what to do with their spare time.

Various social trends are relevant. For example, there is evidence that the Canadian consumer's tastes are shifting to a preference for services as status symbols. Travel, culture, health and beauty, and higher education have partially replaced durable goods as status symbols in the minds of many consumers. Other trends include a growing emphasis on financial security, which has expanded the market for insurance, banking, and investment services; greater stress on health, which has led to a greater demand for exercise programs, dental, medical, and hospital services; and the changing attitude toward credit, which has expanded the demand for the services of banks and other lending agencies.

The Greenskeeper Inc., a Service Specialist

PLANT LEASING AND MAINTENANCE PROGRAMMES

Greenskeeper Sales, Leasing & Maintenance is THE strategic answer to those sad, dusty plastic replicas of foliage that follow so many failures. It is specifically designed for the commercial or industrial environment and will, with the intelligent use of refreshingly alive greenery, give you more relaxed, impressive surroundings.

Here at the Greenskeeper we understand the problems of owning and maintaining healthy plants. The Greenskeeper staff has years of experience and success in creating indoor plant arrangements that rival nature's own settings.

the Greenskeeper Inc.

Source: The Greenskeeper Inc.

Attitudes toward some services change slowly, however. One study of the attitudes of homemakers toward the use of personal services such as home cleaning and window washing observed that homemakers resisted using some services because they felt that purchasing personal services violated the virtues of hard work and self-reliance which are part of the homemaker's traditional image, although they recognized the time and effort using these services would save.[11]

**Political and
Legal Environment**

Service businesses are more closely regulated than most other forms of private enterprise. There are few service firms that are not subject to some special form of government regulation in addition to the usual taxes and anti-combines legislation. For example, many services are subject to restrictions on promotion and price discrimination. Airline fares are subject to the approval of the Canadian Transport Commission; a railway must ensure that its rates do not contravene federal legislation, and adding or dropping a route is subject to hearings. Even hair stylists must be licensed in most provinces.

Marketers of services must recognize the impact of government on their competitive strategies. Regulation affects the marketing of services in at least three significant ways:

1. It typically reduces the range of competition; as this occurs, the intensity of competition is typically reduced.
2. It reduces a marketer's array of options and introduces certain rigidities into the marketing process.
3. Because the decisions of the regulatory agency are binding, part of the marketing decision process must be to predict the actions of the regulatory agency and to influence these actions in regulatory hearings and through lobbying.[12]

Many service industries are regulated at the national level by special government agencies such as the National Energy Board, the Canadian Radio-Television and Telecommunications Commission, and the Canada Deposit Insurance Corporation, to name a few. Other services — insurance and real estate — are traditionally regulated at provincial and local levels. In addition, many personal and business services are restricted at provincial and local levels by special fees or taxes, certification, and licensing. Often included in this category are the legal and medical professions, barbers and beauticians, funeral directors, accountants, engineers, and other professions.

**Technological
Environment:
Productivity
Remains a Problem**

Historically, a large proportion of the economic growth in Canada has resulted from increases in **productivity** — *the output produced by each worker*. Technological developments accounted for significant increases in productivity in the past. The invention of the combine harvester almost tripled the output of the average wheat farmer, and Henry Ford's innovations made it possible to reduce the cost of an average car by 50 percent. How are increases in productivity accomplished in a service economy?

Theodore Levitt argues that service marketers should assume a "manufacturing" attitude. "Instead of looking to the service workers to improve results by greater exertion of animal energy, managers must see what kinds of organizations, incentives, technology, and skills could improve overall productivity."[13]

Levitt cites McDonald's as the ultimate example of how service can be industrialized:

> Each variety of McDonald's hamburger is in a colour-coded wrapper. Parking lots are sprinkled with brightly painted, omnivorous trash cans that even the most chronic litterer finds difficult to ignore. A special scoop has been devised for French fries so that each customer will believe he is getting an over-flowing portion, while actually receiving a uniform ration. Employee discretion is eliminated; everything is organized so that nothing can go wrong.[14]

The manufacturing attitude is already evident in many service firms. Conversion of such businesses as dry cleaners and car washes from hand labour to automatic equipment has increased output per worker. The introduction of wide-bodied jets by the airlines enables them to fly twice as many passengers with the same number of high-salaried pilots and flight engineers. The development of multiple-unit motion picture theatres with a single refreshment stand, ticket-selling booth, and projection room reduced necessary floor space and the number of people needed to operate them.[15] For small personal loans, some banks have shifted from analysis by loan officers to a simple "scorecard" to evaluate prospective borrowers (one point for having a telephone, five points for home ownership, five points for several years of steady employment, and so on). The challenge to service marketers is to produce gains in productivity without sacrificing the quality of service.

Competitive Environment

The competitive environment for services is a paradox. For many service industries, competition comes not from other services but from goods manufacturers or government services. Internal competition is almost nonexistent in some service industries. Price competition is severely limited in such areas as transportation, communication, and legal and medical services. Moreover, many important service producers like hospitals, educational institutions, and religious and welfare agencies are not even operating for a profit in the business sense. Finally, many service industries are difficult to enter; they may require a major financial investment or special education or training or may be restricted by government regulations.

Competition from Goods   Direct competition between goods and services is inevitable since competing goods and services often provide the same basic satisfactions. Consumers may satisfy their service requirements by substituting goods. Competition has become greater because manufacturers, recognizing the changing desires of consumers, are building services and added conveniences into their products. Wash-and-wear clothing has replaced some laundry and dry cleaning services; improved appliances have reduced the need for domestic employees; and television competes with motion pictures and other forms of entertainment. Consumers often have a choice between goods and services that perform the same general function.

Competition from Retailers and Manufacturers The entry of retailers and manufacturers into consumer and service markets is also increasing the intensity of competition for the service dollar. Large retailers such as Eaton's, Woodwards, and The Bay are providing services such as optical centres and automobile repair facilities that go far beyond traditional department store offerings. Sears has been a leader in the trend to diversify into services with its entry into insurance (Allstate). Eaton's and others have travel agencies and provide financial services. These large retailers have apparently decided that the mass merchandising of consumer services is possible and profitable.

Competition from Government An expanded number of services are now provided by all levels of government. Some services can only be provided by government agencies, but others compete with privately produced goods and services. Often, the consumption of government services is mandatory, such as contributions to Canada Pension Plan, unemployment insurance, and compulsory education. Private auto insurance companies have been pushed out of some provinces. Current public debates concern how far government should be involved, and how the consumer should pay for such government services.

The Marketing Mix for Service Firms

Satisfying the service needs of buyers requires the development of an effective marketing mix. Service policies and distribution, promotional, and pricing strategies must be combined in an integrated marketing program. This section introduces the marketing mix for service firms.

Service Policies

Like tangible products, services may be classified according to their intended use. Thus all are either consumer services or industrial services. Even when the same service (telephone, gas, and electric services) is sold to both consumer and industrial buyers, a service firm will often have separate marketing groups for each market segment.

Consumer services may also be classified as convenience, shopping, and specialty services. Dry cleaning, shoe repairs, and similar personal services are commonly purchased on a convenience basis. Auto repairs and insurance are services that can involve considerable shopping to compare price and quality. Specialty services, where the consumer will accept no alternatives, may include professional services, such as financial, legal, and medical assistance.

Some service firms have developed new services or diversified their service mix in an attempt to boost sales. Insurance policies for homeowners, vacation package tours, and air-travel family plans all represent examples of expanded service offerings that have received favourable consumer response.

A new service may often be an improved method of delivering an existing service.[16] Figure 11-4 presents a list of service product innovations.

Some important differences between service policies and product policies should be noted. First, because services are intangible, packaging and labelling decisions are very limited. Service marketers are rarely able to use the package to promote their services. Second, the lack of a tangible product limits sampling by service marketers as a means of introducing a new service to the market.

Figure 11-4   Examples of Service Product Innovations

Nature of Service	New Service Product	or	Service Product Improvement
Communications	Communication satellite		Free-standing public telephone
Consulting and business facilitating	Equipment leasing		Overnight TV rating service
Educational	Ecology-management major		New curricula
Financial	Automated bank tellers		Extended banking hours
Health	Treatment with lasers		Intensive care
Household operations	Laundromat		Fuel budget accounts
Housing	Housing for the elderly		Motel swimming pool
Insurance	National health insurance		No-fault insurance
Personal	Physical fitness facilities		
Recreational	Dual cinema		New play
Transportation	Unit train		Flight reservation system

Source: Adapted from *Marketing in the Service Sector* by John Rathmell. Copyright © 1974 by Winthrop Publishers Inc. Reprinted by permission of the publisher.

Pricing Strategy   In service industries, pricing practices are not substantially different from those in goods industries. The service marketer must consider the demand for the service, production, marketing, and administrative costs, and the influence of competition when developing pricing strategies. However, for many services price competition has been limited. Until recently, prices of transportation, communications, and other utilities have been closely regulated by federal, provincial, and local agencies. Business and the public are watching to see how recent deregulation activities will affect pricing in these industries. For many other service firms, such as advertising agencies, there is a traditional pricing structure that is closely followed within the industry.

Price negotiation is an important part of many professional service transactions. Consumer services that sometimes involve price negotiation include auto repairs, foreign travel, and financial and legal assistance. Specialized business services, such as equipment rental, market research, insurance, and maintenance and protection services, are also priced through direct negotiation.

Many firms use variable pricing to overcome the problems associated with the perishable nature of services. The Canadian telephone system is one service organization that has used this approach. Lower rates for long-distance calls are in effect during evening hours and on weekends. Off-season rates at resort hotels and motels are another example.

Distribution Strategy

Channels of distribution for services are usually simpler and more direct than channels of distribution of goods. In part, this is due to the intangibility of services. The marketer of services is often less concerned with storage, transportation, and inventory control, so shorter channels may be employed.

Another consideration is the need for continuing personal relationships between performers and users of many services. Consumers will remain with the same insurance agent, bank, or travel agent if they are reasonably satisfied. Likewise, public accounting firms and lawyers are retained on a relatively permanent basis by industrial buyers.

When marketing intermediaries are used by service firms they are usually agents or brokers. Common examples include insurance agents, securities brokers, travel agents, and entertainment agents.

Promotional Strategy

Promotion is an important aspect of the marketing mix for most services. As with goods, the importance of each particular form of promotion varies for different services.

The *advertising* of services is somewhat more challenging than the advertising of goods since it is more difficult to illustrate intangible services. Several strategies may be used. One is to make the service seem more tangible by personalizing it. This may be done by featuring employees or recognizable entertainment or sports personalities.

A second strategy is to attempt to create a favourable image for the service or the service company. Some of the themes used by service organizations are efficiency, progressiveness, status, and friendliness. For example, advertisements for American Express show its card being used by well-known personalities.

A third advertising strategy is to show the tangible benefits of purchasing an intangible service. An airline shows grandparents greeting a granddaughter as she arrives for a visit; a local bank shows a young couple enjoying a new home purchased through a home mortgage or a retired couple relaxing in Victoria because of a savings plan they had established years ago. These and many similar themes help buyers relate to the benefits of the particular service that they may be unable to visualize.

The desire of many service buyers for a personal relationship with a service seller increases the importance of *personal selling*. In fact, except for a very simple or highly standardized service, personal selling is usually the backbone of service marketing.

Life insurance marketing provides a good illustration of the sales representative's key role. Because insurance is a confusing, complex subject for the average buyer, the agent must be a professional financial adviser who develops a close personal relationship with the client. Life insurance companies and other service firms must develop well-trained, highly motivated sales forces to provide the high-quality, personalized service that customers require. Their success is closely related to their ability to develop such salespeople.

Sales promotion is difficult because services are intangible. Sampling, demonstrations, and physical displays are limited, but service firms often do use premiums and contests. Publicity is also important for many services, especially for entertainment and sports events. Television and radio reports, newspaper articles, and magazine features inform the public of events and stimulate interest. Contributions to charitable causes, employees' service to nonprofit organizations, sponsorship of public events, and similar activities are publicized to influence the public's opinion of the service firm.

Organizational Responsibility for Marketing

In many service firms, the organizational responsibility for marketing may be considerably different than in manufacturing companies. In any company there may be confusion about what marketing is. It is frequently considered to be what the *marketing department does*. Marketing is, however, often carried out by others in the company to some degree. This confusion may be much more acute for service firms than for manufacturing firms and may constitute an organizational dilemma. In many professional service organizations, the marketing department's role may be limited to handling advertising, sales promotion, and some public relations. The "sales force" are those people in direct contact with customers, for example, the branch managers and the tellers in a bank. With the exception of the members of the marketing department, however, the staff is not hired for its marketing know-how but for its ability to produce services. *Yet the person who produces a service must also be able to market that service.* In most cases, what is needed is not professional salespeople but service workers who sell.

The dilemma arises when service firms are insufficiently aware of the need to have personnel who are able to perform adequately both marketing and service-production functions. Furthermore, when the workload is high, too little time may be spent on marketing, which may have very serious long-term consequences for the organization.

Summary

Approximately 40 percent of all personal consumption expenditures go to the purchase of services. Services can be defined as intangible efforts that satisfy consumer needs when efficiently developed and distributed to chosen consumer segments.

The marketing of services has many similarities to the marketing of goods, but there are also some significant differences. Key features of services have implications for marketing:
1. Services are intangible.
2. Services are perishable.
3. Services are often not standardized.
4. Buyers are often involved in the development and distribution of services.

Important aspects of buyer behaviour are different for services as contrasted to goods. These differences may be grouped into three categories: attitudes, needs and motives, and purchase behaviour.

Although service industries have grown substantially, their development of effective marketing programs has been slow. Many service firms have not adopted the marketing concept, while others, such as the insurance companies, are very efficient marketers.

Environmental factors affect service industries the same way they influence goods producers. Marketers of services must be continuously aware of changes in the economic, socio-cultural, political and legal, and competitive environments.

An effective marketing mix is mandatory in the sale of services. Service policies (service industries' versions of product planning) and pricing, distribution, and promotional strategies must all be combined into a co-ordinated marketing mix if the service marketer is to succeed.

Service industries will need to increase their marketing function in order to increase productivity and to attain the maximum profit from the growing demands for their varied services.

5	5	5	5	5	5	5
5	5	5	5	5	5	5
5	5	5	5	5	5	5
5	5	5	5	5	5	5
5	5	5	5	5	5	5
5	5	5	5	5	5	5
5	5	5	5	5	5	5
5	5	5	5	5	5	5
5	5	5	5	5	5	5

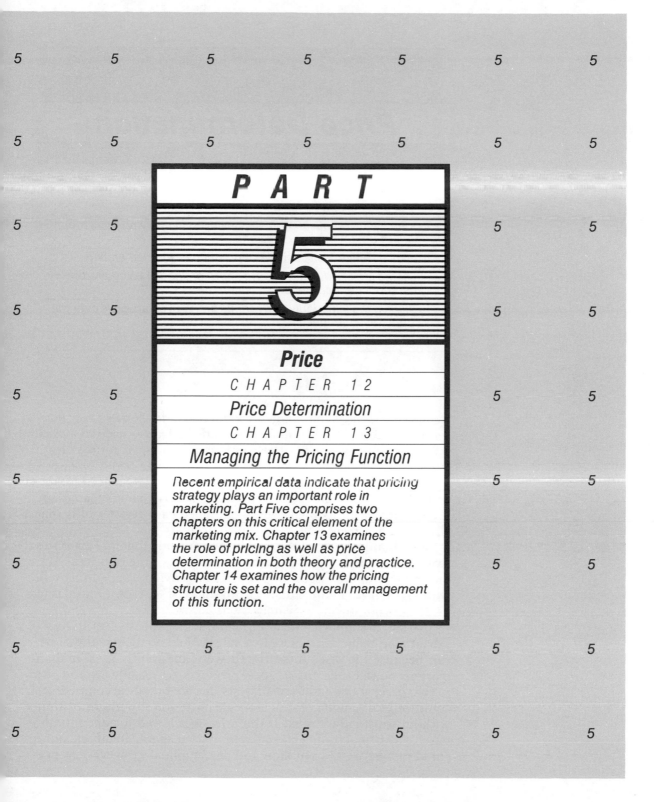

PART

5

Price

CHAPTER 12

Price Determination

CHAPTER 13

Managing the Pricing Function

Recent empirical data indicate that pricing strategy plays an important role in marketing. Part Five comprises two chapters on this critical element of the marketing mix. Chapter 13 examines the role of pricing as well as price determination in both theory and practice. Chapter 14 examines how the pricing structure is set and the overall management of this function.

Price Determination

C H A P T E R   O B J E C T I V E S

1. *To identify the major categories of pricing objectives.*

2. *To explain the concept of elasticity and the determinants of the degree of price elasticity for a product or service.*

3. *To identify the practical problems involved in applying price theory concepts to actual pricing decisions.*

4. *To explain the major cost-plus approaches to price setting.*

5. *To list the major advantages and shortcomings of using break-even analysis in pricing decisions.*

6. *To explain the superiority of dynamic break-even analysis over the basic break-even model.*

7. *To illustrate a pricing model.*

Steinberg, Quebec's third largest food retailer, developed a new marketing strategy which had quite unintended effects — it led to a price war. The strategy was to offer coupons worth 5 percent off future purchases.

Metro-Richelieu, holding second place in the Quebec market, with 900 stores, reacted with a speed that surprised market analysts. It countered with its own offer — stamped cash register bills that allowed a 5 percent rebate on future orders.

IGA Boniprix joined the fray by announcing that its 122 stores would close for a day to allow substantial lowering of prices. And the chain with the largest market share, Provigo, topped them all with an offer of an immediate cash refund of 6 percent on sales in its 250 corporate and privately-owned stores.

All stores supported their strategies with expensive multimedia advertising campaigns. Increased sales would not help in the short-run because the discounts offered were apparently greater than margins on sales. Profits on food products are usually around one to two percent and industry analysts doubted that the competitors could offer discounts of 5 percent or more for any length of time without substantial losses. If the price war lasted for one month, based on normal profits and current market share, Steinberg alone could lose between $3 million and $3.5 million. However, despite the unintended effects of its strategy, Steinberg was optimistic that in the long-term the strategy would result in more customers and increased profits.[1]

Marketers must carefully consider the effects of pricing decisions, because such decisions are usually very visible in the marketplace. In addition, competitors can counter them with amazing speed, and this may be very costly to an entire industry. Consumers may benefit at first but perhaps not in the long-run, as marketers will eventually try to recoup their losses.

The Conceptual Framework

Part Four examined the first critical element of a firm's marketing mix: the determination of the products and services to offer the market target. Part Five focuses upon price — the second element of the marketing mix. Determination of profitable and justified prices is the result of pricing objectives and various approaches to setting prices. These topics are discussed in this chapter. The following chapter focuses upon management of the pricing function and discusses pricing strategies, price-quality relationships, and both industrial pricing and the pricing of public services. The starting place for examining pricing strategy is to understand the meaning of the term *price*.

Price is *the exchange value of a good or service, the value of an item being what it can be exchanged for in the marketplace.* In earlier times, the price of an acre might have been twenty bushels of wheat, three cattle, or a boat. Price is a measure of what one must exchange in order to obtain a desired good or service. When the barter process was abandoned in favour of a monetary system, price became the amount of money required to purchase an item. As David Schwartz has pointed out, contemporary society uses a number of terms to refer to price:

> Price is all around us. You pay *rent* for your apartment, *tuition* for your education, and a *fee* to your physician or dentist.
>
> The airline, railway, taxi, and bus companies charge you a *fare*; the local utilities call their price a *rate*; and the local bank charges you *interest* for the money you borrow.
>
> The price for taking your car on the ferry to Prince Edward Island or Vancouver Island is a *toll*, and the company that insures your car charges you a *premium*.
>
> Clubs or societies to which you belong may make a special *assessment* to pay unusual expenses. Your regular lawyer may ask for a *retainer* to cover her services.
>
> The "price" of an executive is a *salary*; the price of a salesperson may be a *commission*; and the price of a worker is a *wage*.
>
> Finally, although economists would disagree, many of us feel that *income taxes* are the price we pay for the privilege of making money![2]

All products have some degree of *utility*, or want-satisfying power. While one individual might be willing to exchange the utility derived from a colour television for a vacation, another may not be willing to make that exchange. Prices are a mechanism that allows the consumer to make a decision. In contemporary society, of course, prices are translated into monetary terms. The consumer evaluates the utility derived from a range of possible purchases and then allocates his or her exchange power (in monetary terms) so as to maximize satisfaction. Pricing may be the most complicated aspect of the marketing manager's job. It is difficult to determine the price needed to realize a profit. But an even greater problem is that of determining the meaning of price and its role in society.

The Importance of Price as an Element of the Marketing Mix

Ancient philosophers recognized the importance of price to the functioning of the economic system. Early written accounts refer to attempts to develop a fair, or just, price. Their limited understanding of time, place, and possession utilities, however, thwarted such efforts.

Today, price still serves as a means of regulating economic activity. The employment of any or all of the four factors of production (land, labour, capital, and entrepreneurship) is dependent upon the prices received by each. For an individual firm, prices (along with the corresponding quantity that will be sold) represent the revenue to be received. Prices, therefore, influence a company's profit as well as its use of the factors of production.

A widely cited 1964 study by Jon G. Udell found that executives ranked pricing as the sixth in a long list of factors in achieving marketing success.[3] When Udell's factors were reorganized into the four major marketing mix variables, price ranked third — ahead only of distribution.

Figure 12-1   Relative Importance of Marketing Variables: A Comparison of the Udell Study and the Boone and Kurtz Study

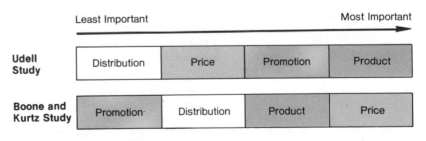

But times have changed. When Udell conducted his study, prices were relatively constant. A 1979 study of marketing executives, conducted when inflation was high, concluded that pricing ranked as the single most important marketing mix variable.[4] Product planning and management was a close second, while distribution strategy and promotional decisions ranked third and fourth respectively. Figure 12-1 compares the Udell findings to those of the later study by Boone and Kurtz.

Pricing Objectives

Pricing objectives are a crucial part of a means–end chain from overall company objectives to specific pricing policies and procedures (see Figure 12-2). The goals of the firm and the marketing organization provide the basis for the development of pricing objectives, which must be clearly established before pricing policies and procedures are implemented.

A firm may have as its primary objective the goal of becoming the dominant supplier in the domestic market. Its marketing objective might then be to achieve maximum sales penetration in all sales regions. The related pricing goal would be sales maximization. This means–end chain might lead to the adoption of a low price policy implemented through provision of the highest cash and trade discounts in the industry.

Pricing objectives vary from firm to firm. Xerox wants its earnings to grow 15 percent annually. Eaton Corporation aspires to rank either first or second in market share in each market in which it

Figure 12-2   The Role of Pricing Objectives in Contemporary Marketing

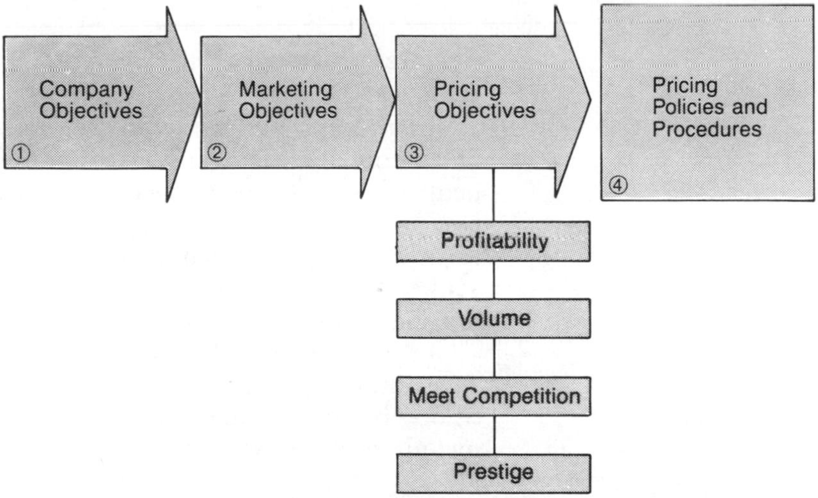

Figure 12-3   Primary and Secondary Pricing Objectives of Firms

Pricing Objective	As Primary Objective	As Secondary Objective	As Either Primary or Secondary Objective
Meeting competitive price level	38.3	43.0	81.3
Specified rate of return on investment	60.9	17.2	78.1
Specified total profit level	60.2	17.2	77.4
Increased market share	31.3	42.2	73.5
Increased total profits above previous levels	34.4	37.5	71.9
Specified rate of return on sales	47.7	23.4	71.1
Retaining existing market share	31.3	35.9	67.2
Serving selected market segments	26.6	39.1	65.7
Creation of a readily identifiable image for the firm and/or its products	21.9	41.4	63.3
Specified market share	15.6	40.6	56.2
Other	5.5	—	5.5

The column header spans *Percentage of Respondents Ranking the Item*.

Source: *Pricing Objectives and Practices in American Industry: A Research Paper.* ©1979 by Louis E. Boone and David L. Kurtz; all rights reserved.

operates. Burroughs has targeted a 15 percent increase in revenue each year.[5]

In a recent U.S. study, marketers were to identify the primary and secondary pricing objectives of their companies. Meeting competitive prices was most often mentioned, but many marketers ranked two profitability-oriented objectives higher: a specified rate of return on investment and specified total profit levels. These two objectives ranked first and second as *primary* pricing objectives. The findings are shown in Figure 12-3.

Pricing objectives can be classified into four major groups: 1) profitability objectives; 2) volume objectives; 3) meeting competition objectives; and 4) prestige objectives. Profitability objectives include profit maximization and target return goals.

Profitability Objectives   In classical economic theory, the traditional pricing objective has been to *maximize profits*. The study of microeconomics is based upon certain assumptions: that buyers and sellers are rational, and that rational behaviour is an effort to maximize gains and minimize losses. In terms of actual business practice, this means that profit maximization is the basic objective of individual firms.

Profits, in turn, are a function of revenue and expenses:

$$\text{Profits} = \text{Revenues} - \text{Expenses}$$

And revenue is determined by the selling price and the quantity sold:

$$\text{Total Revenue} = \text{Price} \times \text{Quantity Sold}$$

Price, therefore, should be increased up to the point where it causes a disproportionate decrease in the number of units sold. A 10 percent price increase that results in only an 8 percent cut in volume adds to the firm's revenue. However, a 10 percent hike that causes an 11 percent sales decline reduces total revenue.

Economists refer to this approach as *marginal analysis*. They identify the point of **profit maximization** as where *the addition to total revenue is just balanced by an increase in total cost.* The basic problem centres on the difficulty in achieving this delicate balance between marginal revenue and marginal cost. As a result, relatively few firms actually achieve an objective of profit maximization. A significantly larger number prefer to direct their efforts toward goals that are more easily implemented and measured.

Consequently, target return objectives have become quite common in industry, particularly among the larger firms where public pressure may limit consideration of the profit maximization objective. Automobile companies are an example of this phenomenon. **Target return objectives** may be *either short-run or long-run goals and usually are stated as a percentage of sales or investment.* A company, for instance, may seek a 15 percent annual rate of return on investment or an 8 percent rate of return on sales. A specified return on investment was the most commonly reported pricing objective in Figure 12-3. Goals of this nature also serve as useful guidelines in evaluating corporate activity. One writer has aptly expressed it: "For management consciously accepting less than maximum profits, the target rate can provide a measure of the amount of restraint. For firms making very low profits, the target rate can serve as a standard for judging improvement."[6] Furthermore, they are more likely to result in a more stable and planned profit pattern for the company. This contrasts with a profit maximization approach, which can be very unstable.

Target return objectives offer several benefits to the marketer. As noted above, they serve as a means for evaluating performance. They also are designed to generate a "fair" profit, as judged by management, stockholders, and the general public as well.

Volume Objectives

Some writers argue that a better explanation of actual pricing behaviour is William J. Baumol's belief that firms attempt to **maximize sales** within a given profit constraint. In other words, they set *a minimum floor at what they consider the lowest acceptable profit level* and then seek to maximize sales (subject to this profit constraint) in the belief that *increased sales are more important to the long-run competitive picture*. The company will continue to expand sales as long as their total profits do not drop below the minimum return acceptable to management.

Another volume-related pricing objective is the **market share** objective — that is, the goal set as *the control of a specific portion of the market for the firm's product.* The company's specific goal can be to maintain or increase its share of a particular market. For example, a firm may desire to increase its 10 percent share of a particular market to 20 percent. As Figure 12-3 indicates, almost two-thirds of all responding firms list retaining existing market share as either a primary or secondary pricing objective.

Some firms with high market shares may even prefer to reduce their share at times because the possibility of government action in the area of monopoly control has become more important in recent years. Courts have used market share figures in their evaluation of cases involving alleged monopolistic practices.

The PIMS Studies   Market share objectives can be critical to the achievement of other objectives. High sales, for example, may mean more profit. The extensive *Profit Impact of Market Strategies (PIMS)* project conducted by the Marketing Science Institute analysed more than 2000 firms and revealed that two of the most important factors influencing profitability were product quality and market share.

The link between market share and profitability is dramatically demonstrated in Figure 12-4. Firms enjoying more than 40 percent of a market achieved a pre-tax return on investment averaging 32.3 percent. By contrast, firms with a minor market share of less than 10 percent generate pre-tax investment returns of 13.2 percent. The underlying factor in this relationship appears to be the operating experience and lower overall costs of high-market-share firms as compared with competitors who possess smaller shares of the market.[7] However, there remains some question: Does profitability come from market share per se, or are both profitability and market share related to a sound marketing strategy over time?

Figure 12-4   Relationship of Market Share to Return on Investment (ROI)

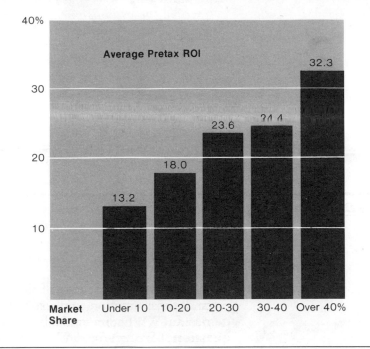

Source: Reprinted by permission from Robert D. Buzzell and Frederik D. Wiersema, "Successful Share-Building Strategies," *Harvard Business Review* (January–February 1981), p. 137.

Henry Allesio has warned marketers not to place too much stress on market share because of the foregoing findings. He correctly points out that marketing strategy should include a conscious recognition of what a firm's real source of comparative advantage is, as well as the delivered cost (not just manufactured cost) of products.[8] Not everyone can obtain market share predominance, but most can still do very well in the market.

Meeting Competition as a Pricing Objective

Status quo objectives — *objectives based on the maintenance of stable prices* — are the basis of the pricing philosophy for many enterprises. This philosophy usually stems from a desire to minimize competitive pricing action. The maintenance of stable prices allows the firm to concentrate its efforts on non-price elements of the marketing mix such as product improvement or promotion. For a long time the automobile producers de-emphasized price competition in their advertisements in favour of developing product features that differentiated their products from the competition. Even today, status quo objectives remain a significant factor in pricing.

Prestige Objectives   Another category of pricing objectives unrelated to either profitability or sales volume is that of prestige objectives. **Prestige objectives** involve *the establishment of relatively high prices in order to develop and maintain an image of quality and exclusiveness.* Such objectives reflect marketers' recognition of the role of price in the creation of an overall image for the firm and its products and services. It appears that Birks and Holt Renfrew follow this strategy. And Rolls-Royce has opted for a higher price image with its Cabriolet convertible model, priced at approximately $150 000. While some marketers set relatively high prices in order to maintain a prestige image with their consumers, others prefer the opposite approach of developing a low-price image among customers.

Price Determination

There are two general ways to look at the determination of price. One is theoretical price derivation; the other is the cost-plus type of approach, which in numerous variations and combined with an eye on demand and the competition, characterizes actual business practice.

During the first part of this century most formal discussion of price determination emphasized the classical concepts of supply and demand. (Whether actual business practice followed this is another question.) Since World War II the emphasis has shifted to a cost-oriented approach to pricing. The advantage of hindsight allows us to see that both concepts have certain flaws in practice. Most firms use a combination of both in their pricing decisions.

There is, however, another aspect that is often overlooked. *Custom, tradition, and social habit* also play an important role in price determination. Numerous examples of **customary pricing** exist. The candy-makers' attempt to hold the line on the traditional 5-cent candy bar led to considerable reductions in the size of the product. Eventually almost all vending machines were supplied with larger 10-cent bars, and the shrinking process began again. Similar practices have prevailed in the marketing of soft drinks.

At some point, someone had to set the *initial* price. Sustained inflation has also created a need for periodically reviewing the firm's price structures.

The remainder of this chapter will discuss the traditional and current concepts of price determination. Finally, we shall deal with the question of how best to tie these concepts together so as to develop a more realistic approach to pricing.

Price Determination in Economic Theory

The microeconomic approach, or price theory, assumes a profit maximization objective and leads to the derivation of correct equilibrium prices in the marketplace. Price theory considers both supply and demand factors and thus is a more complete analysis than what is typically found in practice.

Demand refers to a schedule of the amounts of a firm's product or service that consumers will purchase at different prices during a specific period. *Supply* refers to a schedule of the amounts of a product or service that will be offered for sale at different prices during a specified time period. These schedules may vary for different types of market structures.

Market Structures There are four types of market structures; pure competition, monopolistic competition, oligopoly, and monopoly. Very briefly, **pure competition** is *a market structure where there is such a large number of buyers and sellers that no one of them has a significant influence on price*. Other characteristics of pure competition include a homogeneous product and ease of entry for sellers, and complete and instantaneous information.

This marketing structure is largely theoretical in contemporary society; however, some uncontrolled sectors of the agricultural commodity sector exhibit many of the characteristics of such a market, and provide the closest example of it.

Monopolistic competition is also *a market structure with a large number of buyers and sellers*. However, in this market there is *some degree of heterogeneity in product and/or service and usually geographical differentiation*. The existence of differentiation allows the marketer some degree of control over price. Most retail stores fall into this category, which partially explains why small retailers can exist with 5 to 10 percent higher prices than their larger competitors.

An **oligopoly** is *a market structure in which there are relatively few sellers*. Each seller may affect the market, but no one seller controls it. Examples are the automobile, steel, tobacco, and petroleum-refining industries. Because of high start-up costs, new competitors encounter significant entry barriers. **Oligopsony** is the other side of the coin: *a market where there are only a few buyers*.

A **monopoly** is *a market structure with only one seller of a product with no close substitutes*. Anti-combines legislation has tended to eliminate all but *temporary* monopolies, such as those provided by patent protection, and *regulated* monopolies, such as the public utilities (telephone, electricity, gas). Regulated monopolies are granted by government in markets where competition would lead to an uneconomic duplication of services. In return for this monopoly, government regulates the monopoly rate of return through regulatory bodies such as the Canadian Transport Commission, the Canadian Radio-Television and Telecommunications Commission, the National Farm Products Marketing Council, and provincial public utility regulatory commissions.

Revenue, Cost and   Within each of these market structures the elements of demand, costs,
Supply Curves   and supply must be considered. The demand side of price theory is
concerned with **revenue curves**. *Average revenue* (AR) is obtained
by dividing *total revenue* (TR) by the *quantity* (Q) associated with
these revenues:

$$AR = \frac{TR}{Q}$$

The average revenue line is actually the demand curve facing
the firm. *Marginal revenue* (MR) is the change in total revenue (ΔTR)
that results from selling an additional unit of output (ΔQ). This can
be shown as:

$$MR = \frac{\Delta TR}{\Delta Q}$$

In order to complete the analysis, the supply curves must be determined for each of these market situations. A firm's cost structure
determines its supply curves. Let us examine each of the cost curves
applicable to price determination.

Average cost (AC) is obtained by dividing total cost by the quantity (Q) associated with these costs. *Total cost* (TC) is composed of
both fixed and variable components. *Fixed costs* are those costs that
do not vary with differences in output, while *variable costs* are those
that change when the level of production is altered. Examples of
fixed costs include executive compensation, depreciation, and
insurance. Variable costs include raw materials and the wages paid
production workers.

Average variable cost (AVC) is simply the total variable cost
(TVC) divided by the related quantity. Similary, *average fixed cost*
(AFC) is determined by dividing total fixed costs (TFC) by the related
quantity. **Marginal cost** (MC) is the change in total cost (ΔTC) that
results from producing an additional unit of output (ΔQ). Thus, it
is similar to *marginal revenue*, which is the change in total revenue
resulting from the production of an incremental unit. The point of
profit maximization is where marginal costs are equal to marginal
revenues.

These cost derivations are shown in the following formulas:

$$AC = \frac{TC}{Q} \qquad AFC = \frac{TFC}{Q}$$

$$AVC = \frac{TVC}{Q} \qquad MC = \frac{\Delta TC}{\Delta Q}$$

The resulting *cost curves* are shown in Figure 12-5. The marginal cost curve (MC) intersects the average variable cost curve (AVC)
and average cost curve (AC) at the minimum points.

In the short run a firm will continue to operate even if the price falls below AC, provided it remains above AVC. Why is this rational market behaviour? If the firm were to cease operations after the price fell below AC, it would still have some fixed costs, but *no* revenue. Any amount received above AVC can be used to cover fixed costs. The manager is acting rationally by continuing to produce as long as price exceeds AVC since this is minimizing losses. If price falls below AVC the manager would cease operation because continued operation would result in real losses from out-of-pocket costs per unit, with no control of fixed costs. The **supply curve**, therefore, is *the marginal cost curve above its intersection with* AVC since this is the area of rational pricing behaviour for the firm.

Figure 12-5   Cost Curves

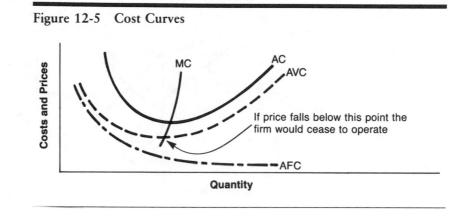

How, then, are prices set in each of the product market situations? Figure 12-6 shows how prices are determined in each of the four product markets. The point of profit maximization (MC = MR) sets the equilibrium output (Point A), which is extended to the AR line to set the equilibrium price (Point B). In the case of pure competition, AR = MR, so price is a predetermined variable in this product market.

The Concept of Elasticity in Pricing Strategy

Although the intersection of demand and supply curves determines the equilibrium price for each of the market structures, the specific curves vary. To understand why, it is necessary to understand the concept of elasticity.[9]

Elasticity is *a measure of responsiveness of purchasers and suppliers to changes in price.* The *price elasticity of demand* is the percentage change in the quantity of a product or service demanded, divided by the percentage change in its price. A 10 percent increase in the price of eggs that results in a 5 percent decrease in the quantity of eggs demanded yields a price elasticity of demand for eggs of 0.5.

Figure 12-6   Price Determination in the Four Product Markets

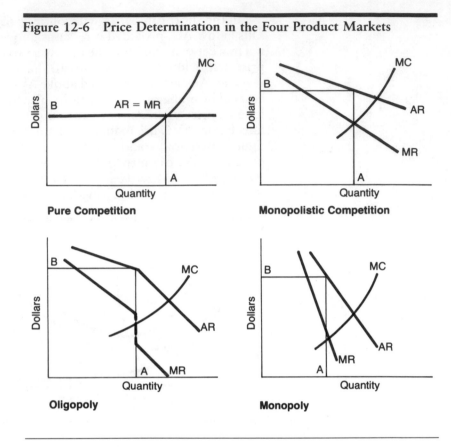

The *price elasticity of supply* of a good is the percentage change in the quantity of a product or service supplied, divided by the percentage change in its price. If a 10 percent increase in the price of milk brings about a 22 percent increase in the quantity supplied, the change yields a price elasticity of supply for milk of 2.2.

Elasticity Terminology Consider a case in which a one percent change in price causes more than a one percent change in the quantity supplied or demanded. Numerically, that means an elasticity greater than one. When the elasticity of demand or supply is greater than one, it is termed *elastic*.

If a one percent change in price results in less than a one percent change in quantity, a good's elasticity of supply or demand will be numerically less than one and is called *inelastic*. The demand for eggs in the example above is inelastic. The demand for gasoline is relatively inelastic. During 1979, retail gasoline prices rose 50 percent, but gasoline sales fell by only about 8 percent.

An extreme case occurs when the quantity supplied or demanded does not change at all when the price changes. Then the supply or demand is called perfectly inelastic.

The case in which a one percent change in price results in exactly a one percent change in quantity is called *unit* (or *unitary*) *elasticity*.

Elasticity and Revenue

There is an important relationship between the elasticity of demand and the way that total revenue changes as the price of a product or service changes. Suppose Montreal wants to find a way to raise more money for the public transportation system. One possible fund-raising method is to change the transit fare, but should it be raised or lowered? The correct answer depends on the elasticity of demand for subway rides. A 10 percent decrease in fares is sure to attract more riders, but unless there is more than a 10 percent increase in riders, total revenue will fall. A 10 percent increase in fares will bring in more money per rider, but if more than 10 percent of the riders are lost, revenue will fall. A price cut will increase revenue only if demand is elastic, and a price increase will raise revenue only if demand is inelastic.

Practical Problems in Applying Price Theory

From the viewpoint of the marketer, price theory concepts are sometimes difficult to apply in practice. What are their practical limitations?

1. Many firms do not attempt to profit-maximize. Economic analysis is subject to the same limitations as the assumptions upon which it is based — for example, the proposition that all firms attempt to maximize profits.

2. It is difficult to estimate demand curves. Modern accounting procedures provide the manager with a clear understanding of his or her cost structure. The manager, therefore, can readily comprehend the supply side of the price equation. But it is difficult to estimate demand at various price levels. Demand curves must be based upon market research estimates that are often not as exact as cost figures. Although the demand element can be identified, it is often difficult to measure in the real-world setting.

3. Inadequate training and communications hinder price theory in the real world. Many businesspersons lack the formal training in economics to be able to apply its concepts to their own pricing decisions. On the other hand, many economists remain essentially theorists devoting little interest or effort to real-world pricing situations. This dual problem significantly hinders the use of economic theory in actual pricing practice.

Price Setting in Practice

The practical limitations inherent in price theory have forced practitioners to turn to other techniques. Actual price determination tends to be based upon some form of the cost-plus approach. For many years government contracts with suppliers called for payments of all expenses plus a set profit, usually stated as a percentage of the cost of the project. (These cost-plus contracts, as they were known, have now been abandoned in favour of competitive bidding or specifically negotiated prices.)

Cost-plus pricing uses some *base cost figure per unit to which is added a markup to cover unassigned costs and to provide a profit.* The only real difference in the multitude of cost-plus techniques is the relative sophistication of the costing procedures employed. For example, the local clothing store may set prices by adding a 40 percent markup to the invoice price charged by the supplier. This markup is expected to cover all other expenses, as well as permit the owner to earn a reasonable return on the sale of the garments.

In contrast to this rather simple pricing mechanism, a large manufacturer may employ a pricing formula that requires a computer to handle the necessary calculations for a sophisticated costing procedure. But in the end the formula still requires someone to make a decision about the markup. The clothing store and the large manufacturer may be vastly different with respect to the *cost* aspect, but they are remarkably similar when it comes to the *markup* side of the equation.

The above discussion demonstrates one of the problems associated with cost-oriented pricing. "Costs do not determine prices, since the proper function of cost in pricing is to determine the profit consequences of pricing alternatives."[10] Unfortunately, this is not always understood by some marketers.

Full-Cost Pricing

The two most common cost-oriented pricing procedures are the full-cost method and the incremental-cost method. *Full-cost pricing* uses all relevant variable costs in setting a product's price. In addition, it considers an allocation of the fixed costs that cannot be directly attributed to the production of the specific item being priced. Under the full-cost method, if job order 515 in a printing plant amounts to 0.000127 percent of the plant's total output, then 0.000127 percent of the firm's overhead expenses are allocated to this job. This approach, therefore, allows the pricer to recover all costs plus the amount added as a profit margin.

The full-cost approach has two basic deficiencies. First, there is no consideration of the demand for the item or its competition. Perhaps no one wants to pay the price that the firm has calculated. Second, any method of allocating overhead, or fixed expenses, is arbitrary and may be unrealistic. In manufacturing, overhead allocations are often tied to direct labour hours. In retailing, the mechanism is sometimes floor area in each profit centre. Regardless of the technique, it is difficult to show a cause-and-effect relationship between the allocated cost and most products.

Incremental-Cost Pricing
One way to overcome the arbitrary allocation of fixed expenses is by *incremental-cost pricing*, which attempts to use only those costs directly attributable to a specific output in setting prices. For example, consider a small manufacturer with the following income statement.

Sales (10 000 units at $10)		$100 000
Expenses		
Variable	$50 000	
Fixed	40 000	90 000
Net Profit		$ 10 000

Suppose that the firm is offered a contract for an additional 5000 units. Since the peak season is over, these items can be produced at the same average variable cost. Assume that the labour force would be idle otherwise. In order to get the contract, how low could the firm price its product?

Under the full-cost approach the lowest price would be $9 each. This is obtained by dividing the $90 000 in expenses by an output of 10 000 units. The full-cost pricer would consider this a profitless situation. One study indicated that this method of calculation and the subsequent decision was typical of many small businesses: "A common practice is to use full costs, not as a flexible point at which the price is to be set, but as a floor below which the price will not be allowed to fall — a reference point to which flexible markups are added."[11]

The incremental approach, on the other hand, would permit a price of anywhere from $5.01 upwards depending on the competition. If competition was strong, a price of $5.10 would be competitive. This price would be composed of the $5 variable cost related to each unit of production, plus a 10 cents per unit contribution to fixed expenses and overhead. With these conditions of sale, note the revised income statement:

Sales (10 000 at $10 plus 5 000 at $5.10)		$125 500
Expenses		
Variable (15 000 × $5)	$75 000	
Fixed	40 000	115 000
Net Profit		$ 10 500

Profits were increased under the incremental approach. Admittedly, the illustration is based on two assumptions: 1) the ability to isolate markets so that selling at the lower price would not affect the price received in other markets; and 2) the absence of certain legal restrictions on the firm. The example, however, does show that profits can sometimes be enhanced by using the incremental approach.

Limitations of Cost-Oriented Pricing

While the incremental method eliminates one of the problems associated with full-cost pricing, it fails to deal effectively with the basic malady: *cost-oriented pricing does not adequately account for product demand.*

The problem of estimating demand is as critical to these approaches as it is to classical price theory. To the marketer, the challenge is to find some way of introducing demand analysis into cost-plus pricing. It has also been pointed out that:

> A well-reasoned approach to pricing is, in effect, a comparison of the impact of a decision on total sales receipts, or revenue, and on total costs. It involves the increase or decrease in revenue and costs, not just of the product under consideration, but of the business enterprise as a whole.[12]

Markups, Markdowns, and Turnover

A frequent criticism of pricing practices is that decision-makers have consistently attempted to develop rigid procedures by which prices can be derived in a largely mechanical fashion. These efforts often produce inappropriate prices for specific market situations because they ignore the creative aspects of pricing. Markup policies are an example of this problem. A **markup** is *the amount a producer or channel member adds to cost in order to determine the selling price*. It is typically stated as either a percentage of the selling price or of cost. The formulas used in calculating markup percentages are as follows:

$$\text{Markup Percentage on Selling Price} = \frac{\text{Amount Added to Cost (the Markup)}}{\text{Price}}$$

$$\text{Markup Percentage on Cost} = \frac{\text{Amount Added to Cost (the Markup)}}{\text{Cost}}$$

Consider an example from retailing. Suppose an item selling for $1.00 has an invoice cost of $0.60. The total markup is $0.40. The markup percentages would be calculated as follows:

$$\text{Markup Percentage on Selling Price} = \frac{\$0.40}{\$1.00} = 40\%$$

$$\text{Markup Percentage on Cost} = \frac{\$0.40}{\$0.60} = 67\%$$

To determine selling price when only cost and markup percentage on selling price are known, the following formula is utilized:

$$\text{Price} = \frac{\text{Cost in Dollars}}{100\% - \text{Markup Percentage on Selling Price}}$$

In the example cited above, price could be determined as $1.00:

$$\text{Price} = \frac{\$.60}{100\% - 40\%} = \frac{.60}{60\%} = \$1.00.$$

Similarly, the markup percentage can be converted from one basis (selling price or cost) to the other by using the following formula:

$$\frac{\text{Markup Percentage}}{\text{on Selling Price}} = \frac{\text{Markup Percentage on Cost}}{100\% + \text{Markup Percentage on Cost}}$$

$$\frac{\text{Markup Percentage}}{\text{on Cost}} = \frac{\text{Markup Percentage on Selling Price}}{100\% - \text{Markup Percentage on Selling Price}}$$

Again, using the data from the example above, the following conversions can be made:

$$\frac{\text{Markup Percentage on}}{\text{Selling Price}} = \frac{67\%}{100\% + 67\%} = \frac{67\%}{167\%} = 40\%$$

$$\frac{\text{Markup Percentage on}}{\text{Cost}} = \frac{40\%}{100\% - 40\%} = \frac{40\%}{60\%} = 67\%$$

Markdowns   A related pricing issue that is particularly important to retailers is markdowns. Markups are based partially on executive judgements about the prices consumers are likely to pay for a given product or service. If buyers refuse to pay the price, however, the marketer must take a **markdown**, a reduction in the price of the item. For purposes of internal control and analysis, the markdown percentage is computed as follows:

$$\text{Markdown Percentage} = \frac{\text{Markdown}}{\text{``Sale'' (New) Price}}$$

Suppose no one was willing to pay $1.00 for an item and the marketer decided to reduce the price to $.75. The markdown percentage would be:

$$\text{Markdown Percentage} = \frac{\$.25}{\$.75} = 33\frac{1}{3}\%$$

From a customer's viewpoint, this is only a 25% reduction, and is known as the "off-retail percentage." This is the percentage which should be quoted in advertisements. Markdowns are also used for evaluative purposes. For instance, department managers or buyers in a large department store could be evaluated partially on the basis of the average markdown percentage on the product lines for which they are responsible.

Turnover   All too often, traditional markup and markdown percentages lead to competitive inertia within an industry. Standard percentages are too frequently applied to all items in a given category regardless of factors such as demand.

A method for avoiding competitive inertia is to use flexible markups that vary with **stock turnover** — *the number of times the average inventory is sold annually*. The figure can be calculated by one of the following formulas. When inventory is recorded at retail:

$$\text{Stock Turnover} = \frac{\text{Sales}}{\text{Average Inventory}}$$

When inventory is recorded at cost:

$$\text{Stock Turnover} = \frac{\text{Cost of Goods Sold}}{\text{Average Inventory}}$$

Store A, with $100 000 in sales and an average inventory at $20 000 (at retail), would have a stock turnover of 5. Store B, with $200 000 in sales, a 40 percent markup rate, and an average inventory of $30 000 (at cost), would have a stock turnover of 4.

Store A	Store B
Stock Turnover $= \dfrac{\$100\ 000}{\$20\ 000} = 5$	$\$200\ 000$ Sales $-80\ 000$ Markup (40 percent) $\$120\ 000$ Cost of Goods Sold Stock Turnover $= \dfrac{\$120\ 000}{\$30\ 000} = 4$

While most marketers recognize the importance of turnover, they often use it more as a measure of sales effectiveness than as a pricing tool. However, it can be particularly useful in setting markup percentages if some consideration is given to consumer demand.

Figure 12-7 indicates the relationship between stock turnover and markup. Above-average turnover, such as for grocery products, are generally associated with relatively low markup percentages. On the other hand, higher markup percentages typically exist in such product lines as jewellery and furniture where relatively lower annual stock turnover is common and inventory and overhead costs must be covered through higher margins.

Figure 12-7   Relationship between Markup Percentage and Stock Turnover

Stock Turnover Rate in Relation to the Industry Average	Markup Percentage in Relation to the Industry Average	Product Example
High	Low	Soft Drinks
Average	Average	Motor Oil
Low	High	Sports Cars

Break-even Analysis   **Break-even analysis** is *a means of determining the number of products or services that must be sold at a given price in order to generate sufficient revenue to cover total costs.* Figure 12-8 shows calculation of the break-even point graphically. The total cost curve includes both fixed and variable segments, and total fixed cost is represented by a horizontal line. Average variable cost is assumed to be constant per unit as it was in the example used for incremental pricing.

The break-even point is the point at which total revenue (TR) just equals total cost (TC). It can be found by using the following formulas:

$$\text{Break-even Point (in Units)} = \frac{\text{Total Fixed Cost}}{\text{Per Unit Selling Price} - \text{Average variable cost}}$$

$$= \frac{\text{Total Fixed Cost}}{\text{Per Unit Contribution to Fixed Cost}}$$

$$\text{Break-even Point (in Dollars)} = \frac{\text{Total Fixed Cost}}{1 - \dfrac{\text{Variable Cost per Unit}}{\text{Selling Price}}}$$

In our earlier example, a selling price of $10 and an average variable cost of $5 resulted in a per unit contribution to fixed costs of $5. This figure can be divided into total fixed costs of $40 000 to obtain a break-even point of 8000 units, or $80 000 in total sales revenue:

$$\text{Break-even Point (in Units)} = \frac{\$40\ 000}{\$10 - \$5} = \frac{\$40\ 000}{\$5} = 8000 \text{ units}$$

$$\text{Break-even Point (in Dollars)} = \frac{\$40\ 000}{1 - \dfrac{\$5}{\$10}} = \frac{\$40\ 000}{0.5} = \$80\ 000$$

$$\text{Break-even Profit Point (in Dollars)} = \frac{\$40\ 000 + 10\% \text{ on Sales } (\$8000)}{1 - \dfrac{\$5}{\$10}} = \frac{\$48\ 000}{.5} = \$96\ 000$$

Break-even analysis is an effective tool for marketers in assessing the required sales in order to cover costs and achieve specified profit levels. It is easily understood by both marketing and nonmarketing executives and may assist in deciding whether required sales levels for a certain price are in fact realistic goals. Extending this analysis a bit further, a simple profit breakdown is also shown in the example. If a 10 percent profit on sales were desired, sales of $96 000 would be required. More data would be needed if a return on investment, or some other measure was used as a profitability target. However, it is not without shortcomings.

First, the model assumes that costs can be divided into fixed and variable categories. Some costs, such as salaries and advertising outlays, may be either fixed or variable depending upon the particular situation. In addition, the model assumes that per unit variable costs do not change at different levels of operation. However, these may vary as a result of quantity discounts, more efficient utilization of the work force, or other economies resulting from increased levels of production and sales. Finally, the basic break-even model does not consider demand. It is a cost-based model and does not directly address the crucial question of whether consumers will actually purchase the product at the specified price and in the required quantities to break even or to generate profits. The challenge of the marketer is to modify break-even analysis and the other cost-oriented approaches to pricing in order to introduce demand analysis. Pricing must be examined from the buyer's perspective. Such decisions cannot be made in a management vacuum in which only cost factors are considered.

Toward Realistic Pricing

Traditional economic theory considers both costs and demand in the determination of an equilibrium price. The dual elements of supply and demand are balanced at the point of equilibrium. In actual industry practice, however, most pricing approaches are largely cost-oriented. Since purely cost-oriented approaches to pricing violate the marketing concept, modifications are required in order to add demand analysis to the pricing decision.

Consumer research of such issues as degree of price elasticity, consumer price expectations, existence and size of specific market segments, and perceptions of strengths and weaknesses of substitute products is necessary for developing sales estimates at different prices. Since much of the resultant data involves perceptions, attitudes, and future expectations, such estimates are likely to be less precise than cost estimates.

The Dynamic Break-even Concept

In Figure 12-8, the break-even analysis was based upon the assumption of a constant $10 retail price regardless of quantity. What happens when different retail prices are considered? **Dynamic break-even analysis** *combines the traditional break-even analysis model with an evaluation of consumer demand.*

Figure 12-9 summarizes both the cost and revenue aspects of a number of alternative retail prices. The cost data are based upon the costs utilized earlier in the basic break-even model. The expected unit sales for each specified retail price are obtained from consumer research. The data in the first two columns of Figure 12-9 represent a demand schedule by indicating the number of units consumers are expected to purchase at each of a series of retail prices. This data

Figure 12-8   Break-even Chart

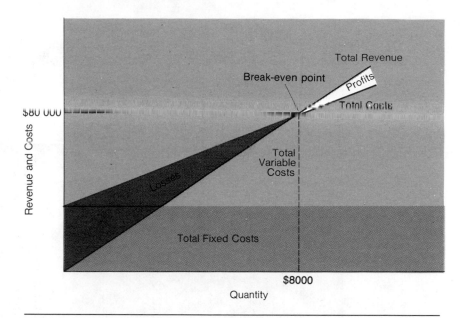

can be superimposed onto a break-even chart in order to identify the range of feasible prices for consideration by the marketing decision-maker. This is shown in Figure 12-10.

As Figure 12-10 indicates, the range of profitable prices exists from a low of approximately \$8 (TR_4) to a high of \$12 (TR_2), with a price of \$10 (TR_3) generating the greatest projected profits. Changing the retail price produces a new break-even point. At a relatively high \$14 retail price, the break-even point is 4445 units; at a \$10 retail price the break-even point is 8000 units; and at a \$6 price, 40 000 units must be sold in order to break even.

Figure 12-9   Revenue and Cost Data for Dynamic Break-even Analysis

	Revenues			Costs		
Price	Quantity Demanded	Total Revenue	Total Fixed Cost	Total Variable Cost	Total Cost	Total Profit (or Loss)
\$14	3 000	\$ 42 000	\$40 000	\$ 15 000	\$ 55 000	(\$13 000)
12	6 000	72 000	40 000	30 000	70 000	2 000
10	10 000	100 000	40 000	50 000	90 000	10 000
8	14 000	112 000	40 000	70 000	110 000	2 000
6	26 000	156 000	40 000	130 000	170 000	(14 000)

Figure 12-10   Dynamic Break-even Chart Reflecting Costs and Consumer Demand

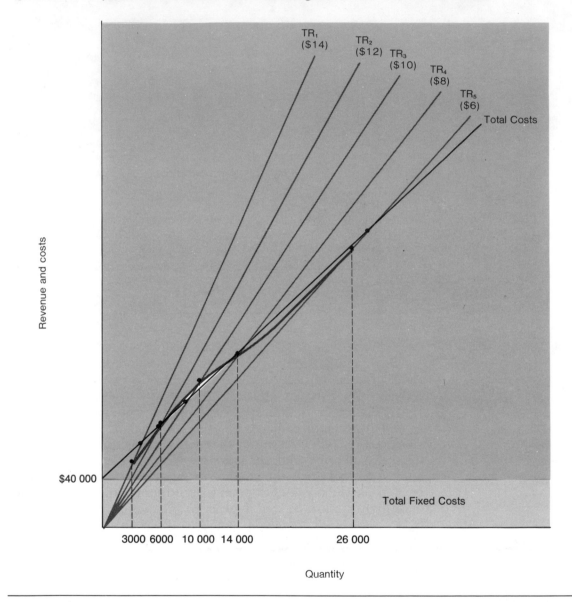

The contribution of dynamic break-even analysis is that it forces the pricing decision-maker to consider whether the consumer is likely to purchase the required number of units of a product or service that will achieve break-even at a given price. It demonstrates that a larger number of units sold does not necessarily produce added profits, since — other things equal — lower prices are necessary to stimulate added sales. Consequently, it necessitates careful consideration of both costs and consumer demand in determining the most appropriate price.

A Pricing Decision Procedure   A product which is new to the world, as opposed to being merely new to the company, passes through distinctive stages in its life cycle. The appropriate pricing policy is likely to be different at each stage.[13] Perhaps the most difficult task is establishing an initial price for the product. In later stages of the product life cycle, pricing is complicated enough, but strategic decisions hinge largely on decisions to meet or beat competition in various ways.

G. David Hughes has suggested a pricing procedure that is especially appropriate for new products but which can be used for new-to-the-company market entries as well (see Figure 12-11). It takes into account many of the points considered in this chapter.[14]

Establish the range of acceptable prices. The first step is to establish a price range that is consistent with corporate values, objectives, and policies. The pricing policies of top executives who are risk-takers may be different from those of risk-averters. The range of prices will be predicated on the company's desire to establish a discount image or a quality image. Similarly, a decision to use a prestige channel of distribution will determine channel discount structures, which in turn will be reflected in a final price.

Set price for a planned target market. As with virtually all marketing mix decisions, the pricing process has to be developed with a specific market target in mind. Given some estimate of the demand curve for the target segment, the price strategist attempts to identify the price that will maximize sales.

Estimate demand for the brand. This price is then positioned against competitive prices to determine expected market share. If this share is too small, the strategist will go back to the generic demand (i.e., primary demand, or those needs which can be met by a product category) and select a new price.

Estimate competitor's reactions. Once a price is selected which provides what seems to be an acceptable sales volume, the next task is to estimate how competitors will react. A very low price may cause a price war in an oligopoly. An exceptionally high price may attract lower priced competition. If either of these responses would destroy the basic marketing strategy, the strategist must go back and select a new price.

Consider public policy implications. Unfavourable reactions from the public may take many forms. Provincial or federal authorities may look on a given price strategy in a monopoly-type situation as unconscionable and therefore subject to legislation or regulation. Consumerists may regard a price as excessive and boycott all of the

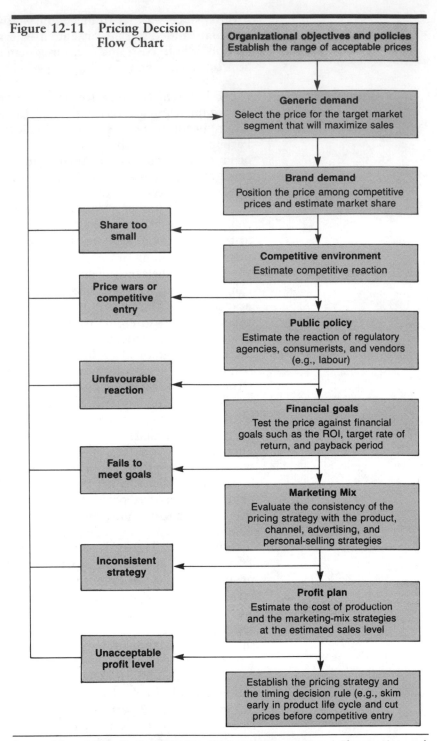

Figure 12-11   Pricing Decision Flow Chart

Organizational objectives and policies
Establish the range of acceptable prices

Generic demand
Select the price for the target market segment that will maximize sales

Brand demand
Position the price among competitive prices and estimate market share

Share too small

Competitive environment
Estimate competitive reaction

Price wars or competitive entry

Public policy
Estimate the reaction of regulatory agencies, consumerists, and vendors (e.g., labour)

Unfavourable reaction

Financial goals
Test the price against financial goals such as the ROI, target rate of return, and payback period

Fails to meet goals

Marketing Mix
Evaluate the consistency of the pricing strategy with the product, channel, advertising, and personal-selling strategies

Inconsistent strategy

Profit plan
Estimate the cost of production and the marketing-mix strategies at the estimated sales level

Unacceptable profit level

Establish the pricing strategy and the timing decision rule (e.g., skim early in product life cycle and cut prices before competitive entry

Source: Adapted from G. David Hughes, *Marketing Management: A Planning Approach* (Reading: Addison-Wesley Publishing Company, 1978), p. 325.

company's products. Labour unions may regard a price increase as an indication that the company can now afford to raise wages.

Test the price against financial goals. The next test is to see if the pricing strategy will meet financial goals such as return on investment (ROI), target rate of return on sales, or a payback period. Failure to meet financial goals sends the pricing strategist back to the generic-demand curve to select a new price for analysis. In actual practice, the strategist will probably have tested the price against the financial goals before proceeding to the positioning of the price among other brands, because rough calculations can be based on previous experience. In fact, it is desirable to make profit plans as early as the concept stage during new-product development. These plans can be continually updated as the product passes through the development stages.

Evaluate its congruence in the mix. The selected price must be evaluated in terms of the product, channel, advertising, and personal-selling strategies that will be used in the market segment in question. The role of price in the marketing mix should be specifically identified, and all elements of the mix must blend together. Any inconsistencies must be reconciled by altering the price or one of the other elements of the mix.

A low price is appropriate when the product category is at the mature stage in its cycle. A low price may also be appropriate when there is little promotion, the product is mass-produced, market coverage is intense, production is capital intensive, technological change is slow, the product is needed to complete the product line, few services are offered, the product is disposable, or the life cycle is short.[15]

Develop a profit plan. The cost of production and the cost of the marketing-mix strategy at the estimated sales level provide inputs for the profit plan. An inadequate profit may send the strategist back to the setting of a new price or to the reduction of the cost of other elements in the marketing mix.

Finalize actual price and timing. The last stage in the process is to establish the final price. This is done in light of the preceding steps, but it also takes into specific consideration the actual prices of competing products. For example, the profit plan calculation might indicate a price of $71.87, but the final price offered to the market might be $69.95. This might be chosen for psychological reasons (it sounds less expensive), or better to meet the prices of competitors. If a high-priced skimming strategy (described in Chapter 13) has been chosen, a timing decision should also be reached in order to be ready to cut prices when predetermined conditions occur.

Summary   Price—the exchange value of a good or service—is important because it regulates economic activity as well as determines the revenue to be received by an individual firm. As a marketing mix element, pricing is one of those grey areas where marketers struggle to develop a theory, technique, or rule of thumb on which they can depend. It is a complex variable because it contains both objective and subjective aspects. It is an area where precise decision-making tools and executive judgement meet.

Pricing objectives should be the natural consequence of overall organizational goals and more specific marketing goals. They can be classified into four major groupings: 1) profitability objectives, including profit maximization and target return; 2) volume objectives, including sales maximization and market share; 3) meeting competition objectives; and 4) prestige objectives.

Prices can be determined by theoretical or cost-oriented approaches. Economic theorists attempt to equate marginal revenue and marginal cost. Elasticity is an important element in price determination. The degree of consumer responsiveness to changes in price is affected directly by the availability of substitutes and inversely to the availability of complementary goods. It is also affected by whether a product or service is a necessity or a luxury, the portion of a person's budget being spent, and the time perspective under consideration.

Price determination in practice frequently emphasizes costs. Break-even analysis and the use of markups are essentially cost-plus approaches to pricing.

A more realistic approach to effective price decisions is to integrate both buyer demand and costs. Dynamic break-even analysis is a method for accomplishing this task.

CHAPTER 13

Managing the Pricing Function

1. To explain how pricing decisions are organized.

2. To describe how prices are quoted.

3. To identify the various pricing policy decisions that must be made by the marketer.

4. To compare skimming and penetration pricing.

5. To explain the relationship between price levels, advertising expenditures, and profitability.

6. To contrast negotiated prices and competitive bidding.

7. To explain the importance of transfer pricing.

8. To describe pricing in the public sector.

The Conceptual Framework

Chapter 12 introduced the concept of price and its role in the economic system and in marketing strategy. It concluded with a discussion of useful decision models for pricing strategy. There are, however, several other important aspects of pricing.

This chapter will consider who should be responsible for the pricing decision and how prices are quoted, and will discuss various aspects of pricing policies. Finally, other pricing practices such as negotiated prices, competitive bidding, and the pricing of public services are considered.

Organization for Pricing Decisions

In translating pricing objectives into pricing decisions, there are two major steps to follow. First some person or group must be assigned responsibility for making pricing decisions and administering the pricing structure. Then that person or group must set the overall pricing structure — that is, the selected price and the appropriate discounts for channel members as well as for various quantities and for geographic and promotional considerations.

A recent survey of marketing executives found that the people or groups most commonly chosen to *set* price structures were 1) a pricing committee composed of top executives, 2) the president of the company, and 3) the chief marketing officer. According to the same survey, the pricing structure is *administered* most often by marketers. As Figure 13-1 indicates, the chief marketing officer was the responsible person in 51 percent of the firms surveyed. In all, marketers administered the pricing structure in over 68 percent of

Figure 13-1   Executives Responsible for Setting and Administering Price Structures

Executives Responsible for Setting Price Structures

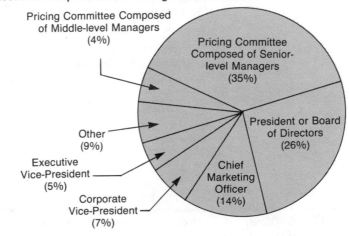

Executives Responsible for Administering Price Structures

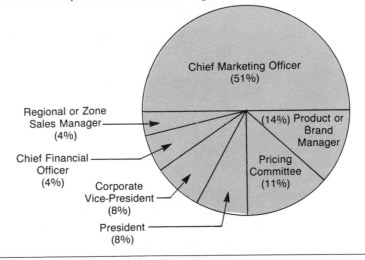

the companies, a result that is consistent with industry's attempt to implement the marketing concept.

Price Quotations

How prices are quoted depends on many factors, such as cost structures, traditional practice in the particular industry, and the policies of individual firms. In this section we shall examine the reasoning and methodology behind price quotations.

The basis upon which most price structures is built is the **list price**, *the rate normally quoted to potential buyers.* List price is usually determined by one or a combination of the methods discussed in Chapter 12. The sticker prices on new automobiles are good examples. They show the list price for the basic model, then add the list price for the options that have been included.

Discounts, Allowances, and Rebates

The amount that a consumer pays — the **market price** — may or may not be the same as the list price. In some cases discounts or allowances reduce the list price. List price is often used as the starting point from which discounts that set the market price are derived. Discounts can be classified as cash, quantity, or trade.

Cash discounts are those *reductions in price that are given for prompt payment of a bill.* They are probably the most commonly used variety. Cash discounts usually specify an exact time period, such as "2/10, net 30." This would mean that the bill is due within 30 days, but if it is paid in 10 days, the customer may subtract 2 percent from the amount due. Cash discounts have become a traditional pricing practice in many industries. They are legal provided that they are granted all customers on the same terms. Such discounts were originally instituted to improve the liquidity position of sellers, lower bad-debt losses, and reduce the expenses associated with the collection of bills. Whether these advantages outweigh the relatively high cost of capital involved in cash discounts depends upon the buyer's need for liquidity as well as alternative sources (and costs) of funds.

Trade discounts, which are also called *functional discounts*, are *payments to channel members or buyers for performing some marketing function normally required of the manufacturer.* These are legitimate as long as all buyers in the same category, such as wholesalers and retailers, receive the same discount privilege. Trade discounts were initially based on the operating expenses of each trade category, but have now become more of a matter of custom in some industries. An example of a trade discount would be "40 percent, 10 percent off list price" for wholesalers. In other words, the wholesaler passes the 40 percent on to his or her customers (retailers) and keeps the 10 percent discount as payment for activities such as storing and transporting. The price to the wholesaler on a $100 000 order would be $54 000 ($100 000 less 40% = $60 000 less 10%).

Quantity discounts are *price reductions granted because of large purchases*. These discounts are justified on the grounds that large-volume purchases reduce selling expenses and may shift a part of the storing, transporting, and financing functions to the buyer. Quantity discounts are lawful provided they are offered on the same basis to all customers.

Figure 13-2   A Noncumulative Quantity Discount Schedule

Units Purchased	Price
1	List price
2–5	List price less 10 percent
6–10	List price less 20 percent
over 10	List price less 25 percent

Quantity discounts may be either noncumulative or cumulative. *Noncumulative quantity discounts* are one-time reductions in list price. For instance, a firm might offer the discount schedule in Figure 13-2. *Cumulative quantity discounts* are reductions determined by purchases over a stated time period. Annual purchases of $25 000 might entitle the buyer to an 8 percent rebate, while purchases exceeding $50 000 would mean a 15 percent refund. These reductions are really patronage discounts since they tend to bind the customer to one source of supply.

Allowances are similar to discounts in that they are deductions from the price the purchaser must pay. The major categories of allowances are trade-ins and promotional allowances. **Trade-ins** are often used in the sale of durable goods such as automobiles. They *permit a reduction without altering the basic list price* by deducting from the item's price an amount for the customer's old item that is being replaced. **Promotional allowances** are *attempts to integrate promotional strategy in the channel*. For example, manufacturers often provide advertising and sales-support allowances for other channel members. Automobile manufacturers have offered allowances to retail dealers several times in recent years to permit dealers to lower prices while maintaining their margins.

Rebates are *refunds by the seller of a portion of the purchase price*. They have been used most prominently by automobile manufacturers eager to move models during periods of slow sales. Wardair has also used rebates. Wardair promised warm weather for its Florida charter customers and backed the promise with a $5 rebate for each day of less than 22°C weather.[1] Manufacturers' rebates are sometimes used to stimulate sales of small appliances such as coffee brewers.

Geographic Considerations   Geographic considerations are important in pricing when the shipment of heavy, bulky, low unit-cost materials is involved. Prices may be quoted with either the buyer or seller paying all transportation charges or with some type of expense sharing.

> The way in which this problem is handled can greatly influence the success of a firm's marketing program by helping to determine the scope of the geographic market area the firm is able to serve, the vulnerability of the firm to price competition in areas located near its production facilities, the net margins earned on individual sales of the product, the ability of the firm to control or influence resale prices of distributors, and how difficult it is for salesmen in the field to quote accurate prices and delivery terms to their potential customers.[2]

The seller has several alternatives in handling transportation costs.

F.O.B. plant or *F.O.B. origin* pricing provides a price that does not include any shipping charges. *The buyer must pay all the freight charges.* The seller pays only the cost of loading the merchandise aboard the carrier selected by the buyer. The abbreviation F.O.B. means *Free on Board*. Legal title and responsibility pass to the buyer once the purchase is loaded and a receipt is obtained from the representative of the common carrier.

Prices may also be shown as F.O.B. origin — freight allowed. *The seller permits the buyer to subtract transportation expenses from the bill.* The amount the seller receives varies with the freight charges charged against the invoice. This alternative, called **freight absorption**, is commonly used by firms with high fixed costs (who need to maintain high volume) because it permits a considerable expansion of their market, since a competitive price is quoted regardless of shipping expenses.

The same price (including transportation expenses) is quoted to all buyers when a **uniform delivered price** is the firm's policy. Such pricing is the exact opposite of F.O.B. prices. This system is often compared to the pricing of a first-class letter, which is the same across the country. Hence, it is sometimes called *postage-stamp pricing*. The price that is quoted includes an *average* transportation charge per customer, which means that distant customers are actually paying a lesser share of selling costs while customers near the supply source pay what is known as *phantom freight* (the average transporation charge exceeds the actual cost of shipping).

In **zone pricing**, which is simply a modification of a uniform delivered pricing system, *the market is divided into different zones and a price is established within each*. Canadian parcel post rates depend upon zone pricing. The primary advantage of this pricing policy is that it is easy to administer and enables the seller to be more competitive in distant markets. Figure 13-3 shows how a marketer in Winnipeg might divide its market into geographic segments. All customers in zone 1 would be charged $10 per unit freight, while more distant customers would pay freight costs based on the zone in which they are located.

Figure 13-3   Zone Pricing for a Winnipeg Firm

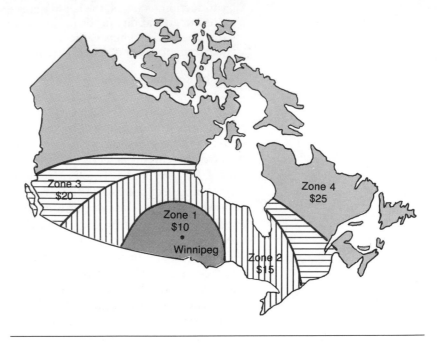

Pricing Policies

Pricing policies are an important ingredient in the firm's total image. They provide the overall framework and consistency needed in pricing decisions. A **pricing policy** is a *general guideline based upon pricing objectives that is intended for use in specific pricing decisions.* Decisions concerning price structure generally tend to be more technical in nature than those concerning price policies. Price structure decisions take the selected price policy as a given, and specify the discount structure details. Price policies have a greater strategic importance, particularly in relation to competitive considerations. They are the bases on which pricing decisions are made.

Many businesses would be well advised to spend more managerial effort in the establishment and periodic review of their pricing policies. Some years ago, a top executive aptly referred to the study and determination of prices as "creative pricing":

Few businessmen, I am sure, would deny that every well-run business should have a price policy. We give a great deal of thought and planning to our engineering, manufacturing, advertising, and sales promotion policies. Certainly the same kind of careful study and planning should be directed toward the formulation of those price policies that will best serve the various long-run objectives of our businesses. I call pricing based on such a well-formulated policy "creative pricing." There are probably better ways of saying it, but this term comes pretty close to describing what I believe to be the true function of pricing.[3]

Pricing policies must deal with varied competitive situations. The type of policy is dependent upon the environment within which the pricing decision must be made. The types of policies to be considered are new-product pricing, price flexibility, relative price levels, price lining, and promotional prices. They should all be arrived at through the use of a pricing procedure similar to those described in Chapter 12.

Psychological Pricing

Psychological pricing is based upon *the belief that certain prices or price ranges are more appealing to buyers than others.* There is, however, no consistent research foundation for such thinking. Studies often report mixed findings. Prestige pricing, mentioned in Chapter 12, is one of many forms of psychological pricing.

Odd pricing is a good example of the application of psychological pricing. *Prices are set ending in numbers not commonly used for price quotations.* A price of $16.99 is assumed to be more appealing than $17 (supposedly because it is a lower figure).

Originally odd pricing was used to force clerks to make change, thus serving as a cash control device within the firm. Now it has become a customary feature of contemporary price quotations. For instance, one discounter uses prices ending in 3 and 7 rather than 5, 8, or 9, because of a belief that customers regard price tags of $5.95, $6.98, $7.99 as *regular* retail prices, while $5.97 and $6.93 are considered *discount* prices.

Unit Pricing

Consumer advocates have often pointed out the difficulty of comparing consumer products that are available in different-size packages or containers. Is an 800 g can selling for 75 cents a better buy than two 450 g cans priced at 81 cents or another brand that sells three 450 g cans for 89 cents? The critics argue that there should be a common way to price consumer products.

Unit pricing is a response to this problem. Under unit pricing all prices are stated *in terms of some recognized unit of measurement* (such as grams and litres) *or a standard numerical count.* There has been considerable discussion about legislating mandatory unit pricing. The Consumers' Association of Canada has endorsed unit pricing, and many of the major food chains have adopted it.[4]

Some supermarket chains have come to regard the adoption of unit pricing as a competitive tool upon which to base extensive advertising. However, unit pricing has not been particularly effective in improving the shopping habits of the urban poor. Others argue that unit pricing significantly increases retail operating costs.

The real question, of course, is whether unit pricing improves consumer decisions. One study found that the availability of unit prices resulted in consumer savings and that retailers also benefitted when unit pricing led to greater purchases of store brands. The study concluded that unit pricing was valuable to both buyer and seller and that it merited full-scale usage.[5] Unit pricing is a major pricing policy issue that must be faced by many firms.

New-Product Pricing

The pricing of new products is a crucial question for marketers. The initial price that is quoted for an item may determine whether or not the product will eventually be accepted in the marketplace. The initial price also may affect the amount of competition that will emerge.

Consider the options available to a company pricing a new product. While many choose to price at the *level of comparable products*, some select other alternatives (see Figure 13-4). A **skimming pricing** policy chooses *a relatively high entry price*. The name is derived from the expression "skimming the cream." One purpose of this strategy is to allow the firm to recover its development costs quickly. The assumption is that competition will eventually drive the price to a lower level, as was the case, for example, with electric toothbrushes.

A skimming policy, therefore, attempts to maximize the revenue received from the sale of a new product before the entry of competition. Ballpoint pens were introduced shortly after World War II at a price of about $20. Today the best-selling ballpoint pens are priced at less than $1. Other examples of products that have been introduced using a skimming policy include television sets, Polaroid cameras, videocassette recorders, home computers, and pocket calculators. Subsequent price reductions allowed the marketers of these products to appeal to additional market segments that are more price sensitive.

A skimming strategy permits the marketer to control demand in the introductory stages of the product's life cycle and to adjust its productive capacity to match demand. A danger of low initial price for a new product is that demand may outstrip the firm's production capacity, resulting in consumer and intermediary complaints and possibly permanent damage to the product's image. Excess demand occasionally results in poor quality products as the firm strives to

Figure 13-4 The Market for Product X

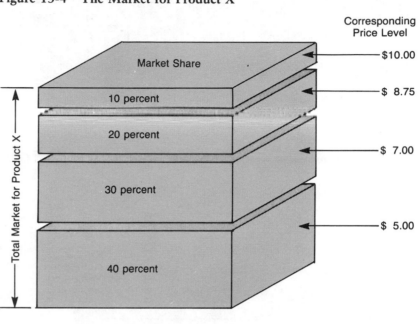

satisfy consumer desires with inadequate production facilities.

During the late growth and early maturity stages of the product life cycle the price is reduced for two reasons: 1) the pressure of competition and 2) the desire to expand the product's market. Figure 13-4 shows that 10 percent of the market for Product X would buy the item at $10, while another 20 percent would buy at $8.75. Successive price declines will expand the firm's market as well as meet new competition.

A skimming policy has one chief disadvantage: it attracts competition. Potential competitors, who see the innovating firms make large returns, also enter the market. This forces the price even lower than where it might be under a sequential skimming procedure. However if a firm has patent protection — as Polaroid had — or a proprietary ability to exclude competition, it may use a skimming policy for a relatively long period. Figure 13-5 indicates that 14.4 percent of the respondents in a recent pricing study used a skimming policy. Skimming also appears to be more common in industrial markets than in consumer markets.

Penetration pricing is the opposite policy in new-product pricing. It results in *an entry price for a product lower than what is believed to be the long-term price.* The pricing study shown in Figure 13-5

Figure 13-5   Use of New-Product Pricing Strategies

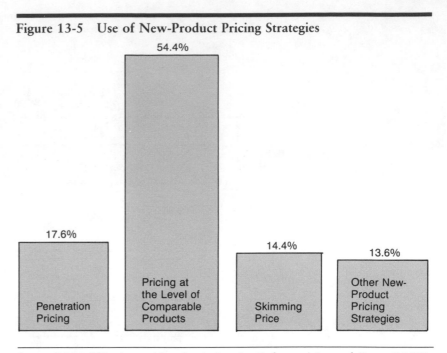

suggests that penetration pricing is used more often in consumer markets. Soaps and toothpastes are often good examples of this kind of pricing.

The premise is that an initially lower price will help secure market acceptance. Since the firm later intends to increase the price, brand popularity is crucial to the success of a penetration policy. One advantage of such a policy is that it discourages competition from entering since the prevailing low price does not suggest the attractive returns associated with a skimming policy.

Penetration pricing is likely to be used in instances where demand for the new product or service is highly elastic and large numbers of consumers are highly price sensitive. It is also likely to be used in instances where large-scale operations and long production runs result in substantial reductions in production and marketing costs. Finally, penetration pricing may be appropriate in instances where the new product is likely to attract strong competitors when it is introduced. Such a strategy may allow it to reach the mass market quickly and capture a large share of the market before the entry by competitors.

The key decision, of course, is when to move the price to its intended level. Consumers tend to resist price increases; therefore, correct timing is essential. The solution depends upon the degree of brand loyalty that has been achieved. Brand loyalty must be at the point where a price increase would not cause a disproportionate decrease in customers. A series of modest price changes, rather than a single large hike, also can retain customers.

A firm may, of course, decide to use neither a skimming nor a penetration price. It may try to price a new product at the point where it is intended to sell in the long run. All three new-product pricing strategies are common, but it can be seen from Figure 13-5 that this last strategy was chosen in 54 percent of new-product pricing situations.

Most Canadian Retailers Follow a One-Price Policy

Source: Reprinted by permission of Newspaper Enterprise Association.

Price Flexibility   Marketing executives must also determine company policy with respect to **flexible pricing**. Is the firm going to have just one price or pursue *a variable price policy in the market*? As a generalization, *one-price policies* characterize situations where mass selling is employed, and *variable pricing* is more common where individual bargaining typifies market transactions, for example, the purchase of a car.

A one-price policy is common in Canadian retailing since it facilitates mass merchandising. For the most part, once the price is set, the manager can direct his or her attention to other aspects of the marketing mix. Flexible prices, by contrast, are found more in wholesaling and industrial markets. This does not mean that price flexibility exists only in manufacturing industries. A study of the retail home appliance market concluded that persons who had purchased identical products from the same dealer had often paid different prices for them. The primary reasons for the differences were customer knowledge and bargaining strength.[6]

While variable pricing has the advantage of flexibility in selling situations, it may result in conflict with the Combines Act provisions. It may also lead to retaliatory pricing on the part of competitors, and it is not well received by those who have paid the higher prices.

Relative Price Levels

Another important pricing policy decision concerns the relative price level. Are the firm's prices to be set above, below, or at the prevailing market price? In economic theory this question would be answered by supply and demand analysis. However, from a practical viewpoint, marketing managers *administer* prices. In other words, cost-oriented pricing allows them the option of subjectively setting the markup percentages. Chapter 12 provided a framework for determining markups, but the decision-maker must still develop a basic policy in regard to relative price levels.

Following the competition is one method of negating the price variable in marketing strategy, since it forces competition to concentrate on other factors. Some firms choose to price below or above competition. These decisions are usually based on a firm's cost structure, overall marketing strategy, and pricing objectives.

Price Lining

Most companies sell a varied line of products. An effective pricing strategy should consider the relationship among the firm's products rather than viewing each in isolation. Specifically, **price lining** is *the practice of marketing merchandise at a limited number of prices*. For example, a clothier might have a $150 line of men's suits and a $225 line. Price lining is used extensively in retail selling; the old five-and-ten-cent stores were run this way. It can be an advantage to both retailer and customer. Customers can choose the price range they wish to pay, then concentrate on all the other variables, such as colour, style, and material. The retailer can purchase and offer specific lines rather than a more generalized assortment.

Price lining requires that one identify the market segment or segments to which the firm is appealing. For example, "Samsonite sees its market not as all luggage, but as the 'medium-priced, hard-side' portion of the luggage trade."[7] The firm must decide how to *line* its product prices. A dress manufacturer might have lines priced at $39.95, $59.95, and $89.95. Price lining not only simplifies the administration of the pricing structure, but also alleviates the confusion of a situation where all products are priced separately. Price lining is really a combined product/price strategy.

One problem with a price-line decision is that once it is made, retailers and manufacturers have difficulty in adjusting it. Rising costs, therefore, put the seller in the position of either changing the price lines, with the resulting confusion, or reducing costs by production adjustments, which opens the firm to the complaint that "XYZ Company's merchandise certainly isn't what it used to be!"

Promotional Prices

A **promotional price** is *a lower-than-normal price used as an ingredient in a firm's selling strategy.* In some cases promotional prices are recurrent, such as the annual shoe store sale: "Buy one pair of shoes, get the second for one cent." Or a new pizza restaurant may have an opening special to attract customers. In other situations a firm may introduce a promotional model or brand to allow it to compete in another market.

Most promotional pricing is done at the retail level. One type is loss leaders, *goods priced below cost to attract customers* who, the retailer hopes, will then buy other regularly priced merchandise. The use of loss leaders can be effective.

> Probably one of the best innovators of this pricing method was Cal Mayne. He was one of the first men to systematically price specials and to evaluate their effect on gross margins and sales. Mayne increased sales substantially by featuring coffee, butter, and margarine at 10 percent below cost. Ten other demand items were priced competitively and at a loss when necessary to undersell competition. Still another group of so-called secondary demand items were priced in line with competition. Mayne based his pricing policy on the theory that a customer can only remember about 30 prices. Keep prices down on these items and the customer will stay with you.[8]

The ethical or moral implications of this practice are not being considered here. Some studies have indeed reported considerable price confusion on the part of consumers. One study of consumer price recall reported that average shoppers misquoted the price they last paid for coffee by over 12 percent, toothpaste by over 20 percent, and green beans by 24 percent. While some people hit the prices exactly, others missed by several hundred percent.[9]

Three potential pitfalls should be considered when one faces a promotional pricing decision:

1. The Combines Investigation Act may prohibit some types of promotional pricing practices. (See Chapter 2.)
2. Some consumers are influenced little by price appeals, so promotional pricing will have little effect on them.[10]
3. Continuous use of an artificially low rate may result in it being accepted as customary for the product. For example, poultry, which was used as a loss leader during the 1930s and 1940s, later suffered from this phenomenon.

The Price–Quality Concept

One of the most researched aspects of pricing is the relationship between price and the consumer's perception of the product's quality. In the absence of other cues, price is an important indication for the consumer in the perception of the product's quality.[11]

The higher the price, the better the buyer believes the quality of the product to be. One study asked 400 people what terms they associated with the word *expensive*. Two-thirds of the replies were related to high quality, such as *best* and *superior*.[12] The relationship between price and perceived quality is a well-documented fact in contemporary marketing.

Probably the most useful concept in explaining price–quality relationships is the idea of **price limits**. It is argued that consumers have *limits within which product quality perception varies directly with price*. A price below the lower limit is regarded as too cheap, while one above the higher limit means it is too expensive. Most consumers do tend to set an acceptable price range when purchasing goods and services. The range, of course, varies, depending upon consumers' socio-economic characteristics and buying dispositions. Consumers, nonetheless, should be aware that price is not necessarily an indicator of quality. Alberta Consumer and Corporate Affairs summarized seven price-quality research studies, six covering *Consumer Reports* analyses of 932 products between 1940 and 1977, and one for 43 products tested by *Canadian Consumer* between 1973 and 1977. It found that while there was a positive relationship between price and quality, the correlation was low (Spearman rank correlation = .25). In addition, about 25 percent of products tested had a negative price-quality relation. That is, products ranked lower in performance had higher prices than products deemed superior by the Canadian and U.S. consumer testing organizations.[13]

Negotiated Prices and Competitive Bidding

Many situations involving government and industrial procurement are not characterized by set prices, particularly for nonrecurring purchases such as a defence system for the armed forces. Markets such as these are growing at a fast pace. Governmental units now spend nearly half of Canada's GNP!

Competitive bidding is a process by which buyers request potential suppliers to make price quotations on a proposed purchase or contract. *Specifications* give a description of the item (or job) that the government or industrial firm wishes to acquire. One of the most important tasks in modern purchasing management is to describe adequately what the organization seeks to buy. This generally requires the assistance of the firm's technical personnel, such as engineers, designers, and chemists.

Competitive bidding strategy should employ the concept of *expected net profit*, which can be stated as:

$$\text{Expected Net Profit} = P\,(\text{Bid} - \text{Costs})$$

where P = the probability of the buyer accepting the bid.

Consider the following example. A firm is contemplating the submission of a bid for a job that is estimated to cost $23 000. One executive has proposed a bid of $60 000; another, $50 000. It is estimated that there is a 40 percent chance of the buyer accepting bid 1 ($60 000) and a 60 percent chance that bid 2 ($50 000) will be accepted. The expected net profit formula indicates that bid 2 would be best since its expected net profit is the higher.

Bid 1
$$ENP = 0.40 (\$60\ 000 - \$23\ 000)$$
$$= 0.40 (\$37\ 000)$$
$$= \$14\ 800$$

Bid 2
$$ENP = 0.60 (\$50\ 000 - \$23\ 000)$$
$$= 0.60 (\$27\ 000)$$
$$= \$16\ 200$$

The most difficult task in applying this concept is in the estimation of the probability as to the likelihood a certain bid will be accepted. But this is not a valid reason for failing to quantify one's estimate. Prior experience can often provide the foundation for such estimates.

In some cases industrial and governmental purchasers use *negotiated contracts* instead of inviting competitive bidding for a project. In these situations, the terms of the contract are set through talks between the buyer and a seller. Where there is only one available supplier or where contracts require extensive research and development work, negotiated contracts are likely to be employed.

Some provincial and local governments permit their agencies to negotiate purchases under a certain limit, say, $500 or $1000. This policy is an attempt to reduce cost since obtaining bids for relatively minor purchases is expensive and there is little prospect of large savings to the agency involved.

The fear that inflation may have unknown effects on the economic viability of prices has become a major deterrent to companies bidding for or negotiating contracts. One response has been to include an **escalator clause** that allows the seller *to adjust the final price based upon changes in the costs of the product's ingredients between the placement of the order and the completion of construction or delivery of the product.* Such clauses typically base the adjustment calculation on the cost-of-living index or a similar indicator. While an estimated one-third of all industrial marketers use escalator clauses in some of their bids, they are most commonly used with major projects involving long time periods and complex operations.

The Transfer Pricing Problem

One pricing problem peculiar to large-scale enterprises is that of determining an internal **transfer price** — that is, *the price for sending goods from one company profit centre to another.* As a company expands, it usually needs to decentralize management. Profit centres are then set up as a control device in the new decentralized operation. **Profit centres** are *any part of the organization to which revenue and controllable costs can be assigned, such as a department.*

In large companies the centres can secure many of their resource requirements from within the corporate structure. The pricing problem becomes what rate should Profit Centre A (maintenance department) charge Profit Centre B (sales department) for the cleaning compound used on B's floors? Should the price be the same as it would be if A did the work for an outside party? Should B receive a discount? The answer to these questions depends upon the philosophy of the firm involved.

The transfer pricing dilemma is an example of the variations that a firm's pricing policy must deal with. Consider the case of UDC-Europe, a Universal Data Corporation subsidiary that itself has 10 subsidiaries. Each of the 10 is organized on a geographic basis, and each is treated as a separate profit centre. Intercompany transfer prices are set at the annual budget meeting. Special situations, like unexpected volume, are handled through negotiations by the subsidiary managers. If complex tax problems arise, UDC-Europe's top management may set the transfer price.[14]

Pricing in the Public Sector

The pricing of public services has also become an interesting, and sometimes troublesome, aspect of contemporary marketing.

Traditionally, government services either were very low-cost or were priced using the full-cost approach: users paid all costs associated with the service. In more recent years there has been a tendency to move toward incremental or marginal pricing, which considers only those expenses specifically associated with a particular activity. However, it is often difficult to determine the costs that should be assigned to a particular activity or service. Governmental accounting problems are often more complex than those of private enterprise.

Another problem in pricing public services is that taxes act as an *indirect* price of a public service. Someone must decide the relative relationship between the direct and indirect prices of such a service. A shift toward indirect tax charges (where an income or earnings tax exists) is generally a movement toward charging on the *ability-to-pay* rather than the *use* principle.

The pricing of any public service involves a basic policy decision as to whether the price is an instrument to recover costs or a technique for accomplishing some other social or civic objective. For example, public health services may be priced near zero so as to encourage their use. On the other hand, parking fines in some cities are high so as to discourage use of private automobiles in the central business district. Pricing decisions in the public sector are difficult because political and social considerations often outweigh the economic aspects.

Summary The main elements to consider in setting a pricing strategy are the organization for pricing decisions, pricing policies, price-quality relationships, negotiated prices, competitive bidding, transfer pricing, and pricing in the public sector. Methods for quoting prices depend on factors such as cost structures, traditional practices in a particular industry, and politics of individual firms. Prices quoted can involve list prices, market prices, cash discounts, trade discounts, quantity discounts, and allowances such as trade-ins, promotional allowances, and rebates.

Shipping costs often figure heavily in the pricing of goods. A number of alternatives exist for dealing with these costs: F.O.B. plant, when the price does not include any shipping charges; freight absorption, when the buyer can deduct transportation expenses from the bill; uniform delivered price, when the same price — including shipping expenses—is charged to all buyers; and zone pricing, when a set price exists within each region.

Pricing policies vary among firms. Among the most common are psychological pricing; unit pricing; new-product pricing, which includes skimming pricing and penetration pricing; price flexibility; relative pricing; price lining; and promotional pricing.

The relationship between price and consumer perception of quality has been the subject of much research. A well-known and accepted concept is that of price limits — limits within which the perception of product quality varies directly with price.

Sometimes, prices are negotiated through competitive bidding, a situation in which several buyers quote prices on the same service or good. At other times, prices depend on negotiated contracts, a situation in which the terms of the contract are set through talks between a particular buyer and seller.

A phenomenon of large corporations is transfer pricing, in which a company sets prices for transferring goods or services from one company profit centre to another.

The pricing of public services has become a troublesome aspect of marketing. It involves decisions on whether the price of a public service serves as an instrument to recover costs or as a technique for accomplishing some other social or civic purpose.

6   6   6   6   6   6   6

6   6   6   6   6   6   6

6   6   6   6   6   6   6

6   6   6   6   6   6   6

6   6   6   6   6   6   6

6   6   6   6   6   6   6

6   6   6   6   6   6   6

6   6   6   6   6   6   6

6   6   6   6   6   6   6

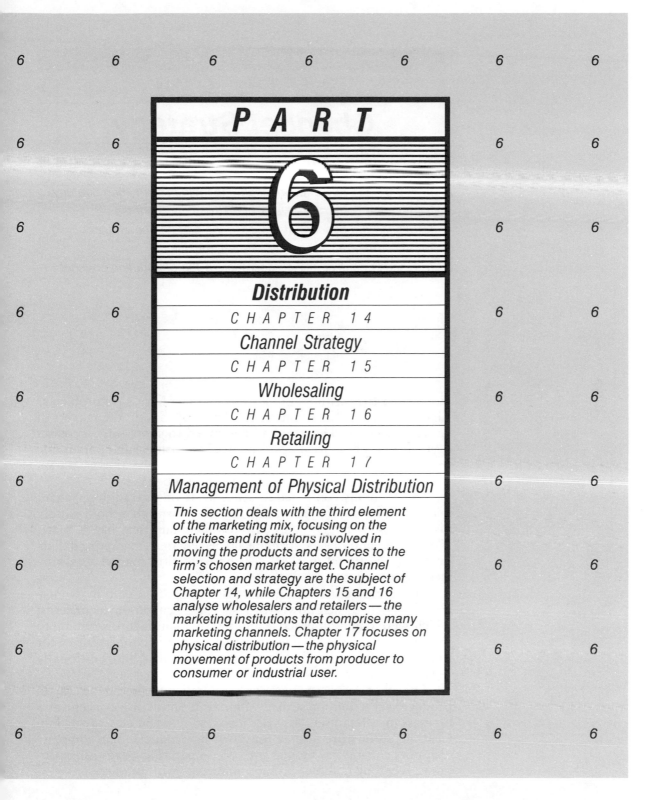

P A R T

6

Distribution

CHAPTER 14

Channel Strategy

CHAPTER 15

Wholesaling

CHAPTER 16

Retailing

CHAPTER 17

Management of Physical Distribution

This section deals with the third element of the marketing mix, focusing on the activities and institutions involved in moving the products and services to the firm's chosen market target. Channel selection and strategy are the subject of Chapter 14, while Chapters 15 and 16 analyse wholesalers and retailers — the marketing institutions that comprise many marketing channels. Chapter 17 focuses on physical distribution — the physical movement of products from producer to consumer or industrial user.

CHAPTER 14

Channel Strategy

1. To relate channel strategy to the other variables of the marketing mix.
2. To explain the role of distribution channels in marketing strategy.
3. To describe the various types of distribution channels.
4. To explain the concept of power in the distribution channel.
5. To outline the major channel strategy decisions.
6. To discuss conflict and co-operation in the distribution channel

How can a firm with an 80 percent market share have problems? That was exactly the situation for Binney & Smith, the makers of Crayola crayons. The firm had continued to show sales increases over the years because of a strong market position and population growth. Binney & Smith remained complacent even after its market target — children — began to decline in numbers.

The company continued to concentrate on its traditional channel — selling to the education market through school-supply distributors. It largely ignored mass merchandisers like K-mart, Woolworth, and Zellers, spending 60 percent of its marketing dollars on their traditional market. Yet the education market was only yielding 30 percent of sales.

The manufacturer acquired a poor reputation with mass merchandisers. It turned down requests for extended payment terms which were common practice among toy manufacturers selling to these large retailers. In addition, promotions were timed wrong for the consumer market because Binney & Smith had traditionally regarded its product as nonseasonal.

Since then, new management has drastically altered the crayon producer's distribution strategy. Binney & Smith now concentrates on mass merchandisers. Its sales force has distributed Crayola Fun Centres, an in-store display for 37 of its products. The company also puts substantial monies into a co-operating advertising program, whereby it shares promotional costs with retailers.

The success of their new distribution strategy is quite evident. Their plant is running three shifts a day. In fact, the company has decided to expand its capacity.

The Conceptual ***Framework***	Basic channel strategy — such as the decisions reached by Binney & Smith — is the starting point for a discussion of the distribution function and its role in the marketing mix. This chapter covers such basic issues as the role and types of distribution channels; power in the distribution channel; channel strategy decisions; and conflict and co-operation in the channel of distribution. Chapters 15 and 16 deal with wholesaling and retailing, the marketing institutions in the distribution channel. Chapter 17 ends Part 6 with a discussion of physical distribution. The starting point of this section is to look at what marketers call distribution channels.

Carson luggage is made in Ottawa, Staedtler pens and erasers come from Germany, plywood is produced in British Columbia, and Timex watches are assembled in Toronto. All are sold throughout Canada. In each case, some method must be devised to bridge the gap between producer and consumer. Distribution channels provide the purchaser with a convenient means of obtaining the products that he or she wishes to buy. **Distribution channels** (also called **marketing channels**) are *the paths goods — and title to these goods —follow from producer to consumer.*[1] Specifically, the term *channels* refers to the various marketing institutions and the interrelationships responsible for the flow of goods and services from producer to consumer or industrial user. Intermediaries are the marketing institutions in the distribution channel. A **marketing intermediary**, or **middleman**, is *a business firm operating between the producer and the consumer or industrial purchaser.* The term therefore *includes both wholesalers and retailers.*

Wholesaling is *the activities of persons or firms who sell to retailers, other wholesalers, and industrial users but not significant amounts to ultimate consumers.* The terms *jobber* and *distributor* are considered synonymous with wholesaler in this book.

Confusion can result from the practices of some firms that operate both wholesaling and retailing operations. Sporting goods stores, for example, often maintain a wholesaling operation in marketing a line of goods to high schools and colleges as well as operating retail stores. For the purposes of this book, we will treat such operations as two separate institutions.

A second source of confusion is the misleading practice of some retailers who claim to be wholesalers. Such stores may actually sell at wholesale prices and can validly claim to do so. However, *stores that sell products purchased by individuals for their own use and not for resale* are by definition **retailers**, not wholesalers.

The Role of Distribution Channels in Marketing Strategy

Distribution channels play a key role in marketing strategy since they provide the means by which goods and services are conveyed from their producers to consumers and users. The importance of distribution channels can be explained in terms of the utility that is created and the functions that are performed.

Utility Created by Marketing Channels

Marketing channels create three types of utility: time, place, and ownership (or possession). *Time* utility is created when marketing channels have products and services available for sale when the consumer wants to purchase them. *Place* utility is created when products and services are available where consumers want to buy them. *Ownership* utility is created when title to the goods passes from the manufacturer or intermediary channel member to the purchaser.

Swimwear provides a good illustration of how the distribution channel can create time utility. Swimwear for the coming spring and summer has already been produced in the months of December and January and is en route to retail stores throughout the nation. Swimwear manufacturers' success or failure depends on consumer reactions to new colours, styles, and fabrics that are decided on months earlier. But the swimsuits are ready in the store for the first warm day in April that customers decide to shop for them. Similarly, this textbook is available before the beginning of classes.

The provision of place utility is illustrated by flight insurance vending machines in airport terminals, a stock of *TV Guides* near a supermarket checkout counter — or this book in your bookstore rather than in the publisher's warehouse in suburban Toronto.

The offices of a real estate broker or lending institution are often used to create ownership utility. Legal title and possession of a new home is often transferred to a buyer in these settings.

The Functions Performed by Distribution Channels

The distribution channel performs several functions in the overall marketing system.[2] These include facilitating the exchange process; sorting to alleviate discrepancies in assortment; standardizing transactions; holding inventories; and the search process.[3]

Facilitating the Exchange Process

The evolution of distribution channels began with the exchange process described in Chapter 1. As market economies grew, the exchange process itself became complicated. With more producers and more potential buyers, intermediaries came into existence to facilitate transactions by cutting the number of marketplace contacts. For example, if ten orchards in the Okanagan Valley each sell to six supermarket chains, there are a total of 60 transactions. If the producers set up and market their apples through a co-operative, the number

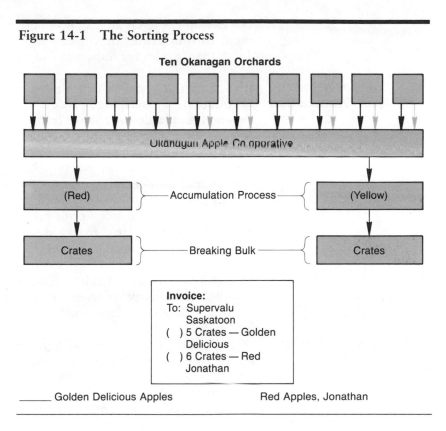

Figure 14-1   The Sorting Process

Ten Okanagan Orchards

Okanagan Apple Co operative

(Red) — Accumulation Process — (Yellow)

Crates — Breaking Bulk — Crates

Invoice:
To: Supervalu
    Saskatoon
( ) 5 Crates — Golden
    Delicious
( ) 6 Crates — Red
    Jonathan

_____ Golden Delicious Apples   Red Apples, Jonathan

of contacts declines to 16. This process is described in detail in Chapter 15.

Sorting to Alleviate Discrepancies in Assortment

Another essential function of the distribution channel is to adjust discrepancies in assortment. For economic reasons, a producer tends to maximize the quantity of a limited line of products, while the buyer needs a minimum quantity of a wide selection of alternatives. Thus, there is a discrepancy between what the producer has to offer and what the customers want. **Sorting** is *the process that alleviates discrepancies in assortment by re-allocating the outputs of various producers into assortments desired by individual purchasers.*

Figure 14-1 shows an example of the sorting process. First, an individual producer's output is divided into separate homogeneous categories such as the various types and grades of apples. These apples are then combined with the similar crops of other orchards, a process known as *accumulation*. These accumulations are broken down into smaller units or divisions, such as crates of apples. This is often called *breaking bulk* in marketing literature. Finally, an assortment is built for the next level in the distribution channel.

For example, the Okanagan co-operative might prepare an assortment of four crates of Golden Delicious and six crates of Red Johnathan apples for Supervalu supermarket in Saskatoon.

Standardizing the Transaction

If each transaction in a complex market economy was subject to negotiation, the exchange process would be chaotic. Distribution channels standardize exchange transactions in terms of the product, such as the grading of apples into types and grades, and the transfer process itself. Order points, prices, payment terms, delivery schedules, and purchase lots tend to be standardized by distribution channel members. For example, supermarket buyers might have on-line communications links with the co-operative cited in Figure 14-1. Once a certain stock position is reached, more apples would automatically be ordered from either the co-operative's current output or its cold storage.

Holding Inventories

Distribution channel members hold a minimum of inventories to account for economies of scale in transporting and to provide a buffer for small changes in demand.

The Search Process

Distribution channels also accommodate the search behaviour of both buyers and sellers. (Search behaviour was discussed earlier in Chapter 7). Buyers are searching for specific products and services to fill their needs, while sellers are attempting to find what consumers want. A college student looking for some Golden Delicious apples might go to the fruit section of Supervalu in Saskatoon. Similarly, the manager of that department would be able to provide the Okanagan co-operative with information about sales trends in his or her marketplace.

Types of Distribution

Literally hundreds of marketing channels exist today; however, there is no one marketing channel that is superior to all others. "Best" for Electrolux vacuum cleaners may be direct from manufacturer to consumer through a sales force of 1000 men and women. The "best" channel for frozen French fries may be from food processor to agent intermediary to *merchant wholesaler* (a wholesaler who takes title) to supermarket to consumer. Instead of searching for a "best" channel for all products, the marketing manager must analyse alternative channels in the light of consumer needs and competitive restraints to determine the optimum channel or channels for the firm's products.[4]

Even when the proper channels have been chosen and established, the marketing manager's channel decisions are not ended. Channels, like so many of the other marketing variables, change, and today's ideal channel may prove obsolete in a few years.

For example, the typical channel for motor oil until the 1960s was from oil company to company-owned service stations, because most oil was installed there. But a significant number of oil purchases are now made by motorists in automotive supply stores, discount department stores, and even supermarkets, as today many motorists install motor oil themselves. Others use rapid oil-change specialty shops. And the channel for Shell, Esso, Texaco, Quaker State, and Castrol must change to reflect these changes in consumer buying patterns.

Figure 14-2 depicts the major channels available for marketers of consumer and industrial products. In general, industrial products channels tend to be shorter than consumer goods channels due to geographic concentrations of industrial buyers, a relatively limited number of purchasers, and the absence of retailers from the chain. The term retailer refers to consumer goods purchases. Service channels also tend to be short because of the intangibility of services and the need to maintain personal relationships in the channel.

Consumer Goods

Direct Channel The simplest, most direct marketing channel is not necessarily the best, as is indicated by the relatively small percentage of the dollar volume of sales that moves *directly from the producer to the consumer*. Less than 5 percent of all consumer goods are candidates for the producer to consumer channel. Dairies, Tupperware, Avon cosmetics, and numerous mail-order houses are examples of firms whose marketing moves directly from manufacturer to the ultimate consumer.

Traditional Channel The traditional marketing channel for consumer goods is *from producer to wholesaler to retailer to user*. It is the method used by literally thousands of small manufacturers or companies producing limited lines of products and by as many or more small retailers. Small companies with limited financial resources utilize wholesalers as immediate sources of funds and as a marketing arm to reach the hundreds of retailers who will stock their products. Smaller retailers rely on wholesalers as *buying specialists* to ensure a balanced inventory of goods produced in various regions of the world.

The wholesaler's sales force is responsible for reaching the market with the producer's output. Many manufacturers also use sales representatives to call on the retailers to assist in merchandising the line. These representatives serve the manufacturer as sources of market information and influence, but will generally not make the sales transaction. If they do initiate a sale, they give it to a wholesaler to complete.

Figure 14-2   Alternative Distribution Channels

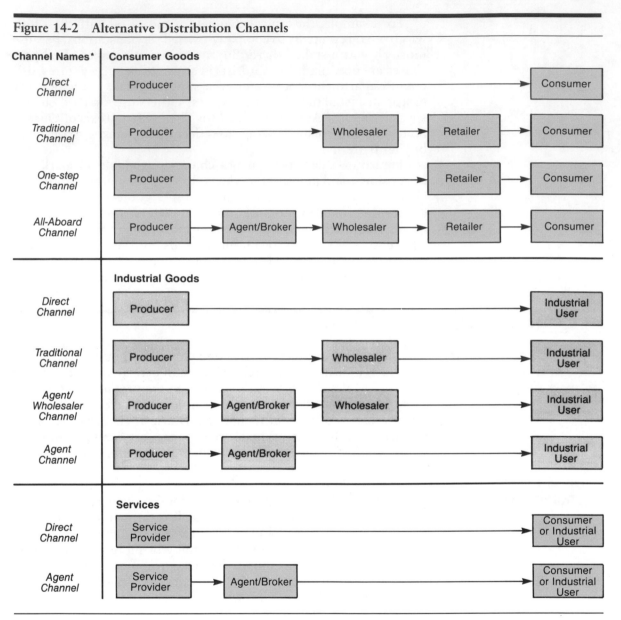

*These descriptive terms were suggested by Lewis Presner, Durham College, Oshawa, Ontario.

One-Step Channel   This channel is being used more and more, and in many instances it has taken the place of the traditional channel. When large retailers are involved, they are willing to take on many functions performed by the wholesaler — consequently, goods move *from producer to retailer to consumer.*

All-Aboard Channel   Probably the longest channel is *from producer to agent to wholesaler to retailer to consumer.* Where products are produced by a large number of small companies, a unique intermediary — the agent or broker — appears to perform the basic function of bringing buyer and seller together. **Agents** are, in fact, *wholesaling intermediaries, but they differ from the typical wholesaler in that they do not take title to the goods.* They merely represent the producer or the regular wholesaler (who does take title to the goods) in seeking a market for the producer's output or in locating a source of supply for the buyer.

Consider a canner of vegetables in Ontario that has 6000 cases of string beans to sell. The firm informs the food brokers (agents) regularly used in various provinces of this fact. A broker in the Maritimes ascertains that the Maritime supermarket chain Sobey's will buy 800 cases. The broker takes the order, informs the canner, and if the price is acceptable, the canner ships the order to Sobey's. The canner bills Sobey's and sends a commission cheque (approximately 3 percent of the sale price) to the food broker for the service of bringing buyer and seller together.

Industrial Products

Direct Channel   Direct channels are much more important in the industrial goods market than in the consumer market; here, most major installations and accessory equipment — and many of the fabricated parts and raw materials — are marketed through *direct contacts between producer and user.*

Traditional Channel   Characteristics in the industrial market often lead to the utilization of *wholesalers between the manufacturer and industrial purchaser.* The term **industrial distributor** is commonly used in the industrial market to refer to those *wholesalers who take title to the goods they handle.* These wholesalers are involved in the marketing of small accessory equipment and operating supplies, such as building supplies, office supplies, small hand tools, and office equipment. For example, in an effort to orient its own sales force toward high-priority computer products, IBM has turned to industrial distributors. The IBM industrial distributors sell only two products: a moderately priced display terminal and a desk-top printer. IBM continues to sell its entire product line, but it concentrates on items with higher priority.[5]

Agent/Wholesaler Channel

Small producers often use a channel to market their offerings through an *agent and a wholesaler to the industrial user*. The agent wholesaling intermediary, often called a manufacturer's representative or manufacturer's agent, serves as an independent sales force in contacting large, scattered wholesalers and some key industrial buyers. For example, a manufacturer of specialty industrial tapes might use agents to sell to industrial wholesalers and to encourage the wholesaler's sales force to push the product to industrial users.

Agent Channel

Where the unit sale is small, merchant wholesalers must be used to cover the market economically. By maintaining regional inventories, they can achieve transportation economies by stockpiling goods and making the final small shipment over a small distance. But where the unit sale is large and transportation costs account for a small percentage of the total product costs, the *producer to agent to industrial user* channel may be employed. The agent wholesaling intermediaries become, in effect, the company's sales force. For example, a producer of special castings might engage agents who are already calling on potential customers with other lines to represent them as well.

Services

Direct Channel

Distribution of services to both consumers and industrial users is usually simpler and more direct than for industrial and consumer goods. In part, this is due to the intangibility of services; the marketer of services does not often have to worry about storage, transportation, and inventory control; shorter channels, often direct *from service provider to consumer or industrial user*, are typically used.

Many services can only be performed on a direct basis, and personal relationships between performers and users are very important. Consumers will remain clients of the same bank, automobile repair shop, or hair stylist as long as they are reasonably satisfied. Likewise, public accounting firms and attorneys are retained on a relatively permanent basis by industrial buyers.

Agent Channel

When *service providers use marketing intermediaries to reach consumers or industrial users*, these are usually *agents* or *brokers*. Common examples include insurance agents, securities brokers, travel agents, and entertainment agents.

For instance, travel and hotel packages are sometimes created by intermediaries and then marketed at the retail level by travel agents to both vacationers and firms wanting to offer employee incentive awards.

A Special Note on Channel Strategy for Consumer Services

A dominant reason for patronage of many consumer services, such as banks, motels, and auto rental agencies, is convenient location. It is absolutely essential that careful consideration be given to selecting the retail site. For example, banks are being sensitive to consumers' needs when they locate branches in suburban shopping centres and malls. The installation of automated electronic tellers that enable customers to withdraw funds and to make deposits when a bank's offices are closed is a further example of attempts to provide convenience.

Multiple Channels

An increasingly common phenomenon is the use of more than one marketing channel for similar products. These *multiple channels* (or dual distribution) are utilized when the same product is marketed both to the ultimate consumer and industrial users. Dial soap is distributed through the traditional grocery wholesaler to food stores to the consumer, but a second channel also exists, from the manufacturer to large retail chains and motels that buy direct from the manufacturer. Competition among retailers and other intermediaries striving to expand lines, profitability, and customer service has created these multiple channels.

In other cases, the same product is marketed through a variety of types of retail outlets. A basic product such as a paintbrush is carried in inventory by the traditional hardware store; it is also handled by such nontraditional retail outlets as auto accessory stores, building supply outlets, department stores, discount houses, mail-order houses, supermarkets, and variety stores. Each retail store may utilize a different marketing channel.

Firestone automobile tires are marketed:
1. directly to General Motors, where they serve as a fabricated part for new Chevrolets;
2. through Firestone stores, company-owned retail outlets;
3. through franchised Firestone outlets;
4. from the factory to tire jobbers to retail gas stations.

Each channel enables the manufacturer to serve a different market.

Reverse Channels

While the traditional concept of marketing channels involves movement of products and services from producer to consumer or industrial user, there is increasing interest in reverse channels. **Reverse channels** are *the paths goods follow from consumer to manufac-*

turer or to marketing intermediaries. William G. Zikmund and William J. Stanton point out several problems in developing reverse channels in the *recycling* process.

> The recycling of solid wastes is a major ecological goal. Although recycling is technologically feasible, reversing the flow of materials in the channel of distribution — marketing trash through a "backward" channel — presents a challenge. Existing backward channels are primitive, and financial incentives are inadequate. The consumer must be motivated to undergo a role change and become a producer — the initiating force in the reverse distribution process.[6]

Reverse channels will increase in importance as raw materials become more expensive, and as additional laws are passed to control litter and the disposal of packaging materials such as soft-drink bottles. In order for recycling to succeed, four basic conditions must be satisfied:

1. a technology must be available that can efficiently process the material being recycled;
2. a market must be available for the end product — the reclaimed material;
3. a substantial and continuing quantity of secondary product (recycled aluminum, reclaimed steel from automobiles, recycled paper) must be available;
4. a marketing system must be developed that can bridge the gap between suppliers of secondary products and end users on a profitable basis.[7]

In some instances, the reverse channel consists of traditional marketing intermediaries. In the soft-drink industry, retailers and local bottlers perform these functions. In other cases, manufacturers take the initiative by establishing redemption centres. A concentrated attempt by the Reynolds Metals Company in one area permitted the company to recycle an amount of aluminum equivalent to 60 percent of the total containers marketed in the area. Other reverse-channel participants may include community groups, which organize "clean-up" days and develop systems for rechannelling paper products for recycling, and specialized organizations developed for waste disposal and recycling.

Reverse Channels for Product Recalls and Repairs   Reverse channels are also used for product recalls and repairs. Ownership of some products (like tires) is registered so that proper notification can be sent if there is a product recall. In the case of automobile recalls, owners are advised to have the problem corrected at their dealership. Similarly, reverse channels have been used for repairs to some products. The warranty for a small appliance may specify that if repairs are needed in the first 90 days, the item should be returned to the dealer. After that period, the product should be returned to the factory. Such reverse channels are a vital element of product recalls and repair procedures.

Facilitating Agencies in the Distribution Channel

A **facilitating agency** *provides specialized assistance for regular channel members (such as producers, wholesalers, and retailers) in moving products from producer to consumer.* Included in the definition of facilitating agencies are transportation companies, warehousing firms, financial institutions, insurance companies, and marketing research companies.

Power in the Distribution Channel

Some marketing institutions must exercise leadership in the distribution channel if it is to be an effective aspect of marketing strategy. Decisions must be made and conflicts among channel members resolved. Channel leadership is a function of one's power within the distribution channel.

Bases of Power

Researchers have identified five bases of power: reward power, coercive power, legitimate power, reference power, and expert power.[8] All of these bases can be used to establish a position of channel leadership.[9]

Reward Power   If channel members can offer some type of reward, such as the granting of an exclusive sales territory or franchise, to another member, then they possess reward power.

Coercive Power   The threat of economic punishment is known as coercive power. A manufacturer might threaten an unco-operative retailer with loss of its dealership, or a giant retailer like Eaton's might use its market size as a significant base of power against its suppliers in its distribution channel.

Legitimate Power   Distribution channels that are linked contractually provide examples of legitimate power. A franchise might be contractually required to perform such activities as maintaining a common type of outlet, contributing to general advertising, and remaining open during specified time periods.

Referent Power   Referent power stems from an agreement among channel members as to what is in their mutual best interests. For instance, many manufacturers maintain dealer councils to help resolve potential problems in distribution of a product or service. Both parties have a mutual interest in maintaining effective channel relationships.

Expert Power   Knowledge is the determinant of expert power. A manufacturer might assist a retailer with store layout or advertising based on its marketing expertise with the product line.

Channel Leadership Leadership in the marketing channel typically falls to the most powerful member. At various times and under certain circumstances channel members will utilize one or more of the foregoing bases of power to influence relationships and channel procedures. The *dominant and controlling member of the channel* is called the **channel captain**.[10] Historically, the role of channel captain belonged to the manufacturer or wholesaler, since retailers tended to be both small and localized. However, retailers are increasingly taking on the role of channel captain as large chains assume traditional wholesaling functions and even dictate product design specifications to the manufacturer.

Manufacturers as Channel Captains Since manufacturers typically create new-product and service offerings and enjoy the benefits of large-scale operations, they fill the role of channel captain in many marketing channels. Examples of such manufacturers include Armstrong Cork, General Electric, Sealy Mattress Co., and Black & Decker.

Retailers as Channel Captains Retailers are often powerful enough to serve as channel captains in many industries. Larger chain operations may bypass independent wholesalers and utilize manufacturers as suppliers in producing the retailers' private brands at quality levels specified by the chains. Major retailers such as The Bay, Eaton's, Woodward's, Canadian Tire, Sears, and Provigo serve as leaders in many of the marketing channels with which they are associated.

Wholesalers as Channel Captains Although the relative influence of wholesalers has declined since 1900, they continue to serve as vital members of many marketing channels. Large-scale wholesalers, such as the Independent Grocers' Association (IGA), serve as channel captains as they assist independent retailers in competing with chain outlets.

Channel Strategy Decisions Marketers face several channel strategy decisions. The selection of a specific distribution channel is the most basic of these, but the level of distribution intensity and the issue of vertical marketing systems must also be addressed.

Selection of a Distribution Channel What makes a direct channel (manufacturer to consumer) best for the Fuller Brush Company? Why do operating supplies often go through both agents and merchant wholesalers before being purchased by the industrial firm? Why do some firms employ multiple channels for the same product? The firm must answer many such questions when it determines its choice of marketing channels. The choice is based upon an analysis of the market, the product and the producer, and various competitive factors. Each is often of critical importance, and all are often interrelated.

Market Factors   A major determinant of channel structure is whether the product is intended for the consumer or the industrial market. Industrial purchasers usually prefer to deal directly with the manufacturer (except for supplies or small accessory items), but most consumers make their purchases from retail stores. Products sold to both industrial users and the consumer market usually require more than one channel.

The geographic location and the needs of the firm's potential market will also affect channel choice. Direct sales are possible where the firm's potential market is concentrated in a few regions. Industrial production tends to be concentrated in a relatively small geographic region, making direct contact possible. The small number of potential buyers also increases the feasibility of direct channels. Consumer goods are purchased by every household everywhere. Since consumers are numerous and geographically dispersed, and purchase a small volume at a given time, intermediaries must be employed to market products to them efficiently.

In Canada, population distribution is an extremely influential factor in channel decisions. For example, the markets for fishing nets are on the two coasts, with smaller markets on the Great Lakes, Lake Winnipeg, and a few other large lakes. The Rockies and the Canadian Shield effectively divide markets and strongly offset channels of distribution. Our relatively smaller and widely dispersed centres of population tend to result in less specialized wholesaling and retailing institutions than in the United States and other developed, heavily populated countries. This, of course, may limit the range of channel opportunities available to the marketing manager.

Order size will also affect the marketing channel decision. Manufacturers are likely to employ shorter, more direct channels in cases where retail customers or industrial buyers place relatively small numbers of large orders. Retail chains often employ buying offices to negotiate directly with manufacturers for large-scale purchases. Wholesalers may be used to contact smaller retailers.

Shifts in consumer buying patterns also influence channel decisions. The desire for credit, the growth of self-service, the increased use of mail-order houses, and the greater willingness to purchase from door-to-door salespeople all affect a firm's marketing channel.

Product Factors   Product characteristics also play a role in determining optimum marketing channels. *Perishable products*, such as fresh produce and fruit, and fashion products with short life cycles, *typically move through relatively short channels* direct to the retailer or to the ultimate consumer. Old Dutch Potato Chips are distributed by company salespeople-truck drivers direct to the retail shelves. Each year Hines & Smart Corporation ships over 2 million kg of live lobsters by air, in specially designed insulating containers, directly to restaurants and hotels throughout North America.

Complex products, such as custom-made installations or computer equipment, are typically sold direct from the manufacturer to the buyer. As a general rule, *the more standardized a product, the longer the channel will be.* Such items will usually be marketed by wholesalers. Also, products requiring regular service or specialized repair services usually avoid channels employing independent wholesalers. Automobiles are marketed through a franchised network of regular dealers whose employees receive regular training on how to service their cars properly.

Another generalization concerning marketing channels is that *the lower the unit value of the product, the longer the channel.* Convenience goods and industrial supplies with typically low unit prices are frequently marketed through relatively long channels. Installations and more expensive industrial and consumer goods go through shorter, more direct channels.

Producer Factors

Companies with adequate resources — financial, marketing, and managerial — will be less compelled to utilize intermediaries in marketing their products.[11] A financially strong manufacturer can hire its own sales force, warehouse its products, and grant credit to the retailer or consumer. A weaker firm relies on intermediaries for these services (although some large retail chains may purchase all of the manufacturer's output, making it possible to bypass the independent wholesaler). Production-oriented firms may be forced to utilize the marketing expertise of intermediaries to replace the lack of finances and management in their organization.

A firm with a broad product line is better able to market its products directly to retailers or industrial users since its sales force can offer a variety of products to the customers. Larger total sales allow the selling costs to be spread over a number of products and make direct sales more feasible. The single-product firm (remember the discussion in Chapter 10 of Monsanto and its single consumer good, All?) often discovers that direct selling is an unaffordable luxury.

The manufacturer's need for control over the product will also influence channel selection. If aggressive promotion for the firm's products at the retail level is desired, the manufacturer will choose the shortest available channel. For new products the manufacturer may be forced to implement an introductory advertising campaign before independent wholesalers will handle the item.

Competitive Factors

Some firms are forced to develop unique marketing channels because of inadequate promotion of their products by independent intermediaries. Avon concentrated on house-to-house selling rather than being directly involved in the intense competition among similar lines of cosmetics in traditional channels. This radical departure from the traditional channel resulted in tremendous sales by the firm's thousands of neighbourhood salespeople. Similarly, Honeywell discovered about 15 years ago that its $700 home security system, Concept 70, was being inadequately marketed by the traditional wholesaler-to-retailer channel and switched to a direct-to-home sales force.

Figure 14-3 summarizes the factors affecting the choice of optimal marketing channels and shows the effect of each characteristic upon the overall length of the channel.

Figure 14-3   Factors Affecting Choice of Marketing Channels

Factor	Channels Tend to Be Shorter When:
Market Factors	
Consumer market or industrial market	Users are in industrial market
Geographic location of market target	Customers are geographically concentrated
Customer service needs	Specialized knowledge, technical know-how, and regular service needs are present
Order size	Customers place relatively large orders
Product Factors	
Perishability	Products are perishable, either because of fashion changes or physical perishability
Technical complexity of product	Products are highly technical
Unit value	Products have high unit value
Producer Factors	
Producer resources — financial, managerial, and marketing	Manufacturer possesses adequate resources to perform channel functions
Product line	Manufacturer has broad product line to spread distribution costs
Need for control over the channel	Manufacturer desires to control the channel
Competitive Factors	
Need for promotion to channel members	Manufacturer feels that independent intermediaries are inadequately promoting products

Determining Distribution Intensity

Adequate market coverage for some products could mean one dealer for each 50 000 people. On the other hand, Procter & Gamble defines adequate coverage for Crest toothpaste as almost every supermarket, discount store, drugstore, and variety store plus many vending machines.

Intensive Distribution

Producers of convenience goods who attempt to provide saturation coverage of their potential markets are the prime users of **intensive distribution**. Soft drinks, cigarettes, candy, and chewing gum are available in convenient locations to enable the purchaser to buy with a minimum of effort.

Bic pens can be purchased in thousands of retail outlets in Canada. TMX Watches of Canada Ltd. uses an intensive distribution strategy for its Timex watches. Consumers may buy a Timex in many jewellery stores, the traditional retail outlet for watches. In addition, they may find Timex in discount houses, variety stores, department stores, hardware stores, and drugstores.

Mass coverage and low unit prices make the use of wholesalers almost mandatory for such distribution. An important exception to this generalization is Avon Products, which operates direct to the consumer through a nationwide network of neighbourhood salespeople who purchase directly from the manufacturer, at 60 percent of the retail price, and service a limited area with cosmetics, toiletries, jewellery, and toys.

It must be remembered that while a firm may wish intensive distribution, the retailer or industrial distributor will only carry products that make a profit. If demand is low the producer may have to settle for less than complete market coverage.

Selective Distribution

As the name implies, **selective distribution** involves *the selection of a small number of retailers to handle the firm's product line.* By limiting its retailers, the firm may reduce its total marketing costs, such as those for sales force and shipping, while establishing better working relationships within the channel. This practice may also be necessary to give the retailers an incentive (through having a product available to a limited number of sellers) to carry the product and promote it properly against many competing brands. Co-operative advertising (where the manufacturer pays a percentage of the retailer's advertising expenditures and the retailer prominently displays the firm's products) can be utilized to mutual benefit. Marginal retailers can be avoided. Where product service is important, dealer training and assistance is usually forthcoming from the manufacturer. Finally, price-cutting is less likely since fewer dealers are handling the firm's line.

Exclusive Distribution   When *manufacturers grant exclusive rights to a wholesaler or retailer to sell in a geographic region*, they are practising **exclusive distribution**, which is an extreme form of selective distribution. The best example of exclusive dealership is the automobile industry. For example, a city of 100 000 might have a single Toyota dealer or one Cadillac agency. Exclusive dealership arrangements are also found in the marketing of some major appliances and in fashion apparel. Powerful retailers may also negotiate to acquire exclusive distribution.

Some market coverage may be sacrificed through a policy of exclusive distribution, but this is often offset through the development and maintenance of an image of quality and prestige for the products, with more active attention by the retailer to promote them, and the reduced marketing costs associated with a small number of accounts. Producers and retailers co-operate closely in decisions concerning advertising and promotion, inventory to be carried by the retailers, and prices.

The Legal Problems of Exclusive Distribution   The use of exclusive distribution presents a number of potential legal problems. Three problem areas exist — exclusive dealing, tied selling, and market restriction. Each will be examined briefly.

Exclusive dealing *prohibits a marketing intermediary* (either a wholesaler or, more typically, a retailer) *from handling competing products*. Through such a contract the manufacturer is assured of total concentration on the firm's product line by the intermediaries. For example, an oil company may consider requiring all dealers to sign a contract agreeing to purchase all of their accessories from that company.

The legal question is covered in Part IV of the Combines Investigation Act, which prohibits exclusive dealing by a major supplier if it is likely to:

1. impede entry into or expansion of a firm in the market;
2. impede introduction of a product into or expansion of sales of a product in the market; or
3. have any other exclusionary effect in the market, with the result that competition is or is likely to be lessened substantially.[12]

A second problem area is **tied selling**. In this case *a supplier might force a dealer who wishes to handle a product to also carry other products from the supplier or to refrain from using or distributing someone else's product*. Tied selling is controlled by the same provision as exclusive dealing.

The third legal issue of exclusive distribution is the use of **mar-**

ket restriction. In this case *suppliers restrict the geographic territories for each of their distributors.* The key issue is whether such restrictions substantially lessen competition. If so, the Restrictive Trade Practices Commission has power to order the prohibition of such practices. For example, a *horizontal territorial restriction*, where retailers or wholesalers agree to avoid competition in products from the same manufacturer, would likely be declared unlawful.

Vertical Marketing Systems

The traditional marketing channel has been described as a "highly fragmented network in which vertically aligned firms bargain with each other at arm's length, terminate relationships with impunity, and otherwise behave autonomously."[13] This potentially inefficient system of distributing goods in some industries is gradually being replaced by **vertical marketing systems** — *"professionally managed and centrally programmed networks preengineered to achieve operating economies and maximum impact."* In other words, a vertical marketing system (VMS) is the use of various types of economic power to attain maximum operating efficiencies, deep market penetration, and sustained profits. Vertical marketing systems produce economies of scale through their size and elimination of duplicated services. Three types prevail: corporate, administered, and contractual. They are depicted in Figure 14-4.

Corporate System

When there is single ownership of each stage of the marketing channel, a *corporate vertical marketing system* exists. Holiday Inn owns a furniture manufacturer and a carpet mill. Bata Shoes owns a retail chain of shoe stores. Many McDonald's food outlets are corporate-owned.

Administered System

Channel co-ordination is achieved through the exercise of economic and "political" power by a dominant channel member in an *administered vertical marketing system.* Canadian General Electric has a network of major appliance dealers who aggressively display and promote the line because of its strong reputation and brand. Although independently owned and operated, these dealers co-operate with the manufacturer because of the effective working relationships enjoyed over the years and the profits to be realized from selling the widely known, well-designed, broad range of merchandise.

Contractual System

The most significant form of vertical marketing is the *contractual vertical marketing system.* It accounts for nearly 40 percent of all retail sales. Instead of the common ownership of channel components that characterizes the corporate VMS or the relative power relationships of an administered system, the contractual VMS is char-

Figure 14-4   Three Types of Vertical Marketing Systems

Type of System	Description	Examples
Corporate	Channel owned and operated by a single organization	Bata Shoes Firestone Sherwin-Williams Singer McDonald's (partial)
Administered	Channel dominated by one powerful member who acts as channel captain	Kodak General Electric Corning Glass
Contractual	Channel co-ordinated through contractual agreements among channel members	*Wholesaler-Sponsored Voluntary Chain:* IGA Canadian Tire Independent Druggists Alliance (IDA) Allied Hardware *Retail Co-operative:* Associated Grocers *Franchise Systems:* McDonald's (partial) Century 21 Real Estate AAMCO Transmissions Coca-Cola bottlers Ford dealers

acterized by formal agreements between channel members. In practice there are three types of agreements: the wholesaler-sponsored voluntary chain, the retail co-operative, and the franchise.

Wholesaler-Sponsored Voluntary Chain

The wholesaler-sponsored voluntary chain represents an attempt by the independent wholesaler to preserve a market for the firm's products through the strengthening of the firm's retailer customers. In order to enable the independent retailers to compete with the chains, the wholesaler enters into a formal agreement with a group of retailers, whereby the retailers agree to use a common name, have standardized facilities, and purchase the wholesaler's products. The wholesaler often develops a line of private brands to be stocked by the members of the voluntary chain. A common store name and similar inventories allow the retailers to achieve cost savings on advertising, since a single newspaper advertisement promotes all retailers in the trading area. IGA, with a membership of approximately 800 food stores, is a good example of a voluntary chain.

Retail Co-operatives   A second type of contractual VMS is the retail co-operative, which is established by a group of retailers who set up a wholesaling operation better to compete with the chains. A group of retailers purchase shares of stock in a wholesaling operation and agree to purchase a minimum percentage of their inventory from the firm. The members may also choose to use a common store name, such as Home Hardware, and develop their own private brands in order to carry out co-operative advertising.

Buying groups like wholesaler-sponsored chains and retail co-operatives are not a new phenomenon in the Canadian distribution industry. They date back at least 50 years, some having evolved from the co-operative movement of the early years of the century. Under the Combines Investigation Act, suppliers may charge different prices for different volumes of purchases, so long as these prices are available to all competing purchasers of articles of like quantity and quality. And suppliers have done so; it is common practice to offer volume rebates. Thus buying groups improved the small retailers' bargaining position with their suppliers, thus increasing competition for their large rivals.

A phenomenon is now occurring in the retail food industry. Buying groups which originally existed to enable small retailers and wholesalers to compete on a more equitable basis with the large chains have now themselves become as large as the chains. At the same time the chains have been coming together to form their own even larger groups. The result is that there are now five groups representing some 14 000 stores, and accounting for about 85 percent of all retail food sales in Canada: Foodwide of Canada (Loblaws and Provigo), Volume 1 (Dominion and Steinberg), IGA-Safeway, United Grocery Wholesales, and Independent Wholesale Grocers. This recent development leads to the concern that while buying groups may improve the balance of market power in some areas, there is a possibility of abuse of this power in others.[14]

Franchising   A third type of contractual VMS is the **franchise**. A franchise is *an agreement whereby dealers (franchisees) agree to meet the operating requirements of a manufacturer or other franchiser.* The dealer typically receives a variety of marketing, management, technical, and financial services in exchange for a specified fee.

Although franchising attracted considerable interest beginning in the late 1960s, the concept actually began 100 years earlier when the Singer Company established franchised sewing machine outlets. Early impetus for the franchising concept came after 1900 in the automobile industry.[15] The soft-drink industry is another example of franchising, but in this case the contractual arrangement is between the syrup manufacturer and the wholesale bottler.

The franchising form that created most of the excitement both in retailing and on Wall Street in the late 1960s was the retailer franchise system sponsored by the service firm. McDonald's Corporation is an excellent example of such a franchise operation. McDonald's brought together suppliers and a chain of hamburger outlets. It provided a proven system of retail operation (the operations manual for each outlet weighs over a kilogram) with a standardized product and ingenious promotional campaigns. This enabled the offering of lower prices through the franchiser's purchasing power on meat, buns, potatoes, napkins, and other supplies. In return the franchisee pays a fee for the use of the name (over $150 000 for McDonald's) and a percentage of gross sales. Other familiar examples include Hertz, Avis, Kentucky Fried Chicken, Pizza Hut, and Weight Watchers.

McDonald's has several stores in operation in every major centre and has expanded its menu to include such items as Egg McMuffin, hotcakes, scrambled eggs, and McChicken. These efforts are aimed at obtaining even more of the millions of dollars Canadians spend annually in restaurants. Almost one-third of all meals

Figure 14-5   How Franchising Branches Out

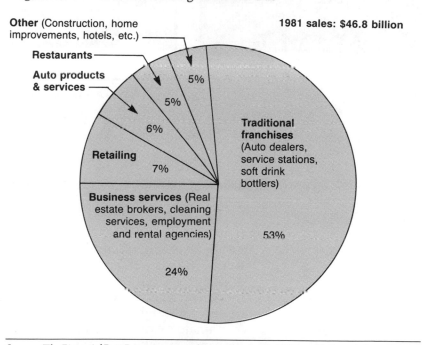

Source: *The Financial Post Report on Franchising*, October 8, 1983, p. S1, from information provided by Statistics Canada, Merchandising & Services Division.

Typical Franchise Advertisements

Source: *The Financial Post Special Report on Franchising*, October 8, 1983, p. S15.

are eaten in restaurants, and the rate is expected to grow to 50 percent within the next five to ten years.

Fast-food franchising has already proven itself in the international market. In Tokyo, London, Rome, and Paris, McDonald's hamburgers are consumed daily. Kentucky Fried Chicken has opened nearly 500 restaurants in Canada and in such locations as Manila and Munich, Nice and Nairobi. In some countries adjustments to the North American marketing plans have been made to match local needs. Although their menu is rigidly standardized in Canada, McDonald's executives approved changes to the menu in outlets in France. Kentucky Fried chicken replaced French fries with mashed potatoes to satisfy their Japanese customers.

Although many franchises have proven extremely profitable, the infatuation with the franchising concept and the market performance of franchise stocks have lured dozens of newcomers into the market. Lacking experience and often with a well-known celebrity's name as their sole asset, many of these firms have disappeared almost as quickly as they entered the market.[16]

The median investment for a franchise varies tremendously from one business area to another. A pet-sitting franchise might sell for as low as $9500, whereas a restaurant franchise will likely average over $250 000. The great bulk of the nation's franchises are in the "traditional" franchise areas such as auto dealers, service stations, and soft-drink bottlers. Figure 14-5 shows the proportion of sales accounted for by the various franchise categories.

Despite the many franchise opportunities available, there are few specific regulations with respect to the proper disclosure of information to prospective franchisees. It is worthwhile to carefully evaluate the opportunity before investing.

VMS—whether in the form of corporate, administered, or contractual systems — are already becoming a dominant factor in the consumer goods sector of the Canadian economy. Over 60 percent of the available market is currently in the hands of retail components of VMS.

The Distribution Channel: Conflict and Co-operation

Distribution channels must be organized and regarded as a systematic co-operative effort if operating efficiencies are to be achieved. Yet channel members often perform as separate, independent, and even competitive forces. Too often, marketing institutions within the channel believe it extends only one step forward or backward. They think in terms of suppliers and customers rather than of vital links in the total channel.

Channel conflict can evolve from a number of sources:

> A manufacturer may wish to promote a product in one manner . . . while his retailers oppose this. Another manufacturer may wish to get information from his retailers on a certain aspect relating to his product, but his retailers may refuse to provide this information. A producer may want to distribute his product extensively, but his retailers may demand exclusives. A supplier may force a product onto its retailers, who dare not oppose, but who retaliate in other ways, such as using it as a loss leader. Large manufacturers may try to dictate the resale price of their merchandise; this may be less or more than the price at which the retailers wish to sell it. Occasionally a local market may be more competitive for a retailer than is true nationally. The manufacturer may not recognize the difference in competition and refuse to help this channel member. There is also conflict because of the desire of both manufacturers and retailers to eliminate the wholesaler.[17]

Types of Conflict   Two types of **channel conflict**—horizontal or vertical—may occur. *Horizontal* conflict occurs between channel members at the same level—two or more wholesalers or two or more retailers. Such conflict may occur between intermediaries of the same type, such as two competing discount stores or several retail florists. More often, however, horizontal conflict occurs between different types of intermediaries who handle similar products. The retail druggist competes with variety stores, discount houses, department stores, convenience food stores, and mail-order houses, all of which may be supplied by the manufacturer with identical branded products. Consumer desires for convenient, one-stop shopping have led to multiple channels and the use of numerous outlets for many products. A major function of manufacturers' sales personnel is to attempt to resolve horizontal conflict and to maintain distribution. Some such conflict is inevitable since the retail or wholesale firms are competing for one or more market segments.

Vertical conflict occurs between channel members at different levels—between wholesalers and retailers or between manufacturers and wholesalers or retailers. Vertical conflict occurs frequently and is often the more severe form of conflict in the channel. Conflict may occur between manufacturers and retailers when retailers develop private brands to compete with the manufacturers' brands, or when manufacturers establish their own retail stores or create a mail-order operation in competition with retailers. Conflict between manufacturers and wholesalers may occur in cases where the manufacturer attempts to bypass the wholesaler and make direct sales to retailers or industrial users. In other instances, wholesalers may promote competitive products.

A third type of vertical conflict may occur between wholesalers and retailers. Retailers may believe that wholesalers are failing to offer credit or to allow returns on the same basis as is being provided for other types of retail outlets. Wholesalers may complain that retailers are making sales to institutions that previously dealt directly with the wholesaler. A wholesaler in the sporting goods field may argue that sales by retail sporting goods outlets directly to local school systems are unfairly competing with its own sales force.[18]

Achieving Co-operation among Channel Members   The basic antidote to channel conflict is effective co-operation among channel members. In general, channels have more harmonious relationships than conflicting ones; if they did not, the channels would have ceased to exist long ago. Co-operation is best achieved by considering all channel members as part of the same organization. Achievement of this co-operation is the prime responsibility of the channel captain, who must provide the leadership necessary to ensure efficient functioning of the channel. However, complete harmony is almost never achieved, nor will it be in a competitive system.

Summary   Distribution channels refer to the various marketing institutions and the interrelationships responsible for the physical and title flow of goods and services from producer to consumer or industrial user. Wholesaling and retailing intermediaries (or middlemen) are the marketing institutions in the distribution channel.

Distribution channels bridge the gap between producer and consumer. By making products and services available when and where the consumer wants to buy, and by arranging for transfer of title, marketing channels create time, place, and possession utility.

Distribution channels also perform such specific functions as 1) facilitating the exchange process; 2) sorting to alleviate discrepancies in assortment; 3) standardizing the transaction; 4) holding inventories; and 5) accommodating the search process.

A host of alternative distribution channels are available for makers of consumer products, industrial products, and services. They range from contacting the consumer or industrial user directly to using a variety of intermediaries. Multiple channels are also increasingly commonplace today. A unique distribution system—the reverse channel—is used in recycling, product recalls, and in some service situations.

Channel leadership is primarily a matter of relative power within the channel. There are five bases for power: reward power, coercive power, legitimate power, referent power, and expert power. The channel leader that emerges is called the channel captain.

Basic channel strategy decisions involve channel selection, the level of distribution intensity, and the use of vertical marketing systems. The selection of a distribution channel is based on market, product, producer, and competitive factors. The decision on distribution intensity involves choosing from among intensive distribution, selective distribution, or exclusive distribution. The issue of vertical marketing systems also has to be explored by the marketing manager. There are three major types of vertical marketing systems: corporate, administered, and contractual, this third including wholesaler-sponsored chains, retail co-operatives, and franchises.

Channel conflict is a problem in distribution channels. There are two types of conflict: horizontal, between channel members at the same level; and vertical, between channel members at different levels. Marketers should work toward co-operation among all channel members as the remedy for channel conflict.

CHAPTER 15

Wholesaling

1. To relate wholesaling to the other variables of the marketing mix.

2. To identify the functions performed by wholesaling intermediaries.

3. To explain the channel options available to a manufacturer who desires to bypass independent wholesaling intermediaries.

4. To identify the conditions under which a manufacturer is likely to assume wholesaling functions rather than use independents.

5. To distinguish between merchant wholesalers and agents and brokers.

6. To identify the major types of merchant wholesalers and instances where each type might be used.

7. To describe the major types of agents and brokers.

At 9:15 a.m. George Martin enters the Save-Easy supermarket in Miramichi Mall on King George Highway, in Newcastle, New Brunswick. He introduces himself to the store manager, and registers in a sign-in book kept near the loading dock. Martin goes first to the deli section where he finds that a label from a brand of cheese his company represents has fallen off. He heats it with a lighter and sticks it back on the package. Martin then deals with the problem of a damaged package of shrimp cocktail and notes that the brands of onion dip and orange juice he is responsible for are out of stock.

The rest of Martin's day is similar. He issues a credit for a spoiled package of ham at the IGA on Chaplin Island Road. At Sobey's on Pleasant Street, the dairy manager complains that the meat company that Martin represents has been shipping its frankfurters, salami, and knockwurst too near the "best before" date when they will have to be removed from sale. Later, he meets the manager of a dairy section at a supermarket in Chatham where there is limited refrigerated space. The manager is upset with him because some fruit punch was shipped with defective seals, and Martin promises to look into the situation.

What does George Martin do for a living? He is a retail sales supervisor for a large food broker that represents many national brands. Food brokers, who account for about 50 percent of all food items sold to food retailers, are classified as wholesaling intermediaries. And wholesaling is the focus of this chapter.

Wholesaling is the initial marketing institution in most channels of distribution from manufacturers to consumer or industrial user. Chapter 14 introduced the basic concepts of channel strategy, primarily from the point of view of the manufacturer. Attention now shifts to the institutions within the distribution channel.

Wholesaling intermediaries are a critical element of the marketing mixes of many products, but many intermediaries are also separate business entities with their own marketing mixes. A good starting point for the discussion is to look at the terminology used in wholesaling.

The Conceptual Framework

Wholesaling involves the activities of persons or firms who sell to retailers and other wholesalers or to industrial users, but not in significant amounts to ultimate consumers. The term **wholesaler** (or **merchant intermediary**) is applied only to *those wholesaling intermediaries who take title to the products they handle*. **Wholesaling intermediaries** (or wholesaling middlemen) is a broader term that describes not only *intermediaries who assume title*, but also *agents and brokers who perform important wholesaling activities without taking title to the goods*. Under this definition, then, a wholesaler is a *merchant intermediary*.

Wholesaling Functions

The route that goods follow on the way to the consumer or industrial user is actually a chain of marketing institutions—wholesalers and retailers. Only 3 percent of the dollar volume of all goods sold to the ultimate consumer is purchased directly from the manufacturer. The bulk of all products sold passes through these marketing institutions.

An increasing number of consumer complaints about high prices is heard each year. The finger of guilt is often pointed at wholesalers and retailers, the intermediaries who allegedly drive prices up by taking "high profits." Discount stores often advertise that their prices are lower since they buy direct and eliminate the intermediaries and their profits. Chain stores often assume wholesaling functions and bypass the independent wholesalers.

Are these complaints and claims valid? Are wholesaling intermediaries anachronisms doomed to a swift demise? Answers to these questions can be formulated by considering the functions and costs of these marketing intermediaries.

Wholesaling Intermediaries Provide a Variety of Services

A marketing institution will continue to exist only so long as it fulfils a need by performing a required service. Its death may be slow, but it is inevitable if other channel members discover that they can survive without it. Figure 15-1 examines a number of possible ser-

Figure 15-1   Possible Wholesaling Services for Customers and Producers-Suppliers

Service	Services Provided for	
	Customers	**Producer-Suppliers**
Buying Anticipates customer demands and possesses knowledge of alternative sources of supply; acts as purchasing agent for customers.		
Selling Provides a sales force to call upon customers thereby providing a low-cost method of servicing smaller retailers and industrial users.		▓
Storing Provides a warehousing function at lower cost than most individual producers or retailers could provide. Reduces the risk and cost of maintaining inventory for producers, and provides customers with prompt delivery services.	▓	▓
Transporting Customers receive prompt delivery in response to their demands, reducing their inventory investments. Wholesalers also break-bulk by purchasing in economical carload or truckload lots, then reselling in smaller quantities to their customers, thereby reducing overall transportation costs.	▓	▓
Providing Market Information Serves as important marketing research input for producers through regular contacts with retail and industrial buyers. Provides customers with information about new products, technical information about product lines, reports on activities of competitors, industry trends, and advisory information concerning pricing changes, legal changes, and so forth.	▓	▓
Financing Aids customers by granting credit that might not be available were the customers to purchase directly from manufacturers. Provides financial assistance to producers by purchasing goods in advance of sale and through prompt payment of bills.	▓	▓
Risk-Taking Assists producers by evaluating credit risks of numerous distant retail customers and small industrial users. Extension of credit to these customers is another form of risk-taking. In addition, the wholesaler responsible for transportation and stocking goods in inventory assumes risk of possible spoilage, theft, or obsolescence.	▓	▓

vices provided by wholesaling intermediaries. It is important to note that numerous types of wholesaling intermediaries exist and that not all of them provide every service listed in Figure 15-1. Producer-suppliers and their customers, who rely on wholesaling intermediaries for distribution, select those intermediaries providing the desired combination of services.

The listing of possible services provided by wholesaling intermediaries clearly indicates the provision of marketing utility — time, place, and ownership — by these intermediaries. The services also reflect the provision of the basic marketing functions of buying, selling, storing, transportation, risk-taking, financing, and market information.

The critical marketing functions — transportation and convenient product storage; reduced costs of buying and selling through reduced contacts; market information; and financing — form the basis of evaluating the efficiency of any marketing intermediary. The risk-taking function is present in each of the services provided by the wholesaling intermediary.

Transportation and Product Storage

Wholesalers transport and store products at locations convenient to customers. Manufacturers ship products from their warehouses to numerous wholesalers, who then ship smaller quantities to retail outlets convenient to the purchaser. A large number of wholesalers and most retailers assume the inventory function (and cost) for the manufacturer. The retailer benefits through the convenience afforded by local inventories, and the manufacturer's cash needs are reduced since the firm's products are sold directly to the wholesaler or retailer.

At the wholesale level costs are reduced through large purchases from the manufacturer. The wholesaler receives quantity discounts from the manufacturer and reduced transportation rates since economical carload or truckload shipments are made to the wholesaler's warehouses. At the warehouse the wholesaler breaks bulk into smaller quantities and ships to the retailer over a shorter distance than would be the case if the manufacturer filled the retailer's order directly from a central warehouse.

Cost Reductions

Costs are often lowered when intermediaries are used, since the sales force of the retailer or wholesaler can represent many manufacturers to a single customer. As Figure 15-2 indicates, the number of transactions between manufacturers and their customers are markedly reduced through the introduction of an intermediary (a wholesaler or retailer). Reduced market contacts can lead to lowered marketing costs. By adding a wholesaling intermediary, the number of transactions in this illustration is reduced from 16 to 8, thereby creating economies of scale by providing an assortment of

Figure 15-2   Achieving Transaction Economy with Wholesaling Intermediaries

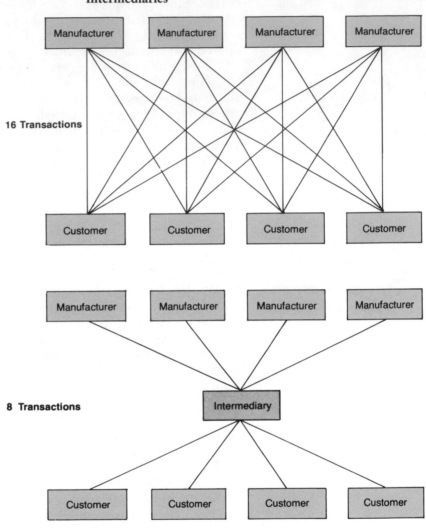

goods with greater utility and at lower cost than without such an intermediary.

Source of Information   Because of their central position between the manufacturer and retailers or industrial buyers, wholesalers serve as important information links. Wholesalers provide their retail customers with useful information about new products. In addition they supply manufacturers with information concerning market reception of their product offerings.

Source of Financing   Wholesalers also provide a financing function. Wholesalers often provide retailers with goods on credit. By purchasing products on credit, retailers can minimize their cash investments in inventory and pay for most of their purchases as the goods are being sold. This allows them to benefit from the principle of *leverage*; a minimum investment inflates their return on investment. A retailer with an investment of $1 million and profits of $100 000 will realize a return on investment (ROI) of 10 percent. But if the necessary invested capital can be reduced to $800 000 through credit from the wholesaler, and if the $100 000 profits can be maintained, the retailer's ROI increases to 12.5 percent.

Figure 15-3   Median Net Profits of Selected Wholesalers

Kind of Business	Net Profit as a Percentage of Net Sales*	Annual Turnover Rate**
Automotive parts and supplies	3.7	4.2
Beer and ale	2.5	14.3
Confectionery	1.4	13.0
Dairy products	1.4	43.1
Drugs, proprietaries, and sundries	1.9	7.6
Electrical appliances, TV and radio sets	1.9	7.4
Footwear	2.7	6.5
Furniture	3.7	8.6
Groceries, general line	1.5	6.2
Hardware	3.8	5.9
Meat products	0.9	39.6
Paper and paper products	3.1	10.3
Petroleum and petroleum products	1.5	32.0
Tires and tubes	2.2	6.7
Tobacco and tobacco products	.9	17.5

* After provision for federal income taxes   ** Net sales to inventory

Source: "The Ratios," *Dun's Business Month* (Feb. 1983), pp. 116–17. Reprinted with the special permission of *Dun's Business Month*, Feb. 1983. Copyright 1983, Dun & Bradstreet Publications Corporation.

Wholesalers of industrial goods provide similar services for the purchasers of their goods. In the steel industry, intermediaries called metal service centres currently market approximately one-fifth of the steel shipped by Canadian mills. Such a centre may stock as many as 6500 items for sale to many of the thousands of major metal users who buy their heavy usage items in large quantities directly from the steel mills, but who turn to service centres for quick delivery of special orders and other items used in small quantities.

While an order from the mills may take 90 days for delivery, a service centre can usually deliver locally within 24 to 48 hours. Such service reduces the investment needed in stock.

Who Should Perform Distribution Channel Functions?

While wholesaling intermediaries often perform a variety of valuable functions for their producer, retailer, and other wholesale clients, these functions could be performed by other channel members. Manufacturers may choose to bypass independent wholesaling intermediaries by establishing networks of regional warehouses, maintaining large sales forces to provide market coverage, serving as sources of information for their retail customers, and assuming the financing function. In some instances, they may decide to push the responsibility for some of these functions through the channel on to the retailer or the ultimate purchaser. Large retailers who choose to perform their own wholesaling operations face the same choices.

A fundamental marketing principle is that marketing functions must be performed by some member of the channel; they may be shifted, but they cannot be eliminated. Either the larger retailers who bypass the wholesaler and deal directly with the manufacturer will assume the functions previously performed by wholesaling intermediaries, or these functions will be performed by the manufacturer. Similarly, a manufacturer who deals directly with the ultimate consumer or with industrial buyers will assume the functions of storage, delivery, and market information previously performed by marketing intermediaries. Intermediaries themselves can be eliminated from the channel, but the channel functions must be performed by someone.

The potential gain for the manufacturer or retailer who might be considering bypassing wholesaling intermediaries is reflected in Figure 15-3. The table shows the potential savings that could be realized *if* channel members performed the wholesale functions as efficiently as the independent wholesaling intermediary. Such savings, indicated in the net profit column, could be used to reduce retail prices, to increase the profits of the manufacturer or retailers, or both. Note, however, the low profit rates on sales earned by most wholesalers. High turnover is necessary to provide adequate returns on investment.

Types of Wholesaling Intermediaries

As mentioned previously, various types of wholesaling intermediaries are present in different marketing channels. Some provide a wide range of services or handle a broad line of products, while others specialize in a single service, product, or industry. Figure 15-4 classifies wholesaling intermediaries based on two characteristics: *ownership*, whether the wholesaling intermediary is independent, manufacturer-owned, or retailer-owned; and *title flows*, whether

Figure 15-4   Major Types of Wholesaling Intermediaries

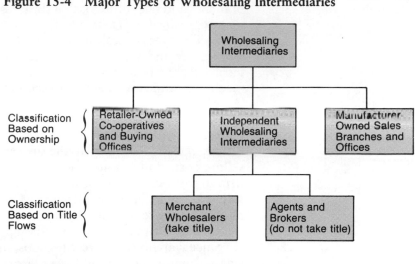

title passes from the manufacturer to the wholesaling intermediary or not. There are, in turn, three basic types of ownership: 1) independent wholesaling, which can be merchant wholesalers who do take title to goods or agents and brokers who do not, 2) manufacturer-owned sales branches and offices, and 3) retailer-owned co-operatives and buying offices.

Manufacturer-Owned Facilities

Increasing volumes of products are being marketed directly by manufacturers through company-owned facilities. There are several reasons for this trend. Some products are perishable; some require complex installation or servicing; others need more aggressive promotion; still others are high unit-value goods that the manufacturer wishes to control through the channel directly to the purchaser. Among the industries that have largely shifted from the use of independent wholesaling intermediaries to company-owned channels are paper, paint, lumber, construction materials, piece goods, and apparel manufacturers.[1] More than 50 percent of all industrial goods are sold directly to users by the manufacturer, and slightly more than one-third of *all* products are marketed through manufacturer-owned channels.[2]

This does not mean that independent wholesalers are being squeezed out. Their numbers are in the thousands, and their volume of trade in the billions of dollars.

Sales Branches and Offices   The basic distinction between sales branches and sales offices is that the **sales branch** of a company *carries inventory, and orders are processed to customers from available stock*. The branch duplicates the storage function of the independent wholesaler and serves as an office for sales representatives in the territory. Sales branches are prevalent in the marketing of commercial machinery and equipment, petroleum products, motor vehicles, and chemicals.

A **sales office**, by contrast, *does not carry stock but serves as a regional office for the firm's sales personnel*. Maintenance of sales offices in close proximity to the firm's customers assists in reducing selling costs and in improving customer service. The listing of the firm in the local telephone directory and yellow pages may result in sales for the local representative. Many buyers will choose to telephone the office of a supplier of a needed product rather than take the time to write letters to distant suppliers.

Since warehouses represent a substantial investment in real estate, smaller manufacturers and even larger firms developing new sales territories may choose to use **public warehouses**. They are *independently owned storage facilities*. For a rental fee the manufacturer may arrange to store its inventory in one of the nation's many public warehouses for shipment by the warehouse to customers in the area. The warehouse owner will break bulk (divide up a carload or truckload), package inventory into smaller quantities to fill orders, and will even bill the purchaser for the manufacturer. The public warehouse can even provide a financial service for the manufacturer by issuing a warehouse receipt for the inventory. The receipt can then be used as collateral for a bank loan.

Other Outlets for the Manufacturer's Products   In addition to the use of a sales force and regionally distributed sales branches, manufacturers will often market their products through trade fairs and exhibitions and merchandise marts. **Trade fairs** or **trade exhibitions** are *periodic shows where manufacturers in a particular industry display their wares for visiting retail and wholesale buyers*. The Montreal toy show and the Toronto, Montreal, and Calgary furniture shows are annual events for both manufacturers and purchasers of toys and furniture.

A **merchandise mart** provides space for *permanent exhibitions where manufacturers rent showcases for their product offerings*. One of the largest is Place Bonaventure in Montreal, which is approximately a block square and is several storeys high. Thousands of items are on display there. A retail buyer can compare the offerings of dozens of competing manufacturers and make many purchase decisions in a single visit to a trade fair or merchandise mart.

Independent Wholesaling Intermediaries

As has been mentioned earlier, there are many independent wholesaling intermediaries. Figure 15-5 shows that they are flourishing. They perform vital functions in the marketing of goods and services, and their role and categorization should be understood clearly. These intermediaries may be divided into two categories: **merchant wholesalers**, who *take title to the goods*, and **agents and brokers**, who *may take possession of the goods, but who do not take title*. Merchant wholesalers account for 82.9 percent of all sales handled by independent wholesalers. As Figure 15-6 indicates, they can be further classified as full- or limited-function wholesalers.

Figure 15-5   Independent Wholesale Trade by Type of Operation

Type of Operation	Number of Establishments	Volume of Trade (billions of $)	Percentage of Volume of Trade
Merchant Wholesalers	27 526	109.6	82.9
Agents and Brokers	6 468	29.6	17.1
Total	33 994	117.6	100.0

Source: Statistics Canada, *Merchandising Business Survey*, Wholesaler Merchants, *1979; Agents and Brokers, 1980; Market Research Handbook, 1983.* By permission of the Minister of Supply and Services Canada.

Figure 15-6   Classification of Independent Wholesaling Intermediaries

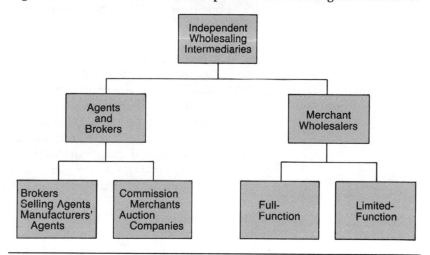

Full-function merchant wholesalers provide a complete assortment of services for the retailers or industrial purchasers. They store merchandise in convenient locations, thus allowing their customers to make purchases on short notice. To minimize their inventory requirements, they usually maintain a sales force who regularly call on retailers, make deliveries, and extend credit to qualified buyers. In the industrial goods market the full-function merchant wholesaler (often called an *industrial distributor*) usually markets machinery, less expensive accessory equipment, and supplies.

Full-function merchant wholesalers prevail in industries where retailers are small and carry large numbers of relatively inexpensive items, none of which is stocked in depth. The hardware, drug, and grocery industries have traditionally been serviced by them.

A unique type of service wholesaler emerged after World War II as supermarkets began to stock high-margin nonfood items. Since the supermarket manager possessed no knowledge of such products as toys, housewares, paperback books, records, and health and beauty items, the **rack jobber** provided the necessary expertise. This wholesaler *provides the racks, stocks the merchandise, prices the goods, and makes regular visits to refill the shelves.* In essence, the rack jobber rents space from the retailer on a commission basis. Rack jobbers have expanded into drug, hardware, variety, and discount stores.

Since full-function merchant wholesalers perform a large number of services, their costs are sometimes as high as 20 percent of sales. Attempts to reduce the costs associated with dealing with the full-function wholesaler have led to the development of a number of *limited-function* intermediaries.

Four types of limited-function merchant wholesalers are: cash-and-carry wholesalers, truck wholesalers, drop shippers, and direct-response wholesalers.

Cash-and-carry wholesalers perform most wholesaling functions except financing and delivery. They first appeared on the marketing stage in the grocery industry during the Depression era of the 1930s. In an attempt to reduce costs, retailers drove to the wholesaler's warehouse, paid cash for their purchases, and made their own deliveries. By eliminating the delivery and financing functions, cash-and-carry wholesalers were able to reduce operating costs to approximately 9 percent of sales.

Although feasible in servicing small stores, such wholesalers have generally proven unworkable for the large-scale operation. The chain store manager is unwilling to perform the delivery function, and the cash-and-carry operation typically operates today as one department of a regular full-service wholesaler. This type of wholesaler, however, has proven quite successful in the United Kingdom; 600 cash-and-carry operations produce over $1 billlion in sales a year. However, as the U.K. grocery industry moves toward large supermarkets such as Tesco and Sainsbury's in the 1980s, the volume of cash-and-carry operations is expected to diminish.

Truck wholesalers, or *truck jobbers, market perishable food items*, such as bread, tobacco, potato chips, candy, and dairy products. They make regular deliveries to retail stores and simultaneously perform the sales, delivery, and collection functions. The relatively high cost of operating a delivery truck and the low dollar volume per sale account for relatively high operation costs of 15 percent. The truck wholesaler does provide aggressive promotion for these product lines.

The **drop shipper** *takes orders from customers and places them with producers who ship directly to the customer.* Although drop shippers take title to the products, they never physically handle — or even see — the goods. Since they perform no storage or handling function, their operating costs are a relatively low 4 to 5 percent of sales.

The drop shipper operates in fields where the product is bulky and customers make purchases in carload lots. Since transportation and handling costs represent a substantial percentage of the total cost of such products as coal and lumber, the drop shipper does not maintain an inventory and thereby eliminates the expenses of loading and unloading carload shipments. Their major service is in developing a complete assortment for customers. For example, drop shippers constitute a highly skilled group of sellers of lumber products out of British Columbia. While the major forest product firms, such as MacMillan-Bloedel and British Columbia Forest Products, have their in-house lumber traders, independent drop shippers compete head-to-head with them in selling the output of independent sawmills to eastern Canada and the United States.

The **direct-response wholesaler** is a limited-function merchant wholesaler who *relies on catalogues rather than a sales force to contact retail, industrial, and institutional customers.* Purchases are made by mail or telephone by relatively small customers in outlying areas. Mail-order operations are found in the hardware, cosmetics, jewellery, sporting goods, and specialty food lines, as well as in general merchandise.

Figure 15-7 compares the various types of merchant wholesalers in terms of services provided. Full-function merchant wholesalers and truck wholesalers are relatively high-cost intermediaries because of the number of services they perform, while cash-and-carry wholesalers, drop shippers, and direct-response wholesalers provide fewer services and have relatively low operating costs.

Agents and Brokers   A second group of independent wholesaling intermediaries — the agents and brokers — may or may not take possession of the goods but they *never take title* to them. They normally perform fewer services than the merchant wholesalers and are typically involved in bringing together buyers and sellers. Agent

Figure 15-7   Services Provided by Merchant Wholesalers

Services	Full-Function Wholesalers	Limited-Function Wholesalers			
		Cash-and-Carry Wholesalers	Truck Wholesalers	Drop Shippers	Direct-response Wholealers
Anticipates customer needs	Yes	Yes	Yes	No	Yes
Carries inventory	Yes	Yes	Yes	No	Yes
Delivers	Yes	No	Yes	No	Yes (by mail)
Provides market information	Yes	Rarely	Yes	Yes	No
Provides credit	Yes	No	No	Yes	Sometimes
Assumes ownership risk by taking title	Yes	Yes	Yes	Yes	Yes

wholesaling intermediaries may be classified into five categories—commission merchants, auction companies, brokers, selling agents, and manufacturers' agents.

Commission merchants predominate in the marketing of agricultural products. The **commission merchant** *takes possession when the producer ships goods to a central market for sale.* The commission merchant acts as the producer's agent and receives an agreed-upon fee when a sale is made. Since customers will make inspections of the products and prices may fluctuate, the commission merchant is given considerable latitude in making decisions. The owner of the goods may specify a minimum price, but the commission merchant will sell them on a "best price" basis. The commission merchant deducts the appropriate fee from the price and the balance is remitted to the original seller.

A valuable service in such markets as used cars, livestock, antiques, tobacco, works of art, fur, flowers, and fruit is performed by agent wholesaling intermediaries known as **auction houses**. They *bring buyers and sellers together in one location and allow potential buyers to inspect the merchandise before purchasing.* A commission, often based on the sale price, is charged by the auction company for its services. Auction houses tend to specialize in merchandise categories such as agricultural products and art. Sotheby's is a world-famous auction house specializing in arts and related products.

The task of **brokers** is to *bring buyers and sellers together.* They operate in industries characterized by a large number of small suppliers and purchasers—real estate, frozen foods, and used machinery, for example. They may represent either buyer or seller in a given transaction, but not both. The broker receives a fee from the client when the transaction is completed. The service performed is finding buyers or sellers and negotiating for exchange of title. The operating expense ratio for the broker may be as low as 2 percent and rises depending on the services performed.

Because brokers operate on a one-time basis for sellers or buyers, they cannot serve as an effective marketing channel for manufacturers seeking regular, continuing services. A manufacturer who seeks to develop a more permanent channel utilizing agent wholesaling intermediaries must evaluate the use of the selling agent or the manufacturers' agent.

For small, poorly financed, production-oriented manufacturers, the **selling agent** may prove an ideal marketing channel. These wholesaling intermediaries have even been referred to as independent marketing departments, since they are *responsible for the total marketing program for the firm's product line*. They typically have full authority over pricing decisions and promotional outlays, and they often provide financial assistance for the manufacturer. The manufacturer can concentrate on production and rely on the expertise of the selling agent for all marketing activities.

Selling agents are common in the textile, coal, and lumber industries. Their operating expenses average about 3 percent of sales.

Instead of a single selling agent, a manufacturer may use a number of manufacturers' agents. A **manufacturers' agent** is essentially *an independent salesperson who works for a number of manufacturers of related but noncompeting products* and receives a commission based on a specified percentage of sales. Manufacturers' agents can be thought of as an independent sales force. Although some commissions may be as high as 20 percent of sales, they usually average between 6 and 7 percent. Unlike the selling agent, who may be given exclusive world rights to *market* a manufacturer's product, the manufacturers' agent *sells* in a specified territory.

Manufacturers' agents reduce their selling costs by spreading the cost per sales call over a number of different products. An agent in the plumbing supplies industry may represent a dozen different manufacturers.

Producers may develop their marketing channels through the use of manufacturers' agents for several reasons. First, when they are developing new sales territories the costs of adding new salespersons to "pioneer" new territories may be prohibitive. The agents, who are paid on a commission basis, can perform the sales function in the new territories at a much lower cost to the manufacturer.

Second, firms with unrelated lines may need to employ more than one channel. One line of products may be marketed through the company's sales force. A second, unrelated line might be marketed through independent manufacturers' agents. This is particularly common where the unrelated product line is a recent addition and the regular sales force has no experience with the products.

Finally, small firms with no existing sales force may turn to manufacturers' agents in order to have access to the market. A newly organized firm producing pencil sharpeners may use office equipment and supplies manufacturers' agents to reach retail outlets and industrial purchasers.

Although the importance of selling agents is now very limited because of the desire of manufacturers to have better control of their marketing programs, the volume of sales by manufacturers' agents has increased substantially since that date.

Retailer-Owned Facilities

Retailers have also assumed numerous wholesaling functions in attempts to reduce costs or to provide special service. Independent retailers have occasionally banded together to form buying groups in order to achieve cost savings through quantity purchases. Other groups of retailers have established retailer-owned wholesale facilities as a result of the formation of a co-operative chain. Larger chain retailers often establish centralized buying offices to negotiate large-scale purchases directly with manufacturers for the members of the chain. This was discussed in Chapter 14. The various types of agents and brokers are compared in Figure 15-8.

Independent Wholesaling Intermediaries — A Durable Marketing Institution

Many marketing observers of the 1920s felt that the end had come for the independent wholesaling intermediaries as chain stores grew in importance and attempted to bypass them. From 1929 to 1939 the independents' sales volume dropped, but it has increased again since then.

Figure 15-5 shows how the relative numbers and shares of total independent wholesale trade volumes have changed over two recent years. While this period has seen a more important role for company-owned channels, it is also true that independent wholesaling intermediaries are far from obsolete. Their continued importance is evidence of the ability of independent wholesaling intermediaries

Figure 15-8   Services Provided by Agents and Brokers

Services	Commission Merchants	Auction Houses	Brokers	Manufacturers' Agents	Selling Agents
Anticipates customer needs	Yes	Some	Some	Yes	Yes
Carries inventory	Yes	Yes	No	No	No
Delivers	Yes	No	No	Infrequently	No
Provides market information	Yes	Yes	Yes	Yes	Yes
Provides credit	Some	No	No	No	Some
Assumes ownership risk by taking title	No	No	No	No	No

to adjust to changing conditions and changing needs. Their market size proves their ability to continue to fill a need in many marketing channels.

Summary   Wholesaling is one of the two major institutions that make up many firms' marketing channels. (The second is retailing.) Wholesaling includes the activities of persons or firms selling to retailers and other wholesalers or to industrial users but who do not sell in significant amounts to ultimate consumers.

Three types of wholesaling intermediaries are manufacturer-owned facilities, independent wholesaling intermediaries, and retailer-owned co-operatives. In this last category are merchant wholesalers and agents and brokers. Merchant wholesalers take title to goods they handle. Agents and brokers may take possession, but do not take title to the goods. Merchant wholesalers include full-function wholesalers, cash-and-carry wholesalers, rack jobbers, truck jobbers, drop shippers, and mail-order wholesalers. Since they do not take title, commission merchants, auction companies, brokers, selling agents, and manufacturers' agents are classified as agent wholesaling intermediaries.

The operating expenses of wholesaling intermediaries vary considerably, depending on the number of services provided and the costs involved. These services may include storage facilities in conveniently located warehouses, market coverage by a sales force, financing for retailers and sometimes manufacturers, market information for retailers and manufacturers, transportation, and management services, sales training, and merchandising assistance and advice for retailers.

While the percentage of wholesale trade by manufacturer-owned facilities has increased since 1958, independent wholesaling intermediaries continue to account for a significant proportion of total wholesale trade. They accomplish this by continuing to provide desired services to manufacturers and retailers.

CHAPTER 16

Retailing

1. To relate retailing to the other variables of the marketing mix.

2. To outline the decision framework for retailing.

3. To distinguish between limited-line retailers and general merchandise retailers.

4. To identify and explain each of the five bases for categorizing retailers.

5. To identify the major types of mass merchandisers.

6. To explain the types of nonstore retailing.

7. To distinguish between chain and independent retailers and to identify several industries dominated by chains.

8. To contrast the three types of planned shopping centres.

They are as ubiquitous as fast-food outlets. Indeed, they may become to retailing in the 1980s what fast food was in the 1970s — a high growth area where entrepreneurs big and small can cash in on the changing tastes and needs of consumers. In the making is nothing short of a revolution. Some 500 home-video stores are now in business in Toronto where two years ago there were virtually none. And the revolution has found its way into all major centres and smaller cities across the country as the consumer appetite for video-cassette recorders and the movies and entertainment that they can provide grows more voracious.

Yet even as future home-video kings are opening up business for as little investment as $30 000, many operators are finding the fledgling business a minefield of risks. Some home-video stores are out of the picture within several months, their owner-managers left to wonder what went wrong.

Plenty can go wrong. Along with the usual start-up problems of undercapitalization, poor location and the like, the home-video entrepreneur is faced with the challenge of identifying just what business he or she is in. Is it a cassette-machine renting business? Should there be an emphasis on sales of equipment?

Competition is growing because franchise operators are entering the home-video market, as are the big mass merchandisers. The Bay, Eaton's, Simpson's, Loblaws, Dominion Stores, Consumers

Distributing, and K-mart are all feeling out the home-video market.

In addition to the growing competition, there is still high uncertainty as to which VCR technology will be popular in the future. The retailer who will make it in the long run will have to be very sensitive to the current market needs as well as the many cross-currents of change which are becoming evident in this retailing business.[1]

The Conceptual Framework

Retailing is the third aspect of distribution to be considered here. Chapter 14 introduced basic concepts in channel strategy. Wholesaling intermediaries were discussed in Chapter 15. This chapter explores retailing, which often links the consumer with the rest of the distribution channel.

In a very real sense, retailers *are* the marketing channel for most consumers, since consumers have little contact with manufacturers and almost none with the wholesaling intermediaries. As a result, the services provided — location, store hours, quality of salespeople, store layout, selection, and returns, among others — often figure even more importantly than the physical product in developing consumer images of the products and services offered.

Retailers are both customers and marketers in the channel. They market products and services to ultimate consumers, and also are the consumers for wholesalers and manufacturers. Because of their critical location in the channel, retailers may perform an important feedback role in obtaining information from customers and transmitting it to manufacturers and other channel members.

Retailing is the "last step of the marketing channel" for the consumer goods manufacturer. Whether the manufacturer has established a company-owned chain of retail stores or uses several of the thousands of retail stores in Canada, the success of the entire marketing strategy rides with the decisions of consumers in the retail store.

Retailing may be defined as *all the activities involved in the sale of products and services to the ultimate consumer.* Retailing involves not only sales in retail stores, but also several forms of nonstore retailing. These include telephone and direct-response sales, automatic merchandising, and direct house-to-house solicitations by salespersons.

Evolution of Retailing

Early retailing can be traced to the voyageurs, to the establishment of trading posts by the Hudson's Bay Company and others, and to pack peddlers who literally carried their wares to outlying settlements. After the trading post days, the Hudson's Bay and other retailers evolved into the institution known as the *general store.* The general store was stocked with general merchandise to meet the needs of a small community or rural area. Here customers could buy clothing, groceries, feed, seed, farm equipment, drugs, spectacles, and candy. The following account provides a good description of this early retail institution:

> The country store was in many respects a departmental store on a small scale, for a well-equipped store contained a little of everything. On one side were to be seen shelves well filled with groceries, crockery-ware, and a few patent medicines, such as blood purifiers, painkillers, and liniments; on the other side, a well assorted stock of dry goods, including prints, woollens, muslins, calico, cottons, etc. At the back, a lot of hardware, comprising nails, paints, oils, putty, glass, and garden tools, as well as an assortment of boots and shoes — from the tiny copper-toe to the farmer's big cowhide. In the back room, at the rear end of the store, were to be found barrels of sugar and New Orleans molasses, crates of eggs, and tubs of butter and lard. With this miscellaneous mixture — tea, coffee, dry goods, codfish, and boots and shoes — the odour of the country store was truly a composite one, and trying to the olfactory organs of the visitor. The country merchant was usually a man in good circumstances, for he was obliged in most cases to give a year's credit, the farmers paying their bills in the fall of the year, after the "threshing" or the "killing"; their only source of revenue at any other time being from butter and eggs, which their wives took to the country store, usually once a week, and exchanged for store goods. Perhaps there was no more popular place of meeting than the country store. After the day's work was over, it was customary for many of the men in the neighbourhood, especially the farmers' hired men, who had no other place of amusement to go to, to gather here. Even if they did not have occasion to buy anything, they would drop in for a few minutes to while away the time; have a chat, see someone they wished, hear politics discussed, and generally learn all the latest news. The society of the country store had a peculiar fascination for many of them, for there generally happened to be some one there who was gifted with the faculty of cracking jokes, telling funny yarns, or interesting stories; besides it was a comfortable place, especially on the long winter evenings, when they would gather around the big box stove, lounge on the counters, sit on the boxes and barrels, puff away at their pipes, chew tobacco, and chaff one another to their heart's content.[2]

The basic needs that caused the general store to develop also doomed this institution to a limited existence. Since the general storekeepers attempted to satisfy the needs of customers for all types of "store-bought" goods, they carried a small assortment of each good. As the villages grew, the size of the market was large enough to support stores specializing in specific product lines, such as groceries, hardware, dry goods, and drugs. Most general stores either converted into more specialized limited-line stores or closed. But the general store did, and in some rural areas still does, fill a need for its customers. General stores are still operated profitably in less developed countries where income levels cannot support more specialized retailers, and in some isolated parts of Canada as well.

Innovation in Retailing

Retailing operations are remarkable illustrations of the marketing concept in operation. The development of new retail innovations can be traced to attempts to better satisfy particular consumer needs.

As consumers demand different bundles of satisfactions from retailers, new institutions emerge to meet this demand. The supermarket appeared in the early 1930s to meet consumer desires for lower prices. Convenience food stores today meet the consumer's desire for convenience in purchasing and after-hours availability. Discount houses and catalogue stores reflect consumer demands for lower prices and a willingness to give up services. Department stores provide a wide variety of products and services to meet the demands of their clientele. Vending machines, door-to-door retailers, and mail-order retailing offer buyer convenience. Planned shopping centres provide a balanced array of consumer goods and services and include parking facilities for their customers. Canada's 162 000 retailing establishments are involved in developing specific marketing mixes designed to satisfy chosen market targets.[3]

The Framework for Decisions in Retailing

The retailer's decision-making process, like the producer's and wholesaler's, centres upon the two fundamental steps of 1) analysing, evaluating, and ultimately selecting a *market target*, and 2) development of a *marketing mix* designed to satisfy the chosen market target profitably. In other words, the retailer must develop a product or service offering to appeal to the chosen consumer group, set prices, and choose a location and method of distribution. Finally, the retailer has to develop a promotional strategy.

The Market Target

Like other marketers, retailers must start by selecting the market target to which they wish to appeal. Marketing research is often used in this aspect of retail decision-making. For example, retailers entering new countries, or even new markets in the same country, have been surprised that the same target market as in the home location apparently does not exist. Canadian Tire expanded to the larger U.S. market with the purchase of White Stores, Inc., but has found that U.S. market acceptance of virtual carbon copies of the successful Canadian stores has been very slow.[4] Marketing research will help a company adjust to a new environment faster.

Sometimes a retailer finds it necessary to shift market targets. For example, stores established to serve specialty markets such as skiers or snowmobiles have found that lack of snow or changes in consumer recreation habits have forced them to expand or change their offerings to serve more viable target markets. Market selection is as vital an aspect of retailers' marketing strategy as it is for any other marketer.

Product/Service Strategy

Retailers must also determine and evaluate their offerings with respect to:
1. general product/service categories
2. specific lines
3. specific products
4. inventory depth
5. width of assortment.

The starting point is to assess their positions in the product/service matrix (shown in Figure 16-2, which appears later in this chapter), which relates convenience, shopping, and specialty retailers to convenience, shopping, and specialty goods. Other marketing factors can influence product and/or service offerings. For instance, the discount-price policies of warehouse supermarkets force these retailers to restrict their product offerings to 1500 to 1700 items, compared to the 15 000 found in traditional supermarkets.[5]

Product strategy evolves to meet competition as well as changing consumer needs. Smaller specialty food stores developed an intriguing version of the old-time bulk-food grocery store. The new version offered quality products that could be purchased in exactly the amount desired by consumers. Furthermore, it was a novel idea. It combined the concept of self-service within a relatively intimate store atmosphere, *and* was economical.

Many supermarkets have now added similar bulk food facilities. They have done so to be competitive with the smaller shops, as well as to try to differentiate themselves from their larger rivals. Competition, as well as demand, has forced such modifications to product strategy despite the fact that it is more inconvenient for a large mass retailer to handle bulk foods.

Retail Pricing Strategy

Pricing is another critical element of the retailing mix. The essential decisions concern relative price levels. Does the store want to offer higher-priced merchandise (as Holt Renfrew does) or lower-priced items (like Zellers)? Some of the larger department stores such as Eaton's have clearly opted for a higher-price strategy, but try simultaneously to serve some of the lower-priced market targets with basement and warehouse outlets.

Other pricing decisions concern markups, markdowns, loss leaders, odd pricing, and promotional pricing. The retailer is the channel member with direct responsibility for the prices paid by consumers. As Chapters 12 and 13 pointed out, the prices that are set play a major role in buyer perceptions of the retail market.

Location and Distribution Decisions

Real estate professionals often point out that location may be the determining factor in the success or failure of a retail business. A store must be in an appropriate location for the type and price of merchandise carried. Small service outlets such as dry cleaners have discovered that there is a difference between being on the "going to work" side of a busy street and the "going home" side. Other retailers have found success in small strip neighbourhood shopping centres that are close to where people live. These centres continue to flourish despite the advent of larger suburban community shopping centres.[6]

Retail Trade Area Analysis

Retail trade area analysis refers to *studies that assess the relative drawing power of alternative retail locations.* For example, shoppers might be polled as to where they live, how they get to the stores they shop at, how long it takes, how often they shop, and the like. Similarly, the credit charges of an existing store might be plotted to show what its service area is.

Another technique to use is the law of retail gravitation, sometimes called Reilly's law after its originator, William J. Reilly.[7] The **law of retail gravitation**, originally formulated in the 1920s, *delineates the retail trade area of a potential site on the basis of distance between alternative locations and relative populations.* The formula is:

$$\text{Breaking Point in km from A} = \frac{\text{km between A and B}}{1 + \sqrt{\dfrac{\text{Population of B}}{\text{Population of A}}}}$$

Assume a retailer is considering locating a new outlet in Town A or Town B, which are located 60 km from each other. The population of A is 80 000 and the population of B, 20 000. One of the questions that concerns the retailer is where people living in a small rural community located on the highway between the two towns 25 km from B are likely to shop.

According to the law of retail gravitation, these rural shoppers would most likely shop in A even though it was 10 km further away than B. The retail trade area of A extends 40 km toward B, and the rural community was located only 35 km away.

$$\text{Breaking Point in km from A} = \frac{60}{1 + \sqrt{\dfrac{20\ 000}{80\ 000}}} = \frac{60}{1 + \sqrt{.25}} = \frac{60}{1.5} = 40$$

The formula can be applied inversely to find B's trade area, yielding a figure of 20 km, which falls 5 km short of the rural community.

$$\text{Breaking Point in km from B} = \frac{60}{1 + \sqrt{\frac{80\ 000}{20\ 000}}} = \frac{60}{1 + \sqrt{4}} = \frac{60}{3} = 20 \text{ km}$$

The complete trade area for A or B could be found by similar calculations with other communities.

The application of this technique is limited in an area of urban sprawl, regional shopping centres, and consumers who measure distances in terms of travel time. As a result, a contemporary version of retail trade analysis has been offered by David Huff.

Huff's work is an interurban model that assesses the likelihood that a consumer will patronize a specific shopping centre. Trading areas are expressed in terms of a series of probability contours. The probability that a consumer will patronize a specific shopping centre is viewed as a function of centre size, travel time, and the type of merchandise sought. Practical application of such models, however, are difficult. They are more often used for structuring decision-making than as a precise, predictive tool.

Other Distribution Decisions   Retailers are faced with a variety of other distribution decisions, largely in order to ensure that adequate quantities of stock are available when consumers want to buy. The definition of "adequate" will vary with the service strategy of the retailer. Since the cost of carrying inventory is high, a high-margin full-service retailer will likely have a greater depth and range of merchandise than a low-margin, limited-line, high-volume outlet.

Retail Image and Promotional Strategy

Retail image refers to *the consumer's perception of a store and of the shopping experience it provides.* Promotional strategy is a key element in determining the store's image with the consumer. Another important element is the amenities provided by the retailer — the so-called "atmospherics."

Promoting a store with screaming headlines about fantastic once-in-a-lifetime sale prices creates a substantially different image than using a subdued, tasteful illustration of clothing of obvious style and elegance. Similarly, walking into a discount store redolent of caramel popcorn produces an image dramatically different from that of entering a beautifully carpeted boutique.

Regardless of how it is accomplished, the objective of retailer promotional strategy should be to position the consumer's perception of the store in line with other elements of the retailing mix: retail image should match the market target that is selected.

Categorizing Retailers by Retailing Strategy

The nation's retailers come in a variety of forms. Since new types of retail operations continue to evolve in response to changing demands of their markets, no universal classification has been devised. The following characteristics or bases can be used in categorizing them:
1. shopping effort expended by customers
2. services provided to customers
3. product lines
4. location of retail transactions
5. form of ownership.

Any retailing operation can be classified using these five bases. A 7 – Eleven food store may be classified as a convenience store (category 1); self-service (category 2); relatively narrow product lines (category 3); in-store retailing (category 4); and a member of a corporate chain (category 5). Figure 16-1 illustrates the bases for classifying retail operations.

Figure 16-1   Bases for Classifying Retailers

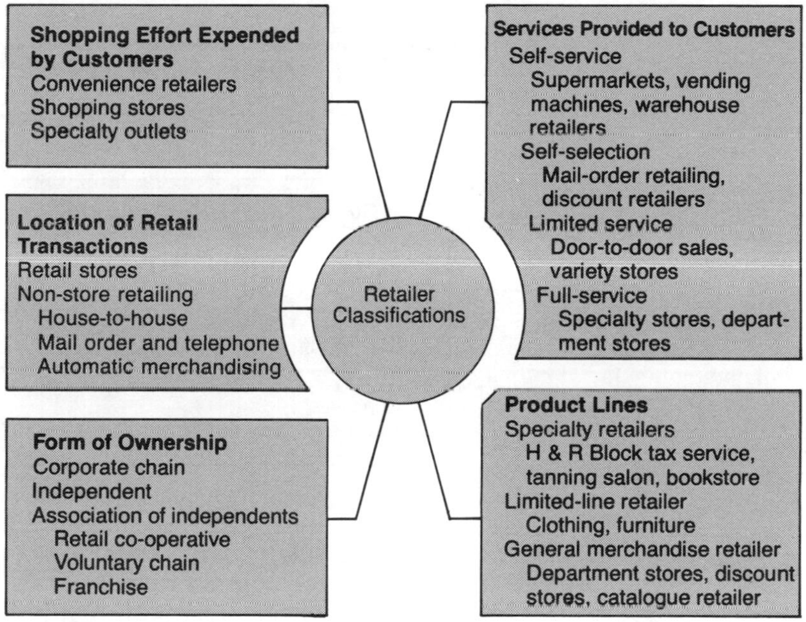

Retailers Classified by Shopping Effort

A three-way classification of consumer goods based on consumer purchase patterns in securing a particular product or service was presented in Chapter 9. This system can be extended to retailers by considering the reasons consumers shop at a particular retail outlet. The result is a classification scheme in which retail outlets, like consumer goods, are categorized as convenience, shopping, or specialty.[8] The type of retail outlet has a significant influence on the marketing strategies the retailer should select. *Convenience retailers* focus on convenient locations, long store hours, rapid checkout service, and adequate parking facilities. Small food stores, gasoline retailers, and some barber shops may be included in this category.

Shopping stores typically include furniture stores, appliance retailers, clothing outlets, and sporting goods stores. Consumers will compare prices, assortments, and quality levels of competing outlets before making a purchase decision. Managers of shopping stores attempt to differentiate their outlets through advertising, window displays and in-store layouts, knowledgeable salespeople, and appropriate merchandise assortments.

Specialty retailers provide some combination of product lines, service, and reputation that results in consumers' willingness to expend considerable effort to shop there. Holt Renfrew and Birks have developed a sufficient degree of preference among many shoppers to be categorized as specialty retailers.

Figure 16-2   Matrix of Consumer Purchase Behaviour

Goods	Retailers		
	Convenience	Shopping	Specialty
Convenience	1	4	7
Shopping	2	5	8
Specialty	3	6	9

A Product/Retailer Matrix

By cross-classifying the product and retailer classifications, a matrix is created representing nine possible types of consumer purchase behaviour. This matrix is shown in Figure 16-2.

Behaviour patterns in each numbered cell can be described as:

1. *Convenience store–convenience good*. The consumer purchases the most readily available brand of the product at the nearest store.
2. *Convenience store–shopping good*. The consumer chooses a product from among the assortment carried by the most accessible store.

3. *Convenience store–specialty good*. The consumer purchases a favoured brand from the nearest store carrying it.
4. *Shopping store–convenience good*. The consumer is indifferent to the brand purchased; shopping is done among competing stores to secure the best service or price.
5. *Shopping store–shopping good*. The consumer makes comparisons among store-controlled factors and factors associated with the product or brand.
6. *Shopping store–specialty good*. The consumer purchases only a favourite brand but shops among a number of stores to obtain the best service or price for it.
7. *Specialty store–convenience good*. The consumer trades only at a specific store and is indifferent to the brand purchased.
8. *Specialty store–shopping good*. The consumer trades only at a specific store and chooses a product from among the assortment carried by it.
9. *Specialty store–specialty good*. The consumer has a strong preference for both a particular store and a specific brand.

This matrix gives a realistic picture of how people buy. The most exclusive specialty store carries handkerchiefs, and many supermarkets have gourmet food departments. The cross-classification system should help the retailer develop appropriate marketing strategies to satisfy particular market segments. The retailer who chooses cells 8 and 9 must seek to develop an image of exclusivity and a good selection of widely accepted competing brands. The same retailer must also carry an assortment of specialty goods, such as high-fashion clothing and expensive perfumes.

Retailers Classified by Services Provided

Some retailers seek a differential advantage by developing a unique combination of service offerings for the customers who compose their market target. Retailing operations may be classified according to the extent of the services they offer. Figure 16-3 indicates the spectrum of retailer services from virtually no services (self-service) to a full range of customer services (full-service retailers).

Since the self-service and self-selection retailers provide few services to their customers, retailer location and price are important factors. These retailers tend to specialize in staple and convenience goods that are purchased frequently by customers and require little product service or advice from retail personnel.

The full-service retail establishments focus more on fashion-oriented shopping goods and specialty items and offer a wide variety of services for their clientele. As a result, their prices tend to be higher than those of self-service retailers due to the higher operating costs associated with the services.

Figure 16-3   Classification of Retailers on the Basis of Customer Service Levels

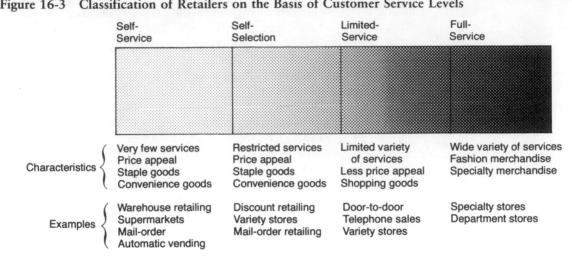

Source: Adapted from *Retailing Management: A Planning Approach*, p. 12, by Larry D. Redinbaugh. Copyright © 1976 McGraw-Hill Book Company. Used with the permission of McGraw-Hill Book Company.

Retailers Classified by Product Lines

A commonly used method of categorizing retailers is to consider the product lines they handle. Grouping retailers by product lines produces three major categories: limited-line stores, specialty stores, and general merchandise retailers. Figure 16-4 shows changing shopping patterns by comparing retail trade for type of outlet in 1975 and 1980.

Limited-Line Retailers

A large assortment of a single line of products or a few related lines of goods are offered in **limited-line stores**. Their development paralleled the growth of towns when the population grew sufficiently to support them. These operations include such retailers as furniture stores, hardware stores, grocery stores and supermarkets, appliance stores, and sporting goods stores. Examples of limited-line stores include Sherwin-Williams (paints), Leon's and House of Teak (furniture), Radio Shack (home electronics), Agnew Surpass and Bata (shoes), Calculator World (electronic calculators), D'Allaird's (ready-to-wear), and Coles (books).

These retailers choose to cater to the needs of a specific market target—people who want to select from a complete line in purchasing a particular product. The marketing vice-president of one limited-line firm summarized the limited-line retailer's strategy this way: "Sears can show customers three types of football, but we can show them 40.[9] Most retailers are in the limited-line category.

Figure 16-4   Retail Trade by Type of Outlet

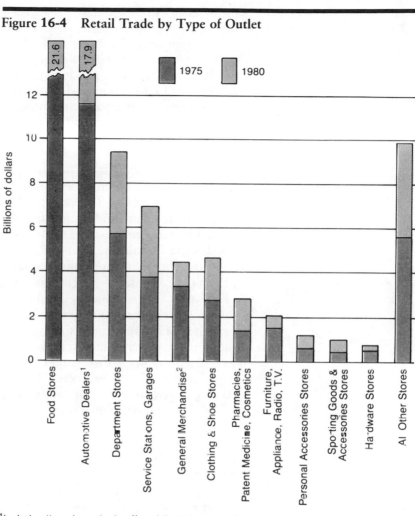

[1] Includes "used car dealers" and "auto parts and accessories stores."

[2] Includes "general stores" and "variety stores."

Source: Statistics Canada: The Conference Board of Canada.

Source: *Handbook of Canadian Consumer Markets, 1982*, The Conference Board of Canada, p. 192.

The Supermarket   Until the 1920s, food purchases were made at full-service grocery stores. Store personnel filled orders (often from a shopping list presented to them), provided delivery services, and often granted credit to their customers. The supermarket eliminated these services in exchange for lower prices, and it quickly revolutionized food shopping in Canada and much of the world.

A **supermarket** can be defined as *a large-scale, departmentalized retail store offering a large variety of food products* such as meats, produce, dairy products, canned goods, and frozen foods in addition to various nonfood items. It operates on a *self-service* basis and emphasizes price and adequate parking facilities. Supermarket customers typically shop once or twice a week and make fill-in purchases between each major shopping trip. Although supermarkets account for only 1546 of the 31 310 food stores in Canada (1977 figures), they have a large percentage of total food sales. In combination with the convenience stores (Becker's, Mac's Milk, etc.) their sales reached nearly 60 percent of all food sales in 1977. The largest supermarket chains in Canada are Provigo, Canada Safeway, stores owned by George Weston Ltd. (Loblaws, Super Valu, and Westfair Foods) and Dominion Stores.[10]

In recent years supermarkets have become increasingly competitive. One Ontario supermarket attempted to increase its share of the market through a well-publicized price-cutting program. The ramifications were quickly felt in other areas of the country where branches of competing chains operate. Retaliation by other supermarkets was swift, and temporary price cuts ensued — as well as reductions in profits. Supermarket profits average only about 1 percent of sales after taxes. However, a high turnover of 20–26 times per year provides attractive returns on investment.

With a razor-thin profit margin, supermarkets compete through careful planning of retail displays in order to sell more merchandise per week and reduce the amount of investment in inventory. Product location is studied carefully in order to expose the consumer to as much merchandise as possible (and increase impulse purchases). In an attempt to fight the fast-food threat — the tendency of consumers to eat many of their meals outside the home — supermarkets have begun to feature their own delicatessens and bakeries, and to devote ever increasing portions of their stores to nonfood items. Nonfood products such as toys, toiletries, magazines, records, over-the-counter drugs, and small kitchen utensils are carried for two reasons: 1) consumers have displayed a willingness to buy such items in supermarkets, and 2) supermarket managers like them because they have a higher profit margin than the food products. Non-food sales have grown substantially as a percentage of supermarket sales.

Another change is an increased emphasis on warehouse stores, box stores (carrying a very limited line of high-volume items which customers carry out in discarded boxes), and food barns. All of these provide fewer items within a narrower range of size and brand options than conventional supermarkets.[11]

Specialty Stores   A **specialty store** typically *handles only part of a single line of products*. However, this narrow line is stocked in considerable depth. Such stores include meat markets, shoe stores, bakeries, furriers, and luggage shops. Although some of these stores are operated by chains, most are run as independent small-scale operations. The specialty store is perhaps the greatest stronghold of the independent retailer, who can develop expertise in providing a very narrow line of products for his or her local market.

Specialty stores should not be confused with specialty goods, for the specialty store typically carries convenience and shopping goods. The label "specialty" comes from the practice of handling a specific, narrow line of merchandise.

General Merchandise Retailers

Department Stores   The department store is actually a series of limited-line and specialty stores under one roof. A **department store**, by definition, is *a large retail firm handling a variety of merchandise* that includes men's and boy's wear, women's wear and accessories, household linens and dry goods, home furnishings, appliances, and furniture. It serves the consumer by acting as a one-stop shopping centre for almost all personal and household items.

A distinguishing feature of the department store is indicated by its name. The entire store is *organized around departments* for the purposes of service, promotion, and control. A general merchandising manager is responsible for the entire store's product planning. Reporting to the merchandising manager are the buyers who manage each department. The buyers typically run the departments almost as independent businesses and are given considerable discretion in merchandising and layout decisions. Acceptance of the retailing axiom that "well-purchased goods are half sold" is indicated in the department manager's title of *buyer*. The buyers, particularly those in charge of high-fashion departments, spend a considerable portion of their time making decisions concerning the inventory to be carried in their departments.

The department store has been the symbol of retailing since the turn of the century. It started in Canada with Timothy Eaton in 1869, when he purchased the 4 m-wide dry-goods store and stock of William Jennings for $6500. Eaton established a one-price, cash policy (instead of bargaining and paying in produce) and formulated the famous "goods satisfactory or money refunded" guarantee. By 1929, half the retail sales in Canada were made at Eaton's.

Today, almost every urban area in Canada has one or more department stores associated with its downtown area and its major shopping areas. Department stores have had a major impact in many cities. For example, as recently as 1969, Eaton's received 40 percent of every retail dollar (except groceries) in Winnipeg.

The impact of department stores on urban life is not confined to

Canada. Such stores are, of course, widespread in the United States. European shoppers associate London with Harrod's, Paris with Au Printemps, and Moscow with GUM. Myer is the dominant department store in both Melbourne and Sydney.

Department stores are known for offering their customers a wide variety of services such as charge accounts, delivery, gift wrapping, and liberal return privileges. In addition, approximately 50 percent of their employees and some 40 percent of their floor space are devoted to nonselling activities. As a result, department stores have relatively high operating costs, averaging between 45 and 60 percent of sales.

Department stores have faced intense competition in the past 30 years. Their relatively high operating costs make them vulnerable to such new retailing innovations as discount stores, catalogue merchandisers, and hypermarkets (discussed later in this section). In addition, department stores are typically located in downtown business districts and experience the problems associated with limited parking, traffic congestion, and urban migration to the suburbs.

Department stores have displayed a willingness to adapt to changing consumer desires. Addition of bargain basements and expansion of parking facilities were attempts to compete with discount operations and suburban retailers. Also, department stores have followed the movement of the population to the suburbs by opening major branches in outlying shopping centres. Canadian department stores have led other retailers in maintaining a vital and dynamic downtown through modernization of their stores, extended store hours, emphasis on attracting the trade of tourists and people attending conventions, and focusing on the residents of the central cities. For example, the first new major downtown department store in more than 20 years in North America was opened by Eaton's in Vancouver in 1973, followed in 1977 by the 108 500 m^2 Eaton Centre in downtown Toronto. The complex has over 300 boutiques, restaurants, and stores along a three-level 260 m long shopping mall, in addition to Eaton's and nearby Simpsons anchor stores.

Retail firms that offer an extensive range and assortment of low-priced merchandise are called variety stores. Some examples are Woolworth and Stedmans. The nation's variety stores account for only about 1.2 percent of all retail sales.[12] Variety stores are not as popular as they once were. Many have evolved into or been replaced by other retailing categories such as discounting.

Mass merchandising has made major inroads on department store sales during the past two decades by emphasizing lower prices for well-known brand-name products, high turnover of goods, and reduced services. **Mass merchandisers** often stock a *wider line of products than department stores*, but they usually do not offer the depth of assortment in each line. Major types of mass merchandisers are discount houses, hypermarkets, and catalogue retailers.

Discount Houses— Limited Services and Lower Prices.   The birth of the modern **discount house** came at the end of World War II when a New York operation named Masters discovered that a very large number of customers were willing to shop at a store that *did not offer such traditional retail services* as credit, sales assistance by clerks, and delivery, *in exchange for reduced prices*. Within a very brief period retailers throughout the country followed the Masters formula and either changed over from their traditional operations or opened new stores dedicated to discounting. At first the discount stores were primarily involved with the sale of appliances, but they have spread into furniture, soft goods, drugs, and even food.

Discount operations had existed in previous years, but the early discounters usually operated from manufacturers' catalogues, with no stock on display and often a limited number of potential customers. The new discounters operated large stores, advertised heavily, emphasized low prices on well-known brands, and were open to the public. Elimination of many of the "free" services provided by traditional retailers allowed the discount operations to reduce their markups to 10 to 25 percent below their competitors. And consumers, who had become accustomed to self-service by shopping at supermarkets, responded in great numbers to this retailing innovation. Conventional retailers such as Kresge and Woolworth joined the discounting practice by opening their own K-mart and Woolco stores.

As the discount houses move into new product areas, a noticeable increase in the number of services offered as well as a corresponding decrease in the discount margin is evident. Carpets are beginning to appear in discounters' stores, credit is increasingly available, and many discounters are even quietly dropping the term *discount* from their name. Even though they still offer fewer services, their operating costs are increasing as they become similar to the traditional department stores. Some have even moved into the "best" shopping areas, and now offer such name brands as Seiko watches, Puma running shoes, and Pentax cameras.

Hypermarkets — Shopping Centres in a Single Store. A relatively recent retailing development has been the introduction of **hypermarkets** — giant *mass merchandisers who operate on a low-price, self-service basis and carry lines of soft goods and groceries*. Hypermarkets are sometimes called superstores, although this latter term has also been used to describe a variety of large retail operations. The *hypermarché*, or hypermarket, began in France and has since spread to Canada and the United States to a limited degree. The Hypermarché Laval outside Montreal was the first to open and had 19 500 m² of selling space (11 to 15 times the size of the average supermarket) and 40 checkouts. A typical hypermarket is like a shopping centre in a single store. It sells food, hardware, soft goods, building materials, auto supplies, appliances, and prescription drugs, and has a restaurant, beauty salon, barber shop, bank branch, and bakery. More than 1000 of these superstores are currently in operation throughout the world. It appears that they are more popular in Europe than in North America. This is likely because North America already had many large, well-developed shopping centres before the hypermarket concept arrived.

Catalogue Retailers   One of the major growth areas in retailing in the past decade has been that of catalogue retailing. **Catalogue retailers** *mail catalogues to their customers and operate from a showroom* displaying samples of their products. Orders are filled from a backroom warehouse. Price is an important factor for catalogue store customers, and low prices are made possible by few services, storage of most of the inventory in the warehouse, reduced shoplifting losses, and handling products that are unlikely to become obsolete, such as luggage, small appliances, gift items, sporting equipment, toys, and jewellery. The largest catalogue retailer in Canada is Consumers Distributing. (Mail-order catalogue retailing is discussed later in this chapter.)

Retailers Classified by Location of Retail Transaction	A fourth method of categorizing retailers is by determining whether the transaction takes place in a store. While the overwhelming majority of retail sales occur in retail stores, non-store retailing is important for many products. Non-store retailing includes direct house-to-house sales, mail-order retailing, and automatic merchandising machines. These kinds of sales account for about 2.5 percent of all retail sales.
House-to-House Retailing	One of the oldest marketing channels was built around direct contact between the retailer seller and the customer at the home of the customer — *house-to-house retailing*. It provides maximum convenience for the consumer and allows the manufacturer to control the firm's marketing channel. House-to-house retailing is a minor part of the retailing picture with less than 1 percent of all retail sales.

House-to-house retailing is conducted by a number of different merchandisers. Manufacturers of such products as bakery and dairy products and newspapers utilize this channel. Firms whose products require emphasis on personal selling and product demonstrations may also use it. Such products and services would include, for example, cosmetics (Avon), vacuum cleaners (Electrolux), household brushes (Fuller Brush Company), encyclopedias (World Book), and insurance.

Some firms, such as Tupperware, and Stanley Home Products, use a variation called *party-plan selling* where a customer gives a party and invites several neighbours and friends. During the party a company representative makes a presentation of the products, and the host or hostess receives a commission based on the amount of products sold. Another version depends heavily on the *personal influence network* and "positive thinking" techniques — for example, Amway and Shaklee. Friends and acquaintances are recruited to recruit others and sell merchandise. A commission scheme on sales made by recruits makes it generally more profitable for sponsors to aggressively solicit recruits than sell themselves.

The house-to-house method of retailing would appear to be a low-cost method of distribution. No plush retail facilities are required; no investment in inventory is necessary; and most house-to-house salespersons operate on a commission basis. In fact, this method is an extremely high-cost approach to distribution. Often the distribution cost of a product marketed through retail stores is half that of the same product retailed house-to-house. High travel costs, the problems involved in recruiting and training a huge sales force that generally has a high turnover, nonproductive calls, several layers of commissions, and the limited number of contacts per day result in high operating expenses.

Mail-Order Retailing   The customers of *mail-order merchandisers* can order merchandise by mail, by telephone, or by visiting the mail-order desk of a retail store. Goods are then shipped to the customer's home or to the local retail store.

Figure 16-5   Factors Contributing to the Success of Mail-Order Catalogues

Socio-Economic Factors	External Factors	Competitive Factors
More women joining the work force	Rising costs of gasoline	Inconvenient store hours
Population growing older	Availability of WATS (800) lines	Unsatisfactory service in stores
Rising discretionary income	Expanded use of credit cards	Difficulty of parking, especially near downtown stores
More single households	Low-cost data processing	"If you can't beat 'em join 'em" approach of traditional retailers
Growth of the "me generation"	Availability of mailing lists	

Source: John A. Quelch and Hirotaka Takeuchi, "Nonstore Marketing: Fast Track or Slow?" *Harvard Business Review* (July–August 1981), p. 77. Reprinted by permission of the *Harvard Business Review*. Copyright © 1981 by the President and Fellows of Harvard College; all rights reserved.

Figure 16-5 identifies a number of socio-economic, external, and competitive factors that have contributed to the growing consumer acceptance of catalogue retailing.

Many department stores and specialty stores issue catalogues to seek telephone and mail-order sales and to promote in-store purchases of items featured in the catalogues. Among typical department stores, telephone, and mail-generated orders account for 15 percent of total volume during the Christmas season.[13]

Mail-order selling began in Canada in 1894 when Eaton's distributed a slim 32-page booklet to rural visitors at the Canadian National Exposition in Toronto. That first catalogue contained only a few items, mostly clothing and farm supplies. Simpsons soon followed, and mail-order retailing became an important source of products in isolated Canadian settlements.

Even though mail-order sales represent only a small percentage of all retail sales, it is an important channel for many consumers who desire convenience and a large selection of colours and sizes.

With the demise of the Eaton's catalogue sales operations in 1976, apparently due to a failure to introduce effective cost and inventory control measures, Simpsons-Sears became the one major mail-order catalogue marketer left in Canada. Sales have been strong. Catalogue sales contributed at least a third to Simpsons-Sears' $3.1 billion in sales in 1982. Simpsons-Sears now has nearly 1300 catalogue sales offices across Canada and produces 11 catalogues a year, with a combined distribution of 45 million.[14]

Mail-order houses offer a wide range of products — from novelty items (Regal Gifts) to sporting equipment (S.I.R.). The growing number of working women, increasing time pressures, and a decline in customer service in some department stores augur well for catalogue sales.

Automatic Merchandising

Automatic vending machines — the true robot stores — are a good way to purchase a wide range of convenience goods. These machines accounted for over $363 million in sales in Canada.[15] Approximately 122 000 vending machines are currently in operation throughout the country.

While automatic merchandising is important in the retailing of some products, it represents less than 1 percent of all retail sales. Its future growth is limited by such factors as the cost of machines and the necessity for regular maintenance and repair. In addition, automatically vended products are confined to convenience goods that are standardized in size and weight with a high rate of turnover. Prices for some products purchased in vending machines are higher than store prices for the same products.

Retailers Classified by Form of Ownership

The fifth method of classifying retailers is by ownership. The two major types are corporate chain stores and independent retailers. In addition, independent retailers may join a wholesaler-sponsored voluntary chain, band together to form a retail co-operative, or enter into a franchise arrangement through contractual agreements with a manufacturer, wholesaler, or service organization. Each type has its special characteristics.

Chain Stores

Chain stores are *groups of retail stores that are centrally owned and managed and handle the same lines of products.* The concept of chain stores is certainly not new; the Mitsui chain was operating in Japan in the 1600s. Woolworth's, Zellers, The Bay, and Reitman's have operated in Canada for many years.

The major advantage possessed by chain operations over independent retailers is economies of scale. Volume purchases through a central buying office allow such chains as Safeway and Dominion to obtain lower prices than independents. Since a chain such as Safeway has hundreds of retail stores, specialists in layout, sales training, and accounting systems may be used to increase efficiency. And advertising can be effectively used. An advertisement in a national magazine for Eaton's promotes every Eaton's store in Canada.

Chains account for approximately one-third of all retail stores and their dollar volume of sales amounts to 44 percent of all retail sales. At the present time, chains dominate four fields: department stores, with virtually 100 percent of department store sales; variety stores, with 82.6 percent of all variety sales; shoe stores, with 68 percent of all retail shoes sales; and food stores, with 55 percent of all retail food sales.[16] Figure 16-6 lists the 25 largest retailers in Canada.

Many of the larger chains have expanded their operations to the rest of the world. Sears now has branch stores in Spain, Mexico, and several countries in South America. Safeway operates supermarkets in Germany, the United Kingdom, and Australia. Bowring's has expanded internationally, as has Marks & Spencer. Direct retailers such as Avon and Tupperware have sales representatives in Europe, South America, and Southeast Asia.

Independent Retailers

Even though most retailers are small independent operators, the large chains dominate a number of fields. As Figure 16-7 indicates, about 13 percent of all stores in Canada have sales of less than $100 000 each year. The Canadian retailing structure can be characterized as a very large number of small stores, a sizeable number of medium-size stores, and a very small number of large stores. Even

Figure 16-6   The Top 25 Retailers, 1984

Top 25 Retailers, 1984	Operating Revenue ($000)	Type
1. George Weston	8,254,700	food distributor
2. Loblaw Companies	6,419,400	food distributor
3. Hudson's Bay	4,829,325	department store
4. Provigo	3,891,151	food distributor
5. Steinberg	3,452,275	food distributor
6. Sears Canada	3,440,744	department store
7. Canada Safeway	3,437,683	food distributor
8. Oshawa Group	2,434,985	food distributor
9. Argcen Holdings	2,218,856	food distributor
10. Canadian Tire	2,108,594	specialty store
11. F. W. Woolworth	1,733,697	department store
12. Kelly Douglas & Co.	1,702,045	food distributor
13. Woodward's	1,091,162	department store
14. Westfair Foods	1,057,756	food distributor
15. K mart Canada	1,004,197	department store
16. Consumers Distributing	898,916	specialty store
17. Dylex	822,404	clothing store
18. Empire	755,753	food distributor
19. Sobeys Stores	672,603	food distributor
20. Silcorp	479,162	food distributor
21. Gendis	474,005	department store
22. Grafton Group	420,654	clothing store
23. Reitmans (Canada)	282,347	clothing store
24. Marks & Spencer Canada	276,648	clothing store
25. Becker Milk	257,226	food distributor

though only about 3 percent of all stores have annual sales of $1 million or more, they account for nearly one-half of all retail sales in Canada.

Independents have attempted to compete with chains in a number of ways. Some independents were unable to do so efficiently and went out of business. Others have joined retail co-operatives, wholesaler-sponsored voluntary chains, or franchise operations as described in Chapter 14. Still others have remained in business by exploiting their advantages of flexibility in operation and knowledge of local market conditions. The independents continue to represent a major part of Canadian retailing.

Figure 16-7   Retail Trade in Canada by Sales Size of Establishments

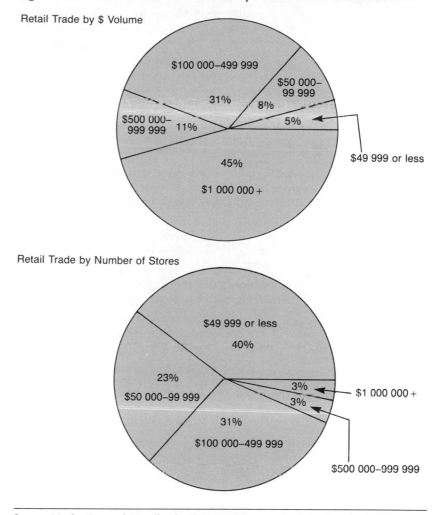

Source: *Market Research Handbook*, CS 63-224 (Ottawa: Statistics Canada, 1977), pp. 146–147. By permission of the Minister of Supply and Services Canada.

Significant Developments Affecting Retailing Strategy

Two developments that have significantly altered retailing strategy in recent decades are the development of the planned shopping centre and the practice of scrambled merchandising. Both have a significant impact on the retail environment in Canada.

Planned Shopping Centres

A pronounced shift of retail trade has been developing since 1950 away from the traditional downtown retailing districts and toward suburban shopping centres. A **planned shopping centre** is a *group of retail stores planned, co-ordinated, and marketed as a unit* to shoppers in a particular geographic trade area. These centres have followed population shifts to the suburbs and have focused on correcting many of the problems involved in shopping in the downtown business districts. Ample parking and locations away from the downtown traffic congestion appeal to the suburban shopper. Additional hours for shopping during the evenings and on weekends facilitate family shopping.

Types of Shopping Centres

There are three types of planned shopping centres. The smallest and most common is the *neighbourhood shopping centre*, which is most often composed of a supermarket and a group of smaller stores such as a drugstore, a laundry and dry cleaner, a small appliance store, and perhaps a beauty shop and barbershop. Such centres provide convenient shopping for perhaps 5000 to 15 000 shoppers who live within a few minutes' commuting time of the centre. Such centres typically contain five to 15 stores whose product mix is usually confined to convenience goods and some shopping goods.

Community shopping centres typically serve 20 000 to 100 000 persons in a trade area extending a few kilometres in each direction. These centres are likely to contain 15 to 50 retail stores, with a branch of a local department store or a large variety store as the primary tenant. In addition to the stores found in a neighbourhood centre, the community centre is likely to have additional stores featuring shopping goods, some professional offices, and a branch of a bank.

The largest planned centre is the *regional shopping centre*, a giant shopping district of at least 30 000 m² of shopping space, usually built around one or more major department stores and as many as 300 smaller stores. In order to be successful, regional centres must be located in areas where at least 150 000 people reside within 30 minutes' driving time of the centre. Characteristically, they are temperature-controlled, enclosed facilities. The regional centres provide the widest product mixes and the greatest depth of each line.

Such a centre is the West Edmonton Mall, located in Jasper Place, a suburb of Edmonton. Said to be the largest shopping centre in the world, the West Edmonton Mall is located in a densely populated area and is easily accessible to both vehicular and pedestrian traffic. Catering to a relatively affluent suburban clientele, the stores at this mall offer a variety of quality merchandise to their customers.

Planned shopping centres account for approximately 40 percent of all retail sales in Canada. Their growth has slowed in recent years, however, as the most lucrative locations are occupied and the market for such centres appears to have been saturated in many regions. Recent trends have developed toward the building of smaller centres in smaller cities and towns.

Scrambled Merchandising   A second fundamental change in retailing has been the steady deterioration of clear-cut delineations of retailer types. Anyone who has attempted to fill a prescription recently has been exposed to the concept of scrambled merchandising — *the retail practice of carrying dissimilar lines to generate added sales volume*. The large mass-merchandising drugstore carries not only prescription and proprietary drugs, but also gifts, hardware, housewares, records, magazines, grocery products, garden supplies, even small appliances. Gasoline retailers now sell bread and milk; supermarkets carry antifreeze, televisions, cameras, and stereo equipment. Two-thirds of all toothpaste purchases are made in supermarkets. It has been estimated that fully one-fourth of all retail stores are at least partially involved in selling tires, batteries, and other automobile parts and accessories.[17]

Scrambled Merchandising Is Common in Modern Retailing

"No used cars? What kind of a drugstore is this anyway?"

Source: Masters Agency

Scrambled merchandising was born out of retailers' willingness to add dissimilar merchandise lines in order to offer additional higher-profit lines as well as to satisfy consumer demands for one-stop shopping. It complicates manufacturers' channel decisions because attempts to maintain or increase the firm's market share mean, in most instances, that the firm will have to develop multiple channels to reach the diverse retailers handling its products.

The Wheel-of-Retailing Hypothesis

M. P. McNair attempted to explain the patterns of change in retailing through what has been termed the **wheel of retailing**. According to this hypothesis, new types of retailers gain a competitive foothold by offering lower prices to their customers through the reduction or elimination of services. Once they are established, however, they evolve by adding more services and their prices gradually rise. Then they become vulnerable to a new low-price retailer who enters with minimum services — and the wheel turns.

Most of the major developments in retailing appear to fit the wheel pattern. Early department stores, chain stores, supermarkets, and discount stores all emphasized limited service and low prices. In most of these instances price levels have gradually increased as services have been added.

There have been some exceptions, however. The development of suburban shopping centres, convenience food stores, and vending machines were not built around low-price appeals. However, the wheel pattern has been present often enough in the past that it should serve as a general indicator of future developments in retailing.

The Retail Life Cycle

Closely related to the wheel hypothesis is the concept of the **retail life cycle**. The notion of "life cycle" was applied earlier to households and to products. It is also possible to apply the concept of "introduction–growth–maturity–decline" to retail institutions. Figure 16-8 applies the retail life cycle concept to a number of institutions and identifies the approximate stage in the life cycle of each institution.

Retailers have demonstrated that it is possible to extend the length of their life cycles through adaptation to changing environments. Such institutions as supermarkets and variety stores reached the maturity stage in their life cycles several decades ago, but have continued to function as important marketing institutions by adapting to changing consumer demands and by adjusting to meet changing competitive situations. Variety stores have countered the sales inroads of discount houses by becoming more price-competitive and by providing greater depth in their product lines. Supermarkets

Figure 16-8   Life Cycles of Selected Retail Institutions

Institutional Type	Period of Fastest Growth	Period from Inception to Maturity (Years)	Stage of Life Cycle
General store	1800–1840	100	Decline
Specialty store	1820–1840	100	Maturity
Variety store	1870–1930	50	Decline
Mail-order house	1915–1950	50	Maturity
Corporate chain	1920–1930	50	Maturity
Discount store	1955–1975	20	Maturity
Supermarket	1935–1965	35	Maturity
Shopping centre	1950–1965	40	Maturity
Gasoline station	1930–1950	45	Maturity
Convenience store	1965–1975	20	Maturity
Fast-food store	1960–1975	15	Maturity
Hypermarket	1973–	–	Early growth
Warehouse retailer	1970–1980	10	Late growth
Catalogue showroom	1970–1980	10	Late growth

Source: Joseph Barry Mason and Morris L. Mayer, *Modern Retailing: Theory and Practice* (Dallas: Business Publications, 1978), p. 58. © 1978 by Business Publications, Inc. Adapted with permission.

have taken such steps as offering generic brands at lower prices, developing departments of gourmet foods to counter the competition of specialty food retailers, and adding non-food items to meet the demand for one-stop shopping convenience.

The Future of Retailing

A number of trends are currently emerging that may greatly affect tomorrow's retailer. One is the possibility of **teleshopping** — *ordering merchandise that has been displayed on home television sets or computers*. Cable television currently reaches 57 percent of Canadian homes, and as it grows it has the potential of revolutionizing many retail practices by the early 1990s, when interactive teleshopping through cable television should be possible. A similar concept is shopping through an interactive personal computer. In Manitoba the Grassroots system, which uses Telidon technology, enables farmers to obtain precise weather reports for their farm locality. This same system is linked with several retailers including the Bay, Sears, Sports Mart, and Compu store. Selected items are listed, along with prices, and orders can be placed through the computer network. Sears and S.I.R., a sporting goods catalogue retailer, both offer customers the opportunity of placing a catalogue order through the Grassroots system after browsing through the printed catalogue. Similarly, patrons may use the system to order tickets for the Jets hockey games.

Teleshopping obviously offers an exciting new dimension for retailing, but it is not without its drawbacks. A survey conducted for *Marketing News* found that only 10 percent of 2163 respondents expressed positive attitudes about teleshopping. Reasons for the low acceptance varied, but included a desire to inspect the product personally, preference for going out to shop, and the fear of being tempted to purchase unneeded items.[18]

Teleshopping via an interactive cable system is likely to be most effective for products where sight, feel, smell, and personal service are not important in the purchase decision.[19] Consumer resistance is not the only problem for the future development of teleshopping. There are also cable operator barriers and cost barriers.[20]

Consumer Barriers

Teleshopping faces several consumer barriers. The *Marketing News* survey reported little interest in shopping via interactive cable television. Several other consumer-related questions have been raised:

1. Given the range of other programming, will consumers watch catalogue programs?
2. How can catalogue programs overcome the advantages of printed catalogues?
3. What can be done about the impersonal nature of teleshopping?
4. How can consumer perceptions of higher prices be handled?
5. Will consumers be willing to use an electronic funds transfer system?

All of these questions must be resolved if teleshopping is to be a successful retail innovation.

Technical Barriers

Few cable operators now have interactive capability and many of the remaining ones cannot be converted. One system that does seem to be working is the Tella Digest of the Toronto Real Estate Board. This is an on-line, interactive system for user-friendly communications. There are also two significant operator-related obstacles to the development of teleshopping. Cable operators may resist catalogue programming because of their perception of consumer resistance to advertising. Cable operators have concentrated on subscription revenue rather than advertising revenues in the past.

Cost Barriers

Teleshopping also faces significant cost barriers. Catalogue marketers would have to absorb production costs, but would not have the ability to divide it over as many viewers as television, for example. Since the programming would be essentially advertising, a method of paying the cable operator, either by buying air time or giving the operators a commission on the orders received through the interactive cable setup, would have to be arranged. These costs are expected to be significant when compared to other forms of retailing.

Regardless of the barriers, teleshopping will become a regular part of the retailing environment in the next decade, where it is cost efficient. In fact, the wheel of retailing seems to be rolling again.

Other Growth Areas   In the future, retail executives believe that catalogue stores, direct mail, discount houses, and telephone selling are likely to offer growth opportunities. Medium-size discount stores may be giving way to extremely large hypermarket discounters on one hand and specialty stores on the other. The furniture warehouse retailer (such as Leon's) is regarded as a major threat to established furniture outlets. In addition, grocery, drug, and other limited-line retailers are likely to generate new competition for the consumers' general merchandise business.

A renewed emphasis upon the pleasurable aspects of shopping is another trend that should accelerate in the next few years. Department stores are placing increased emphasis on boutiques and specialty shops within the department store itself. This will allow them to provide more individualized service and to appeal to specific kinds of customers.

The future of specialty stores appears bright. They accounted for 40 percent of the general merchandise market in the 1970s, and their share is expected to increase to 48 percent by the mid-1980s. However, the *number* of small, independent specialty stores is expected to continue to decline. Those that survive will become stronger and will generate the increase in sales volume.

Summary   Retailers are vital members of the distribution channel for consumer products. They play a major role in the creation of time, place, and ownership utility. Retailers can be categorized on five bases: 1) shopping effort expended by customers; 2) services provided to customers; 3) product lines; 4) location of retail transactions; and 5) form of ownership.

Retailers — like consumer goods — may be divided into convenience, shopping, and specialty categories based upon the efforts shoppers are willing to expend in purchasing products. A second method of classification categorizes retailers on a spectrum ranging from self-service to full-service. The third method divides retailers into three categories: limited-time stores, which compete by carrying a large assortment of one or two lines of products; specialty stores, which carry a very large assortment of only part of a single line of products; and general merchandise retailers, such as department stores, variety stores, and such mass merchandisers as discount houses, hypermarkets, and catalogue retailers — all handling a wide variety of products.

A fourth classification method distinguishes between retail stores and non-store retailing. While more than 97 percent of total retail sales in Canada takes place in retail stores, such non-store retailing as house-to-house retailing, mail-order establishments, and automatic merchandising machines are important in marketing many types of products.

A fifth method of classification categorizes retailers by form of ownership. The major types include corporate chain stores, independent retailers, and independents who have banded together to form retail co-operatives or to join wholesaler-sponsored voluntary chains or franchises.

Chains are groups of retail stores that are centrally owned and managed and that handle the same lines of products. Chain stores dominate retailing in four fields: department stores, variety stores, food stores and shoe stores. They account for more than a third of all retail sales.

Retailing has been affected by the development of planned shopping centres and the practice of scrambled merchandising. Planned shopping centres are a group of retail stores planned, co-ordinated, and marketed as a unit to shoppers in their geographic trade area. Shopping centres can be classified as neighbourhood, community, and regional centres. Another significant development is scrambled merchandising, the practice of carrying dissimilar lines in an attempt to generate additional sales volume.

The evolution of retail institutions has generally been in accordance with the wheel of retailing, which holds that new types of retailers gain a competitive foothold by offering lower prices to their customers through the reduction or elimination of services. Once they are established, however, they add more services and their prices generally rise. Then they become vulnerable to the next low-price retailer. The evolution of retail institutions can also be explained in terms of a retail life cycle. One form of retailing that is at the introductory stage or beginning growth stage is teleshopping conducted through interactive cable television.

CHAPTER 17

Management of Physical Distribution

1. To relate physical distribution to the other variables of the marketing mix.

2. To explain the role of physical distribution in an effective marketing strategy.

3. To describe the objectives of physical distribution.

4. To discuss the problem of suboptimization in physical distribution.

5. To identify and compare the major components of a physical distribution system.

6. To relate the major transportation alternatives to such factors as energy efficiency, speed, dependability, and cost.

While other companies struggled to stay afloat in the economic recession of the early 1980s, Canadian Tire has continued to rack up healthy sales. On top of that, the firm has actually increased inventory turnover by 40 percent since 1977 — during a period when inventory turnover in the retail industry was dropping steadily.

One of the major reasons for the firm's enviable financial position is its sophisticated physical distribution (PD) system. Says Canadian Tire president Dean Muncaster: "PD represents a major opportunity for cost savings. In order to maintain a competitive position in the market and keep profits up, it is important to have the most cost-effective PD system."

As soon as a clerk rings up a sale on the electronic cash register in a Canadian Tire store, the inventory number is automatically routed through an on-line computer network to the store's order sheet at the company's Toronto distribution centre. As the orders come in, warehouse stock is automatically allocated, ensuring that in-store inventory is kept at the proper levels. Price tags, scheduling sheets, and routing stickers are also printed at this time. Merchandise is replaced within three to four days of being sold and emergency orders can be filled in half a day.

Each morning, pre-planned loads based on data on volume and mass are obtained from the computer. The scheduling staff goes through all of the orders until they have enough volume to fill 62 m³, the equivalent of a truckload, in order to "maximize the cube" — use the available volume to its full capacity. Canadian Tire's two PD centres work together to consolidate orders going to the same area or store.

The company also wishes to maximize equipment usage — it has more than 80 tractors and 650 trailers which move goods all over the country. Therefore, when Canadian Tire is delivering it tries to pick up its own supplies, creating a backhaul situation for greater efficiency.

In addition to maximizing cube in Canadian Tire's trucks, the computer also improves warehouse productivity. A warehouse employee who must locate a particular product asks the computer to find the shortest route to the goods. The computer allows the company to control its labour costs, which account for about 80 percent of the company's PD expenses.

The company recognizes that while a sophisticated PD program is important, a competent manager is needed to make the system work. Canadian Tire's experience demonstrates the benefits of a well-designed and sophisticated physical distribution system under the direction of a competent PD manager.[1]

The Conceptual Framework

Chapters 14 through 16 dealt with the basic concepts of distribution channels and the marketing institutions within them. Yet there is another side to the distribution function. Effective marketing requires that products be physically moved within the channel of distribution. This chapter focuses specifically on the physical flow of goods. Improving customer service through more efficient physical distribution remains an important aspect of any organization's marketing strategy. In addition, this efficiency improvement means substantial cost savings.

Physical distribution or **logistics** is one of marketing's most innovative and dynamic areas. It involves a broad range of activities concerned with *efficient movement of finished products from the end of the production line to the consumer.* Physical distribution activities include such crucial decision areas as customer service, inventory control, materials handling, protective packaging, order processing, transportation, warehouse site selection, and warehousing.

Importance of Physical Distribution

Increased attention has been focused in recent years on physical distribution activities, largely because these activities represent a major portion — almost half — of total marketing *costs.*

Management's traditional focal point for cost-cutting has been production. Historically, this began with the industrial revolution of the 1700s and 1800s, when businesses emphasized efficient production, stressing their ability to decrease production costs and improve the output levels of production facilities and workers. But managers have begun to recognize that production efficiency has reached a point at which it is difficult to achieve further cost savings. More and more managers are turning to physical distribution activities as a possible area for cost savings.

In a recent year, Canadian industry spent about $39 billion on transportation, $23 billion on warehousing, $23 billion on the costs of maintaining inventory, and $6 billion on administering and managing these aspects of physical distribution. Physical distribution now accounts for more than 24.5 percent of the nation's gross national product and is the second largest cost item for most companies.[2]

Physical Distribution and Consumer Satisfaction

A second—and equally important—reason for the increased attention on physical distribution activities is the role they play in providing *customer service*. By storing products in convenient locations for shipment to wholesale and retail customers, firms create time utility. Place utility is created primarily by transportation. These major contributions indicate the importance of the physical distribution component of marketing.

Customer satisfaction is heavily dependent upon reliable movement of products to ensure availability. Eastman Kodak Company committed a major marketing error in the late 1970s when it launched a multimillion-dollar advertising campaign for its new instant camera before adequate quantities had been delivered to retail outlets. Many would-be purchasers visited the stores and, when they discovered that the new camera was not available, bought a Polaroid camera instead.

By providing consumers with time and place utility, physical distribution contributes to implementing the marketing concept. Robert Woodruff, former president of Coca-Cola, emphasized the role of physical distribution in his firm's success when he stated that his organization's policy is to "put Coke within an arm's length of desire."

Components of the Physical Distribution System

The study of physical distribution is one of the classic examples of the systems approach to business problems. The basic notion of a system is that it is a set of interrelated parts. The word is derived from the Greek word *systema*, which means an organized relationship among components. The firm's components include such interrelated areas as production, finance, and marketing. Each component must function properly if the system is to be effective and if organizational objectives are to be achieved.

A **system** may be defined as *an organized group of parts or components linked together according to a plan to achieve specific objectives*. The physical distribution system contains the following elements:

1. Customer service: What level of customer service should be provided?
2. Transportation: How will the products be shipped?
3. Inventory control: How much inventory should be maintained at each location?
4. Materials handling: How do we develop efficient methods of handling products in the factory, warehouse, and transport terminals?
5. Order processing: How should orders be handled?
6. Warehousing: Where will the products be located? How many warehouses should be utilized?

These components are interrelated, and decisions made in one area affect the relative efficiency of other areas. Attempts to reduce transportation costs by utilizing low-cost, relatively slow water transportation will probably reduce customer service and may increase inventory costs, since the firm may be required to maintain larger inventory levels to compensate for longer delivery times. The physical distribution manager must balance each component so that no single aspect is stressed to the detriment of the overall functioning of the distribution system.[3]

The Objective of Physical Distribution

The objective of a firm's physical distribution system is *to produce a specified level of customer service while minimizing the costs involved in physically moving and storing the product* from its production point to the point where it is ultimately purchased. To achieve this, the physical distribution manager makes use of three basic concepts that are vital to effective logistics management: 1) the total-cost approach, 2) the avoidance of suboptimization, and 3) the use of cost trade-offs.

Total-Cost Approach

The premise that *all relevant factors in physically moving and storing products should be considered as a whole and not individually* forms the basis of the **total-cost approach**. Thus, the following business functions should be included: 1) transportation, 2) warehousing, 3) warehouse location, 4) inventory control systems, 5) materials handling, 6) internal information flows, 7) customer service standards, and 8) packaging. All these cost items are considered as a whole when attempting to meet customer service levels at minimum cost.

The Problem of Suboptimization

The total-cost approach requires that all physical distribution elements must be considered as a whole rather than individually. Sometimes this does not happen. **Suboptimization** is a condition in which *the manager of each physical distribution function attempts to minimize costs, but, due to the impact of one physical distribution task on the others, the results are less than optimal.* One writer explains suboptimization using the analogy of a football team made up of numerous talented individuals who seldom win games. Team members hold league records in a variety of skills: pass completions, average distance gained per rush, blocked kicks, and average gains on punt returns. Unfortunately, however, the overall ability of the team to accomplish the organizational goal — scoring more points than the opponents — is rarely achieved.[4]

Why does suboptimization occur frequently in physical distribution? The answer lies in the fact that each separate logistics activity is often judged by its ability to achieve certain management objectives, some of which are at cross-purposes with other objectives. Sometimes, departments in other functional areas take actions that cause the physical distribution area to operate at less than full efficiency. Psychological factors often come into play here. For example, a product manager might think to herself, "cartons are bought out of my department's budget, so we'll only buy standard, non-reinforced ones. We don't care if the warehouse staff complain — breakages are their problem, not ours. We'll look good because this department kept costs down." Counteracting this type of attitude is the responsibility of top management who must convince junior management that they are serious about total cost (which means not complaining about the cost of cartons to one department head and about breakages to the other).

Effective management of the physical distribution function requires some cost trade-offs. Some functional areas of the firm will experience cost increases while others will have cost decreases resulting in the minimization of total physical distribution costs. Of course, the reduction of any physical distribution cost assumes that the level of customer service will not be sacrificed.[5]

Cost Trade-offs

The third fundamental concept of physical distribution is the use of **cost trade-offs**. This approach assumes that *some functional areas of the firm will experience cost increases while others will have cost decreases.* The result will be that total physical distribution costs will be minimized. At no time will the established level of customer service be sacrificed. By thinking in terms of the cost trade-offs shown in Figure 17-1, management should minimize the total of these costs rather than attempt to minimize the cost of each component.

Figure 17-1   Cost Trade-offs Required in a Physical Distribution System

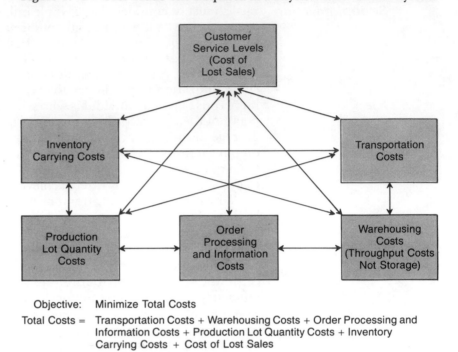

Objective: Minimize Total Costs

Total Costs =   Transportation Costs + Warehousing Costs + Order Processing and
                Information Costs + Production Lot Quantity Costs + Inventory
                Carrying Costs + Cost of Lost Sales

Source: Douglas Lambert and Robert Quinn, "Increase Profitability by Managing the
Distribution Function," *Business Quarterly*, Spring 1981, p. 59.

Adapted from: Douglas M. Lambert, *The Development of an Inventory Costing
Methodology: A Study of the Cost Associated with Holding Inventory* (Chicago, Illinois:
The National Council of Physical Distribution Management, 1976), p. 7.

For example, the Gillette Company, the world's largest producer
of safety razors, was faced with an ever expanding assortment of
products due to its expansion into a broad range of toiletry products.
To produce good customer service, Gillette shipped by air freight,
but this proved to be very expensive. Through a detailed study of
its distribution system, Gillette discovered that its problem was inefficient order processing. By simplifying the paperwork involved, it
was able to reduce the time required to process new orders. Gillette
was then able to return to lower-cost surface transportation and
still meet previous delivery schedules. The cost trade-off here was
that the order-processing costs *increased* and transportation costs
decreased, and the net result was that total logistics costs decreased.

The integration of these three basic concepts — the total-cost approach, the avoidance of suboptimization, and the use of cost tradeoffs—*forms what is commonly referred to as the physical distribution concept.* It should be noted that the real uniqueness of the physical distribution concept is not in the individual functions, since each function is performed anyway. Rather, it stems from the integration of all of these functions into a unified whole, the objective of which is providing an established level of customer service at the lowest possible distribution costs.

Organizational Considerations

The integration of these functions into a unified system is a very difficult organizational problem. In most companies that have not yet recognized the physical distribution concept, logistics functions are dispersed throughout the company. Figure 17-2 illustrates how physical distribution objectives might conflict in a typical company.

Unifying the physical distribution activities involves shifting functions from the other departments to form the new logistics division. Departments are reluctant to give up their jurisdiction over procedures. Too often when a new physical distribution department is finally established, the traffic manager receives the new title of director of physical distribution but in effect does little more than he or she previously did. Senior management must take the necessary organizational steps to see that enough power is given to the physical distribution manager to make the appropriate changes within the system. It must be clearly recognized that *some* costs may increase in order to decrease the cost of physical distribution in total

Customer Service Standards

Customer service standards are *the quality of service that the firm's customers will receive.* For example, a customer service standard for one firm might be that 60 percent of all orders will be shipped within 48 hours after they are received, 90 percent in 72 hours, and all orders within 96 hours.

Setting the standards for customer service to be provided is an important marketing decision. Inadequate customer service levels may mean dissatisfied customers and loss of future sales.

Physical distribution departments must delineate the costs involved in providing proposed standards. A conflict may arise when sales representatives make unreasonable delivery promises to their customers in order to obtain sales. In many cases such customer service requirements are so costly to the firm, because of the need for additional inventory or the use of premium-cost transportation, that the orders prove unprofitable.

Figure 17-2   Physical Distribution Organization in a Typical Manufacturing Company

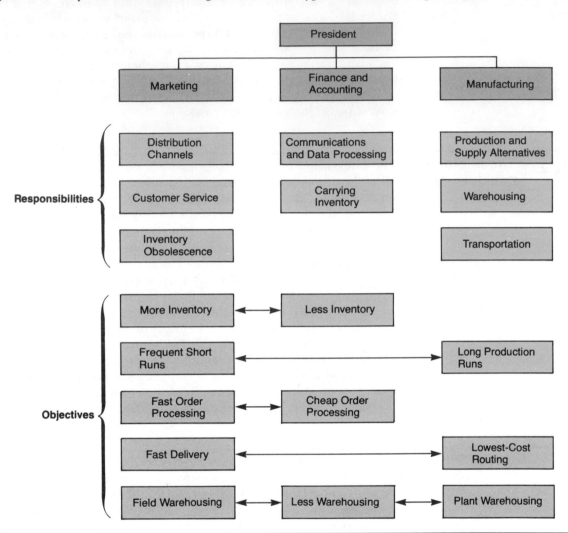

In an attempt to increase its share of the market, a major manufacturer of highly perishable food items set a 98 percent service level; that is, 98 percent of all orders were to be shipped the same day they were received. To meet this extremely high level of service, the firm leased warehouse space in 170 different towns and cities and kept large stocks in each location. The large inventories, however, often meant the shipment of dated merchandise. Customers interpreted this practice as evidence of a low-quality product — or poor "service."[6]

Customer service standards must include both time and consistency of performance. *Time* refers to the percentage of customer orders that can be filled from existing inventory and the amount of time between the receipt of an order and its delivery. *Performance consistency* refers to the organization's dependability in meeting delivery schedules; in shipping the right amount and type of merchandise, damage-free; and in following special instructions.[7] Figure 17-3 indicates specific objectives that might be developed

---

Figure 17-3   Customer Service Standards

Service Factor	Objectives
Order-Cycle Time	To develop a physical distribution system capable of effecting delivery of the product within eight days from the initiation of a customer order: • transmission of order — one day • order processing (order entry, credit verification, picking, and packing) — three days • delivery — four days.
Dependability of Delivery	To ensure that 95 percent of all deliveries will be made within the eight-day standard and that under no circumstances will deliveries be made earlier than six days nor later than nine days from the initiation of an order.
Inventory Levels	To maintain inventories of finished goods at levels that will permit: • 97 percent of all incoming orders for class A items to be filled • 85 percent of all incoming orders for class B items to be filled • 70 percent of all incoming orders for class C items to be filled.
Accuracy in Order Filling	To be capable of filling customer orders with 99 percent accuracy.
Damage in Transit	To ensure that damage to merchandise in transit does not exceed 1 percent.
Communications	To maintain a communication system that permits salespersons to transmit orders on a daily basis and that is capable of accurately responding to customer inquiries on order status within four hours.

Source: David T. Kollat, Roger D. Blackwell, and James F. Robeson, *Strategic Marketing* (New York: Holt, Rinehart and Winston, 1972), p. 316. Copyright © 1972 by Holt, Rinehart and Winston, Inc. Reprinted by permission of Holt, Rinehart and Winston, Inc.

for each factor involved in customer service. It also illustrates the importance of co-ordinating order processing, transportation, inventory control, and the other components of the physical distribution system in achieving these service standards.

Physical Distribution System Components

The establishment of acceptable levels of customer service provides the physical distribution department with a standard by which actual operations may be compared. The physical distribution system should be designed to achieve these standards by minimizing the total costs of the following components: 1) transportation, 2) warehouses and their location, 3) inventory control, 4) order processing, and 5) materials handling. Relative costs for major components are illustrated in Figure 17-4.

Figure 17-4   Relative Costs of Physical Distribution Components

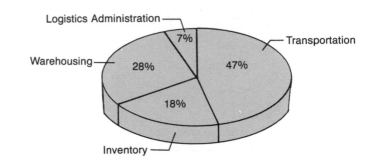

Source: Andrew M. Schell and Jim Heuer, "Creating a PD Strategy For a Rebounding Economy," *Canadian Transportation and Distribution Management* (November 1983), p. 79.

Transportation Considerations[8]

The transportation system of Canada is a regulated industry, much like the phone and electricity industries. In fact, the courts have often referred to the transport modes as public utilities. The federal government plays a twofold role in affecting transportation services. One is promotional, to ensure growth and development of the transportation appropriate to need; the other is regulatory. This includes economic regulation of rates and services and the application of technical regulations to meet safety requirements. The National Transportation Act defines a national transportation policy for Canada with a view to achieving maximum efficiency in all available modes of transportation at the lowest cost. (Whether this is being accomplished is highly arguable.) The Act established the Canadian Transport Commission (CTC) to be responsible for the air, rail, pipeline, and inland water components of the transportation industry. In the case of road transport, the federal government establishes motor vehicle safety standards, and other regulation of motor vehicle activities is controlled by provincial and territorial governments.

In general, the purpose of the Act is to develop the industry while protecting the public against excessive or discriminatory charges.

Rate Determination

One of the most difficult problems facing the physical distribution manager when choosing a transportation service is determining the correct rate or cost of the service. The complexity is related to **tariffs** — the *price lists that are used to determine shipping charges*. There are hundreds of these tariff books. Rate regulation in Canada provides only formulas for minimum and maximum rates. The wide range inside these limits is left to the private managements of the modal carriers. The manager must find the proper mixture of value of service and cost of service considerations, a mixture that recognizes all the varying conditions that can be found in the operation of the competing modal carriers. Fortunately, physical distribution managers only have to master the rate system for the range of goods handled by their own firms. Consequently, they may avoid wading through the total tariff maze.

There are two basic freight rates: class and commodity. Of the two rates, the class rate is the higher. The **class non-carload rate** is *the standard rate that is found for every commodity moving between any two destinations*. The **commodity rate** is sometimes called a special rate, since it is *given by carriers to shippers as a reward for either regular use or large-quantity shipments*. It is used extensively by the railways and the inland water carriers.

Classes of Carriers

Freight carriers are classified as common, contract, and private. **Common carriers** have been called the "backbone" of the transportation industry. They are *for-hire carriers that serve the general public*. Their rates and services are regulated, and they cannot conduct their operations without the appropriate regulatory authority's permission. Common carriers exist for all the modes of transport.

Contract carriers are *for-hire transporters that do not offer their services to the general public*. Instead they establish specific contracts with certain customers and operate exclusively for the industry. Most contract carriers operate in the motor freight industry. These carriers are subject to much less regulation than the common carriers.

Private carriers are not for-hire carriers. *The operators only transport products for a particular firm* and may not solicit other transportation business. Since transportation is solely for the carrier's own use, there is no rate-of-service regulation.

Figure 17-5   The Major Modes of Transportation

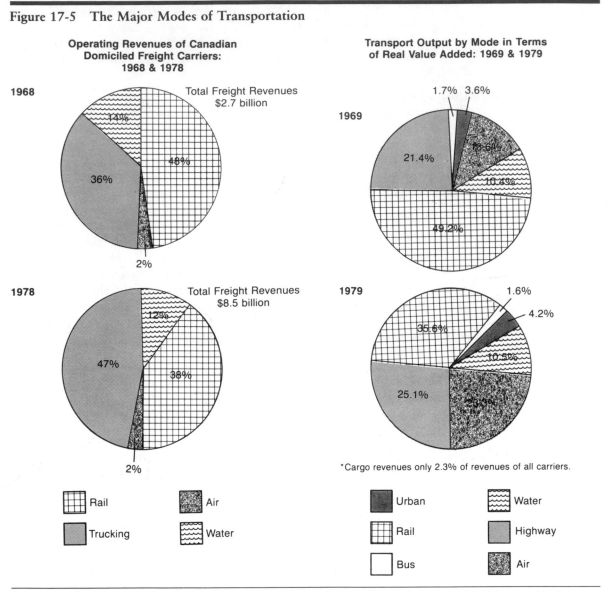

Note: The above charts do not include the following parts of the transport sector — pipelines, taxi cabs, highway and bridge maintenance, and other — and these amounted to roughly one-fifth of the total transport sector in 1977. Services incidental to water transport are included under Water.

Source: *Transport Review* (Ottawa: Canadian Transport Commission, March 1981), pp. 15, 19.

**Transportation
Alternatives**

The physical distribution manager has five major transportation alternatives. These are railways, trucking, water carriers, pipelines, and air freight. Figure 17-5 compares the major modes according to their operating revenues and the real value added (for a discussion of the value added concept, see Chapter 10). The water carriers' percentage has been roughly stable over the years, while the railways have experienced a significant percentage decrease. Air mode shipments have increased substantially, from 12.6 percent in 1967 to 20.4 percent in 1977.

**Railways — The Back-
bone of the Industry**

The largest transporter (as measured by tonne-kilometres) of freight continues to be the railways. They are one of the most efficient modes for the movement of bulk commodities over long distances.

The railways have launched a drive in recent years to improve their service standards and capture a larger percentage of manufactured and other higher-value products. To reach their improved service standards, they have introduced a number of innovations. One is called *ACI (Automatic Car Identification)*. All rail cars and locomotives are equipped with a 13-line reflective label. The railway companies have positioned hundreds of scanners throughout Canada that can interpret these labels as they pass by at speeds as high as 130 km/h. These scanners "read" the labels and report to a central computer the car number and the name of the railway, allowing each railway to tell its customers at all times the exact location and status of their shipments.

Railways are also making extensive use of unit trains to provide time and cost savings for their customers. A unit train is used exclusively by a single customer who negotiates lower rates for its shipments. Specially designed single-usage unit trains are operated by Canadian National to haul coal for Japanese steel companies. The railway hauls a trainload of coal from interior British Columbia to the Roberts Bank Seaport, Vancouver, and then returns empty for another run, providing rapid low-cost transport. In Ontario, a unit train carries iron ore pellets from Temagami to a Hamilton steel mill, with cars loading from silos in 30 seconds and unloading over furnace bins in 60 seconds.

The Canadian railway system is showing transporters how to apply the marketing concept. It is stressing improved service to its shippers. In response to the need for a more efficient method of transporting various commodities, specialized new rail cars of different configurations have been designed. Most of us recognize the yellow and brown tubular cars used to haul the millions of tonnes of grain Canada exports annually. The new car has lowered the shipping costs significantly, since fewer steps in loading and unloading are required.

Motor Carriers —
Flexible and Growing

The trucking industry has shown dramatic growth over recent decades. Its prime advantage over other modes is relatively fast, consistent service, for both large and small shipments. For this reason truckers concentrate on manufactured products, as opposed to the railways, which haul more bulk products and raw materials. Truckers, therefore, receive greater revenue per tonne shipped as compared to the railways (4.9 cents per tonne-kilometre to the railway's 1.3 cents in a recent year). In 1978, for-hire motor carriers accounted for 47 percent of the total operating revenues of all Canadian domiciled freight carriers (Figure 17-5).

Trucking's primary appeal to shippers is superior service, and the industry is working diligently to maintain this advantage. The Kwikasair trucking company is currently running schedules that just a few years ago would have seemed impossible. At one time it took seven to 10 days for a coast-to-coast truckload shipment. Kwikasair Express now offers three-day service between Montreal or Toronto and Vancouver.

Water Carriers — Slow
but Cheap

There are basically two types of water carriers — the inland or barge lines and the ocean deep-water ships. Barge lines are very efficient transporters of bulk commodities.

Ocean-going ships operate on the Great Lakes, between Canadian port cities, and in international commerce. The international water freight bill for 1981 was $633 million, with domestic water transport billings totalling $634 million.[9]

Pipelines — One-Way
Transporters

Even though the pipeline industry is second only to the railways in number of tonne-kilometres transported, many people are barely aware of its existence. Pipelines serve one-way traffic, making them extremely efficient transporters of natural gas and oil products. They are highly automated and involve low labour costs, as is demonstrated by the fact that they can turn a profit on an average revenue per tonne-kilometre of a little less than 0.2 cents. Oil pipelines haul two types of commodities: crude (unprocessed) oil and refined products, such as gasoline and kerosene. A second generation of pipeline is the "slurry" pipeline, where a product such as coal is ground up into a powder, mixed with water, and transported in suspension. A third generation will carry capsules that could contain a variety of products in a liquid medium.

Air Freight — Fast but
Expensive

The use of air freight has been growing significantly. In 1961 Canadian airlines flew about 39 million tonne-kilometres. By 1977, this figure had jumped to 453 million tonne-kilometres. However, air freight is still a relatively small percentage of the total tonne-kilometres shipped.

Figure 17-6   Comparing the Transport Modes

Factor	Rank 1	2	3	4	5
Speed	Air carriers	Motor carriers	Railways	Water carriers	Pipelines
Dependability in meeting schedules	Pipelines	Motor carriers	Railways	Water carriers	Air carriers
Cost	Water carriers	Pipelines	Railways	Motor carriers	Air carriers
Frequency of shipments	Pipelines	Motor carriers	Air carriers	Railways	Water carriers
Availability in different locations	Motor carriers	Railways	Air carriers	Water carriers	Pipelines
Flexibility in handling products	Water carriers	Railways	Motor carriers	Air carriers	Pipelines

Source: Based on a discussion in James L. Heskitt, Nicholas A. Glaskowsky, Jr., and Robert M. Ivie, *Business Logistics* (New York: Ronald Press, 1973), pp. 113-118. Used with permission.

Because of air freight's relatively high cost, it is used primarily for very valuable or highly perishable products. Typical products include watches, computers, furs, fresh flowers, high-fashion clothing, and live lobsters. Air carriers market their services effectively by stressing that firms can offset the higher transportation costs with reduced inventory holding costs and faster customer service.

Figure 17-6 ranks the five transport modes on several bases.

Freight Forwarders— Transportation Intermediaries

Since their function is to *consolidate shipments*, **freight forwarders** can be considered *transportation intermediaries*. They do this because the transport rates on LTL (less than truckload) and LCL (less than carload) shipments are significantly higher, on a per-unit basis, than on TL (truckload) and CL (carload) shipments. Freight forwarders consolidate shipments and charge their customers a rate per unit that is less than the LTL or LCL rate but greater than the TL or CL. They receive their profits by paying the TL or CL rate to the carriers. The advantage to the shipper, in addition to lower costs on small shipments, is faster delivery service than LTL and LCL shipments receive.

Supplemental Carriers

The physical distribution manager also has available a number of auxiliary or supplemental carriers that specialize in the transportation of relatively small shipments. These include bus freight service and the post office.

**Intermodal
Co-ordination**

Transport modes often combine their services to give the shipper the service and cost advantages of each mode. The most widely accepted form of intermodal co-ordination is *piggyback*. This technique involves placing the entire highway trailer on a rail flatcar and performing the majority of the intercity movement via the railway. The pickup and delivery of the shipment is performed by the motor carrier involved.

The combination of truck and rail service generally provides the shipper with both faster service and lower rates, since trucks are used where they are most efficient, for pickup and delivery, and the rails are used where they are best suited, as high-volume transporters of bulk shipments. Shipper acceptance of piggybacking has been tremendous. In 1960 fewer than 11 000 piggyback rail cars were shipped. By 1977 more than 240 000 cars were involved.

Another form of intermodal co-ordination is motor carriers with air carriers, called *birdyback*. Again, the truckers perform the pickup and delivery and the air carriers perform the long haul. In addition, truckers, railways, and water carriers have developed a form of intermodal co-ordination called *fishyback*. In fact, ferries are used for most goods moving to and from Newfoundland, Prince Edward Island, and Vancouver Island.

Warehousing

Two types of warehouses exist: storage warehouses and distribution warehouses. **Storage warehouses** store products for moderate to long periods of time in an attempt *to balance supply and demand* for producers and purchasers. They are used most often by firms whose products are seasonal in supply or demand.

Distribution warehouses are designed *to assemble and then redistribute products*. The object is to keep the products on the move as much as possible. Many distribution warehouses or centres achieve their operational objective of having the goods in the warehouse less than one day.

To save transportation costs, manufacturers have developed central distribution centres. A manufacturer in Kitchener, Ontario, with customers in Manitoba, Saskatchewan, and Alberta could send each customer a direct shipment. But since each places small orders, the transportation charges for the individual shipments are relatively high. A feasible solution is to use a "break-bulk" centre, probably Regina in this case. (See Figure 17-7.) A *consolidated shipment may be sent to such a central distribution centre, and then smaller shipments made* for delivery to the individual customers in the area. Such centres are known as **break-bulk warehouses**.

Another type of distribution centre *brings together shipments from various points or sources going to one point and consolidates these into one shipment* — the **make-bulk centre**. For example, a

Figure 17-7   Break-Bulk and Make-Bulk Centres

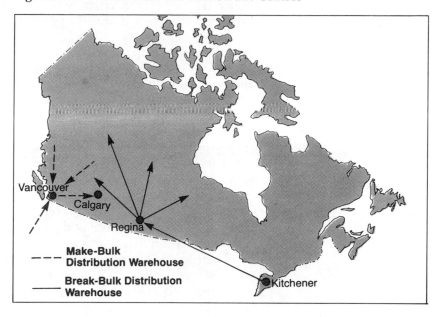

giant retailer such as Safeway Stores may have several satellite production facilities in a given area. Each production plant can send shipments to a storage warehouse in Calgary. However, this again would result in an excessive number of small, expensive shipments. Therefore, a make-bulk distribution centre is created in Vancouver, as illustrated in Figure 17-7. Each supplier sends its shipment to the Vancouver make-bulk point, and all shipments bound for Calgary are consolidated into more economical shipments.

Automated Warehouses   Warehouses lend themselves exceptionally well to automation, with the computer as the heart of the operation. An outstanding example of the automated warehouse of the future is the Aerojet-General Industrial Systems Division warehouse in Frederick, Maryland. This huge warehouse is operated entirely by a single employee who gives instructions to the facility's governing computer. The computer operates the fully automated materials handling system and also generates all the necessary forms.[10]

Although automated warehouses may cost as much as $10 million, they can provide major savings to such high-volume distributors as grocery chains. Some current systems can select 10 000 to 300 000 cases per day of up to 3000 different items. They can "read" computerized store orders, choose the correct number of cases, then move them in the desired sequence to loading docks. Such ware-houses reduce labour costs, worker injuries, pilferage, fires, and breakage and assist in inventory control.

Location Factors   A major decision that each company must make is the number and location of its storage facilities. While this is a very complex question, the two general factors involved are the costs of warehousing and materials handling and the costs of delivery from the warehouse to the customer. The first set of costs are subject to economies of scale; therefore, their cost, on a per-unit basis, decreases as volume increases. Delivery costs, on the other hand, increase as the distance increases from the warehouse location to the customer to be served.

These cost items are diagrammed in Figure 17-8. The asterisk in Figure 17-8 marks the ideal area of coverage for each warehouse. This model is a useful tool in deciding the proper number of ware-houses if decentralization is desired.

The specific location of the firm's warehouses is another very complicated problem. Factors that must be considered include municipal and provincial taxes; laws and regulations; availability of a trained labour force; police and fire protection; access to the various transport modes; attitude of the community toward the pro-posed warehouse; and the cost and availability of public utilities such as electricity and natural gas.

Figure 17-8   Factors Influencing the Number of Warehouses

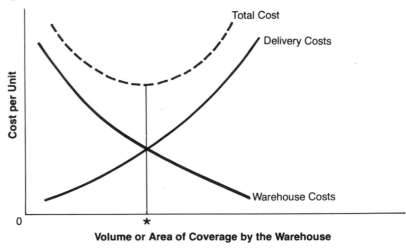

Order Processing   Like customer service standards, order processing is a logistics-type function. The physical distribution manager is concerned with order processing because it directly affects the firm's ability to meet its customer service standards. If a firm's order processing system is inefficient, the company may have to compensate by using costly premium transportation or increasing the number of field warehouses in all major markets.

Order processing typically consists of four major activities: a credit check; recording the sale, such as crediting a sales representative's commission account; making the appropriate accounting entries, and locating the item, shipping, and adjusting inventory records. *An item that is not available for shipment* is known as a **stock-out**, which requires the order-processing unit to advise the customer of the situation and of the action the company plans to take.[11]

Inventory Control Systems

Inventories have been referred to as the "graveyard of Canadian businesses." This title is earned because this aspect of business is often regarded as unimportant, and therefore it is basically ignored — *with deadly results*.

What many managers fail to realize is the significant expense involved in holding inventory over a period of time. Most current estimates of inventory holding costs are 25 percent per year. This means that $1000 of inventory held for a single year costs the company $250. Inventory costs include such expenses as storage facilities, insurance, taxes, transportation, handling costs, depreciation, lost interest opportunities, and possible obsolescence of the goods in inventory.

Figure 17-9   The EOQ Model

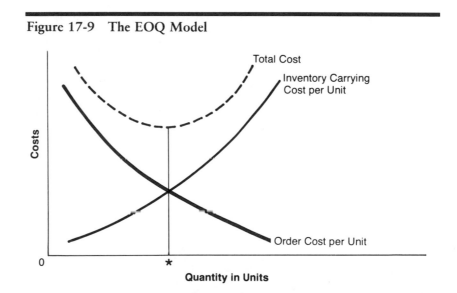

Inventory control analysts have developed a number of techniques that aid the physical distribution manager in effectively controlling inventory. The most basic is the **EOQ** (**economic order quantity**) **model**. This technique *emphasizes a cost trade-off between two fundamental costs involved with inventory. Inventory holding costs* increase with the addition of more inventory. *Order costs*, those involved in placing an order, decrease as the quantity ordered increases. As Figure 17-9 indicates, these two cost items are then "traded off" to determine the optimum order quantity of each product.

The EOQ point in Figure 17-9 is the point at which total cost is minimized. By placing an order for this amount as needed, firms can minimize inventory cost.

How the EOQ Is Calculated   The size of the investment in inventory has prompted managers to develop scientific methods of determining the correct balance between the costs of holding goods available in inventory and order costs. The following formula has been developed for determining the economic order quantity:

$$EOQ = \sqrt{\frac{2RS}{IC}}$$

where EOQ = the economic order quantity (in units)
       R = the annual rate of usage
       S = the cost of placing an order
       I = the annual inventory carrying cost percentage
       C = the cost per unit

In the above formula, R is an estimate based upon the demand forecast for the item. S is calculated from the firm's cost records. I is also an estimate, based upon the costs of such items as depreciation, handling, insurance, interest, storage, and taxes. Since the costs of the item may vary over time, C is also likely to be an estimate. By inserting specific data into the formula, the EOQ can be determined. Consider, for example, the following data:

$$R = 5500 \text{ units}$$
$$S = \$7.50$$
$$I = 20 \text{ percent}$$
$$C = \$12.90$$

$$EOQ = \sqrt{\frac{(2)\,(5500)\,(7.50)}{(.20)\,(12.90)}}$$
$$= 178.82$$

Although the EOQ has been calculated at approximately 179 units, other factors should be taken into account. Truckload or railway carload shipments may consist of 200 units. In certain instances, the purchasing firm may discover that the units are shipped in special containers consisting of 175 units. In such cases, the EOQ may be adjusted to match these conditions and an order for 175 or 200 units, rather than the calculated 179 units, may be placed.

Once the EOQ has been determined, specific re-order points are determined by considering such factors as the lead time required for receiving an order once it has been placed and the average daily demand. If the necessary lead time is seven days and average daily sales consist of five units, orders must be placed when the available inventory reaches 35 units. Since demand may fluctuate, most organizations add a certain amount of inventory called *safety stock* to compensate for such demand fluctuations. In the above instance, a predetermined safety stock of five units would mean that new orders would be placed when the inventory level drops to 40 units.

Managers use the EOQ as a powerful tool in making rational decisions about inventory. Additionally, the EOQ has become a widely used technique as managers attempt to minimize the costs of ordering and maintaining inventory.

Materials Handling Systems

All of the activities associated in *moving products among the manufacturer's plants, warehouses, and transportation company terminals* are called **materials handling**. The materials handling system must be thoroughly co-ordinated, for both intra- and intercompany activities. The efficiency of plants and warehouses is dependent on an effective system.

Two important innovations have developed in the area of materials handling. One is known as **unitizing** — *combining as many packages as possible into one load*, preferably on a pallet. A pallet is a standard-size platform, generally made of wood, on which products are transported. It is designed to be lifted by forklift trucks. Utilizing can be done by using steel bands to hold the unit in place or by shrink packaging. Shrink packages are constructed by placing a sheet of plastic over the unit and then heating it so that when it cools, the plastic shrinks and holds the individual packages securely together. Unitizing has the advantages of requiring less labour per package, promoting faster movements, and reducing damage and pilferage.

The second innovation is **containerization**, the *combination of several unitized loads*. A container is typically a box 2.4 m wide, 2.4 m high, and 3, 6, 9, or 12 m in length. Such containers allow ease of intertransport mode changes. Thus, a container of oil rig parts could be loaded in Edmonton, sent by high-speed through-train to Montreal, and then on to Saudi Arabia by sea.

Containerization markedly reduces the time involved in loading and unloading ships. Container ships can often be unloaded in less than 24 hours — a task otherwise requiring up to two weeks. In-transit damage has also been reduced since individual packages are not handled en route to the purchaser, and pilferage is greatly reduced.

International Physical Distribution

Canada has experienced rapid growth in international trade since World War II. In 1982 Canadian merchandise exports totalled approximately $81.4 billion, of which manufactured goods accounted for $56.7 billion, crude products and fuels another $14.8 billion, and food, beverages, and tobacco approximately $9.9 billion. Total imports for 1981 amounted to 67.4 billion.[12] This unparalleled growth of international commerce has placed new responsibilities on many firms' physical distribution departments.

A major problem facing international marketers is the pile of paperwork involved in exporting products. Over a hundred different international trade documents representing more than a thousand separate forms must be completed for each international shipment. As a result, documentation for the average export shipment requires approximately 36 employee-hours; for the average import shipment, it is 27 employee-hours. Paperwork alone now accounts for approximately 7 percent of the total value of Canadian international trade.[13] Many physical distribution departments are not large enough to employ international specialists to deal with these complexities, so this work is subcontracted to *foreign freight forwarders*, wholesaling intermediaries who specialize in physical distribution outside Canada.

A significant facilitating factor for the export business has been the advent of containerization and container ships. Shipping companies now use container ships that can make a round trip between Halifax, Bremerhaven, and Rotterdam in 14 days. Only four days are needed for each crossing of the Atlantic, and another six for the three port calls.[14] This speed allows Canadian exporters to provide competitive delivery schedules to European markets.

The largest volume of our shipments, however, still comprises agricultural products and raw materials (lumber and minerals). The importance of these basic commodities to Canada has resulted in specialized, complex systems at various ports for handling them.

Summary   Physical distribution, as a system, consists of six elements: 1) customer service, 2) transportation, 3) inventory control, 4) materials handling, 5) order processing, and 6) warehousing. These elements are interrelated and must be balanced for a smoothly functioning distribution system. The physical distribution department is one of the classic examples of the systems approach to business problems. Three basic concepts of the systems approach — the total-cost approach, the avoidance of suboptimization, and cost trade-offs — combine to form the physical distribution concept.

The goal of a physical distribution department is to produce a specified level of customer service while minimizing the costs involved in physically moving and storing the product from its production point to the point where it is ultimately purchased.

The physical distribution manager has available five transportation alternatives: railways, motor carriers, water carriers, pipelines, and air freight. In addition, intermodal transport systems are available and increasingly used.

Other elements of the physical distribution department include warehousing and warehouse location, inventory control systems, materials handling systems, customer service standards, and order processing. Efficient international physical distribution allows a firm to compete more effectively in foreign markets.

Physical distribution, by its very nature, involves keeping track of thousands of details, such as transport rates, inventory locations, and customer locations. The computer is a necessary and invaluable tool for the logistics manager.

7   7   7   7   7   7   7

7   7   7   7   7   7   7

7   7   7   7   7   7   7

7   7   7   7   7   7   7

7   7   7   7   7   7   7

7   7   7   7   7   7   7

7   7   7   7   7   7   7

7   7   7   7   7   7   7

7   7   7   7   7   7   7

7 7 7 7 7 7 7
7 7 7 7 7 7 7
7 7 7 7
7 7 7 7
7 7 7 7
7 7 7 7
7 7 7 7 7 7 7
7 7 7 7 7 7 7

Promotional Strategy

CHAPTER OBJECTIVES

1. To relate the communications process to promotional strategy.

2. To explain the concept of the promotional mix and its relationship to the marketing mix.

3. To indentify the primary determinants of a promotional mix.

4. To contrast the two major alternative promotional strategies.

5. To list the objectives of promotion.

6. To explain the primary methods of developing a promotional budget.

7. To defend promotion against the public criticisms that are sometimes raised.

Effective advertising programs stake out places in our memories and can be considered as signs of the times. The slogan, "Only in Canada — pity" is an advertising theme which helped to make Red Rose tea famous. The theme was the work of John Cronin and Peter Matthews from the advertising agency J. Walter Thompson, Ltd.

Brooke Bond, the tea company whose Red Rose brew is now inextricably linked with the "only in Canada" slogan, used the Cronin-Matthews brainchild from 1970 to 1982. This is one of the longest-running campaigns in Canadian television advertising history.

Marlene Hore, JWT's Toronto-based national creative director and a Red Rose ad writer from 1975 to 1981, says the ads, comparing Red Rose to highly respected British tea, were among the first of their kind.

"Consumer research showed British tea was the gold standard, so a number of campaigns were developed to tap the Britishness of the tea," Hore says. "At the same time, we knew that Canadians did not want to be lectured about the merits of tea by David Niven or Terry Thomas."

Instead, the 1970 ads borrowed characters from the then-popular British serial, *The Forsyte Saga*, and had them test the upstart Canadian blend. Throughout the duration of the "Only in Canada" series, Hore says, the ads played on the stereotype of the stiff-upper-lipped British tea snob.

The much-lauded Red Rose ads garnered the advertising world's top prizes. Among them were Canada's Clio and Cannes' bronze advertising awards. In spite of this success, Brooke Bond have finally adopted a new slogan, "the perfect cup of tea," instead of the long-lived "pity" slogan. Explains Hore: "Times change."[1]

**The Conceptual
Framework**

Red Rose tea benefited from a well-designed advertising strategy that was brought to life through ingenuity and creativity. This is the essence of successful promotion. **Promotion**, the fourth variable in the marketing mix, can be defined as *the function of informing, persuading, and influencing the consumer's purchase decision*. Figure 18-1 depicts the relationship between the firm's promotional strategy and the other elements of the overall marketing strategy in accomplishing organizational objectives and producing utility for the consumer.

The marketing manager sets the goals and objectives of the firm's promotional strategy in accordance with overall organizational objectives and the goals of the marketing organization. Then, based on these goals, the various elements of the strategy — personal selling, advertising, sales promotion, publicity, and public relations — are formulated in a co-ordinated promotion plan. This becomes an integral part of the total marketing strategy for reaching selected consumer segments. Finally, the feedback mechanism, in such forms as marketing research and field reports, closes the system by identifying any deviations from the plan and by suggesting modifications for improvement.

Promotional strategy is closely related to the process of communications. A standard definition of *communications* is the transmission of a message from a sender to a receiver. **Marketing communications**, then, are *those messages that deal with buyer-seller relationships*. Marketing communications is a broader term than

---

Figure 18-1   Integrating the Promotional Plan into the Total Marketing Mix

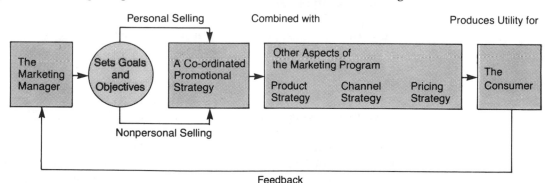

promotional strategy since it includes word-of-mouth and other forms of unsystematic communication. A planned promotional strategy, however, is certainly the most important part of marketing communications.

The Communications Process

Figure 18-2 shows a generalized communication process using terminology borrowed from radio and telecommunications. The sender is the *source* of the communications system since he or she seeks to convey a *message* (a communication of information or advice or a request) to a *receiver* (the recipient of the communication). The message must accomplish three tasks in order to be effective:

1. It must *gain the attention* of the receiver.
2. It must *be understood* by both the receiver and the sender.
3. It must *stimulate* the needs of the receiver and *suggest* an appropriate method of satisfying these needs.[2]

The message must be *encoded*, or translated into understandable terms, and transmitted through a communications medium. *Decoding* is the receiver's interpretation of the message. The receiver's response, known as *feedback*, completes the system. Throughout the process, *noise* can interfere with the transmission of the message and reduce its effectiveness.

In Figure 18-3 the marketing communications process is applied to promotional strategy. The marketing manager is the sender in the system. The message is encoded in the form of sales presentations, advertisements, displays, or publicity releases. The *transfer mechanism* for delivering the message may be a salesperson, the advertising media, or public relations channel.

The decoding step involves the consumer's interpretation of the sender's message. This is the most troublesome aspect of marketing communications since consumers often do not interpret a promotional message in the same way as does its sender. As receivers are likely to decode messages based upon their own frames of reference or individual experiences, the sender must be careful to ensure that the message is encoded to match the target audience.

Feedback is the receiver's response to the message. It may take the form of attitude change, purchase, or nonpurchase. In some instances, firms may use promotion to create a favourable attitude toward its new products or services. Such attitude changes may result in future purchases. In other instances, the objective of the promotional communication is to stimulate consumer purchases. Such purchases indicate positive responses to the firm, its product/service offerings, its distribution channels, its prices, and its promotion. Even nonpurchases can serve as feedback to the sender. They may result from ineffective communication in that the message was not believed, not remembered, or failed to persuade the receiver that

Figure 18-2   A Generalized Communications Process

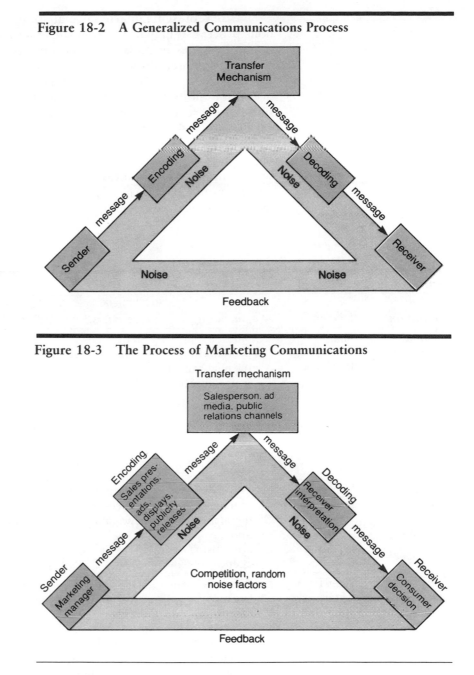

Figure 18-3   The Process of Marketing Communications

the firm's products or services are superior to its competitors. Feedback can be obtained from field sales reports and such techniques as marketing research studies.

Noise represents interference at some stage in the communications process. It may result from such factors as competitive promotional messages being transmitted over the same communications channel, misinterpretation of a sales presentation or an advertising message, receipt of the promotional message by the wrong person, or random noise factors, such as people conversing during a television commercial or leaving the room.

Figure 18-4 illustrates the steps in the communications process with several examples of promotional messages. Although the types of promotion vary from a highly personalized sales presentation to such nonpersonal promotion as television advertising and two-for-one coupons, each form of promotion goes through each stage in the communications model.

Figure 18-4   Examples of Marketing Communications

Type of Promotion	Sender	Encoding	Transfer Mechanism	Decoding by Receiver	Feedback
Personal selling	Sharp Business Products	Sales presentation on new model office copier	Sharp sales representative	Office manager and employees in local firm discuss Sharp sales presentation and those of competing suppliers.	Order placed for the Sharp copier
Two-for-one coupon (sales promotion)	Wendy's Hamburgers	Wendy's marketing department and advertising agency	Coupon insert to weekend newspaper	Newspaper reader sees coupon for hamburger and saves it.	Hamburgers purchased by consumers using the coupon
Television advertising	Walt Disney Enterprises	Advertisement for a new family entertainment animated movie is developed by Disney's advertising agency	Network television during programs with high percentage of viewers under 12 years old	Children see ad and ask their parents to take them; parents see ad and decide to take children.	Movie ticket purchased

Components of the Promotional Mix

The promotional mix, like the marketing mix, involves the proper blending of numerous variables in order to satisfy the needs of the firm's market target and achieve organizational objectives. While the marketing mix is comprised of product, price, promotion, and distribution elements, the promotional mix is a subset of the overall marketing mix. In the case of the promotional mix, the marketing manager is attempting to achieve the optimal blending of various promotional elements in order to accomplish promotional objectives. The components of the **promotional mix** are *personal selling and nonpersonal selling (including advertising, sales promotion, and public relations).*

Personal selling and advertising are the most significant elements since they usually account for the bulk of a firm's promotional expenditures. However, all factors contribute to efficient marketing communications. A detailed discussion of each of these elements is presented in the chapters that follow. Here only a brief definition will be given in order to set the framework for the overall discussion of promotion.

Personal Selling

Personal selling may be defined as *a seller's promotional presentation conducted on a person-to-person basis with the buyer.* It is a direct face-to-face form of promotion. Personal selling was also the original form of promotion. Today it is estimated that 600 000 people in Canada are engaged in this activity.

Nonpersonal Selling

Nonpersonal selling is divided into advertising, sales promotion, and public relations. Advertising is usually regarded as the most important of these forms.

Advertising may be defined as *paid nonpersonal communication through various media by business firms, nonprofit organizations, and individuals who are in some way identified with the advertising message and who hope to inform or persuade members of a particular audience.*[3] It involves the mass media, such as newspapers, television, radio, magazines, and billboards. Business has come to realize the tremendous potential of this form of promotion, and during recent decades advertising has become increasingly important in marketing. Mass consumption makes advertising particularly appropriate for products that rely on sending the same promotional message to large audiences.

Sales promotion includes *"those marketing activities other than personal selling and mass media advertising, and publicity, that stimulate consumer purchasing and dealer effectiveness*, such as displays, shows and expositions, demonstrations, and various nonrecurrent selling efforts not in the ordinary routine."*[4] Sales promotion is usually practised together with other forms of advertising to emphasize, assist, supplement, or otherwise support the objectives of the promotional program.

Public relations is *a firm's communications and relationships with its various publics.* These publics include the organization's customers, suppliers, shareholders, employees, the government, the general public, and the society in which the organization operates. Public relations programs can be either formal or informal. The critical point is that every organization, whether or not it has a formalized, organized program, needs to be concerned about its public relations.

In comparison to personal selling, advertising, and even sales promotion, expenditures for public relations are usually low in most firms. Therefore, *publicity* concerning a company's products or affairs is an important part of an effective public relations effort. It is information disseminated through the public media at no cost. It is generally achieved by placing commercially significant news or obtaining favourable presentation of company or product in a published medium. Since they don't pay for it, companies have little control over the publication by the press of "good" or "bad" company news. But for this very reason, a consumer may find this type

Figure 18-5   Comparing Alternative Promotional Techniques

Type of Promotion	*Personal or Nonpersonal*	*Cost*	*Advantages*	*Disadvantages*
Advertising	Nonpersonal	Relatively inexpensive per contact	Appropriate in reaching mass audiences; allows expressiveness and control over message	Considerable waste; difficult to demonstrate product; difficult to close sales; difficult to measure results
Personal selling	Personal	Expensive per contact	Permits flexible presentation and gains immediate response	Costs more than all other forms per contact; difficult to attract qualified salespeople
Sales promotion	Nonpersonal	Can be costly	Gains attention and has immediate effect	Easy for others to imitate
Public relations	Nonpersonal	Relatively inexpensive; publicity is free	Has high degree of believability	Not as easily controlled as other forms

Source: Adapted from David J. Rachman and Elaine Romano, *Modern Marketing* (Hinsdale, Ill.: The Dryden Press, 1980), p. 450. Adapted by permission of the publisher.

of news source more believable than if the news were disseminated directly by the sponsor.

As Figure 18-5 indicates, each type of promotion has both advantages and disadvantages. Even though personal selling has a relatively high cost per contact, there is less wasted effort than in such nonpersonal forms of promotion as advertising. In addition, it is often more flexible than the other forms, since the salesperson can tailor the sales message to meet the unique needs — or objections — of each potential customer.

On the other hand, advertising is an effective means of reaching mass audiences with the marketer's message. Sales promotion techniques are effective in gaining attention, and public relations efforts such as publicity frequently have a high degree of believability compared to other promotional techniques. The task confronting the marketer is to determine the appropriate blend of each of these techniques in marketing the firm's products and services.

Factors Affecting the Promotional Mix

Since quantitative measures to determine the effectiveness of each component of the promotional mix in a given market segment are not available, the choice of a proper mix of promotional elements is one of the most difficult tasks facing the marketing manager. Factors affecting the promotional mix are: 1) nature of the market; 2) nature of the product; 3) stage in the product life cycle; 4) price; and 5) funds available for promotion.

Nature of the Market

The marketer's target audience has a major impact upon the type of promotion to use. In cases where there is a limited number of buyers, personal selling may prove highly effective. However, markets characterized by a large number of potential customers scattered over a large geographic area may make the cost of contact by personal salespeople prohibitive, and in such instances, advertising may be extensively used. The type of customer also affects the promotional mix. A market target made up of industrial purchasers or retail and wholesale buyers is more likely to require personal selling than one consisting of ultimate consumers.

Nature of the Product

A second important factor in determining an effective promotional mix is the product itself. Highly standardized products with minimal servicing requirements are less likely to depend upon personal selling than higher priced custom products that are technically complex and require servicing. Consumer goods are more likely to rely heavily upon advertising than industrial goods. Within each product category, promotional mixes vary.

Figure 18-6   A Reminder Advertisement Used in the
Maturity Stage of the Product Life Cycle

Source: Reproduced by permission of General Foods Corporation, © 1981.

For instance, installations typically involve heavy reliance upon
personal selling compared to the marketing of operating supplies.
Convenience goods rely heavily upon manufacturer advertising, and
personal selling plays a small role. On the other hand, personal selling is often more important in the marketing of shopping goods,
and both personal selling and nonpersonal selling are important in
the marketing of specialty goods. Finally, personal selling is likely
to be more important in the marketing of products characterized by
trade-ins.

Stage in the
Product Life Cycle
The promotional mix must also be tailored to the stage in the prod-
uct life cycle. In the introductory stage, heavy emphasis is placed on

personal selling to inform the marketplace of the merits of the new product or service. Salespeople contact marketing intermediaries to secure interest and commitment to handle the new product. Trade shows and exhibitions are frequently used to inform and educate prospective dealers and ultimate consumers. Any advertising at this stage is largely informative, and sales promotional techniques, such as samples and cents-off coupons, are designed to influence consumer attitudes and stimulate initial purchases.

As the product or service moves into the growth and maturity stages, advertising becomes more important in attempting to persuade consumers to make purchases. Personal-selling efforts continue to be directed at intermediaries in an attempt to expand distribution. As more competitors enter the marketplace, advertising stresses product differences in an attempt to persuade consumers to purchase the firm's brand. Reminder advertisements begin to appear in the maturity and early decline stages. Figure 18-6 is an example of a reminder ad used for Kool-Aid.

Price   Price of the product or service is a fourth factor in the choice of promotional mixes. Advertising is a dominant mix component for low unit value products due to the high costs per contact for personal selling. The cost of an industrial sales call, for example, is now estimated at over $105.[5] As a result, it has become unprofitable to promote lower value products and services through personal selling. Advertising, by contrast, permits a low promotional expenditure per sales unit, since it reaches mass audiences. For low value consumer products, such as chewing gum, colas, and snack foods, advertising is the only feasible means of promotion.

Funds Available for   A very real barrier to implementing any promotional strategy is the
Promotion   size of the promotional budget. A 30-second television commercial costs an average packaged goods company $86 000[6] to shoot, and one showing during a Grey Cup game can cost $6000 or more. Even though the message is received by millions of viewers and the cost per contact is relatively low, such an expenditure would exceed the entire promotional budget of thousands of firms. For many new, smaller firms, the cost of mass advertising is prohibitive, and they are forced to seek less expensive, less efficient methods. Neighbourhood retailers may not be able to advertise in metropolitan newspapers or on local radio and television stations; apart from personal selling, their limited promotional budgets may be allocated to an eye-catching sign, one of the most valuable promotional devices of a small retailer.

Figure 18-7 summarizes the factors influencing the determination of an appropriate promotional mix.

Figure 18-7   Factors Influencing the Promotional Mix

	Emphasis on	
Factor	Personal Selling	Advertising
Nature of the Market		
Number of buyers	Limited number	Large number
Geographic concentration	Concentrated	Dispersed
Type of customer	Industrial purchaser	Ultimate consumer
Nature of the Product		
Complexity	Custom-made, complex	Standardized
Service requirements	Considerable	Minimal
Type of good	Industrial	Consumer
Use of trade-ins	Trade-ins common	Trade-ins uncommon
Stage in the Product Life Cycle		
	Introductory and early growth stages	Latter part of growth stages and maturity and early decline stages
Price	High unit value	Low unit value

Promotional Strategy — Pull or Push

Essentially, there are two promotional policies that may be employed: a pulling strategy and a pushing strategy. A **pulling strategy** is *a promotional effort by the seller to stimulate final-user demand*, which then exerts pressure on the distribution channel. The plan is to build consumer demand for the product by means of advertising so that channel members will have to stock the product to meet that demand. If a manufacturer's promotional efforts result in shoppers requesting the retailer to stock an item, they will usually succeed in getting that item on the retailer's shelves, since most retailers want to stimulate repeat purchases by satisfied customers. A pulling strategy may be required to motivate marketing intermediaries to handle a product when they already stock a large number of competing products. When a manufacturer decides to use a pulling strategy, personal selling is often largely limited to contacting intermediaries, providing requested information about the product, and taking orders. Advertising and sales promotion are the most commonly used elements of promotion in a pulling strategy.

By contrast, a **pushing strategy** relies more heavily on personal selling. Here, the objective is the *promotion of the product to the members of the marketing channel rather than to the final user.* This can be done through co-operative advertising allowances, trade discounts, personal selling efforts by the firm's sales force, and other

Figure 18-8 Relative Importance of Advertising and Selling

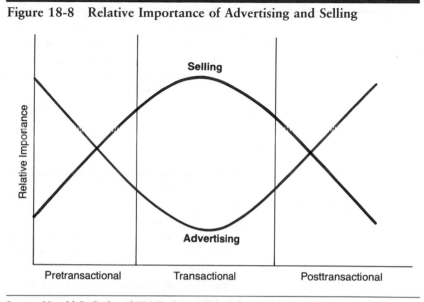

Source: Harold C. Cash and W.J.E. Crissy, "The Salesman's Role in Marketing," *The Psychology of Selling*, Vol. 12 (Personnel Development Associates, Box 3005, Roosevelt Field Station, Garden City, NY 11530). Reprinted by permission.

dealer supports. Such a strategy is designed to produce marketing success for the firm's products by motivating representatives of wholesalers and/or retailers to spend a disproportionate amount of time and effort in promoting these products to customers.

While these are presented as alternative policies, it is unlikely that very many companies will depend entirely upon either strategy. In most cases a mixture of the two is employed.

Timing is another factor to consider in the development of a promotional strategy. Figure 18-8 shows the relative importance of advertising and selling in different periods of the purchase process. During the pretransactional period (before the actual sale) advertising is usually more important than personal selling. It is often argued that one of the primary advantages of a successful advertising program is that it assists the salesperson in approaching the prospect. Personal selling becomes more important than advertising during the transactional phase of the process. In most situations personal selling is the actual mechanism of closing the sale. In the post-transactional stage advertising regains primacy in the promotional effort. It serves as an affirmation of the customer's decision to buy a particular good or service as well as a reminder of the product's favourable qualities, characteristics, and performance.

Promotion Objectives   Management has always found that determining exactly what it expects promotion to achieve is a perplexing problem. Generally, promotional strategy should be oriented toward achieving clearly stated, measurable communications objectives.

What specific tasks should promotion accomplish? The answer to this question varies with the situation. However, the following can be considered objectives of promotion: 1) to provide information; 2) to increase demand; 3) to differentiate the product; 4) to accentuate the value of the product; and 5) to stabilize sales. Note that it is generally too simplistic to state the objective of advertising and promotion in terms of "increasing sales."

Providing Information   The traditional function of promotion was to inform the market about the availability of a particular product. Indeed, a large part of modern promotional effort is still directed at providing product information to potential customers. An example of this is the typical university or college extension course program advertisement appearing in the newspaper. Its content emphasizes informative features, such as the availability of different courses. Southam Business Publications has employed an interesting idea in advertising to potential business advertisers. It shows the back of a station wagon covered with bumper stickers, then makes the point: "To communicate effectively, deal with one idea at a time." By doing this, it educates potential advertisers, as well as showing how Southam can help.

Figure 18-9   Promotion Can Help Marketers Achieve Demand Objectives

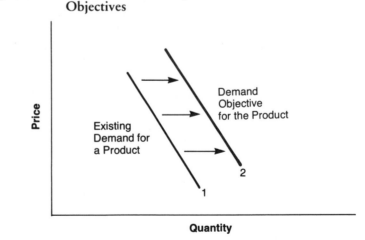

Source: *Principles of Marketing: The Management View*, 3d ed., by Richard H. Buskirk. Copyright © 1961, 1966, 1970, by Holt, Rinehart and Winston, Inc. Adapted and reprinted by permission of Holt, Rinehart and Winston, Inc.

Figure 18-10   Using Advertising to Stimulate Demand

Source: Courtesy of Cadbury Schweppes Powell.

The informative function often requires repeated customer exposures. For instance, "in a . . . study concerning customer acceptance of a new durable good, it was found that . . . at least several months were required after introduction (and accompanying promotion) before consumers became generally aware of the item and somewhat familiar with its characteristics."[7]

Stimulating Demand   The primary objective of most promotional efforts is to increase the demand for a specific brand of product or service. This can be shown by using the familiar demand curves of basic economics (see Figure 18-9). Successful promotion can shift demand from schedule 1 to schedule 2, which means that greater quantities can be sold at each possible price level. Cadbury Schweppes Powell accomplished this with its "Thick" bars (see Figure 18-10), in a campaign that brought the chocolate bar to a position among the top five brands in the Canadian market.[8] The Thick bars were introduced in test markets in Vancouver, then in Ontario. The advertising series used such slogans as "Birds of a Feather Thick Together," "Great Minds Thick Alike," and "Chop Thicks." The ads have been very successful in the three years since they were first run. They not only won an award, but their success in influencing the market spawned a number of 'thick' competitors. Cadbury's latest slogan, therefore, is "the thick of the crop."

Differentiating the Product

Product differentiation is often an objective of the firm's promotional effort. Homogeneous demand, represented by the horizontal line in Figure 18-11, means that consumers regard the firm's output as no different from that of its competitors. In such cases the individual firm has no control over such marketing variables as price. A differentiated demand schedule, by contrast, permits more flexibility in marketing strategy, such as price changes.

For example, McCain's, a producer of high-quality frozen vegetables, advertises the dependable high quality and good taste of its products. This differentiates these products from others. Consequently some consumers wanting these attributes are willing to pay a higher price for McCain's than they would for other brands. Similarly, the high quality and distinctiveness of Cross pens are advertised, resulting in Cross's ability to ask and obtain a price 100 times that of some disposable pens. With the exception of commodities, most products have some degree of differentiation, resulting in a downward-sloping demand curve. The angle of the slope varies somewhat according to the degree of product differentiation.

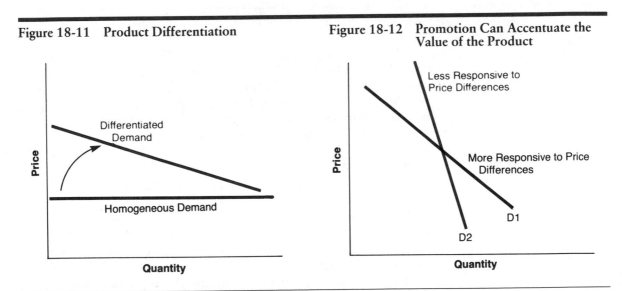

Figure 18-11 Product Differentiation

Figure 18-12 Promotion Can Accentuate the Value of the Product

Source: *Markets and Marketing: An Orientation*, by Lee E. Preston (Glenview, Ill.: Scott, Foresman, 1970), p. 196. Copyright © 1970 by Scott, Foresman and Company. Adapted by permission.

Accentuating the Value of the Product

Promotion can point out more ownership utility to buyers, thereby accentuating the value of a product. The good or service might then be able to command a higher price in the marketplace. For example, status-oriented advertising may allow some retail clothing stores to command higher prices than others. The demand curve facing a prestige store may be less responsive to price differences than that of a competitor without a quality reputation. The responsiveness to price differences is shown in Figure 18-12.

Stabilizing Sales

A company's sales are not uniform throughout the year. Fluctuations can be caused by cyclical, seasonal, or other reasons. Reducing these variations is often an objective of the firm's promotional strategy. Lee E. Preston states:

> Advertising that is focused on such attitudinal goals as "brand loyalty" and such specific sales goals as "increasing repeat purchases" is essentially aimed at stabilizing demand. The prominence of such goals in the current literature and in advertising planning discussions suggests that stabilizing demand and insulating the market position of an individual firm and product against unfavourable developments is, in fact, one of the most important purposes of promotional activity at the present time. [9]

Budgeting for Promotional Strategy

Promotion budgets can differ not only in amount but also in composition. Industrial firms generally invest a larger proportion of their budgets for personal selling than for advertising, while the reverse is usually true of most producers of consumer goods.

A simple model showing the productivity of promotional expenditures is shown in Figure 18-13. In terms of sales revenue, initial expenditures on promotion usually result in increasing returns. There appear to be some economies associated with larger promotional expenditures. These economies result from such factors as the cumulative effects of promotion and repeat sales.

Evidence suggests that sales initially lag behind promotion for structural reasons (filling up the retail shelves, low initial production, lack of buyer knowledge). This produces a threshold effect, where there are no sales but lots of initial investment in promotion. A second phase might produce returns (sales) proportional to a given promotion expenditure; this would be the most predictable range. Finally, the area of diminishing returns is reached when an increase in promotional expenditure does not produce a proportional increase in sales.

For example, an initial expenditure of $40 000 may result in the sale of 100 000 product units for a consumer goods manufacturer. An additional $10 000 expenditure may then sell 30 000

Figure 18-13   Promotion–Sales Curve

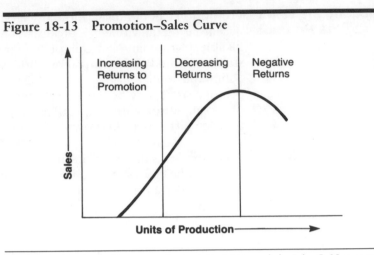

Source: *The Marketing Economy: An Analytical Approach*, by John C. Narver and Ronald Savitt, p. 294. Copyright © 1971 by Holt, Rinehart and Winston, Inc. Reprinted by permission of Holt, Rinehart and Winston, Inc.

more units of the item. And a further $10 000 may produce another 35 000-unit sale. The cumulative effect of the expenditures and repeat sales have resulted in increasing returns to the promotional outlays. However, as the advertising budget moves from $60 000 to $70 000, the marginal productivity of the additional expenditure may fall to 28 000 units. At some later point, no increase, or an actual decrease in units, may occur with additional expenditures. As competition intensifies, markets become saturated, and media effectiveness decreases because of increased noise in communications channels.

To test the thesis that there is a saturation point for advertising, Anheuser-Busch once quadrupled its advertising budget in several markets. After three months the company's distributors demanded an advertising cut. Many claimed that beer consumers came into their stores saying, "Give me anything *but* Bud."[10]

Establishing a Budget   Theoretically, the optimal method of allocating a promotion budget is to expand it until the cost of each additional increment equals the additional incremental revenue received. In other words, the most effective allocation procedure is to increase promotional expenditures until each dollar of promotion expense is matched by an additional dollar of profit (see Figure 18-13). This procedure—called *marginal analysis* — results in the maximization of the input's productivity. The difficulty arises in identification of this optimal point. It requires a precise balancing of marginal expenses for promotion and the resulting marginal receipts.

The more traditional methods of allocating a promotional budget are by percentage of sales, fixed sum per unit, meeting competition, and task-objective methods.

Percentage of sales is a very common way of allocating promotion budgets. The percentage can be based on either past (such as the previous year) or forecasted (current year) sales. While the simplicity of this plan is appealing, it is not an effective way of achieving the basic promotional objectives. Arbitrary percentage allocations (whether applied to historical or future sales figures) fail to allow the flexibility that is required. Furthermore, such reasoning is circular, for the advertising allocation is made dependent upon sales, rather than vice versa, as it should be. Consider, for example, the implications of a decline in sales.

The *fixed sum per unit* approach differs from percentage of sales in only one respect: it applies a predetermined allocation to each sales or production unit. This also can be set on either a historical or a forecasted basis. Producers of high-value consumer durable goods, such as automobiles, often use this budgeting method.

Another traditional approach is simply to match competitors' outlays—in other words, *meet competition*—on either an absolute or a relative basis. However, this kind of approach usually leads to a status quo situation at best, with each company retaining its percentage of total sales. Meeting the competition's budget does not necessarily relate to the objectives of promotion and, therefore, seems inappropriate for most contemporary marketing programs.

The **task-objective method** of developing a promotional budget is based upon a sound evaluation of the firm's promotional objectives, and is thus better attuned to modern marketing practices. It involves two sequential steps.

1. The organization must *define the realistic communication goals* the firm wants the promotional mix to accomplish — for example, a 25 percent increase in brand awareness, or a 10 percent rise in consumers who realize that the product has certain specific differentiating features. The key is to specify quantitatively the objectives to be accomplished. They then become an integral part of the promotional plan.

2. The organization must *determine the amount (as well as type) of promotional activity required to accomplish each of the objectives* that have been set. These units combined become the firm's promotion budget.

A crucial assumption underlies the task-objective approach: that the productivity of each promotional dollar is measurable. That is why the objectives must be carefully chosen, quantified, and accomplished through promotional efforts. Generally, an objective like "We wish to achieve a 5 percent increase in sales" is an ill-conceived marketing objective because a sale is the culmination of the effects of *all* elements of the marketing mix. Therefore, an appropriate promotional objective might be "To make 30 percent of the target market aware of the facilities available at the health spa."

A study by the Marketing Science Institute found that many firms do not keep adequate records of promotional expenditures, nor do they attempt to test alternative promotional efforts.[11]

While promotional budgeting is always difficult, recent research studies, and more frequent use of computer-based models, make it less of a problem than it has been in the past.

Measuring the Effectiveness of Promotion

It is widely recognized that part of a firm's promotional effort is ineffective. John Wanamaker, a successful nineteenth-century retailer, once observed: "I know half the money I spend on advertising is wasted; but I can never find out which half."

Measuring the effectiveness of promotional expenditures has become an extremely important research question, particularly among advertisers. Studies aimed at this measurement dilemma face several major obstacles, among them the difficulty of isolating the effect of the promotion variable.

Most marketers would prefer to use a **direct-sales results test** to measure the effectiveness of promotion. This test attempts to *ascertain for each dollar of promotional outlay the corresponding increase in revenue.* The primary difficulty is controlling the other variables operating in the marketplace. A $1.5-million advertising campaign may be followed by an increase in sales of $20 million. However, this may be more because of a sudden price hike by the leading competitor than because of the advertising expenditure. Therefore, advertisers are turning to establishing and assessing achievable, measurable objectives.

With the increasing sophistication of marketing analysts, analytical techniques, and computer-based marketing information systems, banks of historical data on promotional expenditures and their effects are being subjected to ever more scrutiny. More and more is being learned about measuring and evaluating the effects of promotional activity. While the technical literature in marketing reveals much of what is happening in this critical area, firms are reluctant to release much of this information. Not only do they wish to keep their proprietary (privately held) information about how the market works to themselves for competitive reasons, but they do not want competitors knowing the methods and decision routines used in planning promotional activity.

Other methods of assessing promotion effectiveness include inquiries about the product, determination of change in attitudes toward the product, and improvement in public knowledge and awareness. One indicator of probable advertising effectiveness would be the elasticity or sensitivity of sales to promotion based on historical data concerning price, sales volume, and advertising expenditures.

It is difficult for the marketer to conduct research in a controlled environment like that which can be set up in other disciplines. The difficulty in isolating the effects of promotion causes many to abandon all attempts at measurement. Others, however, turn to indirect evaluation. These researchers concentrate on the factors that are quantifiable, such as recall (how much is remembered about specific products or advertisements) and readership (the size and composition of the audience). The basic problem here is that it is difficult to relate these variables to sales. Does extensive ad readership actually lead to increased sales? Another problem is the high cost of research in promotion. To assess the effectiveness of promotional expenditures correctly may require a significant investment.

The Value of Promotion

Promotion has often been the target of criticism. A selection of these would include the following:

"Promotion contributes nothing to society."
"Most advertisements and sales presentations insult my intelligence."
"Promotion 'forces' consumers to buy products they cannot afford and do not need."
"Advertising and selling are economic wastes."
"Salespersons and advertisers are usually unethical."

Consumers, public officials, and marketers agree that all too often many of these complaints are true. Some salespersons do use unethical sales tactics. Some product advertising is directed at consumer groups that can least afford to purchase the particular item. Many television commercials do contribute to the growing problem of cultural pollution.

While promotion can certainly be criticized on many counts, it is important to remember that it plays a crucial role in modern society. This point is best explained by looking at the importance of promotion on the business, economic, and social levels.

Business Importance

Promotional strategy has become increasingly important to business enterprises — both large and small. The long-term rise in outlays for promotion is well documented and certainly attests to management's faith in the ability of promotional efforts to produce additional sales. It is difficult to conceive of an enterprise that does not attempt to promote its product or service in some manner or another. Most modern institutions simply cannot survive in the long run without promotion. Business must communicate with the public.

Nonbusiness enterprises have also recognized the importance of this variable. The Canadian government is now the largest advertiser in Canada, promoting many programs and concepts. Religious organizations have acknowledged the importance of promoting what they do. Even labour organizations have used promotional channels to make their viewpoints known to the public at large. In fact, promotion now plays a larger role in the functioning of non-profit organizations than it ever has in the past. Figure 18-14 effectively points out the power of advertising in the case of a public appeal.

Economic Importance   Promotion has assumed a degree of economic importance, if for no other reason than that it is an activity that employs thousands of people. More importantly, however, effective promotion has allowed society to derive benefits not otherwise available. For example, the criticism that "promotion costs too much" views an individual expense item in isolation. It fails to consider the possible effect of promotion on other categories of expenditures.

Promotion strategies that increase the number of units sold permit economies in the production process, thereby lowering the production costs assigned to each unit of output. Lower consumer prices then allow these products to become available to more people. Similarly, researchers have found that advertising subsidizes the informational content of newspapers and the broadcast media.[12] In short, promotion pays for many of the enjoyable entertainment and educational aspects of contemporary life, as well as lowering product costs.

Social Importance   Criticisms such as "most promotional messages are tasteless" and "promotion contributes nothing to society" sometimes ignore the fact that there is no commonly accepted set of standards or priorities existing within our social framework. We live in a varied economy characterized by consumer segments with differing needs, wants, and aspirations. What is tasteless to one group may be quite informative to another. Promotional strategy is faced with an "averaging" problem that escapes many of its critics. The one generally accepted standard in a market society is freedom of choice for the consumer. Customer buying decisions will eventually determine what is acceptable practice in the marketplace.

Promotion has become an important factor in the campaigns to achieve such socially oriented objectives as stopping smoking, family planning, physical fitness, and the elimination of drug abuse. Promotion performs an informative and educational task that makes it extremely important in the functioning of modern society. As with everything else in life, it is how one uses promotion, not the using itself, that is critical.

Figure 18-4   An advertisement sponsored by a non-profit organization

Brian has kidney failure. It bloats his small body with harmful fluids and poisons. It's robbed him of energy.

For Brian, life depends on routine dialysis treatments to cleanse his blood. Someday he may receive a successful kidney transplant.

But preventing kidney disease and making successful transplants requires research which costs money... a lot of money.

Buddy, can you spare a donation? To donate call-toll-free 1-800-268-7742, operator #77.

THE KIDNEY FOUNDATION OF CANADA

Help put us out of business.

Summary   This chapter has provided an introduction to promotion, the fourth variable in the marketing mix (product, pricing, distribution, and promotional strategies). Promotional strategy is closely related to the marketing communications system, which includes the elements of sender, message, encoding, transfer mechanism, decoding, receiver, feedback, and noise. The major components of promotional strategy are personal selling and nonpersonal selling (advertising, sales promotion, and public relations). These elements are discussed in the two chapters that follow.

Developing an effective promotional strategy is a complex matter. The elements of promotion are related to the type and value of the product being promoted, the nature of the market, the stage of the product life cycle, and the funds available for promotion, as well as to the timing of the promotional effort. Personal selling is used primarily for industrial goods, for higher-value items, and during the transactional phase of the purchase decision process. Advertising, by contrast, is used primarily for consumer goods, for lower-value items, and during the pretransactional and posttransactional phases.

A pushing strategy, which relies on personal selling, attempts to promote the product to the members of the marketing channel rather than the final user. A pulling strategy concentrates on stimulating final-user demand, primarily in the mass media through advertising and sales promotion.

The five basic objectives of promotion are to 1) provide information, 2) stimulate demand, 3) differentiate the product, 4) accentuate the value of the product, and 5) stabilize sales.

There are several methods used in establishing promotional budgets. However, the task-objective method makes the most sense and promises best management of promotional resources.

Although the target of much criticism, promotion plays an important role in the business, economic, and social activity of the country.

CHAPTER 19

Advertising, Sales Promotion, and Public Relations

CHAPTER OBJECTIVES

1. To explain the current status and historical development of advertising.

2. To identify the major types of advertising.

3. To list and discuss the various advertising media.

4. To explain how advertising effectiveness is determined.

5. To outline the organization of the advertising function.

6. To describe the process of creating an advertisement.

7. To identify the methods of sales promotion.

8. To explain the role of public relations and publicity.

When developing an advertising strategy, firms sometimes choose not to put much emphasis on individual products. Honda has chosen this strategy, and will emphasize its corporate image rather than details about products for at least the next year.

The first of Honda's magazine ads was purely corporate in emphasis. It featured a blank piece of graph paper, with the headline: "This is how a Honda engineer starts his day." On television, the Civics are described in a general way — only the silhouettes of the cars are shown — to emphasize the new look. The 30-second spot, called "The new car" is designed to convey the message that Honda has "taken another innovative step, established the benchmark again." That is why the shapes are shown, rather than individual features.

Coupled with this general image-building strategy, the company will also carry some detailed advertisements on each car. This will be done through the efforts of its dealers, as well as other magazine advertisements and outdoor billboards. Honda has clearly developed a strategy which they feel will best serve them in the market position in which they find themselves. The execution of the various elements of the advertising program seems to be well-balanced, and to fit in well with their overall strategy.[1]

The Conceptual Framework	As explained in Chapter 18, promotion consists of both personal and nonpersonal elements. In this chapter the nonpersonal elements of promotion — advertising, sales promotion, and public relations — are examined. These elements play a critical role in the promotional mixes of thousands of organizations.

For most organizations, advertising represents the most important type of nonpersonal promotion. This chapter examines advertising objectives and the importance of planning for advertising. Also discussed are the different types of advertisements and media choices. Both retail advertising and manufacturer (national) advertising are discussed and the alternative methods of assessing the effectiveness of an advertisement are examined. Sales promotion and public relations — including publicity — are also discussed.

Advertising

If you sought to be the next prime minister of Canada, you would need to communicate with every possible voting Canadian. If you had invented a new calculator and went into business to sell it, your chances of success would be slim without informing and persuading students and businesses of the usefulness of your calculator. In these situations you would discover, as have countless others, that you would need to use *advertising* — to communicate to buyers or voters. In the previous chapter, advertising was defined as a paid, nonpersonal communication through various media by business firms, nonprofit organizations, and individuals who are in some way identified in the advertising message and who hope to inform or persuade members of a particular audience.

Today's widespread markets make advertising an important part of business. Since the end of World War II, advertising and related expenditures have risen faster than gross national product and most other economic indicators. Furthermore, about 8500 people are employed in advertising, according to Statistics Canada.[2]

Four advertisers — the Government of Canada, Procter & Gamble, Labatt's, and Molson's — spent over $30 million each for advertising in 1983. Figure 19-1 ranks the top advertisers in Canada.

Figure 19-1   The Top 50 National Advertisers, 1984

Company Name	Total $
1. Government of Canada	95,767,946
2. Procter & Gamble	46,339,143
3. John Labatt	37,581,241
4. The Molson Companies	35,297,759
5. Dart and Kraft	32,489,845

Figure 19-1, cont'd.

Company Name	Total $
6. Government of Ontario	32,086,361
7. Rothmans of Canada	31,045,579
8. General Motors of Canada	30,011,258
9. Nabisco Brands	24,471,874
10. General Foods	22,945,590
11. Unilever	21,830,065
12. Ford Motor of Canada	20,364,261
13. American Home Products	18,327,314
14. Kellogg Salada Canada	17,787,386
15. Government of Quebec	17,781,235
16. Chrysler Canada	17,640,849
17. Canadian Pacific	17,341,827
18. Imperial Oil	15,580,595
19. Warner Lambert Canada	15,500,551
20. Coca-Cola	14,335,015
21. Imasco Holdings Canada	14,216,971
22. McDonald's Restaurants Canada	13,608,806
23. Gillette Canada	12,097,653
24. The Thomson Group	11,939,927
25. Bristol-Myers Canada	11,880,576
26. Rowntree Mackintosh Canada	11,297,038
27. Dairy Bureau of Canada	11,045,297
28. Pepsico	10,905,944
29. Canada Packers	10,733,553
30. Kodak Canada	10,627,891
31. Sears Canada	10,600,922
32. Ralston Purina Canada	10,481,771
33. CKR	10,419,209
34. IBM Canada	9,859,007
35. Bell Enterprises Canada Inc.	9,360,472
36. Eaton's of Canada	9,300,706
37. Quakers Oats Co. of Canada	9,274,361
38. Canadian Tire Corporation	9,243,044
39. Johnson and Johnson	9,002,141
40. Union Carbide Canada	8,959,164
41. Kimberly-Clark of Canada	8,944,850
42. Gulf Canada	8,678,255
43. Nissan Automobile Co. of Canada	8,666,836
44. Canadian Imperial Bank of Commerce	8,533,066
45. Nestlé Enterprises	8,527,154
46. Telecom Canada	8,180,212
47. General Mills Canada	7,950,696
48. Bank of Montreal	7,724,703
49. Honda Canada	7,575,819
50. George Weston	6,904,644

It is particularly noteworthy that governments, both federal and provincial, are such a major force in Canadian advertising. The government is the nation's largest advertising spender. It spent over twice as much as the number two spender, Procter & Gamble. About $224 is spent on advertising each year for every person in Canada.[3]

Advertising expenditures vary among industries and companies. Cosmetics companies are often cited as an example of firms that spend a high percentage of their funds on advertising and promotion. Management consultants Schonfeld & Associates studied more than 4000 firms and calculated their average advertising expenditures as a percentage of both sales and gross profit margin. Estimates for selected industries are given in Figure 19-2. Wide differences exist among industries. Advertising spending can range from one fifth of one percent in an industry like iron and steel foundries to more than 7 percent of sales in the detergent industry.

Industry in general has become somewhat advertising-oriented as other elements of promotion have grown relatively more expensive. But advertising's future potential remains a matter of conjecture, although it may be determined by the environmental framework within which it operates. The role of advertising in Canadian society attracts considerable public interest today.

Figure 19-2   Estimates of Average Advertising to Sales in Ten Industries

Industry	Advertising and Promotion as Percentage of Sales, 1982
Soap, detergent	7.1%
Beer, ale	6.9%
Toy, sporting goods	6.9%
Cigarette	6.4%
Restaurant	3.1%
Photographic equipment and supply	2.7%
Household furniture	1.9%
Chemicals, allied industries	1.3%
General building contractor	0.6%
Iron and steel foundry	0.2%

Source: Schonfeld & Associates, Inc., 120 S. La Salle St., Chicago 60603, (312) 236-5846.

Historical Development   Some form of advertising products has probably existed since the development of the exchange process.[4] Most of the early advertising was vocal. Criers and hawkers sold various products, made public announcements, and chanted advertising slogans like the now familiar:

> One-a-penny, two-a-penny, hot-cross buns
> One-a-penny, two for tuppence, hot-cross buns

Signs were also used in early advertising. Most were symbolic and used to identify products or services. In Rome a goat signified a dairy; a mule driving a mill, a bakery; a boy being whipped, a school.

Later the development of the printing press greatly expanded advertising's capability. A 1710 advertisement in the *Spectator* billed one dentifrice as "the Incomparable Powder for cleaning of Teeth, which has given great satisfaction to most of the Nobility and Gentry in England."

Many early newspapers carried advertising on their first page. Most of the advertisements would be called classified ads today — spouses looking for wandering partners, householders looking for servants, and the like. However, some future national advertisers also began to use newspaper advertising at this time.

The first advertising agency was organized in the United States in 1841. Originally, these agencies were simply brokers who sold advertising space. In their competition for business they gradually began to offer additional services like advertising research, copywriting, and advertising planning.

Claude C. Hopkins used a large-scale consumer survey concerning home-baked beans before launching a campaign for Van Camp's Pork and Beans in the early 1900s. Hopkins claimed that home-baked beans were difficult to digest, and suggested that consumers should try Van Camp's beans. He used "reason-why copy" to show the reasons why someone should buy the product.

Some of the early advertising promoted products of questionable value, such as patent medicines. As a result, a reformist movement developed in advertising during the early 1900s, and some newspapers began to screen their advertisements. Magazine publisher Cyrus Curtis began rejecting certain types of advertising, such as medical copy that claimed cures and advertisements for alcoholic beverages. These improvements established the springboard for the further growth in advertising that many of the industry's forefathers thought impossible.

One identifying feature of advertising in the last half of the twentieth century is its concern for researching the markets that it attempts to reach. Originally, advertising research dealt primarily with media selection and the product. Then, advertisers became increasingly concerned with aiming their messages more specifically through determining the appropriate *demographics* (such characteristics as the age, sex, and income level of potential buyers). Now, understanding consumer behaviour has become an important aspect of advertising strategy. Psychological influences on purchase decisions — often called *psychographics* — can be useful in describing potential markets for advertising appeals. As described in Chapter 4, these influences include such factors as lifestyle and personal attitudes. Increased knowledge in these areas has led to improved advertising decisions.

THE BORN LOSER

Copyright © 1983, Newspaper Enterprise Association

The emergence of the marketing concept, with its emphasis on a company-wide consumer orientation, saw advertising take on an expanded role as marketing communications assumed greater importance in business. Advertising provides an efficient, inexpensive, and fast method of reaching the much sought-after consumer. Its extensive use now rivals that of personal selling. Advertising has become a key ingredient in the effective implementation of the marketing concept.

Advertising Objectives

Traditionally the objectives of advertising were stated in terms of direct sales goals. A more realistic approach, however, is to view advertising as having communications objectives that seek *to inform, persuade, and remind* potential customers of the product. Advertising seeks to condition the consumer so that he or she has a favourable viewpoint toward the promotional message. The goal is to improve the likelihood that the customer will buy a particular product. In this sense, advertising illustrates the close relationship between marketing communications and promotional strategy.

In instances where personal selling is the primary component of a firm's marketing mix, advertising may be used in a support role to assist the salespeople. Much of Avon's advertising is aimed at assisting the neighbourhood salesperson by strengthening the image of Avon, its products, and its salespeople. The well-known advertisement for McGraw-Hill Magazines, shown in Figure 19-3 illustrates the important role advertising can play in opening doors for the sales force by preparing customers for the sales call.

Advertising Planning   Advertising planning begins with effective research. Research results allow management to make strategic decisions, which are then translated into tactical execution such as budgeting, copywriting,

Figure 19-3   Use of Advertising to Assist Personal Selling

Source: Reprinted with permission of McGraw-Hill Publications Company.

scheduling, and the like. Finally, there must be some feedback mechanism for measuring the effectiveness of the advertising. The elements of advertising planning are shown in Figure 19-4.

There is a real need for following a sequential process in advertising decisions. Novice advertisers are often guilty of being overly concerned with the technical aspects of advertisement construction, while ignoring the more basic steps such as market analysis. The type of advertisement that is employed in any particular situation is related in large part to the planning phase of this process.

Figure 19-4   Elements of Advertising Planning

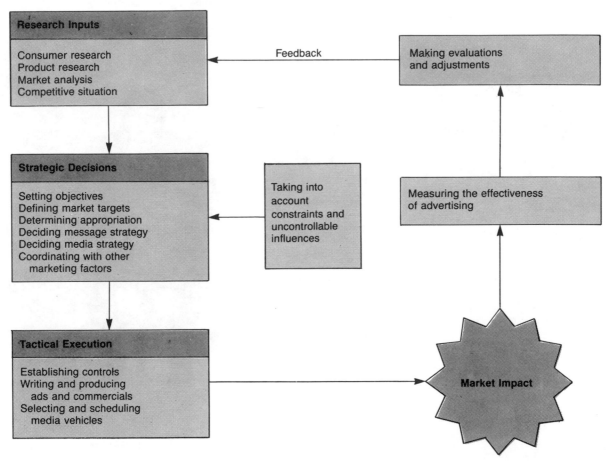

Source: Adapted from *Advertising: Its Role in Modern Marketing*, p. 202, by S. Watson Dunn and Arnold M. Barban. Copyright © 1982 by CBS College Publishing. Reprinted by permission.

Positioning   The concept of positioning was discussed in Chapter 5. It involves the development of a marketing strategy aimed at a particular segment of the market in order to achieve a desired position in the mind of the prospective buyer. As Professors David A. Aaker and J. Gary Shansby point out, a variety of positioning strategies is available to the advertiser. An object can be positioned:

1. By attributes. (Crest is a cavity fighter.)
2. By price/quality. (Sears is a value store.)
3. By competitor. ("Avis is only number two in rent-a-cars, so why go with us? We try harder.")
4. By application. (Gatorade is for quick, healthful energy after exercise and other forms of physical exertion.)
5. By product user. (Mercedes-Benz automobiles are for discriminating executives.)
6. By product class. (Carnation Instant Breakfast is a breakfast food.)[5]

Types of Advertisements   Essentially, there are two basic types of advertisements: product and institutional. These can each be subdivided into informative, persuasive, and reminder categories.

Product advertising deals with *the nonpersonal selling of a particular good or service.* It is the type we normally think of when the subject of advertising comes up in a conversation. **Institutional advertising**, by contrast, is concerned with *promoting a concept, idea, or philosophy, or the goodwill of an industry, company, or organization.* It is often closely related to the public relations function of the enterprise. An example of institutional advertising by Alcan appears in Figure 19-5.

Informative Product Advertising   All advertising seeks to influence the audience, as does any type of communication. **Informative product advertising** *seeks to develop demand through presenting factual information on the attributes of the product and/or service.* For example, an advertisement for a new type of photocopy machine would attempt to persuade through citing the various unique product and/or service features of that copier. Informative product advertising tends to be used in the promotion of new products since a major requirement in such cases is to announce availability and characteristics which will satisfy needs. Thus it is often seen in the introductory stages of the product life cycle. Figure 19-6 shows an advertisement for Mastercard which uses a factual approach to persuade people to use that service.

Persuasive Product Advertising   In **persuasive product advertising** *the emphasis is on the use of words and/or images to try to create an image for a product and to influence attitudes about it.* In contrast to informative product advertis-

Figure 19-5   An Example of Institutional Advertising

Source: *Maclean's* (May 7, 1984), Inside-back Cover.

ing, this type of advertising contains little objective information. Figure 19-7 shows an advertisement for Quaker cookie mix. While it gives a little objective information, the main thrust is persuasion. Coke and Pepsi use persuasive techniques in their lifestyle advertisements featuring a group of happy people enjoying the product. Persuasive advertising is generally used more in the growth period and to some extent in the maturity period of the product life cycle.

Figure 19-6   An Example of Informative Product Advertising

Reminder-Oriented Product Advertising

The goal of **reminder-oriented product advertising** is *to reinforce previous promotional activity by keeping the name in front of the public*. It is used in the maturity period as well as throughout the decline phase of the product life cycle. An example of a reminder-oriented slogan is Esso's well-known "we help to make you better." The general relationship between the type of advertising and the stage of the life cycle is illustrated in Figure 19-8.

Figure 19-7   An Example of Persuasive Product Advertising

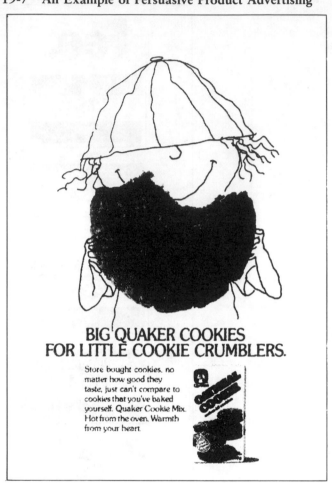

Informative Institutional
Advertising

This approach seeks to increase public knowledge of a concept, idea, philosophy, industry, or company. In the early 1980s the oil industry was experiencing a degree of unfavourable publicity. Gulf Oil's communications director said, "We decided we had a story to tell."[6] Consequently, the company tripled its corporate advertising budget to $3 million and undertook an extensive program to educate the public about the contributions of the company to society. Other firms, such as Volkswagen have continuously advertised their innovativeness and reliability. An example of a recent Volkswagen institutional advertisement is shown in Figure 19-9.

Figure 19-8   Relationship Between Advertising and the Product Life Cycle

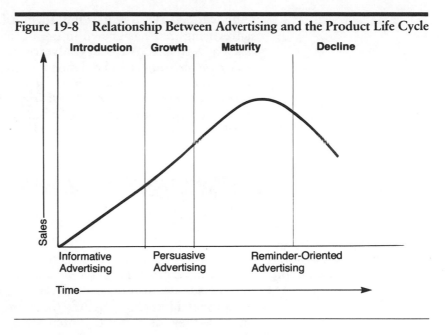

Figure 19-9   An Example of Informative Institutional Advertising

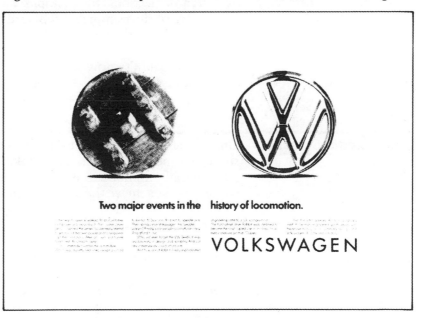

Advocacy Advertising One form of persuasive institutional advertising that has grown in use during the past decade is advocacy advertising. **Advocacy advertising**, sometimes referred to as *cause advertising*, can be defined as *any kind of paid public communication or message, from an identified source and in a conventional medium of public advertising, which presents information or a point of view bearing on a publicly recognized controversial issue*.[7] Such advertising is designed to influence public opinion, to affect current and pending legislation, and to gain a following.

Advocacy advertising has long been utilized by such nonprofit organizations as Mothers Against Drunk Driving (MADD), Planned Parenthood, "right to life" anti-abortion groups, and the National Citizen's Coalition.

Persuasive Institutional Advertising

When a firm or advertising agency wishes *to advance the interests of a particular institution within a competitive environment*, it often uses **persuasive institutional advertising**. Examples of persuasive institutional advertising include the efforts of Canada and others to increase their shares of the intensely competitive tourism market.

Reminder-Oriented Institutional Advertising

Reminder-oriented institutional advertising, like reminder-oriented product advertising, is used *to reinforce previous promotional activity*. In most elections, for example, early persuasive (issue-directed) advertising of the nominee is replaced by reminder-oriented advertising during the closing weeks of the campaign. Examples of this type of institutional advertising abound in the media. The 3M ad "Maybe you didn't know we made all these products. There's more too!" is an example.

Media Selection

One of the most important decisions in developing an advertising strategy is media selection. A mistake at this point can cost a company literally millions of dollars in ineffectual advertising. Media strategy must achieve the communications goals mentioned earlier.

Research should identify the market target to determine its size and characteristics and then match the target with the audience and effectiveness of the available media. The objective is to achieve adequate media coverage without advertising beyond the identifiable limits of the potential market. Finally, alternative costs are compared to determine the best possible media purchase.

These are numerous types of advertising media, and the characteristics of some of the more important ones will be considered here.[8] The advantages and disadvantages of each are shown in Figure 19-10.

Figure 19-10 Advantages and Disadvantages of the Various Advertising Media

Media	Advantages	Disadvantages
Newspapers	Flexibility Community prestige Intense coverage Reader control of exposure Co-ordination with national advertising Merchandising service	Short lifespan Hasty reading Poor reproduction
Magazines	Selectivity Quality reproduction Long life Prestige associated with some magazines Extra services	Lack of flexibility
Television	Great impact Mass coverage Repetition Flexibility Prestige	Temporary nature of message High cost High mortality rate for commercials Evidence of public lack of selectivity
Radio	Immediacy Low cost Practical audience selection Mobility	Fragmentation Temporary nature of message Little research information
Outdoor Advertising	Communication of quick and simple ideas Repetition Ability to promote products available for sale nearby	Brevity of the message Public concern over aesthetics
Direct Mail	Selectivity Intense coverage Speed Flexibility of format Complete information Personalization	High cost per person Dependency on quality of mailing list Consumer resistance

Source: Based on S. Watson Dunn and Arnold M. Barban, *Advertising: Its Role in Modern Marketing*, 5th ed. (Hinsdale, Ill.: The Dryden Press, 1982), pp. 513–577.

Newspapers About 32 percent of Canada's total advertising revenues, the largest share received by any of the media, is spent on advertising in newspapers.[9] The primary advantages of newspapers are flexibility (advertising can be varied from one locality to the next), community prestige (newspapers have a deep impact on the community), intense coverage (in most places about nine out of ten homes can be reached by a single newspaper), and reader control of exposure to the advertising message (unlike audiences of electronic media, readers can refer back to newspapers). The disadvantages are a short lifespan, hasty reading (the typical reader spends only 20–30 minutes on the newspaper), and poor reproduction.

Magazines   Magazines are divided into such diverse categories as consumer magazines, farm and business publications, and directories. They account for about 15 percent of all advertising. The primary advantages of periodical advertising are: selectivity of market targets; quality reproduction; long life; the prestige associated with some magazines; and the extra services offered by many publications. The primary disadvantage is that periodicals lack the flexibility of newspapers, radio, and television. The leading magazines in Canada are shown in Figure 19-11.

Figure 19-11   15 Leading Magazines in Canada

Rank	Magazine	Average Circulation (000)
1	TV Times	1 644
2	Chatelaine (E & F)	1 374
3	Homemaker's Magazine	1 336
4	Reader's Digest	1 335
5	TV Guide Magazine	877
6	Maclean's/L'Actualité	863
7	Starweek	836
8	Quest	713
9	Legion Magazine	513
10	Marquee	510
11	Leisure Ways	376
12	Canadian Living	369
13	Time	331
14	United Church Observer	302
15	City Woman	301

Source: *The Canadian Media Directors' Council Media Digest* (1983/84), pp. 38–39.

Television   Television is the fastest growing advertising medium ever. It is now second to newspapers with about 18 percent of the total advertising volume. Television advertising can be divided into three categories: network, national spot, and local spot. The Canadian Broadcasting Corporation, the Canadian Television Network, and Global Television are the three national networks. Network advertising usually accounts for over two-thirds of the total television advertising expenditures. A national "spot" refers to non-network broadcasting used by a general advertiser (for example, Black & Decker might choose to place an advertisement in several cities across the country, without buying time from a total television network). Local spots, primarily used by retailers, consist of locally developed and sponsored commercials. Television advertising offers the following advantages: impact, mass coverage, repetition, flexibility, and prestige. The disadvantages include high costs, high mortality rates for commercials, some evidence of public distrust, and lack of selectivity.

Radio Advertisers using the medium of radio can also be classified as network or local advertisers. Radio accounts for about 11 percent of total advertising volume. The advantages of radio advertising are immediacy (studies show most people regard radio as the best source for up-to-date news); low cost; flexibility; practical, low-cost audience selection; and mobility (radio is an extremely mobile broadcast medium). Radio's disadvantages include fragmentation (for instance, Montreal has about 19 AM and FM stations), the unavailability of the advertising message for future reference, and less research information than for television.

Direct Mail Sales letters, postcards, leaflets, folders, broadsides (larger than folders), booklets, catalogues, and house organs (periodical publications issued by an organization) are all forms of direct mail advertising. The advantages of direct mail include selectivity, intensive coverage, speed, format flexibility, complete information, and the personalization of each mailing piece. Direct mail purchasers also tend to be consistent buyers by mail.[10] A disadvantage of direct mail is its high cost per reader. Direct mail advertising is also dependent upon the quality of the mailing list. Often those unfamiliar with the efficacy of direct mail condemn it all as "junk mail." They are very surprised to find that many people respond positively to direct mail. In fact, marketing research surveys consistently show a majority who say they prefer to receive it. Effectively used, direct mail is a successful and lucrative marketing tool.

Outdoor Advertising Posters (commonly called billboards), painted bulletins or displays (such as those that appear on building walls), and electric spectaculars (large illuminated, sometimes animated, signs and displays) make up outdoor advertising. This form of advertising has the advantages of quickly communicating simple ideas, repetition, and the ability to promote products that are available for sale nearby. Outdoor advertising is particularly effective in metropolitan and other high-traffic areas. Disadvantages of the medium are the brevity of its message and public concern over aesthetics, however, a simple message can be extremely powerful, as seen in Figure 19-12.

An Advertisement Used by the Canadian Direct Mail/Marketing Association

This symbol assures you there is order in the mail order business

Mail Order

When you see it printed on advertising mail or in mail order ads in publications, you know that it's from someone you can trust. So when you shop by mail, you know you'll receive exactly what you ordered.

The symbol shows that the seller is a member of the Canadian Direct Mail/Marketing Association. We insist that members abide by a tough 14-point code of ethics and follow the highest standards of practice or they get kicked out.

Our members work for publishers, mail order catalogues, book clubs, fund raisers, department stores, financial institutions, insurance firms, schools, government, etc. They represent about 80% of the direct marketing industry.

But we know that there are some mail order people who don't always treat customers properly. That's why the CDM/MA has set up a Task Force to investigate customer complaints.

If you've had poor treatment from a mail order seller, after trying to resolve the problem with the seller, write us about your experience. Give us as much information as possible. We'll get after them for you, member or non-member and we will do our best to resolve the problem for you.

Or, write us if you want your name taken off (or added on to) the mailing lists of our members; we call this our Mail Preference Service. It's been in operation since 1975. The score to date is 3,274 people wanted off and 1,440 wanted on.

Write us, too, if you'd like a free copy of our highly informative brochure "Direct Mail and You". It discusses some controversial points about advertising mail.

For copies, write to:
CDM/MA,
130 Merton Street,
Toronto, Ontario M4S 1A4.

**Canadian
Direct Mail/Marketing
Association**

Figure 19-12   An Award-Winning Billboard

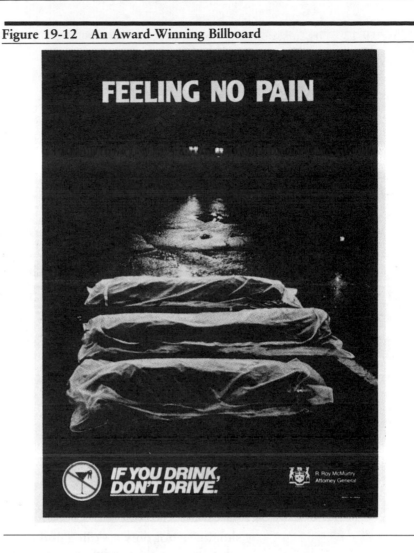

***Organizing the
Advertising Function***

While the ultimate responsibility for advertising decisions often rests
with top marketing management, the organization of the advertising function varies among companies. A producer of a technical
industrial product may be served by a one-person operation primarily
concerned with writing copy for trade publications. A consumer
goods company, on the other hand, may have a large department
staffed with advertising specialists.

   The advertising function is usually organized as a staff department reporting to the vice-president (or director) of marketing.
The *director of advertising* is an executive position heading the
functional activity of advertising. The individual filling this slot

Figure 19-13   Organization Chart for a Large Advertising Agency

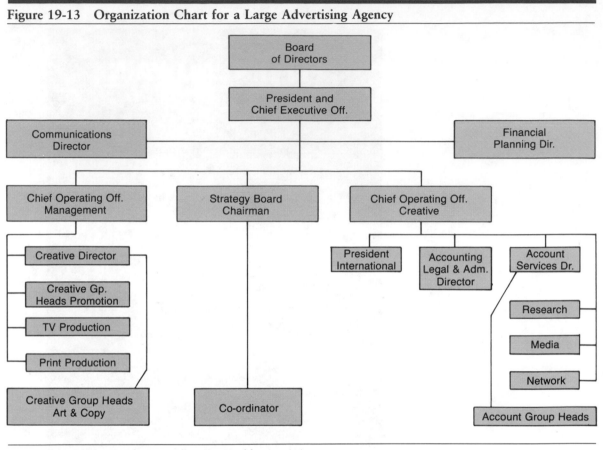

Source: Copyright © 1981 by Marsteller, Inc. Used by permission.

should be not only a skilled and experienced advertiser; he or she must also be able to communicate effectively within the organization. The success of a firm's promotional strategy depends upon the advertising director's willingness and ability to communicate both vertically and horizontally. The major tasks typically organized under advertising include advertising research, art, copywriting, media analysis, and, in some cases, sales promotion.

Advertising Agencies   Many advertisers also make use of an independent advertising agency. The **advertising agency** is *a marketing specialist firm that assists the advertiser in planning and preparing its advertisements.* There are several reasons why advertisers use an agency for at least a portion of their advertising. Agencies are typically staffed with highly qualified specialists who provide a degree of creativity and objectivity that is difficult to maintain in a corporate advertising department. In some cases the use of an agency reduces the cost of advertising since the agency does not require many of the fixed expenses associated with internal advertising departments. Effective use of an advertising agency requires a close relationship between advertiser and agency.

Figure 19-13 shows the organization chart for a large advertising agency. While the titles may vary from agency to agency, the major operational responsibilities can be classified as creative services, account management, research, and promotional services.

J. Walter Thompson Company is the largest advertising agency with worldwide billings of over $900 million. Seven agencies have world billings in excess of $500 million. Figure 19-14 shows the leading Canadian advertising agencies.

Figure 19-14   Canada's Top 15 Advertising Agencies

Rank	Company (head office)	Revenue ($ million) 1984	1983	Number of offices	Number of employees
1	J. Walter Thompson Co. (Toronto)	26.4	24.0	7	447
2	MacLaren Advertising (Toronto)	24.4	21.6	4	389
3	McKim Advertising Ltd. (Toronto)	22.5	19.4	5	390
4	Foster Advertising Ltd. (Toronto)	20.9	20.0	4	503
5	Ogilvy & Mather Canada Ltd. (Toronto)	17.8	13.5	6	238
6	Vickers & Benson Co. (Toronto)	15.6	10.7	2	320
7	Young & Rubicam Ltd. (Toronto)	15.2	12.2	5	225
8	Baker Lovick Ltd. (Toronto)	14.9	12.6	6	223
9	McCann-Erickson Advertising of Canada Ltd. (Toronto)	13.0	9.9	3	200
10	Ronalds-Reynolds & Co. (Toronto)	12.5	9.9	2	206
11	Cossette Communications Marketing (Montreal)[2]	12.3	9.2	3	215
12	Saffer Cravit & Freedman Advertising Ltd. (Toronto)[2]	11.8	9.0	3	200
13	Hayhurst Advertising Ltd. (Toronto)[2]	10.3	11.2	3	182
14	Leo Burnett Co. (Toronto)	9.9	9.1	2	147
15	Grey Advertising Ltd. (Toronto)	9.3	7.0	2	138

[1]Revenue is generally comprised of revenue from commissionable media (usually 15%) and fees negotiated with clients it should be noted that 11 of the 15 agencies have included figures from associated or subsidiary companies, such as public relations, graphic design shops, retail boutiques, sales promotion, radio and television products, and print operations. However, J. Walter Thompson, McKim Advertising, Hayhurst and Vickers & Benson did not include figures from Canadian associates or subsidiaries.

[2]The fiscal year for Cossette Communications and Hayhurst Advertising ends Sept. 30 and April 30 for Saffer Cravit.

Source: Financial Post 500 (Summer, 1985), p. 216.

**Creating an
Advertisement**

The final step in the advertising process is the development and preparation of an advertisement that should flow logically from the promotional theme selected. It should thus be a complementary part of the marketing mix, with its role in total marketing strategy carefully determined. In addition, major factors to consider when preparing an advertisement are its creativity, its continuity with past advertisements, and possibly its association with other company products.

What should an advertisement accomplish? Regardless of the exact appeal that is chosen, an advertisement should 1) gain attention and interest, 2) inform and/or persuade, and 3) eventually lead to buying action.

Gaining attention should be productive. That is, the reason for gaining consumers' attention should be to instil some recall of the product. Consider the case of the Gillette Company, which had a chimpanzee shave a man's face in a commercial. After tests in two cities, one Gillette man observed, "Lots of people remembered the chimp, but hardly anyone remembered our product. There was fantastic interest in the monkey, but no payoff for Gillette."[11] The advertisement gained the audience's attention but it failed to lead to buying action. An advertisement that fails to gain and hold the receiver's attention is ineffectual.

Information and persuasion is the second factor to consider when creating an advertisement. For example, insurance advertisements typically specify the features of the policy and may use testimonials in attempting to persuade prospects.

Stimulating buying action, however, is often difficult since an advertisement cannot actually close a sale. Nevertheless, if the first two steps have been accomplished, the advertising has likely been well worthwhile. Too many advertisers fail to suggest how the receiver of the message can buy the product if he or she so desires. This is a shortcoming that should be eliminated.

**Celebrity Testimonials:
Advantages and
Disadvantages**

In their attempts to improve the effectiveness of their advertising, a number of marketers utilize celebrities to present their advertising messages.[12] Well-known current examples include Wayne Gretzky for 7-Up, Gary Carter for Chrysler, James Garner and Mariette Hartley for Polaroid, and Bill Cosby for Jell-O pudding.

The primary advantage of using big-name personalities is that they may improve product recognition in a promotional environment filled with hundreds of competing 20- and 30-second commercials. (Advertisers use the term *clutter* to describe this situation.) In order for this technique to succeed, the celebrity must be a credible source of information for the item being sold. Most advertisers believe that celebrity advertisements are ineffective where there is no reasonable relationship between the celebrity and the advertised product or service.

Canada is currently very sports- and celebrity-oriented.[13] Therefore, there is opportunity for firms profitably to sponsor athletes or sporting events. However, such promotion should clearly be an adjunct to existing promotional programs. There are several principles that corporate sponsors should consider before getting involved. First, they must be selective and specific. A market target should be pinpointed, and a sport or celebrity carefully matched to that target and objective. Second, sports interest trends should be followed carefully. Too often firms get involved without assessing the strength of the trend. Third, they must be original, looking for a special focus. Is it possible to come up with a unique concept? Fourth, firms should analyse the result, short- and long-term. Sponsorship is a business decision that should pay off in profits.

Comparative Advertising

Comparative advertising *makes direct promotional comparisons with leading competitive brands.* The strategy is best employed by firms that do not lead the market. Most market leaders prefer not to acknowledge that there are competitive products. Procter & Gamble and General Foods, for instance, traditionally have devoted little of their huge promotional budgets for comparative advertising. But many firms do use it extensively. An estimated 23 percent of all radio and television commercials make comparisons to competitive products. Here are some examples:

- Scope mouthwash prevents "medicine breath," but Listerine is never mentioned.
- Minute Maid lemonade is better than the "no-lemon lemonade," a reference to General Foods' Country Time brand.
- Suave antiperspirant will keep you just as dry as Ban Ultra Dry does and for a lot less.
- Nationwide, more Coca-Cola drinkers prefer the taste of Pepsi.

Marketers who contemplate using comparative advertising in their promotional strategies should take precautions to assure that they can substantiate their claims, because comparison advertising has the potential of producing lawsuits. Advertising experts disagree about this practice's long-term effects. The conclusion is likely to be that comparative advertising is a useful strategy in a limited number of circumstances.[14]

Retail Advertising

Retail advertising is all advertising by stores that sell goods or services directly to the consuming public. While accounting for a sizeable portion of total advertising expenditures, retail advertising varies widely in its effectiveness. One study showed that consumers were often suspicious of retail price advertisements. Responses to such advertisements were affected by perceptions of the source, nature of the message, and shopping experience.[15]

The basic problem is that advertising is often treated as a secondary activity, particularly in smaller retail stores. Store managers in these stores are usually given the responsibility of advertising as an added task to be performed along with their normal functions. Advertising agencies have traditionally been used rarely by retailers.

More recently, however, larger retailers have been spending more than ever on advertising, and they are going to agencies to buy the needed expertise.[16] One reason for this is that Canadians spend 42 percent of their consumer dollars in chain stores. Consequently, there is great incentive to promote a chain store nationally, as well as to stress its private brands.

Co-operative advertising is *a sharing of advertising costs between the retailer and the manufacturer or wholesaler*. For example, General Mills may pay 50 percent of the cost of the 50 cm^2 of a chain's weekly newspaper ad that features a Betty Crocker cake mix special.

Co-operative advertising resulted initially from the newspapers' practice of offering lower rates to local advertisers than to national advertisers. Later, co-operative advertising was seen as a method of improving dealer relations. From the retailer's viewpoint, co-op advertising permits a store to secure additional advertising that it would not otherwise have.

Assessing the Effectiveness of an Advertisement	For many firms, advertising represents a major expenditure, so it is imperative to determine whether a campaign is accomplishing its promotional objectives. The determination of advertising effectiveness, however, is one of the most difficult undertakings in marketing. It consists of two primary elements — pre-testing and post-testing.[17]
Pre-testing	**Pre-testing** is *the assessment of an advertisement's effectiveness before it is actually used*. It includes a variety of evaluative methods. To test magazine advertisements, the ad agency Batten, Barton, Durstine & Osborn cuts ads out of advance copies of magazines and then "strips in" the ads it wants to test. Interviewers later check the impact of the advertisements on the readers who receive free copies of the revised magazine.

Another ad agency, McCann-Erickson, uses a "sales conviction test" to evaluate magazine advertisements. Interviewers ask heavy users of a particular item to pick which of two alternative advertisements would "convince" them to purchase it.

Potential radio and television advertisements are often screened by consumers who sit in a studio and press two buttons — one for a positive reaction to the commercial, the other for a negative one.

Sometimes, proposed ad copy is printed on a postcard that also offers a free product; the number of cards returned is viewed as an indication of the copy's effectiveness. "Blind product tests" are also often used, in which people are asked to select unidentified products on the basis of available advertising copy. Mechanical means of assessing how people read advertising copy are yet another method. One mechanical test uses a camera that photographs eye movement to see how people read ads; the results help determine headline placement and advertising copy length. These are but a few examples of the many methods of pre-testing developed by advertisers.

Post-testing   Post-testing is *the assessment of advertising copy after it has been used*. Pre-testing is generally a more desirable testing method than post-testing because of its potential cost savings. But post-testing can be helpful in planning future advertisements and in making adjustments to current advertising programs.

In one of the most popular post-tests, the *Starch Readership Report*, interviewers ask people who have read selected magazines whether they have read various ads in them. A copy of the magazine is used as an interviewing aid, and each interviewer starts at a different point in the magazine. For larger ads, respondents are also asked about specifics such as headlines and copy. All readership or recognition tests assume that future sales are related to advertising readership.

Unaided recall tests are another method of post-testing advertisements. Here, respondents are not given copies of the magazine but must recall the ads from memory. Interviewers for the Gallup and Robinson market-research firm require people to prove they have read a magazine by recalling one or more of its feature articles. The people who remember particular articles are given cards with the names of products advertised in the issue. They then list the ads they remember and explain what they remember about them. Finally, the respondents are asked about their potential purchase of the products. A readership test similar to the Starch test concludes the Gallup and Robinson interview. Other firms use telephone interviews the day after a commercial appears on television in order to test brand recognition and the effectiveness of the advertisement.

Inquiry tests are another popular form of post-test. Advertisements sometimes offer a free gift, generally a sample of the product, to people who respond to the advertisement. The number of inquiries relative to the cost of the advertisement is then used as a measure of effectiveness. Split runs allow advertisers to test two or more ads at the same time. Under this method, a publication's production run is split in two; half the magazines use Advertisement A, and half use Advertisement B. The relative pull of the alternatives is then determined by inquiries.

Regardless of the exact method used, marketers must realize that pre-testing and post-testing are expensive and must, therefore, plan to use them as effectively as possible.

Sales Promotion Methods

The second type of nonpersonal selling is sales promotion. **Sales promotion** may be defined as *those marketing activities, other than personal selling, advertising, and publicity, that stimulate consumer purchasing and dealer effectiveness*. It includes such activities as displays, shows and exhibitions, demonstrations, and various non-recurrent promotional efforts not in the ordinary routine.[18]

Sales promotional techniques may be used by all members of a marketing channel: manufacturers, wholesalers, and retailers and are typically targeted at specific markets. For example, a manufacturer such as Texize Corporation might combine trial sample mailings of a new spot remover to consumers with a sales contest for wholesalers and retailers who handle the new product. In both instances, the sales promotion techniques are designed to supplement and extend the other elements of the firm's promotional mix.

Firms that wish to use sales promotion can choose from various methods—point-of-purchase advertising, specialty advertising, trade shows, samples, coupons and premiums, contests, and trading stamps. More than one of these options may be used in a single promotional strategy, but probably no promotional strategy has ever used all of the options in a single program. While they are not mutually exclusive, promotions are generally employed on a selective basis.

Point-of-Purchase Advertising

Displays and demonstrations that seek to promote the product at a time and place closely associated with the actual decision to buy are called **point-of-purchasing advertising**. The in-store promotion of consumer goods is a common example. Such advertising can be extremely useful in carrying forward a theme developed in another element of promotional strategy. A life-size display of a celebrity used in television advertising, for instance, can become a realistic in-store display. Another example is the L'eggs store displays that completely altered the pantyhose industry.

Specialty Advertising

Specialty advertising is a sales promotion medium that *utilizes useful articles to carry the advertiser's name, address, and advertising message* to reach the target customers.[19] The origin of specialty advertising has been traced to the Middle Ages, when wooden pegs bearing the names of artisans "were given to prospects to be driven into their walls and to serve as a convenient place upon which to hang armor."[20]

Examples of contemporary advertising specialties carrying a firm's name include calendars, pencils, pens, paperweights, matchbooks, personalized business gifts of modest value, pocket diaries, shopping bags, memo pads, ash trays, balloons, measuring sticks, key rings, glasses, and hundreds of other items.

Advertising specialties help reinforce previous or future advertising and sales messages. An A. C. Nielsen survey found that both the general public and business were more likely to purchase from firms using specialty advertising.[21]

When Gulf Metals Industries added aluminum and copper drill bits to its vast existing selection of products, the sales department sought an effective way to bring the new products to the attention of purchasing agents in the foundry industry. The challenge was to highlight the bits, thus allowing them to stand out from the rest of the company's products — as well as those of competitors — during the introduction period. The sales department turned to specialty advertising to accomplish their mission.

Playing on the idea of "two bits," Gulf Metals embedded two clusters of the new copper and aluminum bits alongside a quarter in a clear paperweight. The highly distinctive gift-reminders were delivered either in person by the salespeople or through the mail. Once in the purchasing agents' offices, these conversation piece specialties served to remind the recipients again and again of the Gulf Metals sales message. An entire year's production capacity of the new metal bits was sold during the first two months of the campaign.[22]

Trade Shows
To influence channel members and resellers in the distribution channel, it has become a common practice for a seller to participate in a *trade show*, exposition, or convention. These shows are often organized by an industry's trade association and may be part of the association's annual meeting or convention. Vendors serving the particular industry are invited to the show to display and demonstrate their products for the association's membership. An example would be the professional meetings attended by college professors in a given discipline where the major textbook publishers exhibit their offerings to the channel members in their marketing system. Shows are also used to reach the ultimate consumer. Home and recreation shows, for instance, allow businesses to display and demonstrate home-care, recreation, and other consumer products to the entire community.[23] Originally such shows were used for demonstration purposes only, but now many go beyond the display format and sell merchandise to the public.

Samples, Coupons, and Premiums
The distribution of samples, coupons, and premiums is probably the best-known sales promotion technique. *Sampling* is a free distribution of an item in an attempt to obtain consumer acceptance. This may be done on a door-to-door basis, by mail, through demonstrations, or insertion into packages containing other

products. Sampling is especially useful in promoting new products.

Coupons offer a discount, usually some specified price reduction, from the next purchase of a product. Coupons are readily redeemable with retailers, who also receive an additional handling fee. Mail, magazine, newspaper, or package insertion are standard methods of distributing coupons.

Figure 19-15   Coupon Redemption Rates by Method of Distribution

Method of Distribution	Redemption Rate (percent)
Newspapers	39.6
In/on pack	30.0
Magazines	14.0
Direct mail	10.8
Sunday supplements	7.9
Free-standing inserts	7.7

Source: Adapted from Richard H. Aycrigg, "A New Look at Coupons," *The Nielsen Researcher* (November 1, 1976), p. 6. Reprinted by permission.

Premiums, bonus items given free with the purchase of another product, have proved to be effective in getting consumers to try a new product or a different brand. Service stations, for example, use glassware, ice scrapers, and beach balls to convince noncustomers to try their brand. Premiums are also used to obtain direct mail purchases. The value of premium giveaways runs into millions of dollars each year.

Contests   Firms may sponsor contests to attract additional customers, offering substantial cash or merchandise prizes to call attention to their products. A company might consider employing a specialist in developing this type of sales promotion because of the variety and complexity of schemes available.

Trading Stamps   Trading stamps are a sales promotion technique, similar to premiums, that offer additional value in the product being purchased. Whether the consumer benefits depends upon the relative price levels. In Canada the use of trading stamps is almost nonexistent, mainly for legal reasons.

Public Relations   The previous chapter defined *public relations* as the firm's communications and relationships with its various publics, including customers, suppliers, stockholders, employees, the government, and the society in which it operates. While public relations expenditures are small relative to those for personal selling, advertising, and even sales promotion, public relations does provide an efficient indirect communications channel for promoting a company's products.

Modern public relations efforts were preceded by the publicity releases of the early entertainment promoters such as P. T. Barnum. Later, industry recognized the need to provide public information as well as to develop public understanding and goodwill. Companies began to develop internal public relations departments to improve their public image. Today, all of these objectives have merged into current public relations practice.

The public relations program has broader objectives than the other aspects of promotional strategy. It is concerned with the prestige and image of all parts of the organization. An example of a nonmarketing-oriented public relations objective would be a company's attempt to gain favourable public opinion during a long strike, or a "Don't sell your shares" plea to stockholders during a financial acquisition attempt by another firm. As a result, the public relations department is not usually placed within the structure of the marketing organization. In fact, many writers advocate having it report directly to the president. However, public relations activities invariably have an impact on promotional strategy.

Publicity   The part of public relations that is most directly related to promoting a firm's products or services is publicity. **Publicity** can be defined as *the nonpersonal stimulation of demand by placing commercially significant news about it in a published medium or obtaining favourable presentation of it upon radio, television, or stage that is not paid for by an identified sponsor.*[24] Designed to familiarize the general public with the characteristics, services, and advantages of a product, service, or organization, publicity is an information activity of public relations. Publicity is not entirely cost-free: while expenses are minimal in comparison to other forms of promotion, they include the salaries of marketing personnel assigned to creating and submitting publicity releases, printing and mailing, and other related items.

Some publicity is done to promote a company's image or viewpoint, but a significant part is to provide information about products, particularly new ones. Since many consumers tend to accept the authenticity of a news story more readily than they do an advertisement's, publicity releases covering products are often sent to media editors for possible inclusion in newspapers, magazines, and the like. In many cases, such information is valuable to a newspaper or magazine writer, and is eventually published. Some of these releases are used almost word for word to fill voids in the publication, while others are incorporated into regular features. In either case, the use of publicity releases is a valuable supplement to advertising.

Public relations is now considered to be in a period of major growth as a result of increased environmental pressure for better communication between industry and the public. Many top executives are becoming involved. Lee Iacocca's efforts to publicize the justification for federal loan guarantees for Chrysler Corporation are an illustration. A survey of 185 chief executives concluded that 92 percent of them spend more time on public relations now than they did five years ago. And nearly 40 percent of the respondents reported that public relations accounted for 25 to 50 percent of their time.[25]

Some critics assert that the publication of product publicity is directly related to the amount of advertising revenue coming from a firm. But this is not the case at most respected newspapers and periodicals. The story is told that some years ago a bus company executive was enraged at a cartoon appearing in a newspaper that told of a character having numerous problems on a bus trip. The executive threatened to cancel future advertisements in the newspaper unless the cartoon strip was stopped or changed immediately. The newspaper's curt reply was, "One more such communication from you and the alternative of withdrawing your advertising will no longer rest with . . . your company. . . ."[26]

Today, public relations has to be considered an integral part of promotional strategy even though its basic objectives extend far beyond just attempting to influence the purchase of a particular good. While this is difficult to measure, public relations programs, especially their publicity aspects, make a significant contribution to the achievement of promotional goals.

Summary

Advertising, sales promotion, public relations, and publicity — the nonpersonal selling elements of promotion — are not merely twentieth-century phenomena. Advertising, for instance, can trace its origin to very early times. Today, these elements of promotion have gained professional status and are vital policies of most organizations, both profit and nonprofit.

Advertising (a nonpersonal sales presentation usually directed to a large number of potential customers) should generally seek to achieve communications goals rather than direct sales objectives. It strives to inform, persuade, and remind the potential consumer of the product or service being promoted.

Advertising planning starts with effective research, which permits the development of a strategy. Tactical decisions about copy and scheduling are then made. Finally, advertisements are evaluated, and appropriate feedback is provided to management. There are six basic types of advertisements:

1. informative product advertising
2. persuasive product advertising
3. reminder-oriented product advertising
4. informative institutional advertising
5. persuasive institutional advertising
6. reminder-oriented institutional advertising

One of the most vital decisions in developing an advertising strategy is the selection of the mix of newspapers, periodicals, television, radio, outdoor advertising, and direct mail to be employed to attract the attention of the target market.

The major tasks of advertising departments are advertising research, art, copywriting, media analysis, and sales promotion. Many advertisers use independent advertising agencies to provide them with the creativity and objectivity missing in their own organizations and to reduce the cost of advertising. The final step in the advertising process is developing and preparing the advertisement.

The principal methods of sales promotion are point-of-purchase advertising; specialty advertising; trade shows; samples, coupons, and premiums; contests; and trading stamps. Public relations and publicity also play major roles in developing promotional strategies.

CHAPTER 20

Personal Selling and Sales Management

1. *To explain the factors affecting the importance of personal selling in the promotional mix.*
2. *To identify the three basic sales tasks.*
3. *To list the characteristics of successful salespersons.*
4. *To outline the steps in the sales process.*
5. *To describe the major problems faced by sales managers.*
6. *To list the functions of sales management.*

The Conceptual Framework

Personal selling was defined in Chapter 18 as a seller's promotional presentation conducted on a person-to-person basis with the buyer. Selling is an inherent function of any business enterprise. Accounting, engineering, personnel management, and other organizational activities are useless unless the firm's product can be sold to someone. Thousands of sales employees bear witness to selling's importance in the Canadian economy. While advertising expenses in the average firm may represent from 1 to 3 percent of total sales, selling expenses are likely to equal 10 to 15 percent of sales. In many firms, personal selling is the single largest marketing expense.

As Chapter 18 pointed out, personal selling is likely to be the primary component of a firm's promotional mix when customers are concentrated geographically; when orders are large; when the products or services are expensive, technically complex, and require special handling; when trade-ins are involved; when channels are short; and when the number of potential customers is relatively small. Figure 20-1 summarizes the factors affecting personal selling's importance in the overall promotional mix.

Selling has been a standard part of business for thousands of years.[1] The earliest peddlers were traders who had some type of ownership interest in the goods they sold after manufacturing or importing them. In many cases, these people viewed selling as a secondary activity.

Selling later became a separate function. The peddlers of the eighteenth century sold to the farmers and settlers of the vast North American continent. In the nineteenth century, salespeople called "drummers" sold to both consumers and marketing intermediaries. These early settlers sometimes employed questionable sales practices and techniques and earned an undesirable reputation for themselves and their firms. Some of this negative stereotype remains today. But for the most part, selling is far different from what it was in earlier years

Figure 20-1   Factors Affecting the Importance of Personal Selling in the Promotional Mix

	Personal Selling is likely to be more important when:	*Advertising* is likely to be more important when:
consumer is:	geographically concentrated, relatively small numbers;	geographically dispersed, relatively large numbers;
product is:	expensive, technically complex, custom-made, special handling required, trade-ins frequently involved;	inexpensive, simple to understand, standardized, no special handling, no trade-ins;
price is:	relatively high;	relatively low;
channels are:	relatively short.	relatively long.

Sales Tasks

The sales job has evolved into a professional occupation. Today's salesperson is more concerned with helping customers select the correct product to meet their needs than with simply selling whatever is available. Modern professional salespeople advise and assist customers in their purchase decisions. Where repeat purchases are common, the salesperson must be certain that the buyer's purchases are in his or her best interest or else no future sales will be made. The interests of the seller are tied to those of the buyer.

Not all selling activities are alike. While all sales activities assist the customer in some manner, the exact tasks that are performed vary from one position to another. Three basic sales tasks can be identified: 1) order processing, 2) creative selling, and 3) missionary sales.

These tasks can form the basis for a sales classification system. It should be observed, however, that most sales personnel do not fall into any single category. Instead, we often find salespersons performing all three tasks to a certain extent. A sales engineer for a computer firm may be doing 50 percent missionary sales, 45 percent creative selling, and 5 percent order processing. In other words, most sales jobs require their incumbents to engage in a variety of sales activities. However, most selling jobs are classified on the basis of the primary selling task that is performed. We shall examine each of these selling tasks.

Order Processing

Order processing is most often typified by selling at the wholesale and retail levels. Salespeople who handle this task must do the following:

1. *Identify customer needs:* for instance, a soft-drink route salesperson determines that a store that carries a normal inventory of 40 cases has only seven cases left in stock.
2. *Point out the need* to the customer: the route salesperson informs the store manager of the inventory situation.
3. *Complete (or write up) the order:* the store manager acknowledges the situation; the driver unloads 33 cases; the manager signs the delivery slip.

Order processing is part of most selling jobs and becomes the primary task where needs can be readily identified and are acknowledged by the customer. Selling life insurance is usually not simple order processing. However, one insurance company reported that during a period of civil unrest in Belfast, Northern Ireland, one of their representatives, Danny McNaughton, sold 208 new personal accident income-protection policies in a week. McNaughton averaged one sale every 12 minutes of his working day.[2] Apparently, the need for insurance was readily recognized in Belfast.

Creative Selling

When a considerable degree of analytical decision-making on the part of the consumer is involved in purchasing a product, the salesperson must skilfully solicit an order from a prospect. To do so, creative selling techniques must be used. New products often require a high degree of **creative selling**. The seller *must make the buyer see the worth of the item*. Creative selling may be the most demanding of the three tasks.

Missionary Sales

Missionary sales are an indirect type of selling; people *sell the goodwill* of a firm and provide the customers with technical or operational assistance. For example, a toiletries company salesperson may call on retailers to look after special promotions and overall stock movement, although a wholesaler is used to take orders and deliver merchandise. In more recent times, technical and operational assistance, such as that provided by a systems specialist, have also become a critical part of missionary selling.

Characteristics of Successful Salespeople

The saying "Salespeople are born, not made" is untrue. Most people have some degree of sales ability. Each of us is called upon to sell others his or her ideas, philosophy, or personality at some time. However, while some individuals adapt to selling more easily than others, selling is not an easy job; it involves a great deal of practice and hard work.

Effective salespersons are self-motivated individuals who are well prepared to meet the demands of the competitive marketplace. The continuing pressure to solve buyers' problems requires that salespeople develop good work habits and exhibit considerable initiative.

Successful sales representatives are not only self-starters, they are knowledgeable businesspersons. Sales personnel are also in the peculiar position of having their knowledge tested almost continually. Sales success is often a function of how well a salesperson can handle questions. Salespeople must know their company, products, competition, customers, and themselves. They must also be able to analyse customer needs and fit them with products and services which satisfy those requirements.

Feedback: The Responsibility of Every Salesperson

There is *one function that all sales personnel perform* — providing sales intelligence to the marketing organization.[3] Chapter 18 noted that field sales reports are a part of the feedback generated within the marketing system. Since the sales force is close to the market, it is often the best (and most reliable) source of current marketing information, upon which management decisions are made.

The marketing intelligence provided by field sales personnel is copious and varied. Sales personnel can provide timely, current assessments of competitive efforts, new product launches, customer reactions, and the like. Marketing executives should nurture and implement this valuable information source.

The Sales Process

What, then, are the steps involved in selling? While the terminology may vary, most authorities agree on the following sequence:
1. prospecting and qualifying
2. approach
3. presentation
4. demonstration
5. handling objections
6. closing
7. follow-up

Prospecting, *the identification of potential customers*, is difficult work involving many hours of diligent effort. Prospects may come from many sources: previous customers, friends and neighbours, other vendors, nonsales employees in the firm, suppliers, and social and professional contacts. New sales personnel often find prospecting frustrating, since there is usually no immediate payback. But without prospecting there are no future sales. For example, in the marketing of various types of adhesive tapes for industrial use, a representative of a tape manufacturing company, perhaps a manufacturers' agent, must seek out potential users of these specialty tapes. Prospecting is a continuous process because there will always be a loss of some customers over time, which must be compensated for by the emergence of new customers or the discovery of potential customers who have never been contacted before. Many sales management experts consider prospecting to be the very essence of the sales process.

Qualifying — *determining that the prospect is really a potential customer* — is another important sales task. Not all prospects are qualified to become customers. Qualified customers are people with both the money and the authority to make purchase decisions. A person with an annual income of $10 000 may wish to own a $75 000 house, but this person's ability to actually become a customer has to be questioned. Similarly, a parent with six children may strongly desire a two-seater sports car, but this would probably not be a practical purchase as the sole family vehicle.

Approach   Once the salesperson has identified a qualified prospect, he or she collects all available information relative to the potential buyer and plans an **approach** — *the initial contact of the salesperson with the prospective customer*. Figure 20-2 suggests that the relative aggressiveness of a sales approach usually varies inversely with the repeat-

Figure 20-2   The Sales Aggression Spectrum with Ecological Determinants

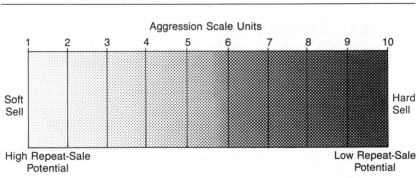

Source: Adapted from Barry J. Hersker, "The Ecology of Personal Selling," *Southern Journal of Business* (July 1970), p. 44. Reprinted by permission.

sale potential of the prospect. In other words, the lower the repeat-sale potential, the harder the approach is likely to be and vice versa. All approaches should be based on comprehensive research. The salesperson should find out as much as possible about the prospect. Retail salespeople often cannot do this in advance, but they can compensate by asking leading questions to learn more about the prospect's purchase preferences. Industrial marketers have far more data available, and they should make use of it before scheduling the first interview.

Presentation   When the salesperson *gives the sales message to a prospective customer*, he or she makes a **presentation**. The seller describes the product's major features, points out its strengths, and concludes by citing illustrative successes. The seller's objective is to talk about the product or service in terms meaningful to the buyer — benefits, rather than technical specifications. Thus the presentation is the stage where the salesperson relates product features to customer needs.

The presentation should be clear and concise, and should emphasize the positive. For example, consider how, many years ago, a young college president presented an *idea* to industrialist Andrew Carnegie:

> One of the buildings of Wooster University burned down one night. On the following day the youthful, boyish-looking president, Louis E. Holden, started to New York City to see Andrew Carnegie. Without wasting a minute in preliminaries he began: "Mr. Carnegie, you are a busy man and so am I. I won't take up more than five minutes of your time. The main building of Wooster University burned down night before last, and I want you to give us $100 000 for a new one." "Young man," replied the philanthropist, "I don't believe in giving money to colleges." "But you believe in helping young men, don't you?" urged President Holden. "I'm a young man, Mr. Carnegie, and I'm in an awful hole. I've gone into the business of manufacturing college men from the raw material and now the best part of my plant is gone. You know how you would feel if one of your big steel mills were destroyed right in the busy season." "Young man," responded Mr. Carnegie, "raise $100 000 in thirty days and I'll give you another." "Make it sixty days and I'll go you," replied Dr. Holden. "Done," assented Mr. Carnegie. Dr. Holden picked up his hat and started for the door. As he reached it, Mr. Carnegie called after him, "Now remember, it's sixty days only." "All right, sir, I understand." Dr. Holden's call had consumed just four minutes. The required $100 000 was raised within the specified time, and when handing over his check, Mr. Carnegie said, laughing, "Young man, if you ever come to see me again, don't stay so long. Your call cost me just $25 000 a minute."[4]

One type of sales presentation is the **canned approach** originally developed by John H. Patterson of National Cash Register Company during the late 1800s. This is *a memorized sales talk* used to ensure uniform coverage of the points deemed important by management. While canned presentations are still used in such areas as door-to-door *cold canvassing*, most professional sales forces have long since abandoned their use. The prevailing attitude is that flexible presentations allow the salesperson to account for motivational differences among prospects. Proper planning, of course, is an important part of tailoring a presentation to each particular customer.

Demonstration   Demonstrations can play a critical role in a sales presentation. A demonstration ride in a new automobile allows the prospect to become involved in the presentation. It awakens customer interest in a manner that no amount of verbal presentation can achieve. Demonstrations supplement, support, and reinforce what the sales representative has already told the prospect. The key to a good demonstration is planning. A unique demonstration is more likely to gain a customer's attention than a "usual" sales presentation. But such a demonstration must be well planned and executed if a favourable impression is to be made. One cannot overemphasize that the salesperson should check and recheck all aspects of the demonstration prior to its delivery.

Handling Objections   A vital part of selling involves handling objections. It is reasonable to expect a customer to say, "Well, I really should check with my family," or "Perhaps I'll stop back next week," or "I like everything except the colour." A good salesperson, however, should use each objection as a cue to provide additional information to the prospect. In most cases an objection such as "I don't like the bucket seats" is really the prospect's way of asking what other choices or product features are available. A customer's question reveals an interest in the product. It allows the seller an opportunity to expand a presentation by providing additional information.

Closing   The moment of truth in selling is the **closing**, for this is when *the salesperson asks the prospect for an order*. A sales representative should not hesitate during the closing. If he or she has made an effective presentation, based on applying the product to the customer's needs, the closing should be the natural conclusion.

A surprising number of sales personnel have difficulty in actually asking for an order. But to be effective they must overcome the difficulty. Methods of closing a sale include the following:

1. The *alternative-decision technique* poses choices to a prospect where either alternative is favourable to the salesperson. "Will you take this sweater or that one?"

2. The *SRO (standing room only) technique* is used when a prospect is told that a sales agreement should be concluded now, because the product may not be available later.
3. *Emotional closes* attempt to get a person to buy through appeal to such factors as fear, pride, romance, or social acceptance.
4. *Silence* can be used as a closing technique since a discontinuance of a sales presentation forces the prospect to take some type of action (either positive or negative).
5. *Extra-inducement closes* are special incentives designed to moti vate a favourable buyer response. Extra inducements may include quantity discounts, special servicing arrangements, or a layaway option.

Follow-up   The *postsales activities* that often determine whether a person will become a repeat customer constitute the sales **follow-up**. To the maximum extent possible, representatives should contact their customers to find out if they are satisfied with their purchases. This step allows the salesperson to reinforce psychologically the person's original decision to buy. It gives the seller an opportunity, in addition to correcting any sources of discontent with the purchase, to secure important market information, and to make additional sales. Automobile dealers often keep elaborate records on their previous customers. This allows them to remind individuals when they might be due for a new car. One successful travel agency never fails to telephone customers upon their return from a trip. Proper follow-up is a logical part of the selling sequence.

Effective follow-up also means that the salesperson should conduct a critical review of every call that is made. One should ask, "What was it that allowed me to close that sale?" or "What caused me to lose that sale?" Such continual review results in significant sales dividends.

Retail Selling   For the most part, the public is more aware of retail selling than of any other form of personal selling. In fact, many writers have argued that a person's basic attitude toward the sales function is determined by his or her impression of retail sales personnel.

Retail selling has some distinctive features that require its consideration as a separate subject. The most significant difference between it and its counterparts is that the customer *comes to* the retail salesperson. This requires that the retailer effectively combine selling with a good advertising and sales promotion program that draws the customer into the store. Another difference is that while store employees are sales personnel in one sense, they are also retailers in the broader dimension. Selling is not their only responsibility.

Retail sales personnel should be well versed in store policy and procedures. Credit, discounts, special sales, delivery, layaway, and return policies are examples of the type of information that the salesperson should know. *Uninformed sales personnel* are one of the major complaints voiced by today's customer.

The area of retail selling exhibiting the greatest potential for improvement is the greeting. The standard "May I help you?" seems totally out of place in contemporary marketing, and yet it is interesting to observe the number of retail salespeople who still use this outdated approach. "May I help you?" invites customer rejection in the form of the standard reply, "No thanks, I'm just looking." A better method is to use a merchandise-oriented greeting such as "The fashion editors say that this will be the most popular colour this fall." The positive approach helps to orient the customer toward the merchandise or display.

Two selling techniques particularly applicable to retailing are selling up and suggestion selling. **Selling up** is the technique of *convincing the customer to buy a higher-priced item than he or she originally intended.* An automobile salesperson may convince a consumer to buy a more expensive model than the person intended to buy. An important point is that the practice of selling up should always be used within the constraints of the customer's real needs. If the salesperson sells the customer something that he or she really does not need, the potential for repeat sales by that seller is substantially diminished.

Suggestion selling *seeks to broaden the customer's original purchase* with related items, special promotions, and/or holiday and seasonal merchandise. Suggestion selling, too, should be based upon

Figure 20-3   Operational and Administrative Abilities Required for Sales Organization Jobs

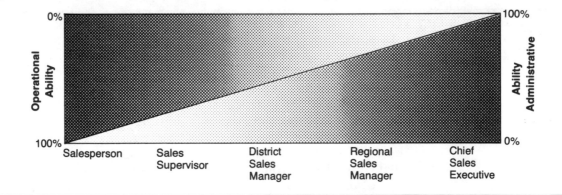

Source: Thomas R. Wotruba, *Sales Management Planning, Accomplishment, and Evaluation* (New York: Holt, Rinehart and Winston, 1971). Reprinted by permission of the author.

the idea of helping the customer recognize true needs rather than selling the person unwanted merchandise. Suggestion selling is one of the best methods of increasing retail sales and should be practised by all sales personnel.

Managing the Sales Effort

Contemporary selling requires that **sales management** effort be exerted in the direction of *securing, maintaining, motivating, supervising, evaluating, and controlling an effective field sales force.* The sales manager is the link between the salesperson, customers and prospects, and the firm's management. The sales manager has professional responsibilities in both directions. Most sales management jobs require some degree of both operational (or sales-oriented) ability and administrative (or managerial) ability. The higher one rises in the sales management hierarchy, the more administrative ability and the less operational ability is required to perform the job. Figure 20-3 diagrams this relationship.

Problems Faced by Sales Management

Sales executives face a variety of management problems. However, with few exceptions, these problems have remained largely the same over the years. Poor utilization of time and failure to plan sales effort were reported as the leading problems in both the 1959 and the 1979 surveys cited earlier in this chapter. Other current major problem areas and their 1959 rankings are shown in Figure 20-4.

Figure 20-4   Major Sales Management Problems

Problem Area	1979 Ranking	1959 Ranking
Poor utilization of time and failure to plan sales effort	1	1
Inadequacy in sales training	2	21
Wasted time in office by salespeople	3	6
Too few sales calls during hours	4	3
Inability to overcome objections	5	5
Indifferent follow-up	6	7
Lack of sales creativity	7	2
Meeting competitive pricing	8	15
Lack of sales drive and motivation	9	8
Recruiting and selecting personnel	10	11

Source: "Significant Trends," *Sales & Marketing Management* (October 15, 1979), p. 102. Reprinted by permission from *Sales & Marketing Management.* Copyright 1979.

Sales Management:
Functions

The sales manager performs seven basic managerial functions: 1) recruitment and selection, 2) training, 3) organization, 4) supervision, 5) motivation, 6) compensation, and 7) evaluation and control.

Recruitment and
Selection

The initial step in building an effective sales force involves recruiting and selecting good personnel. Sources of new salespeople include community colleges, trade and business schools, colleges and universities, sales personnel in other firms, and people at present employed in nonsales occupations, including a company's own nonsales employees.

Not all of these areas are equally productive. One of the problem areas seems to be the reluctance of high school guidance counsellors to convey to the students the advantages of a selling career. A successful career in sales offers satisfaction in all the five areas that a person generally looks for when deciding on a profession:

1. Opportunity for advancement: Studies have shown that successful sales representatives advance rapidly in most companies. Advancement can come either within the sales organization or laterally (to a more responsible position in some other functional area of the firm).
2. High earnings: The earnings of successful salespersons compare favourably to the earnings of successful people in other professions. In fact, over the long run, sales earnings often exceed those of most other professional occupations.
3. Personal satisfaction: One derives satisfaction in sales from achieving success in a competitive environment and from helping people satisfy their wants and needs.
4. Security: Contrary to what many students believe, selling provides a high degree of job security. Experience has shown that economic downturns affect personnel in sales less than those in most other employment areas. In addition, there is a continuing need for good sales personnel. Figure 20-5 shows the median employment situation for some sales occupations.

Figure 20-5   Employment in Sales

	Persons Employed in 1975	Annual Average Job Openings 1975 to 1982
Manufacturers' and Wholesale Salespersons	70 000	1 400
Retail Salespersons	304 000	11 000

Source: Department of Manpower and Immigration, *Careers in Sales*, 1976, p. 30.

5. Independence and variety: Most often salespersons really operate as "independent" businesspeople (or as managers of sales territories). Their work is also quite varied and provides an opportunity for involvement in numerous business functions.

Salesperson selection is important because 1) it requires a substantial investment in money and management time, and 2) selection mistakes are detrimental to customer relations and performance of the sales force as a whole, as well as being costly to correct.

Selection of salespeople is more than a set of procedural steps. It is a *process*, in which the several steps are interrelated and independent. Each of the steps must be considered as a further refinement of a matching and screening process, a hurdle to be overcome.

The selection process for sales personnel is outlined in Figure 20-6. An application screening is followed by an initial interview. If there is sufficient interest, in-depth interviewing is conducted. Next, the company may use testing in their procedure. This step could include aptitude, intelligence, interest, knowledge, or personality tests. References are then checked to guarantee that job candidates have represented themselves correctly. A physical examination is usually included before a final hiring decision is made.

Figure 20-6   Steps in the Sales Personnel Selection Process

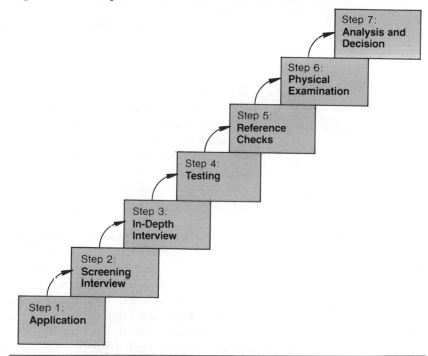

This process indicates that sales managers use several types of *tools* in selecting new sales personnel. Interviews are considered the most helpful selection tool, although they are the most costly. In contrast, experienced managers rate intelligence, aptitude, and personality tests considerably lower.

Training

To shape new sales recruits into an efficient sales organization, management must conduct an effective training program. The principal methods used in sales training are lectures, role-playing, and on-the-job training.

Sales training is also important for veteran salespeople. Most of this type of training is done in an informal manner by sales managers. A standard format is for the sales manager to travel with a field sales representative periodically, then compose a critique of his or her work afterward. Sales meetings are also an important part of training for experienced personnel.

Organization

Sales managers are responsible for the organization of the field sales force. General organizational alignments, which are usually made by top marketing management, can be based upon geography, products, types of customers, or some combination of these factors. Figure 20-7 presents simplified organization charts showing these alignments.

A product sales organization would have specialized sales forces for each major category of products offered by the firm. A customer organization would use different sales forces for each major type of customer served. For instance, a plastics manufacturer selling to the automobile, small appliance, and defence industries might decide that each type of customer requires a separate sales force.

The individual sales manager then has the task of organizing the sales territories within his or her area of responsibility. Generally, the territory allocation decision should be based upon company objectives, personnel qualifications, work-load considerations, and territory potential.

Supervision

A source of constant debate among sales managers is the supervision of the sales force. It is impossible to pinpoint the exact amount of supervision that is correct in each situation since this varies with the individuals involved. However, there is probably a curvilinear relationship between the amount of supervision and organizational performance (see Figure 20-8). The amount of supervision input increases sales output to some point, after which additional supervision tends to retard further sales growth.

Figure 20-7   Basic Approaches to Organizing the Sales Force

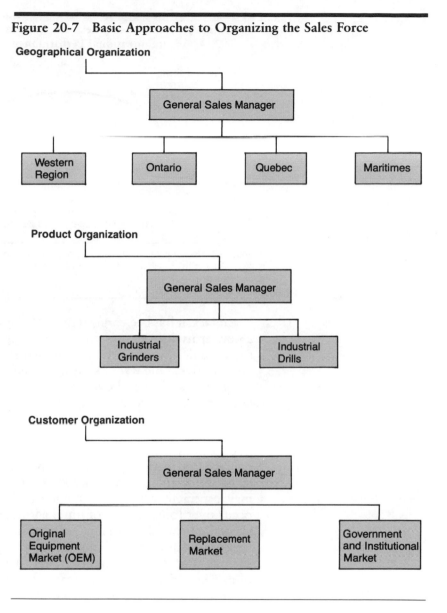

The key to effective supervision is clear communications with the sales force. This, of course, involves effective listening on the part of the sales manager. Sales personnel who clearly understand messages from management and who have an opportunity to express their concerns and opinions to their supervisors are usually easier to supervise and motivate.

Figure 20-8   Relationship Between Amount of Supervision and
Organizational Performance

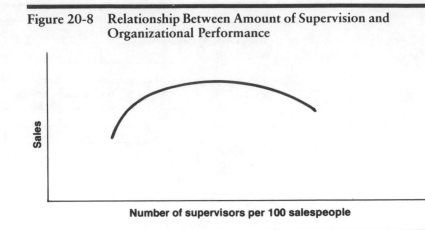

Number of supervisors per 100 salespeople

Source: *Management of the Personal Selling Function* by Charles S. Goodman. Copyright © 1971 by Holt, Rinehart and Winston, Inc. Reprinted by permission of Holt, Rinehart and Winston.

In fact, it has been argued that sales management has now entered a new era with the new emphasis being placed upon total human resource development. All personnel should be developed to their full abilities. One writer states, "In the long run, the total development approach may be desirable not only for humanistic reasons but also from a profit standpoint."[5]

Motivation   The sales manager's responsibility for motivating the sales force cannot be glossed over. Because the sales process is a problem-solving one, it often leads to considerable mental pressures and frustrations. Sales are often achieved only after repeated calls on customers and may, especially with new customers and complex technical products, occur over long periods of time. Motivation of salespeople usually takes the form of debriefing, information sharing, and both psychological and financial encouragement. Appeal to emotional needs, such as ego needs, recognition, and peer acceptance are examples of psychological encouragement. Monetary rewards, bonuses, club memberships, paid travel arrangements, and so forth are financial incentives.

Compensation   Monetary rewards are an important factor in human motivation, and, not surprisingly, the compensation of sales personnel is a critical matter to managers. Basically, sales compensation can be determined on a commission plan, a straight salary plan, or some combination.[6]

A **commission** is *a payment directly tied to the sales or profits achieved by a salesperson*. For example, a salesperson might receive a

5 percent commission on all sales up to a specified quota, then 7 percent on sales beyond the quota. Commissions provide maximum selling incentive but may cause the sales force to short-change nonselling activities such as completing sales reports, delivering sales promotion materials, and normal account servicing.

A **salary** is *a fixed payment made on a periodic basis* to employees, including some sales personnel. A firm that has decided to use salaries rather than commissions might pay a salesperson a set amount every week, for example. Benefits of using salaries exist for both management and sales personnel. A straight salary plan allows management to have more control over how sales personnel allocate their efforts, but it reduces the incentive to expand sales. As a result, compensation programs combining features of both salary and commission plans have been accepted in many industries.

Evaluation and Control. Perhaps the most difficult of the tasks required of sales managers are evaluation and control. The basic problems are setting standards and finding an instrument to measure sales performance. Sales volume, profitability, and investment return are the usual means of evaluating sales effectiveness. They typically involve the use of a **sales quota**—*a specified sales or profit target a salesperson is expected to achieve*. A particular sales representative might be expected to sell $300 000 in Territory 414 during a given year, for example. In many cases, the quota is tied to the compensation system.

Regardless of the key elements in the program for evaluating salespeople, the sales manager needs to follow a formalized system of decision rules.[7] The purpose of this system is to supply information to the sales manager as a basis for action.

What the sales manager needs to know are the answers to three general questions. First, what are the rankings of the salesperson's performance relative to the predetermined standards? In determining this ranking, full consideration should be given to the effect of uncontrollable variables on sales performance. It is preferable that each adjusted ranking be stated in terms of a percentage of the standard. This simplifies evaluation and makes it easier to convert the various rankings into a composite index of performance.

Second, what are the strong points of the salesperson? One way to answer this question is to list areas of the salesperson's performance where he or she has surpassed the respective standard. Another way is to categorize a salesperson's strong points under three aspects of the work environment.[8]

1. *Task*, or the technical ability of the salesperson. This is manifested in knowledge of the product (end uses), customer, and company, as well as selling skills.

2. *Process*, or the sequence of work flow. This pertains to the actual sales transaction — the salesperson's application of technical ability, and his or her interaction with customers. Personal observation is a frequently used technique for measuring process performance. Other measures are sales calls, expenses, and invoice lines.
3. *Goal*, or end results or output of sales performance. Usually this aspect of the salesperson's work environment will be stated in terms of sales volume and profits.

The third and final question is, what are the weaknesses or negatives in the performance of the salesperson in question? These should be listed or categorized as much as the salesperson's strong points. An evaluation summary for a hypothetical salesperson appears in Figure 20-9.

In making the evaluation summary the sales manager should follow a set procedure.

Figure 20-9   An Evaluation Summary

Performance evaluation summary

Name: J. D. Martin
Territory: Northern Saskatchewan
Time period covered: 1st Quarter 198__

Salesperson's ability
Strong points
1. Has extensive product knowledge, knows end uses.
2. Keeps up to date on company pricing policies.

Weaknesses
1. Does not have in-depth knowledge of customer requirements.

Selling proficiency
Strong points
1. Exceeded by 20 percent the standard for sales/ call.
2. Exceeded by 12 percent the standard for sales calls/day.
3. Exceeded by 8 percent the standard for invoice lines/order.

Weaknesses
1. Overspending of expense monies (14 percent).
2. Overaggressive in selling tactics.

Sales results
Strong points
1. Exceeded sales quota by 3 percent.
2. Exceeded new account quota by 6 percent.

Weaknesses
1. Turnover of customers amounted to 5 percent.
2. Repeated delay in report submission.

Source: H. Robert Dodge, *Field Sales Management* (Dallas: Business Publications, Inc., 1973), pp. 337–38.

1. Each aspect of sales performance for which there is a standard should be measured separately. This helps to avoid the *halo effect*, whereby the rating given on one aspect is carried over to other aspects.
2. Each salesperson should be judged on the basis of actual sales performance rather than potential ability. This emphasizes the importance of rankings in evaluation.
3. Each salesperson should be judged on the basis of sales performance for the entire period under consideration rather than particular incidents. The sales manager as the rater should avoid reliance on isolated examples of the salesperson's prowess or failure.
4. Each salesperson's evaluation should be reviewed for completeness and evidence of possible bias. Ideally this review should be made by the immediate superior of the sales manager.

While the evaluation step includes both revision and correction, the attention of the sales manager must necessarily focus on correction. This is defined as the adjustment of actual performance to predetermined standards. Corrective action with its obvious negative connotations poses a substantial challenge to the typical sales manager.

Summary   Personal selling is the seller's promotional presentation conducted on a person-to-person basis with the buyer. It is inherent in all business enterprises. The earliest sellers were known as peddlers, and some of the negative stereotyping associated with them remains today.

Three basic selling tasks exist: order processing, creative selling, and missionary selling. The successful salesperson is self-motivated and prepared to meet the demands of the competitive marketplace.

The basic steps involved in selling are 1) prospecting and qualifying, 2) approach, 3) presentation, 4) demonstration, 5) handling of objections, 6) closing, and 7) follow-up.

Retail selling is different from other kinds of selling, primarily in that the customer comes to the salesperson. Also, salespeople in stores are concerned with responsibilities other than selling. Two selling techniques particularly applicable to retailing are selling up and suggestion selling.

Sales management involves seven basic functions: 1) recruitment and selection, 2) training, 3) organization, 4) supervision, 5) motivation, 6) compensation, and 7) evaluation and control. Poor utilization of time and lack of planned sales effort rank as the leading problems faced by sales management today.

Careers in Marketing

The more one knows about business, careers, and employment trends when entering the labour force, the better. Business administration is now one of the most popular programs for university and college students, and completion of one or more marketing courses is a good step toward preparing for the job marketplace.

The marketing of goods and services plays a vital role in our economy. Occupations necessary to get the marketing tasks done constitute a significant and interesting aspect of the overall employment picture. This appendix discusses marketing careers, emphasizing 1) the kinds of positions available, with brief descriptions of the responsibilities attached to each; 2) the necessary academic and other preparation for marketing employment; and 3) marketing employment trends and opportunities.

Extensive and Varied Career Opportunities

This text has examined the great extent and diversity of the components of the marketing function. The types of marketing occupations required to perform these tasks are just as numerous and diverse. Indeed, with the growth of our industrial society, marketing occupations too have become more complex and specialized. The student intending to pursue a marketing career may be bewildered at the range of employment opportunities in marketing. How does one find one's way through the maze of marketing occupations and concentrate on those possibilities that most match one's interests and talents? Gaining a knowledge of the different positions and the duties required of each is a convenient starting point.

Marketing personnel are described as either sales-force personnel or marketing-staff personnel. Marketing-staff personnel include persons employed in such service and staff functions as advertising, product planning, marketing research, public relations, purchasing, and distribution management. The precise nature of their responsibilities and duties varies from organization to organization and industry to industry. Marketing tasks may be undertaken in-house by the company marketing personnel, or they may be subcontracted to outside sources. Indeed, there is a whole host of agencies available to support the in-house marketing effort. Among them are advertising agencies, public relations firms, and marketing research agencies. Marketing employment is found in a variety of organizations — manufacturing firms, nonprofit organizations such as art galleries, distributive enterprises such as retailers and wholesalers, service suppliers, and advertising and research agencies.

All these organizations have managerial marketing positions. The specific management duties vary with the size of the organization, the nature of its business, and the extent to which marketing operations are departmentalized or centralized. Marketing management jobs generally require the individual to formulate and to assist in the formulation of the organization's marketing policies and to plan, organize, co-ordinate, and control marketing operations and resources. Some of the typical management positions (actual titles or designations may differ) and descriptions of their responsibilities follow.

The Chief Marketing Executive   The person who oversees all the marketing activities and is ultimately responsible for the success of the marketing function is the chief marketing executive. All other marketing executives report through channels to this person.

The Product Manager   The person in charge of marketing operations for a particular type of product — such as clothing, building materials, or appliances — is the product manager. This person also assumes responsibilities for some or all of the functions described as falling under the chief executive's authority, but only insofar as they pertain to particular products.

The Brand Manager   The brand manager has a position similar to the product manager but only with regard to a specific brand. Sometimes the two position titles are used interchangeably.

The Marketing Research Director   The marketing research director determines the marketing research needs of the organization, and plans and directs various stages of the marketing research projects: the formulation of the problem, research design, data collection, analysis, and interpretation of results. On the basis of these studies, the director also helps formulate marketing strategies for the organization.

The Sales Manager   The sales manager is responsible for managing the sales force. Some of the sales manager's specific duties include establishing sales territories, deploying the sales force, recruiting and hiring the sales force, sales training, and setting sales quotas.

The Advertising Manager

The advertising manager plans and arranges for the promotion of the company's products or services. Particular duties encompass formulating advertising policy, selecting advertising agencies, evaluating creative promotional ideas, and setting the advertising budget.

The Public Relations Officer

The public relations officer directs all activities required to project and maintain a favourable image for the organization. These may include arranging press conferences, exhibitions, news releases, and the like. Some firms divide the duties of the public relations officer between a customer or consumer affairs officer and a press information officer.

The Purchasing or Procurement Manager

The purchasing manager is in control of all purchasing and procurement activities pertaining to the acquisition of merchandise, equipment, and materials for the organization.

The Retail Buyer

The retail buyer is responsible for the purchase of merchandise from various sources — like manufacturers, wholesalers, and importers — for resale through retail outlets. Often the buyer also plans and manages the retail selling activities of a department.

The Wholesale Buyer

The wholesale buyer buys products from manufacturers, importers, and others for resale through wholesale outlets. Duties are similar to those for the retail buyer but within the specific context of wholesale distribution.

The Physical Distribution Manager

All the varied activities of the physical distribution function — transportation, warehousing, inventory control, and so forth— are co-ordinated by the physical distribution manager. The trend for companies to consolidate physical distribution activities under a single managerial hierarchy has resulted in a significant increase in the importance of the position.

The discussion thus far has placed the spotlight on the upper management level. Depending on the company size, there may be several levels of management under any of the categories described above. Also, for every management position, there are several other marketing occupations that involve personnel in the "doing" of the specific tasks that are supervised and controlled by the managers. The exact number of these personnel varies considerably from organization to organization. In the area of marketing research, for instance, employees are engaged in field work, information collection, editing, coding, tabulation, and other statistical analyses of the data.

In advertising, the advertising copywriter gathers information on the products and customers or likely customers, and then writes copy — creating headlines, slogans, and text for the advertisements; the media planner is more often than not a time and space buyer, specializing in determining which advertising media will be most effective; the advertising layout person decides the exact layout of illustrations and copy that make up the finished advertisement.

The majority of people in marketing work in sales. Sales representatives are engaged at the manufacturing, wholesale, or retail level. Their job descriptions vary somewhat with the type of product being sold and the level of distribution being serviced. Sales positions are a common entry point for people desiring promotion to marketing management positions.

Preparing for a Career in Marketing

What are the educational or other requirements necessary to obtain a marketing job? What are the typical positions in which one might commence a marketing career? What are the usual patterns of progression to a top spot in the marketing function?

Top-ranking executives in the Canadian marketing field state that education and experience are important criteria in corporate hiring for marketing positions. Most large firms now prefer candidates with a college education, and express particular interest in the graduate who holds a degree in business administration or a bachelor of commerce degree with a minor in marketing. Also, community college graduates in business and marketing have an advantage in gaining a position in the marketing field. But business education is not enough. Business graduates must also be well-rounded individuals with good communications skills and an understanding of their society and culture such as may be gained through a knowledge of literature, history, and other more general subjects. This will enable them to be more effective in the long run.

Although companies strongly suggest that academic preparation is significant, any experience the marketing student has or can acquire in the business or specific marketing fields is a decided benefit in launching a career in marketing. But firms also rely on company training programs to equip the individual with a knowledge of the company's products and policies. The entry point for a marketing career is not as clear-cut as for some other business positions. This is partly because marketers do not have to "article" as do many accountants. It is also because there is such a wide variety of marketing positions. This lack of specificity is sometimes confusing. However, virtually all graduates quickly find themselves in challenging and interesting roles. One common starting point is in sales, but movement into marketing staff and managerial positions is common. Moreover, top marketing executive positions can be reached at relatively young age.

The Marketing Employment Outlook

Canada Employment and Immigration furnishes some data on employment on different occupations. However, with few exceptions, marketing staff positions are not detailed separately but rather are grouped within an overall administrative category.

Experience indicates, however, that the demand for individuals in the categories we have listed is relatively steady, and is a function of the growth and turnover in business in general. There does appear to be an increasing demand for people in marketing research. Furthermore, it is our opinion that there is a small but growing desire on the part of advertising agencies to hire university graduates with marketing training. More and more nonprofit organizations are looking for marketing people as well.

As we have mentioned, a very large entry point for many marketing positions is sales. Many firms wish future managers to have some sales experience. University graduates starting in sales normally find these positions much more interesting and challenging than they had imagined.

Salaries in the Marketing Profession

Figure 1 shows the range of salaries of eight middle-management positions on a national basis in Canada. It can be seen that marketing and sales positions compare favourably with other functions. (The graph shows the top end of the salary range for each percentage group; thus 50 percent of top marketing personnel earn $50 000 or less, and 25 percent earn between $50 000 and $61 000.)

Figure 2 shows the compensation ranges for various top marketing and sales positions. These data illustrate the earnings potential in marketing careers. From the student's viewpoint, starting salary ranges can be estimated from looking at the lower ranges in Figures 1 and 2.

Figure 1   Range of Salaries of Middle Management Positions

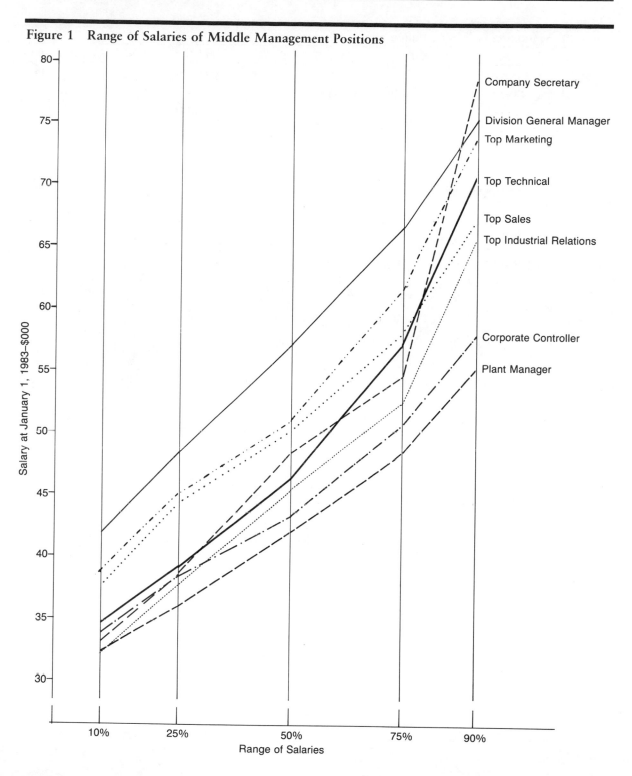

Figure 2   Marketing Positions: Range of Salaries, January 1, 1983

	10%	25%	50%	75%	90%	Average
Division Sales Manager	33 500	38 000	43 824	50 400	55 000	44 789
Regional Sales Manager	30 000	34 068	38 200	42 485	47 519	38 675
District Sales Manager	24 284	28 300	32 200	39 000	46 459	33 931
Division Marketing Manager	32 620	38 489	44 000	49 159	57 300	44 216
Top Advertising/Sales Promotion Manager	28 540	30 080	36 400	43 400	51 596	37 680
Marketing Research Manager	26 196	30 750	38 210	43 350	51 060	37 665
Product/Brand Manager	27 460	31 096	35 000	38 100	41 486	34 509

Source: *Management Compensation in Canada* (Toronto: Sobeco Group Inc., 1983), p. 67.

Notes

Part 1

Chapter 1

[1] Based on James Walker, "New Look for Marks & Spencer," *Financial Times of Canada*, September 26, 1983, p. 3.

[2] Peter F. Drucker, *The Practice of Management* (New York: Harper & Row, 1954), p. 37.

[3] Joseph P. Guiltinan and Gordon W. Paul, *Marketing Management* (New York: McGraw-Hill, 1982), pp. 3–4.

[4] "AMA Board Approves New Marketing Definition," *Marketing News* (Chicago: American Marketing Association, March 1, 1985), p. 1.

[5] See Lynn J. Loudenback, "Social Responsibility and the Marketing Concept," *Atlanta Economic Review* (April 1972), pp. 38–39.

[6] M. Kubr, ed., *Management Consulting: A Guide to the Profession* (Geneva: International Labour Organization, 1977), pp. 188–189.

[7] Richard P. Bagozzi, "Marketing as an Organized Behavioral System of Exchange," *Journal of Marketing* (October 1974), p. 77.

[8] *Ibid.*

[9] Wroe Alderson, *Marketing Behavior and Executive Action* (Homewood, Ill.: Richard D. Irwin, 1962), p. 292.

[10] T. G. Povey, "Spotting the Salesman Who Has What It Takes," *Nation's Business* (July 1972), p. 70.

[11] Robert J. Keith, "The Marketing Revolution," *Journal of Marketing* (January 1960), p. 36.

[12] *Ibid.*

[13] Theodore Levitt, *Innovations in Marketing* (New York: McGraw-Hill, 1962), p. 7.

[14] *Annual Report* (New York: General Electric, 1952), p. 21.

[15] Richard P. Bagozzi, "Marketing as an Organized Behavioral System of Exchange," *Journal of Marketing* (October 1974), p. 77.

[16] Theodore Levitt, "Marketing Myopia," *Harvard Business Review* (July–August 1960), pp. 45–56.

[17] "An About-Face in TI's Culture," *Business Week*, July 5, 1982, p. 77.

[18] *The Financial Post 500,* June 1983, p. 130.

[19] Adapted from M. Kubr, ed., *Management Consulting: A Guide to the Profession* (Geneva: International Labour Organization, 1977).

Chapter 2

[1] Adapted from Ian Anderson, "Switching Allegiances: Why the Breakup of US Telephone Markets is Wiring up Canadians," *Canadian Business*, Oct. 1983, pp. 15–20.

[2] M. Dale Beckman, "What Businessmen Know About Government and Legislative Intent," *The Canadian Marketer* (Fall 1973), pp. 13–17.

3 This section has been adapted and updated from a section in M. Dale Beckman and R. H. Evans, "Social Control of Business Through the Federal Department of Consumer and Corporate Affairs," by D. H. Henry, *Marketing: A Canadian Perspective* (Scarborough, Ont.: Prentice-Hall, 1972), pp. 102–129.
4 Donald N. Thompson, "Competition Policy and Marketing Regulation," in Donald N. Thompson and David S. R. Leighton, eds., *Canadian Marketing, Problems and Prospects* (Toronto: Wiley Publishers of Canada, 1973), p. 14.
5 As reported in the *Toronto Star*, December 16, 1972, January 5, 1973, and January 6, 1973.
6 James Walker and Alan D. Gray, "$1 Million Ad Fine Signal to Retailers," *Financial Times*, July 1983, Vol. 72, no. 6, p. 14.
7 *Annual Report: Director of Investigation and Research, Combines Investigation Act*, March 31, 1983 (Ottawa: Consumer and Corporate Affairs Canada).
8 David Thompson, "Rising to The Challenge," *Marketing*, May 2, 1983, p. 13.
9 Laurence P. Feldman, "Societal Adaptation: A New Challenge for Marketing," *Journal of Marketing* (July 1971), pp. 54–60.
10 This is suggested in Leslie M. Dawson, "Marketing Science in the Age of Aquarius," *Journal of Marketing* (July 1971), pp. 66–72.
11 Lawrence Stessin, "Incidents of Culture Shock Among American Businessmen Overseas," *Pittsburgh Business Review* (November–December 1971), p. 3. Reprinted by permission.
12 These examples are from "Why a Global Market Doesn't Exist," *Business Week*, December 9, 1970, pp. 140, 142, 144. Reprinted by special permission; © 1970 by McGraw-Hill, Inc. All rights reserved.

Part 2

Chapter 3

1 Adapted from Sandy Fife, "Creative Appliance Puts Kettle Sales on Boil," *Financial Times*, May 9, 1983, pp. 23–24.
2 Alfred D. Chandler, Jr., *Strategy and Structure* (Cambridge, Mass.: MIT Press, 1962), p. 13.
3 "Strategic Planning Should Occupy 30 to 50 Percent of CEO's Time: Schanck," *Marketing News*, June 1, 1979, p. 1.
4 Derek F. Abell, "Strategic Windows," *Journal of Marketing* (July 1978), pp. 21–26.
5 Philippe Haspeslagh, "Portfolio Planning: Uses and Limitations," *Harvard Business Review* (January–February 1982), pp. 58–73.
6 David S. Hopkins, *The Marketing Plan* (New York: The Conference Board, Inc., 1981), p. 34.
7 Some of the ideas expressed here are from an address by D. D. Monieson published in "Effective Marketing Planning: An Overview," *Executive Bulletin No. 8.* (Ottawa: The Conference Board in Canada, 1978).
8 See Walter Kiechel III, "Corporate Strategies Under Fire," *Fortune*, December 27, 1982, pp. 34–39.
9 Robert S. Wheeler, "Marketing Tales with a Moral," *Product Marketing* (April 1977), p. 43.
10 The discussion of these strategies is based on David W. Cravens, "Marketing Strategy Positioning," *Business Horizons* (December 1975), pp. 53–61.
11 "Toyota Motor: Hedging Autos with a Move into Housing," *Business Week*, November 13, 1978, pp. 162–65.
12 This discussion is adapted from Arthur G. Bedeian and William F. Glueck, *Management,* 3rd ed. (Hinsdale, Ill.: The Dryden Press, 1983), pp. 229–233.

Chapter 4

[1] This section relies heavily on Harry H. Hiller, *Canadian Society: A Sociological Analysis* (Scarborough, Ont.: Prentice-Hall of Canada Ltd., 1976), pp. 13–37.
[2] R. T. Gajda, "The Canadian Ecumene—Inhabited and Uninhabited Areas," *Geographical Bulletin*, 15 (1960), p. 6.
[3] T. R. Weir, "Population Changes in Canada, 1867–1967," *The Canadian Geographer*, 2, 4 (1967), p. 198.
[4] Larry H. Long, "On Measuring Geographic Mobility," *Journal of the American Statistical Association* (September 1970).
[5] Kenneth Runyon, *Consumer Behavior* (Columbus, Ohio: Charles E. Merrill, 1980), p. 35.
[6] Based on Statistics Canada Catalogue 62-544, and the Conference Board of Canada Statistics: *Handbook of Consumer Markets*, current data bank.
[7] *Changes in Income in Canada, 1970–1980*, Statistics Canada, Catalogue 99-941.
[8] Reported in "Research on Food Consumption Values Identifies Four Market Segments: Finds 'Good Taste' Still Tops," *Marketing News*, May 15, 1981, p. 17. Used by permission of the American Marketing Association.
[9] See "Lifestyle Research: A Lot of Hype, Versus Little Performance," *Marketing News*, May 14, 1982, Section 2, p. 5.
[10] David T. Kollat, Roger D. Blackwell, and James F. Robeson, *Strategic Marketing* (New York: Holt, Rinehart and Winston, 1972), p. 192.
[11] Dik Warren Twedt, "How Important to Marketing Strategy is the 'Heavy User'?" *Journal of Marketing* (January 1964), pp. 71–72.
[12] Martin L. Bell, *Marketing: Concepts and Strategy* (Boston: Houghton Mifflin, 1979), p. 129.
[13] Daniel Yankelovich, "New Criteria for Market Segmentation," *Harvard Business Review* (March–April 1964), p. 83–90.
[14] Susan Chace, "Marketing Grows More Vital for Desktop Computer Sales," *The Wall Street Journal*, October 22, 1982, 27.

Chapter 5

[1] Adapted from Tessa Wilmott, "Bread Company on the Rise," *The Financial Post*, November 26, 1983, p. 25.
[2] This section is based on materials written by J. D. Forbes, University of British Columbia.
[3] Fred Rothenberg, "Saturday-Night Television Isn't What It Used to Be," *The Seattle Times*, July 31, 1982, p. B 8.
[4] "Small Clothes Are Selling Big," *Business Week*, November 16, 1981, pp. 152, 156.
[5] Jennifer Alter, "Toothbrush Makers' Lament: Who Notices?" *Advertising Age*, October 4, 1982, p. 66.
[6] Philip Kotler and Ravi Singh, "Basic Marketing Strategy for Winning Your Marketing War," *Marketing Times* (November/December 1982), pp. 23–24. This article is reprinted by permission from the *Journal of Business Strategy*, Vol. 1, No. 3, Winter 1981, Copyright © 1981, Warren, Gorham and Lamont, Inc., 210 South St., Boston, Mass. 02111. All rights reserved.
[7] A similar analysis is suggested in Robert M. Fulmer, *The New Marketing* (New York: Macmillan, 1976), pp. 34–37; Philip Kotler, *Marketing Management* (Englewood Cliffs, N.J.: Prentice-Hall, 1976), pp. 141–151; and E. Jerome McCarthy, *Basic Marketing* (Homewood, Ill.: Richard D. Irwin, 1975), pp. 111–126.

8 A good example of this systematic approach to identifying a precise market target appears in Richard P. Carr, Jr., "Developing a New Residential Market for Carpeting: Some Mistakes and Successes," *Journal of Marketing* (July 1977), pp. 101–2.

9 "Properly Applied Psychographics Add Marketing Luster," *Marketing News*, November 12, 1982, p. 10.

Chapter 6

1 Adapted from John Powers, "Credit Success of Kodak Disc Camera to Research," *Marketing News*, January 21, 1983, pp. 8–9.

2 Committee on Definitions, *Marketing Definition: A Glossary of Marketing Terms* (Chicago, American Marketing Association, 1960), p. 17. Italics added.

3 "Include Marketing Research in Every Level of Corporate Strategic Planning," *Marketing News*, September 18, 1981, Section 2, p. 8.

4 John A. Gonder, "Marketing Research in Canada," *Cases & Readings in Marketing* (Toronto: Holt, Rinehart and Winston, 1974), p. 221.

5 Jo Marney, "Beyond the 6 P's of Marketing Research," *Marketing*, April 25, 1983, p. 8.

6 Estimate based on Frances Phillips, "Why It Pays to be a Pollster," *The Financial Post*, June 4, 1983, p. 1.

7 Bertram Schoner and Kenneth P. Uhl, *Marketing Research: Information Systems and Decision Making* (New York: John Wiley & Sons, Inc., 1975), p. 199.

8 The classification and definitions of marketing research companies are based on William G. Zikmund, *Exploring Marketing Research* (Hinsdale Ill.: The Dryden Press, 1982), pp. 79–81.

9 Reported in Priscilla A. La Barbera and Larry J. Rosenberg, "How Marketers Can Better Understand Consumers," *MSU Business Topics* (Winter 1980), p. 29.

10 "Marketing Oriented Lever Uses Research to Capture Bigger Dentrifice Market Shares," *Marketing News*, February 10, 1978, p. 9.

11 "Marquee," *The Seattle Times*, May 16, 1982, p. H 4.

12 Zikmund, *Exploring Marketing Research*, pp. 216–217.

13 John F. Cooney, "In Their Quest for Sure Fire Ads, Marketers Use Psychological Tests to Find Out What Grabs You," *The Wall Street Journal*, April 12, 1979, p. 40.

14 "Many Researchers Prefer Interviewing by Phone," *Marketing News*, July 14, 1978, p. 8.

15 Reported in A. B. Blankenship, "Listed versus Unlisted Numbers in Telephone-Survey Samples," *Journal of Advertising Research* (February 1977), pp. 39–42.

16 Douglas R. Berdie and John F. Anderson, "Mail Questionnaire Response Rates: Updating Outmoded Thinking," *Journal of Marketing* (January 1976), pp. 71–73; A. Marvin Roscoe, Dorothy Lang, and Jagdish N. Sheth, "Follow-up Methods, Questionnaire Length, and Market Differences in Mail Surveys," *Journal of Marketing* (April 1975), pp. 20–27; and Richard T. Hise and Michael A. McGinnis, "Evaluating the Effect of a Follow-up Request on Mail Survey Results," *Akron Business and Economic Review* (Winter 1974), pp. 19–21.

17 *The Wall Street Journal*, June 28, 1972, p. 1.

18 This discussion follows William G. Zikmund, *Exploring Marketing Research* (Hinsdale, Ill.: The Dryden Press, 1982), pp. 377–393. Used by permission.

19 Donald F. Cox and Robert E. Good, "How to Build a Marketing Information System," *Harvard Business Review* (May–June 1967), p. 147.

20 "Marketing Intelligence Systems: A DEW Line for Marketing Men," *Business Management* (January 1966), p. 32.

[21] "Marketing Management and the Computer," *Sales Management*, August 20, 1965, pp. 49–60.

[22] Donald F. Cox and Robert E. Good, "How to Build a Marketing Information System," *Harvard Business Review* (May–June 1967), p. 152.

Part 3

Chapter 7

[1] Dean Rotbart, "Chinese Accountants Find that America Is Hard to Figure," *The Wall Street Journal*, June 5, 1981, pp. 1, 12.

[2] This definition is adapted from James F. Engel and Roger D. Blackwell, *Consumer Behaviour*, 4th ed. (Hinsdale, Ill.: The Dryden Press, 1982), p. 9.

[3] "Learning How to Please the Baffling Japanese," *Fortune*, October 5, 1981, p. 122.

[4] Engel and Blackwell, *Consumer Behavior*, 4th ed., p. 72.

[5] Daniel Yankelovich, "New Rules," *The Seattle Times*, November 1, 1981, pp. F 1, F 4. Excerpted from the book, *New Rules: Searching for Self-Fulfillment in a World Turned Upside Down* by Daniel Yankelovich. Copyright 1981, Daniel Yankelovich. Distributed by Los Angeles Times Syndicate.

[6] Engel and Blackwell, *Consumer Behavior*, 4th ed., p. 75.

[7] Robert Linn, "Americans Turn Deaf Ear to Foreign Tongues," *Orlando Sentinel Star*, November 1, 1981.

[8] *Wall Street Journal*, March 9, 1977, p. 1.

[9] Leon G. Schiffman and Leslie Lazar Kanuk, *Consumer Behavior* (Englewood Cliffs, N.J.: Prentice-Hall, 1978), p. 390.

[10] *Advertising Age*, April 1, 1974.

[11] Charles Winich, "Anthropology's Contributions to Marketing," *Journal of Marketing* (July 1961), p. 59.

[12] Edward T. Hall, "The Silent Language in Overseas Business," *Harvard Business Review* (May–June 1960), p. 89.

[13] Patricia L. Layman, "In Any Language, the Beauty Business Spells Success," *Chemical Week*, September 17, 1975, p. 26.

[14] N. R. Kleinsfield, "This is One Story with Teeth in It — False Ones, That Is," *The Wall Street Journal*, August 18, 1975, p. 1.

[15] Gail Chaisson, "The French Market Today," *Marketing*, June 1, 1981, pp. 11, 14.

[16] Eleine Saint-Jacques and Bruce Mallen, "The French Market under the Microscope," *Marketing*, May 11, 1981, p. 10.

[17] Gail Chaisson, "The French Market Today," *Marketing*, June 1, 1981, p. 11. And Statistics Canada, Catalogue 63-005 and 13-201.

[18] Canadian Royal Commission on Bilingualism and Biculturalism.

[19] Based on Jan Morin and Michel Ostiguy, "View From the Top," *Marketing*, June 1, 1981, p. 28.

[20] Adapted from Eleine Saint-Jacques and Bruce Mallen, "The French Market under the Microscope," *Marketing*, May 11, 1981, pp. 12–13.

[21] M. Cloutier, "Marketing in Quebec," Industrial Marketing Research Association Conference, Toronto, March 1978.

[22] Del I. Hawkins, Kenneth A. Coney, and Roger J. Best, *Consumer Behaviour: Implications for Marketing Strategy* (Dallas: Business Publications, 1980), pp. 181–82. The quotation is adapted from S. E. Asch, "Effects of Group Pressure upon the Modification and Distortion of Judgments," in *Readings in Social Psychology*, eds. E. E. MacCoby et al. (New York: Holt, Rinehart and Winston, 1958), pp. 174–83.

23 Francis S. Bourne, *Group Influence in Marketing and Public Relations* (Ann Arbor, Mich.: Foundation for Research on Human Behavior, 1956).

24 John W. Slocum, Jr., and H. Lee Mathews, "Social Class and Income as Indicators of Consumer Credit Behaviour," *Journal of Marketing* (April 1970) pp. 69–74.

25 Charles M. Schaninger, "Social Class Versus Income Revisited: An Empirical Investigation," *Journal of Marketing Research* (May 1981), pp. 192–208.

26 Elihu Katz and Paul F. Lazarfield, *Personal Influence* (New York: Free Press, 1957), p. 32.

27 James F. Engel and Roger D. Blackwell, *Consumer Behavior*, 4th ed., pp. 176–182.

28 "Business Shifts Its Sales Pitch for Women," *U.S. News & World Report*, July 9, 1981, p. 46; and Margaret LeRoux, "Exec Claims Most Ads to Women Miss the Mark," *Advertising Age*, May 21, 1979, p. 24.

29 George J. Szybillo, Arlene K. Sosanie, and Aaron Tenebein, "Should Children Be Seen but Not Heard?" *Journal of Advertising Research* (December 1977), pp. 7–13.

30 Lester Rand, *The Rand Youth Poll*, 1981.

Chapter 8

1 Adapted from James Walker, "Changing Consumer Patterns Fuel Sunday Debate," *Financial Times of Canada*, November 14, 1983, pp. 4–5.

2 A. H. Maslow, *Motivation and Personality* (New York: Harper & Row, Publishers, 1954), pp. 370–396.

3 A. H. Maslow, *Motivation and Personality* (New York: Harper & Row, 1954), p. 382.

4 E. E. Lawlor and J. L. Suttle, "A Causal Correlational Test of the Need Hierarchy Concept," *Organizational Behaviour and Human Performance* 3 (1968), pp. 12–35.

5 George Katona, *The Powerful Consumer* (New York: McGraw-Hill, 1960), p. 132.

6 Burt Schorr, "The Mistakes: Many New Products Fail Despite Careful Planning, Publicity," *The Wall Street Journal*, April 5, 1961, pp. 1, 22.

7 Steuart Henderson Britt, "How Weber's Law Can Be Applied to Marketing," *Business Horizons* (February 1975), pp. 21–29.

8 John Brooks, "The Little Ad That Isn't There," *Consumer Reports* (January 1958), pp. 7–10.

9 Richard P. Barthol and Michael J. Goldstein, "Psychology and the Invisible Sell," *California Management Review* (Winter 1959), p. 34.

10 David Krech, Richard S. Crutchfield, and Egerton L. Ballachey, *Individual in Society* (New York: McGraw-Hill Book Company, 1962), Chapter 2.

11 C. E. Osgood, G. J. Suci, and P. H. Tannenbaum, *The Measurement of Meaning* (Urbana: University of Illinois Press, 1957).

12 George S. Day, "Using Attitude Change Measures to Evaluate New Product Introductions," *Journal of Marketing Research* (November 1970), pp. 474–482.

13 Frederick E. Webster, Jr., and Frederick Von Pechmann, "A Replication of the 'Shopping List' Study," *Journal of Marketing* (April 1970), pp. 61–63.

14 This section is based on Michael L. Rothschild and William C. Gaidis, "Behavioral Learning Theory: Its Relevance to Marketing and Promotion," *Journal of Marketing* (Spring 1981), pp. 70–78.

15 John Koten, "For Kellogg, the Hardest Part Is Getting People Out of Bed," *The Wall Street Journal*, May 27, 1982, p. 27.

16 B. M. Campbell, "The Existence of Evoked Set and Determinants of its Magnitude in Brand Choice Behavior," in *Buyer Behavior: Theoretical and*

Empirical Foundations, eds. John A. Howard and Lonnie Ostrom (New York: Alfred A. Knopf, Inc., 1973), pp. 243–44.

[17] James Engel, David Kollat, and Roger Blackwell, *Consumer Behaviour,* 3d ed. (Hinsdale: Dryden Press, 1978), p. 369.

[18] Leon Festinger, *A Theory of Cognitive Dissonance* (Stanford, Calif.: Stanford University Press, 1958), p. 3.

[19] These categories were originally suggested in John A. Howard, *Marketing Management: Analysis and Planning* (Homewood, Ill.: Richard D. Irwin, 1963). The discussion here is based on Donald R. Lehmann, William L. Moore, and Terry Elrod, "The Development of Distinct Choice Process Segments over Time: A Stochastic Modelling Approach," *Journal of Marketing* (Spring 1982), pp. 48–50.

Part 4

Chapter 9

[1] Bruce Gates, "Smart 'Super Machines' to Invade Copier Market," *The Financial Post*, November 5, 1983, p. s10.

[2] *Ibid.*

[3] "Videodiscs: The Expensive Race to Be First," *Business Week*, September 15, 1975, pp. 58–66.

[4] Alan Freeman, "Will People Buy Toothpaste that Doesn't Come in a Tube?" *The Wall Street Journal*, June 3, 1982, p. 25.

[5] This section relies on George S. Day, "The Product Life Cycle: Analysis and Application Issues," *Journal of Marketing* (Fall 1981), pp. 60–65.

[6] Ben M. Enis, Raymond LaGarce, and Arthur E. Prell, "Extending the Product Life Cycle," *Business Horizons* (June 1977), pp. 46–56.

[7] William Qualls, Richard W. Olschavsky, and Ronald E. Michaels, "Shortening the PLC — An Empirical Test," *Journal of Marketing* (Fall 1981), pp. 76–80.

[8] Rolando Pilli and Victor J. Cook, "A Test of the Product Life Cycle as a Model of Sales Behavior," *Marketing Science Institute Working Paper* (November 1967) and "Validity of the Product Life Cycle," *The Journal of Business* (October 1969), pp. 385–400. This research is reviewed in William S. Sachs and George Benson, *Product Planning and Management* (Tulsa, Okla.: PennWell Books, 1981), p. 80.

[9] Stephen Grover, "Record Business Slumps as Taping and Video Games Take Away Sales," *The Wall Street Journal*, February 18, 1982, p. 25.

[10] Ennis et al., op. cit.

[11] Bill Abrams, "Warring Toothpaste Makers Spend Millions Luring Buyers to Slightly Altered Products," *The Wall Street Journal*, September 9, 1981, p. 33.

[12] Gail Bronson, "Baby Food It Is, but Gerber Wants Teen-Agers to Think of It as Dessert," *The Wall Street Journal*, July 17, 1981, p. 29.

[13] Karger, "5 Ways to Find New Uses — Re-Evaluate Your Old Products," p. 18.

[14] Alan Freeman, "Levi Unit Tries to Give Jeans Limited Appeal," *The Wall Street Journal*, August 11, 1981, p. 25.

[15] "Good Products Don't Die, P&G Chairman Declares," *Advertising Age*, November 1, 1976, p. 8.

[16] Everett M. Rogers and F. Floyd Schoemaker, *Communication of Innovations* (New York: The Free Press, 1971), pp. 135–157.

[17] Gillette Spends $17.4 Million to Introduce Aapri, Gain Foothold in Skin Care Market," *Marketing News*, May 29, 1981, p. 6.

18 Walter P. Gorman III and Charles T. Moore, "The Early Diffusion of Color Television Receivers into a Fringe Market Area," *Journal of Retailing* (Fall 1968), pp. 46–56.

19 James Coleman, Elihu Katz, and Herbert Menzel, "The Diffusion of an Innovation Among Physicians," *Sociometry* (December 1957), pp. 253–270.

20 Bryce Ryan and Neal Gross, "The Diffusion of Hybrid Seed Corn in Two Iowa Communities," *Rural Sociology* (March 1943), pp. 15–24.

21 Joseph Barry Mason and Danny Bellenger, "Analyzing High-Fashion Acceptance," *Journal of Retailing* (Winter 1974), pp. 79–88.

22 Ronald Marks and Eugene Hughes, "Profiling the Consumer Innovator," in *Evolving Marketing Thought for 1980*, (eds.) John H. Summey and Ronald D. Taylor (New Orleans: Southern Marketing Association, 1980), pp. 115–118; Elizabeth Hirschman, "Innovativeness, Novelty Seeking and Consumer Creativity," *Journal of Consumer Research* (December 1980), pp. 283–295; and Richard W. Olshavsky, "Time and the Rate of Adoption of Innovations," *Journal of Consumer Research* (March 1980), pp. 425–428.

23 This three-way classification of consumer goods was first proposed by Melvin T. Copeland. See his book, *Principles of Merchandising* (New York: McGraw-Hill Book Company, 1924), Chapters 2–4. For a more recent discussion of this classification scheme, see Richard H. Holton, "The Distinction between Convenience Goods, Shopping Goods and Specialty Goods," *Journal of Marketing* (July 1958), pp. 55–56.

Chapter 10

1 Adapted from Edward Greenspon, "K-Tel Moves on From Records to Video Games," *The Financial Post*, June 25, 1983, pp. 1–2.

2 Nancy Giges, "Nestlé's Chief's Mission: Pick Winners, Ax Losers," *Advertising Age*, September 7, 1981, p. 64.

3 Polaroid's product development strategies are described in "Polaroid: Turning Away from Land's One Product Strategy," *Business Week*, March 2, 1981, pp. 108–112.

4 Bill Abrams, "Despite Mixed Record, Firms Still Pushing for New Products," *The Wall Street Journal*, November 12, 1981, p. 25.

5 Douglas R. Scase, "Chrysler Is Upbeat as Market Share Rises, but Some Doubt It Can Maintain Success," *The Wall Street Journal*, April 22, 1982, p. 33.

6 Howard Rudnitakey, "Snap Judgments Can Be Wrong," *Forbes*, April 12, 1982.

7 Roger Leigh Lawton and A. Parasuraman, "So You Want Your New Product Planning to Be Productive," *Business Horizons* (December 1980), pp. 29–34; and Roger Calantone and Robert G. Cooper, "New Product Scenarios: Prospects for Success," *Journal of Marketing* (Spring 1981), pp. 48–60.

8 Carol J. Loomis, "P & G Up Against Its Wall," *Fortune*, February 23, 1981, pp. 49–54.

9 Abrams, "Despite Mixed Record, Firms Still Pushing for Products," p. 25.

10 David S. Hopkins, *New Product Winners and Losers* (New York: The Conference Board, Inc., 1980).

11 Abrams, "Despite Mixed Record, Firms Still Pushing for Products," p. 25.

12 This list is adapted from Roger Calantone and Robert G. Cooper, "New Product Scenarios: Prospects for Success," *Journal of Marketing* (Spring 1981), p. 49.

13 Robert G. Cooper, "The Myth of the Better Mousetrap: What Makes a New Product a Success?" *The Business Quarterly* (Spring, 1981), pp. 71, 72.

14 "Seven-Up Uncaps a Cola — And an Industry Feud," *Business Week*, March 22, 1982, pp. 98, 100.

[15] Abrams, "Despite Mixed Record Firms Still Pushing for Products," p. 25.

[16] David Gordon and E. Edward Blevins, "Organizing for Effective New-Product Development," *Journal of Business* (December 1978), pp. 21–26; and James Rothe, Michael Harvey and Walden Rhines, "New Product Development under Conditions of Scarcity and Inflation," *Michigan Business Review* (May 1977), pp. 16–22.

[17] Reported in Ann M. Morrison, "The General Mills Brand of Manager," *Fortune*, January 12, 1981, pp. 99–107.

[18] Jacob M. Duker and Michael V. Laric, "The Product Manager: No Longer on Trial," in *The Changing Marketing Environment: New Theories and Applications*, (eds.) Kenneth Bernhardt, Ira Dolich, Michael Etzel, William Kehoe, Thomas Kinnear, William Perrault, Jr., and Kenneth Roering (Chicago: American Marketing Association, 1981), pp. 93–96; and Peter S. Howsam and G. David Hughes, "Product Management System Suffers from Insufficient Experience, Poor Communication," *Marketing News*, June 26, 1981, Section 2, p. 8.

[19] This discussion is based on Richard M. Hill and James D. Hlavacek, "The Venture Team: A New Concept in Marketing," *Journal of Marketing* (July 1972) pp. 44–50.

[20] Richard M. Hill and James D. Hlavacek, "The Venture Team: A New Concept in Marketing," *Journal of Marketing* (July 1972), p. 50.

[21] Adapted from John R. Rockwell and Marc C. Particelli, "New Product Strategy: How the Pros Do It," *Industrial Marketing* (May 1982), p. 50.

[22] Rockwell, op. cit.

[23] *Wall Street Journal*, March 26, 1974, p. 1.

[24] Reported in Edward Buxton, *Promise Them Anything* (New York: Stein and Day, 1972), p. 101.

[25] Quoted in Mary McCabe English, "Marketers: Better than a Coin Flip," *Advertising Age*, February 9, 1981, p. S–15. Copyright 1981 by Crain Communications, Inc. Reprinted by permission.

[26] Dylan Landis, "Durable Goods for a Test?" *Advertising Age*, February 9, 1981, pp. S–18, S–19.

[27] Lee Adler, "Time Lag in New-Product Development," *Journal of Marketing* (January 1966), p. 17.

[28] Spencer Klaw, "The Soap Wars: A Strategic Analysis," *Fortune* (June 1963), pp. 122ff.

[29] Committee on Definitions, *Marketing Definitions: A Glossary of Marketing Terms* (Chicago: American Marketing Association, 1960), pp. 9–10.

[30] A Worldwide Brand for Nissan," *Business Week*, August 24, 1981, p. 104.

[31] John Koten, "Mixing with Coke over Trademarks is Always a Fizzle," *The Wall Street Journal*, March 9, 1978.

[32] *Business Week*, February 20, 1960, p. 71.

[33] Meir Statman and Tyzoon T. Tyebjee, "Trademarks, Patents, and Innovation in the Ethical Drug Industry," *Journal of Marketing* (Summer 1981), pp. 71–81.

[34] Bill Abrams, "Brand Loyalty Rises Slightly, but Increase Could Be Fluke," *The Wall Street Journal*, February 7, 1982, p. 21.

[35] "Name Game," *Time*, August 31, 1981, p. 41.

[36] Frances Phillips, "Private Label Appliances Vie with National Brands," *The Financial Post*, Aug. 13, 1983, p. 12.

[37] Osama Al-Zand and Joseph Ditton, "Development of Performance of Generic Foods in Canada, *Food Market Commentary*, Vol. 5, No. 1, March 1983, p. 23.

[38] Private Brands Get More Public Attention," *Marketing*, August 29, 1983, p. 1.

[39] Frances Phillips, "New Packaging Looks are Making Some Products Winners," *The Financial Post*, June 4, 1983, p. 24.

40 "Packaging Linked to Ad's Effect," *Advertising Age*, May 3, 1982, p. 63.
41 Bill Abrams and David P. Garino, "Package Design Gains Stature as Visual Competition Grows," *The Wall Street Journal*, August 6, 1981.
42 Robert Ball, "Warm Milk Wakes Up the Packaging Industry," *Fortune*, August 7, 1982, pp. 78–82.

Chapter 11

1 Adapted from Robert L. Perry, "Telecom Takes to The Airwaves for Business," *The Financial Post*, Sept. 17, 1983, p. 39.
2 Some of the material in this chapter is adapted from Eugene M. Johnson, "The Selling of Services" in Victor P. Buell (ed.), *Handbook of Modern Marketing* (New York: McGraw-Hill, 1970), pp. 12–110 to 12–120.
3 Theodore Levitt, "Marketing Intangible Products and Product Intangibles," *Harvard Business Review* (May–June 1981), pp. 94–102. The example is from pp. 96–97.
4 This section is based on Eugene M. Johnson, "Are Goods and Services Different? — An Exercise in Marketing Theory," unpublished DBA dissertation, Washington University, 1969, pp. 83–205. Used by permission.
5 William R. George, "The Retailing of Services — A Challenging Future," *Journal of Retailing* (Fall 1977), pp. 89–90.
6 Sidney P. Feldman and Merline C. Spencer, "The Effect of Personal Influence in the Selection of Consumer Services," in *Marketing and Economic Development*, (ed.) Peter D. Bennett (Chicago: American Marketing Association, 1967), p. 440.
7 Theodore Levitt, "Marketing Myopia," *Harvard Business Review* (July–August 1961), pp. 45–56.
8 William R. George and Hiram C. Barksdale, "Marketing Activities in the Service Industries," *Journal of Marketing* (October 1974), p. 69.
9 *Ibid.*, p. 65.
10 Colin Clark, *The Conditions of Economic Progress*, 3rd ed. (London: Macmillan, 1957), pp. 490–491.
11 William R. Darden and Warren A. French, "Selected Personal Services: Consumer Reactions," *Journal of Retailing* (Fall 1972), pp. 42–48.
12 Blaine Cooke, "Analyzing Markets for Services," in Victor P. Buell (ed.), *Handbook of Modern Marketing* (New York: McGraw-Hill Book Company, 1970), pp. 2–44.
13 The 'Big Mac' Theory of Economic Progress," *Forbes*, April 15, 1977, p. 137. See also Theodore Levitt, "The Industrialization of Service," *Harvard Business Review* (September–October 1976), pp. 63–75.
14 Levitt, "The Industrialization of Service," p. 70.
15 Dan R. E. Thomas, "Strategy Is Different in Service Business," *Harvard Business Review* (July–August 1978), p. 160.
16 John M. Rathmell, *Marketing in the Service Sector* (Cambridge, Mass.: Winthrop Publishers, 1974), p. 61.

Part 5

Chapter 12

1 Adapted from "Steinberg Strategy Starts Price War," *Marketing*, March 21, 1983, p. 15.
2 Adapted from *Marketing Today* by David J. Schwartz, copyright © 1981 by Harcourt Brace Jovanovich, Inc. Reprinted by permission of the publisher.

[3] Jon G. Udell, "How Important Is Pricing in Competitive Strategy?" *Journal of Marketing* (January 1964), pp. 44–48.

[4] "Pricing Objectives and Practices in American Industry: A Research Report," © 1979 by Louis E. Boone and David L. Kurtz; all rights reserved.

[5] These objectives are reported in Bro Uttal, "Xerox Is Trying Too Hard," *Fortune*, March 13, 1978, p. 84; Ralph E. Winter, "Corporate Strategists Giving New Emphasis to Market Share, Rank," *Wall Street Journal*, February 3, 1978, p. 1; and Bro Uttal, "How Ray MacDonald's Growth Theory Created IBM's Toughest Competitor," *Fortune*, January 1977, p. 96.

[6] Robert A. Lynn, *Price Policies and Marketing Management* (Homewood, Ill.: Richard D. Irwin, 1967), p. 99.

[7] Robert D. Buzzell and Frederick D. Wiersema, "Successful Share-Building Strategies," *Harvard Business Review* (January–February 1981), pp. 135–144.

[8] Henry Allesio, "Market Share Madness," *Strategic Marketing* (Fall 1982), p. 76.

[9] This section is adapted from Edwin G. Dolan, *Basic Economics*, 3d ed. (Hinsdale, Ill.: The Dryden Press, 1983); and Richard H. Leftwich, *The Price System and Resource Allocation* (Hinsdale, Ill.: The Dryden Press, 1979), pp. 55–56. Reprinted by permission of Holt, Rinehart & Winston.

[10] Theodore E. Wentz, "Realism in Pricing Analysis," *Journal of Marketing* (April 1966), p. 26.

[11] W. Warren Haynes, "Pricing Decisions in Small Business," *Management Research Summary* (Washington, D.C.: Small Business Administration, 1966), p. 1.

[12] *Ibid.*, p. 2.

[13] Joel Dean, "Techniques for Pricing New Products and Services," in Victor P. Buell and Carl Heyel, eds., *Handbook of Modern Marketing* (McGraw-Hill Book Company, 1970), pp. 5–51.

[14] This section has been adapted from G. David Hughes, *Marketing Management: A Planning Approach* (Reading: Addison-Wesley Publishing Company, 1978), pp. 324–326.

[15] W. J. E. Crissy and R. Boewadt, "Pricing in Perspective," *Sales Management*, June 15, 1971.

Chapter 13

[1] Katrinka W. Leefmans, "Business Bulletin," *Wall Street Journal*, December 20, 1979, p. 1.

[2] Donald V. Harper, *Price Policy and Procedure* (New York: Harcourt Brace Jovanovich, 1966), p. 204. By permission of the author.

[3] Fred C. Foy, "Management's Part in Achieving Price Respectability," *Competitive Pricing* (New York: American Management Association, 1958), pp. 7–8.

[4] Victor Grostern, "Unit Pricing: A Case for Adoption and Use," *Canadian Consumer* (December 1975), p. 28–29.

[5] J. Edward Russo, "The Value of Unit Price Information," *Journal of Marketing Research* (May 1977), pp. 193–201.

[6] Walter J. Primeaux, Jr., "The Effect of Consumer Knowledge and Bargaining Strength on Final Selling Price: A Case Study," *Journal of Business* (October 1970), pp. 419–426.

[7] Robert A. Lynn, *Price Policies and Marketing Management* (Homewood, Ill.: Richard D. Irwin, 1967), p. 143.

[8] Bernie Faust, William Gorman, Eric Oesterle, and Larry Buchta, "Effective Retail Pricing Policy," *Purdue Retailer* (Lafayette, Indiana: Department of Agricultural Economics, 1963), p. 2.

9 Karl A. Shilliff, "Determinants of Consumer Price Sensitivity for Selected Supermarket Products: An Empirical Investigation," *Akron Business & Economic Review* (Spring 1975), pp. 26–32.

10 John F. Willenborg and Robert E. Pitts, "Perceived Situational Effects on Price Sensitivity," *Journal of Business Research* (March 1977), pp. 27–38.

11 J. Douglass McConnell, "An Experimental Examination of the Price-Quality Relationship," *Journal of Business* (October 1968), pp. 439–444.

12 James H. Myers and William H. Reynolds, *Consumer Behavior and Marketing Management* (Boston: Houghton-Mifflin Company, 1967), p. 47.

13 *Market Spotlight* (Edmonton: Alberta Consumer and Corporate Affairs, March 1979).

14 M. Edgar Barret, "Case of the Tangled Transfer Price," *Harvard Business Review* (May–June 1977), p. 22.

Part 6

Chapter 14

1 Committee on Definitions, *Marketing Definitions: A Glossary of Marketing Terms* (Chicago: American Marketing Association, 1960), p. 10.

2 This section is adapted by permission from Louis W. Stern and Adel I. El-Ansary, *Marketing Channels*, 2d ed. (Englewood Cliffs, N.J.: Prentice-Hall, Inc., 1982) pp. 6–11.

3 These functions were developed in Wroe Alderson, "Factors Governing the Development of Marketing Channels," in *Marketing Channels for Manufactured Products*, (ed.) Richard M. Clewitt (Homewood, Ill.: Richard D. Irwin, 1954), pp. 5–22.

4 Wilke English, Dale M. Lewison, and M. Wayne DeLozier, "Evolution in Channel Management: What Will Be Next?" in *Proceedings of the Southwestern Marketing Association*, (eds.) Robert H. Ross, Frederic B. Kraft, and Charles H. Davis (Wichita, Kansas, 1981), pp. 78–81.

5 James A. White, "IBM Expands Outside Its Sales Channel," *The Wall Street Journal*, October 7, 1981, p. 2.

6 William G. Zikmund and William J. Stanton, "Recycling Solid Wastes: A Channels-of-Distribution Problem," *Journal of Marketing* (July 1971), p. 34.

7 Donald A. Fuller, "Aluminum Beverage Container Recycling in Florida: A Commentary," *Atlanta Economic Review* (January–February 1977), p. 41.

8 These bases were identified in John R. P. French, Jr., and Bertram Raven, "The Bases of Social Power," in *Group Dynamics: Research and Theory*, 2d ed., (eds.) Darwin Cartwright and Alvin Zandler (Evanston, Ill.: Row, Putnam, 1960), pp. 607–623. The list originally came from *Studies in Social Power* (ed.) Darwin Cartwright (Ann Arbor: University of Michigan, 1959), pp. 612–613.

9 The discussion that follows is based on Bert Rosenbloom, *Marketing Channels: A Management Overview*, 2d ed. (Hinsdale, Ill.: The Dryden Press, 1983).

10 Bruce J. Walker and Donald W. Jackson, Jr., "The Channels Manager: A Needed New Position," in *Proceedings of the Southern Marketing Association*, (eds.) Robert S. Franz, Robert M. Hopkins, and Al Toma (New Orleans, La., November 1978), pp. 325–328.

11 Robert E. Weigand, "The Marketing Organization, Channels, and Firm Size," *The Journal of Business* (April 1963), pp. 228–236.

12 Combines Investigation Act, Part IV. 1, 31.4, 1976.

13 Bert C. McCammon, Jr., "The Emergence and Growth of Contractually Integrated Channels in the American Economy," in Peter D. Bennett (ed.),

Marketing and Economic Development (Chicago: American Marketing Association, 1965), p. 496. This section is based on material in this paper, pp. 496–515.

[14] Adapted from Lawson A. W. Hunter, "Buying Groups," *Agriculture Canada: Food Market Commentary*, Vol. 5, No. 4, p. 15.

[15] Thomas G. Marx, "Distribution Efficiency in Franchising," *MSU Business Topics* (Winter 1980), p. 5.

[16] Leonard L. Berry, "Is It Time to Be Wary about Franchising?" *Arizona Business Bulletin* (October 1970), pp. 3 9.

[17] Bruce Mallen, "A Theory of Retailer-Supplier Conflict, Control, and Cooperation," *Journal of Retailing* (Summer 1963), p. 26. Reprinted with permission.

[18] *Educators Conference Proceedings*, (eds.) Neil Beckwith, Michael Houston, Robert Mittelstaedt, Kent B. Monroe, and Scott Ward (Chicago: American Marketing Association, 1970), pp. 495–499; Michael Etgar, "Sources and Types of Intra Channel Conflict," *Journal of Retailing* (Spring 1979), pp. 61–78; and Louis W. Stern and Torger Reve, "Distribution Channels as Political Economies," *Journal of Marketing* (Summer 1980), pp. 52–64.

Chapter 15

[1] James R. Moore and Kendell A. Adams, "Functional Wholesaler Sales Trends and Analysis," Edward M. Mazze (ed.), *Combined Proceedings* (Chicago: American Marketing Association, 1976), pp. 402–405.

[2] Louis P. Bucklin, *Competition and Evolution in the Distributive Trades* (Englewood Cliffs, N.J.: Prentice-Hall, 1972), p. 214.

Chapter 16

[1] Adapted from Susan Hoeschen, "Selling the Home Video Revolution," *The Financial Times of Canada*, January 24, 1983, p. 2.

[2] *Pen Pictures of Early Pioneer Life in Upper Canada* by a "Canuck," Coles Canadiana Collection (Toronto: Coles Publishing Company, 1972), pp. 80–82.

[3] Gerald Albaum, Roger Best, and Del Hawkins, "Retailing Strategy for Customer Growth and New Customer Attraction," *Journal of Business Research* (March 1980), pp. 7–19; and Bert Rosenbloom, "Strategic Planning in Retailing: Prospects and Problems," *Journal of Retailing* (Spring 1980), pp. 107–120.

[4] Frances Phillips, "Canadian Tire Finds Texas Trail a Bit Bumpy," *The Financial Post*, March 26, 1983, p. 18.

[5] Bill Abrams, "New Worry for Manufacturers: Growth of Warehouse Outlets," *The Wall Street Journal*, May 28, 1981, p. 29.

[6] Clayton Sinclair, "The New Priorities for Shopping Centres," *Financial Times of Canada*, March 21, 1983, p. 12.

[7] The following discussion of Reilly and Huff's work is adapted from Joseph Barry Mason and Morris Lehman Mayer, *Modern Retailing: Theory and Practice* (Plano, Tex.: Business Publications, Inc., 1978), pp. 486–489.

[8] This section is adapted from Louis P. Bucklin, "Retail Strategy and the Classification of Consumer Goods," *Journal of Marketing* (January 1963), pp. 50–55, published by the American Marketing Association.

[9] "Sears' Identity Crisis," *Business Week*, December 8, 1975, p. 54.

[10] *The Financial Post 500*, June 1983, p. 110.

11 D. Richard and G. Hewston, "More on Canadian Food Retailers: Some Recent Observations," *Food Market Commentary* (March 1983), p. 18.
12 Statistics Canada; The Conference Board of Canada, *Handbook of Canadian Consumer Markets*, 1982, p. 190.
13 John A. Quelch and Hirotaka Takeuchi, "Nonstore Marketing: Fast Track or Slow?" *Harvard Business Review* (July–August 1981), p. 75.
14 Quoted by a Sears executive in Toronto (Mr. Knox).
15 *Vending Machine Operators* (Ottawa: Statistics Canada, 1982), Catalogue 63–213.
16 *Department Store Sales by Regions* (Ottawa: Statistics Canada, 1982) Catalogue 63–005.
17 William R. Davidson, "Changes in Distributive Institutions," *Journal of Marketing* (January 1970), p. 8.
18 "Only 10% of Consumers Interested in Shopping at Home Via 2-Way TV," *Marketing News*, May 29, 1981, pp. 1, 3.
19 Malcolm P. McNair and Eleanor G. May, "The Next Revolution of the Retailing Wheel," *Harvard Business Review* (September–October 1978), pp. 81–91.
20 The discussion that follows is adapted from Quelch and Takeuchi, "Nonstore Marketing: Fast Track or Slow?" pp. 80–83.

Chapter 17

1 Adapted from Michelle Ramsay, "Boosting Inventory Turns the Canadian Tire Way," *Canadian Transportation and Distribution Management* (November 1983), p. 33–34.
2 Andrew M. Schell and Jim Heur, "Creating a PD Strategy for a Rebounding Economy," *Canadian Transportation and Distribution Management* (November 1983), p. 79.
3 David P. Herron, "Managing Physical Distribution for Profits," *Harvard Business Review* (May–June 1979), pp. 121–32.
4 Warren Rose, *Logistics Management* (Dubuque, Iowa: Wm. C. Brown, 1979), p. 4.
5 James M. Daley and Zarrell V. Lambert, "Toward Assessing Trade-Offs by Shippers in Carrier Selection Decisions," *Journal of Business Logistics,* vol. 2, no. 1 (1980), pp. 35–54.
6 Robert E. Sabath, "How Much Service Do Customers Really Want?" *Business Horizons* (April 1978), pp. 26–32.
7 David T. Kollat, Roger D. Blackwell, and James F. Robeson, *Strategic Marketing* (New York: Holt, Rinehart and Winston, 1972), p. 315.
8 *Canada Year Book 1976/77* (Ottawa: Statistics Canada, 1977), pp. 731–732.
9 *Water Transportation* (Ottawa: Statistics Canada, 1981), Catalogue 54–205.
10 The Ultimate in Automation," *Transportation and Distribution Management* (January 1970), p. 38.
11 Based on James C. Johnson and Donald F. Wood, *Contemporary Physical Distribution and Logistics,* 2nd ed. (Tulsa, Okla.: Penn Well Books, 1982), p. 66.
12 *Summary of External Trade*, (Ottawa: Statistics Canada, 1982), Catalogue 65-001.
13 "Reducing Paperwork," *Transportation and Distribution Management* (November 1971), p. 15.
14 Robert L. Dausend, "Containerization — Stimulus to World Trade," *Transportation and Distribution Management* (January 1972), pp. 15–16.

Part 7

Chapter 18

[1] Adapted from "What Makes an Ad Package Stand Test of Time," *The Financial Post*, January 28, 1984, p. A13.

[2] Wilbur Schramm, "The Nature of Communication Between Humans," in *The Process and Effects of Mass Communication*, rev. ed. (Urbana: University of Illinois Press, 1971), pp. 3–53.

[3] S. Watson Dunn and Arnold M. Barban, *Advertising: Its Role in Modern Marketing* (Hinsdale, Ill.: The Dryden Press, 1982), p. 7.

[4] Committee on Definitions, *Marketing Definitions: A Glossary of Marketing Terms* (Chicago: American Marketing Association, 1960), p. 20. Italics added.

[5] "Market Research Facts and Trends" (Maclean-Hunter Research Bureau, 1981), p. 1.

[6] Frances Phillips, "Advertisers Seek Ways to Curb the Cost of TV Ads," *The Financial Post*, May 19, 1984, p. 14.

[7] Terrence V. O'Brien, "Psychologists Take a New Look at Today's Consumer," *Arizona Review* (August–September 1970), p. 2.

[8] "Cadbury Gets Back in the Thick of the Action," *Marketing*, June 1, 1981, p. 1.

[9] *Markets and Marketing: An Orientation* by Lee E. Preston (Glenview, Ill.: Scott, Foresman and Company, 1970), p. 198. Copyright © 1970 by Scott, Foresman and Company. Reprinted by permission of the publisher.

[10] Charles G. Burch, "While the Big Brewers Quaff, the Little Ones Thirst," *Fortune*, November 1972, p. 107.

[11] Reported in *Marketing Science Institute Research Briefs* (December 1975), p. 1.

[12] Francis X. Callahan, "Does Advertising Subsidize Information?" *Journal of Advertising Research* (August 1978), pp. 19–22.

Chapter 19

[1] Rob Wilson, "Honda's Corporate Drive," *Marketing*, October 17, 1983, p. 1.

[2] *A Report on Advertising Revenues in Canada* (Toronto: Maclean-Hunter Research Bureau, 1978), p. 3.

[3] Francis Phillips, "Bring Back The Good Old Days," *The Financial Post 500*, Summer, 1984, p. 200.

[4] This section follows in part the discussion in S. Watson Dunn and Arnold Barban, *Advertising: Its Role in Modern Marketing*, 3rd ed. (Hinsdale, Ill.: The Dryden Press, 1974), p. 5.

[5] David A. Aaker and J. Gary Shansby, "Positioning Your Product," *Business Horizons* (May/June 1982), p. 62. Reprinted by permission of the publisher.

[6] "Gulf to Tell a $3-Million Story," *Marketing*, May 25, 1981, p. 1.

[7] *Controversy Advertising: How Advertisers Present Points of View in Public Affairs; A Worldwide Study by the International Advertising Association* (New York: Communication Arts Books, 1977), p. 18.

[8] The discussion of various advertising media is adapted from material in S. Watson Dunn and Arnold Barban, *Advertising: Its Role in Modern Marketing*, 5th ed. (Hinsdale, Ill.: Dryden Press, 1982), pp. 512–591.

[9] The 1980 advertising volume percentages for the four major media (newspapers, television, magazines, and radio) are estimated by Maclean-Hunter Research Bureau, Toronto.

10 Patrick Dunne, "Some Demographic Characteristics of Direct Mail Purchasers," *Baylor Business Studies* (July 1975), pp. 67–72.

11 William M. Carley, "Gillette Co. Struggles as Its Rivals Slice at Fat Profit Margin," *The Wall Street Journal*, February 2, 1972, p. 1. Reprinted by permission.

12 Hershey H. Friedman and Linda W. Friedman, "Does the Celebrity Endorser's Image Spill Over to the Product?" *The Journal of Business* (May 1980), pp. 31–36.

13 This section is based on Jamie Wayne, "No Easy Way To Sports Promotion," *Financial Post*, February 7, 1981, p. 15.

14 Bill Abrams, "Comparative Ads Are Getting More Popular, Harder Hitting," *The Wall Street Journal*, March 11, 1982, p. 27.

15 Joseph N. Fry and Gordon H. McDougall, "Consumer Appraisal of Retail Price Advertisements," *Journal of Marketing* (July 1974), pp. 64–67.

16 This section is based on Tony Thompson, "Retail Advertisers 'Enter 20th Century,' " *Advertising Age*, October 13, 1980, p. 51.

17 This section is based on S. Watson Dunn and Arnold Barban, *Advertising: Its Role in Modern Marketing*, 4th ed. (Hinsdale, Ill.: Dryden Press, 1978), pp. 287–310.

18 Committee on Definitions, *Marketing Definitions: A Glossary of Marketing Terms* (Chicago: American Marketing Association, 1960), p. 20.

19 This definition is adapted from "How to Play Championship Specialty Advertising," (Chicago: Specialty Advertising Association International, 1978).

20 Walter A. Gaw, *Specialty Advertising* (Chicago: Specialty Advertising Association, 1970), p. 7.

21 *Specialty Advertising Report* (Second Quarter 1979), pp. 1–2.

22 "Gulf Metals Find Little Bits Count," *Specialty Advertising Report*, Vol. VII. No. 3, p. 2, published by the Specialty Advertising Information Bureau, Chicago, Ill.

23 Thomas V. Bonoma, "Get More Out of Your Trade Shows," *Harvard Business Review* (January–February 1983), pp. 75–83.

24 Committee on Definitions, *Marketing Definitions: A Glossary of Marketing Terms* (Chicago: American Marketing Association, 1960), p. 18.

25 The data in this section is from Alvin P. Sanoff, "Image Makers Worry about their Own Images," *U.S. News & World Report*, August 13, 1979, pp. 57–59; "The Corporate Image: PR to the Rescue," *Business Week*, January 22, 1979, pp. 46–50, 54, 56, 60–61; and Fred Kirsch, "No Slick Tricks in One-Man P.R. Firm," *Detroit News*, April 17, 1978, pp. 1-C, 3-C.

26 Gene Harlan and Alan Scott, *Contemporary Public Relations: Principles and Cases* (Englewood Cliffs, N.J.: Prentice-Hall, 1955), p. 36.

Chapter 20

1 The remainder of this section is based on David L. Kurtz, "The Historical Development of Selling," *Business and Economic Dimensions* (August 1970), pp. 12–18.

2 Reported in "Sell, Sell, Sell," *The Wall Street Journal*, September 14, 1971, p. 1.

3 Joel Saegert and Robert J. Hoover, "Sales Managers and Sales Force Feedback: Information Left in the Pipeline," *Journal of the Academy of Marketing Science* (Winter/Spring 1980), pp. 33–39.

4 Quoted in James Samuel Knox, *Salesmanship and Business Efficiency* (New York: The Gregg Publishing Company, 1922), pp. 243–244.

[5] Leslie M. Dawson, "Toward a New Concept of Sales Management," *Journal of Marketing* (April 1970), p. 38.

[6] The advantages and disadvantages of the commission, salary, and combination plans are adapted by permission from John P. Steinbrink, "How to Pay Your Sales Force," *Harvard Business Review* (July–August 1978), p. 113. Copyright © 1978 by the President and Fellows of Harvard College; all rights reserved.

[7] This section is adapted from H. Robert Dodge, *Field Sales Management* (Dallas: Business Publications, Inc., 1973), pp. 337–38.

[8] Fremont A. Shull, Jr., Andre L. Delbecq, and L. L. Cummings, *Organizational Decision Making* (New York: McGraw-Hill, 1970), p. 215.

Glossary

Note: Number in parentheses indicates chapter where term first appears.

Absolute advantage In international marketing, the relative position of a nation that is the sole producer of a product or that produces the product more cheaply than other nations can.

Accelerator principle The disproportionate impact that changes in consumer demand has upon industrial market demand.

Accessory equipment (9) Capital items such as typewriters, hand tools, small lathes, and adding machines. They are usually less expensive and shorter-lived than installations.

Active exporting In international marketing, the activities of a firm that has made a commitment to seek export business.

Administered vertical marketing system (14) A VMS in which channel co-ordination is achieved through the exercise of economic and political power by the dominant member. *See also* Channel captain.

Adoption process The various decisions a consumer makes about a new product. The consumer adoption process has several identifiable stages: awareness, interest, evaluation, trial, and adoption.

Advertising (18, 19) A nonpersonal sales presentation usually directed to a large number of potential customers.

Advertising agency (19) Independent businesses used to assist advertisers in planning and implementing advertising programs.

Advocacy advertising (19) A paid public communication or message that presents information or a point of view bearing on a publicly recognized controversial issue.

Agent wholesaling middleman (14, 15) A middleman who performs wholesaling functions but does not take title to the products handled. Sometimes called *agent*.

AIO statements (4) *See* Psychographics.

Approach (20) The step in the sales process that involves the initial contact between seller and buyer.

Area sampling (19) Used when population lists are unavailable for sampling. Blocks instead of individuals are selected at random. Then everyone on the selected block is interviewed or, in some cases, respondents are randomly selected from each designated block.

Asch phenomenon (7) An occurrence first documented by the psychologist S. E. Asch, which illustrates the effect of the reference group on individual decision-making.

Aspirational group (7) A sub-category of a reference group where the member desires to associate with a group.

Attitude (8) One's enduring favourable or unfavourable evaluations, emotional feelings, or pro or con action tendencies.

Auction house (15) An agent wholesaling middleman who brings buyers and sellers of such products as used cars, livestock, antiques, and tobacco together in one location and allows potential buyers to inspect the merchandise physically before purchasing.

Average cost (12, 13) Obtained by dividing total cost by the quantity associated with these costs.

Average fixed cost (12, 13) Determined by dividing total fixed costs by the related quantity.

Average revenue (12, 13) Obtained by dividing total revenue by the related quantity. The average revenue line is actually the demand curve facing the firm.

Average variable cost (12, 13) The total variable costs divided by the related quantity.

Balance of payments The money flow into or out of a country.

Balance of trade The relationship between a nation's exports and imports.

Bartering The exchange of one product for another instead of for money.

Benefit segmentation (4) Dividing a population into homogenous groups based on the benefits the consumer expects to derive from the product.

Bid (13) In the industrial market, a written sales proposal from a vendor to a firm that wants to purchase a good or service.

Bottom line Business jargon referring to the overall profitability measure of performance.

Brand (10) A name, term, sign, symbol, design, or some combination used to identify the products of one firm and to differentiate them from competitive offerings.

Brand insistence (10) The ultimate stage in brand acceptance when consumers will accept no alternatives and will search extensively for the product.

Brand name (10) That part of the brand consisting of words or letters making up a name used to identify and distinguish the firm's offerings from those of competitors. The brand name is that part of the brand that may be vocalized.

Brand preference (10) The second stage of brand acceptance. Based on previous experience with the product, consumers will choose it rather than a competitor's — if it is available.

Brand recognition (10) The first stage of brand acceptance, when the consumer is able to identify a specific brand.

Break-bulk centre (17) A central warehouse where economical carload and truckload shipments are disassembled and then redistributed to numerous customers over shorter distances at the higher less-than-carload or--truckload rates.

Break-even analysis (12) A tool for assessing the profit consequences of alternative prices. The *break-even point* (in units) equals total fixed cost divided by the per-unit contribution to fixed cost.

Broadening concept An idea introduced by Philip Kotler and Sidney J. Levy, suggesting that marketing is a generic function to be performed by all organizations.

Broker (15) An agent wholesaling middleman who facilitates marketing operations by bringing together small, geographically dispersed sellers and buyers.

Buyer's market (1) A market with an abundance of goods and services.

Buying centre Refers to everyone who participates — in some fashion — in an industrial buying action.

Canadian Transport Commission (17) Established by the National Transportation Act, it is responsible for the air, rail, pipeline, and water components of the transportation industry.

Canned approach (20) A memorized sales presentation used to ensure uniform coverage of the points deemed important by management.

Cannibalizing (10) A product that takes sales from another offering in a product line. Marketing research should take steps to see that cannibalizing is minimized or at least anticipated.

Capital items Long-lived business assets that must be depreciated over time.

Cartel A monopolistic organization of firms.

Cash-and-carry wholesaler (15) A merchant wholesaler who does not offer credit and delivery services.

Cash discount (13) Deduction from list price that is given for prompt payment of a bill.

Casual exporting The activities of a firm that takes a passive level of involvement in international marketing.

Catalogue retailer (16) A merchant who operates from a showroom displaying samples of the product line. Customers order from the store's catalogue and orders are filled from a warehouse, usually on the premises.

Census (6) Collection of marketing data from all possible sources.

Chain stores (16) Groups of retail stores centrally owned and managed, and handling the same lines of products.

Channel captain (14) The dominant member of each channel, who assumes the responsibility for obtaining cooperation among the individual channel members.

Channel conflict (14) Competition between channel members.

Channels of distribution (14) *See* Marketing channels.

Charter (9) A document drawn up by a manufacturing firm specifically defining the functions, operating procedures, and other guidelines for a venture team. Also known as a *venture team charter*.

Class action A legal suit brought by private citizens on behalf of a group of consumers for damages caused by unfair business practices.

Closed sales territories (14) Restricted geographic selling regions ordered by a manufacturer for its distributors.

Closing (20) The step in the sales process when the salesperson actually asks the prospect for an order.

Cluster sample (6) A sampling technique where areas or clusters are selected, then all or a sample within them become respondents.

Cognitions (8) An individual's knowledge, beliefs, and attitudes about certain events.

Cognitive dissonance (8) The postpurchase anxiety that occurs when an imbalance exists among a person's cognitions (knowledge, beliefs, and attitudes).

Cold canvassing (20) Unsolicited sales calls upon a random group of people; the prospecting and qualifying effort is minimal.

Combination plan (20) A method of compensating sales personnel by using a base salary along with a commission incentive.

Combines Investigation Act (2) Canada's major legislation regulating business relationships (e.g. monopolies) and business practices. It deals with pricing, advertising, exclusive dealing, and other practices.

Commission (20) Payment directly tied to the sales or profits achieved by a salesperson.

Commission merchant (15) An agent wholesaling middleman who exercises physical control over and negotiates the sale of goods that he or she handles.

Commodity rate (17) Sometimes called a special rate, since it is given by carriers to shippers as a reward for either regular use or large quantity shipments.

Common carrier (17) A regulated carrier who offers transportation services to all shippers.

Common market In international marketing, a format for multinational economic integration involving a customs union and continuing efforts to standardize trade regulations of all governments. *See also* Customs union.

Communications (18) The transmission of a message from a sender (or source) to a receiver (or recipient).

Community shopping centre (16) A group of 15 to 50 retail stores, often including a branch of a department store as the primary tenant. This type of centre typically serves 20 000 to 100 000 persons within a radius of a few kilometres.

Comparative advantage (20) In international marketing, the relative position of a nation that can produce one particular product more efficiently than it can produce alternative products.

Comparative advertising (19) A type of persuasive product advertising that makes direct comparisons with competitive brands.

Competitive bidding (13) A process by which buyers request potential suppliers to make price quotations on a proposed purchase or contract.

Competitive environment (2) The interactive process that occurs in the marketplace.

Component parts and materials (9) In the industrial market, the finished industrial goods that actually become part of the final product.

Concentrated marketing (5) An extreme form of differentiated marketing, where a firm selects one segment of the total market and devotes all of its marketing resources to satisfying this single segment.

Concept testing (10) The evaluation of a product idea prior to the actual development of the physical product in the new-product development process.

Consumer behaviour (7, 8) The acts and decision processes involved in obtaining and using goods and services.

Consumer goods (4) Products destined for use by the ultimate consumer and not intended for resale or further use in producing other goods.

Consumer innovator (9) The first purchaser of new products and services.

Consumer market Individuals who purchase goods and services for personal use.

Consumer rights The rights to safety, to be informed, to choose, and to be heard.

Consumerism A demand that marketers give greater attention to consumer wants and desires in making their decisions.

Containerization (17) The combination of several unitized loads of products into a single load, facilitating intertransport changes in transportation modes.

Contract carrier (17) A carrier that establishes specific contracts with a few customers and does not offer its services to the general public.

Contractual vertical marketing system (14) A VMS where channel co-ordination is achieved through formal agreements between channel members. The three types of contractual systems are wholesaler-sponsored voluntary chains, retail co-operatives, and franchise organizations.

Control charts Diagrams that plot a firm's actual performance against established limits.

Convenience goods (9) Those items the consumer wants to purchase frequently, immediately, and with little effort, such as milk, bread, and gasoline. Convenience goods are usually branded and are low-priced.

Convenience retailer (16) One who sells to the ultimate consumer and focusses chiefly on a central location, long store hours, rapid checkout, and adequate parking facilities.

Convenience sample (6) A nonprobability sample based on the selection of readily available respondents.

Co-operative advertising (19) A program in which advertising costs are shared between retailers and the manufacturer or vendor.

Corporate vertical marketing system (14) A VMS created through single ownership of each stage in the marketing channel.

Cost-plus pricing (12) An approach to price determination using cost as the base to which a profit factor is added.

There are two cost-plus pricing procedures: *full-cost* pricing, which uses all relevant variable costs in setting a product's price, and the *incremental approach*, which considers only those costs directly attributable to a specific output.

Cost trade-offs (17) The "total system" approach to physical distribution, whereby some functional areas of the firm will experience cost increases while others will have cost reductions, but the result will be that *total* physical distribution costs will be minimized.

Coupon (19) A sales promotion technique that offers a discount from the next purchase of a product.

Creative selling (20) A basic sales task that characterizes purchases involving a considerable degree of analytical decision-making on the part of the consumer.

Cues (8) Any objects existing in the environment that determine the nature of the response to a drive.

Culture (7) A learned way of life including values, ideas, and attitudes that influence consumer behaviour.

Customary pricing (12) Price-setting by custom or tradition in the marketplace.

Customer service standards (17) The quality of service that the firm's customers will receive.

Customs union In international marketing, a format for multinational economic integration that sets up a free trade area for member nations and a uniform tariff for nonmember nations.

Decoding (18) The consumer's interpretation of the sender's message.

Demand curve (12) A schedule relating the quantity demanded to specific prices. It is the average revenue line.

Demand variability (10) In the industrial market, the impact of derived demand on the demand for interrelated products used in producing consumer goods.

Demarketing (2) The process of cutting consumer demand for a product back to a level that can reasonably be supplied by the firm.

Demographics (9) The characteristics of potential buyers; for example, age, sex, and income level.

Demographic segmentation (7) Dividing a population into homogeneous groups based on characteristics such as age, sex, and income level.

Demonstration (20) The step in the selling process when the salesperson actually involves the prospect in the presentation by allowing him or her to use, test, or experiment with the product.

Department store (16) A large retailer organized into separate departments for purposes of promotion, service, and control. A department store typically stocks a wide variety of shopping and specialty goods, including women's ready-to-wear and accessories, men's and boys' wear, piece goods, and home furnishings.

Depreciation The accounting concept of charting a portion of a capital item as a deduction against the company's annual revenue for purposes of determining its net income.

Derived demand In the industrial market, the demand for an industrial product that is linked to demand for a consumer good.

Detailers (20) Special representatives of firms in the health-care industry, who familiarize physicians and hospitals with the firms' products.

Devaluation When a nation reduces the value of its currency in relation to gold or some other currency.

Differentiated marketing (5) The development of different marketing programs for each segment of the total market.

Diffusion process (9) The way in which new products are adopted by customers in a particular community or social system.

Direct-sales results test (18) A tool for measuring the effectiveness of promotional expenditures, by ascertaining the increase in revenue per dollar spent.

Disassociative group (7) A sub-category of a reference group, one in which an individual does not want to be identified with by others.

Discount house (16) A retail operation that competes on the basis of price appeal by operating on a relatively low markup and minimal customer services.

Discretionary income (6) That part of total income that remains after expenditures for necessities.

Distribution channel (14) Refers to the various marketing institutions and their interrelationships responsible for the physical and title flow of goods and services from producer to consumer or industrial user.

Distribution strategy (1) An element of marketing decision-making dealing with the physical handling of goods and the selection of marketing channels.

Distribution warehouse (17) A place to assemble and then redistribute products. The objective of the distribution warehouse is to facilitate rapid movement of products to the purchasers rather than to serve as a storage facility.

Distributor *See* Wholesaler.

Drive (8) Any strong stimulus that impels action.

Drop shipper (15) A merchant wholesaler who sells for delivery by the producer direct to the buyer. The shipper usually does not carry inventories but consolidates orders to be filled by several producers.

Dumping Situations where products are sold at significantly lower prices in a foreign market than in a nation's own domestic market.

Ecology The relationship between people and their environment.

Economic environment (2) A setting of complex and dynamic business fluctuations that historically tended to follow a four-stage pattern: 1) recession, 2) depression, 3) recovery, and 4) prosperity.

Economic order quantity (EOQ) (17) The optimum order quantity of each product. The optimum point is determined by balancing the costs of holding inventory and the costs involved in placing orders.

Ecumene (6) Inhabited space; in Canada, this is mainly the East-West strip of land adjacent to the American border.

Elasticity (12) A measure of responsiveness of purchasers and suppliers to a change in price.

Embargo A complete ban of certain products.

Encoding (18) Translating a message into terms understandable to a receiver.

Engel's Laws (4) An early spending behaviour study published by a German statistician, Ernst Engel. He advanced three generalizations about the spending resulting from increases in family income: 1) a smaller percentage of expenditures would go for food; 2) the percentage spent on housing and household operations and clothing will remain constant; and 3) the percentage spent on other items will increase.

EOQ *See* Economic Order Quantity.

Escalator clause (13) In pricing, part of many bids allowing the seller to adjust the final price, based upon changes in the costs of the product's ingredients, between the placement of the order and the completion of construction or delivery of the product.

Ethics *See* Marketing ethics.

Evaluation and control The various assessments that marketers employ to determine whether all phases of a marketing program have been effective.

Evaluative criteria (8) In consumer decision-making, the features considered in a consumer's choice of alternatives.

Evoked set (8) In consumer decision-making, the number of brands that a consumer actually considers before making a purchase decision.

Exchange control When firms gaining foreign exchange by exporting must sell their foreign exchange to a control authority, while importers must buy foreign exchange from the same organization. Exchange control is a method of regulating foreign trade.

Exchange process (1) The process by which two or more parties give something of value to one another to satisfy felt needs.

Exchange rate The rate at which a nation's currency can be exchanged for other currencies or gold.

Exclusive dealing (14) A contract prohibiting a middleman from handling competing products. Such a contract is legal except in those cases where it has the effect of "substantially lessening competition or tending to create a monopoly."

Exclusive distribution (14) An extreme form of selective distribution wherein the manufacturer grants exclusive rights to a wholesaler or retailer to sell in a geographic region.

Expected net profit (13) A concept employed in competitive bidding strategy. Expected net profit equals the probability of the buyer accepting the bid *times* the bid price *minus* related costs.

Expense item Industrial products and services that are used within a short period of time.

Experience curve The idea that higher market shares reduce costs because of factors like learning advantages, increased specialization, higher investment, and economies of scale.

Experiment (6) A scientific investigation in which a researcher controls or manipulates a test group or groups and compares the results with that of a control group that did not receive the controls or manipulations.

Exploratory research (6) Research designed to give the researcher an intelligent understanding of the problem area and some insights into its causes and effects.

Exporting Selling goods and services abroad.

External data (8) In marketing research, the type of secondary data that comes from sources outside a firm.

Fabricated parts and materials (10) Industrial goods that actually become a part of the final product.

Facilitating agencies (14) Institutions, such as insurance companies, banks, and transportation companies, that provide specialized assistance to channel members in moving the product from producer to consumer.

Fads (9) Fashions with abbreviated life cycles. Examples include disco, punk, and new wave.

Family brand (10) A brand name that is used for several products made by the same firm, such as General Electric or Johnson & Johnson.

Family life cycle (4) The process of family formulation and dissolution. The stages of the cycle include the bachelor stage, young married couples with no children, young married couples with children, older married couples with dependent children, older married couples with no children at home, and solitary survivors.

Fashions (9) Currently popular products that tend to follow recurring life cycles.

FCN treaties Friendship, commerce, and navigation treaties that include many aspects of world marketing.

Feedback (18) Information about receiver response to messages. This data is returned to the sender.

Fiscal policy (2) The use of taxation and government spending as a means of controlling the economy.

Fixed costs (12) Costs that do not vary with differences in output, such as depreciation and insurance.

Fixed sum per unit (18) A budget allocation method under which a predetermined promotional amount is allocated, either on an historical or forecasted basis.

Flanker brands (10) The introduction of new products into the market in which the company has established positions in an attempt to increase overall market share. For example, Butcher's Blend Dry Dog Food is Ralston Purina's flanker to their Dog Chow line.

Flexible pricing (13) A pricing policy allowing variable prices.

F.O.B. plant (13) A price quotation that does not include any shipping charges. The abbreviation refers to Free on Board. The buyer must pay all freight charges. Also called *F.O.B. origin*.

F.O.B. plant with freight allowed (13) A price quotation where the seller permits the buyer to deduct transportation expenses from the invoice.

Focus group interview (6) A marketing research information-gathering procedure that typically brings eight to 12 individuals together in one location to discuss a given subject.

Follow-up (20) The step in the sales process that concerns postsales activities.

Foreign freight forwarders (17) Transportation middlemen who specialize in physical distribution outside Canada.

Foreign licensing In international marketing, an agreement between a firm and a foreign company, whereby the foreign company produces and distributes the firm's goods in the foreign country.

Form utility (1) Created when raw materials are converted into finished products.

Franchise (14) An agreement whereby dealers (franchisees) agree to meet the operating requirements of a manufacturer or other franchiser.

Free trade area In international marketing, economic integration among participating nations, without any tariff or trade restrictions.

Freight absorption (13) A pricing system under which the buyer of goods may deduct shipping expenses from the cost of the goods.

Freight forwarder (17) A wholesaling middleman who consolidates shipments from several shippers to enable them to achieve the cost savings of truckload or carload shipments.

Full-cost pricing (12) A pricing procedure in which all costs are considered in setting a price, allowing the firm to recover all of its costs and realize a profit.

Full-function merchant wholesaler (17) A wholesaling middleman who provides a complete assortment of services for retail customers, including storage, regular contacts through a sales force, delivery, credit, returns privileges, and market information.

Full service research supplier (6) An independent marketing research firm that contracts with a client to conduct the complete marketing research project. They define the problem or conceptual stage; work through the research, design, data collection, and analysis stages; and prepare the final report to management.

Functional accounts Income statement expense categories representing the purpose for which an expenditure is made.

GATT *See* General Agreement on Tariffs and Trade.

General Agreement on Tariffs and Trade (GATT) An international trade accord that has sponsored various tariff negotiations.

General merchandise retailer (16) A retail store that carries a wide variety of product lines, all of which are stocked in some depth. General merchandise retailers would include department stores, variety stores, and many discount houses.

Generic name (10) A commonly used word that is descriptive of a particular type of product, such as cola or nylon.

Generic product (10) A food or household item characterized by plain labels, little or no advertising, and no brand name.

Geographic segmentation (4) Dividing a population into homogeneous groups on the basis of location.

Goods – services continuum (11) A method of presenting the differences and similarities among goods and services.

Gross margin percentage An evaluative technique indicating the percentage of revenues available for covering expenses and earning a profit after the payment of the production costs of products sold during a certain time period.

House-to-house retailing (16) Direct contact between the retailer-seller and the customer at the home of the customer.

Hypermarket (16) A giant mass-merchandising retail outlet that operates on a low-price, is self-service, and carries lines of soft goods and groceries. Also called *hypermarché*.

Hypothesis (6) A tentative explanation about some specific event. A hypothesis is a statement about the relationship between variables and carries clear implications for testing this relationship.

Iceberg principle A theory that suggests that important evaluative information is often hidden by collected data when it exists in a summary format.

Idea marketing The identification and marketing of a cause to chosen consumer segments.

Importing Purchasing foreign goods and raw materials.

Import quota A restriction on the amount of goods in a specific product category that may enter a country.

Impulse goods (9) Products for which the consumer spends little time in conscious deliberation in making a purchase decision. Such products are often displayed near cash registers in retail stores to induce spur-of-the-moment consumer purchases.

Incremental-cost pricing (12) A pricing procedure in which only the costs directly attributable to a specific output are considered in setting a price.

Individual brand (10) The strategy of giving each item in a product line its own brand name, rather than identifying it by a single name used for all products in the line. An example would be the many detergents marketed by Procter & Gamble — Tide, Cheer, Oxydol, and so on. *See also* Family brand.

Individual offerings (10) One of the primary components of a product mix, it consists of single products.

Industrial distributor (9) A wholesaling middleman who operates in the industrial goods market and typically handles small accessory equipment and operating supplies.

Industrial goods (4) Products that are used directly or indirectly in producing other goods for resale.

Industrial goods market A marketplace made up of customers who purchase goods and services for use in producing other products for resale. Examples include manufacturers, utilities, government agencies, retailers, wholesalers, contractors, mining firms, insurance and real estate firms, and institutions, such as schools and hospitals.

Inflation (2) A generally rising price level resulting in reduced purchasing power for the consumer.

Informative institutional advertising (19) Advertising intended to increase public knowledge of a concept, idea, philosophy, industry, or company.

Informative product advertising (19) Advertising intended to develop initial demand for a product.

Input-output models (3) Quantitative forecasting techniques first developed by Wassily Leontif which show the impact on supplier industries of production changes in a given industry and which can be utilized in measuring the impact of changing demand in any industry throughout an economy.

Installations (9) A firm's major capital assets such as factories and heavy machinery. They are relatively long-lived and are expensive. Their purchase represents a major decision for a company.

Institutional advertising (19) Promoting a concept, idea, philosophy, or goodwill of an industry, company, or organization.

Intangible products (11) Products best illustrated by services such as legal advice or a medical examination.

Intensive distribution (14) Practised by marketers of convenience goods who attempt to provide saturation coverage of a given market with their products.

Intermediary (14) A business firm operating between the producer and the consumer or industrial purchaser. Both wholesaler and retailer are included in the definition of intermediary.

Internal secondary data (6) In marketing research, the type of information that is found in records of sales, product performances, sales force activities, and marketing costs.

Inventory adjustments (10) Changes in the amounts of raw materials or goods in process a manufacturer keeps on hand.

Inventory turnover An evaluative figure showing how many times the average value of a firm's stock of merchandise is sold in a year.

Jobber (14) *See* Wholesaler.

Job-order production (14) A production system in which products are manufactured to fill customers' orders.

Joint demand In the industrial market, the demand for

an industrial good as related to the demand for another industrial good that is necessary for the use of the first item.

Joint venture A foreign enterprise jointly held with a national of the country involved.

Judgement sample (6) A nonprobability sample of people with a specific attribute.

Jury of executive opinion (3) A qualitative sales forecasting method which combines and averages the outlook of top executives from such functional areas as finance, production, marketing, and purchasing.

Just price (12) A concept held by the early philosophers. Essentially, they believed that there was one fair price for each good or service.

Label (10) The descriptive part of the package, which usually contains the brand name or symbol, name and address of the manufacturer or distributor, product composition and size, and recommended uses of the product.

Law of retail gravitation (18) Sets the retail trade area of a potential site on the basis of mileage between alternative locations and relative populations.

Learning (8) Any change in behaviour as a result of experience.

Life-cycle costing In the industrial market, the cost of using a product over its lifetime.

Lifestyle (4) The mode of living of consumers.

Limited-function merchant wholesaler (15) A wholesaling middleman who reduces the number of services provided to retail customers and also reduces the costs of servicing such customers.

Limited-line store (16) A retail store that competes with larger stores by offering a complete selection of a narrow line of merchandise such as clothing, hardware, shoes, or sporting goods.

Line extension (10) A new product that is closely related to existing product lines.

List price (13) The rate that is normally quoted to potential buyers. It is the basis upon which most price structures are built.

Local-content law In international marketing, laws specifying the portion of a product that must come from domestic sources.

Loss leader (13) A good priced at less than cost in order to attract customers who may then buy other regularly priced merchandise.

Mail order wholesaler (15) Limited-function merchant wholesalers who utilize catalogues instead of a sales force

to contact their customers in an attempt to reduce operating expense.

Make-bulk centre (17) A central warehouse where individual small shipments of products are shipped small distances at high freight rates, reassembled into economical carload or truckload quantities, and then shipped over longer distances to a large customer or to a storage warehouse.

Manufacturers' agent (15) An agent wholesaling middleman who markets a line of related but noncompeting products for a number of manufacturers. The agent usually operates on a contractual basis and covers a limited territory.

Marginal analysis (12, 18) A budgeting procedure, the objective of which is to allocate the same amount for an expenditure (such as promotion) that the expenditure will generate in profits.

Marginal cost (12) The change in total cost that results from producing an additional unit of output.

Marginal revenue (12, 18) The change in total revenue that results from selling an additional unit of output.

Markdown (12) A reduction in the price of an item.

Market (4) Customers who possess purchasing power and both the willingness and the authority to buy.

Market price (13) The amount a consumer or middleman pays for a product.

Market segmentation (4, 7) Companies producing numerous separate products and designing different marketing mixes to satisfy smaller homogeneous segments of the total market.

Market share The percentage of a submarket controlled by a particular seller. The attainment of a specific market share is a common primary objective advocated by many companies.

Market share objective (12) Pricing objective linked to achieving and maintaining a stated percentage of the market for a firm's product or service.

Market target (5) A specific segment of the overall potential market that has been analysed and selected by the firm. The firm's marketing mix will be directed toward satisfying this chosen consumer segment.

Market target decision analysis (5) The evaluation of potential market segments by dividing the overall market into homogeneous groupings. Cross-classifications may be based on such variables as type of market, geographic location, use frequency, and demographic characteristics.

Marketing (1) The development and efficient distribution of goods, services, ideas, issues, and concepts for chosen consumer segments.

Marketing audit A thorough, objective evaluation of an organization's marketing philosophy, goals, policies, procedures, practices, and results.

Marketing channels (1, 14) The path a good or service follows from producer to final consumer.

Marketing communications (18) Messages that deal with buyer-seller relationships.

Marketing concept (1) A managerial philosophy of consumer orientation. The marketing concept holds that all planning begins with an analysis of the consumer and that all company decisions are based upon profitable satisfaction of consumer wants.

Marketing cost analysis The evaluation of such items as selling costs, billing, warehousing, advertising, and delivery expenses, to determine the profitability of particular customers, territories, and product lines. It involves classifying accounting data into *functional* accounts (by the purpose for which each expenditure was made) rather than the traditional *natural* accounts, such as salaries and supplies.

Marketing ethics The marketer's standards of conduct and moral values.

Marketing functions (1) Buying, selling, transporting, storing, grading, financing, entrepreneurial risk-taking, and marketing information.

Marketing Information System (MIS) (6) A systematic approach to providing relevant information to decision-makers on a continual basis.

Marketing institutions (14) Include such middlemen as retailers and wholesalers.

Marketing mix (1) The blending of the elements of product planning, price, distribution strategy, and promotion to satisfy chosen consumer segments.

Marketing myopia (1, 11) A term coined by Theodore Levitt that identifies his thesis that top executives in many industries have failed to recognize the scope of their businesses. Levitt argues that they lack a marketing orientation.

Marketing planning (3) The implementation of planning activity as it relates to the achievement of marketing objectives.

Marketing research (6) The systematic gathering, recording, and analysing of data about problems relating to the marketing of goods and services.

Marketing strategy (3) The overall company program for selecting a particular market segment and then satisfying the segment through the careful use of the elements of the marketing mix.

Mark-on (12) Markup compared against cost of a product, expressed as a percentage.

Markup (12) The amount that is added to cost to determine the selling price.

Maslow's hierarchy (8) A classification of needs whereby priority is assigned to the basic needs that must be at least partially satisfied before proceeding to the next order of needs. The hierarchy proceeds from physiological needs to safety to social needs to esteem to self-actualization.

Mass merchandisers (16) Retailers stocking a wider line of products than department stores, but in less depth.

Material handling (17) All the activities associated in moving products among the manufacturer's plants, warehouses, and transportation company terminals.

Membership groups (7) A sub-category for a reference group, where the members of the reference group belong to, say, a country club.

Merchandise mart (15) A permanent exhibition facility where manufacturers rent showcases for their product offerings and display them for visiting retail and wholesale buyers.

Merchant wholesaler (15) A wholesaler middleman who takes *title* to products.

Message (18) Information transmitted by a (marketing) communication system.

Middleman *See* Intermediary.

Misleading advertising (2) A false statement of any kind made to the public about products or services.

Missionary sales (20) A basic sales task. It is an indirect type of selling that can be subclassified into selling the goodwill of a firm and providing the customer with technical or operational assistance.

Missionary salesperson (14) A manufacturer's representative who assists wholesalers and retailers in becoming more familiar with the firm's products and aids in store displays and promotional planning.

Modified breakeven analysis (12) A pricing technique that combines the traditional breakeven analysis model with an evaluation of consumer demand.

Modified rebuy A situation where industrial purchasers are willing to re-evaluate their available options in a repurchase of the same product or service. Lower prices, faster delivery, or higher quality may be buyer desires in this type of purchase situation.

Monetary policy (2) Various techniques used by the Bank of Canada to control the money supply and interest rates as a means of controlling the economy.

Monopolistic competition (12) A market situation where a large number of sellers offer a heterogeneous product. The existence of product differentiation allows the marketer some degree of control over price. This situation is characteristic of most retailing.

Monopoly (12) A market situation with only one seller of a product with no close substitutes. Anti-combines legislation has attempted to eliminate all but *temporary* monopolies, such as those provided by patent protection, and *regulated* monopolies, such as the public service companies.

Motive (8) An internal tension state that directs individuals toward the goal of satisfying a felt need.

MRO items (9) Supplies for an industrial firm, so called because they can be categorized as maintenance items, repair items, or operating supplies.

Multinational corporation A firm that operates in several countries and literally views the world as its market.

National brands (10) Those offered by manufacturers. In fact, they are sometimes called *manufacturer's brands*.

National Transportation Act (17) Defines transportation policy in Canada.

Natural accounts Expense categories traditionally listed on an organization's income statement. An example is salary expenses.

Need (8) The lack of something useful; a discrepancy between a desired state and the actual state.

Negotiated contract (10) Sometimes used in industrial and governmental purchases when there is only one available supplier and/or contracts requiring extensive research and development work.

Neighbourhood shopping centre (16) A geographical cluster of stores, usually consisting of a supermarket and about 5 to 15 smaller stores. The centre provides convenient shopping for 5 000 to 15 000 shoppers in its vicinity.

Net profit percentage An evaluative technique reflecting the ratio of net profits to net sales for an organization.

New-product department (9) A separate, formally organized division that is involved with new-product development on a permanent, full-time basis.

New product committee (10) An inter-disciplinary group on temporary assignment that works through functional departments. Its basic task is to coordinate and integrate the work of these functional departments on some specific project.

New task buying Refers to first time or unique industrial purchase situations that require considerable effort on the part of the decision makers.

Noise (20) Interruptions in a communications system.

Nonprobability sample (6) Sample chosen in an arbitrary

fashion in which each member of the population does not have a representative chance of being selected.

Nonprofit organization A firm whose primary objective is something other than the return of a profit to its owners.

Observational study (6) Conducted by actually viewing (either by visual observation or through mechanical means such as hidden cameras) the overt actions of the respondent.

Odd pricing (13) A type of psychological pricing that uses prices with odd endings, such as $16.99, $17.95, and $18.98. Originally, odd pricing was initiated to force clerks to make change, thus serving as a cash control device within the firm.

Oligopoly (12) A market situation with relatively few sellers, such as in the automobile, steel, tobacco, and petroleum-refining industries. There are significant entry barriers to new competition due to high start-up costs.

Open dating Shows the last possible date that a perishable or semiperishable food item may be sold.

Operating expense ratio An evaluative technique that combines both selling and general expenses and compares them with overall net sales.

Opinion leader (7) An individual in any group who is the trendsetter. The opinion of such individuals is respected, and they are often sought out for advice. Opinion leaders serve as information sources about new products.

Order processing (20) Selling at the wholesale and retail levels; specifically, identifying customer needs, pointing out the need to the customer, and completing the order.

Organization marketing Marketing by *mutual benefit organizations* (churches, labour unions, and political parties), *service organizations* (colleges, universities, hospitals, museums), and *government organizations* (military services, police and fire departments, post office) that seeks to influence others to accept the goals of, receive the services of, or contribute in some way to that organization.

Ownership utility (1, 14) Created by marketers when *title* to products is transferred to the consumer at the time of purchase.

Party-plan selling (16) A distribution strategy under which a company's representative makes a presentation of the product(s) in a party setting. Orders are taken and the host or hostess receives a commission or gift based on the amount of sales.

Penetration pricing (12) A new-product pricing policy that uses an entry price lower than what is believed to be the long-term price. The premise is that an initially lower price will help secure market acceptance.

Perception (8) The meaning we attribute to stimuli coming through our five senses.

Perceptual screen (8) The perceptual filter through which messages must pass.

Person marketing Marketing efforts designed to cultivate the attention, interest, and preference of a market target toward a person. Person marketing is typically employed by political candidates and celebrities.

Personal selling (18, 20) A seller's promotional presentation conducted on a person to person basis with the buyer.

Persuasive institutional advertising (19) Used to advance the interests of a particular institution within a competitive environment.

Persuasive product advertising (19) A competitive type of advertising that attempts to develop demand for a particular product or brand.

Phantom freight (13) In a uniform delivered price system, the amount by which the average transportation charge exceeds the actual cost of shipping for customers near the supply source.

Physical distribution (17) Activities concerned with efficient movement of finished products from the producer to the consumer. These activities include freight transportation, warehousing, materials handling, protective packaging, inventory control, order processing, plant and warehouse site selection, market forecasting, and customer service. Also known as logistics.

PIMS study (12) Acronym for Profit Impact of Market Strategies, a project that discovered that market share and return-on-investment figures are closely linked.

Place utility (1, 14) Created by marketers having products available *where* the consumer wants to buy.

Planned obsolescence A policy of producing products with only a limited life span. This can occur where the producer uses materials of lower cost without any compensating benefits to the consumer such as lower prices or better performance characteristics.

Planned shopping centre (16) A group of retail stores owned, co-ordinated, and marketed as a unit.

Planning (3) The process of anticipating the future and determining the course of action to achieve company objectives.

Point-of-purchase advertising (19) Displays and demonstrations that seek to promote the product at a time and place closely associated with the actual decision to buy.

Political and legal environment (2) Component of the marketing environment consisting of laws and interpretation of laws that require firms to operate under competitive conditions and to protect consumer rights.

Pollution A broad term that is usually defined as "making unclean"; it can be categorized as either *environmental* (water and air) or *cultural* (aesthetic and intellectual) pollution.

Population (6) The total group that the researcher wants to study. For a political campaign, the population would be eligible voters.

Positioning (5) A marketing strategy that concentrates on particular market segments rather than attempting a broader appeal. It attempts to introduce the product into the mind of the potential customer by relating it to competitive products, as exemplified by 7-Up's "Uncola" campaign, relating 7-Up as an alternative to cola beverages.

Possession utility (1, 14) *See* Ownership utility.

Posttesting (19) The assessment of an advertisement after it has been used.

Posttransactional phase (4) The time span after the actual sale.

Premium (19) A bonus item given free with the purchase of another product.

Presentation (20) The step in the sales process when the salesperson gives the sales message. Typically, the representative describes the product's major characteristics, points out its advantages, and concludes by citing examples of customer satisfaction.

Prestige goals (12) In pricing policy, adopting relatively high prices so as to maintain a prestige or quality image with consumers.

Pretesting (19) The assessment of an advertisement's effectiveness before it is actually used.

Pretransactional period (4) The time span prior to the actual sale.

Price (12) The exchange value of a good or service.

Price elasticity of demand (12) A measure of responsiveness of purchasers to changes in price; calculated as the percentage change in the quantity of a product or service demanded divided by the percentage change in its price.

Price elasticity of supply (13) A measure of responsiveness of suppliers to changes in price; calculated as the percentage change in the quantity of a product or service supplied divided by the percentage change in price.

Price flexibility (13) The policy of maintaining a variable price for a product in the market.

Price limits (12) A concept that consumers have a price range within which product quality perception varies directly with price. A price below the lower limit is regarded as "too cheap," while one above the higher limit means it is "too expensive."

Price lining (13) The practice of marketing merchandise at a limited number of prices.

Pricing objectives (12, 13) The goals a company seeks to reach through implementation of its pricing strategy.

Pricing policy (13) A general guideline based upon pricing objectives and intended for use in specific pricing decisions.

Pricing strategy (1) An element of marketing decision-making dealing with the methods of setting profitable and justified prices.

Primary data (6) Data collected for the first time during a marketing research study.

Private brand (10) A line of merchandise offered by a wholesaler or retailer under its own label such as Eaton's Birkdale, Eatonia, and Tecomaster brands.

Private carrier (17) A freight carrier who only transports products for the firm's use and who cannot legally solicit the transportation business of anyone else.

Probability sample (6) A sample in which every member of the population has an equal chance of being selected.

Producers Industrial customers who purchase goods and services for the production of other goods and services.

Product (9) A bundle of physical, service, and symbolic characteristics designed to produce consumer want satisfaction.

Product advertising (19) The nonpersonal selling of a particular good or service.

Product deletion (9) The elimination of marginal items from a firm's product line.

Product life cycle (9) The path of a product from introduction to deletion. The stages of the product life cycle include introduction, growth, maturity, and decline.

Product line (10) A series of related products.

Product manager (10) The management officer assigned to one product or product line with complete responsibility for determining objectives and establishing marketing strategies.

Product mix (10, 5) The assortment of product lines and individual offerings available from a marketer.

Product positioning (10) Refers to the consumer's perception of a product's attributes, use, quality, and advantages and disadvantages.

Product strategy (1) An element of marketing decision-making comprising package design, branding, trademarks, warranties, guarantees, product life cycles, and new-product development.

Profit centre (13) Any part of an organization to which revenue and controllable costs can be assigned.

Profit Impact of Market Strategies (12) *See* PIMS study.

Profit margin on sales An evaluative figure showing the percentage of each sales dollar that remains after costs and taxes.

Profit maximization (12) The traditional pricing objective of classical economic theory. The assumption is that all firms need to maximize their gains or minimize their losses. In actual practice, few, if any, firms meet this goal.

Promotion (18) The function of informing, persuading, and influencing the consumer's purchase decision.

Promotional allowance (13) An advertising or sales promotional grant by a manufacturer to other channel members in an attempt to integrate promotional strategy within the channel.

Promotional mix (18) The blending of personal selling and nonpersonal selling (including advertising, sales promotion, and public relations) by marketers in an attempt to accomplish promotional objectives.

Promotional price (13) A price that is used as a part of a firm's selling strategy.

Promotional strategy (1) An element of marketing strategy involving personal selling, advertising, and sales promotion tools.

Prospecting (20) The step in the selling process that involves identification of potential customers.

Psychographics (4) Behavioural profiles of consumers, developed from analysis of activities, interests, opinions, and lifestyles, that may be used to segment consumer markets.

Psychological pricing (13) The belief that certain prices or price ranges are more appealing to buyers than others.

Psychophysics (8) The relationship between the actual physical stimulus and the corresponding sensation produced in the individual.

Public relations (18, 19) A firm's communications and relationships with its various publics, including customers, suppliers, stockholders, employees, the government, and the society in which it operates.

Public responsibility committee A permanent group within the board of directors of a firm that considers matters of corporate social responsibility.

Public warehouse (15) An independently owned storage facility that will store and ship products for a rental fee.

Publicity (18, 19) The segment of public relations directly related to promoting a company's products or services.

Pulling strategy (18) A promotional effort by the seller to stimulate final user demand, which then exerts pressure on the distribution channel. The plan is to build consumer demand for the product that is recognizable to channel members, who will then seek to fill this void.

Pure competition (12) A market situation in which there is such a large number of buyers and sellers that no one of them has a significant influence on price. Other characteristics include a homogeneous product and ease of entry for sellers resulting from low start-up costs. The closest examples exist in the agricultural sector.

Pushing strategy (19) A promotional effort directed toward the members of the marketing channel. This can be done through co-operative advertising allowances, trade discounts, personal selling, and other dealer support.

Qualifying (20) The step in the sales process that seeks to determine whether a prospect can become a customer. In most cases financial resources are a determining factor.

Quantity discount (13) A price reduction granted because of large purchases. Such as discount can be either *cumulative* (based on purchases over a stated period of time) or *non-cumulative* (one-time reduction in list price).

Quota (20) A specified sales or profit target that a salesperson is expected to achieve.

Quota sample (6) A nonprobability sample that is divided so that different segments or groups are represented in the total sample.

Rack jobber (15) A wholesaler who markets specialized lines of merchandise to retail stores and provides the services of merchandising and arrangement, maintenance, and stocking of display racks.

Rate of return on common equity An evaluative figure showing how successful a firm has been in earning returns on stockholders' investments.

Rate of return on total assets An evaluative figure showing the firm's net profit after taxes as measured against the total assets.

Raw materials (9) Industrial goods used in producing the final products such as *farm* products (wheat, cotton, milk) or *natural* products (copper, iron ore, and coal). Since most raw materials are graded, the purchaser is assured of a standardized product with uniform quality.

Rebate (13) A refund of a portion of the purchase price, usually granted by the manufacturer of a product.

Receiver (18) The person(s) a message is directed toward in a communications system.

Reciprocity The practice of giving favourable consideration to suppliers who are also purchasers of the firm's products.

Recycling The re-use of such items as packaging materials. Recycling provides a new source of raw materials and alleviates a major factor in environmental pollution. The major problem in recycling is getting the used materials from the consumer back to the manufacturer.

Reference groups (7) Groups with which a person identifies and to which his or her behaviour patterns are oriented.

Referral sample (6) Referred to as the Snowball Sample. It is a sample which is done in waves as more respondents with the requisite characteristics are identified.

Regional shopping centre (16) The largest type of planned cluster of retail stores, usually involving one or more major department stores and as many as 200 other stores. A centre of this size is typically located in an area with at least 250 000 people within 30 minutes driving time of the centre.

Reinforcement (8) The reduction in drive that results from a proper response.

Reminder-oriented institutional advertising (19) Used to reinforce previous promotional activity on the behalf of an institution, concept, idea, philosophy, industry, or company.

Reminder-oriented product advertising (19) Used to reinforce previous promotional activity by keeping the name of the product in front of the public.

Research design (6) A comprehensive plan for performing a marketing research study.

Response (8) The consumer's reaction to cues and drive.

Retail advertising (19) All nonpersonal selling by stores that offer goods or services directly to the consuming public.

Retail co-operative (14) A contractual agreement between a group of retailers where, in order to compete with chain operations, each retailer purchases stock in a retail-owned wholesaling operation and agrees to purchase a minimum percentage of supplies from the operation.

Retail image (16) Refers to the consumer's perception of a store and the shopping experience it provides.

Retail life cycle (16) The concept that retail institutions pass through a series of stages in their existence—introduction, growth, maturity, and decline.

Retail trade area analysis (16) Refers to studies that assess the relative drawing power of alternative retail locations.

Retailer (14) A middleman who sells products that are purchased by persons for their own use and not for resale.

Retailing (16) The activities of persons and firms selling to the ultimate consumer.

Return on investment (ROI) (13, 15) The rate of profit (net profit/sales) multiplied by turnover (sales/investment).

Revaluation When a nation adjusts its currency upward relative to gold or some other currency.

Reverse channel (14) The path goods follow from consumer to manufacturer, in an effort to recycle used products or by-products. *See also* Recycling.

Reverse reciprocity The practice of extending supply privileges to firms that provide needed supplies.

ROI *See* Return on investment.

Role (7) The rights and duties expected by other members of the group of the individual in a certain position in the group.

Safety stock (17) In inventory control, a certain quantity of merchandise kept on hand to protect a firm from fluctuations in demand and to prevent depletion of inventory.

Salary (20) Fixed payment made on a periodic basis to employees, including salespersons.

Sales analysis The study of internal sales data. It involves breaking aggregate data down into its component parts in order to obtain more meaningful information.

Sales branch (15) An establishment maintained by a manufacturer that serves as a warehouse for a particular sales territory, thereby duplicating the services of independent wholesalers.

Sales force composite (3) A qualitative sales forecasting method in which sales estimates are based upon the combined estimates of the firm's sales force.

Sales forecast (3) An estimate of sales, in dollars or physical units, for a specified future period under a proposed marketing plan or program and under an assumed set of economic and other forces outside the unit for which the forecast is made. The forecast may be for a specified item of merchandise or for an entire line.

Sales management (20) Management effort exerted in the direction of securing, maintaining, motivating, supervising, evaluating, and controlling an effective sales force.

Sales maximization (12) The pricing philosophy analysed by William J. Baumol, an economist. Baumol believes that many firms attempt to maximize sales within a profit constraint.

Sales office (15) An establishment maintained by a manufacturer that serves as a regional office for salespersons. The sales office, unlike the sales branch, does not carry inventory.

Sales promotion (18, 20) Assorted, one-time, and somewhat extraordinary nonpersonal selling activities (other than advertising).

Sales quota A standard of comparison used in sales analysis. It is the level of expected performance by which actual results are compared.

Sample (8) A representative group.

Sampling (19) Free distribution of a product in an attempt to secure consumer acceptance resulting in future purchases.

Scrambled merchandising (16) The attempts of retailers to satisfy consumer demands for convenient one-stop shopping by carrying a variety of seemingly unrelated products; for example, antifreeze in supermarkets.

Secondary data (6) Information that has been published previously.

Selective distribution (14) The use of a small number of retailers to handle the firm's product or product line.

Selective perception (8) People's awareness of only those incoming stimuli they wish to perceive.

Self-concept (8) The way people picture themselves, which influences the manner in which they act as consumers.

Seller's market (1) A market with a shortage of goods and services.

Selling agent (15) An agent wholesaling middleman who markets the products of a manufacturer. The selling agent has full authority over pricing decisions and promotional outlays and often provides financing for the manufacturer.

Selling expense ratio An evaluative technique revealing the relationship between selling expenses and total net sales.

Selling up (20) The technique of convincing a customer to buy a higher-priced item than he or she originally intended. The practice of selling up should always be used within the constraints of the customer's real needs.

Semantic differential (8) An attitude-scaling device that uses a number of bipolar adjectives, such as hot and cold.

Sender (18) The source of a message in a communications system.

Services (11) Intangible products such as tax advice, management consulting, and hair care. Services are included in the marketing definition of products.

Shaping (8) The process of applying a series of rewards and reinforcement so that more complex behaviour can evolve over time.

Shopping centre (16) A geographical cluster of retail stores, collectively handling a varied assortment of goods designed to satisfy purchase needs of consumers within the area of the centre.

Shopping goods (9) Products purchased by the consumer only after he or she has made comparison of competing goods on such bases as price, quality, style, and colour.

Shopping goods may be classified as either *homogeneous* (where the consumer views them as essentially the same) or *heterogeneous* (where the consumer sees significant differences in quality and styling).

SIC codes *See* Standard Industrial Classifications.

Simple random sample (8) A sample chosen in such a way that every member of the group has an equal chance of being selected.

Single-line store *See* Limited-line store.

Skimming price (13) A new-product pricing policy that uses a relatively high entry price.

Social and ethical considerations (12) A pricing objective based on certain factors of society and ethics. A sliding-scale fee schedule is an example.

Social class (7) The relatively permanent divisions in a society into which individuals or families are categorized based on prestige and community status.

Social responsibility The duty of business to be concerned with the quality of life as well as its quantity.

Societal – cultural environment (2) A marketer's relationship with society in general.

Sorting (14) The contribution of distribution channels in securing a balanced stock of goods available to match the needs of customers. It consists of accumulating, allocating, assorting, and sorting out goods.

Specialty advertising (19) A sales promotion medium that utilizes useful articles carrying the advertiser's name, address, and advertising message. These include calendars, pens, and matchbooks.

Specialty goods (9) Products that possess unique characteristics so as to cause the consumer to make a special effort to obtain them. Specialty goods are typically high-priced and frequently are branded.

Specialty retailer (16) One who provides a combination of product lines, service, and/or reputation in an attempt to attract customer preference.

Specialty store (16) A retail store that handles only part of a single line of products such as a meat market, a men's shoe store, or a millinery shop.

Specifications (9) In the industrial market, a written description of a product or a service needed by a firm. Prospective bidders use this description initially to determine whether they can manufacture the product or deliver the service, and subsequently to prepare a bid.

Speculative production (14) A production system based on management's estimate of future demand for its products. Products are produced in advance of orders for them.

SSWD (4) Market segment composed of single, separated, widowed, and divorced people.

Stagflation (2) A situation where an economy has high unemployment and a rising price level at the same time.

Standard Industrial Classification (SIC) A series of industrial classifications developed by the federal government for use in collecting detailed statistics for each industry. These classifications are called *SIC codes*.

Status (7) An individual's relative position in a group.

Status quo objectives (12) In pricing strategy, goals based on the maintenance of stable prices.

Stock out (17) An item that is not available for shipment.

Stock turnover (12) The number of times the average inventory is sold annually.

Storage warehouse (17) The traditional warehouse where products are stored prior to shipment. Often storage warehouses are used to balance supply and demand problems of the producing firm.

Straight rebuy A recurring industrial purchase decision where an item that has performed satisfactorily is purchased again by a customer.

Strategic business units (SBU) (3) Related product groupings or classifications within a multi-product firm, so structured for optimal planning purposes.

Strategic planning (3) The process of determining an organization's primary objectives, and allocating funds and proceeding on a course of action to achieve those objectives.

Strategic window (3) The limited periods during which the "fit" between the key requirements of a market and the particular competencies of a firm is at an optimum.

Stratified sample (6) A probability sample that is constructed so that randomly selected sub-samples of different groups are represented in the total sample.

Subculture (7) A separate and distinct segment of the prevailing culture.

Subliminal perception (8) Communication at the subconscious level of awareness.

Suboptimization (17) A condition where individual objectives are accomplished at the cost of accomplishing the broader objectives of the total organization.

Suggestion selling (20) Broadening the customer's original purchase with related items, special promotions, and/or holiday and seasonal merchandise.

Supermarket (16) A large-scale, departmentalized retail store offering a large variety of food products, such as meats, produce, dairy products, canned goods, and frozen foods.

It operates on a self-service basis and emphasizes price and adequate parking facilities.

Supplies (10) Industrial goods that are considered regular expense items necessary in the daily operation of a firm, but that do not become part of the final product. Supplies include *maintenance*, *repair*, and *operating* items.

Supply curve (17) A schedule relating the quantity offered for sale to specific prices. It is the marginal cost curve above its intersection with the average variable cost curve.

Survey study (8) Asks respondents to answer questions in order to obtain information on attitudes, motives, and opinions. There are three types of surveys: telephone, mail, and personal interview.

Syndicated service (6) An organization that offers to provide a standardized set of data on a regular basis to all who wish to buy it.

System (17) An organized group of parts or components linked together according to a plan to achieve specific objectives.

Systematic sample (6) A probability sample that takes every Nth item on a list.

Tactical planning (3) The implementation of activities necessary in the achievement of a firm's objectives.

Tangible products Goods (rather than services, such as legal advice or a medical examination).

Target return objectives (12) Either short-run or long-run, they are the profit goals a firm seeks to reach. Typically, they are stated as a percentage of sales or investment.

Tariffs (17) Official publications listing the rates for shipping various commodities. This term is also used to identify taxes on imports.

Task objective method (18) A sequential approach to allocating promotional budgets. The organization must 1) define the particular goals that it wants the promotional mix to accomplish and 2) determine the amount (as well as type) of promotional activity required to accomplish each of the objectives that have been set.

Technological environment (2) The applications of knowledge based upon discoveries in science, inventions, and innovations to marketing.

Teleshopping (16) A new type of shopping made possible by cable television whereby the shopper can order merchandise that has been displayed on his or her television set.

Tertiary industries (11) A term that has been used to identify the service industries.

Test marketing (6, 10) Selection of a specific city or area considered reasonably typical of the total market and the introduction of a new product in this area complete with a total promotional campaign. The results of such a program largely determine whether the product will be introduced on a larger scale.

Tied selling (14) An agreement requiring a middleman who wishes to become the exclusive dealer for a manufacturer's products to also carry other of the manufacturer's products in inventory. The legality of a tying contract is based on whether it restricts competitors from major markets.

Time utility (1, 14) Created by marketers having products available *when* the consumer wants to buy.

Tokyo Round A series of international trade negotiations intended to reduce the amount of tariffs throughout the world.

Total-cost approach (17) This approach to physical distribution advocates considering all distribution-related factors as a whole, rather than by individual cost item.

Trade discount (13) A payment to a channel member or buyer for performing some marketing function normally required of the manufacturer. Also called *functional discount*.

Trade fair or trade exhibition (15) A periodic show where manufacturers in a particular industry display their wares for visiting retail and wholesale buyers.

Trade-in (13) An allowance often used in selling durable goods such as automobiles. A trade-in permits a price reduction without altering the basic list price.

Trade industries Organizations such as retailers and wholesalers who purchase for resale to others.

Trademark (10) A brand that has been given legal protection and has been granted solely to its owner. Thus the trademark includes not only pictorial design but also the brand name.

Trade show *See* Trade fairs and trade exhibitions.

Trading stamps (19) Sales promotion premiums offered by some retailers. These stamps may be exchanged for items of value at specified redemption centres.

Transactional phase (4) The point in time when a sale is actually closed.

Transfer mechanism (18) In marketing communications, the means of delivering a message.

Transfer pricing (13) Charges for goods sent from one profit centre to another within the same company.

Trend analysis (3) A quantitative sales forecasting method in which estimates of future sales are determined through statistical analyses of historical sales patterns.

Trigger pricing system In international marketing, a protective measure taken by a country to combat the practice of dumping. When a price level for a commodity dips below a preordained figure, it sets off an immediate investigation by a government agency. *See also* Dumping.

Truck wholesaler (17) A wholesaler who specializes in the marketing of perishable food items and making regular deliveries to retail stores. Also called *trade jobber*.

Turnover (12) The number of times the average inventory is sold annually. The turnover rate is often frequently used as a sales efficiency measure.

Tying agreement (14) An understanding between a dealer and a manufacturer that requires the dealer to carry the manufacturer's full product line in exchange for an exclusive dealership.

Undifferentiated marketing (5) When firms produce only one product and attempt to match it to their consumers with a single marketing mix.

Uniform delivered price (13) The same price (including transportation expenses) quoted to all buyers. The price that is quoted includes an "average transportation charge" per customer. This is sometimes called *postage stamp pricing*.

Unitizing (17) The combination of smaller packages into a single load, often on a pallet. It requires less labour in materials handling, promotes faster product movement, and reduces damage and pilferage.

Unit pricing (13) Pricing items in terms of some recognized unit of measurement, such as kilogram, litre, or standard numerical count.

Unit trains (17) A time- and money-saving service provided by railroads to large-volume customers, in which a train is loaded with the shipments of only one company and transports solely for that customer.

Universal product code (10) Special codes on packages that can be read by optical scanners. The scanner can print the item and its price on a sales receipt and simultaneously maintain a sales and inventory record for the retailer or shipper.

Utility (1) The want-satisfying power of a good or service.

Value added by manufacturing (10) The difference between the price charged for a manufactured good and the cost of the raw materials and other inputs.

Variable costs (12) Costs that change when the level of production is altered, such as raw materials and the wages paid to operative employees.

Venture team (10) An organizational arrangement combining representatives from marketing, engineering, and financial accounting who are responsible for development of new products and services. The venture team is physically separated from the permanent organization and is linked directly with top management for high-level support.

Vertical Marketing Systems (VMS) (14) Networks that are professionally managed, centrally programmed, and pre-engineered in order to attain operating economies and maximum impact in the channel.

Voluntary chains *See* Wholesaler-sponsored voluntary chain.

Want satisfaction A state of mind achieved when a consumer's needs have been met as the result of a purchase.

Warranty (9) A guarantee to the buyer that the manufacturer or retailer will replace a defective product or refund its purchase price during a specified period of time.

Weber's Law (8) The proposition that the higher the initial intensity of a stimulus, the greater the amount of the change in intensity that is necessary in order for a difference to be noticed.

Wheel-of-retailing (16) A hypothesis by Malcolm McNair to explain changes in retailing. McNair contended that new types of retailers enter the marketplace by offering lower prices and fewer services and gradually increase the number of services and prices, thereby becoming vulnerable to new types of low-price retailers.

Wholesaler (15) A wholesaling middleman who takes title to the goods that he or she handles. The terms *jobber* and *distributor* are synonymous with wholesaler.

Wholesaler-sponsored voluntary chain (14) A contractual agreement between a group of retailers and a wholesaler to enable the retailers to compete with chain operations.

Wholesaling (14) The activities of firms selling to retailers, other wholesalers, and industrial users, but who do not sell to the ultimate consumer.

Wholesaling middleman (15) A broad term that includes wholesalers (those wholesaling middlemen who take title to the products they handle) and also the agents and brokers who perform wholesaling activities but do not take title to the goods.

Zone pricing (13) A uniform delivered price quoted by geographical regions.

Index

CHAPTER ONE

Review Questions

1. What are the four types of utility? With which is marketing concerned?
2. How does the text definition of marketing differ from the definition proposed by the American Marketing Association?
3. Relate the definition of marketing to the concept of the exchange process.
4. Contrast the production era and the sales era.
5. In what ways does the marketing era differ from the previous eras?
6. Explain the concept of marketing myopia. Why is it likely to occur? What steps can be taken to reduce the likelihood of its occurrence?
7. What did the General Electric annual report mean when it said it was introducing the marketer at the beginning rather than at the end of the production cycle?
8. What are the parameters of the marketing concept?
9. Identify the major variables of the marketing mix.
10. What are the components of the marketing environment? Why are these factors not included as part of the marketing mix?

Discussion Questions and Exercises

1. What types of utility are being created in the following examples?
   a. One-hour cleaners
   b. 7-Eleven convenience food store
   c. Michelin Tire factory in Nova Scotia
   d. Annual boat and sports equipment show in local city auditorium
   e. Regional shopping mall
2. How would you explain marketing and its importance in the Canadian economy to someone not familiar with the subject?
3. Identify the product and the consumer market in each of the following:
   a. Local cable television firm
   b. Vancouver Canucks hockey team
   c. Planned Parenthood
   d. Milk Marketing Board
4. Suggest methods by which the following organizations might avoid marketing myopia by correctly defining their industries:
   a. Atari Computer Division   d. Petro-Canada
   b. First Choice (pay television)   e. Bank of Nova Scotia
   c. Northern Alberta Railway
5. Give two examples of firms you feel are in the following eras:
   a. Production era   c. Marketing era
   b. Sales era   Defend your answer.

CHAPTER TWO

Review Questions

1. Identify and briefly describe the five components of the marketing environment.
2. Explain the types of competition faced by marketers.
3. What are the steps involved in developing a competitive strategy?
4. How does inflation affect marketing activity?
5. How did the Great Depression influence marketing legislation?
6. Trace the evolution of Consumer and Corporate Affairs Canada into an "activist watchdog" of marketing practices. Then evaluate the department's degree of success.
7. What are the major economic factors affecting marketing decisions?
8. Distinguish between inflation and stagflation. In what ways do they affect marketing?
9. Indentify the ways in which the technological environment affects marketing activities.
10. Explain how the socio-cultural environment influences marketing.

Discussion Questions and Exercises

1. Give an example of how each of the environmental variables discussed in this chapter might affect the following firms:
   a. Eastern Provincial Airlines
   b. Local aerobics exercise centre
   c. Swiss Chalet franchise
   d. Avon Products
   e. Sears catalogue department
   f. Local television station
2. Comment on the following statement: The legal framework for marketing decisions is basically a positive one.
3. Can the consumerism movement be viewed as a rejection of the competitive marketing system? Defend your answer.
4. As a consumer, do you favour laws permitting resale price maintenance agreements? Would your answer vary if you were the producer of Sony television sets? If you were the retailer of Sony television sets? Why or why not?
5. Would a gas station that sold gasoline to a city's police department for one cent a litre less than its price for other customers be in violation of the Combines Investigation Act? Why? Explain your answer.

CHAPTER THREE

1. Distinguish between strategic planning and tactical planning.
2. Contrast marketing planning at different levels in the organization.
3. Identify the steps in the marketing planning process.
4. Explain the concept of the strategic window. Give an example.
5. Differentiate among *cash cows, dogs, stars,* and *question marks* in the BCG matrix.
6. Outline the five marketing strategies that can be employed by marketers.
7. Identify and discuss the major external and internal influences on marketing strategy.
8. Compare and contrast each of the major types of forecasting methods.
9. Explain the steps involved in the forecasting process.
10. Suggest methods for forecasting sales for newly introduced products.

Discussion Questions and Exercises

1. Give two examples of products currently in each of the following quadrants of the BCG matrix:
   a. Cash cow   c. Star
   b. Dog   d. Question mark
   Suggest marketing strategies for each product.
2. Relate the discussion of the development of Creative Appliance Corp. to the model of the marketing planning process shown in Figure 3-3.
3. Discuss the advantages and shortcomings of basing sales forecasts exclusively on estimates developed by the firm's sales force.
4. Assume that growth in industry sales will remain constant for Year 6, the coming year. Forecast company sales for Year 6 based upon the following data:
   Year 1: $320 000
   Year 2: $350 000
   Year 3: $340 000
   Year 4: $380 000
   Year 5: $580 000
   What assumptions have you made in developing your forecast?
5. Which forecasting technique do you feel is most appropriate for each of the following:
   a. Bayer aspirin
   b. Royal Winnipeg Ballet
   c. Office supplies retailer
   d. Fender guitars

CHAPTER FOUR

Review Questions

1. Explain why each of the four components of a market is needed for a market to exist.
2. Bicycles are consumer goods; iron ore is an industrial good. What about trucks — are they consumer goods or industrial goods? Defend your answer.
3. Identify and briefly explain the bases for segmenting consumer markets.
4. Identify the major population shifts that have occurred in recent years. How do you account for these shifts?
5. Explain and describe the use of AIO questions.
6. Why is demographic segmentation the most commonly used approach to marketing segmentation?
7. How can lifestyles be used in market segmentation?
8. Explain the use of product usage rates as a segmentation variable.
9. What market segmentation base would you recommend for the following:
   a. Professional soccer team
   b. Porsche sports car
   c. Capitol Records
   d. Scope mouthwash
10. Identify and briefly explain the bases of segmenting industrial markets.

Discussion Questions and Exercises

1. Match the following bases for market segmentation with the items below:
   a. Geographic segmentation
   b. Demographic segmentation
   c. Psychographic segmentation
   d. Benefit segmentation
   _____1. A government-financed study divided households into five categories of eating patterns: meat eaters; healthy eaters; conscientious eaters; "in a dither" eaters; and on the go eaters.
   _____2. A department store chain decides to emphasize suburban rather than downtown outlets.
   _____3. "7-Up, clear, crisp with no caffeine."
   _____4. A catalogue retailer targets its catalogues at 25- to 54-year-old working women with household incomes of $34 000.
2. The 1988 Calgary Winter Olympics will be extensively televised. What types of products would most likely benefit from advertis-

ing associated with the games? Will they appeal to more than one market segment?

3. Prepare a brief report on the future growth prospects of the geographical area in which you live.

4. Explain why the household growth rate is more than double the increase in population.

5. Canadian census data reveal that a significant number of Canadians have a mother tongue other than English or French (mother tongue is defined as the language first learned and still understood). Some of the larger language groups are Italian (529 000 people), German (523 000), Ukrainian (292 000), and Chinese (224 000). How could a marketer use this demographic information?

CHAPTER FIVE

Review Questions

1. Outline the basic features of a single-offer strategy.
2. Outline the basic features of a multi-offer strategy.
3. Outline the rationale of market matching strategies.
4. What are the primary determinants of product market strategy selection?
5. List and describe the five stages of the market segmentation process.
6. What is meant by market target decision analysis?
7. Show how market target decision analysis can help select market segments that the firm should attempt to reach.
8. Illustrate how the four consumer-oriented segmentation bases can be used in market target decision analysis.
9. Illustrate how the three industrial market segmentation bases can be used in market target decision analysis.
10. How can market target decision analysis be used to assess a product mix?

Discussion Questions and Exercises

1. What can be learned from the Corporate Foods example at the beginning of the chapter? Discuss.
2. Prepare a term paper on an actual firm employing marketing segmentation in the development of its marketing strategy.
3. Identify the conditions where a single-offer market matching strategy would be appropriate and those where a multi-offer would be.
4. Prepare a report that traces an actual company's experience as it moved through the various market segmentation stages.
5. Assess a firm's actual product mix using market target decision analysis.

CHAPTER SIX

Review Questions

1. Outline the development and current status of the marketing research function.
2. Explain the services offered by different types of marketing research suppliers.
3. List and explain the various steps in the marketing research process.
4. Distinguish between primary and secondary data.
5. What advantages does the use of secondary data offer the marketing researcher? What potential limitations exist in using such data?
6. Distinguish among surveys, experiments, and observational methods of data collection.
7. Illustrate each of the three methods for gathering survey data. Under what circumstances should each be used?
8. Explain the differences between probability and nonprobability samples and the various types of each.
9. Distinguish between marketing research and marketing information systems.
10. What is the current status of marketing information systems?

Discussion Questions and Exercises

1. Prepare a brief two to three page report on a syndicated marketing research service. Explain how this data is used by marketing decision-makers.
2. Collect from secondary data the following information:
   a. retail sales in Windsor, Ontario
   b. number of persons over 65 in Moncton, New Brunswick
   c. earnings per share for International Business Machines Corporation last year.
   d. bituminous coal production in Canada
   e. consumer price index for a given month
   f. number of households earning more than $35 000 in your home town or city
3. Look up the "Survey of Buying Power" data for your community or one nearby. What marketing implications can be drawn from these situations?
4. James Roe, the vice-president of Gadget Electronics, a medium-to-large Canadian company, refuses to involve himself with the activities of his marketing research staff. He explains that he has hired competent professionals for the research department, and he does not plan to meddle in their operation. Critically evaluate Roe's postion.

5. You have been asked to determine the effect on Gillette of Schick's introduction of a revolutionary new blade that is guaranteed to give a hundred nick-free shaves. Outline your approach to the study.

CHAPTER SEVEN

Review Questions

1. What are the two primary determinants of behaviour according to Lewin?
2. List the steps in the consumer behaviour process.
3. Explain the interpersonal determinants of consumer behaviour.
4. How does culture influence buying patterns?
5. Identify the two major cultures in Canada. How do their consumption patterns differ?
6. Describe the Asch phenomenon.

Discussion Questions and Exercises

1. Relate a recent purchase you made to the consumer decision process shown in Figure 7-1.
2. Discuss the cultural values or norms that have had the greatest effect on your purchase behaviour.
3. For which of the following products is reference-group influence likely to be strong?
   a. Rolex watch   e. Portable radio
   b. Skis   f. Personal computer
   c. Shaving lather   g. Electric blanket
   d. 10-speed bicycle   h. Contact lenses
4. Identify the opinion leaders in a group to which you belong. Why are these people the group's opinion leaders?
5. List two product purchases for which the influence of the following family members might be most important:
   a. Mother   d. Teenage son
   b. 6-year-old child   e. Teenage daughter
   c. Father   f. 2-year-old child

CHAPTER EIGHT

Review Questions

1. What are the personal determinants of consumer behaviour?
2. How do needs and motives influence consumer behaviour?
3. Explain the concept of perception. Consider perceptual screens, selective perception, Weber's Law, and subliminal perception in your explanation.

4. How do attitudes influence consumer behaviour? How can negative attitudes be changed?
5. Describe the steps that occur in learning.
6. How can learning theory be applied to marketing strategy?
7. Differentiate among the four components of the self-concept: ideal self, looking-glass self, self-image, and real self.
8. Outline the steps in the consumer decision process.
9. Describe internal and external research.
10. Differentiate among routinized response behaviour, limited problem solving, and extended problem solving.

Discussion Questions and Exercises

1. Using Maslow's classification system, which needs are being referred to in the following advertising slogans:
   - "No caffeine. Never had it. Never will." (7-Up)
   - Swedish engineering. Depend on it. (SAAB)
   - A blending of art and machine. (Jaguar)
   - The best bed a body can buy. (Simmons)
   - "Don't leave home without it." (American Express Card)
2. Poll your friends about subliminal perception. How many believe that marketers can control consumers at a subconscious level? Report the results of this survey to your marketing class.
3. Find examples of shaping procedures being used in marketing applications.
4. Outline your own ideal self, looking-glass self, self-image, and real self.
5. Taking a recent shopping experience, analyse your attitudes as related to your consumer behaviour. Be sure your assessment considers all three components of an attitude.

CHAPTER NINE

Review Questions

1. Describe the total product concept.
2. Draw and explain the product life-cycle concept.
3. Outline the various forms that the traditional product life cycle might take.
4. Suggest several means by which the life cycle of a product (such as Scotch tape) can be extended.
5. Identify and briefly explain the stages in the consumer adoption process.
6. Describe each of the determinants of the rate of adoption.
7. Why is the basis used for categorizing industrial goods different from that used for categorizing consumer goods?

8. Compare a typical marketing mix for convenience goods with a mix for specialty goods.
9. Outline the typical marketing mix for a shopping good.
10. Discuss the marketing mix for the various types of industrial goods.

Discussion Questions and Exercises

1. Select a specific product in each stage of the product life cycle (other than those shown in the text). Explain how the marketing strategies might vary by life-cycle stage for each product.
2. Trace the life cycle of a recent fad. What marketing strategy implications can you draw from your study?
3. Home burglar alarm systems using microwaves are the fastest-growing product in the home-security market. Such systems operate by filling rooms with microwave beams, which set off alarms when an intruder intercepts one of them. What suggestions can you make to accelerate the rate of adoption for this product?
4. Classify the following consumer goods:
   a. Furniture
   b. Puma running shoes
   c. Felt-tip pen
   d. Swimsuit
   e. Nissan sports car
   f. Binaca breath freshener
   g. *Hockey News* magazine
   h. Original oil painting
5. Classify the following products into the appropriate industrial goods category. Briefly explain your choice for each product.
   a. Calculators
   b. Land
   c. Light bulbs
   d. Wool
   e. Paper towels
   f. Nylon
   g. Airplanes
   h. Tires

CHAPTER TEN

Review Questions

1. What is meant by a product mix? How is the concept used in making effective marketing decisions?
2. Why do most business firms market a line of related products rather than a single product?
3. Explain the new-product decay curve.
4. Outline the alternative organizational structures for new-product development.
5. Identify the steps in the new-product development process.
6. What is the chief purpose of test marketing? What potential problems are involved in it?
7. List the characteristics of an effective brand name. Illustrate each characteristic with an appropriate brand name.

8. Identify and briefly explain each of the three stages of brand loyalty.
9. What are the objectives of modern packaging?
10. Explain the chief elements of the Hazardous Products Act.

---

1. General Foods gave up on Lean Strips, a textured vegetable protein strip designed as a bacon substitute, after eight years of test marketing. Lean Strips sold well when bacon prices were high but poorly when they were low. General Foods hoped to offer a protein analogue product line that also included Crispy Strips, a snack and salad dressing item. Consumers liked the taste of Crispy Strips but felt it was too expensive for repeat purchases, and the product was abandoned before Lean Strips' demise. General Foods decided to concentrate on new product categories instead of on individual items like Lean Strips. What can be learned from General Food's experience with Lean Strips?
2. A firm's new-product idea suggestion program has produced a design for a portable car washer that can be attached to a domestic garden hose. Outline a program for deciding whether the product should be marketed by the firm.
3. Campbell Soup Company's Belgian candy company, Godiva Chocolates, introduced a designer line called "Bill Blass Chocolates." The premium chocolates sold for $14 per pound. Relate this action to the material discussed in Chapter 11.
4. Exxene, a $1 million manufacturer of antifog coatings for goggles, was sued for trademark infringement by Exxon Corp. The oil company giant claimed that it had nearly exclusive rights to the letters *EXX* regardless of what followed it. Four and a half years later, a jury awarded Exxene $250 000 in damages instead. Exxon filed an appeal. Relate this case to the discussion of trademarks.

CHAPTER ELEVEN

1. Explain why services are difficult to define.
2. How is a goods-services continuum useful in defining the term *service*?
3. Outline the proportions of the consumer dollar spent on products and services.
4. Describe the evolution of the service sector.

5. Explain the classification of services on the bases of reliance on equipment and relative skills of service personnel.
6. Identify and outline the key features of services.
7. How does Levitt's marketing myopia thesis relate to service industries?
8. What is the status of the marketing concept in service industries?
9. Explain how Colin Clark's concept describes the growth of service industries.
10. Cite major differences in the marketing strategies of firms producing goods and firms producing services.

Discussion Questions and Exercises

1. Prepare a brief report on the marketing activities conducted by a local lawyer, and a local insurance broker. In addition, compare and contrast the two. What generalizations can be reached from your study?
2. Describe the last service you purchased. What was your impression of the way in which the service was marketed? How could the firm's marketing effort have been improved?
3. Commonwealth Holiday Inns of Canada has tried to overcome the problems of a service industry by stressing consistency in their product offering. The slogan "The best surprise is no surprise" is an illustration of Holiday Inn's effort to provide a service of consistently reliable quality. What is your opinion of Holiday Inns' approach to the consistency problem faced by all varieties of services?
4. Outline a marketing mix for the following service firms:
   a. local radio station
   b. independent insurance agency
   c. janitorial service
   d. funeral home
5. Identify three or four service firms and propose methods by which their productivity can be improved. Point out any potential problems with your proposal.

CHAPTER TWELVE

Review Questions

1. Identify the four major categories of pricing objectives.
2. Categorize each of the following into a specific type of pricing objective:
   a. 8 percent increase in market share
   b. 5 percent increase in profits over previous year
   c. prices no more than 5 percent higher than prices quoted by independent dealers

d. 20 percent return on investment (before taxes)
e. highest prices in product category to maintain favourable brand image
f. follow price of most important competitor in each market segment

3. What are the major price implications of the PIMS studies? Suggest possible explanations for the relationships discovered by the studies.

4. What market situations exist for the pricing of the following products:

a. telephone service e. potatoes
b. Candu nuclear reactors f. dishwashers
c. golf clubs   g. tape recorders
d. steel   h. skis

5. Explain the concept of elasticity.

6. What are the practical problems involved in attempting to apply price theory concepts to actual pricing decisions?

7. Explain the advantages of using incremental cost pricing rather than full cost pricing. What potential drawbacks exist?

8. Explain the relationship between markups and stock turnover rates.

9. Explain the primary benefits of using break-even analysis in price determination. What are the shortcomings of the basic break-even model?

10. In what ways is dynamic break-even analysis superior to the basic model?

Discussion Questions and Exercises

1. A retailer has just received a new kitchen appliance invoiced at $28. The retailer decides to follow industry practice for such items and adds a 40 percent markup percentage on selling price. What retail price should the retailer assign to the appliance?

2. If a product has a markup percentage on selling price of 28 percent, what is its markup percentage on cost?

3. An economic downturn in the local area has seriously affected sales of a retailer's line of $150 dresses. The store manager decides to mark these dresses down to $125. What markdown percentage should be featured in advertising this sale item?

4. A store with an average inventory of $50 000 (at cost) operates on a 40 percent markup percentage on selling price. Annual sales total $750 000. What is the stock turnover rate?

5. What is the break-even point in dollars and units for a product with a selling price of $25, related fixed costs of $126 000, and per unit variable costs of $16?

CHAPTER THIRTEEN

1. Who in the organization is most likely to be responsible for setting a price structure? Who is most likely to administer a price structure?
2. How are prices likely to be quoted?
3. Contrast the freight absorption and uniform delivered pricing systems.
4. List and discuss the reasons for establishing price policies.
5. What are the benefits derived from utilizing a skimming approach to pricing?
6. Under what circumstances is penetration pricing most likely to be used?
7. When does a price become a promotional price? What are the pitfalls in promotional pricing?
8. What is the relationship between prices and consumer perceptions of quality?
9. Contrast negotiated prices and competitive bidding.
10. What types of decisions must be made in the pricing of public services? What role could escalator clauses play in this area?

1. What type of new-product pricing would be appropriate for the following items:
   a. a new deodorant
   b. a fuel additive that increases fuel efficiency by 50 percent
   c. a new pattern of fine china
   d. a new ultrasensitive burglar, smoke, and fire alarm
   e. a new video game
2. How are prices quoted for each of the following:
   a. a CP Air ticket to Montreal
   b. an aluminum siding installation by a local contractor
   c. a new jogging suit from a sportswear retailer
   d. a new Nissan pick-up truck
3. Comment on the following statement: Unit pricing is ridiculous because everyone ignores it.
4. Prepare a list of arguments that might be used in justifying a negotiated contract instead of requiring competitive bids.
5. What criteria should be considered for transfer pricing in a large corporation like Westinghouse Electric?

CHAPTER FOURTEEN

1. What types of products are most likely to be distributed through direct channels?
2. Which marketing channel is the traditional channel? Give some reasons for its frequent use.
3. Why would manufacturers choose more than one channel for their products?
4. Explain the concept of power in the distribution channel.
5. Under what circumstances is the retailer likely to assume a channel leadership role?
6. Explain and illustrate the major factors affecting distribution channel selection.
7. Why would any manufacturer deliberately choose to limit market coverage through a policy of exclusive coverage?
8. Explain and illustrate each type of vertical marketing system.
9. What advantages does franchising offer the small retailer?
10. In what ways could the use of multiple channels produce channel conflict?

1. Chipwich, an ice cream and chocolate-chip cookie snack, is marketed via vendor carts as well as supermarkets. Relate Chipwich's distribution strategy to the material presented in this chapter.
2. Which degree of distribution intensity is appropriate for each of the following:
   a. *Maclean's*
   b. Catalina swim wear
   c. Irish Spring soap
   d. Johnson outboard motors
   e. Cuisinart food processors
   f. Kawasaki motorcycles
   g. Waterford crystal
3. Outline the distribution channels used by a local firm. Why were these particular channels selected by the company?
4. Prepare a brief report on the dealer requirements for a franchise that has units in your area.
5. One generalization of channel selection mentioned in the chapter was that low unit value products require long channels. How can you explain the success of a firm (such as Avon) that has a direct channel for its relatively low unit value products?

CHAPTER FIFTEEN

1. Distinguish between a wholesaler and a retailer.
2. In what ways do wholesaling intermediaries assist manufacturers? How do they assist retailers?

3. Explain how wholesaling intermediaries can assist retailers in increasing their return on investment.
4. Distinguish between sales offices and sales branches. Under what conditions might each type be used?
5. What role does the public warehouse play in distribution channels?
6. Distinguish merchant wholesalers from agents and brokers.
7. Why is the operating expense ratio of the merchant wholesaler higher than that of the typical agent or broker?
8. In what ways are commission merchants and brokers different?
9. Distinguish between a manufacturers' agent and a selling agent.
10. Under what conditions would a manufacturer utilize manufacturers' agents for a distribution channel?

| *Discussion Questions and Exercises* | |

Discussion Questions and Exercises

1. Match each of the following industries with the most appropriate wholesaling intermediary:

_____ Groceries	a. Drop shipper
_____ Potato chips	b. Truck wholesaler
_____ Coal	c. Auction house
_____ Grain	d. Manufacturers' agent
_____ Antiques	e. Full-function merchant wholesaler
	f. Commission merchant

2. Comment on the following statements: Drop shippers are good candidates for elimination. All they do is process orders. They don't even handle the goods.
3. Prepare a brief five page report on a wholesaler in your local area.
4. The term *broker* also appears in the real estate and securities fields. Are these brokers identical to the agent wholesaling intermediaries described in this chapter?
5. Interview someone who works at a local wholesaling firm. Report to the class on this person's job within the wholesaling sector.

CHAPTER SIXTEEN

Review Questions

1. Discuss the evolution of retailing.
2. Outline the framework for decisions in retailing.
3. Outline the five bases for categorizing retailers.
4. How are limited-line and specialty stores able to compete with such general merchandise retailers as department stores and discount houses?
5. Identify the major types of general merchandise retailers.

6. Give reasons for the success of discount retailing in Canada.
7. Identify and briefly explain each of the types of non-store retailing operations.
8. Why has the practice of scrambled merchandising become so common in retailing?
9. Compare the retail life cycle concept with the wheel-of-retailing hypothesis.
10. Discuss the current development and potential for teleshopping.

1. Computers are one of the fastest growing aspects of retailing. Computer outlets include Radio Shack, Computerland, Computer Connection, MicroAge, and Computer Innovations. Relate this growth to the concepts discussed in Chapter 17.
2. Xerox and IBM have recently opened stores to serve small businesses and professionals like attorneys, physicians, dentists, and chartered accountants. How would you classify these stores?
3. Assume that a retailer was considering opening an outlet in Town A, population 144 000. The retailer wanted to know how far his trade area would extend toward Town B (population 16 000), 72 km away. Apply the law of retail gravitation to the retailer's problem.
4. List several examples of the wheel of retailing in operation. List examples that do not conform to the wheel hypothesis. What generalizations can be drawn from this exercise?
5. What is your assessment of the future of teleshopping through interactive cable television?

CHAPTER SEVENTEEN

1. Why was physical distribution one of the last areas in most companies to be carefully studied and improved?
2. Outline the basic reasons for the increased attention to physical distribution management.
3. What are the basic objectives of physical distribution?
4. What is the most effective organization for physical distribution management? Explain.
5. What factors should be considered in locating a new distribution warehouse?
6. Who should be ultimately responsible for determining the level of customer service standards? Explain.
7. Outline the basic strengths and weaknesses of each mode of transport.

8. Under what circumstances are freight forwarders used?
9. Identify the major forms of intermodal co-ordination and give an example of a product that is likely to use each type.
10. Determine the EOQ (economic order quantity) for the following situation:

    A firm has calculated the cost of placing orders at $4.60 per order. The annual cost of carrying the product in inventory is estimated to be 22 percent. Cost per unit estimates for the next 12 months are $8.40. Annual usage rates are estimated to be 11 500.

Discussion Questions and Exercises

1. Comment on the following statement: The popularity of physical distribution management is a fad; ten years from now it will be considered a relatively unimportant function of the firm.
2. Prepare a brief report on career opportunities in physical distribution.
3. Suggest the most appropriate method of transportation for each of the following products and defend your choices:
   a. Iron ore
   b. Dash detergent
   c. Heavy earth-moving equipment
   d. Crude oil
   e. Orchids
   f. Lumber
4. Develop an argument for the increased use of intermodal co-ordination. Present your argument to the class.
5. Which mode of transport do you believe will experience the greatest tonne-kilometre percentage growth during the 1980s? Why?

CHAPTER EIGHTEEN

Review Questions

1. Relate the steps in the communications process to promotional strategy.
2. Explain the concept of the promotional mix and its relationship to the marketing mix.
3. Identify the major determinants of a promotional mix and describe how they affect the selection of an appropriate blending of promotional techniques.
4. Compare the five basic objectives of promotion. Cite specific examples.
5. Explain the concept of noise in marketing communications and its causes.
6. Under what circumstances should a pushing strategy be used in promotion? When would a pulling strategy be effective?
7. What are the primary objectives of promotion?

8. Identify and briefly explain the alternative methods for developing a promotional budget.
9. How should a firm attempt to measure the effectiveness of its promotional efforts?
10. Identify the major public criticisms sometimes directed toward promotion. Prepare a defence for each criticism.

Discussion Questions and Exercises

1. "Perhaps the most critical promotional question facing the marketing manager concerns when to use each of the components of promotion." Comment on this statement, and relate your response to the goods classification, product value, marketing channels, price, and the timing of the promotional effort.
2. What mix of promotional variables would you use for each of the following?
   a. Champion spark plugs
   b. Weedeater lawn edgers
   c. a management consulting service
   d. industrial drilling equipment
   e. women's sports outfits
   f. customized business forms
3. Develop a hypothetical promotion budget for the following firms. Ignore dollar amounts by using percentage allocations to the various promotional variables (such as 30 percent to personal selling, 60 percent to advertising, and 10 percent to public relations).
   a. Tilden Rent-A-Car
   b. Commonwealth Holiday Inns
   c. a manufacturer of industrial chemicals
   d. Great West Life Insurance Company
4. Should doctors, dentists, and lawyers be prohibited from promoting their services through media like direct mail and newspaper advertisements? How do these professionals currently promote their services?
5. When paperback book sales suffered a downturn, several of the major publishers adopted new promotional strategies. One firm began using 30-cents-off coupons to promote its romance series. Another company, on the other hand, established a returns policy that rewarded dealers with high sales. The new policy also contained penalties to discourage low volume by retail book outlets. Relate these promotional strategies to the material discussed in this chapter.